בתודה ובהוקרה

לרבנו הרב, לקרן

לכל בני משפחתם, ולכל משפחת המכון

"כי מלאה הארץ דעה את השם כמים לים מכסים"

לעילוי נשמת

צבי בן יוסף ז״ל

אהרון דב בן יואל ז״ל

לברכה, בריאות, הצלחה, אושר ועושר
והתפתחות רוחנית

אסתר בת יוסף ומרים

ליוסף בן שלמה ושרה

וחנה בת הרמן ואנליז

לכל האחים והאחיות ובני משפחותיהם

לילדינו

יוסף, מיכל, אסתר, שירי

יעל, מרים, דוד ושרה

מאחלים

יהודה בן צבי ואסתר

רחל בת יוסף וחנה

INTRODUCTION TO THE INDEX

Creating an index to a text as large as the Zohar is a daunting task, and one that, without the computer, would have occupied several people for a lifetime. It is analogous to the indexing of a major encyclopedia --- which, considering that the Zohar is indeed a spiritual encyclopedia, is just what one would expect. In order to keep the index to a manageable length we had to first ask ourselves what its principal purpose should be. Thus, the principle purpose of this index is to enable readers quickly to locate in the complete text of the English Zohar where a specific term or name occurs. To achieve just this objective in fewer than 600 pages meant that we had to make certain sacrifices. This is thus not a scholarly index inasmuch as the specific usage of a term throughout the text is not defined. The index merely tells the reader the names of the various volumes and the verse numbers therein where the term can be found employed in any context. To do more would have been to increase the size of the index by a factor of ten or more. In practical terms, this would have meant providing a separate index for each volume of the text.

Our second principal objective, however, was to create a single index for the entire English Zohar in one volume. Therefore detailed definitions were ruled out. Limitations of space have also meant that some readers less familiar with the text will be surprised to find no mention in the index of the more common Kabbalistic terms. For example, there is no listing for 'Sfirot' or 'Hashem' or 'Holy One'. Such startling omissions may be explained by referring the reader to the listing for 'Light', which occupies four pages in the index. The ubiquity throughout the text of certain terms is so extensive that any indexing of them would have been redundant. Barely a page of the Zohar fails to mention 'Sfirot' or 'Hashem' or 'the Holy One, blessed be He.' Similarly, it has been assumed that the reader will understand that, to the extent it is a commentary on Torah, any given volume of the Zohar will be replete with references to events or persons in the section of Torah under discussion. Thus, in the case of 'Noah', for example, where the name is mentioned frequently in the Zohar portion named Noach, not every verse is individually identified. Yet by indicating 'Noah' to be present in, say, verses '212-216' does not necessarily mean that the name itself will be found in every verse, but that 'Noah' himself is under discussion in each of those consecutive verses.

We consider the above sacrifices to be far outweighed by the utility of the index as it now stands. The fact that this monumental task was completed in such a relatively brief time is evidence in itself to the guiding force of the

Light, whose influence was felt on so many occasions where problems seemed insurmountable, whose loving grace never failed to provide the energy and encouragement that made an often tedious task seem vital and urgent. If there are flaws in the index, they are human ones. Where it succeeds, the credit is due only to the One from Whom all good proceeds.

Using the Index

To find if a term has been indexed, first look it up in the 'Content of Index' section preceding the index proper. If it is not found there, either it does not exist in the text, or else it is too ubiquitous throughout to warrant indexing, as mentioned above. Having found the term you wish to look up, proceed to the page number given. There you will find occurrences of the term listed as verse or paragraphs numbers under the volume or volumes in which it is mentioned or which refer to it. For example, the term 'Adamah (soil)' gives you the English meaning of the Hebrew term in parentheses and refers you to page 10 of the index, where you find that it occurs in the Zohar only in verse 36 of the portion or volume named Beresheet B and in verses 117 and 118 of the portion or volume named Mishpatim. Since it has been assumed that only readers unable to easily read Hebrew-Aramaic will be using the English Zohar, those Hebrew names or terms more commonly known in their anglicized forms --- such as 'Noah', 'Moses' or 'Mount Ararat' --- are given only in the English form. If you do not find, say, 'Yitro' listed, simply refer to 'Jethro'. Where a volume of the Zohar has been titled Noach, for example, the title will remain Noach although the biblical personage is referred to as 'Noah'. This is to preserve the integrity of the original text and to acknowledge that, in the Zohar, a person's name need not always refer merely to a character in the scriptural drama. It can and does frequently refer to something whose echoes in eternity far outlast the reverberating span of a human life --- even the resounding echoes of those prodigious spans enjoyed by some of the Prophets and Patriarchs.

APPLYING THE POWER OF THE ZOHAR

The Zohar is a book of great mystical power and wisdom. It is Universally recognized as the definitive work on the Kabbalah – and it is also so Much more.

The Zohar is a wellspring of spiritual energy, a fountainhead of metaphysical power that not only reveals and explains, but literally brings blessing, protection, and well-being into the lives of all those who read or peruse its sacred texts. All that is required is worthy desire, the certainty of a trusting heart, and an open and receptive mind. Unlike other books, including the great spiritual texts of other traditions, The Zohar is written in a kind of code, through which metaphors, parables, and cryptic language at first conceal but ultimately reveal the forces of creation.

As electrical current is concealed in wire and cable before disclosing itself as an illuminated light bulb, the spiritual Light of the Creator is wrapped in allegory and symbolism throughout the Aramaic text of the Zohar. And while many books contain information and knowledge, the Zohar both expresses and embodies spiritual Light. The very letters on its pages have the power to bring spiritual wisdom and positive energy into every area of our lives.

As we visually scan the Aramaic texts and study the accompanying insights that appear in English, spiritual power is summoned from above – and worlds tremble as Light is sent forth in response.

It's primary purpose is not only to help us acquire wisdom, but to draw Light from the Upper Worlds and to bring sanctification into our lives. Indeed, the book itself is the most powerful of all tools for cleansing the soul and connecting to the Light of the Creator. As you open these pages, therefore, do not make understanding in the conventional sense your primary goal.

Although you may not have a knowledge of Aramaic, look first at the Aramaic text before reading the English. Do not be discouraged by difficulties with comprehension. Instead, open your heart to the spiritual transformation the Zohar is offering you.

Ultimately, the Zohar is an instrument for refining the individual soul – for removing darkness from the earth – and for bringing well being and blessing to our fellow man.

Its purpose is not only to make us intellectually wise, but to make us spiritually pure.

כרך כג

מפתח עניינים

Vol. XXIII

Index

CONTENT OF INDEX

Page	Subject
1	Aaron
2	Aba and Ima
3	Abarim
4	Abel
	Abihu
	Abimelech
	Abraham
6	Abram
7	Absalom, son of David
	Abyss
8	Acacia
	Achaz
	Achish
	Achitofel
	Adam Kadmon
	Adam
10	Adamah (soil)
	Adder
	Adiel (spirit)
	Adiriel (spirit)
	Adiririyah (spirit)
	Adiriyah Sanug'ya (spirit)
	Adonai
11	Adrahinael (spirit)
	Adrianus
	Afrira (spirit)
	Agirison (spirit)
	Agrat
	Ahab
	Ahadiel (spirit)
	Ahadoriya (spirit)
12	Ahaniel (spirit)
	Ahasuerus
	Ahava (spirit)
	Ahiel (spirit)
	Ahiman
	Ahimelech
	Ahinael (angel)
	Air
13	Almond
	Almond (Aaron's staff)
	Almond tree
	Alms
	Alphabet
14	Altar
15	Amalek
16	Amalekim

Page	Subject
16	Amen
17	Amidah (standing prayer)
	Amminadab
	Amon
	Amorites
	Amrafel
	Amram
18	Anael (spirit)
	Anah
	Anakim
	Anatot
	Ancient of Days (Atik Yomin)
	Anfiel (spirit)
	Angel of Death
19	Angels
22	Anger
	Angerayon (spirit)
	Aniel (spirit)
	Animals
23	Anointment
24	Apples
	Arab
	Arad
25	Aram
	Aram Tzova
	Aramaic
26	Arami
	Aravah
	Aravot
	Arich Anpin
	Ariel (supernal minister)
	Aries
	Ark of the covenant
	Ark of the testimony
	Ark
27	Arka (ground)
28	Armageddon
	Arnon
	Arrows
	Arvit (evening prayer)
	Asael
	Asher
	Asherah
	Asimon (spirit)
29	Asirta (spirit)
	Asisaniyah (spirit)
	Asiyah

CONTENT OF INDEX

Page	Subject
30	Askara (spirit)
	Asmodeus
	Ass
	Assir
	Assyrians
	Astiriya (spirit)
31	Astrology
32	Atad
33	Atariel (spirit)
	Atarim
	Atbash cipher
	Atik yomin (ancient of days)
	Atika Kadisha
34	Atik-Yomin
	Atonement
35	Attributes of Mercy, Thirteen
	Atzilut
36	Av (month)
	Avadon
	Awl
	Aya
	Aza
	Azael (supernal minister)
37	Azariah
	Azazel
	Azpiel (spirit)
	Azriel
	Azuzyah (spirit)
	Baal
	Baal Pe'or
	Babel
38	Baby
	Babylon
	Babylonians
39	Balaam
	Baladan (dog)
	Balak
40	Balsam
	Balsam tree
	Banners
41	Baraithas
	Barak (spirit)
	Barhiel (spirit)
	Bastard
	Bathsheba
	Beans
42	Beard

Page	Subject
42	Beasts
44	Becher, son of Benjamin
	Beginning
	Bela, son of Benjamin
	Belshazzar
	Ben Azai
	Ben Zoma
	Benaiah (Bnayahu)
	Benjamin
	Beor
45	Beth-El
	Bethuel
	Bezalel
	Bilaam
	Bilhah
	Birds
46	Birth
	Birthright
	Blasphemy
	Blessing
49	Blind
	Bliss
	Blood
50	Bloodshed
	Blossom
51	Blue
	Boards
	Boaz
	Body
54	Boel (angel)
	Bone
55	Book of Adam
	Book of Asmodeus
	Book of Dumah
	Book of Enoch
	Book of Formation
	Book of King Solomon
56	Book of Life
	Book of Memories
	Book of Remembrance
	Book of secrets of Enoch
	Book of the generations Adam
	Book of the physician Kartana
	Booth
	Bozrah
	Brain
57	Brass

CONTENT OF INDEX

Page	Subject
57	Bread of Affliction
58	Bread
59	Breastplate
	Breath
60	Bride
61	Brit (covenant)
63	Briyah
64	Bullocks
	Bush
	Butler
	Button
	Caesarea
	Cain
65	Caleb
	Camels
	Camp
66	Canaan
	Canaanite
	Candles
68	Canopy wedding (chupah)
	Cantillation
	Carmel
	Castration
	Cave of Machpelah
	Caves
69	Celestial Yeshivah
	Census
	Chachmiel (supernal minister)
	Chagai
	Chair
	Chalchaliel (spirit)
	Chaldeans
70	Chalitzah
	Chambers
71	Chaniel (spirit)
	Chariot
73	Chasdiel (spirit)
	Chasdihael (spirit)
	Chassadim
75	Chassidim
	Chayah
	Chayot
	Chebar (river)
	Cherubim (Cherubs)
76	Chidekel (river)
	Children
77	Chirah

Page	Subject
77	Chizkiel (supernal minister)
	Cholam
	Chupah (wedding canopy)
78	Chut Hashani (spirit)
	Ciphers
	Circumcision
79	Citron (etrog)
	Clay
	Cloud
80	Coffin
81	Colors
82	Comets
	Community of Yisrael
	Compassion
83	Congregation
84	Constellation
	Converts
85	Copper
	Coriander
	Corn
	Corners
86	Correction (Tikun)
87	Correction
88	Court
89	Courtyard
	Covenant (Brit)
91	Cows
	Cozbi, daugher of Zur
	Craftsmanship
	Creation
94	Crocodiles
	Crowns
96	Crystal
	Cubits
	Cup of Benediction
97	Cup of Salvation
	Cup
	Curse
98	Curtain
99	Dahariel (spirit)
	Dan
	Daniel
100	Darkness
102	Daughter
103	David
105	Deaf
	Death

CONTENT OF INDEX

Page	Subject
107	Death and the Afterlife
109	Death of Rabbi Shimon
	Deborah (prophetess)
	Deeds
111	Deer
	Deities
	Deity of the Illuminating Jewels
	Demons
112	Destruction
113	Dew
114	Diamond
	Dibri
	Dinah
	Diphtheria
	Directions
116	Disease
	Divorce
	Do'eg
	Doe
	Dog
	Dogs
117	Donkeys
	Door
118	Doorpost
119	Dots
	Doves
120	Dreams
121	Drought
	Drunkenness
	Dryness (tziyah)
	Dryness
	Dumah (angel)
	Dust
122	Dwellings
123	Eagle
124	Ears
125	Earth (eretz)
	Earth
128	East
129	Echad (one)
	Eden
130	Edom
131	Edomites
	Efron
	Eggs
	Egypt
133	Egyptians

Page	Subject
134	Eheyeh
	Ein sof (Infinity)
135	Eitan
	Elazar
	Eldad
	Electrum
	Eleh (these)
	Eli
136	Eliezer
	Elihu
	Elijah
137	Elim
	Elimelech
	Elisha
	Elisheba
	Emasculation
	Emet (truth)
138	End of Days
	Endless
	Endlessness
	Enoch
	Enosh
139	Ephod
	Ephraim
	Epilepsy
	Er
	Eretz (earth)
	Esau
141	Esophagus
	Esther
	Etrog (citron)
	Eunuchs
	Eve
142	Evening prayer (Arvit)
	Evil Inclination
143	Evil
146	Evyatar
	Exile
148	Expulsion from the Garden of Eden
	Eyebrows
	Eyes
150	Ezekiel
151	Ezrachite
152	Face
154	Faith
155	Falsehood (sheker)
	Famine

CONTENT OF INDEX

Page	Subject
156	Fasting
	Fear
159	Female
161	Female Waters (Mayin Nukvin)
	Fetus
	Field
162	Fifty
	Figs
	Fingernails
	Fingers
163	Fire
165	Firmaments
167	First Fruits
	Firstborn
168	Fish
	Flame
169	Flax
	Flesh
171	Flood
	Flow
173	Flower
	Flowers
	Food
174	Footstool (earth)
175	Forehead
	Foreigner
	Foreskin
176	Form
177	Fragrance
178	Freedom
	Freezing
	Frogs
179	Fruit
180	Furnace
	Gabriel (angel)
181	Gad
	Gadiel (spirit)
	Gadrihael (spirit)
	Gai (valley)
	Gall
	Gallim
	Gamgima (spirit)
	Garden of Eden
182	Garments
184	Gates
185	Gazelle
	Gazriel (supernal minister)

Page	Subject
186	Gedariah (spirit)
	Gehazi
	Gehenom (hell)
187	Gemini
	Gera
	Gey (valley)
	Gezar Dinaya (spirit)
	Gezuriyah (spirit)
	Giants
	Giborim
	Gideon
188	Gilboa mountains of
	Gilgal
	Girdle
	Gizzard
	Glass
	Goats
	Goblet
189	Gods
	Gog and Magog
	Gold
190	Golden Calf
191	Golden Calves
	Gomer
	Gonorrhea
	Good Inclination
	Goshen
	Grades
195	Grass
	Grasshoppers
	Grave
	Greece
	Ground (Arka)
	Ground
197	Guilt
	Gutters
	Gzardia (spirit)
	Habakkuk
198	Hadar
	Hadarniel (angel)
	Hadriel (spirit)
	Hagar
	Hail
	Hair
199	Hallel
	Ham
200	Haman

CONTENT OF INDEX

Page	Subject
200	Hamor
	Hananiah
	Hands
202	Haran
	Hariel (spirit)
203	Harlotry
	Hatred
204	Havdalah
	Hawk
	Head
206	Health
207	Heart
208	Heaven
210	Heavens
212	Heave-offering
	Heber
	Hebrew Alphabet
213	Hebrew letters
215	Hebron
	Heel
	Heifer
216	Heiman (spirit)
	Hell (Gehenom)
217	Hephzibah
	Heshbon
	Hezekiah
	Hidden book (Safra De'tzniuta)
218	High Priest
	Hind
	Hips
	Hire
219	Hittites
	Holiness (Kedushah)
221	Holyland
222	Holy Name
223	Holy of Holies
224	(Holy) Temple
	Honey
225	Horeb
	Horses
	Hosea
	Hosts
227	House
	Hundred
228	Hyssop
	Idolatry
230	Idra Raba

Page	Subject
230	Igael (spirit)
	Igeret
	Illness
	Ima
	Images
231	Immanuel
	Incense
	Incest
232	Infertility
	Infinite
	Infinity (Ein Sof)
233	Infinity
	Intercourse
	Ira
	Iriel (spirit)
234	Iron
	Isaac
236	Isaiah
	Ish Boshet
	Ishmael
	Israel
237	Issachar
	Itai
	Itamar
	Ivtzan
	Izhar
	Jacob
240	Jealousy
241	Jehoiada (Yehoyada)
	Jehoshaphat
	Jered
	Jeremiah
243	Jericho
	Jeroboam
	Jerusalem
244	Jerusalem, celestial
	Jerusalem, terrestrial
	Jesse
	Jesurun
245	Jethro
	Joab
	Job
246	Jokshan
	Jonah
247	Jordan river
	Joseph
248	Joshua

CONTENT OF INDEX

Page	Subject
249	Josiah
	Jubilee
250	Judah
251	Judges
	Judgment
255	Juniper
	Jupiter
	Kaddish
	Kadmiel (spirit)
	Kadshiel (supernal minister)
	Kaftziel (spirit)
	Karshiel (spirit)
256	Kartana (physician)
	Kasiriyah (spirit)
	Katfira
	Kedumiel (supernal minister)
	Kedumiyah (spirit)
	Kedushah (Holiness)
258	Kemuel (angel)
	Kenites
	Kesher
	Kestimon (spirit)
	Keter
259	Keturah
	Key
260	Kiddush
	Kidneys
	Kidron
	Kingdom
261	Kiryat Arba
	Kisses
262	Klipot (shells – negativity)
263	Knife
	Koh
	Kohath
	Kolyah
	Korah
	Kozbi
	Krashihael (spirit)
	Kraspihael (spirit)
264	Kriat Sh'ma
	Krishiel (spirit)
	Ktatarihael (spirit)
	Kushite
	Laban
	Labyrinth
	Ladder

Page	Subject
265	Laisha
	Lambs
	Lamp
	Lamps
266	Land of Yisrael
	Laws of Priests
267	Leah
	Leaven
	Leaves
	Lebanon
268	Lemuel
	Lentils
	Leopard
	Lepers
	Leprosy
269	Levana (spirit)
	Leviathan
	Levirate marriage
	Levites
270	Light
273	Lights
275	Likenesses
276	Lilit
277	Lily
	Linen
	Lintel
278	Lion
279	Lips
280	Liver
	Living creatures
281	Lock
	Locusts
	Loins
	Lot
282	Love
284	Lulav
	Lungs
	Lupinus
	Luz
	Maassiyah
	Machalat
	Machlon
	Machpelah
	Mah (what)
285	Mahalalel
	Maidens
	Malachi

Page Subject

285 Male
287 Male Waters (Mayin Duchrin)
Malkam
Malkiel (spirit)
Mamre
Mandrakes
288 Manna
Manoah
Mara
Marah
Marriage
289 Mars
Mata (angel)
Matana
Match-making
Matred
290 Matron
Matzoh
Mayin Duchrin (male waters)
Mayin Nukvin (female waters)
291 Mazal
Meal Offering
292 Meals
Medicine
Meditation
293 Mehetabel
Mehitavel
Mei zahab
Meidad
Melchizedek
Menashe, King of Judah
Menorah
Mercury
294 Mercy
296 Merit
297 Merodach Baladan
Mesopotamia
Messiah, the
298 Metatron
299 Methuselah
Mezahab
Mezuzah
Mi (who)
300 Michael (angel)
Midianites
301 Midnight
Midyan

Page Subject

302 Milcah
Milk
Minchah
303 Miracle
304 Miriam
Mirror
305 Misarsaniyah (spirit)
Mishael
Mishnah
Moab
306 Mochin
307 Moon
309 Mordecai
Moreh
Morning
310 Moses
313 Mount Ararat
Mount Ebal
Mount Gerizim
Mount Hor
Mount Horeb
314 Mount Moriah
Mount of Olives
Mount Sinai
Mount Zion
315 Mountains
316 Mozniya (spirit)
Myriads
Myrrh
317 Myrtle
Naamah
Nabal
Nadab and Abihu
Nadab
Naftali
Nahshon
318 Nakedness
Naomi
Nathan
Navot
Nazarites
Nebaioth
Nebo
319 Nebuchadnezzar
Necho
Nefesh (soul)
320 Nefilim

CONTENT OF INDEX

Page	Subject
320	Negev
	Neshamah (soul)
321	Neshiyan (oblivion)
	Nesira (spirit)
	Nest
322	Netzach
	Niatziriel (spirit)
	Nile
	Nimrod
	Nineveh
	Ninth of Av (month)
	Nishyah (forgetfulness)
	Noah
323	Nod
	Nogah (spirit)
	North
324	Nose
325	Nukva
327	Nuts
	Oath
328	Obadiah
	Oblivion (neshiyan)
	Ocean
	Offering
330	Offering, daily
	Og
	Oil
331	Olive
	Omer
332	Onan
	One (echad)
	Onimta
	Onkelus
	Oral Law
	Oriel (lion)
	Orlah
	Ornaments
333	Orpah
	Other Side
335	Oved
	Ox
336	Padael (angel)
	Paddan-Aram
	Palanquin
	Palm tree
337	Partzufim
	Passover

Page	Subject
337	Patchiel (spirit)
	Patriarchs
339	Peace
340	Peace-offering
	Pearls
341	Pedael (spirit)
	Peniel
	Peor
	Peretz
	Persimmon
	Pesagniyah (spirit)
	Petachiyah (spirit)
	Pharaoh, the
342	Philistines
	Physician Kartana
	Pillar
343	Pillar of Cloud
344	Pillar of fire
	Pinchas
	Pipes
	Pishon (river)
345	Pitut (spirit)
	Plagues
	Planets
346	Plants
	Point
347	Poison
	Pole
	Pomegranate
348	Poor
	Potiphar
	Pottage
	Pox
	Praise
350	Prayer
352	Precepts
354	Pregnancy
	Priests
355	Prison
356	Prophecy
	Prophets
358	Prosecution
	Punishment
359	Purification
360	Purple
361	Queen of Sheba
	Rabbi Akiva

CONTENT OF INDEX

Page	Subject
361	Rabbi Shimon, death of
	Rachel
362	Rachmiel (angel)
	Ragshiel (supernal minister)
	Rahav
	Rain
363	Rainbow
	Rama
	Ramah
	Rape
	Raphael (angel)
	Ratzon
364	Ravens
	Raziel (supernal minister)
	Rebecca
	Red
365	Red cow
366	Red Sea
	Redemption and salvation
367	Refael (angel)
	Refaim
	Rehoboth
	Reincarnation
368	Remarriage
	Remember and Keep
	Repentance
369	Reptile
	Resurrection
370	Reuben
	Revenge
371	Rib
	Righteous
375	Ring
	River Jordan
	River of Fire (Dinur)
	Rivers
377	Robbers
	Rock
378	Rocks
	Rod
379	Rods
	Rome
	Rooster
	Rope
380	Rosh Hashanah
	Ruach (soul)
381	Rumiel (supernal minister)

Page	Subject
381	Ruth
	Saadiel (spirit)
	Sabbatical year
382	Sachsicha (spirit)
	Sacrifice
383	Safsirita (spirit)
	Sahadiel (spirit)
	Sakafortaya (spirit)
	Salt
384	Samael
385	Samson
	Samuel
386	Sanctification
	Sanctuary
387	Sandalfon
388	Sanegoryah (spirit)
	Sangadiel (spirit)
	Sangirya (spirit)
	Sanhedrin
	Sansaniya (spirit)
	Sanuriya (spirit)
	Sapir (spirit)
	Sapphire
389	Sarah
390	Sartaya (spirit)
	Satan, the
	Saturn
	Saul
391	Scales
	Sea of Galilee
	Sea of Kineret
	Sea of Suf
	Seal
392	Seas
393	Seasons
	Sefer Yetzirah (Book of Formation)
	Seir
394	Semen
	Sennacherib
	Serach
	Seraph
	Seraphel (spirit)
	Seraphim
395	Serpent
396	Seth
	Seven
398	Seventeen

CONTENT OF INDEX

Page	Subject
398	Seventy
400	Seventy-Two
	Shabbat
402	Shachniel (spirit)
	Shadai
403	Shades
	Shadow
	Shamashiel (spirit)
404	Shamayim (heaven)
	Shamiel (supernal minister)
	Shamshiel (spirit)
	Sharon
	Shavuot
	Shechem
	Shechinah
407	Sheep
408	Shekels
	Sheker (falsehood)
	Shelah, son of Judah
	Shells (Klipot)
409	Shelomith
	Sh'ma Yisrael
410	Sheol
	Shepherd
411	Sheshai
	Shevna
412	Shield
	Shields
	Shiloh
	Shim'i
413	Ships
	Shittim
	Shmayahel (spirit)
	Shmini Atzeret
	Shoe
	Shofar
414	Shewbread
	Shua
	Shunamit
	Sichon
	Sihon
	Silence
415	Silkworm
	Silver
416	Simeon
	Sin
418	Sinai

Page	Subject
419	Sinew
	Singing
420	Sin-offering
421	Sisera
	Sisra
	Sixth day, the
	Skatufa (spirit)
	Skin
422	Slavery
423	Smoke
	Snow
424	Sodom and Amorah (Gomorrah)
	Sodomy
	Soil (adamah)
	Soil
	Solomon
425	Sorcery
426	Sotah
	Soul (nefesh)
427	Soul (neshamah)
428	Soul (Ruach)
429	Soul, the
432	Soulmates
	South
433	Spears
	Spices
434	Spies
	Spinal Chord
	Spinning
435	Spleen
	Spoons
	Srayah
	Staff
	Standing prayer (Amidah)
436	Stariel (spirit)
	Stars
437	Staturiyah (spirit)
	Sterilization
	Stone
438	Stones
439	Stork
	Streams
440	Strength
441	Sturiyah (angel)
	Substance (yesh)
442	Suffering
	Sugadyah (spirit)

Page	Subject
442	Suicide
	Sukkot
443	Sun
444	Supernal book
	Supernal forms
	Suriyah (spirit)
	Sword
445	Tabernacle
446	Table
447	Tablets
448	Tahariel (angel)
	Talit
	Talmai
	Tamar
	Tammuz
	Tanya
	Tarmod
	Taskifa (spirit)
	Taurus
	Teardrops
	Temple, the
450	Temple, destruction of
	Ten
452	Ten commandments
	Tents
453	Terah, Abraham's father
	Terah
	Testimony
454	Tetragrammaton
455	Tevel (world)
456	Tfilin
	These (eleh)
457	Thigh
	Thirteen
458	Thirteen Attributes of Mercy
459	Thorns
	Thought
460	Thread
461	Threshing
	Throne
462	Tikun (correction)
463	Tishrei (month)
	Tithing
464	Torah
468	Tower
	Trachea
	Tree

Page	Subject
470	Tree of Knowledge of Good and Evil
	Tree of Life
472	Tribes
	Truth (emet)
473	Tubal-Cain
	Tulip
	Tumiel (spirit)
	Tumihael (spirit)
	Tumim
	Turtle
	Turtledove
	Twelve
475	Twelve stones
	Twelve tribes of Israel
	Twins
476	Tzadikim (righteous)
	Tzadkiel (supernal minister)
	Tzadok
	Tzaftzafiyah (spirit)
	Tzalmon (spirit)
	Tzarfat
	Tzelyah
	Tzidon
	Tzipor
.	Tziporah
	Tzitzit
477	Tziyah (dryness)
	Tzruyah
	Unity
478	Universe
479	Urfaniel (spirit)
	Uriah the Hittite
	Uriah
	Uriel (angel)
480	Urim
	Uzziah
	Valley (gey)
	Valley
	Vanity
481	Venus
	Vertebrae
	Vessels
482	Vine
	Vineyard
483	Vineyards
	Virgin
	Vision

Content of Index

Page Subject

484 Voice
Void
485 Vow
Wagons
Walls
486 Walnut
War
487 Washing
488 Watchman
Water
490 Waters
492 Well
493 Wells
West
494 Whale
What (Mah)
Wheat
Wheel
White
496 Who (mi)
Wicked
498 Wickedness
500 Widow
Willow
501 Wind
502 Windows
Wine
503 Winepress
Wisdom
505 Witchcraft
506 Witnesses
507 Wolves
Womb
Women
509 Wood
Wool
World (tevel)
510 World to Come, the
512 Worlds
513 Worm
Wormwood
Wrapping
Wreath
Written Law
514 Yaahadonahi (spirit)
. Yachin

Page Subject

514 Year
515 Yechidah
516 Yechonyah
Yehadaniel (spirit)
Yehadriel (spirit)
Yehirael (spirit)
Yehodiam
Yehodiyah (spirit)
Yehosheva
Yehotzedek
Yemim
Yesh (substance)
Yeshivah
517 Yetzirah
518 Yibum
Yiftach
Yishai
Yisrael Saba
519 Yisrael-Saba and Tevunah
Yoach
Yofiel (supernal minister)
Yom Kippur
520 Yud Hei Vav Hei (YHVH)
522 Yumbrus
Yunus
Zachar
Zahariel (spirit)
Zarka
Zebulun
Zechariah
Zechut (spirit)
523 Zedekiah
Zeh (this, masc.)
Zeir Anpin
529 Zelophehad
Zerach
Zevuliel (spirit)
Zibeon
Zilpah
Zimran
Zimri
Zion
530 Zodiac
Zohar
Zot (this, fem.)

AARON

Acharei Mot
1, 2, 5, 6, 9, 10, 12, 19-22, 26, 28-30, 38, 39, 41, 43, 44, 53, 68-70, 84, 97, 98, 111, 116, 120, 121, 355
Balak
386, 392
Bechukotai
9
Beha'alot'cha
1, 22, 38, 42, 48, 146
Behar
10, 27
Bemidbar
15
Beresheet A
46, 147
Beresheet B
293
Beshalach
29, 31, 121, 153, 280, 283, 466
Bo
117, 186
Chayei Sarah
68, 129
Chukat
1, 21, 22, 35, 37-40, 53, 62-67, 69, 87
Ekev
19, 38
Emor
1-3, 11-13, 81, 236, 260a, 260b, 262, 263, 265, 270, 275, 279, 289
Ha'azinu
175
Ki Tetze
24, 56, 79, 120
Ki Tisa
47, 49, 64, 69-73, 75-79, 83, 86, 88, 90-97, 107
Korach
3, 14, 20, 22, 26, 27
Lech Lecha
58
Metzora
23, 24
Mishpatim
145
Naso
81, 135, 144, 155
Noach
281, 309
Pekudei
72, 176, 259, 306, 307, 312-315, 317, 318, 321, 322, 363, 365, 776
Pinchas
6, 11, 34, 74, 128, 130, 232, 342, 575, 632, 765, 814, 824, 838
Shemot
56, 196, 197, 262, 331, 333-335, 338
Shlach Lecha
14, 111-113, 115, 315, 316
Shmini
29, 30, 31, 34-38, 45, 53, 56, 57, 60, 64, 98
Shoftim
23
Tazria
71, 87, 123, 128, 135
Tetzaveh
1, 2, 4, 34, 35, 38, 104
Trumah
40, 404, 405, 406, 407, 461, 462, 541, 746

Tzav
15-17, 34, 42, 98, 99, 134, 135, 152, 153, 162, 164, 165, 171, 172, 177, 181
Vaera
67, 82, 84, 85, 87, 88, 97, 99, 104, 117-121, 125, 126, 128, 129, 142, 175
Vaetchanan
13, 14
Vayakhel
157, 473, 474, 480
Vayechi
35, 133, 383, 419, 420
Vayelech
2, 3
Vayera
120, 123, 127, 494
Vayeshev
267
Vayetze
29
Vayikra
18, 32, 104, 114, 128, 165, 330, 335, 337, 392, 415
Yitro
1, 249, 253

ABA AND IMA

Acharei Mot
87, 101-103, 114, 165, 166, 168, 169, 171-173, 237, 374, 377-379, 382
Balak
18, 48, 49, 50, 119, 121, 123, 124, 156, 157, 332, 340, 344, 347, 433, 437-439, 507
Beha'alot'cha
20, 21, 24, 29, 30
Bemidbar
34, 62-64
Beresheet A
31, 32, 34, 108, 109, 160-168, 203, 243, 244, 247, 256, 277, 279, 282, 306, 307, 316, 317, 328, 332, 334, 360, 362, 370, 373, 374
Beresheet B
136, 166, 202, 213, 232, 235, 236, 238-241
Beshalach
144, 160, 162, 163, 172, 255
Bo
126
Chayei Sarah
65, 120, 138, 160
Chukat
27, 28, 31, 50
Ekev
10, 36
Emor
21, 25, 69, 87-91, 102-105, 111, 114, 115, 117, 134, 170, 173, 195, 224, 226, 250, 255, 256, 258, 259
Ha'azinu
33, 41, 47, 48, 63, 72, 75, 81-86, 89-90, 94, 108, 109, 116, 118-120, 124, 129, 162, 167, 180, 188, 189, 193, 205
Idra Raba
37, 183, 324
Kedoshim
37-43, 51, 54, 61, 70, 131
Ki Tetze
50, 52, 67, 86, 88, 93, 100, 106, 125-127
Ki Tisa
102

Korach
9, 10, 52, 56
Lech Lecha
13, 212, 311, 366, 367, 445
Miketz
32
Mishpatim
12, 13, 83, 137, 184, 378, 433, 435, 467, 523, 525 -532, 537, 563
Naso
90, 126
Noach
21, 84, 128, 159, 245, 332 -334
Pekudei
9, 10, 92, 95, 127, 293, 732, 772, 952
Pinchas
31, 222, 438, 513, 521, 648, 654, 678, 690, 717, 719, 754, 766-768, 770, 814, 833, 841
Prologue
17, 80
Safra Detzniuta
10, 12, 13, 22-24, 26, 31, 32, 38, 44, 53, 59, 60, 72, 73
Shemot
191,192
Shlach Lecha
54, 87, 90, 91, 138
Shmini
58, 65, 117
Tetzaveh
15, 25, 36, 63, 98, 102, 116, 124, 135
Trumah
5, 7, 9, 10, 11, 125, 127, 128, 132, 133, 155, 184-186, 191, 195-198, 203, 204, 206, 249, 330, 354, 355, 357-359, 379, 380, 394, 534, 535, 577, 585, 625, 629, 694, 718, 719, 720, 725, 759, 823
Tzav
35, 54, 62, 63, 87, 157
Vaera
103, 112, 189
Vaetchanan
21, 43, 45, 46, 48, 59
Vayakhel
214, 255, 256, 262, 279, 397, 419, 423, 428
Vayechi
35, 131-133, 217, 221, 224, 284, 569, 612, 632, 633, 648, 735
Vayelech
48
Vayera
8, 12, 350
Vayeshev
107
Vayetze
4, 6, 33, 151, 152, 161, 208, 210, 213, 232
Vayigash
131, 132
Vayikra
2, 17, 37-39, 44, 94, 168-171, 196, 197, 248, 250, 256, 258, 260, 280, 284, 286, 288, 341, 448
Yitro
96, 97, 256, 359, 360, 386, 396, 462, 487, 489, 559

ABARIM

Shlach Lecha
9

ABEL

Acharei Mot
357, 369
Bemidbar
4
Beresheet A
285, 455, 456, 458
Beresheet B
331-333, 337-339, 341, 346, 348-350
Bo
32, 144
Idra Raba
156, 326, 328, 338, 344
Kedoshim
55, 116, 119, 120
Lech Lecha
16
Pekudei
203-205
Tazria
44
Tetzaveh
44
Trumah
761, 763, 765, 766

ABIHU

Acharei Mot
6, 10, 11, 19-22, 24, 25, 69, 97, 98
Pinchas
11, 35d, 71-74
Shmini
36, 37, 52, 55, 61
Tzav
156
Vaera
86, 87
Vayikra
64, 65, 67

ABIMELECH

Balak
1
Bechukotai
12, 13
Beshalach
27
Lech Lecha
137, 138
Mishpatim
37
Toldot
98, 101, 102
Trumah
253
Vayera
346, 347, 351, 352, 358, 365, 366
Vayetze
21
Vayikra
105

ABRAHAM

Acharei Mot
12, 13, 17, 146, 147, 184, 385
Balak
51, 52, 128, 145, 146, 228, 301, 350, 354, 393
Beha'alot'cha
29, 34, 35, 37, 39, 40, 92
Behar
4, 63, 64, 69, 70, 73
Bemidbar
5, 52, 58
Beresheet A
140, 196, 197, 220, 221, 223,

433, 467
Beresheet B
25, 61, 133, 186, 365
Beshalach
13, 52-54, 96, 158, 172, 198 -200, 247, 248, 338, 432
Bo
12-14, 29, 30, 88, 90, 91, 106, 111, 114, 123, 134, 155, 156, 164, 201, 212
Chayei Sarah
20, 26, 36, 41, 46, 48, 51, 52, 54, 60, 88-94, 98, 99, 100, 101, 103- 110, 116, 118-121, 138-142, 151, 154, 156, 157, 162, 164, 170, 177, 184, 185, 187, 196, 198, 200, 215-218, 225, 238, 245, 249, 252-264
Chukat
26, 86, 87, 90
Ekev
17, 62
Emor
187, 189, 195-200, 217, 218, 221, 269, 276, 279, 281, 289
Ha'azinu
210, 225, 228, 237, 244
Idra Raba
59, 97, 153, 231, 312
Kedoshim
77
Ki Tetze
16, 17, 18, 19, 20, 27, 28, 50, 71, 88, 89, 112, 135, 136, 140
Ki Tisa
30, 37, 39, 52, 54
Lech Lecha
1, 3, 16, 17, 22, 27, 28, 33-40, 50, 56, 58-65, 68, 72-76, 107, 110, 111, 113, 118, 119, 122, 123, 126, 138, 140, 141, 142, 143, 160-162, 170, 176, 178, 179, 191, 192, 197, 199-201, 215-219, 223, 224, 226, 227, 234-236, 242, 253, 254, 255, 257, 270-272, 274 -276, 288, 289, 290, 293, 295, 320, 321, 322, 326, 338-343, 374, 382, 383, 426, 437, 439, 442, 454, 455, 457-459, 461, 466
Metzora
8, 62
Miketz
67, 98, 226-228, 230, 232
Mishpatim
23, 41, 295-297, 301, 391, 473, 475, 476, 481, 484
Naso
33, 190, 191, 192
Noach
13, 14, 24, 84, 179, 282, 300, 374
Pekudei
6, 8, 192, 476, 712, 714, 715, 719, 720, 800-802, 805
Pinchas
35b, 35c, 64, 65, 70, 83, 87, 97, 98, 99, 100, 207, 232, 329, 344, 368, 387, 482, 483, 487, 498, 558, 560, 567, 575, 579, 580, 582, 590, 615, 651, 652, 657, 677, 844, 845
Prologue
46, 48, 163, 177, 178, 179, 184
Shemot
120, 150, 169, 210, 249, 290, 387
Shlach Lecha
29, 117, 122, 133, 134, 135,

168, 169, 171, 187, 284, 303, 340
Shmini
9, 31, 42-44, 48, 88
Tazria
181, 182, 184
Tetzaveh
24, 41, 115
Toldot
7, 8, 9, 13, 18, 22, 32, 33, 40, 46, 72, 73, 79, 86, 88, 94, 96, 98, 101-103, 119-121, 164, 169, 182, 194, 197, 207
Trumah
49, 123, 308, 353, 364, 733, 815, 816, 817, 911, 919
Tzav
48, 49, 76, 94, 95, 96, 112, 187
Vaera
1, 13, 14, 17, 19, 21, 28, 32, 51, 73, 74, 180, 196, 197, 199, 200
Vaetchanan
46, 47, 69, 70, 140, 141
Vayakhel
62, 66, 111, 215, 379
Vayechi
19, 20, 35, 38, 47, 49, 67, 93, 119, 123, 177, 218, 220, 223, 266, 269, 276, 277, 278, 302, 330, 357, 359, 374, 432-435, 437, 516, 517, 539, 574, 649, 772, 783, 789, 790, 802
Vayera
5-7, 9-14, 17, 22, 28, 29, 50, 51, 54, 57, 60, 69, 71-75, 89, 90, 93, 95, 102-104, 106, 107, 109-112, 114, 115, 119, 132, 133, 137, 141, 142, 143, 144, 148-150, 159-161, 164 -166, 168 -172, 174, 175, 177, 181-183, 185, 187, 188, 190 -192, 199-202, 204, 205, 207, 208, 211, 213, 218, 219, 221 -224, 228, 236, 252, 256, 266, 304-306, 312, 313, 330, 333, 342, 343-345, 347-349, 352, 353, 357, 359-363, 365, 366, 407, 411, 437, 438, 461-466, 468, 469, 470, 484, 489-503, 505-508, 512, 513
Vayeshev
46, 48, 76, 102, 110, 161, 186, 200, 204
Vayetze
21, 22, 33, 51, 59-62, 153, 158, 172, 262, 296, 354, 372, 373, 381-383
Vayigash
1, 8, 44
Vayikra
32, 116, 191, 192, 216, 224, 225, 295, 305, 308, 329, 381, 399, 400, 435, 449
Vayishlach
13, 54, 55, 56, 60, 67, 111, 143, 172, 225, 226, 228
Yitro
58, 249, 253, 289, 349, 351, 352, 380, 395, 406, 423, 425, 432, 461

ABRAM

Beresheet A
277
Bo
164
Chayei Sarah
19

Idra Raba
231
Lech Lecha
13, 16-18, 20, 21, 36, 41, 42, 46, 48, 49, 57, 58, 60, 66-68, 72, 74, 80, 81, 84, 85, 86, 88, 90, 106, 109, 114, 137, 138, 140, 143, 144, 161, 162, 166, 167, 169, 174, 176, 179, 180, 191, 234, 242, 243, 261, 270, 271, 273, 280, 288, 296, 319, 326, 327, 338, 339, 340, 342, 357, 437, 438, 472
Noach
300
Pekudei
123
Shlach Lecha
246
Toldot
94
Vaera
196, 199
Vayera
7, 9, 18, 313
Vayishlach
172

ABSALOM, SON OF DAVID

Chayei Sarah
42
Lech Lecha
402, 408
Vayetze
88
Vayikra
407, 408

ABYSS

Acharei Mot
80, 96
Balak
305
Bechukotai
44
Beresheet A
22, 24, 317
Beresheet B
37, 41, 45, 191, 192, 269- 273, 277
Emor
55
Idra Raba
327, 337, 344
Kedoshim
90
Ki Tetze
60, 61, 63, 65
Lech Lecha
237
Metzora
6
Mishpatim
121, 192
Naso
17
Noach
152
Pekudei
38, 146, 147, 149-151, 154, 289, 420
Prologue
68, 156, 252
Shemot
313
Shlach Lecha
185
Trumah
167, 614, 683, 876
Tzav
78, 127, 128

Vaera
109
Vaetchanan
191
Vayakhel
135, 172, 173, 174
Vayechi
137, 445, 446, 682, 684, 711
Vayera
214
Vayikra
242, 316

ACACIA

Balak
33, 42, 45, 137
Ekev
20
Pekudei
251

ACHAZ

Shemot
169
Vayikra
1
Yitro
382

ACHISH

Vayishlach
7, 8

ACHITOFEL

Mishpatim
150

ADAM KADMON

Emor
11

ADAM

Acharei Mot
79, 255, 357, 359, 360, 369, 380
Balak
76, 79, 82, 416, 417, 468
Behar
69-73
Beresheet A
82, 98, 99, 100, 102, 164, 167, 179, 246, 258, 259, 260, 275, 276, 277, 285, 286, 287, 292, 348, 413-417, 419-423, 429, 430-432, 434, 439, 444, 445, 450, 453-455, 458, 461, 464, 470, 472-474
Beresheet B
2-5, 198, 204, 205, 211-214, 220, 221, 286-288, 302, 304, 310-313, 318, 319, 324, 331, 332, 340, 345, 346, 348-351, 358-365, 367, 369-371, 373-376, 379, 407, 410, 412-415, 428, 429, 436, 437
Beshalach
232-238
Bo
148, 151-153, 198, 201, 204-206, 208, 218

Chayei Sarah
39, 40, 41, 43, 47, 68, 72, 88, 89, 105, 106, 108-110, 144, 201, 220

Chukat
44
Ekev
30, 41, 66, 67, 68
Emor
11, 185, 222, 227a, 334, 336 -338
Idra Raba
204, 259, 261, 326, 328
Kedoshim
55, 61-63, 68-70, 118, 119
Ki Tetze
77, 96
Ki Tisa
105, 115, 116
Korach
36
Lech Lecha
16, 95, 104, 142, 300, 301, 331, 332, 335, 344, 345
Metzora
22
Miketz
131
Mishpatim
315, 316, 476, 481
Naso
20, 83, 125, 139-142
Noach
30-35, 37, 38, 88, 119-121, 139-141, 145, 228, 229, 244, 245, 252, 258, 295, 308, 320, 351, 360, 373, 374, 379
Pekudei
168, 169, 202, 203, 205, 207, 208, 278, 304, 341, 454, 474, 836
Pinchas
44, 97, 100, 101, 202, 262, 287, 288, 329, 466, 489, 587, 597, 604, 630, 771
Prologue
97, 148, 235
Safra Detzniuta
15, 38, 41, 46, 48, 57
Shemot
200, 360
Shlach Lecha
42, 53, 105, 133-135
Shoftim
9
Tazria
44, 45, 91, 106-114, 116, 117, 122, 124
Tetzaveh
28
Toldot
2, 84, 92, 131-133, 138, 141-143, 191, 193
Trumah
214, 283, 332-336, 347, 413, 433, 641, 666, 667, 750, 754, 756-760, 763-766, 794, 834
Tzav
38, 68, 146, 150
Vaera
33, 118
Vaetchanan
34, 64, 95
Vayakhel
27-273, 275, 277, 383, 443
Vayechi
237, 240-242, 259, 301, 369, 384, 501, 523, 571, 573, 612, 801, 802, 803
Vayera
1, 4, 114, 377, 393, 458
Vayeshev
246, 247, 267
Vayetze
21, 22, 112, 385

Vayigash
1, 11, 14, 62, 129
Vayikra
17, 137-139, 142, 315-318, 320, 325
Vayishlach
51, 52, 53, 77, 81, 140, 236
Yitro
62, 64, 65, 66, 125, 148, 170, 178, 224, 226, 406, 407

ADAMAH (SOIL)

Beresheet B
36
Mishpatim
117, 118

ADDER

Vayechi
710, 711, 723
Vayishlach
85

ADIEL (SPIRIT)

Pekudei
544

ADIRIEL (SPIRIT)

Beresheet B
59

ADIRIRIYAH (SPIRIT)

Pekudei
694

ADIRIYAH SANUG'YA (SPIRIT)

Pekudei
494, 496, 497, 500, 506-508, 681

ADONAI

Acharei Mot
83, 157, 163, 277, 288, 334, 336, 389
Balak
17, 18, 49, 51, 271
Beha'alot'cha
50
Beresheet A
11, 37, 60, 185, 189, 236, 238, 395
Beshalach
385
Ekev
19, 22, 26, 38, 40, 41, 47, 50, 55, 61
Emor
188
Ha'azinu
137
Idra Raba
67, 123
Ki Tetze
28, 99, 101, 102, 129
Lech Lecha
319
Miketz
18
Mishpatim
382, 446, 448, 548-550, 561
Naso
180
Pekudei
97, 188, 195, 292, 293, 294, 505-507, 779-783, 785, 790
Pinchas
43, 63, 178, 179, 182, 201, 243, 247, 255, 260-262, 268, 271, 280, 281, 282, 283, 289, 294,

297, 307, 308, 311, 312, 320, 322, 323, 330, 333, 334, 335, 337, 340, 342, 404, 405, 432, 434, 483, 489, 611, 616, 621, 630, 688, 712, 719, 742, 746, 758, 759, 809, 810, 811, 812, 815, 839, 860, 864, 865, 867

Safra Detzniuta
19, 21, 40, 41, 52, 58, 73

Shemot
213, 313, 354

Shoftim
4

Toldot
86, 91, 133

Trumah
404

Tzav
88, 137, 139, 141, 149

Vaera
9, 12, 13, 112, 113

Vaetchanan
1, 12, 176, 177, 178, 190

Vayakhel
341, 342, 343, 344

Vayera
58, 60, 64, 65, 69, 70, 96, 229, 235, 277

Vayetze
108

Vayikra
32, 162, 176, 277, 278, 305, 362, 363

ADRAHINAEL (SPIRIT)

Beresheet B
57

Pekudei
510

ADRIANUS

Beshalach
311

AFRIRA (SPIRIT)

Pekudei
905

Prologue
155

AGIRISON (SPIRIT)

Pekudei
872

AGRAT

Mishpatim
377

AHAB

Bo
96

Lech Lecha
177

Trumah
538

Vayakhel
377

Vayera
412

AHADIEL (SPIRIT)

Pekudei
558, 559, 560, 561, 566

AHADORIYA (SPIRIT)

Pekudei
562

AHANIEL (SPIRIT)

Pekudei
504
Vayera
276
Pekudei
687

AHASUERUS

Ki Tetze
2, 6, 7

AHAVA (SPIRIT)

Beresheet B
123, 129, 133

AHIEL (SPIRIT)

Pekudei
561
Vayera
275

AHIMAN

Shlach Lecha
32, 39, 40, 60

AHIMELECH

Noach
87
Pekudei
67, 186

AHINAEL (ANGEL)

Beresheet B
56

AIR

Acharei Mot
165, 360
Balak
2, 20, 156, 161, 174-176, 344, 347, 419, 420
Beha'alot'cha
135
Beresheet A
22, 29, 32-35, 274
Beresheet B
82, 178
Beshalach
134, 230, 445
Bo
46, 47, 55, 143, 203, 204, 241
Chukat
27, 28, 82
Ekev
65
Emor
296
Ha'azinu
115, 116, 118, 154, 155, 167, 178, 200, 238
Idra Raba
21, 37, 38, 91, 156, 181-183, 187, 251, 338, 344
Ki Tetze
58, 119, 140, 145
Lech Lecha
8, 78, 79, 100, 101, 102, 183
Metzora
39
Mishpatim
15, 27, 150, 214, 248, 482
Naso
54
Noach
122-124, 126, 192, 255

Pekudei
109, 110, 135, 136, 338, 340, 407, 505, 546, 573, 638, 665, 666, 670, 790, 864, 930
Pinchas
56, 223, 430, 436, 479, 480, 588, 627, 809
Prologue
76, 88, 89, 109
Safra Detzniuta
6, 26
Shemot
163, 178, 219, 222, 224, 225
Shlach Lecha
152, 153, 217, 218, 221, 229, 231, 239, 250, 287, 288
Shmini
58, 118
Tazria
117
Tetzaveh
92, 94
Trumah
11, 330, 379, 470, 582, 600, 601, 607, 610, 612, 615, 619
Tzav
45, 147
Vaera
33-35, 38-40, 43-48, 50, 88, 97
Vaetchanan
160
Vayakhel
128-134, 136, 137, 146, 470
Vayechi
31, 160, 315, 509
Vayera
52, 71, 73, 94, 171, 305, 382
Vayetze
192, 259, 260
Vayikra
2, 13, 22-25, 280, 431, 432
Vayishlach
134, 136
Yitro
250, 252, 253, 279, 282, 302, 365, 513

ALMOND

Shemot
261, 262
Vayetze
308, 309, 314, 316

ALMOND (AARON'S STAFF)

Shemot
261, 262
Vayetze
308, 309, 314, 316

ALMOND TREE

Shemot
262

ALMS

Vayeshev
28
Vayetze
115, 367

ALPHABET

Acharei Mot
303
Beresheet A
11, 34
Beresheet B
348

Ekev
29, 41
Korach
49
Miketz
241
Mishpatim
298, 359
Noach
22
Pekudei
134, 139, 142, 181, 791
Pinchas
129, 184, 200, 611, 739, 792
Prologue
23, 116
Safra Detzniuta
40
Shlach Lecha
288, 289
Tetzaveh
24, 122
Trumah
102, 106, 110, 113, 114, 477, 616, 618-620, 622, 882
Vayakhel
212
Vayetze
261, 264
Vayikra
155, 157
Yitro
26, 138, 139

ALTAR

Acharei Mot
13, 145, 176, 179, 247, 309
Balak
112, 220, 255, 280, 281, 396, 453, 454, 478, 479
Bechukotai
9
Beha'alot'cha
9, 48-50, 51
Behar
1-5, 28, 40, 43
Bemidbar
31, 35, 60, 61
Beresheet A
424
Beresheet B
25, 210, 211, 411
Beshalach
473-475, 485
Bo
13
Ekev
19
Emor
48, 293
Ha'azinu
148a, 148b, 151
Idra Raba
234
Kedoshim
122
Ki Tisa
88, 90, 93, 94, 95, 96, 97
Korach
25
Lech Lecha
69-71, 82-84, 160, 166, 169, 273, 430, 431, 433
Metzora
12, 63
Mishpatim
225, 304, 451, 491, 524, 573, 574
Naso
197

Noach
13, 97, 109, 118, 120, 121, 127, 157-160, 225, 228, 229, 240
Pekudei
65, 159, 322, 355, 368, 942, 943, 944, 945
Pinchas
32, 205, 212, 216, 342, 422, 438, 528, 529, 755, 795, 801, 886
Prologue
96, 97
Shemot
364, 367-369, 375
Shlach Lecha
87
Shoftim
8
Tetzaveh
60, 70, 76, 139
Toldot
159
Trumah
63, 68, 72, 229, 237, 238, 277, 471, 651
Tzav
6, 21, 23-26, 47, 50, 52, 55, 70, 72, 73, 76-79, 81-88, 109, 114, 128, 129, 131-134, 143, 151
Vayakhel
174, 258, 379, 467, 471, 472, 474
Vayechi
420, 788
Vayera
74, 123, 142, 146, 501, 504, 507
Vayeshev
37, 114
Vayetze
62, 372
Vayikra
53, 63, 197, 314, 414-419, 421, 442
Vayishlach
136, 158-162, 222, 229
Yitro
482, 572

AMALEK

Balak
97, 169, 170, 276
Beresheet A
222-224, 225, 231, 287, 291
Beshalach
436, 437, 441-444, 453-457, 459, 460, 463, 464, 467-469, 471, 472, 485, 486
Emor
266
Kedoshim
59
Ki Tetze
109, 110, 111
Mishpatim
489
Naso
13
Pekudei
191, 295
Pinchas
106, 703, 750
Shlach Lecha
65, 80, 82, 330
Tzav
87
Vayakhel
1, 2, 5, 6

Vayechi
61, 72, 87
Vayikra
127

AMALEKIM

Beresheet A
224, 225, 269

AMEN

Acharei Mot
413
Balak
507
Bechukotai
61
Behar
85
Bemidbar
77
Beresheet B
15, 193, 194, 448
Beshalach
177
Bo
246
Chukat
90
Ekev
5, 6, 21
Emor
144, 340
Idra Raba
4
Ki Tetze
24
Ki Tisa
39
Metzora
60
Mishpatim
206
Naso
199
Noach
67, 68, 388
Pekudei
625, 959
Pinchas
134, 307, 311, 312
Safra Detzniuta
43
Shlach Lecha
95, 348
Toldot
208
Trumah
57, 71, 720, 721
Tzav
181, 193
Vaetchanan
198
Vayakhel
225, 496
Vayelech
36-42, 45, 46, 49
Vayera
422
Vayeshev
285
Vayikra
337, 388
Vayishlach
278
Yitro
38, 488, 498

AMIDAH (STANDING PRAYER)

Balak
198, 200, 205
Bemidbar
73
Beresheet A
189, 244
Chayei Sarah
232, 234, 235
Emor
176
Ki Tetze
45, 49, 129, 132
Mishpatim
114, 395, 396
Pekudei
790, 797, 811
Pinchas
41, 261, 281, 282, 304, 305, 306, 312, 338, 349, 350, 564, 566, 569, 583, 596, 610, 719, 789, 821, 855
Trumah
43, 45, 54, 115-117, 121, 225, 247, 546, 785
Vayakhel
109, 111, 256, 411
Vayechi
394
Vayigash
9
Vayikra
32, 33

AMMINADAB

Chukat
39
Yitro
380

AMON

Miketz
123
Mishpatim
241, 242, 244
Prologue
135
Vayechi
54
Vayera
297, 309, 334, 336, 337
Vayishlach
155, 156

AMORITES

Balak
9, 11, 12, 14, 244
Shlach Lecha
65
Vayakhel
416
Vayera
373

AMRAFEL

Lech Lecha
211

AMRAM

Beresheet B
416
Mishpatim
387, 389, 390
Shemot
183, 185, 335-339

ANAEL (SPIRIT)

Vayakhel
138
Vayera
276
Vayetze
73

ANAH

Vayishlach
260, 263, 264

ANAKIM

Beresheet A
224, 231, 269

ANATOT

Noach
84, 86, 87
Trumah
406
Vayechi
829, 830, 831, 833

ANCIENT OF DAYS (ATIK YOMIN)

Beresheet A
159
Chayei Sarah
130
Ha'azinu
116, 127
Prologue
62, 63, 64, 118, 186
Toldot
151
Vayechi
689
Vayeshev
183

ANFIEL (SPIRIT)

Vayakhel
133, 147

ANGEL OF DEATH

Acharei Mot
136
Balak
13, 363, 368
Behar
40
Beresheet A
266, 440, 460-463, 478, 479
Beresheet B
37, 167, 297, 298, 302, 319, 320, 333, 334, 336, 422
Chayei Sarah
68, 70, 213, 220, 221
Chukat
26
Emor
6
Ki Tetze
58
Ki Tisa
113
Korach
46
Miketz
1, 196
Mishpatim
148, 165, 364, 430, 431
Naso
40, 117

Noach
77, 78, 135, 197, 200, 213, 244
Pekudei
115, 299, 385, 551, 552, 587, 838, 841, 859, 872,
Pinchas
22, 270, 364, 409, 410, 414, 415, 464, 467, 468, 590
Prologue
246
Shemot
349
Shlach Lecha
139, 282
Shmini
118
Toldot
52, 175
Trumah
432, 433, 437, 438, 469, 475, 675, 678, 747, 892
Tzav
61
Vaetchanan
10
Vayakhel
26-28, 30, 32-38, 41, 42, 92, 99, 473
Vayechi
148, 152, 577
Vayera
55, 56, 251, 326, 375, 378
Vayetze
288
Vayigash
80, 87, 114, 115
Vayishlach
47, 191, 192

ANGELS

Acharei Mot
16, 136, 152, 153, 219-221, 264, 265, 303, 350, 359, 363, 388, 391, 392
Balak
13, 16, 25, 26, 42, 47-51, 53, 86, 90, 91, 104, 105, 107, 111, 113, 238, 304-306, 363, 368, 408, 409, 410-413, 416, 419, 420, 427, 428, 431-433, 442, 443, 445, 479
Bechukotai
50
Beha'alot'cha
6-8, 33, 34, 59, 101-103, 112, 118, 121, 124
Behar
18, 33-36, 40, 43, 44
Beresheet A
58, 70, 76, 77, 82, 94, 95, 116, 145, 171, 177-179, 184, 191, 204, 226, 227, 249, 258, 266, 406, 407, 410, 411, 438, 440, 454, 460-465, 467, 468, 472, 474, 478, 479
Beresheet B
3, 11, 19, 37, 39, 41-53, 55, 57 -59, 66-68, 71, 82, 93, 108, 119, 121, 153, 166, 167, 169, 190, 297, 298, 302, 309, 319, 320, 333-336, 361-365, 385, 392, 406, 407, 409, 422-424
Beshalach
25, 35, 64, 134, 138, 140, 146, 147, 149, 150, 153, 155, 157, 159, 165, 172, 174, 184, 190, 231, 237, 260, 261, 298 -301, 303, 316, 365,

372, 376, 420,
Bo
1-3, 65, 101, 201-203, 228
Chayei Sarah
12, 42, 56, 57, 58, 59, 60, 68, 70, 81, 125, 133, 150, 157, 158, 165, 169, 175, 176, 213, 216, 220, 221, 227
Chukat
26, 32, 57
Ekev
24, 34, 67
Emor
6, 8, 78, 90, 92, 109, 113, 136, 186, 222, 315
Ha'azinu
4, 5, 9, 28, 164, 223, 236, 239, 259
Idra Raba
9, 10, 169, 227, 247, 336, 353-355, 357, 361
Kedoshim
42, 55, 62, 90, 92
Ki Tetze
9, 24, 31, 32, 33, 37, 42, 58, 82, 100, 108, 125, 126, 127, 129, 137, 138
Ki Tisa
113
Korach
46, 60
Lech Lecha
8, 84, 97, 100, 123, 136, 138, 216, 218, 289, 290-295, 315 -317, 361, 362, 386, 407
Metzora
2, 8, 11, 12, 34, 52-54, 61, 62
Miketz
1, 40, 124, 135, 196
Mishpatim
2, 123, 148, 165, 235, 236, 263, 335, 336, 364, 391, 417, 419, 422, 426, 430, 431, 445, 455, 458, 460, 465, 476, 496, 551, 555, 557-561
Naso
9, 40, 42, 45, 53, 57, 98, 111, 114, 115, 116, 117, 137, 138, 160, 194
Noach
35, 38, 41, 42, 66, 67, 77-81, 89, 113, 135, 137, 149, 196, 197, 200, 202, 211, 213 -215, 236, 244, 258, 346, 373
Pekudei
115, 140, 167, 212, 219, 220, 299, 357, 385, 466, 490, 523, 524, 551, 552, 555, 563, 564, 569, 571, 577, 579, 581, 582, 587, 711, 767, 768, 780, 791, 838, 841, 845, 859, 872, 880, 883
Pinchas
3, 14, 16, 22, 23, 24, 39, 42, 43, 51, 77, 78, 86, 88, 126, 147, 168, 176, 188, 212, 221, 223, 235, 237, 240, 250, 258, 270, 281, 293, 302, 306, 311, 319, 321, 322, 333, 334, 339, 342, 343, 349, 364, 372, 398, 401, 409, 410, 414, 415, 417, 420, 421, 430, 464, 467, 468, 500, 501, 503, 558, 578, 590, 599, 650, 750, 762, 763, 764, 827, 884
Prologue
56, 66, 110, 111, 131, 137, 138, 150, 152, 155, 160, 176, 216, 217, 220, 221, 246
Safra Detzniuta
69

Shemot
2, 15, 17, 18, 36, 38, 45, 48, 49, 51, 52, 54, 55, 61, 63, 77, 79, 85, 88, 110, 124, 125, 157, 182, 213, 242, 247, 269, 272, 280, 295, 296, 311, 316, 323, 324, 332, 348-352, 359, 360, 383, 388, 390, 396

Shlach Lecha
24, 29, 48, 74, 88, 100, 139, 171, 173, 199, 224, 230, 232, 244, 253, 282, 294, 307, 314, 321

Shmini
78, 79, 118

Tazria
4, 38, 52, 54, 55, 57, 60, 82, 183, 184, 185

Tetzaveh
114

Toldot
8, 37, 38, 41, 47, 48, 52, 72, 162, 163, 164, 165, 166, 170, 175, 201

Trumah
47, 50, 52, 54, 55, 93, 94, 115, 176, 183, 234, 241, 264, 265, 296, 300, 304, 335, 339, 341, 363, 376, 377, 385, 386, 388, 392, 432, 433, 437, 438, 446, 453, 456, 458, 460, 461, 466, 468, 469, 474, 475, 508, 553, 557, 592, 596, 642-644, 675, 678, 681, 691, 697, 747, 807, 816, 824, 825, 863, 865, 866, 867, 869, 870, 872-874, 892

Tzav
8, 58, 61, 125, 126, 128, 129, 130, 138

Vaera
160, 170, 201

Vaetchanan
7, 10, 98, 179, 182, 183, 195

Vayakhel
15, 16, 20, 23, 24, 26, 27, 28, 30, 32-38, 40-42, 46, 51, 54, 55, 92, 99, 108, 142, 208, 260, 284, 296, 298, 301, 302, 309, 324, 354, 378, 380, 435, 461, 473

Vayechi
15, 35, 45, 46, 50, 52, 53, 54, 148, 152, 173, 204, 229, 285, 384, 385, 394, 395, 398, 399, 404, 405, 425, 439, 441, 449, 450, 451, 453, 454, 467-469, 474, 546, 553, 572, 577, 594, 595, 727, 743, 788, 843

Vayelech
5

Vayera
30, 41, 54, 55, 56, 57, 59, 70, 72, 73, 74, 75, 86, 93, 96, 97, 99, 100, 101, 103, 104, 107, 113, 118, 121, 123, 130, 131, 136, 137, 139, 140, 147, 167, 168, 170, 171, 172, 174, 200, 201, 202, 224, 228, 232, 235, 238, 251, 274, 278, 284, 287-289, 326, 346, 362, 367, 369, 370, 373, 374, 375, 378, 411, 412, 414-416, 474, 486, 504-506, 509-511

Vayeshev
77, 78, 84, 85, 88, 159, 199, 200, 210, 212, 244, 245, 246

Vayetze
45, 46, 53, 54, 55, 70, 71, 72, 73, 101, 108, 120, 122, 190,

204, 255, 258, 262, 273, 288, 317, 318, 320, 347, 348, 371, 384, 386, 387, 388, 389, 390, 391
Vayigash
8, 9, 49, 80, 83, 87, 108, 114, 115
Vayikra
9, 11, 14, 22-24, 36, 132, 284, 345, 370, 426, 427, 432, 433, 442
Vayishlach
1, 3, 4, 5, 6, 7, 10, 11, 13, 14, 44, 47, 48, 100-103, 162, 182 -184, 187, 191, 192
Yitro
32, 52, 236, 284, 571, 572

ANGER

Beresheet A
44, 47, 51, 52, 53, 58, 118, 184, 265, 267, 441, 458
Ki Tisa
20, 25, 33, 65, 91, 92
Prologue
129, 138, 144
Tetzaveh
24, 54-58, 60, 61, 101
Vaetchanan
48

ANGERAYON (SPIRIT)

Pekudei
870

ANIEL (SPIRIT)

Pekudei
531

ANIMALS

Balak
8, 80, 495
Beha'alot'cha
116
Behar
44, 46
Beresheet A
80, 121, 123, 285, 291, 302, 432
Beresheet B
66, 286
Beshalach
101
Bo
67, 110, 119, 197, 213,
Emor
48, 59, 61, 72, 185
Ha'azinu
189
Idra Raba
342, 343
Kedoshim
5
Ki Tetze
33
Ki Tisa
49, 67
Lech Lecha
299, 300, 302
Mishpatim
11, 445, 453, 459, 463, 469, 570
Naso
42, 45, 53, 54
Noach
73, 119, 192, 261, 264, 266
Pekudei
1, 338-342, 349, 355, 490, 499,

500, 519, 526-529, 531, 536, 561, 562, 619, 620, 621, 622-628, 637, 640, 642-644, 680, 686, 692, 786, 789, 797
Pinchas
66, 145, 154, 219, 221, 485, 529-532, 534, 538, 540, 543, 547, 563, 692, 697, 699, 700, 703, 705, 708, 715, 718, 719, 728, 729, 740, 764
Prologue
223
Safra Detzniuta
52
Shemot
2, 84, 94, 236, 349
Shlach Lecha
22
Shmini
14, 99, 102-108
Tazria
36, 141
Tetzaveh
111
Trumah
239, 299, 464, 812, 859
Tzav
68, 70, 82, 83
Vaera
96, 170, 189, 190
Vaetchanan
36
Vayakhel
55, 59, 323, 324, 471, 472, 486
Vayechi
621
Vayeshev
72, 243
Vayigash
123, 124, 125, 129
Vayikra
69, 283, 317, 366, 440, 441
Vayishlach
101, 117, 137, 144, 150
Yitro
310

ANOINTMENT

Acharei Mot
34, 46, 87, 88
Balak
438
Beha'alot'cha
99
Behar
27, 38
Beshalach
207, 354
Bo
59
Ekev
56
Emor
10, 12, 14, 21, 25, 154, 290
Ha'azinu
175
Idra Raba
73, 87, 89, 164, 249, 256
Mishpatim
531, 532, 535, 536
Noach
296
Pekudei
129, 557-560, 756
Pinchas
662

Shlach Lecha
111
Shmini
27, 53, 54
Tetzaveh
114
Toldot
21
Trumah
160, 398, 489, 490, 534, 535
Tzav
162, 164, 168, 177
Vayakhel
55
Vayechi
758, 856
Vayeshev
258
Vayigash
45, 86
Vayikra 1
96, 415, 418
Yitro
121

APPLES

Acharei Mot
317, 318
Balak
131, 420
Ekev
4
Emor
124
Ha'azinu
9, 10, 11, 35, 117, 150, 162, 165, 250
Idra Raba
17, 141-147, 159, 186, 254, 289, 290, 327
Lech Lecha
196, 199, 201, 202
Mishpatim
492, 515
Pekudei
57
Pinchas
45, 203, 204, 511, 559
Safra Detzniuta
16, 34
Shemot
264
Shlach Lecha
108, 248, 250, 251
Shmini
80, 82
Toldot
133, 135, 151
Trumah
595
Vaetchanan
66
Vayakhel
181, 252
Vayechi
307, 342, 833
Vayera
36
Vayetze
98, 108
Vayikra
427

ARAB

Shemot
290

ARAD

Emor
260a, 265, 266

Vayelech
2

ARAM

Balak
121, 124, 136, 154, 422, 425
Beresheet A
210
Beresheet B
28, 163,
Chayei Sarah
81
Lech Lecha
277
Pinchas
383, 491
Vayeshev
56
Vayetze
48, 89, 312
Vayishlach
22

ARAM TZOVA

Pinchas
383, 491

ARAMAIC

Acharei Mot
45, 282
Balak
72, 197
Beresheet A
239, 339
Beresheet B
57, 160, 340
Beshalach
61, 284, 401
Bo
149
Chayei Sarah
42, 43
Chukat
71
Emor
71, 288
Idra Raba
19, 151
Kedoshim
41
Ki Tisa
95
Lech Lecha
42, 81, 288, 289, 290, 291
Metzora
23
Mishpatim
1, 197, 272, 489
Pekudei
362
Pinchas
206, 489, 563, 732, 855
Prologue
40, 152, 160
Safra Detzniuta
39, 41
Shlach Lecha
59
Tazria
71, 84, 91
Tetzaveh
70
Toldot
8, 62, 182, 194
Trumah
57, 58, 115, 117, 118, 910
Tzav
14

Vayechi
56, 224, 530
Vayelech
44
Vayera
203, 411
Vayetze
156
Vayikra
177, 445
Vayishlach
34
Yitro
5, 246, 248

ARAMI

Mishpatim
564

ARAVAH

Emor
331
Ki Tetze
145

ARAVOT

Beshalach
267-269
Chayei Sarah
143
Ha'azinu
13
Trumah
709, 710, 711, 796

ARICH ANPIN

Prologue
7

ARIEL (SUPERNAL MINISTER)

Pekudei
583, 585
Vayikra
14

ARIES

Miketz
164

ARK OF THE COVENANT

Beha'alot'cha
128, 132
Beresheet A
212
Pekudei
292, 762, 763, 766, 767, 768
Prologue
17
Shlach Lecha
14
Vayechi
392
Vayelech
21
Vayera
69
Vayetze
108

ARK OF THE TESTIMONY

Shemot
282

ARK

Acharei Mot
51-55, 57

Balak
268, 299, 300
Bechukotai
9
Beha'alot'cha
12-14, 17, 88, 89, 127-133
Behar
19
Bemidbar
29
Beresheet A
212, 337, 394, 395, 398
Beresheet B
137, 242
Chayei Sarah
28
Emor
249
Idra Raba
149
Ki Tetze
57
Korach
38
Mishpatim
30, 470
Noach
1, 5-7, 11, 12, 26, 27, 34, 38, 72, 73, 78, 80, 81, 93, 132, 133, 155, 165-167, 176-178, 181, 194, 200-202, 204, 205, 212, 213, 215, 221, 232, 249, 250, 255, 258, 293, 294, 296, 297, 301
Pekudei
41-43, 124, 256, 257, 258, 292, 340, 341, 409, 755, 756, 762, 763, 766-768
Pinchas
168, 554, 755, 777, 778, 827, 828, 829, 884
Prologue
17
Shemot
189, 213, 282
Shlach Lecha
14, 87, 138
Tetzaveh
143
Trumah
211, 213, 573, 594, 595
Vayakhel
39, 375-377, 381, 383-386, 390, 494
Vayechi
332, 392, 396, 574, 696, 858, 859, 860
Vayelech
20, 21
Vayera
69, 218, 257
Vayeshev
77, 207
Vayetze
34, 35, 108
Vayikra
236, 283
Vayishlach
227

ARKA (GROUND)

Beresheet B
36, 38, 343
Mishpatim
117
Prologue
153
Vayetze
222, 227

ARMAGEDDON

Beshalach
290, 312, 459
Yitro
458

ARNON

Balak
9
Beshalach
251, 255

ARROWS

Toldot
142, 143
Vaetchanan
170
Vayechi
775
Vayeshev
185

ARVIT (EVENING PRAYER)

Ki Tetze
46
Korach
48
Pinchas
207
Trumah
63
Tzav
47
Vaetchanan
84

ASAEL

Chayei Sarah
42

ASHER

Acharei Mot
164, 166-168
Beha'alot'cha
118, 123
Beresheet A
6
Beresheet B
184, 210, 211
Beshalach
42
Emor
158
Mishpatim
69, 202
Pekudei
178
Shlach Lecha
263
Vayechi
527, 541, 542, 543, 729, 751-754, 757, 758
Vayera
68
Vayetze
243
Vayikra
166
Yitro
389

ASHERAH

Beresheet B
210, 211

ASIMON (SPIRIT)

Pekudei
562

Prologue
252
Pekudei
699

ASIRTA (SPIRIT)

Pekudei
919, 920
Pinchas
415

ASISANIYAH (SPIRIT)

Pekudei
694

ASIYAH

Acharei Mot
273
Balak
311, 312
Beha'alot'cha
63
Behar
43
Beresheet A
63, 77, 83, 109, 114, 260, 282, 302, 401, 407, 445
Beresheet B
29, 33, 39, 53, 69, 76, 268, 420
Beshalach
225, 273, 411
Chukat
29
Emor
58, 158
Ha'azinu
187, 190, 195, 224, 228
Idra Raba
20, 177, 179, 340
Kedoshim
57
Ki Tetze
30, 38
Ki Tisa
82
Korach
9
Lech Lecha
214
Mishpatim
5, 11, 336, 351, 352, 403
Noach
61, 62
Pekudei
1, 2, 210, 222, 339, 737
Pinchas
223, 225, 230, 283, 294, 456, 502, 515, 692, 700
Safra Detzniuta
63
Shemot
1, 137, 310
Shlach Lecha
48, 345
Tazria
4
Trumah
175, 176, 287, 493, 494, 495, 531, 532
Tzav
57, 64, 65, 75
Vaera
34, 103
Vaetchanan
21
Vayakhel
136, 137, 142, 143, 275,

283-285, 318
Vayechi
118, 119, 284, 408, 716, 753, 806
Vayera
232
Vayetze
92, 116, 120, 148, 160, 242, 262, 305, 306, 310, 318, 335, 337
Vayikra
149, 152
Yitro
10, 327

ASKARA (SPIRIT)

Pekudei
549, 553, 596, 604, 871, 920

ASMODEUS

Balak
182
Miketz
132
Tazria
16
Trumah
36
Vayikra
322

ASS (DONKEY)

Chayei Sarah
76
Ki Tetze
4, 5, 62
Ki Tisa
84, 85, 88, 100
Miketz
226
Mishpatim
16
Vayechi
31, 582, 588, 590, 626-629, 681, 682, 684, 685, 690
Vayetze
228, 275
Vayishlach
24, 145, 146, 147, 148, 149, 151, 263

ASSIR

Mishpatim
228

ASSYRIANS

Bo
101
Miketz
124
Shemot
94, 95, 100, 129, 260
Shlach Lecha
198
Tazria
124
Vayechi
547

Vayera
415
Vayigash
105

ASTIRIYA (SPIRIT)

Pekudei
854

ASTROLOGY

Acharei Mot
89, 91, 145, 146, 196, 263, 366, 406, 408, 409
Balak
1, 6, 104, 142, 501
Bechukotai
22, 29, 36, 39
Beha'alot'cha
4, 57, 70, 139, 148
Behar
29
Bemidbar
9, 11
Beresheet A
3, 37, 39, 101, 103, 110, 113, 116, 126-128, 153-155, 277, 281, 390, 396, 397, 401-404, 478, 479
Beresheet B
49, 57, 65, 69, 82, 84, 94, 112, 113, 124, 161-164, 211, 296, 297, 302, 303, 306-309, 397
Beshalach
160, 267
Bo
158-160, 169-171, 174, 175, 187
Chayei Sarah
30, 67, 71, 167, 205, 206
Chukat
34, 38-42, 44, 46, 59, 87
Ekev
16, 35, 44, 65
Emor
70, 132, 134, 139, 151, 180, 181, 187, 190, 205, 206, 209, 224, 257, 315
Ha'azinu
14, 15, 17, 204
Idra Raba
149, 150, 362, 363
Kedoshim
45, 46, 63
Ki Tetze
32, 40, 70, 84, 112-114, 116, 117-123
Ki Tisa
6, 10, 110, 111, 115-119
Korach
41
Lech Lecha
27, 114, 223, 224, 322-324, 328, 361, 384, 449
Metzora
8, 60
Miketz
29, 73, 80, 112, 113, 134, 164
Mishpatim
212, 336, 460, 573
Naso
13, 14, 55, 190, 196
Noach
35, 66, 96, 101-106, 108, 129, 149, 169, 245, 247, 251, 319, 361, 362, 364, 365
Pekudei
27, 161, 216, 222, 223, 224, 234, 235, 279, 281, 336, 348, 378, 503, 549, 550, 562, 579, 734, 757, 812, 871, 920, 924, 940, 953
Pinchas
35b, 59, 64, 65, 66, 126, 136, 139, 236, 270, 360, 383, 384, 385, 444, 478, 496, 498, 671, 674-679, 683, 684, 686, 687,

688, 689, 690, 706, 717, 720, 737, 738, 739, 777, 820
Prologue
11, 19, 21, 104, 139, 164
Safra Detzniuta
25
Shemot
1, 14, 101, 107, 155, 159, 174, 191, 305
Shlach Lecha
8, 31, 53, 54, 112, 124, 142, 205, 311
Shmini
1, 9, 50, 90
Shoftim
14, 15
Tazria
16, 62, 76, 77, 78
Tetzaveh
2, 3, 31, 32, 34, 38, 40, 83, 88, 90-92, 116, 118, 122, 124
Toldot
6, 10, 12, 13, 25, 27, 31, 98, 115, 128, 168, 196
Trumah
2, 3, 107, 168, 171, 200, 203, 205, 209, 212, 221, 294, 301, 304, 313, 333, 347, 355, 361, 362, 381, 551, 581, 708, 753, 831, 832, 834-847, 849, 859, 863
Tzav
48
Vaera
24, 130, 134, 135, 159
Vaetchanan
15, 180, 181, 182
Vayakhel
10, 13, 24, 78, 159, 160, 162, 200, 210, 221, 286, 333, 396 -400, 402, 410, 489
Vayechi
208, 276, 281, 286, 288-290, 310, 311, 335, 359, 452, 502, 540, 564, 565, 566, 574, 589, 590, 597, 614, 615, 619, 673, 702, 781, 793, 807, 808, 813, 829-834, 840, 841
Vayelech
4, 5, 6, 12, 14
Vayera
40, 83, 244, 246, 252, 253, 254, 290, 353, 384, 385, 405, 406, 478
Vayeshev
6, 21, 22, 32, 34, 38-40, 42, 44, 45, 47, 48, 55, 63, 68, 152, 196, 198, 200, 203, 272, 275
Vayetze
16, 55, 57, 58, 128, 332, 346, 354, 385
Vayigash
94, 108, 130
Vayikra
132, 135, 184, 354, 371, 379, 380
Vayishlach
12, 57, 64, 75, 80, 90, 93, 94, 137, 163, 240
Yitro
130, 133, 135, 146, 183, 184, 212, 225, 238, 239, 241, 288, 379-384, 402, 505

ATAD

Vayechi
815, 822, 850

ATARIEL (SPIRIT)

Pekudei
684

ATARIM

Emor
265
Vayelech
2

ATBASH CIPHER

Trumah
106, 110, 618

ATIK YOMIN (ANCIENT OF DAYS)

Beresheet A
159
Chayei Sarah
130
Ha'azinu
116, 127
Prologue
62, 63, 64, 118, 186
Toldot
151
Vayeshev
183

ATIKA KADISHA

Acharei Mot
224, 408, 409, 411, 412
Balak
158
Beha'alot'cha
63
Beshalach
172, 180, 181, 215, 372, 386, 395
Emor
295, 299, 300, 302
Ha'azinu
30-34, 36, 37, 38, 39, 41-43, 47-50, 53, 54, 57, 58, 61, 62, 64, 65, 66, 69-72, 74, 76, 77, 90, 94, 95, 98, 100, 108, 109, 114-116, 118, 123, 131, 133, 143, 147, 148b, 149, 151, 163, 165, 166, 167, 175
Idra Raba
14, 17, 19, 233, 244, 245, 249, 278, 283, 284, 289, 290, 293, 298-300, 314, 326
Mishpatim
521, 523, 524, 525, 531
Naso
162, 164, 173,
Prologue
7, 146
Safra Detzniuta
28, 46, 49
Shlach Lecha
36, 91
Trumah
418, 910, 913
Vaetchanan
37, 59, 144
Vayechi
156, 180, 331
Vayetze
30
Vayikra
103, 245-247, 259, 260, 261, 332, 341, 360, 445

Yitro
327, 338, 370, 448, 449, 463, 468, 483

ATIK-YOMIN

Balak
298
Idra Raba
5, 9, 20, 23, 59, 61, 65, 66, 105, 106, 115, 129, 138, 139, 152, 163, 171, 175, 182, 186, 188, 189, 197, 199, 201, 206, 216, 220, 221, 229, 244, 246, 269, 271, 278, 279, 280, 284, 285, 329

ATONEMENT

Acharei Mot
9, 28, 29, 130, 145, 176, 179 -181, 188, 194, 195, 223, 239, 244, 406, 409
Bechukotai
9
Behar
40
Beresheet A
179, 180
Beshalach
10, 71, 474
Bo
12, 160, 176
Chayei Sarah
257
Chukat
35
Emor
157, 223, 224, 228, 248
Kedoshim
10, 122
Korach
27
Lech Lecha
90, 91, 92, 98, 298, 302, 303, 427
Metzora
42
Mishpatim
409
Naso
128, 129, 142, 143
Noach
99, 131, 228
Pekudei
71, 73, 333, 546, 857, 956,
Pinchas
28, 31, 52, 109, 111, 112, 221, 261, 354, 366, 367, 403, 474, 522, 524, 671, 674, 679, 681, 682, 683, 797, 807, 808, 812, 813, 826, 827, 836, 881-884
Prologue
96, 135
Shemot
367, 369
Shmini
29, 46, 47
Tetzaveh
64, 96, 112, 114, 116
Toldot
148
Trumah
113, 157, 160, 473, 707
Tzav
135
Vaera
112
Vayakhel
219, 449, 465, 470, 480, 483

Vayechi
187, 217, 297, 301, 318, 420, 494
Vayera
128, 132, 298, 386, 454
Vayeshev
226, 251
Vayigash
29
Vayikra
72, 164, 190, 250, 256, 293, 300-302, 392, 419, 440
Vayishlach
176
Yitro
301, 479

ATTRIBUTES OF MERCY, THIRTEEN

Tetzaveh
20

ATZILUT

Behar
33-35, 37, 42, 43
Beresheet A
109, 114, 131, 164, 165, 256-259, 263, 271, 272, 302, 401, 470
Beresheet B
39, 53, 55, 130-132, 169, 268, 309
Bo
40, 41, 226, 227
Chayei Sarah
24
Emor
58
Ha'azinu
187, 224,
Idra Raba
179, 304,
Kedoshim
52-54, 56, 57, 70
Ki Tetze
30, 34, 36, 37, 45, 75, 76, 128, 137-139
Korach
9, 10
Lech Lecha
99, 101-103, 212
Mishpatim
3, 5-8, 12, 13, 403, 442, 455
Noach
7, 12, 62, 102, 328, 336
Pekudei
103, 340, 342, 361, 478, 494, 533-535, 665, 667, 672, 711, 729, 732, 740, 749, 752, 755, 756, 757, 763, 764, 769, 770, 771, 789, 795-797, 817, 820, 821, 906
Pinchas
39, 224, 225, 226, 230, 251, 259, 294, 316, 332, 738, 739
Safra Detzniuta
57, 63, 64, 65
Shemot
249, 309, 310
Shlach Lecha
46, 47, 87, 88, 90
Tetzaveh
126, 133
Toldot
151
Trumah
219, 236, 289, 292, 298, 301 -304, 336, 378, 396, 757, 919

Tzav
13, 64, 65, 75
Vaera
34, 103
Vaetchanan
191
Vayakhel
104, 143, 149, 275, 277, 283, 285, 292, 304, 310, 311, 313, 316, 325, 333, 339
Vayechi
285, 397, 568, 572, 753, 806
Vayera
69, 488
Vayeshev
54
Vayetze
45, 160, 163, 166, 236, 337, 363
Vayigash
132
Vayikra
152, 434
Yitro
6

AV (MONTH)

Beresheet A
371
Ekev
17, 36
Lech Lecha
13
Prologue
135
Shemot
193
Shlach Lecha
313
Trumah
159, 162,
Vayishlach
103, 104,
Yitro
241, 486

AVADON

Korach
32
Noach
70
Vayelech
44, 45, 46

AWL

Mishpatim
221, 272, 287, 288, 393
Vaetchanan
19

AYA

Vayishlach
260

AZA

Balak
416, 417, 419, 421-425, 494 -498
Beresheet A
102, 178, 179, 226, 228, 464, 466, 468
Chayei Sarah
81

AZAEL (SUPERNAL MINISTER)

Balak
172, 416, 417, 419, 421-425,

494-498
Beresheet A
102, 178, 179, 226, 228, 464, 466, 468
Beresheet B
353, 423, 424
Chayei Sarah
81
Pinchas
390, 391
Prologue
156
Vayikra
23

AZARIAH

Acharei Mot
14-18
Mishpatim
569
Noach
357
Toldot
123

AZAZEL

Acharei Mot
116, 118, 120, 123, 127, 134, 137
Emor
39, 234-237, 244, 271
Naso
58
Pekudei
944
Pinchas
679, 681
Tetzaveh
100, 104, 138
Toldot
80, 129
Trumah
565
Tzav
42, 43
Vayetze
116

AZPIEL (SPIRIT)

Pekudei
694

AZRIEL

Pekudei
531, 544, 692
Vayakhel
139, 142

AZUZYAH (SPIRIT)

Pekudei
692

BAAL

Beresheet B
210, 211
Pinchas
472, 473, 474
Vayigash
86

BAAL PE'OR

Pinchas
472, 473, 474

BABEL

Beresheet A
224, 349

Ki Tetze
40
Noach
338, 340, 355, 366, 377
Pekudei
324, 371, 372
Shemot
8-13, 59, 75, 91, 142
Trumah
79, 767, 896
Vayakhel
20
Vayera
255
Yitro
26, 513

BABY

Miketz
246, 247

BABYLON

Acharei Mot
182
Balak
287
Bemidbar
24
Beresheet A
224, 349
Bo
45, 164
Emor
22
Ki Tisa
33
Lech Lecha
188, 282, 474, 475
Miketz
203, 205, 234
Noach
335, 338, 355, 366, 377
Pekudei
324, 371, 372
Pinchas
17
Shemot
8-13, 59, 76, 91, 142-144
Shlach Lecha
28
Toldot
188
Trumah
79, 767, 896
Vayakhel
20
Vayechi
23, 313, 576, 578
Vayera
255, 327, 388
Vayeshev
221
Vayetze
47
Vayikra
265
Yitro
26, 513

BABYLONIANS

Pinchas
359, 886
Vayechi
322
Vayishlach
122

BALAAM

Acharei Mot
125
Balak
94, 133, 135, 137, 154, 161, 162, 165, 170, 171, 173-175, 177, 181, 182, 185, 244, 254, 265, 266, 276, 277-281, 284, 285, 286, 287, 288, 291, 292, 304, 305, 323, 324, 338, 387, 389, 390, 393-402, 406, 407, 408, 410, 413, 414, 418, 422-429, 431, 442, 444-446, 448 -453, 456, 457, 458, 459, 461, 462, 471, 472, 473, 474, 475, 481, 482, 483, 484, 485, 486, 487, 490, 493, 494, 498, 499, 500
Bechukotai
1, 5, 6, 8, 10-15
Beha'alot'cha
15
Behar
2
Bemidbar
47, 48, 49

Beresheet A
224
Chayei Sarah
74, 76, 81, 86, 264
Ha'azinu
256, 257, 259, 260
Ki Tetze
110
Ki Tisa
76
Lech Lecha
290, 341
Mishpatim
37
Naso
184, 186
Pekudei
65, 66, 320, 861
Pinchas
390, 652
Shemot
299, 392, 393, 395
Tetzaveh
23
Trumah
860
Vayakhel
3
Vayechi
706, 710
Vayera
346, 486
Vayishlach
22, 23, 28, 30, 32, 33, 36-38, 85, 86, 123
Yitro
43, 46, 48, 50, 51

BALADAN (DOG)

Prologue
97

BALAK

Balak
1, 3, 4, 6, 28, 134, 135, 154, 169, 170, 171, 212, 222, 223, 244, 245, 255, 264, 276, 277, 278, 280-282, 287, 292, 336, 338, 397 -400, 407, 422, 425,

446, 452, 453, 460, 461, 462, 482, 499
Bechukotai
1, 2, 5, 6, 8, 10, 15
Beha'alot'cha
15
Beresheet A
224
Chayei Sarah
81
Ha'azinu
259
Ki Tetze
110
Naso
186
Pekudei
65, 66, 73
Shemot
299, 300
Vayishlach
37

BALSAM

Chukat
28
Emor
52
Idra Raba
357, 362
Pinchas
891
Prologue
109
Safra Detzniuta
17
Shemot
253, 256, 257, 393
Tazria
66
Trumah
19, 20, 21-24, 376, 377, 916
Vaetchanan
142
Vayishlach
217
Yitro
343, 439

BALSAM TREE

Acharei Mot
200
Emor
52
Idra Raba
362
Safra Detzniuta
17
Shemot
253, 256, 257
Tazria
66
Trumah
19, 20, 21, 22, 23, 376

BANNERS

Acharei Mot
52
Balak
46
Behar
25
Beresheet A
249
Beresheet B
95
Beshalach
473, 474, 485

Ki Tisa
32
Lech Lecha
266
Mishpatim
142
Pekudei
27, 54, 111
Toldot
88
Trumah
2, 3, 860
Vayikra
305
Vayishlach
90, 93, 94

BARAITHAS

Chayei Sarah
162
Ha'azinu
13, 15, 16, 17, 18
Pekudei
731, 733, 734, 735, 738, 818
Pinchas
492

BARAK (SPIRIT)

Beresheet B
115, 117, 120
Lech Lecha
391

BARHIEL (SPIRIT)

Pekudei
687
Pekudei
622
Vayera
276

BASTARD

Mishpatim
31, 356
Vayera
419
Vayishlach
264

BATHSHEBA

Chukat
22
Lech Lecha
119, 120, 403
Mishpatim
239, 240
Pinchas
814
Prologue
132, 135
Shlach Lecha
61
Shmini
28
Vayechi
291, 568, 810, 812
Vayetze
90
Vayikra
75, 404, 408

BEANS

Mishpatim
74, 189, 283

BEARD

Acharei Mot
184, 410-412
Balak
438
Beresheet B
110
Beshalach
88, 89
Emor
11, 12
Ha'azinu
38, 41, 49, 58, 59, 61, 64, 78, 90, 94, 108, 109, 117, 165, 166, 168-176
Idra Raba
72-74, 77, 81, 82, 83, 86, 87, 88, 89, 90, 91, 92, 95, 96, 99, 100, 101, 102, 105, 106, 110, 11-115, 117, 120-122, 126, 128-130, 134, 136, 138-141, 147, 148, 150, 153, 155, 159 -165, 233, 247, 249, 250, 254-258, 264, 265, 266-268, 274-278, 282, 288, 289, 291, 294, 304
Mishpatim
144, 145
Naso
126, 127, 162
Pekudei
630
Pinchas
286
Safra Detzniuta
7, 14-17, 33, 34, 36, 37, 56, 66
Shemot
47, 72, 290
Shmini
64
Tazria
124
Tetzaveh
131
Trumah
913
Vayechi
660
Vayera
40
Vayikra
103, 446
Yitro
113, 118, 144, 212

BEASTS

Acharei Mot
75
Balak
8, 80, 297, 355, 395, 449, 450, 451, 492
Bechukotai
26-27
Behar
25, 43
Beresheet A
76, 77, 123, 274, 285, 290, 291, 302, 410, 411, 426
Beshalach
98-99, 101, 110, 230, 263, 269-272
Chayei Sarah
39
Chukat
27, 29, 30
Emor
16, 52, 53, 324

Ha'azinu
198
Idra Raba
342, 343
Ki Tetze
33, 62, 66, 123
Korach
42, 46, 47
Lech Lecha
76, 214, 246, 299
Mishpatim
230, 445, 459, 461, 487, 504, 505, 509, 567, 570
Naso
10, 42, 53, 54, 95, 96, 166, 167
Noah
73, 85, 119-121, 228, 252-254, 258
Pekudei
1, 2, 210, 310, 353, 355, 365, 412, 413, 464, 856, 861, 940, 943, 944
Pinchas
44, 51, 66, 78, 79, 115, 126, 171, 187, 188, 196, 202, 219, 223, 230, 251, 256-260, 262, 264-266, 282-284, 303, 308, 311, 313-319, 329, 335, 339 -341, 348, 407, 408, 419-421, 427, 485, 488, 516, 533, 543, 547, 549, 604, 665, 666, 668, 699, 740, 741, 743, 746, 749, 750, 756, 769, 771, 774, 864
Prologue
232, 235
Safra Detzniuta
50
Shemot
48, 247
Shlach Lecha
18, 21-24, 212, 295
Shmini
15, 20, 22, 98, 102-105, 109, 116
Tazria
112
Toldot
141
Trumah
812
Tzav
44, 45, 70, 75, 83
Vaera
103, 156
Vaetchanan
192, 193, 194
Vayakhel
120, 168, 325, 326, 339, 340, 345, 360, 361, 411
Vayechi
285, 381, 424, 428, 429, 431, 553, 554, 621, 787, 829
Vayera
232, 388
Vayeshev
2, 134, 242, 243
Vayetze
92, 94, 305
Vayigash
71
Vayikra
143
Vayishlach
117, 137, 237
Yitro
225, 478

BECHER, SON OF BENJAMIN

Vayetze
136, 137

BEGINNING

Beresheet A
2, 4, 6-8, 10, 216, 303, 306, 307, 340

BELA, SON OF BENJAMIN

Vayetze
136, 137

BELSHAZZAR

Shlach Lecha
174
Trumah
896

BEN AZAI

Beresheet A
250, 251, 256
Pekudei
669

BEN ZOMA

Beresheet A
250, 251, 256
Pekudei
670
Pinchas
198

BENAIAH (BNAYAHU)

Chayei Sarah
222
Toldot
11
Vayera
209
Vayigash
52

BENJAMIN

Balak
323, 324
Emor
237
Lech Lecha
354
Miketz
133, 162, 185, 209, 214, 215, 216
Mishpatim
201, 484
Shlach Lecha
97
Vayechi
332, 553, 787, 788
Vayelech
24
Vayeshev
95
Vayetze
133-138, 139, 155, 157, 163, 165, 166, 234, 239-241, 246, 247, 249, 250, 292, 380, 389
Vayigash
23, 24, 25, 26, 88
Vayishlach
173, 174, 178, 199, 243

BEOR

Vayishlach
22

BETH-EL

Vayigash
102

BETHUEL

Toldot
16, 18, 50, 51, 52, 207

BEZALEL

Pekudei
8, 36, 47, 53, 55-57, 59, 69, 83, 87, 130, 273-275, 298, 399, 400
Prologue
20, 149
Shlach Lecha
95, 105, 119, 121, 129
Vayakhel
375

BILAAM

see Balaam

BILHAH

Chayei Sarah
256
Trumah
352
Vayeshev
70
Vayishlach
203, 204, 205, 216

BIRDS

Balak
1-6, 133, 135, 159, 212, 215, 216, 218, 219, 221, 296, 307 -309, 352, 361
Beresheet A
123, 274, 308, 406, 407, 410
Chayei Sarah
87
Chukat
30
Emor
16
Ha'azinu
153, 189, 198
Idra Raba
235
Ki Tetze
47, 58, 142
Lech Lecha
358, 363, 415
Metzora
5, 9, 17, 18, 19, 25
Miketz
55, 56, 238
Mishpatim
328, 344, 482, 486, 528
Naso
16, 53, 54
Pekudei
356, 357, 408, 606
Pinchas
53, 56-58, 83, 126, 199, 275, 276, 281, 283, 390, 418, 488, 494, 495, 496, 532, 536, 540, 751, 780-783, 785-787, 790, 791, 831, 841
Prologue
187, 188, 217, 218, 220, 225
Safra Detzniuta
67

Shlach Lecha
140, 151
Shmini
78, 79, 109, 116, 118
Tetzaveh
70
Toldot
183
Trumah
77, 78, 812
Vayakhel
79
Vayechi
93, 94, 121, 122, 123, 135, 136, 137, 142, 182, 183, 185, 186, 360, 509
Vayera
1, 3, 6, 8, 212, 456
Vayeshev
94, 242, 243, 271
Vayetze
176, 235, 337
Vayishlach
132, 134

BIRTH

Beresheet A
8, 30, 70, 223, 369, 455, 465
Chayei Sarah
7, 26, 150
Ki Tisa
6, 24
Lech Lecha
29, 380, 457, 459
Tetzaveh
25
Vayechi
20, 264, 728
Vayera
159, 310, 421
Vayeshev
2, 193
Vayetze
127, 132, 159, 196, 200, 239
Vayishlach
1, 2

BIRTHRIGHT

Balak
14, 15, 143
Mishpatim
310, 311, 312, 337
Toldot
32, 62, 77, 78, 80, 177, 178
Trumah
782
Vayechi
5, 8, 262, 496, 544, 550, 551, 701, 729
Vayeshev
139
Vayetze
156, 187, 281
Vayishlach
219, 221

BLASPHEMY

Beresheet A
432
Beshalach
420
Bo
26

BLESSING

Acharei Mot
35, 37-39, 48, 55, 102-107,

109, 124-126, 146, 149, 153, 175, 180, 186, 197, 247, 316, 328-331, 334, 335

Balak
29, 34, 38-41, 54, 56, 58, 104, 110, 119-126, 134, 145, 147, 197, 265, 266, 341, 439, 440, 460, 461, 463, 481, 483, 507

Bechukotai
19

Beha'alot'cha
23-25, 27, 31, 98

Behar
9, 15, 34, 56, 57, 63

Bemidbar
11-15, 17-20, 54

Beresheet A
65, 128, 130, 196, 199, 244, 439, 475

Beresheet B
52, 61, 97, 136, 193, 232, 234, 370, 375, 420, 421

Beshalach
227, 240, 279, 281, 282, 284, 286, 293, 352, 354, 385-387, 410-412, 415

Bo
40, 44, 57

Chayei
17, 18, 37, 65, 67, 120, 138, 143, 265

Chukat
31, 32, 33, 83

Ekev
1-16, 21-24, 28-31, 37-39, 41 -43, 45, 48, 56, 57, 59, 60, 62-64

Emor
37, 38, 40, 93, 115, 191, 219, 269, 272

Ha'azinu
52, 54, 186, 193, 195, 212, 214

Idra Raba
56, 111, 289, 358

Kedoshim
32, 129

Ki Tetze
5, 19, 24, 45, 97, 132

Ki Tisa
2, 3, 38, 39, 40, 43, 100

Korach
43, 47, 49

Lech Lecha
13, 14, 32, 33, 41, 118, 121, 242, 243, 251, 253, 255-265, 267, 323, 392, 394, 426, 444

Metzora
41

Miketz
140, 141, 142, 204, 222, 240, 254

Mishpatim
189, 310, 311, 337, 395, 396, 414, 428, 450, 464, 494, 545, 546, 547

Naso
10, 61, 80, 147, 152, 153, 159, 160, 165, 168, 169, 174, 178, 179, 184-186, 192, 194, 197, 199

Noach
101, 106-109, 116, 147, 241, 242, 248, 250, 251, 259, 305, 325, 334

Pekudei
28, 29, 31, 33, 43, 82, 84-86, 90, 126, 197, 280, 343, 344, 578, 579, 626, 627, 713, 775, 795,

796, 797, 803-806, 808, 809 -811, 816, 821, 823, 828, 834, 891, 900

Pinchas
34, 37, 63, 68, 180, 191, 192, 261, 297, 304-306, 307, 308, 311, 312, 315, 336, 337, 340, 341, 349, 492, 549, 569, 583, 596, 610, 623, 624, 626, 628, 630, 632, 638, 714, 719, 739, 795, 821, 829, 855, 882

Prologue
99, 126, 171, 172, 259

Safra Detzniuta
41

Shemot
174

Shlach Lecha
213, 297, 302, 338

Shmini
11, 54, 60, 66, 72, 81, 86

Tazria
3, 18, 45, 49, 56, 57, 58, 137

Tetzaveh
25, 89, 102, 139, 140

Toldot
8, 14, 32, 132, 136, 141-143, 146-154, 156, 157, 159, 161, 167, 169, 172-175, 177-179, 185, 186, 187, 188, 194, 198, 199-205

Trumah
23, 34, 45, 49, 115, 116, 121, 166, 168, 169-173, 217-219, 225, 360, 394, 501, 503, 504, 508, 515, 523, 525, 555, 571, 572, 586, 587, 630, 656, 681, 684, 747, 770, 771, 778, 785-788, 791-798, 883

Tzav
99, 102, 109-112, 119, 123, 154, 157, 163, 164, 170, 187, 191

Vaera
4, 61, 91, 92, 112, 141, 194, 195

Vaetchanan
16, 89, 112, 113, 123, 125, 126

Vayakhel
73, 149, 154, 189, 255, 257, 258, 260, 262, 263, 269, 350, 402, 452, 456, 457, 458, 461, 462, 472, 482

Vayechi
9, 34, 64, 71, 225, 371, 372, 375, 376, 377, 385, 395, 397, 398, 405, 406, 408, 415, 418, 439, 440, 464, 467, 468, 477, 486, 489, 490, 491, 493-496, 504, 505, 509-512, 527-530, 540, 542, 543, 551, 552, 555, 559, 636, 674, 675, 709, 715, 717, 720, 721, 750, 778, 780 -783, 795-801, 844, 845, 846, 847, 848

Vayelech
34, 35, 36, 37, 38, 40, 42, 47, 48

Vayera
54, 92, 129, 172, 205, 291, 415, 424, 435, 504

Vayeshev
66, 67, 111, 113, 117, 216, 232

Vayetze
67, 75, 76, 119-121, 151, 181, 198, 201, 204, 206, 211, 213, 214, 277, 281, 299, 302 -304, 309, 310, 323, 324, 325, 385

Vayigash
5, 7, 8, 9, 53, 54, 69, 77, 97
Vayikra
31-33, 41, 61, 63, 75, 104, 133, 161, 183, 203, 205, 217, 246, 260, 288, 289, 291, 294, 314, 382, 418, 419, 448, 449
Vayishlach
21, 41, 42, 113, 126, 127
Yitro
2, 3, 4, 5, 7, 125, 338, 425, 437, 438, 439, 443-448, 450, 457, 548, 549, 554

BLIND

Acharei Mot
316, 368
Beshalach
119
Emor
46, 48, 51
Kedoshim
89, 91, 93
Miketz
236
Mishpatim
426
Naso
55
Noach
194
Pekudei
320
Pinchas
60, 637
Shlach Lecha
211
Toldot
121
Vaetchanan
35
Vayechi
295
Yitro
330

BLISS

Noach
296
Shmini
86
Vayakhel
112, 183
Vayetze
148

BLOOD

Acharei Mot
51, 249, 250
Balak
141, 142, 145, 227, 315, 468, 479
Beha'alot'cha
7-9, 15, 77
Behar
71
Beresheet A
266, 267, 273, 432, 444, 445
Beresheet B
316, 359, 394
Beshalach
120, 215
Bo
74, 77-83, 85, 189, 191, 192, 206
Chukat
24
Emor
61, 62, 130, 162, 249

Ha'azinu
198, 250
Idra Raba
334
Kedoshim
79, 89, 131
Ki Tisa
48
Lech Lecha
298, 302
Metzora
4, 28, 30
Miketz
150
Mishpatim
248, 348, 462, 469, 518, 572-574
Pekudei
437, 458, 690
Pinchas
95, 96, 98-100, 109, 110, 112, 113, 154, 220, 246, 354, 411, 412, 467, 528, 531, 699, 798
Shemot
81, 202, 302, 322, 347, 364-369
Shlach Lecha
238
Shmini
57
Tazria
27, 28
Toldot
5, 29, 60-62, 79, 162, 179, 180
Trumah
494, 804, 814
Tzav
42, 46, 155
Vaera
128, 131, 132, 135-137, 142-144, 167
Vayakhel
403, 404, 405, 406, 407, 408
Vayechi
193, 591, 604, 630
Vayera
40, 131, 380
Vayeshev
72, 113, 140, 141, 142, 154, 183
Vayetze
391
Vayigash
53, 116
Vayikra
129, 130, 221, 222, 274, 326, 344
Vayishlach
150, 250
Yitro
104, 275, 491

BLOODSHED

Beresheet A
265, 266, 267, 291, 445

BLOSSOM

Balak
393, 438
Beha'alot'cha
107
Beshalach
482
Lech Lecha
129
Mishpatim
497
Shlach Lecha
158, 212

BLUE

Matot
1
Mishpatim
461
Shoftim
13
Vaetchanan
99
Vayechi
129

BOARDS

Balak
33, 42, 45
Beshalach
168
Ki Tetze
58
Pekudei
251, 253, 254, 255, 374, 379, 418, 422
Pinchas
259, 312
Shmini
119

Trumah
240, 788, 806, 807, 825, 826, 893, 909
Vayakhel
375, 376
Vayechi
294
Vayera
477
Vayetze
29

BOAZ

Acharei Mot
34, 287
Emor
45
Ki Tetze
98, 121
Lech Lecha
399
Mishpatim
180, 191, 193, 395
Prologue
236
Vaetchanan
126
Vayakhel
451, 452, 453, 456, 457, 463
Vayera
311
Vayeshev
193
Yitro
380, 524 body
Acharei Mot
24, 185, 189, 198, 203, 215, 216, 220, 223, 254, 292, 313, 341, 364, 388

BODY

Balak
5, 43, 44, 53, 54, 159, 182, 322, 349, 370, 371, 382
Beha'alot'cha
20, 44, 53, 61-63, 68, 77, 92, 113, 129, 135, 140, 144
Behar
6, 13, 31-37, 40, 42, 66
Bemidbar
5, 56, 58, 64, 65

Beresheet A
3, 6, 14, 27, 82, 109, 120-123, 144, 149-152, 154, 155, 157, 167, 199, 260, 261, 264, 283, 369, 407, 410, 454, 479, 480
Beresheet B
9, 104, 116, 151, 190, 212, 221, 286, 319, 320, 348, 364
Beshalach
71, 103, 104, 212, 216, 288, 367, 376-378
Bo
70, 86, 88, 195, 197, 203, 213
Chayei Sarah
9, 38, 44, 46-49, 52, 53, 54, 56, 59, 60, 70, 94, 95, 96, 99, 130, 142, 150, 152, 153, 155, 156, 163-165, 174, 176, 177, 179, 182, 183, 185, 186, 187, 192, 193, 197, 201, 203, 204, 207, 208, 211-213, 246
Chukat
13, 36, 37, 39, 46, 62, 70a
Ekev
26, 39
Emor
6-10, 38, 45, 50, 51, 139, 155, 227b, 235
Ha'azinu
67, 68, 89, 92, 119, 120, 123, 133, 156, 157, 161, 169, 183, 185-187, 189-193, 195
Idra Raba
19, 46, 140, 192, 203, 204, 241, 264, 269, 313, 319, 328, 332-340, 342-345
Kedoshim
24, 32, 33, 46, 60, 61-64, 68, 69, 87
Ki Tetze
10, 30, 31, 44, 51, 56, 67, 88, 102, 103, 124, 128, 134, 138
Ki Tisa
103
Korach
19, 37
Lech Lecha
8, 13, 15, 42, 44-47, 51, 53, 78, 81, 85, 89, 90, 96-99, 103, 146-148, 155, 158, 300-302, 348, 349, 350, 351, 422
Metzora
9, 10, 11, 21, 36, 37, 50
Miketz
64, 88, 89, 91, 192, 193, 235
Mishpatim
2, 6, 7, 8, 9, 15, 25, 26, 47, 52, 55, 56, 60, 67, 95, 109, 112, 114-118, 133, 134, 138, 141, 153, 164, 213, 215, 259, 303, 305, 315, 341, 351-353, 418, 419, 426, 433, 434, 442, 451, 454, 455, 457, 476, 480, 499, 530, 534, 535
Naso
40, 50, 51, 53, 56, 106-108, 114, 117-119, 121, 122, 123, 127
Noach
102, 130, 134, 139, 143, 208, 212, 275, 276, 381
Pekudei
69, 83, 87, 118, 201, 219, 220, 342, 414, 458, 463, 476, 671, 677, 731, 746, 747, 749, 752, 764, 766, 768, 816-818, 846, 877, 878, 895, 910, 915 -917, 955

Pinchas
29, 33, 53, 54, 89, 95-100, 109, 110, 112, 113, 124, 126, 145, 152, 167, 169, 170, 173, 174, 177, 179, 188, 193, 215, 220, 224, 244, 251, 265, 267, 274, 275, 280, 281, 293, 299, 302, 309-311, 326, 328, 343, 365, 368, 380, 408, 413, 414, 416, 422, 423, 430, 433, 436, 445, 450, 566, 635, 661, 817, 859, 861, 862, 869
Prologue
59, 93, 117, 188, 190, 222, 232
Safra Detzniuta
5, 12, 15, 22, 51, 68
Shemot
27, 177, 178, 181, 200, 217-219, 224, 225, 245, 368
Shlach Lecha
16, 53, 64, 65, 67, 74, 84, 85, 87, 88, 93, 201, 206, 207, 209, 217, 227, 228, 232, 233, 236-239, 318
Shmini
101, 102, 111
Shoftim
3, 8, 9, 12, 13
Tazria
17, 26, 27, 29, 30, 73, 117, 118, 135, 152
Tetzaveh
9, 18, 28-30, 36, 50, 60, 65, 118, 131, 132
Toldot
3, 12, 24, 35, 37, 40, 48, 49, 50, 51, 53, 57, 58, 59, 62, 64, 68, 71, 89, 90, 107, 117, 163, 164, 197
Trumah
20, 24, 193, 201, 230, 234, 256, 266-268, 276, 279, 281-285, 288, 289, 291-293, 298, 299, 304, 305, 334, 335, 373, 386, 387, 389, 390, 403, 436-438, 453, 454, 456, 457, 458, 459, 463, 464, 493, 494, 522, 524, 558, 559, 576, 579, 583, 591, 611, 614, 664, 665, 710, 722, 751, 752, 758, 764, 875, 885
Tzav
31, 32, 44, 46, 50, 54, 62, 67, 68, 71, 146-148
Vaera
33, 50, 63, 95, 104, 126, 127
Vaetchanan
6, 13, 20, 31, 37, 51, 56, 62-66, 69, 97, 119, 140, 172, 193, 195-197
Vayakhel
16, 44, 46, 48, 70, 71, 81, 91, 94, 96, 97, 121, 122, 188, 192, 206, 209, 271, 329, 369, 370, 383, 388, 390, 404, 405, 409, 453, 491, 492
Vayechi
105, 107, 141, 170-172, 175, 196-200, 206, 207, 222, 224, 253, 258, 259, 269, 288, 324, 328, 336, 337, 343, 346, 347, 348, 360, 362, 363, 497, 650, 651, 653, 654, 659, 660, 669, 679, 680, 697, 698, 732, 741, 742, 762, 766, 769, 770, 783, 785, 793, 847, 856, 857, 858
Vayelech
2-5
Vayera
30, 31, 41, 56, 91, 116, 129,

132, 133, 136, 137, 155, 260, 282, 283, 315-317, 319, 320, 322, 339, 356, 389, 392, 393, 396, 401, 404, 405, 408-410, 479, 482

Vayeshev
26, 27, 28, 33, 36, 39, 51, 52, 61, 62, 64, 88, 114, 115, 122, 123, 136, 156, 159, 161, 162

Vayetze
13, 24, 27, 40, 48, 52, 67, 113, 114, 137, 138, 144, 145, 170, 177, 184, 231, 237, 239, 323, 331

Vayigash
83, 90, 94

Vayikra
74, 93, 96, 101, 130, 151, 209, 263, 316, 365, 441

Vayishlach
13, 82, 83, 86, 100, 101, 102, 111, 116, 194, 198, 210, 262, 263

Yitro
116, 161, 183, 226, 227, 267, 296, 321, 322, 392, 400, 406, 422, 436, 526, 527, 553, 556, 563

BOEL (ANGEL)

Trumah
131, 388

Vayakhel
296, 297

BONE

Acharei Mot
135, 137

Balak
183

Beresheet A
149, 150, 151, 152, 242, 282

Beresheet B
217, 241

Bo
4, 15, 195, 196

Chayei Sarah
50, 164, 178

Ki Tetze
104, 123

Matot
3

Mishpatim
201, 326, 328, 329, 418, 434

Noach
208

Pinchas
160, 161, 166, 728, 736, 761, 811

Shlach Lecha
237, 238, 240

Shoftim
12, 13

Toldot
50, 51, 52, 106, 107

Vaera
127

Vaetchanan
148, 196

Vayechi
329, 492

Vayera
393, 405

Vayishlach
149, 212

BOOK OF ADAM

Acharei Mot
221
Beresheet A
51
Tetzaveh
13, 33
Trumah
85, 317
Vayakhel
46
Vayikra
142
Yitro
176, 212 Book of Agadah
Emor
195, 261 Book of Agadah
Ha'azinu
80, 93, 177 Book of Agadah
Vaetchanan
172 Book of Agadah
Vayechi
218 Book of Agadah
Vayikra
45, 91, 162 Book of Agadah
Yitro
255, 256

BOOK OF ASMODEUS

Balak
182
Trumah
36
Vayikra
322

BOOK OF DUMAH

Chayei Sarah
12

BOOK OF ENOCH

Beresheet A
474-476
Beshalach
232
Ki Tisa
79, 81
Mishpatim
110, 182, 214
Pinchas
454, 527, 684, 776
Tetzaveh
26
Vayikra
150

BOOK OF FORMATION

Ki Tetze
34, 35
Ki Tisa
4
Vayera
274

BOOK OF KING SOLOMON

Acharei Mot
167, 257, 258
Beha'alot'cha
51
Emor
285
Prologue
116, 235
Shlach Lecha
135
Vayechi
331

BOOK OF LIFE

Noach
65, 66

BOOK OF MEMORIES

Noach
65

BOOK OF REMEMBRANCE

Miketz
160
Pekudei
503
Prologue
126, 139
Vaetchanan
99
Vayakhel
100, 101, 437, 439
Vayechi
693

BOOK OF SECRETS OF ENOCH

Tetzaveh
20

BOOK OF THE GENERATIONS OF ADAM

Beresheet A
470-474
Lech Lecha
331
Pinchas
69
Vayechi
369
Yitro
62, 68, 149, 176, 185

BOOK OF THE PHYSICIAN KARTANA

Ha'azinu
248, 253, 254

BOOTH

Emor
264, 268, 270, 271, 276, 277
Pinchas
815, 884
Tetzaveh
62, 134, 135, 136
Vayechi
204
Vayishlach
131, 142

BOZRAH

Emor
17
Vaera
205

BRAIN

Acharei Mot
75
Balak
15
Beresheet A
98, 251
Beresheet B
57

Chayei Sarah
194, 195
Emor
154
Ha'azinu
36, 38, 40, 48, 49, 51, 52, 55, 63-72, 90, 92, 109, 120, 124, 125, 127-130, 138, 152, 156, 158, 183, 195
Idra Raba
21-23, 26, 27, 45, 48, 64, 65, 68, 92-95, 100, 101, 152, 189, 190, 196, 200, 236-242, 269-273, 279, 280, 319, 350
Mishpatim
525, 527
Naso
50
Pekudei
769
Pinchas
97, 126, 153, 167, 204, 209, 211, 213, 220, 247, 248, 265, 273, 275, 276, 296, 402, 407, 408, 426, 428, 437, 438, 664, 876
Prologue
212
Shlach Lecha
84, 85, 87, 88, 89, 90, 91
Shoftim
12
Toldot
58, 60
Trumah
267, 268, 270, 272, 273, 493, 494, 495
Tzav
52, 53, 74
Vaetchanan
37, 40, 41, 42, 43, 44, 97, 174
Vayakhel
7, 122, 162, 226, 310, 360, 412
Yitro
53, 102

BRASS

Beresheet B
64
Mishpatim
202
Pekudei
74, 131, 132, 158-161, 236, 238, 432, 780-782
Pinchas
318
Shemot
33
Trumah
60, 157, 158, 160, 227, 229, 237, 238, 370, 387, 388, 391, 402, 403, 408-410, 412, 831, 842, 902
Tzav
84, 86
Vaera
45
Vayakhel
55, 57, 73
Vayechi
129, 132

BREAD OF AFFLICTION

Beresheet A
378
Beshalach
379
Bo
169, 171, 173-175

Pinchas
737
Tetzaveh
72
Vayetze
219, 227

BREAD

Acharei Mot
31, 75, 353
Balak
30, 57, 69, 70, 71, 74, 83, 92, 137, 194, 397
Beha'alot'cha
23, 146, 147
Behar
29, 57-59
Beresheet A
186, 378
Beresheet B
184
Beshalach
141, 364, 372, 374, 376, 379, 384, 399
Bo
166-169, 171-175, 178
Ekev
18, 19, 21, 22, 28, 29, 45, 47
Emor
110, 123, 131, 146, 182-184, 186, 260a, 278
Ha'azinu
117, 182
Idra Raba
56, 360
Ki Tetze
122
Ki Tisa
58
Korach
49, 50, 55
Lech Lecha
73, 98, 237, 241, 255, 303, 446
Miketz
139, 141, 166
Mishpatim
21, 69, 136, 488, 489, 494, 544
Naso
58, 185, 187
Pekudei
831
Pinchas
81, 219, 265, 345, 446, 598, 599, 600, 601, 608-614, 616, 617, 619, 620, 641, 644, 664, 680, 730, 731, 737-739, 741, 743, 744, 756-759, 761, 762, 797, 889, 890
Prologue
19, 254
Safra Detzniuta
2
Shemot
21-23, 251, 384, 385
Shlach Lecha
68, 276, 297
Shoftim
20
Tetzaveh
49-51, 61, 63, 72, 73, 75, 76, 78
Toldot
41, 45, 46, 63, 144, 148, 157, 164
Trumah
162, 488, 493, 502, 503, 515, 517, 518, 526, 527, 770, 777
Tzav
68, 149, 150

Vaera
138, 139, 141, 153
Vayakhel
61, 63, 462
Vayechi
87, 353, 527, 541, 543, 590, 607, 634-636, 675, 729, 751, 752-756, 793, 845, 848
Vayelech
4
Vayera
74, 115, 226, 236, 289, 291
Vayeshev
164, 166, 269, 270
Vayetze
219, 220, 223, 224, 225, 226, 227, 328, 329, 384
Vayikra
96, 128, 195
Vayishlach
16, 18, 19, 160, 188
Yitro
446

BREASTPLATE

Balak
81
Ha'azinu
211
Pekudei
172, 174, 179, 182-187, 196, 198, 201, 209, 210, 258, 268, 269
Pinchas
712
Trumah
241, 855
Vaetchanan
93

BREATH

Acharei Mot
215, 219
Bechukotai
28
Behar
42, 66
Beresheet A
258, 388
Beresheet B
177
Beshalach
320-323, 325
Bo
143-145
Chayei Sarah
150, 201
Chukat
33, 34
Idra Raba
67, 156, 157, 158, 292, 293, 302
Kedoshim
85
Ki Tisa
6
Korach
17, 19
Lech Lecha
411
Mishpatim
12, 119, 139, 467, 468, 530, 531, 551
Naso
31, 33, 41, 52
Noach
140
Pinchas
160, 268, 271, 365, 371, 405, 431, 432, 435, 781

Safra Detzniuta
73
Shemot
20, 217-219, 225
Shlach Lecha
24, 221
Tazria
76, 77, 81, 98, 99, 100, 116
Tetzaveh
51, 52, 55, 60
Toldot
64
Trumah
59, 371, 735
Tzav
70, 125
Vaera
65, 125
Vayechi
167, 246, 531, 534
Vayera
382, 400
Vayetze
13, 189, 191
Vayigash
12, 18
Vayikra
93, 317
Vayishlach
212

BRIDE

Acharei Mot
187, 282, 283, 285, 377, 378, 383
Balak
30, 88, 127, 128, 231, 271, 272
Bechukotai
57, 59
Beha'alot'cha
3
Beresheet A
367, 416
Beresheet B
214
Beshalach
416
Chayei Sarah
183, 234
Ekev
4, 32, 49, 62
Emor
133, 134, 150, 152, 169, 170, 172, 183, 275
Ha'azinu
84, 85, 86, 205, 228
Ki Tetze
14, 16-19, 43, 44, 72, 79, 82, 83
Ki Tisa
6
Metzora
23
Miketz
32
Mishpatim
372, 373, 457
Naso
193, 194, 195, 196
Noach
289, 291
Pekudei
284, 342
Pinchas
130, 141, 195, 208, 238, 241, 252, 334-337, 348, 416, 504, 527, 552, 553, 557, 558, 606, 792, 794, 804, 805, 844, 855, 879, 887
Prologue
125, 126, 127, 129, 139, 150,

168, 169
Shemot
14, 19, 39, 60, 61, 63, 64, 192
Shlach Lecha
211, 242
Shoftim
23
Tazria
44, 45, 49
Trumah
140, 199, 263, 265, 346, 355, 356, 357, 358, 787-791, 797, 798
Tzav
36, 37, 41, 157
Vaetchanan
147
Vayakhel
479
Vayechi
77, 559, 648, 651, 757
Vayetze
44
Vayikra
26, 28, 29, 31, 32, 33, 41, 44, 46, 183, 318
Vayishlach
223
Yitro
502

BRIT (COVENANT)

Acharei Mot
25-27, 85, 182-184, 301, 307
Balak
34, 51, 97, 128, 268, 349
Bechukotai
52, 53, 54, 55, 56
Beresheet A
56, 149, 204, 216, 217, 287, 358, 360-364, 377, 382, 383, 394-396, 398, 434, 458, 476
Beresheet B
2, 11, 184, 186, 228, 242, 373 -377, 442
Beshalach
44, 96, 200, 291, 292, 349, 358, 360, 361, 464, 469, 473, 474, 478
Bo
123, 172, 188, 191, 246
Chayei Sarah
162, 214, 216
Chukat
16, 88, 90
Ekev
54, 59, 60
Emor
30, 32, 55-57, 63, 128, 130, 148, 162, 167
Ha'azinu
17, 159, 218, 221
Idra Raba
197
Kedoshim
78
Ki Tetze
35, 67, 79, 82, 138
Ki Tisa
45, 46
Lech Lecha
230, 233, 276, 277, 294-296, 326, 338, 342, 343, 385, 386, 388, 389, 391-394, 398-400, 403, 404, 405, 407, 409, 410, 412-414, 426, 431, 432, 438, 442, 456, 469, 472
Miketz
35, 39, 83, 101, 158, 162, 170-172, 245, 247

Mishpatim
217, 381, 406, 407, 410, 450, 458, 572, 573, 574, 581
Naso
20, 75, 76
Noach
2, 3, 5-7, 9, 134, 153-162, 181, 188, 224, 261, 267, 268, 270, 287, 291, 292, 297, 304, 310
Pekudei
83, 87, 221, 262, 263, 277, 308, 310, 636, 690, 731, 761, 763, 766, 768, 836, 855, 860, 902
Pinchas
5, 15, 18, 22, 26, 34, 35a, 35d, 36, 37, 38, 40, 73, 74, 76, 128-131, 140, 142, 174, 193, 231, 232, 394, 433, 449, 450, 456, 457, 482-485, 488-490, 566, 571, 583, 584, 593, 771, 830, 851, 852, 855
Prologue
2, 3, 17, 26, 130-132, 138, 139, 219, 222, 226
Shemot
26-29, 91, 149, 150, 186, 189, 213
Shlach Lecha
66, 118, 119, 154, 167-170
Tazria
31, 32, 33, 34, 36
Tetzaveh
25, 34, 47, 66
Toldot
8, 102
Trumah
23, 40, 41, 169, 355, 576, 617, 778, 779, 789, 793
Tzav
32, 57, 87
Vaera
20, 75-81, 86, 87, 189, 200
Vaetchanan
57, 180
Vayakhel
4, 98, 100, 169, 171, 376, 383-387, 389, 390, 423, 424, 494
Vayechi
68, 74, 107, 187, 224, 253, 265, 268, 315, 373, 374, 379, 381, 392, 393, 405, 408, 439, 482, 561, 562, 642, 644, 645, 666, 667, 753, 760, 776, 786, 858, 859
Vayelech
13, 20
Vayera
6, 22, 50, 51, 118, 121, 122, 140, 304, 305, 355, 447, 448, 451, 476, 511, 512
Vayeshev
14, 81, 102, 104, 129, 171, 212, 215, 216, 218
Vayetze
52, 57, 58, 66, 134, 135, 137, 138, 239, 268, 269, 274, 278, 324, 325
Vayigash
85, 87, 131
Vayikra
33, 34, 214-220, 222-225, 236, 238, 326
Vayishlach
50, 227
Yitro
26, 27, 113, 261, 265, 406, 547, 574

BRIYAH

Acharei Mot
48, 76, 273
Balak
311, 312
Beha'alot'cha
63
Behar
33-35, 37, 42, 43
Beresheet A
63, 77, 83, 109, 110, 114, 164, 165, 166, 180-182, 256, 257, 260, 263, 272, 282, 302, 401, 445, 470
Beresheet B
29, 60, 69, 76, 131, 268, 420
Beshalach
225, 273, 411
Bo
47, 227
Chukat
29
Emor
58, 158
Ha'azinu
187, 189, 190, 195, 224, 228
Idra Raba
20, 177, 179, 340
Kedoshim
52, 56, 57, 61
Ki Tetze
27, 30, 37, 38, 43, 138, 139
Ki Tisa
82
Korach
9
Lech Lecha
214, 449
Miketz
20
Mishpatim
2, 6-8, 11, 61, 336, 403, 415, 442, 443, 455
Noach
61, 62
Pekudei
1, 2, 222, 251, 339, 729, 737, 781, 821, 906
Pinchas
57, 223, 225, 230, 283, 294, 316, 348, 456, 502, 515, 692, 700
Safra Detzniuta
63
Shemot
1, 137, 310
Shlach Lecha
48, 345
Tazria
4
Trumah
94, 114, 138, 175, 176, 235, 286, 287, 340, 343, 361, 393, 396, 493-495, 530, 532, 757, 759
Tzav
57, 64, 65, 75, 172
Vaera
34, 103
Vaetchanan
21
Vayakhel
102, 103, 104, 292
Vayechi
118, 119, 284, 397, 408, 568, 716, 753, 806
Vayera
232

Vayetze
92, 116, 120, 148, 160, 163, 242, 262, 305, 306, 310, 318, 335, 337
Vayikra
36, 149, 152, 434
Yitro
10, 327

BULLOCKS

Miketz
164
Pinchas
664, 672, 677, 806, 826, 827, 832, 833, 880, 884-890

BUSH

Ki Tetze
86, 88, 89
Pekudei
24
Shemot
383, 388-390, 396
Shoftim
9
Vayera
374
Vayetze
273
Vayishlach
6
Yitro
52

BUTLER

Miketz
8
Tetzaveh
101
Vayeshev
241, 253, 257, 265, 268, 272

BUTTON

Vayechi
186

CAESAREA

Toldot
8
Vayechi
183

CAIN

Bemidbar
4
Beresheet A
101, 285, 286, 456, 457, 458, 464, 465
Beresheet B
331-338, 341, 342, 344-346, 349, 350, 353, 354
Idra Raba
284, 326, 327, 328, 337
Kedoshim
55, 116, 119, 120
Naso
16, 17, 18
Pinchas
61
Prologue
153, 154, 158
Tetzaveh
42, 43, 44
Vayechi
22
Vayishlach
261, 262, 263

CALEB

Shlach Lecha
16, 31, 32, 38, 39, 69, 70, 71

CAMELS

Chayei Sarah
170, 172, 176
Emor
222
Miketz
80
Pekudei
301-305, 424, 439, 941
Toldot
207
Vayechi
121
Vayera
144
Vayeshev
54, 56, 61, 62
Vayishlach
59

CAMP

Acharei Mot
152, 339, 341
Balak
114, 224, 228, 229, 392, 426, 466, 468, 475
Bechukotai
33, 35
Beha'alot'cha
7, 33, 34, 36, 102, 103, 105, 112, 115-118, 123-125, 138
Bemidbar
27, 29, 30, 31, 53, 59
Beresheet A
249
Beresheet B
82, 91, 294, 295, 303
Beshalach
62, 98, 110, 111, 146, 147, 150, 154, 159, 172, 178, 179, 199, 209, 217, 420
Bo
101
Chukat
23, 29
Ekev
34
Emor
165, 306, 312
Ha'azinu
31, 223
Idra Raba
337

Kedoshim
42, 73
Ki Tisa
67, 109, 116
Korach
26
Lech Lecha
85, 86
Metzora
54, 61
Miketz
124, 154, 156, 260
Mishpatim
57, 58, 185, 244, 465, 467
Naso
98, 149
Noach
114, 326, 354, 379, 381
Pekudei
300, 327, 328

Pinchas
3, 171, 217, 220, 234, 237, 240, 258, 302, 306, 423, 429, 541, 573, 578
Prologue
128
Shemot
5, 11, 13, 17, 36, 107, 280, 323
Shlach Lecha
88, 173, 290, 316
Tazria
52, 53, 58
Trumah
11, 50, 67, 93-95, 98, 101, 130, 131, 173, 176, 265, 304, 376, 377, 538, 553, 586, 807
Tzav
57
Vaetchanan
163, 166, 182
Vayakhel
10, 36, 139, 142, 145, 285, 352, 411
Vayechi
92, 529, 618, 655, 656, 696, 700, 704, 706, 708, 709, 773
Vayera
415
Vayeshev
202, 282, 283
Vayetze
386, 387, 388, 390, 393
Vayikra
9-14, 17, 19-24, 348, 426
Vayishlach
9, 10, 11, 14, 39, 44, 48, 59, 60, 68
Yitro
235, 236, 238, 316, 383

CANAAN

Balak
257
Chayei Sarah
46, 47
Emor
267, 269
Lech Lecha
18, 25, 27, 34, 49, 68, 88, 179
Mishpatim
66
Shlach Lecha
1, 29
Vaera
20, 79
Vayechi
3, 64, 272, 382, 857
Vayera
109, 415
Vayeshev
1, 15, 20, 52
Vayetze
241

CANAANITE

Chayei Sarah
215
Lech Lecha
81
Vayeshev
150

CANDLES

Acharei Mot
237, 247

Balak
59, 354, 356
Beha'alot'cha
4, 11, 20, 21, 23, 99
Behar
29
Beresheet A
113, 128, 132, 394
Beresheet B
64, 138, 142, 145, 198, 199, 231, 248, 254, 258, 263-265, 268
Beshalach
205, 208, 212
Chayei Sarah
89, 248
Chukat
66
Ekev
7, 10, 31, 36, 65
Emor
15
Ha'azinu
33, 41, 42, 51, 115, 116, 167
Idra Raba
38, 43, 44, 45, 46, 47, 109, 118, 121, 144, 145, 166, 167, 181, 229, 285, 315, 358
Korach
34
Lech Lecha
19, 158, 159, 305, 309, 376, 464
Mishpatim
105, 106, 491
Noach
236, 241, 242
Pekudei
81, 82, 198, 227, 286, 361, 492, 557, 705
Pinchas
115, 116, 131, 248, 252, 323, 364, 406, 538, 540, 542, 820, 824, 850
Prologue
119, 251, 254, 255, 256, 258
Safra Detzniuta
16
Shemot
1, 137, 245
Shlach Lecha
24, 181, 182, 184, 189, 192, 202
Shmini
38
Tazria
16
Tetzaveh
39, 89, 136
Trumah
44, 74, 124, 216, 286, 316, 394, 576, 725, 726, 728, 729, 736, 737, 745, 746, 766, 862, 874, 921
Tzav
13, 50, 52, 54, 136, 152, 165, 168, 172, 189, 190
Vayakhel
87, 118, 260-262, 264, 265, 268, 269, 368, 482
Vayechi
419, 472, 603, 715-717, 792, 853
Vayeshev
55
Vayetze
333
Vayigash
104

Vayishlach
229
Yitro
33, 40, 273, 413

CANOPY WEDDING (CHUPAH)

Beresheet B
22
Beshalach
231
Chayei Sarah
234
Chukat
61
Ekev
32
Lech Lecha
428
Mishpatim
78
Naso
193
Noach
46
Pinchas
335, 337, 339, 553, 879
Prologue
125-128, 130, 143, 168, 169
Trumah
126, 137, 138, 139, 199, 200, 344, 345, 788, 789
Vayechi
77
Vayikra
41

CANTILLATION

Beresheet A
14, 15, 199, 201, 213, 414

CARMEL

Prologue
237, 242
Vayera
388, 389, 392

CASTRATION

Mishpatim
275
Vayechi
760

CAVE OF MACHPELAH

Tetzaveh
24
Trumah
466
Chayei Sarah
88, 93, 111, 112, 116
Lech Lecha
95

CAVES

Balak
387, 504
Bechukotai
52
Beha'alot'cha
20
Beresheet A
26, 27
Beresheet B
13, 411, 412
Beshalach
100
Bo
155, 156

Chayei Sarah
61, 88, 89, 90, 92, 93, 100 -108, 110, 111, 112, 116
Chukat
65, 66
Ha'azinu
182, 201, 233
Idra Raba
153
Lech Lecha
95, 104
Metzora
61
Mishpatim
445
Noach
195
Prologue
188, 252
Shemot
99, 217, 220, 221, 274
Shlach Lecha
39, 94, 98, 109, 110, 128, 132, 133, 136, 285
Tazria
4, 152, 169-171, 178, 179
Toldot
102
Vaera
149
Vaetchanan
162
Vayechi
120, 172, 254, 269, 270, 329 -331, 429, 431, 487, 730, 737, 786, 801, 823, 847, 849, 853, 854
Vayera
308, 409, 457
Vayetze
32, 243
Vayikra
350, 352, 354-356, 366, 384
Vayishlach
234

CELESTIAL YESHIVAH

Prologue
109, 148

CENSUS

Beha'alot'cha
115, 123
Idra Raba
20, 188

CHACHMIEL (SUPERNAL MINISTER)

Vayikra
12

CHAGAI

Naso
148

CHAIR

Prologue
77, 78, 86, 95, 186, 225

CHALCHALIEL (SPIRIT)

Pekudei
689

CHALDEANS

Acharei Mot
13
Vayechi
268

Vayera
18
Vayetze
46, 47

CHALITZAH

Chukat
9, 12
Ki Tetze
103
Vaetchanan
119

CHAMBERS

Acharei Mot
45, 48, 50, 91, 167, 214, 220, 242, 260, 313, 328, 334, 375
Balak
19, 85, 111, 116, 219, 221, 290, 291, 332, 347, 348, 358
Beha'alot'cha
1, 3, 4
Behar
24, 34
Beresheet A
193, 194, 195, 297, 370, 389
Beresheet B
1, 4-10, 12-28, 43, 47, 55-65, 69-73, 75-77, 79, 82-88, 91-95, 98, 99, 101, 102, 104-106, 108 -111, 113-115, 118, 119, 122 -127, 129-139, 141, 142
Beshalach
7, 9, 83
Chayei Sarah
143
Chukat
30, 48
Ekev
40
Emor
171, 212
Ha'azinu
68, 90, 92, 183, 189
Idra Raba
3, 160, 192, 195, 352, 353, 357, 359, 360
Ki Tetze
70
Lech Lecha
310, 311, 312, 313, 425
Miketz
216
Mishpatim
61, 62, 85, 99 106, 107, 153, 248, 336, 529
Naso
189
Noach
124, 125, 127
Pekudei
40, 260, 460, 461, 471-473, 477-484, 486, 488, 489, 492 -497, 507, 509-511, 515 -518, 521, 522, 525, 529, 532 -535, 537, 539, 540, 541, 542, 546, 549, 550, 551, 553, 555-557, 559, 560, 563-567, 571-574, 576, 577, 587, 592 -597, 599, 600, 603-605, 608, 609, 611, 613, 620, 624, 625, 629, 630, 632, 633, 635, 638 -641, 645-651, 658, 661, 665, 667, 678-681, 686, 688, 690, 692, 696, 699, 701, 702, 705, 707, 708, 710-716, 718 -721, 724, 729-731, 734, 735, 740, 742, 743, 746, 748, 749, 750, 752-

759, 761-764, 766, 768- 771, 773, 776, 777, 781, 788-797, 803-805, 807 -809, 811, 815 -824, 834-836, 838, 839, 842 -844, 848, 853, 859, 861, 862, 864 -866, 869, 872, 877, 882, 883, 887, 888, 890, 893, 896, 897, 903, 907-913, 918, 919, 925, 926, 928, 932, 933, 934, 936, 946, 949

Pinchas
61, 250

Prologue
121, 125, 143, 168, 230, 231

Safra Detzniuta
1

Shemot
38, 69, 71, 72, 106-108, 123, 125, 249

Shlach Lecha
89, 104, 138, 257, 265

Shmini
93

Shoftim
12

Trumah
20, 21, 31, 42-45, 114, 119, 120, 122, 133, 138, 340, 343, 361, 440, 445-447, 452, 848

Tzav
124

Vaetchanan
4, 5, 145, 146

Vayakhel
103, 105, 148

Vayechi
154, 584

Vayera
18, 405

Vayeshev
74, 78

Vayikra
3, 36

Yitro
35, 36, 37, 38, 327

CHANIEL (SPIRIT)

Pekudei
531

Vayera
275, 276, 277

CHARIOT

Acharei Mot
38, 177, 194, 251, 276, 395

Balak
157, 179, 299, 356

Beha'alot'cha
40, 45

Behar
25, 42

Beresheet A
70, 82, 88, 89, 134, 176, 194, 264, 295, 337, 371, 466, 467

Beresheet B
19, 167, 255, 257

Beshalach
25, 53, 55, 61-63, 65, 95, 98, 105, 107-111, 113, 128, 155, 156, 164, 168, 173-175, 200, 259, 261-264, 266, 267, 271-273, 340

Bo
218, 229

Chayei Sarah
159, 190, 191-194, 234

Chukat
29, 37, 47, 67
Ekev
67, 74
Emor
7, 101, 125, 186, 188, 203, 260a, 260b, 261, 263
Ha'azinu
17, 29, 106
Idra Raba
6, 169, 247, 363
Kedoshim
77
Ki Tetze
4, 104
Ki Tisa
57
Korach
59, 60
Lech Lecha
72
Miketz
64, 79, 83, 213, 220
Mishpatim
87, 298, 300, 327, 338, 429, 445, 476
Naso
42, 149
Noach
17, 24, 284
Pekudei
2, 35, 75, 109, 128, 159, 210, 237, 253, 295, 348, 357, 372, 375, 397, 473, 491, 505, 769, 777-782, 789, 833
Pinchas
18, 51, 70, 100, 196-198, 200, 202, 223, 248, 263, 270, 303, 304, 310, 317, 334, 338, 341, 343, 344, 408, 604, 611, 655, 666, 749, 774, 863
Safra Detzniuta
67, 71
Shemot
11-13, 40, 45, 47, 48, 50, 51, 57, 59, 107, 123, 124, 213, 240, 241, 259, 260, 272, 275, 280
Shlach Lecha
88, 118, 238, 239, 275
Shmini
42, 94
Tazria
110, 114
Tetzaveh
12, 15, 17, 26, 28-30, 33, 34
Toldot
96
Trumah
103, 105, 107, 110-112, 116, 117, 158, 176, 180, 193, 219, 241, 283, 304, 312, 328-330, 341, 342, 346, 372, 380, 625, 711, 719, 916
Tzav
8, 47, 62, 70, 75
Vaera
9, 10, 17, 23, 34, 68, 108, 175, 195
Vaetchanan
50, 51, 52, 54, 60, 97, 181
Vayakhel
50, 51, 57, 58, 103-105, 175, 185, 210, 211, 213, 231 -233, 260-262, 264, 267, 269, 272, 273, 281, 297, 299, 300, 302, 333, 340, 347, 357, 360, 391, 409, 420, 428, 435, 437, 461, 470, 479
Vayechi
38, 47, 48, 63, 78, 93, 103, 107,

265, 294, 328, 333, 334, 351, 353, 507, 517, 540, 541, 567, 621, 652, 779, 802, 803, 804, 805, 847, 859

Vayera
10, 35, 438, 493

Vayeshev
61, 149

Vayetze
60, 62, 70, 91, 108, 120, 158, 170, 173, 197, 272

Vayigash
66, 67, 83, 123, 129, 133, 134

Vayikra
2, 7, 9, 17, 19, 46, 135, 224, 291, 337, 342, 406

Vayishlach
45, 143, 163

Yitro
6, 17, 67, 128, 129, 182, 225, 319, 324, 327, 383, 406, 540, 545

CHASDIEL (SPIRIT)

Beha'alot'cha
112

Vayera
275

Vayetze
73

CHASDIHAEL (SPIRIT)

Pekudei
696

CHASSADIM

Acharei Mot
47, 49, 87, 91, 116, 146, 149, 153, 154, 237, 251, 316, 319

Balak
5, 80, 88, 89, 158, 159, 231, 439

Beha'alot'cha
23, 30, 33, 37, 120, 125, 132

Bemidbar
17, 36, 56

Beresheet A
7, 33, 40, 43, 85, 312, 322, 332, 344, 378, 381, 467

Beresheet B
47, 73, 79, 130, 131, 233

Beshalach
137, 157, 171, 172, 215, 274, 430, 482

Bo
232

Chayei Sarah
169

Chukat
27, 28, 32, 33

Emor
135, 141, 149, 152, 226, 229, 255, 263

Ha'azinu
33, 35, 39, 42, 45, 106, 116, 117, 118, 120, 123, 142, 148b, 149, 150, 151, 180

Idra Raba
7, 48, 56, 182, 183, 276, 77, 284, 285, 290, 313, 317, 341

Ki Tetze
136

Lech Lecha
10, 233, 236, 241, 242, 337, 363, 412, 459

Metzora
8, 40, 41, 42

Miketz
228

Mishpatim
186, 187, 409, 414, 480, 523, 525
Naso
5, 133
Noach
116
Pekudei
10, 74, 76, 95, 96, 103, 118, 126, 215, 243, 245, 255, 277, 298, 475
Pinchas
14, 15, 32, 141, 179, 184, 283, 309, 314, 335, 337, 349, 365, 370, 401, 402, 404, 405, 407, 505, 513, 567, 598, 648, 674, 689, 715, 718, 878
Prologue
14, 15, 16, 20
Safra Detzniuta
26, 45, 56, 67
Shemot
19, 41, 43-47, 112, 114, 212, 224, 243, 244, 324, 332, 365, 366
Shlach Lecha
4, 151, 155, 156, 161, 162, 284, 308, 326, 333
Shmini
77, 79, 86, 89
Tazria
60, 123
Tetzaveh
145
Toldot
12, 73, 107, 111, 119, 120, 194
Trumah
7, 13, 42, 74, 78, 128, 169, 208, 227, 259, 260, 261, 320, 321, 347, 358, 368, 376, 377, 427, 428, 480, 520, 521, 531, 569, 704, 737, 785, 838, 879, 880, 913
Tzav
37, 44, 55, 76, 88, 178
Vaera
4, 23, 27, 102, 104, 141, 156, 157
Vaetchanan
53
Vayakhel
169, 188, 242, 262, 294, 304, 321, 322, 481, 486, 489
Vayechi
30, 118, 176, 215, 217, 356, 433, 437, 438, 461, 476, 477, 509, 510, 560, 632-634, 660, 662, 727, 767, 791, 792, 794, 799, 837, 840, 846, 848
Vayera
20, 26, 27, 28, 29, 46, 103, 107, 161, 171, 172, 301, 350, 512
Vayeshev
62, 146, 147
Vayetze
2, 12, 17-20, 32, 46, 161, 162, 169, 190, 191, 194, 201, 202, 204-206, 211, 212, 220, 244, 260, 306, 316, 348, 351, 362
Vayigash
15, 41, 45, 64, 65, 101
Vayikra
21, 98, 197, 223, 360, 380
Vayishlach
11, 12, 45, 133, 134, 136, 137, 143, 199
Yitro
224

CHASSIDIM

Acharei Mot
251
Lech Lecha
13
Naso
144
Noach
219
Prologue
20
Vaetchanan
141
Vayechi
215, 433
Trumah
194, 591
Vayechi
5
Vayeshev
275
Vayetze
362
Vayikra
283
Yitro
128

CHAYAH

Beresheet B
67, 68, 71, 78-81, 88-90, 107
109, 115-117, 119, 120, 145,
169, 285, 324
Emor
58
Idra Raba
325
Lech Lecha
76, 112, 161, 193
Mishpatim
77
Naso
36
Pekudei
772, 773
Pinchas
258
Prologue
216, 229
Safra Detzniuta
38

CHAYOT

Beresheet B
66, 71, 78-82, 88, 92, 98,
116, 128-130, 171
Pekudei
519
Pinchas
196
Vayakhel
168

CHEBAR (RIVER)

Prologue
95
Vayetze
46, 47

CHERUBIM (CHERUBS)

Balak
49, 54, 90
Beresheet A
77, 80, 81, 100, 371
Beresheet B
137

Chayei Sarah
95, 194
Ekev
66
Emor
252
Ki Tetze
127
Lech Lecha
104
Naso
104
Pekudei
500
Pinchas
213, 263, 312, 342, 403, 431, 451, 815, 816
Prologue
6
Shlach Lecha
87, 97, 105, 131, 140, 143, 145, 159, 160, 191, 262, 279
Trumah
100, 357, 407, 408, 434, 483, 573, 922, 923
Vayechi
172, 332, 396-398, 449-451, 477, 572
Vayetze
105, 203
Vayishlach
129

CHIDEKEL (RIVER)

Bo
71

CHILDREN

Acharei Mot
173, 285, 363-365
Balak
29, 31, 32, 47, 57, 66-71, 75, 80-84, 87, 92, 103, 106, 109, 113, 114, 119, 126, 131, 335, 361, 362, 364, 365, 367, 374, 379, 380, 381, 383, 487
Bechukotai
10, 42
Bemidbar
33, 40
Beresheet A
474
Beresheet B
221, 330
Beshalach
12, 14, 19, 199
Chayei Sarah
66, 67, 202, 214
Ekev
24, 43
Ha'azinu
229, 231, 232
Idra Raba
123, 232
Kedoshim
55, 132
Ki Tetze
27, 37, 54, 97
Ki Tisa
24
Lech Lecha
320, 322, 329, 426, 439, 446, 449, 471
Mishpatim
12, 18, 21, 43, 47, 59, 60, 78, 118, 120, 130, 131, 134, 157, 185, 258, 320, 333, 352, 355, 371, 383, 474
Naso
73, 190

Noach
13
Pekudei
552, 871, 926, 927
Pinchas
104, 251, 257, 614, 693, 710
Prologue
177, 178, 215
Safra Detzniuta
69
Shemot
78, 190, 198, 203-206, 279, 296
Shlach Lecha
94, 95, 131, 204, 253-256, 259, 260, 317
Shmini
1, 21
Tazria
1, 9, 10, 14, 23-25, 27, 28, 30, 36, 37, 60, 171
Tetzaveh
119
Trumah
406, 407, 633, 689, 803, 893, 908
Vaera
138, 198
Vaetchanan
30, 31, 115, 166
Vayakhel
420
Vayechi
20, 206, 207, 606-608, 626, 637, 642
Vayera
20, 146, 317, 325, 398, 426
Vayeshev
3, 6, 136, 137, 185
Vayetze
135, 267, 366, 367
Vayikra
92, 96, 221, 323, 405, 408
Yitro
162, 495, 552, 554

CHIRAH

Vayeshev
152

CHIZKIEL (SUPERNAL MINISTER)

Vayera
275
Vayikra
20

CHOLAM

Beresheet A
9, 38, 211, 212, 213
Ki Tetze
114
Tetzaveh
12
Vayera 275

CHUPAH (WEDDING CANOPY)

Beresheet B
22
Beshalach
231
Chayei Sarah
234
Chukat
61
Ekev
32

Lech Lecha
428
Mishpatim
78
Naso
193
Noach
46
Pinchas
335, 337, 339, 553, 879
Prologue
125-128, 130, 143, 168, 169
Trumah
126, 137-139, 199, 200, 344, 345, 788, 789
Vayechi
77
Vayikra
41

CHUT HASHANI (SPIRIT)

Beresheet B
125

CIPHERS

Trumah
106, 110, 618

CIRCUMCISION

Acharei Mot
296, 297, 300-302, 305, 307, 309, 310
Balak
15
Beha'alot'cha
7
Behar
6
Beresheet A
217, 361, 362, 364, 383
Beresheet B
428, 429
Beshalach
30, 38, 291, 292, 330, 349, 351, 352, 354, 356, 361-363, 374, 474, 485
Bo
78, 80, 85, 86, 88, 90, 170-174, 188, 189, 191, 192
Chayei Sarah
66
Chukat
86
Emor
53, 57, 58, 61, 62, 130, 131, 162
Ha'azinu
93
Ki Tisa
46
Korach
45
Lech Lecha
271-276, 290, 293, 296, 338, 339, 340, 342, 343, 380-382, 387, 389, 393-398, 426, 427, 430-432, 434, 435, 438, 440-442, 444, 454, 456, 458, 468, 469, 472
Miketz
162, 170, 171, 267
Mishpatim
26, 287, 316, 456, 545, 546, 548, 572
Noach
2, 10, 134, 288
Pekudei
690, 691, 901

Pinchas
484, 583, 830, 853, 855
Prologue
130, 131, 223, 225, 226, 228
Shemot
29, 186, 187
Shlach Lecha
117, 122, 131, 169, 171, 172
Tazria
27, 28, 31, 32, 36
Tetzaveh
25
Trumah
789, 894
Tzav
87
Vaera
20, 200, 201, 202, 203
Vaetchanan
119, 180
Vayakhel
169
Vayechi
50, 66, 67, 88, 107, 379, 603, 760
Vayera
6-11, 13, 17, 18, 51, 54, 60, 61, 69, 93, 95, 97, 160, 161, 244, 248, 304, 305, 306
Vayetze
296
Vayigash
85
Vayikra
215-217, 221, 222, 224-226, 229, 438
Vayishlach
139, 140, 150
Yitro
406, 407, 423, 425

CITRON (ETROG)

Emor
282
Ki Tetze
143, 144, 145
Mishpatim
493, 495, 499
Noach
94, 97
Pinchas
57, 822, 823, 827
Shmini
40
Tzav
108
Vayechi
211, 226, 229, 230
Vayikra
412, 420

CLAY

Tetzaveh
120
Vayera
299, 300, 301
Vayeshev
126, 155
Vayishlach
253

CLOUD

Acharei Mot
51-53, 140, 392
Balak
127, 140, 308
Beha'alot'cha
36, 37, 46
Beresheet A
70, 239, 371, 424

Beshalach
52, 54, 157, 158, 172, 298, 299, 434, 453
Bo
228, 229
Chukat
62, 66
Emor
205, 260a, 260b, 261, 262, 263, 264, 265, 267, 270, 275
Idra Raba
239, 351
Ki Tisa
49, 67
Lech Lecha
8, 39, 218
Miketz
227, 228
Mishpatim
87, 96, 204, 205, 206, 258, 341, 343, 375, 546
Naso
98
Noach
144, 261, 266, 269, 270
Pekudei
163, 285, 392, 519, 957, 958
Pinchas
150, 174, 177, 226, 334, 344, 435, 437, 658, 739, 744, 745, 815
Prologue
209
Shemot
82, 89, 259
Shlach Lecha
113, 114, 173, 213, 242
Toldot
125, 186
Trumah
82, 236, 416, 424, 442, 709, 711, 712, 717-719
Tzav
52, 117
Vayakhel
45, 164, 165, 317, 319, 320
Vayechi
103, 174, 218, 469
Vayelech
1, 2, 45
Vayera
447, 458
Vayetze
290
Vayikra
7, 8, 9, 238, 275, 317
Vayishlach
105, 132, 223, 224, 225, 226
Yitro
250, 288, 294, 295, 296, 308, 311, 312, 351

COFFIN

Beshalach
113
Pekudei
189
Pinchas
18
Trumah
459
Vayakhel
383-388, 494
Vayechi
268, 855, 858, 860
Vayishlach
227

COLORS

Acharei Mot
311, 312, 315, 317, 318
Balak
389, 433, 437
Beha'alot'cha
121, 135
Beresheet A
1, 7, 9, 16, 20, 23, 70-72, 85, 86, 87, 135, 207, 277
Beresheet B
14, 15, 27, 64, 73, 84, 88, 89, 99, 100, 115, 116, 255, 267, 269, 273-276
Beshalach
163, 167, 171, 388, 476, 478, 480
Bo
78, 79, 232
Ekev
61, 70, 71, 72
Emor
251, 333
Ha'azinu
9, 10, 11, 117, 120, 123, 138- 141, 164, 179, 184, 189, 205
Idra Raba
17, 57, 58, 142, 185, 205, 217, 290
Kedoshim
78
Ki Tetze
94, 95
Lech Lecha
7, 101, 196, 201, 340, 341, 459
Matot
1
Metzora
55, 58
Mishpatim
96, 515, 522, 523, 529, 534
Noach
102, 266, 269-271, 289-291, 297, 302, 303
Pekudei
41, 151, 157, 160, 162, 164, 165, 168, 247, 248, 286, 307, 356, 381, 428, 429, 430, 433, 435, 436, 437, 438, 439, 440, 445, 448, 458, 492, 498, 519, 560, 561, 562, 633, 637, 642, 644
Pinchas
34, 35a, 35b, 35c, 37, 38, 40, 41, 68, 251, 254, 255, 266, 313, 318, 344, 583, 584, 629, 822
Prologue
113
Safra Detzniuta
26, 28
Shemot
4, 81, 101, 106, 112, 194, 361
Shlach Lecha
104, 124, 125, 144, 157, 158, 161, 176, 213, 224, 248, 279, 314, 328, 342
Tazria
88, 165
Tetzaveh
14, 94
Trumah
42-45, 52, 77, 82, 158, 159, 162, 229-231, 233, 234, 237, 370, 380, 386, 388, 400, 408, 409, 425, 426, 428-431, 480- 483, 484, 704, 840

Tzav
7
Vaera
22, 23, 24, 26, 27, 28, 29, 106,
108
Vaetchanan
34, 53
Vayakhel
160, 161, 172, 252, 293, 303, 307, 322, 323, 339-341, 348, 354, 362, 414
Vayechi
166, 174, 235, 236, 238, 341, 342, 469-472, 475, 508
Vayera
45-48, 52, 53, 57, 58, 59, 64, 65, 269, 271, 272, 274, 447
Vayeshev
49, 65, 83
Vayetze
17, 117, 309, 315, 316
Vayigash
123
Vayikra
140, 427
Vayishlach
114
Yitro
85-87, 89, 92, 100, 104, 163 -165, 205, 209, 210-212, 225, 228, 230, 310-312, 315, 360, 500, 502, 533, 535, 536, 538

COMETS

Vayechi
286

COMMUNITY OF YISRAEL

Prologue
1, 82

COMPASSION

Balak
17, 18, 89, 124, 228, 229, 259, 260, 262, 329, 331, 352, 366, 408, 410-412, 427, 476
Beresheet A
184
Chukat
3, 13, 84
Emor
37, 52
Ha'azinu
218, 229, 231, 232, 237, 238
Lech Lecha
250
Matot
2, 3, 4
Miketz
119, 152, 184
Mishpatim
53, 225, 230
Pinchas
157, 360, 591, 653, 859
Prologue
234
Tetzaveh
24
Vayechi
410
Vayera
510
Vayeshev
35, 131
Vayishlach
232

CONGREGATION

Acharei Mot
26, 29, 43, 49, 92, 99, 130, 163, 174, 204, 205, 208, 317, 319, 322, 324, 406
Balak
224, 225, 238, 239, 311, 331, 378, 443, 494, 507
Bechukotai
3, 24, 26, 56
Beha'alot'cha
20, 24, 26, 28, 29, 31-33, 35, 46, 63, 73, 149
Behar
1, 4, 5, 14, 15, 62
Bemidbar
25, 26, 27, 40
Beresheet A
57, 339, 424, 449
Beresheet B
184, 186, 297, 308
Beshalach
7, 46, 47, 69, 121, 123, 126, 127, 132, 133, 141, 152
Bo
141, 160, 163, 186, 190
Chayei Sarah
63, 268, 270
Chukat
2, 35, 37, 63, 66, 84
Emor
16, 19, 31, 32, 45, 56, 57, 61 -63, 95-97, 100, 101, 128, 130, 141, 144, 147-149, 152, 153, 156, 165, 168, 225, 250, 257, 261, 264, 265, 275, 295, 330, 331
Ha'azinu
1, 10, 11, 12
Kedoshim
1, 18, 19, 21, 38, 127-129
Ki Tetze
4, 105
Korach
9, 10, 12, 27, 40
Lech Lecha
15, 181, 182, 209, 427
Metzora
8, 15, 19, 36, 39, 41, 42, 43
Miketz
71, 72, 75, 110, 224,
Mishpatim
76, 81, 82, 237, 356, 367, 369, 371, 536, 551, 552, 556, 562, 576
Naso
25, 26, 60, 61, 106, 107, 108, 154
Noach
25, 84
Pekudei
19, 43, 57, 76, 79, 82, 83, 86, 87, 97, 114, 227, 276, 281, 348, 349, 366, 367-369, 372, 376, 387, 402-404
Pinchas
1, 59, 313, 315, 381, 393 -395, 398, 470, 471, 477, 528, 532, 553, 558, 563, 598, 699, 772, 809
Prologue
241, 254, 256, 257, 258, 259
Shemot
14, 15, 39, 56, 139, 176, 180, 199, 200, 233, 248, 385
Shlach Lecha
4, 81, 137, 317
Shmini
9, 28, 29, 37, 38, 39, 40, 41,

51, 52, 71, 72, 80, 81, 82
Tazria
1, 3-5, 8, 13, 29, 41, 46-49, 59, 60, 134, 139, 140
Tetzaveh
25
Toldot
18, 181, 185, 204
Trumah
91, 97, 98, 99, 101, 105, 107, 112, 114, 118, 153, 327, 545, 731, 879, 884
Tzav
1, 19-22, 72, 98, 100, 109, 116, 176, 177, 181, 183
Vaera
72, 141, 150

Vaetchanan
5, 43, 59, 130, 131, 157, 187, 190
Vayakhel
1, 8, 36, 42, 51, 154, 157, 232, 453
Vayechi
84, 181, 232, 233, 351, 416, 477, 543, 563, 568, 586, 596, 604, 629, 633, 655, 676, 677, 680, 693, 730, 731, 732, 737, 748, 750, 753, 759, 764, 824, 826, 827, 846, 848
Vayelech
16, 17
Vayera
120, 123, 253, 396, 438, 439, 441, 442, 446, 448, 449, 451
Vayeshev
106, 216, 217, 252, 263, 264
Vayetze
7, 60, 159, 161, 167, 168, 371
Vayigash
65, 67, 68, 69, 70
Vayikra
29, 31, 39, 46, 48, 56, 60, 75, 81, 82, 100-102, 114, 184, 195, 200, 205, 273, 287, 288, 290, 292-294, 315, 332, 334, 344, 346, 349, 352, 366, 367, 370, 371, 373, 374, 378, 387, 389, 390, 396, 398-402, 419, 423, 426, 436
Vayishlach
45, 66, 94, 179, 267, 270, 272
Yitro
283, 348, 385, 393, 489

CONSTELLATION

Beresheet A
396
Lech Lecha
27, 322, 323, 324, 449
Prologue
139
Vayechi
452
Vayera
83, 244, 246, 252, 254, 290, 353
Vayeshev
34, 198
Vayishlach
240

CONVERTS

Acharei Mot
108, 134, 135, 158, 396

Balak
100
Beresheet A
220
Beresheet B
10, 11, 12, 55
Ekev
46
Kedoshim
50
Ki Tetze
23
Ki Tisa
15, 60, 71
Lech Lecha
59, 60, 200
Mishpatim
23, 26, 88-90, 92, 94, 95, 107, 111, 116, 487
Naso
100, 186
Pekudei
194
Pinchas
469
Prologue
228, 229, 231, 232
Shemot
113, 194
Shlach Lecha
99, 202, 203
Vaera
90, 94, 113
Vayechi
79, 80, 88
Vayera
398
Vayikra
128, 229
Yitro
47, 48, 60, 61, 425

COPPER

Acharei Mot
361
Balak
5
Beresheet B
273
Mishpatim
302
Pekudei
151
Vaera
34, 35, 43, 44, 45, 46

CORIANDER

Balak
420
Beha'alot'cha
134, 135

CORN

Vayechi
3, 11, 353, 356
Vayishlach
19, 41

CORNERS

Acharei Mot
76, 88, 254, 311
Balak
1
Beha'alot'cha
70, 101

Bemidbar
28, 31, 35, 36, 60-62, 64, 65
Beresheet A
118, 203, 297, 408
Beshalach
137, 272, 438
Bo
91
Chukat
15, 47
Ekev
26
Ha'azinu
30, 132, 228
Idra Raba
136, 138, 139, 291, 315, 319
Ki Tetze
46, 47, 71
Ki Tisa
42
Lech Lecha
6, 9, 25, 370
Miketz
94, 98
Naso
80
Noach
38, 264, 345, 352
Pekudei
564, 912, 913
Pinchas
226, 250, 256, 257, 258, 259, 286, 288, 340, 674, 705
Shemot
292
Shlach Lecha
124, 125, 135, 271, 290, 309, 329, 333, 338, 345
Trumah
23, 579
Tzav
77, 78, 79, 83, 164
Vaera
205
Vaetchanan
7
Vayakhel
128
Vayechi
445, 456, 549, 764, 802
Vayera
126, 127, 480
Vayetze
393
Vayigash
109, 110
Vayikra
169, 170, 252
Yitro
225, 271

CORRECTION (TIKUN)

Acharei Mot
105
Balak
274
Bechukotai
20, 42, 43
Beha'alot'cha
53
Beresheet A
234, 250, 252, 273, 280, 281, 332
Beresheet B
16, 157, 184, 187, 362
Bo
50
Idra Raba
1, 170, 178, 300, 330, 349- 351

Korach
3
Lech Lecha
75
Mishpatim
138, 176, 203, 350
Naso
188
Noach
73, 244
Pekudei
381, 484, 491, 752, 765, 878, 955
Pinchas
1, 76, 222, 228, 231, 232, 235, 284, 313, 322, 334, 509, 512, 542, 556, 567, 605, 636, 674, 705, 727, 892
Shlach Lecha
125, 258, 340
Tetzaveh
89
Toldot
146, 148
Trumah
115
Tzav
29, 34, 38, 41, 117
Vaera
126
Vayechi
21, 42, 648, 650, 657, 658
Vayeshev
45, 173, 176
Vayigash
17, 29
Vayikra
115, 256
Vayishlach
159
Yitro
165, 518

CORRECTION

Acharei Mot
25-27, 52, 55, 98, 168, 316
Balak
72, 166, 273, 275, 318
Beha'alot'cha
69
Bemidbar
45, 76
Beresheet A
236, 237, 437, 482
Beresheet B
14, 26, 156, 157, 173, 176, 187, 190, 198, 202, 203, 212, 213, 232, 233, 245, 301, 308, 354, 372, 378, 379, 419, 435
Bo
110, 243
Chukat
56
Ha'azinu
11, 71, 93, 95
Idra Raba
6, 14, 121, 129, 171, 174, 325
Kedoshim
13, 64, 114
Ki Tetze
75
Korach
3
Lech Lecha
75, 351, 410, 453
Miketz
54, 55, 67
Mishpatim
2, 118, 165, 179, 182, 207, 213,

215, 216, 226, 228, 541
Naso
183
Noach
237, 245, 311, 319, 328
Pekudei
122, 219, 259, 413, 415, 417, 539, 541-543, 732, 737, 739 -743, 750
Pinchas
8, 11, 35d, 50, 166, 184, 217, 228, 231, 232, 275, 315, 509, 510, 513, 532, 605, 658, 705, 881
Prologue
162, 163
Safra Detzniuta
64
Shlach Lecha
82, 238
Shmini
31, 32, 46
Tetzaveh
68, 69
Toldot
3, 44, 105, 116, 173
Trumah
69, 343, 361, 754
Tzav
30-32, 34, 40, 117
Vaetchanan
132, 171
Vayakhel
122, 170, 192, 250, 383, 409, 410
Vayechi
141, 218, 475, 570, 573, 679, 725, 751, 756, 768
Vayera
220, 223, 379
Vayetze
14, 76, 106, 161, 231, 237, 250
Vayigash
16
Vayikra
142, 256, 258, 263
Vayishlach
242
Yitro
108, 155, 156, 428, 563

COURT

Acharei Mot
13, 163

Balak
19, 189, 240, 351
Behar
23
Beresheet A
410
Beresheet B
93, 106, 107, 118
Beshalach
16, 52
Bo
116, 206
Chayei Sarah
5, 7, 127, 128
Emor
207, 208
Ha'azinu
134
Idra Raba
227, 329
Kedoshim
49
Lech Lecha
422, 423

Miketz
108
Mishpatim
429, 447, 547
Noach
361
Pekudei
11, 123, 126, 484, 513, 514, 538, 543, 546, 551, 563, 603, 605, 613, 614, 712, 717, 727, 857, 858
Pinchas
353, 355, 356, 358, 468, 686
Shemot
56
Shlach Lecha
86, 89, 140, 143, 159, 163, 164, 243, 244, 249, 257, 258, 260, 262, 271, 279, 299
Shoftim
3, 11, 14, 21, 22
Tetzaveh
84, 128
Trumah
419, 537, 861
Vayakhel
85, 355, 356
Vayechi
132, 362, 546, 591, 598, 635, 748
Vayera
175, 189, 195, 300
Vayeshev
282
Vayetze
31, 83, 267
Yitro
259

COURTYARD

Behar
23
Emor
29
Noach
361
Shlach Lecha
161, 162, 261, 270, 279

COVENANT (BRIT)

Acharei Mot
25-27, 85, 182-184, 301, 307
Balak
34, 51, 97, 128, 268, 349
Bechukotai
52, 53, 54, 55, 56
Beresheet A
56, 149, 204, 216, 217, 287, 358, 360-364, 377, 382, 383, 394-396, 398, 434, 458, 476
Beresheet B
2, 11, 184, 186, 228, 242, 373-377, 442
Beshalach
44, 96, 200, 291, 292, 349, 358, 360, 361, 464, 469, 473, 474, 478
Bo
123, 172, 188, 191, 246
Chayei Sarah
162, 214, 216
Chukat
16, 88, 90
Ekev
54, 59, 60
Emor
30, 32, 55, 56, 57, 63, 128, 130, 148, 162, 167

Ha'azinu
17, 159, 218, 221
Idra Raba
197
Kedoshim
78
Ki Tetze
35, 67, 79, 82, 138
Ki Tisa
45, 46
Lech Lecha
230, 233, 276, 277, 294 -296, 326, 338, 342, 343, 385, 386, 388, 389, 391, 392, 393, 394, 398, 399, 400, 403-405, 407, 409, 410, 412-414, 426, 431, 432, 438, 442, 456, 469, 472
Miketz
35, 39, 83, 101, 158, 162, 170-172, 245, 247
Mishpatim
217, 381, 406, 407, 410, 450, 458, 572, 573, 574, 581
Naso
20, 75, 76
Noach
2, 3, 5-7, 9, 134, 153-162, 181, 188, 224, 261, 267, 268, 270, 287, 291, 292, 297, 304, 310
Pekudei
83, 87, 221, 262, 263, 277, 308, 310, 636, 690, 731, 761, 763, 766, 768, 836, 855, 860, 902
Pinchas
5, 15, 18, 22, 26, 34, 35a, 35d, 36-38, 40, 73, 74, 76, 128-131, 140, 142, 174, 193, 231, 232, 394, 433, 449, 450, 456, 457, 482, 483, 484, 485, 488, 489, 490, 566, 571, 583, 584, 593, 771, 830, 851, 852, 855
Prologue
2, 3, 17, 26, 130-132, 138, 139, 219, 222, 226
Shemot
26-29, 91, 149, 150, 186, 189, 213
Shlach Lecha
66, 118, 119, 154, 167-170
Tazria
31-34, 36
Tetzaveh
25, 34, 47, 66
Toldot
8, 102
Trumah
23, 40, 41, 169, 355, 576, 617, 778, 779, 789, 793
Tzav
32, 57, 87
Vaera
20, 75-81, 86, 87, 189, 200
Vaetchanan
57, 180
Vayakhel
4, 98, 100, 169, 171, 376, 383 -387, 389, 390, 423, 424, 494
Vayechi
68, 74, 107, 187, 224, 253, 265, 268, 315, 373, 374, 379, 381, 392, 393, 405, 408, 439, 482, 561, 562, 642, 644, 645, 666, 667, 753, 760, 776, 786, 858, 859
Vayelech
13, 20

Vayera
6, 22, 50, 51, 118, 121, 122, 140, 304, 305, 355, 447, 448, 451, 476, 511, 512
Vayeshev
14, 81, 102, 104, 129, 171, 212, 215, 216, 218
Vayetze
52, 57, 58, 66, 134, 135, 137, 138, 239, 268, 269, 274, 278, 324, 325
Vayigash
85, 87, 131
Vayikra
33, 34, 214-220, 222-225, 236, 238, 326
Vayishlach
50, 227
Yitro
26, 27, 113, 261, 265, 406, 432, 433, 436, 470, 474, 527, 547, 574

COWS

Acharei Mot
353, 355
Balak
299, 304
Beha'alot'cha
53
Chayei Sarah
27, 28
Chukat
18, 21, 22, 23, 24, 35
Emor
71
Miketz
19, 20, 21
Pekudei
315
Shemot
374, 377
Shmini
29, 46, 48, 51
Trumah
211
Vayera
380
Vayikra
72

COZBI, DAUGHER OF ZUR

Pinchas
6, 21, 462, 481

CRAFTSMANSHIP

Beresheet B
30, 177, 179, 185
Ha'azinu
115
Pekudei
69
Pinchas
508
Prologue
77
Shlach Lecha
250, 262, 279
Tetzaveh
2
Trumah
17, 18, 528

CREATION

Acharei Mot
94, 99, 210, 219, 220, 222, 243, 244, 279, 289, 395
Balak
82, 174, 305, 306, 307, 355,

359, 417, 446, 468, 486
Beha'alot'cha
59, 101
Behar
66
Bemidbar
1, 2, 3
Beresheet A
1, 4, 5, 10, 11, 13, 28, 29, 44-51, 58, 70, 76, 82, 93, 94, 98, 110, 131, 162, 163, 167, 178, 180-182, 194, 197, 214-217, 219, 232, 260, 275, 294, 300, 304, 307, 310, 313, 315-317, 319, 327, 338, 339, 341-345, 347, 348, 351, 358, 364, 374, 393, 405, 408, 412, 417, 419, 420, 425, 426, 428, 438, 441, 442, 461, 468, 470
Beresheet B
1-3, 21, 28, 30, 32, 33, 54, 66, 77, 120, 146, 152, 153, 156, 159, 166-169, 172-175, 178, 180, 185-188, 190, 191, 202, 207, 241, 349, 366-369, 372, 375, 383, 406, 419, 425, 427, 432, 434, 446
Beshalach
96, 109, 112, 217, 233, 261, 459
Bo
39, 47, 49, 54, 104, 129, 153, 213-215, 217, 227, 239
Chayei Sarah
25, 28, 29, 35, 39, 42, 43, 47, 81, 110, 152, 154, 168, 169, 176, 201, 203, 209, 211, 220
Chukat
34
Ekev
49
Emor
3, 4, 55, 112, 218, 227, 283-285, 334
Ha'azinu
34, 79, 114, 212, 220, 225, 226, 228, 234
Idra Raba
13, 172, 301, 305, 347
Kedoshim
7, 29, 34, 40, 57, 61, 62, 68, 69, 108, 109
Ki Tetze
88, 112-115, 118
Ki Tisa
6, 50, 82
Korach
6, 35, 37, 38
Lech Lecha
4, 12, 78, 84, 94, 100, 189, 211, 220, 223, 225, 226, 237, 249, 277, 278, 310, 311, 312, 329, 331, 343, 347, 369, 383
Metzora
28, 58
Miketz
10, 66, 81, 88, 130, 131, 134, 178, 233, 240, 242, 243, 267
Mishpatim
15, 52, 114, 208, 240, 273, 275, 313, 359, 360, 403, 408, 431, 517
Naso
31, 33, 36, 38, 39, 43, 53- 55, 113, 194
Noach
11, 32, 55, 98, 193, 247, 255, 274, 278, 279, 315, 334

Pekudei
6, 12, 13, 14, 38, 98, 105, 127, 138, 202, 208, 211, 213, 214, 216, 218, 267 -270, 272, 273, 355, 525, 549, 638, 714, 743, 792

Pinchas
7, 46, 49, 65, 67, 69, 77, 123, 124, 126, 176, 177, 223, 224, 232, 259, 287, 335, 370, 375, 385, 393, 395, 396, 410, 412, 448, 489, 500, 501, 502, 516, 560, 584, 601, 621, 622, 627, 646, 669, 770, 772, 820, 840, 841, 858, 859, 868, 869, 880

Prologue
1-4, 7, 10-12, 14, 16, 18, 20, 22, 23, 26, 27, 34, 37, 38, 40, 41, 44, 46-48, 56, 72, 73, 75, 76, 77, 82, 101, 108, 117, 132, 145, 151, 152, 159, 167, 176, 189, 195, 201, 219, 224, 226, 229, 235, 237, 243, 247, 248, 249

Safra Detzniuta
7, 8, 43, 48, 58

Shemot
31, 123, 191, 210, 249, 324, 326, 358, 359, 380

Shlach Lecha
40-42, 46, 83, 84, 86, 153, 211, 212, 227

Shmini
1, 2, 3, 29, 44, 56, 72, 75, 76

Tazria
13, 15, 43, 80, 106, 113, 114, 116, 146

Tetzaveh
25, 53, 134, 141

Toldot
2, 30, 33, 42, 45, 47, 59, 61, 92, 113, 182, 196

Trumah
2, 8, 18, 26, 40, 60, 75, 200, 313, 325, 333, 335, 347, 416, 417, 426-428, 430, 433, 454, 469, 470, 472, 478, 480, 528 -530, 533, 543, 561, 618, 635, 637, 638, 639, 640, 644, 701, 702, 749, 755, 793, 795, 817, 834, 894, 913

Tzav
6, 48, 57, 89, 94, 117, 124, 172, 175

Vaera
8, 32, 33, 49, 50, 55, 56, 127, 180

Vayakhel
8, 62, 74-80, 98, 157, 252, 263, 264, 265, 383, 410

Vayechi
43, 44, 58, 63, 108, 165, 212, 213, 237, 241, 368, 435, 437, 444, 445, 446, 447, 483, 497, 499, 518, 539, 586, 630, 631, 648, 649, 772, 852

Vayelech
35

Vayera
1-3, 76, 78, 151, 194, 207, 208, 240, 242, 282, 304, 389, 394, 399, 400, 446, 468, 482, 508

Vayeshev
7, 25, 42, 57, 62, 66, 145, 146, 156, 160, 161, 242, 264

Vayetze
153, 190, 193, 200, 230, 260, 313, 332, 376, 384, 385

Vayigash
1-3, 5-7, 10-12, 14, 41, 42, 62, 64

Vayikra
54, 59, 92, 94, 134, 156, 178,

179, 182-190, 315, 316
Vayishlach
52, 53, 75, 80, 236, 248, 262, 263
Yitro
31, 33, 35, 62, 65-67, 123, 124-126, 129, 176, 183, 249, 253, 368, 369, 378, 398, 399, 441, 478, 479, 484, 519, 542, 553, 560, 569, 570, 574

CROCODILES

Acharei Mot
76
Balak
177
Beresheet A
408
Bo
36-41, 46-51, 53, 56, 58, 60-62, 64, 66-68, 70, 71, 73
Ki Tetze
58, 59
Shmini
76, 77, 119
Toldot
30, 43
Vaera
103, 104, 122, 144

CROWNS

Acharei Mot
93, 94, 100-102, 106, 108, 115, 133, 177, 180, 191, 192, 226 -228, 232, 248, 256, 258, 359, 374
Balak
162, 219, 223, 299, 391, 428, 436-440
Beha'alot'cha
3, 35, 73, 103
Beresheet A
6, 43, 85-87, 201, 202, 204, 229, 305, 318, 319, 354, 373, 374, 454
Beresheet B
2, 7, 26, 27, 77, 93, 97, 101, 150, 233-235, 299, 304, 310, 317, 406
Beshalach
117, 160, 162-164, 167, 172, 187, 190, 207, 208, 210, 215, 224, 227, 275, 296, 297, 301, 418, 419, 440
Bo
76, 80, 85, 87, 91, 92, 108, 120, 122, 127, 147, 161, 164, 232
Chayei Sarah
192, 195
Chukat
12
Ekev
59
Emor
10, 12, 24, 66, 67, 74, 100, 102, 105, 115-117, 127, 134, 147, 150, 153, 169-173, 200, 248, 259, 296
Ha'azinu
30, 41, 64, 86, 88, 89, 97, 119, 180-182
Idra Raba
11, 20, 228, 298, 312, 314, 328, 362
Kedoshim
20, 39, 58, 92
Ki Tetze
71, 74, 116

Ki Tisa
63, 113, 116
Korach
44
Lech Lecha
7, 72, 73, 102, 121, 161, 167, 170, 172, 238, 239, 240, 241, 255, 343, 401, 412, 438, 444, 465
Mishpatim
9, 41, 46, 67, 72, 79, 81, 123, 124, 410, 411, 439, 441, 468, 530
Naso
83, 149, 160, 162
Noach
21, 50, 127, 332, 383
Pekudei
64, 82, 103, 264, 286, 308, 357, 485, 693, 823
Pinchas
269, 331, 332, 336, 452, 510, 563, 569, 572-574, 600, 626, 668, 670-674, 677, 687, 712-714, 754, 824, 832, 848, 852, 873, 877
Prologue
9, 57, 62-64, 66, 82, 114, 125, 126, 142, 143
Safra Detzniuta
11, 22, 23, 47, 53, 54, 60, 72, 73
Shemot
103, 118, 123, 124, 155, 310, 393, 394
Shlach Lecha
53, 146-150, 231, 232, 259, 287, 292, 297, 306
Shmini
8, 13, 25, 27, 31, 40, 45, 52, 54
Shoftim
15
Tazria
4, 68, 97, 124
Tetzaveh
26, 94
Toldot
104, 167, 169
Trumah
20, 32, 33, 43, 46, 48, 59, 98, 99, 106, 165, 167, 168, 173, 182, 286, 293, 311, 312, 319, 326, 327, 333, 377, 396, 537, 578-584, 588, 589, 611, 902, 906, 912, 913, 915, 916
Tzav
58, 62, 167
Vaera
4, 141
Vaetchanan
49, 65, 66, 109, 116, 117, 141, 175, 195
Vayakhel
129, 145, 147, 148, 149, 161, 180, 188, 193, 194, 202, 204, 205, 206, 211, 214, 225, 230, 239, 240, 251, 253, 262, 281, 282, 309, 321, 345, 352, 355, 370, 438, 443, 444, 446, 450, 459, 469, 489
Vayechi
122, 138, 139, 156, 157, 183, 217, 278, 294, 298, 304, 308, 334, 367, 409, 461, 588, 613, 693, 753, 793, 810
Vayera
68, 305, 336, 337, 438, 490, 492, 493
Vayeshev
103, 220

Vayetze
6, 323, 348, 351
Vayigash
5, 16, 38
Vayikra
2, 44, 51, 103, 104, 110, 113, 147, 162, 166, 183, 208, 209, 229, 247, 285, 305, 308, 324, 372, 427
Vayishlach
25, 34, 37, 44, 155, 156, 173, 239, 240
Yitro
187, 285, 334, 339, 350, 355, 356, 359, 360, 362, 390, 402, 414, 424, 462, 465, 505, 511, 539, 540, 546, 548

CRYSTAL

Acharei Mot
315
Beha'alot'cha
135
Idra Raba
17, 185
Lech Lecha
285, 287
Safra Detzniuta
6
Shmini
92
Tazria
125
Trumah
189
Vayechi
331

CUBITS

Balak
43, 255, 322
Beresheet A
205, 206, 320
Chayei Sarah
229, 236
Idra Raba
311, 312, 313
Korach
48
Mishpatim
249
Naso
32
Pekudei
241, 242, 243, 244, 245, 249, 252, 253, 255, 256, 258
Pinchas
169, 302, 626, 830
Prologue
81, 147, 148
Shlach Lecha
133
Toldot
133
Vayetze
174

CUP OF BENEDICTION

Pinchas
623, 630-633, 640, 641
Prologue
2
Shmini
75
Vayera
172

CUP OF SALVATION

Balak
58
Pekudei
515
Pinchas
624
Prologue
2
Trumah
786
Vayechi
845

CUP

Ekev
37, 49, 56-62
Ki Tetze
19
Ki Tisa
37, 38, 39, 40, 41, 76
Lech Lecha
284, 285, 287
Mishpatim
189
Prologue
2, 253, 256
Vayechi
205, 504, 598, 845-848
Vayera
172
Vayetze
201

CURSE

Acharei Mot
125, 331, 349
Balak
120, 121, 123, 125, 133, 134, 136, 186, 232, 249, 252-254, 258, 265, 266, 279, 291, 385, 386, 396, 398, 410, 411, 442, 452, 461, 464, 482, 488
Bechukotai
8, 14, 15, 45, 52
Beha'alot'cha
138
Bemidbar
46, 47, 48, 49
Beresheet A
98, 101, 103, 110, 390, 393, 410, 438
Beresheet B
149, 161, 313, 428-431
Bo
24, 70, 71
Ekev
54
Emor
160, 161, 269, 312, 315, 316, 320, 321, 322, 326
Ha'azinu
153
Kedoshim
89
Ki Tetze
113
Ki Tisa
20
Korach
47
Lech Lecha
33, 41, 42, 68
Metzora
31
Miketz
222, 223, 254

Mishpatim
251, 255, 257, 258
Naso
71, 72, 186
Noach
242, 243, 245, 251, 298, 301, 311, 382
Pekudei
66, 113, 310, 465, 627, 727, 891, 894, 895, 906
Pinchas
34, 375, 442, 587, 642, 643, 884, 886, 887, 889
Prologue
4, 254, 255
Shemot
71
Shlach Lecha
29, 208, 299
Tetzaveh
52
Toldot
45, 138, 139, 141, 142, 148, 149, 160, 196
Trumah
753
Tzav
48
Vaetchanan
103, 182
Vayakhel
200
Vayechi
65, 381
Vayera
34
Vayeshev
44, 111, 113, 119
Vayikra
90, 91, 237
Vayishlach
23, 28, 33, 196, 197
Yitro
4

CURTAIN

Acharei Mot
61, 108, 148
Balak
114
Beresheet B
137, 189
Beshalach
157, 301
Bo
64, 232
Chayei Sarah
131
Ha'azinu
13
Idra Raba
166, 167, 247, 355, 361
Lech Lecha
70, 311
Mishpatim
134
Pekudei
161, 245, 246, 247, 248, 249, 250, 252, 255, 257, 258, 380, 755
Pinchas
19, 201, 301, 312
Prologue
56, 222
Shemot
164, 233, 234, 237, 238
Shlach Lecha
104, 113, 156, 185, 195, 265, 284, 340

Tazria
146
Tetzaveh
16, 135, 136, 137
Toldot
134
Trumah
47, 233, 272, 614, 617, 621, 664, 692, 699, 701, 703, 706, 707, 719, 758, 759, 860
Vayakhel
275, 284, 320, 323, 324, 359, 360, 382
Vayechi
90, 310, 502, 543
Vayeshev
183
Vayigash
56
Yitro
127, 228, 533, 545

DAHARIEL (SPIRIT)

Pekudei
612, 614, 615, 696

DAN

Balak
176, 178, 179
Beha'alot'cha
118, 123, 125
Bemidbar
29, 30, 31, 59
Beresheet A
249, 348
Ki Tisa
100
Lech Lecha
91
Mishpatim
202
Pekudei
37, 69, 178, 298
Shemot
35
Trumah
512
Vayechi
527, 695, 696, 700, 703, 704, 706-709, 711, 723, 724, 774
Vayera
73

DANIEL

Acharei Mot
14
Balak
348
Beresheet A
3, 14, 159, 190, 198, 237
Beresheet B
335
Bo
31
Chayei Sarah
99, 180, 199, 210
Emor
26
Ha'azinu
62, 89, 176, 201
Idra Raba
37, 60, 100, 106, 165, 186, 196, 219, 235, 279, 292, 319, 336, 351
Ki Tetze
74, 129
Metzora
30

Miketz
27, 41, 60, 61, 63, 149
Mishpatim
7, 118, 126, 214, 216, 408, 429, 569, 570, 571
Naso
89, 90, 133, 148, 150, 185
Noach
75, 76
Pekudei
199, 324, 521, 536, 697, 718
Pinchas
179, 227, 282, 496, 655, 690, 840, 867
Prologue
166, 191, 236
Shemot
1, 69, 89, 180, 213, 262, 337
Shlach Lecha
174, 289
Tazria
38
Tetzaveh
42, 145
Toldot
66, 71, 123, 186, 204
Trumah
233, 337, 392, 401, 572, 627, 847, 896, 902, 903
Vaera
24, 43
Vaetchanan
164, 198
Vayakhel
326
Vayechi
20, 50, 162, 186, 224, 689
Vayera
61, 249, 265, 324, 388, 393, 409
Vayeshev
105, 244, 245, 247
Vayetze
50, 79, 108, 349
Vayigash
109
Vayishlach
89, 210, 219
Yitro
304, 334

DARKNESS

Acharei Mot
30, 129, 334
Balak
80, 206, 208, 209, 211, 421, 422, 424, 425, 494, 497
Beha'alot'cha
12, 36, 37, 121
Behar
48, 64, 65, 66
Beresheet A
17, 19, 23, 25, 26, 34, 35, 37, 39, 41, 42, 51, 127, 141, 142, 166, 167, 178, 180-182, 230, 267, 320, 330, 331, 332, 334, 353, 354-357, 369, 371
Beresheet B
35-37, 40, 45, 48, 49, 149, 151, 157, 167, 198, 271, 343, 447
Beshalach
215, 279
Bo
16, 20, 52, 61, 62, 128, 164
Chayei Sarah
103, 106
Chukat
59

Emor
95
Ha'azinu
127, 129
Idra Raba
196, 273
Kedoshim
7
Ki Tetze
63, 114
Ki Tisa
104
Lech Lecha
361
Miketz
1, 2, 8, 25, 26
Mishpatim
126, 186, 234, 343, 344, 403, 474, 546
Naso
40, 44, 45, 55-58, 95, 100
Noach
75, 77, 78, 195, 247, 299
Pekudei
148, 424, 427-435, 445, 448, 542, 790, 867, 934, 940
Pinchas
39, 226, 255, 266, 270, 348, 390, 391, 396, 546, 657, 658, 659, 660, 689, 696, 698, 704, 709, 739, 887, 894
Prologue
1, 53, 54, 153, 154, 156, 195, 196, 197
Safra Detzniuta
7, 8, 45
Shemot
104, 145, 149, 160, 208, 390
Shlach Lecha
94
Shoftim
13
Tazria
54, 62, 63, 75, 96, 101, 105
Tetzaveh
86, 145, 146
Toldot
118, 120, 121
Trumah
29, 41, 61, 79, 101, 264, 265, 431, 532, 618, 619, 682, 683, 702, 747, 748, 859, 908
Tzav
49, 50, 51
Vaera
161
Vayakhel
75, 124, 165, 166, 314, 362, 368, 391
Vayechi
43, 44, 58, 122, 248, 592
Vayera
161, 242, 360, 361, 362, 363, 366
Vayeshev
5, 20, 126, 272
Vayetze
161, 162, 201, 311, 312, 362
Vayigash
109
Vayikra
209, 296
Vayishlach
56, 93, 96, 131, 134, 135, 257
Yitro
51, 288, 294, 295, 296, 351, 352, 543

DAUGHTER

Acharei Mot
25, 110, 171, 173, 231, 234, 282, 285, 324, 355, 357, 369, 379, 383, 393, 395
Balak
48, 50, 74, 76, 93, 94, 99, 284, 293, 331, 395, 426
Bechukotai
26, 47
Beha'alot'cha
80
Behar
16, 65
Bemidbar
64
Beresheet A
179, 192, 269, 270, 286, 350, 355
Beresheet B
205, 206, 214, 355
Beshalach
42, 121, 286, 370
Chayei Sarah
13, 177, 215
Chukat
8, 10, 22
Emor
29, 68, 152, 225, 226, 310
Ha'azinu
75, 83, 87, 89, 112, 113
Idra Raba
180, 312, 317
Kedoshim
41
Ki Tetze
1, 14, 16, 19, 25, 30, 36, 51, 68, 71, 76, 94, 114, 115, 116, 119
Lech Lecha
279, 346, 350, 352
Mishpatim
4, 6-13, 21, 23-26, 28, 32, 41, 54, 63, 64, 124, 132, 134, 373, 401, 415, 467
Naso
49, 85, 130
Noach
84
Pekudei
67, 224, 284, 481
Pinchas
5, 35, 49, 54, 83, 139, 192, 245, 255, 298, 378, 532, 584, 593, 600, 678, 688, 715, 740, 753, 789, 814, 834, 841, 842, 854, 871, 872
Prologue
17, 82, 186
Shemot
26, 34, 35, 170, 172, 180, 183, 191, 192, 195, 200, 202, 336, 338, 339, 377
Shlach Lecha
61, 196, 197, 198, 257, 263, 311, 312, 315, 318
Shmini
28, 56
Tazria
178
Toldot
16, 50, 51, 52, 190
Trumah
6, 161, 358, 725, 729-731, 768
Tzav
27, 29, 30, 32, 35, 57, 64, 109, 157, 160, 161
Vaera
12, 13, 14

Vaetchanan
120, 125
Vayakhel
180, 397
Vayechi
51, 58, 177, 277, 291, 401, 562, 568, 600, 810, 824, 826, 827
Vayera
225, 226, 286, 309, 310, 335, 350, 353, 477, 479
Vayeshev
100, 150, 189
Vayetze
41, 127, 128, 132, 139, 143, 147, 207, 208
Vayikra
75, 92, 94-97, 152, 154, 170 -172, 335, 408, 416
Vayishlach
144, 161
Yitro
395, 396, 432

DAVID

Acharei Mot
58, 213, 214, 238, 276, 279, 348, 382, 394, 395
Balak
17, 18, 38, 96, 98, 100, 101, 104, 111, 157, 179, 186, 187, 191, 193, 195, 196, 198, 204, 212, 252, 255-257, 266, 272, 276, 340-342, 355, 356, 372, 373, 387-390, 393, 469
Bechukotai
19
Beha'alot'cha
60, 90, 91, 93
Bemidbar
56, 57, 58, 66, 68, 71
Beresheet A
63, 117, 118, 119, 145, 147, 187, 189, 216, 234, 283, 304, 348, 399, 449, 471
Beresheet B
17, 31, 358, 359, 420, 421, 443, 444
Beshalach
24, 43, 52, 53, 116, 126, 200, 409, 430
Bo
31, 59, 96
Chayei Sarah
29, 39, 59, 69, 121, 128, 223, 243
Chukat
27, 47, 52
Ekev
27, 64
Emor
100, 101, 102, 129, 227a, 228, 279, 280, 281, 282a, 289
Ha'azinu
17, 106, 168, 182, 249
Idra Raba
64, 207, 257, 259, 262, 264, 266, 319
Kedoshim
73, 74, 95, 106, 107
Ki Tetze
48, 56, 62, 71, 120
Ki Tisa
21
Lech Lecha
59, 64, 65, 118, 119, 121, 134, 135, 171, 214, 215, 232, 244, 245, 246, 266, 306, 307, 308, 327, 344, 345, 370, 374, 375,

401-403, 407, 408, 409, 464, 468
Metzora
43, 58
Miketz
14, 15, 94, 107, 112, 120-122, 127, 150, 151, 244
Mishpatim
77, 143, 144, 175, 177, 179, 184, 191, 193, 194, 230, 238 -241, 244, 245-252, 255, 258 -261, 264, 293, 297, 301, 304, 387, 475, 481, 483-485, 492, 516, 524, 532, 542
Naso
110, 123, 149, 150, 166
Noach
14, 24, 41, 75, 77, 86, 87, 168, 256, 280, 281, 286, 291, 314, 315, 318, 349
Pekudei
10, 67, 90, 91, 96, 186, 217, 231, 233, 235, 276, 278, 370, 372, 376, 377, 394, 412, 602, 671, 837
Pinchas
12, 14, 15, 57, 77, 165, 172, 180, 182, 183, 187, 190, 193, 206, 218, 268, 345, 346, 347, 350, 355, 380, 383, 393, 485, 491, 494, 515, 517, 550, 554 -556, 565, 581, 582, 595, 643, 651, 652, 711, 745, 814, 822, 824, 856, 870
Prologue
104, 124, 132-135, 137, 138, 218
Safra Detzniuta
36, 72
Shemot
131, 160-162, 175, 296, 329, 371, 374
Shlach Lecha
86, 89, 136, 150, 298, 328, 340, 342
Shmini
56, 57, 78, 89, 90
Shoftim
12
Tazria
69, 79, 87, 90, 134, 164
Tetzaveh
24, 43, 136
Toldot
3, 5, 85, 106, 136, 142, 146
Trumah
91, 95, 96, 108, 110, 123, 207, 208, 209, 221, 229, 253-256, 257, 260, 261, 315, 328, 329, 338, 339, 340, 343, 347, 489, 493, 496, 546, 550, 551, 556, 586, 589, 590, 591, 627, 662, 686-688, 728, 785, 808, 809, 823, 830, 833, 874, 881, 882, 914
Tzav
184
Vaera
15, 30, 31, 98, 100, 103, 133, 134, 178, 181
Vaetchanan
7, 31, 51, 52, 53, 148, 152
Vayakhel
64, 65, 97, 152, 377
Vayechi
30, 91, 176, 353, 357, 421, 439, 440, 500-503, 602, 608, 635, 640, 682, 689, 699, 702, 714, 764, 802, 803, 804, 806, 812, 832, 834, 838, 848

Vayelech
10, 11, 31
Vayera
16, 77, 92, 200, 256, 310, 311, 336, 337, 338, 356, 400, 427, 440, 486
Vayeshev
98, 99, 191, 194, 205, 274, 275, 281
Vayetze
35, 37, 38, 39, 40, 57, 78, 79, 88, 89, 90, 158, 167, 219, 253, 254, 350, 351
Vayigash
20, 34, 36-39, 47, 48, 50-52, 89, 90
Vayikra
33, 81, 113, 163, 225, 330, 332, 341, 342, 359, 360, 364, 365, 367, 369, 396, 404, 406-408, 424, 436
Vayishlach
2, 7, 8, 52-57, 61, 64, 72, 118, 155, 156, 243, 267, 268-270, 276, 277
Yitro
16, 17, 40, 100, 102, 107, 111, 113, 209, 212, 213, 221, 360, 380, 563

DEAF

Kedoshim
89
Naso
55
Vayechi
295
Yitro
266, 330

DEATH

Acharei Mot
1, 2, 5, 6, 9, 12, 19-21, 29, 49, 68, 70, 136, 276, 357
Balak
13, 31, 58, 102, 151, 180, 368, 369, 372, 373, 505
Bechukotai
23, 60
Beha'alot'cha
41, 44, 51, 82, 93, 96, 99, 136, 137, 138, 147
Behar
55, 58, 59, 62, 76
Bemidbar
13, 14, 41, 43-45, 67, 73, 74
Beresheet A
153, 154, 157, 172, 180, 246, 254, 255, 257, 262, 266, 291, 292, 320, 337, 392, 404, 433, 435, 438, 440, 448, 450, 458, 461, 462, 463, 482
Beresheet B
37, 47, 78, 114, 167, 173, 198, 254, 267, 286-288, 292, 297, 298, 302, 304, 307, 308, 310, 319-321, 323, 333, 335, 336, 339, 354, 360, 398, 411, 413, 415
Beshalach
12, 13, 16, 26, 28, 35, 79, 97, 184
Bo
21, 22
Chayei Sarah
13, 19, 26, 31, 33, 40, 63, 70, 87, 89, 186, 200, 204, 220, 250
Chukat
9, 26, 35, 56

Ekev
51, 56, 57
Emor
1, 116, 161, 203, 222, 321, 322, 326, 336, 337, 338, 339, 340
Ha'azinu
176, 189, 251, 252
Idra Raba
2, 180, 273, 342
Kedoshim
49, 52, 79, 118
Ki Tetze
10, 13, 39, 59, 65, 66, 76, 80, 122, 134
Ki Tisa
107, 111, 112, 115, 116, 118
Korach
2, 11, 14, 20, 27, 33
Lech Lecha
99, 100, 142, 216, 397
Metzora
4, 37
Miketz
1, 2, 137, 138, 196
Mishpatim
165, 241, 244, 257, 258, 271, 355, 368, 440, 447, 455, 463, 556
Naso
3, 20, 40, 72, 110, 115, 171
Noach
31, 75, 89, 92, 93, 146, 189, 212 -214, 246, 298, 360
Pekudei
90, 116, 203, 299, 302-304, 313, 335, 385, 427, 433, 476, 514, 528, 543, 544, 546, 547, 549, 551, 579, 631, 651, 669, 671, 836-838, 841, 857, 859, 870, 871, 872, 875, 884, 885, 908, 925, 939, 941, 959
Pinchas
19, 75, 206, 267, 338, 364, 409, 410, 412, 414, 415, 417, 464, 466, 467, 468, 472, 480, 482, 488, 521, 584, 590, 591, 731, 746
Prologue
23, 85, 115, 118, 132, 136, 197, 212-214, 246
Shemot
18, 31, 269, 270, 275, 278, 340, 349
Shlach Lecha
3, 13, 42, 52, 53, 54, 100
Shoftim
6, 17, 18
Tazria
167, 183
Tetzaveh
106
Toldot
7, 8, 86, 101, 122, 175, 191
Trumah
135, 230, 231, 292, 296, 332, 333, 335, 431, 432, 433, 437, 438, 470, 548, 587, 760, 854, 865, 888, 889
Tzav
68, 70, 134, 137, 140-142, 156
Vaera
178, 191, 193
Vaetchanan
2, 3, 10, 28, 196
Vayakhel
8, 16, 28, 29, 33, 34, 36, 37, 40, 41, 92, 93, 96, 302, 369,

385, 386, 404, 468, 469, 473, 488, 492
Vayechi
25, 44, 110, 135, 148, 160, 187, 188, 194, 196, 199, 205, 206, 240, 241, 242, 243, 244, 245, 339, 343, 384, 403, 420, 523, 556, 571, 577, 668, 732, 752, 831, 832
Vayelech
8, 29
Vayera
30, 33, 34, 42, 114, 169, 226, 246, 326, 340, 341, 377, 378, 380, 388, 401, 410, 419, 473
Vayeshev
77, 114, 124, 173, 174, 205, 206, 227, 267
Vayetze
109, 178, 179, 180, 286-290, 313, 359
Vayigash
36, 37, 38, 39, 46, 47, 52, 74, 80, 84, 85, 114
Vayikra
235
Vayishlach
47, 77, 83, 140, 173, 174, 198, 200, 204
Yitro
14, 32, 518

DEATH AND THE AFTERLIFE

Acharei Mot
1, 2, 5, 6, 9, 12, 19-21, 29, 49, 68, 70, 136, 276, 357
Balak
13, 31, 58, 102, 151, 180, 368, 369, 372, 373, 505
Bechukotai
23, 60
Beha'alot'cha
41, 44, 51, 82, 93, 96, 99, 136 -138, 147
Behar
55, 58, 59, 62, 76
Bemidbar
13, 14, 41, 43, 44, 45, 67, 73, 74
Beresheet A
153, 154, 157, 172, 180, 246, 254, 255, 257, 262, 266, 291, 292, 320, 337, 392, 404, 433, 435, 438, 440, 448, 450, 458, 461-463, 482
Beresheet B
8, 37, 47, 78, 114, 167, 173, 198, 254, 267, 286-288, 292, 297, 298, 302, 304, 307, 308, 310, 319-321, 323, 333, 335, 336, 339, 354, 360, 398, 411, 413, 415, 416
Beshalach
12, 13, 16, 26, 28, 35, 79, 97, 184
Bo
21, 22
Chayei Sarah
13, 19, 26, 31, 33, 40, 63, 70, 87, 89, 186, 200, 204, 220, 250
Chukat
9, 26, 35, 56
Ekev
51, 56, 57
Emor
1, 116, 161, 203, 222, 321, 322, 326, 336-340
Ha'azinu
176, 189, 251, 252

Idra Raba
2, 180, 273, 342
Kedoshim
49, 52, 79, 118
Ki Tetze
10, 13, 39, 59, 65, 66, 76, 80, 122, 134
Ki Tisa
107, 111, 112, 115, 116, 118
Korach
2, 11, 14, 20, 27, 33
Lech Lecha
51, 54, 99, 100, 131, 142, 163, 216, 397
Metzora
4, 37
Miketz
1, 2, 4, 137, 138, 196
Mishpatim
165, 241, 244, 257, 258, 271, 355, 368, 440, 447, 455, 463, 556
Naso
3, 20, 40, 72, 110, 115, 171
Noach
31, 66, 75, 89, 92, 93, 146, 189, 204, 212-214, 246, 298, 360
Pekudei
90, 116, 203, 299, 302-304, 313, 335, 385, 427, 433, 476, 514, 528, 543, 544, 546, 547, 549, 551, 579, 631, 651, 669, 671, 836-838, 841, 857, 859, 870, 871, 872, 875, 884, 885, 908, 925, 939, 941, 959
Pinchas
19, 22, 26, 75, 206, 267, 338, 364, 409, 410, 412, 414, 415, 417, 464, 466, 467, 468, 472, 480, 482, 488, 521, 584, 590, 591, 731, 746
Prologue
23, 85, 115, 118, 132, 136, 197, 212, 213, 214, 246
Shemot
18, 31, 269, 270, 275, 278, 340, 349
Shlach Lecha
3, 13, 42, 52, 53, 54, 100
Shoftim
6, 17, 18
Tazria
167, 183
Tetzaveh
106
Toldot
7, 8, 86, 101, 122, 175, 191
Trumah
135, 230, 231, 292, 296, 332, 333, 335, 431-433, 437, 438, 470, 548, 587, 760, 854, 865, 888, 889
Tzav
68, 70, 134, 137, 140-142, 156
Vaera
178, 191, 193
Vaetchanan
2, 3, 10, 28, 196
Vayakhel
8, 16, 28, 29, 33, 34, 36, 37, 40, 41, 92, 93, 96, 97, 302, 369, 385, 386, 404, 468, 469, 473, 488, 492
Vayechi
25, 44, 110, 135, 148, 160, 187, 188, 194, 196, 199, 205, 206, 240, 241, 242, 243, 244, 245, 303, 339, 343, 384, 403, 420, 523, 556, 571, 577, 668,

732, 752, 831, 832
Vayelech
8, 29
Vayera
30, 31, 33, 34, 42, 114, 169, 226, 246, 326, 340, 341, 377, 378, 380, 388, 401, 410, 419, 473
Vayeshev
77, 114, 124, 173, 174, 205, 206, 227, 267
Vayetze
109, 178, 179, 180, 286- 290, 313, 359

Vayigash
36-39, 46, 47, 52, 74, 80, 84, 85, 114
Vayikra
210, 235
Vayishlach
47, 77, 83, 140, 173, 174, 198, 200, 204, 209
Yitro
14, 32, 518

DEATH OF RABBI SHIMON

Ha'azinu
23-30, 95-97, 196-201

DEBORAH (PROPHETESS)

Chayei Sarah
13
Ki Tisa
44
Shlach Lecha
200

DEEDS

Acharei Mot
84, 91, 243, 316, 348, 369, 371
Balak
7, 17, 44, 134, 154, 186, 264, 279, 401
Bechukotai
1, 4-7, 10, 28
Beha'alot'cha
9, 10, 41, 42
Behar
11, 44, 53, 54, 67, 69, 70, 75, 82
Bemidbar
38, 69, 71, 72, 73
Beresheet A
324, 460
Beresheet B
42, 47, 105, 186, 389, 390, 400
Beshalach
34, 36, 193, 194, 196, 197, 201, 203, 215, 227, 254-256, 318, 320
Bo
21, 96, 153, 180, 205, 211
Chayei Sarah
71, 72, 73, 78, 108, 119, 129, 130, 138, 197, 198, 199, 203, 204, 207, 208, 257, 258
Chukat
53, 56, 58, 78, 81
Ekev
45, 46, 55
Emor
21, 82, 127, 191, 193, 204, 210, 217, 219, 232, 233, 255, 293
Ha'azinu
107, 131, 211, 223
Idra Raba
135, 199, 200, 211, 295, 346

Kedoshim
53, 54, 65, 83, 101, 117
Ki Tetze
31, 135
Ki Tisa
34, 60
Korach
16, 20, 31, 33, 34, 60
Lech Lecha
47, 50, 53, 77, 88, 117, 155, 208, 327, 330, 351, 352, 378
Metzora
14
Miketz
1, 52-56, 76, 129, 179, 189, 192, 193, 198, 209
Mishpatim
40, 41, 59, 92, 104, 159, 236, 248, 267, 332, 365, 418, 433, 437, 454, 471, 498, 510, 521, 565, 566
Naso
8, 41, 55, 57, 83, 111-114, 122
Noach
15, 39, 42, 44, 63, 189, 352
Pekudei
58, 170, 193, 194, 211, 212, 214, 227, 321, 372, 376, 397, 404, 447, 530, 583, 586, 600, 603, 610, 615, 616, 617, 619, 670, 675, 725, 802, 927, 929
Pinchas
6, 8, 9, 10, 20, 21, 23, 25, 83, 87, 94, 102, 108, 136, 137, 172, 221, 354, 374, 376, 435, 437, 462, 489, 553, 554, 569, 583, 803, 808, 813, 859
Prologue
91, 92, 166, 167
Shemot
60, 163, 167, 168, 170-172, 207, 233
Shlach Lecha
65, 83, 280, 300, 321
Shmini
49
Tazria
11, 12, 21, 24, 33, 89, 126, 141, 143, 179, 180
Tetzaveh
89
Toldot
16, 36, 54, 74, 76, 83, 86, 87, 114, 190
Trumah
24, 307, 308, 309, 343, 386, 632, 726, 879
Tzav
45, 68, 71, 105, 106, 113, 117, 148
Vaera
44, 141, 169
Vaetchanan
32, 47, 184, 185
Vayakhel
18, 33, 96, 121, 127, 301, 308, 309, 372, 387, 410, 455, 464, 488
Vayechi
6, 7, 164, 179, 211, 212, 357, 358, 362, 367, 400, 401, 402, 403, 411, 412, 413, 462, 500, 515, 524, 551, 552, 563, 610, 774
Vayelech
9, 49
Vayera
29, 31, 82, 92, 128, 169, 179, 180, 182, 241, 297, 301, 303,

324, 325, 332, 419
Vayeshev
36, 170, 173, 180, 181, 193, 198, 224, 225, 226, 229, 234, 244, 250-252, 269
Vayetze
53, 113, 119, 135, 188, 260
Vayikra
48, 62, 71, 74, 100, 213, 246, 249, 251, 260, 322, 404
Vayishlach
120, 122, 175, 219
Yitro
71, 80, 194, 209, 220, 246, 283, 285, 307, 355, 550, 553, 555, 562, 564

DEER

Acharei Mot
209
Beha'alot'cha
129
Beresheet A
121
Beresheet B
209
Beshalach
182
Noach
119
Shemot
235, 236
Trumah
179, 224

DEITIES

Lech Lecha
185
Mishpatim
30, 268, 421, 485
Prologue
14, 151, 170
Vayechi
258, 353
Vayeshev
10
Vayishlach
154, 156, 157

DEITY OF THE ILLUMINATING JEWELS

Ki Tisa
7

DEMONS

Acharei Mot
91, 123, 250, 252, 253, 254, 358-362, 367, 405
Bechukotai
25
Beha'alot'cha
119
Behar
43
Beresheet A
64, 102, 104, 105, 291, 401, 456
Beresheet B
113, 186, 187, 188, 190, 192, 333, 346, 351, 353-355, 357
Beshalach
401
Chayei Sarah
135
Ekev
45
Ha'azinu
103

Idra Raba
344
Ki Tetze
7, 8, 30-33, 35, 38, 137, 138
Ki Tisa
57
Korach
37, 60
Metzora
1, 6
Mishpatim
57, 58, 448, 449
Noach
346
Pekudei
205, 457, 847, 920
Pinchas
88, 217, 317, 417, 420, 485, 488, 509, 681, 732, 762, 763
Prologue
68, 157, 251
Safra Detzniuta
46
Shemot
194, 300
Shlach Lecha
3, 120
Tazria
53, 117, 154, 173, 174
Trumah
36, 71, 265, 543, 615
Vaera
116, 168
Vaetchanan
74, 75, 76, 77, 106, 107
Vayakhel
244, 273
Vayechi
289, 424, 583, 682, 684, 706, 711
Vayera
87
Vayikra
243, 279, 425
Vayishlach
24, 34, 75, 79, 82, 185

DESTRUCTION

Acharei Mot
151, 268, 282
Balak
230, 270, 271, 272, 276, 391
Bechukotai
29, 50
Beresheet A
180, 184, 231, 246, 254, 481
Beresheet B
11, 16, 44, 254, 370
Beshalach
249, 252, 311
Chayei Sarah
17
Ekev
33
Idra Raba
202
Kedoshim
50
Korach
47
Lech Lecha
190
Metzora
42
Miketz
112, 150, 216, 220
Mishpatim
66, 451, 479

Noach
50, 52, 54, 66, 113, 178, 198, 206, 228, 241, 243
Pekudei
307, 491, 542, 639, 643, 657, 897, 898
Pinchas
14, 50, 88, 192, 269, 270, 420, 440, 442, 701, 747, 752, 827
Prologue
6, 31, 34
Shemot
31, 62, 125
Shlach Lecha
76, 120, 304
Tetzaveh
97
Trumah
158, 230, 270, 271, 753
Tzav
128
Vaera
168
Vaetchanan
188
Vayakhel
20, 378, 380
Vayechi
100, 380
Vayera
168, 184, 288, 441
Vayeshev
25, 270
Vayetze
14, 85, 359
Vayigash
106
Vayikra
319
Vayishlach
265

DEW

Acharei Mot
218, 251, 291
Balak
225, 231, 420
Bemidbar
19
Beshalach
372, 395
Bo
171
Chayei Sarah
204, 205
Emor
129, 165
Ha'azinu
35, 117
Idra Raba
16, 17, 184, 185, 186
Ki Tisa
49
Lech Lecha
264, 445
Miketz
238
Pekudei
812
Pinchas
288, 300
Prologue
109, 259
Safra Detzniuta
6, 26
Shlach Lecha
111, 166, 227, 255

Tazria
125
Toldot
136, 144, 148-151, 205
Trumah
188, 189, 376, 377, 557
Vaera
127
Vayakhel
48, 92, 287, 304, 305, 347
Vayechi
17, 307, 308, 329-331, 465, 640
Vayera
410, 422
Vayetze
392
Vayigash
78
Vayikra
332
Vayishlach
41
Yitro
249, 338, 343, 370, 448

DIAMOND

Vayechi
287

DIBRI

Emor
310

DINAH

Emor
29
Vayechi
112
Vayeshev
13
Vayishlach
144

DIPHTHERIA

Balak
329
Beresheet A
98

DIRECTIONS

Acharei Mot
31, 83, 87, 120, 246, 254, 296, 311, 329
Balak
6, 78, 86, 226, 263, 309, 311, 313, 314, 320, 322, 335, 340, 348, 411, 412, 433-435, 437, 438, 440, 486, 502
Beha'alot'cha
33, 34, 37-40, 49, 55, 112
Behar
3, 36
Bemidbar
30, 55
Beresheet A
36, 81, 89, 115, 409, 426
Beresheet B
29, 30, 51, 63, 64, 69, 73, 93, 94, 96, 106, 115, 116, 118, 129, 130, 172, 191, 193, 253, 282, 325, 341
Beshalach
138, 139, 315, 483
Bo
50, 239
Chayei Sarah
82, 94, 201

Chukat
28, 30, 33, 46, 52, 67, 77
Ekev
12, 66, 74, 75
Emor
15, 64, 135, 143, 332, 338
Ha'azinu
33, 48, 66, 107, 114, 183, 205
Idra Raba
18, 25, 118, 147, 156, 158, 165-167, 181, 183, 185-187, 190, 192, 255, 272, 273, 276, 334
Kedoshim
1, 74, 116, 120
Ki Tisa
63, 103, 116
Korach
55
Lech Lecha
7, 27, 162, 193, 243, 305, 465
Metzora
40
Miketz
10, 99
Mishpatim
139, 185, 456
Naso
53
Noach
68, 264, 266, 303, 335
Pekudei
38, 76, 104, 111, 133, 135, 141, 142, 178, 215, 218, 229, 259, 264, 297, 307, 391, 411, 511, 562, 566, 583, 622, 649, 655, 692, 912
Pinchas
10, 139, 168, 202, 216, 226, 262, 302, 304, 305, 383, 422, 468, 510, 517, 533, 538, 603, 686, 705, 707, 708, 710, 711, 717, 748, 821, 830, 861
Prologue
43, 81, 117, 144, 149, 219
Safra Detzniuta
67
Shemot
66, 102, 217, 219
Shlach Lecha
124, 180, 183, 190, 252, 272, 315
Shmini
97
Tazria
40, 82
Tetzaveh
8, 14, 21, 95, 99, 135
Trumah
22, 23, 131, 304, 372, 866, 918
Tzav
174
Vaera
33, 34, 35, 47, 108, 127, 130, 158, 186
Vaetchanan
49, 129, 140, 191, 193
Vayakhel
220, 267, 311, 428, 461
Vayechi
154, 162, 283, 317, 350, 653
Vayera
61, 89, 268, 269, 274, 278, 303, 342
Vayeshev
112, 199

Vayetze
2, 132, 160, 162, 202, 233, 258, 262-264, 323
Vayigash
14, 65
Vayikra
11, 13, 14, 164, 282-284, 412, 414
Vayishlach
6, 90, 136, 137
Yitro
226, 412, 543

DISEASE

Beresheet A
98
Prologue
182
Vayechi
363
Vayeshev
30, 162
Vayetze
14

DIVORCE

Acharei Mot
337
Mishpatim
21, 134, 160, 162, 223, 224, 225, 239
Pekudei
685
Pinchas
53
Prologue
133
Vayakhel
430

DO'EG

Mishpatim
150

DOE

Beshalach
274
Bo
98, 99
Mishpatim
283, 485
Pinchas
482
Vayakhel
487

Vayikra
201, 203, 367, 435, 436

DOG

Naso
84, 86, 102, 10
Shlach Lecha
d26, 330

DOGS

Acharei Mot
135-137
Balak
87, 229, 455, 456, 458, 479
Beha'alot'cha
123
Behar
2, 43, 46
Beshalach
22, 29, 49, 441
Bo
129, 195, 196, 198

Emor
49
Kedoshim
5
Ki Tetze
123
Matot
4, 5
Mishpatim
317, 318, 322, 326, 328, 504, 509
Pinchas
218, 485, 486, 525, 680
Prologue
96, 97
Trumah
487-490, 683
Tzav
61, 132, 133
Vayechi
683
Vayikra
431, 437
Vayishlach
99
Yitro
192

DONKEYS

Balak
36, 293, 297, 298, 304, 399, 401, 403, 404, 406, 449
Beha'alot'cha
123
Beresheet B
222
Beshalach
49
Bo
93, 119, 198, 230
Kedoshim
118
Ki Tetze
4, 5
Ki Tisa
84
Mishpatim
18
Pinchas
158, 159, 486, 487
Prologue
74, 80, 86-88, 90
Shemot
56, 67
Tazria
171, 179
Tetzaveh
80
Trumah
536, 539, 544, 680
Tzav
56, 58, 60
Vaera
182, 191
Vayechi
606
Vayikra
354
Yitro
471

DOOR

Acharei Mot
133, 152, 160, 264, 280, 297, 358
Balak
200, 289
Beha'alot'cha
8, 9

Behar
12, 13
Beresheet A
140, 192, 459-461, 477
Beresheet B
340
Bo
81, 84, 89-91, 189, 191
Chayei Sarah
70, 88
Emor
130
Idra Raba
118
Lech Lecha
42, 359
Mishpatim
322
Naso
8, 70
Noach
81, 303, 308
Pekudei
3, 260, 304, 327, 379, 406, 481, 486, 604, 605, 923
Pinchas
773, 776, 812
Prologue
178
Shemot
332
Shlach Lecha
2, 104, 120, 131, 143, 145, 146
Shmini
26
Tetzaveh
51, 121
Toldot
8, 9
Trumah
421, 424, 549
Tzav
170
Vaetchanan
72-77, 98, 100, 106, 107, 108, 109, 116-118, 132
Vayakhel
18, 291, 293, 294, 297, 299, 309, 311, 312, 316, 317, 320, 324, 340, 342, 343, 344, 490, 491
Vayechi
144, 149, 156, 603, 670, 692, 830
Vayera
11-13, 27, 29, 41, 50, 51, 101, 147, 148, 154, 156, 157, 158, 159, 228, 257, 477, 491
Vayeshev
1, 74, 78
Vayigash
85
Vayikra
113, 225, 307, 308, 339
Vayishlach
1, 65, 132, 134, 135, 136, 139, 214
Yitro
306, 412, 419

DOORPOST

Pinchas
484, 488
Trumah
662
Vaetchanan
106, 119, 134, 154, 175

DOTS

Beha'alot'cha
67
Beresheet A
207, 414
Bo
217
Ha'azinu
78
Idra Raba
173, 175, 178
Ki Tetze
114
Mishpatim
554
Pinchas
671, 819
Tetzaveh
9, 11, 12, 18, 26, 27
Trumah
9, 233, 429, 583
Vaera
35
Vayera
98, 310, 311
Vayeshev
95
Vayikra
285
Vayishlach
123
Yitro
86

DOVES

Acharei Mot
92
Balak
357, 358
Beha'alot'cha
88-90, 113
Beshalach
67, 152, 189, 234
Chayei Sarah
141, 142, 150
Ha'azinu
135, 183
Idra Raba
208, 324
Ki Tetze
30, 55, 56
Lech Lecha
181
Mishpatim
204, 486, 523
Naso
75
Pinchas
168, 170, 401, 537, 538, 565, 597
Shemot
247, 248
Shlach Lecha
147, 149, 150
Tazria
44
Toldot
96
Tzav
9, 44, 46
Vayechi
92
Vayera
349
Vayetze
97
Yitro
211

DREAMS

Acharei Mot
361, 362, 365, 368
Balak
84
Beha'alot'cha
80, 86
Beresheet A
324
Beresheet B
267, 347, 354
Beshalach
371
Chukat
8, 12
Emor
22, 23, 73, 222, 300, 303, 304
Ha'azinu
258
Idra Raba
267
Ki Tetze
93, 94
Lech Lecha
148
Metzora
6
Miketz
7, 9, 16, 22, 24, 26-28, 31, 58- 60, 62, 63, 130, 144-153, 155, 183
Mishpatim
22, 37, 127, 152, 261, 465, 539
Naso
173
Pekudei
131, 180, 303, 533, 606, 608, 730, 740, 741, 819, 820, 862, 863, 864, 919, 941
Pinchas
159, 166, 171, 174, 367, 417
Prologue
236
Safra Detzniuta
37
Shemot
256
Shlach Lecha
193, 328
Tazria
117
Tetzaveh
141
Toldot
6
Trumah
158, 230, 295, 331, 332, 337, 388, 470, 481, 902
Vaetchanan
134
Vayechi
124, 146, 158, 332, 350, 593, 594, 595, 596, 598
Vayera
240, 346
Vayeshev
82-94, 253-257, 265, 266, 268272
Vayetze
44, 45, 48-50, 53, 55-58, 70, 71, 75, 122, 386, 387, 388
Vayikra
105, 106, 198, 284, 430-432
Vayishlach
30, 51, 82
Yitro
50, 254, 255, 256

DROUGHT

Acharei Mot
207
Mishpatim
54
Toldot
106, 107
Trumah
305
Vayakhel
278, 314
Vayechi
304, 312, 512
Vayera
393
Vayikra
120

DRUNKENNESS

Noach
239
Vayera
324

DRYNESS (TZIYAH)

Beresheet B
36, 37
Mishpatim
117

DRYNESS

Beresheet B
36
Pekudei
63
Vaera
36, 40, 41, 43, 44

DUMAH (ANGEL)

Acharei Mot
265
Balak
26, 27, 306
Chayei Sarah
11, 12, 56, 57, 58, 59, 60, 95, 96, 99, 134, 155
Ha'azinu
28
Lech Lecha
8, 404, 405, 407
Metzora
11
Naso
114
Noach
66
Pekudei
838, 844, 845, 866
Prologue
131-138
Shemot
318
Toldot
38, 166
Trumah
80, 81, 446
Vayakhel
244
Vayechi
170, 583, 584, 585
Vayikra
375

DUST

Beresheet A
229, 257, 320, 448

Chayei Sarah
11, 29, 30, 31, 43, 53, 57, 60, 97, 99, 105, 173, 199, 201, 203, 204, 207, 210, 270
Ki Tisa
14, 67
Miketz
224, 236
Mishpatim
66, 118, 164, 184, 210, 211, 213-216, 256, 259, 439
Prologue
49
Toldot
33, 34, 49, 67, 68, 71
Vaetchanan
193, 194, 196, 197, 198
Vayechi
167, 340, 345, 348, 465, 835-837, 839
Vayera
134, 136, 236, 249, 253, 260, 324, 377, 389-391, 394, 400, 422, 441, 443, 445, 448, 449
Vayeshev
47, 50, 51, 123, 124, 177, 251
Vayigash
14, 68, 82, 105
Vayishlach
87, 88, 89, 210, 237

DWELLINGS

Acharei Mot
8, 51, 193, 258, 260, 261, 291, 358, 361, 363, 397
Balak
8, 12, 47, 213, 218, 488, 490
Beha'alot'cha
101
Behar
26
Beresheet A
265
Beresheet B
28, 36, 39, 40, 42-48, 50, 52 -55, 59, 94, 184, 288, 341 -343
Beshalach
113, 124, 301
Bo
139, 235, 236, 244
Chayei Sarah
60, 126, 127, 129, 138, 195, 217, 270
Chukat
57
Ekev
43
Emor
157, 220, 276, 329
Ha'azinu
13, 138, 222
Idra Raba
98, 271
Kedoshim
75
Ki Tetze
60
Ki Tisa
115
Lech Lecha
4, 48, 88
Metzora
24
Mishpatim
226, 296, 305, 405, 426, 471, 570

Naso
144
Noach
41, 62, 69, 70, 199, 344
Pekudei
40, 181, 332, 396, 482, 791, 864, 887
Pinchas
151, 275, 455, 498, 593, 732, 871, 874, 876
Prologue
117, 229, 231, 243
Safra Detzniuta
46
Shemot
24, 42, 45, 164, 232
Shlach Lecha
25, 86, 104, 304
Tetzaveh
62, 70
Toldot
57, 61, 100, 150, 194
Trumah
39, 155, 413, 436, 565, 655, 725, 909
Vaetchanan
37, 40, 41, 43, 44, 46-48, 56, 60, 75, 88, 99, 105, 119, 145, 173
Vayakhel
196, 317, 319, 421
Vayechi
53, 73, 112, 150, 174, 365, 765
Vayelech
15
Vayera
184, 320, 345
Vayeshev
93, 112
Vayetze
48, 127
Vayikra
344, 363, 365
Vayishlach
42, 75, 79, 266
Yitro
61, 413, 423, 526

EAGLE

Acharei Mot
76
Balak
437
Beha'alot'cha
101, 112-114, 116, 117
Bemidbar
28
Beresheet A
81-84, 86, 89, 121, 190
Beresheet B
67, 79, 88
Beshalach
269
Bo
204-207
Chukat
29
Ekev
19, 41, 68, 69, 71
Emor
70
Ha'azinu
237, 238
Idra Raba
172, 263

Ki Tetze
77, 111, 119
Korach
57
Mishpatim
15, 341, 342, 343, 344, 345, 445, 476, 481, 483, 486
Naso
42, 54
Noach
265
Pekudei
561, 562
Pinchas
70, 85, 260, 270, 329, 382, 383, 386-392, 398, 407, 408, 419, 492, 494, 533, 536, 539 -541, 543, 545, 597, 604, 617, 620, 666, 749, 769, 863, 864
Prologue
155
Safra Detzniuta
25, 67
Shemot
259
Shlach Lecha
94, 98, 99, 246
Tazria
115
Trumah
526, 894
Tzav
44, 47, 68
Vayakhel
318, 319, 326
Vayetze
73
Yitro
97, 112, 161-163, 225, 279-282, 327

EARS

Balak
36
Bechukotai
50
Behar
31, 42
Beresheet A
170
Beshalach
470
Chayei Sarah
9, 60, 230, 232, 233
Ha'azinu
126, 152-154, 156, 157, 165, 167, 170, 171
Idra Raba
29, 30, 73, 74, 96, 103, 106, 196, 235, 236, 238, 240, 241, 243, 250, 251, 266, 268
Ki Tetze
3
Ki Tisa
1, 71, 73, 74
Lech Lecha
6
Miketz
22, 49, 50
Mishpatim
221, 268, 272, 393, 394, 418, 423, 426, 427, 433, 525
Naso
51
Noach
64
Pekudei
68, 88

Safra Detzniuta
14, 16, 27, 29, 33, 34, 56
Shemot
40
Shlach Lecha
105
Tetzaveh
21, 25, 127
Toldot
2
Trumah
295
Vaetchanan
19, 43, 58
Vayakhel
139, 142, 223
Vayechi
295, 357, 531, 714, 817, 825
Vayeshev
86, 87
Vayetze
26, 311
Yitro
68, 119, 175, 198, 201, 202, 208, 220, 230, 339

EARTH (ERETZ)

Beresheet B
36
Mishpatim
117
Vayechi
19

EARTH

Acharei Mot
16, 50, 54, 63, 78, 83, 96, 115, 144, 145, 156, 174, 175, 205, 218, 219, 230, 251, 255, 258, 261, 285, 290, 291, 294, 301, 303, 314, 319, 376, 377, 401, 402
Balak
47, 55, 56, 58, 78, 82, 102, 105, 130, 138, 153, 259, 264, 304, 306, 362, 377, 419, 447
Beha'alot'cha
7, 100
Behar
17, 25, 49, 79, 80
Bemidbar
4, 29
Beresheet A
12, 17, 37, 41, 65, 74, 75, 78, 79, 92, 93, 110, 116, 131, 158, 181, 185, 214, 216, 217, 219, 222, 224, 225, 227, 229, 231-234, 237-239, 245, 246, 273, 304-309, 311, 312, 317, 318, 322, 323, 328-330, 339, 347, 358, 377, 381, 384, 385, 389, 390, 392, 394, 396, 400, 402, 406, 407, 418, 420, 422- 424, 457, 464, 468, 474, 481, 482
Beresheet B
31, 33-39, 44, 54, 66, 82, 94, 105, 112, 158-162, 165 -169, 171, 175-179, 190, 204, 209, 211, 212, 241, 242, 244, 246, 311, 323, 324, 334, 336, 341-344, 352, 355, 362, 366, 367, 370-373, 375, 385-387, 390, 392-394, 396, 399, 406, 418, 423-425, 427, 430-433, 448
Beshalach
62, 77, 95, 96, 114, 115, 126, 127, 182, 212, 218, 228, 230,

236, 238, 258, 267, 270, 277, 284, 290, 327, 376, 378, 486

Bo
9, 13, 48-50, 52, 66, 72, 75, 104, 105, 108, 137, 147, 150, 174, 177, 180, 200, 203, 218, 220, 228, 246

Chayei Sarah
1, 17, 110, 140, 141, 148, 161, 168, 179, 199, 200, 201, 210, 215, 216, 268

Chukat
31, 34, 58, 59

Ekev
26, 43

Emor
32, 54, 55, 56, 57, 70, 92, 97, 98, 112, 141, 145, 146, 151, 184, 220, 230, 238, 240, 274, 276, 281

Ha'azinu
1, 5-8, 58, 106, 139, 144, 201, 224-226, 231, 234, 242

Idra Raba
9, 42, 54, 120, 153, 186, 210, 271, 339, 345, 346, 347, 349

Kedoshim
8, 9, 20, 29, 61, 64, 73, 80, 106, 119, 124, 125, 129

Ki Tetze
13, 32, 33, 100, 128

Ki Tisa
7, 8, 31

Korach
18, 35

Lech Lecha
4, 22, 33, 41, 63, 94, 159, 180, 226, 243, 249, 253, 277, 310, 311, 312, 316, 317, 343, 362, 383, 391, 392, 420, 430, 431, 433, 469

Miketz
10, 41, 62, 78, 81, 84, 86, 107, 139, 145, 227, 228, 246

Mishpatim
66, 118, 162, 201, 204, 209, 211, 214, 215, 216, 225, 245, 273, 289, 293, 296, 298, 307, 329, 336, 392, 405, 406, 407, 408, 417, 424, 428, 432, 482, 483, 517, 518, 519, 525, 531

Naso
33, 39, 42, 53, 54, 55, 104, 117, 168, 192, 196

Noach
5, 8, 9, 11, 15, 16, 26, 28, 29, 38-41, 44, 45, 55-57, 74, 76, 78, 131, 148, 152, 160, 162, 163, 168-171, 178, 192-194, 202-205, 207, 209-212, 244-246, 248, 251, 252, 260, 263, 270, 292, 302, 307, 319, 323, 349, 350, 358, 367, 372, 377, 388

Pekudei
6, 8, 12, 13, 15, 23, 31, 35, 38, 39, 40, 41, 45, 53, 117, 210, 211, 212, 222, 243, 271, 272, 273, 292, 294, 307, 317, 339, 340, 356, 357, 387, 393, 394, 405, 409, 491, 590, 594, 606, 607, 670, 717, 751, 762, 790, 925, 928, 938, 957, 959

Pinchas
34, 49, 53, 58, 59, 65, 79, 93, 118, 121-124, 126, 127, 146, 177, 193, 202, 223, 227, 228, 245, 270, 291, 304, 305, 373, 396, 414, 420, 444, 543, 575, 588, 589, 600, 621, 626, 633,

657, 674, 678, 718, 720, 778, 841, 852, 855, 867, 871, 877

Prologue
1, 4, 5, 9, 12, 16, 17, 19, 36, 46, 48, 49, 56, 65, 66, 67, 76, 77, 88, 141, 145, 151, 152, 153, 159, 163, 166, 167, 186, 191, 195, 207, 209, 217, 218, 225, 228, 232, 235, 244

Safra Detzniuta
1, 3, 7, 8, 19, 26, 36, 41, 50, 58, 63, 66, 71

Shemot
17, 18, 53, 77, 78, 80, 81, 85, 89, 99-101, 103, 104, 115, 126, 127, 129, 145, 150, 152, 163, 166, 169, 170, 200, 213, 219, 263, 266, 276, 288, 289, 292, 301, 302, 306-308, 321, 322, 324, 327, 348, 359

Shlach Lecha
23, 24, 40, 53, 74, 176, 177, 239, 318, 319, 333, 348

Shmini
5, 9, 15, 44, 77, 79, 90, 100, 102, 103, 106

Shoftim
16, 18, 24

Tazria
13, 21, 22, 23, 67, 68, 81, 84, 113, 175, 187

Tetzaveh
107, 125, 128

Toldot
2, 3, 49, 61, 71, 125, 133, 136, 144, 145, 148, 149, 150, 151, 152, 154, 155

Trumah
1, 18, 30, 41, 49, 75, 114, 182, 197, 237, 263, 264, 265, 268, 269, 273, 315, 355, 417, 434, 449, 458, 475, 478, 495, 529, 530, 531, 537, 561, 583, 589, 618, 622, 634, 639, 667, 770, 799, 813, 825, 829, 832, 838, 841, 906, 907, 913, 916

Tzav
7, 8, 45, 52, 57, 94, 147, 175, 179- 182

Vaera
15, 32, 55, 120, 127, 130, 163, 171-175, 180, 205

Vaetchanan
38, 55, 114, 167, 175, 188, 194, 198

Vayakhel
16, 23, 43, 49, 77, 84, 91, 92, 95, 98, 144, 205, 282, 283, 289, 292, 306, 318, 325, 331, 336, 439

Vayechi
15, 44, 63, 71, 93, 96, 125, 147, 160, 165, 181, 285, 308, 358, 392, 460, 484, 565, 566, 569, 596, 597, 640, 661, 666, 667, 689, 750, 751, 754, 757, 772, 781, 836, 859

Vayelech
16, 20, 29, 30

Vayera
1, 2, 4-7, 19, 25, 41, 43, 58, 76, 94, 122, 133, 136, 152, 207, 208, 230-234, 242, 249, 261, 293, 297, 323, 324, 387, 389, 393, 396, 399, 405, 407, 409, 412, 418, 422, 481, 513

Vayeshev
59, 110, 129, 146, 214, 218, 242, 258

Vayetze
46, 52, 58, 70, 108, 128, 153, 190, 195, 214, 223, 225, 227, 255, 271, 272, 287, 334, 360
Vayigash
11, 12, 18, 32, 41, 42, 48, 49, 94, 108
Vayikra
31, 41-43, 48, 60, 93, 138, 140, 178, 183, 186, 219, 222, 230, 268, 284, 317, 379, 380, 388, 401, 413, 424, 439, 447
Vayishlach
41, 57, 87, 88, 89, 139, 143, 174, 175, 210, 236, 249, 261
Yitro
13, 17, 19, 23, 51, 58, 62, 144, 225, 226, 228, 249, 250, 253, 277, 278, 299, 335, 336, 337, 340, 347, 352, 358, 359, 382, 393, 394, 398-400, 402, 403, 424, 442, 451, 454, 455, 484, 494, 497, 517, 560, 570, 574, 575

EAST

Balak
97, 425, 434
Beha'alot'cha
39, 102, 108, 126
Bemidbar
29, 31, 32, 34-36, 62-64
Beresheet A
81, 89, 413
Beresheet B
51, 71, 81, 82, 90, 147, 189, 343
Beshalach
100, 137, 229, 233
Chayei Sarah
81, 129, 239, 263, 264
Ki Tisa
7, 73
Lech Lecha
7, 162, 175, 178, 211, 215, 219, 221, 222, 223, 224
Miketz
62
Mishpatim
143
Noach
101, 263, 265, 335-337, 361, 365, 366, 384
Pekudei
134, 140, 141, 142, 178, 406, 511, 512, 514, 531, 537, 546, 583, 660, 662, 680, 682, 686, 687, 692, 814
Pinchas
319, 686, 705, 708, 821
Shemot
101, 160, 260
Shlach Lecha
61, 156, 271
Tetzaveh
8, 23
Trumah
22, 75, 250, 251, 252, 604, 610, 612, 615, 838, 843, 844, 846
Tzav
77
Vaera
35, 37, 38, 39, 41, 158
Vayakhel
12, 128, 242, 293, 294, 296, 341, 349, 354
Vayechi

118, 276, 278, 281, 290, 292, 533, 540, 546, 570, 572, 652, 653, 694, 768, 847

Vayera
80, 89, 478

Vayetze
2, 3, 11, 92, 123-125, 170, 262, 264

Vayikra
24, 58, 380

Yitro
383

ECHAD (ONE)

Beresheet A
126, 138

Ekev
52, 55

Ki Tetze
97, 104

Mishpatim
405, 407, 436, 463

Pinchas
183, 300, 397, 453-455, 603, 646, 654, 710, 711, 754, 846, 870, 871

Prologue
204, 205

Shlach Lecha
95

Shoftim
16

Trumah
135, 629

Tzav
142, 144

Vaetchanan
64

Vayetze
315

Vayikra
100

EDEN

Acharei Mot
33, 101, 160, 167, 171, 209, 238, 260, 261, 264, 271, 380, 382

Balak
160, 214

Beha'alot'cha
31

Beresheet A
243, 247, 248, 249, 256, 258, 259, 316, 327, 336, 342, 358, 367, 400, 401, 426, 436, 468

Beresheet B
3, 9, 12, 22, 26, 178, 343, 411, 412, 414

Beshalach
6, 45, 46, 209, 225, 232, 237, 255, 396, 410

Bo
45, 98, 100, 148, 149, 157

Chayei Sarah
49, 52, 88, 95, 143-145, 147149, 206

Chukat
28, 57, 58, 59

Ekev
43, 48

Ha'azinu
29, 48, 67, 70, 79, 80, 85, 96, 205, 226

Idra Raba
23, 38, 39, 135, 189

Kedoshim
18, 75, 92

Korach
34

Lech Lecha
5, 94, 100, 102, 105, 129, 130, 189, 366, 381, 423, 448
Metzora
11
Miketz
19, 78, 87, 113
Mishpatim
67, 85, 88, 89, 105, 106, 166, 296, 297, 539
Noach
4, 5, 35, 38, 140, 141, 145, 302, 336
Pekudei
22, 58, 127, 168, 169, 212, 414, 454, 474, 475, 476, 493, 677, 756, 758, 761
Pinchas
177, 458, 528, 654, 766, 768
Prologue
109
Safra Detzniuta
20, 58
Shemot
1, 14, 46, 61, 99, 106, 108, 109, 118, 120, 121, 177, 178, 193, 218, 219, 223-225, 237, 241, 242, 257, 259, 277
Shlach Lecha
53, 177, 191, 245, 291, 293, 305
Shmini
77
Tazria
68
Toldot
108, 115
Trumah
20, 24, 45, 73, 126, 175-181, 188, 200, 208, 214, 226, 285, 286, 288, 291-293, 298, 300, 303, 318, 355, 413, 433, 434, 436, 437, 438, 466, 535, 557, 723, 740, 742, 823, 830, 878, 880
Tzav
63, 112
Vaera
16, 117, 158
Vaetchanan
4, 58, 64, 146
Vayakhel
19, 21, 22, 23, 145, 184, 185, 188, 213, 272, 273, 275, 277, 282, 292, 296, 300, 302-306, 308-317, 324, 325, 329-334, 336, 338, 339
Vayechi
108, 170, 172, 175, 349, 460, 542, 783, 784
Vayelech
43
Vayera
26, 242, 244, 292, 424
Vayeshev
21, 33, 37, 52
Vayetze
47, 267
Vayigash
64
Vayikra
29, 37, 153, 168, 174, 204, 266, 290, 379
Yitro
64, 95, 326, 341, 362, 485, 486

EDOM

Balak
138, 153, 256, 505

Bechukotai
3
Beresheet A
186
Beshalach
106, 156, 192, 266
Bo
83, 177
Emor
16, 17, 54, 56
Ha'azinu
111
Idra Raba
10, 12, 173, 175, 314
Ki Tetze
121
Ki Tisa
19
Mishpatim
267, 314
Pekudei
324, 380
Pinchas
98, 104, 269, 411, 650
Shemot
75, 76, 90, 92, 95, 145-147, 175
Shoftim
2
Tetzaveh
85, 106
Toldot
188
Vaera
204, 205
Vayakhel
20
Vayechi
290, 578, 591
Vayeshev
207
Vayigash
134
Vayikra
333, 375
Vayishlach
177, 233, 236, 242
Yitro
19, 26

EDOMITES

Balak
231
Trumah
693

EFRON

Chayei Sarah
56, 57, 59, 60, 90, 92, 93, 98, 103, 104

EGGS

Ekev
22, 45, 47
Pinchas
56, 57, 496, 602, 603, 604, 608, 609, 611, 616, 617, 751, 787, 790

EGYPT

Acharei Mot
230, 232, 249, 250, 277, 289, 290
Balak
93, 133, 154, 263, 403, 405, 491, 493, 494, 498
Beha'alot'cha
5, 6, 8, 36, 56, 57, 82

Behar
9, 11, 21, 22, 76
Bemidbar
9
Beresheet A
149, 153, 223, 248, 288
Beshalach
25-28, 30, 37-40, 42, 56, 57, 60-62, 93, 105, 106, 111, 113, 130, 131, 133, 155, 179, 184, 190-199, 201, 203, 204, 206, 213, 219, 266, 293, 294, 313, 353, 361, 374, 376, 404, 405, 443, 481
Bo
30, 38, 64, 74, 76, 82-86, 92, 101, 107, 116, 118, 121, 124, 125, 127, 132, 163-165, 171, 174, 175, 178, 179, 186, 189, 190, 194, 195, 229, 238
Chayei Sarah
19, 146, 147
Chukat
41
Emor
40, 62, 77, 80, 128, 162, 175, 239, 326
Ha'azinu
19, 222
Idra Raba
127, 179
Ki Tetze
17, 18, 28, 56
Ki Tisa
30, 34, 59, 60, 61, 65, 85, 106
Lech Lecha
74, 75, 106, 107, 108, 109, 110, 114, 117, 124, 136, 139, 140, 143, 144, 161, 167, 374, 395, 396
Miketz
12, 13, 15, 16, 19, 29, 37, 38, 39, 57, 64, 65, 67, 68, 82, 84, 93, 102, 104, 105, 172, 174
Mishpatim
10, 95, 377, 477, 482, 483, 490, 492, 531, 542, 572
Naso
98
Noach
81, 206, 355
Pekudei
281, 323, 371, 404, 429, 434
Pinchas
16, 18, 20, 21, 55, 147, 151, 177, 192, 253, 330, 566, 721, 722, 723, 726, 733, 734, 735, 736, 741, 815, 841
Prologue
99, 147, 240
Shemot
1, 5, 8, 13, 14, 19, 21-23, 32-36, 38, 48, 50-52, 54-57, 59, 61, 63, 65, 75, 76, 77, 81-83, 87-89, 91, 93-95, 132, 157, 158, 233, 243, 246, 250, 268, 270-273, 275, 280, 281, 285-287, 295, 296, 299, 300, 314, 317, 318, 320, 322, 323, 340, 341, 344, 345
Shlach Lecha
61, 79, 173, 347, 348
Tazria
111, 160, 161, 185-187
Tetzaveh
48, 50, 72, 75, 83
Toldot
45, 94
Trumah
79, 158, 283, 308, 325, 343, 365,

424, 631, 632, 814, 894, 904
Tzav
57, 59, 60, 134
Vaera
18, 52, 54, 57, 60, 71, 81, 82, 84, 87, 88, 104, 122, 128, 129, 131, 136, 137, 142, 143, 144, 152, 153, 162, 164, 166, 167, 169, 170, 174, 175, 190, 192
Vaetchanan
41, 42, 44, 114, 127, 131, 161, 162, 174, 181, 183
Vayakhel
2, 64, 68, 75, 153, 384, 429, 432, 434, 494
Vayechi
1-4, 9-11, 17, 19, 21-23, 29, 30, 60-63, 73, 75, 76, 109 -112, 115, 245, 255, 256, 258, 267-269, 281, 290, 292, 336, 337, 547, 586, 598, 656, 815, 816, 822, 850, 852, 853, 855, 857, 858, 860
Vayera
18, 99, 292, 293, 344, 348, 351, 357, 414, 415, 416, 479
Vayeshev
14, 24, 103, 104, 130, 149, 195, 203, 206, 209, 241, 253
Vayetze
21, 22, 137, 219, 225, 269
Vayigash
105, 106, 112, 120, 134, 135
Vayikra
127, 427
Vayishlach
25, 150, 234
Yitro
24, 26, 27, 41, 47, 235, 279, 353, 354, 355, 388-390, 396

EGYPTIANS

Acharei Mot
249
Balak
493
Beha'alot'cha
6, 36
Beresheet A
248
Beshalach
38, 55, 181, 190, 192, 206, 229, 260, 264, 327
Bo
82, 120, 125, 161, 196
Emor
130, 239, 306, 312, 318
Ki Tetze
18
Ki Tisa
30, 31, 59, 62, 84
Lech Lecha
113, 114, 115, 117, 133, 141, 143
Mishpatim
376, 377
Naso
66, 68
Noach
53
Pekudei
324
Pinchas
721-727, 729, 733, 734
Prologue
99, 101, 102, 146, 147, 149, 170
Shemot
21, 23, 35, 76, 77, 81, 94, 95,

195, 207, 209, 232, 289, 297, 305, 317
Shlach Lecha
315
Shoftim
20
Tazria
183, 185
Trumah
365
Vaera
131, 170
Vayakhel
77
Vayechi
19, 20, 110, 492, 816, 821, 822, 851
Vayera
293, 371, 416, 463-466
Vayeshev
103, 204, 207
Vayetze
26
Vayigash
135
Vayishlach
148-151
Yitro
47, 354, 390, 422

EHEYEH

Acharei Mot
164-168, 332
Behar
20
Beresheet A
6, 9
Ki Tetze
99
Naso
180
Pinchas
63, 179, 289, 308
Safra Detzniuta
40, 49, 58, 60
Trumah
555
Vayikra
162, 166-168, 174

EIN SOF (INFINITY)

Acharei Mot
75, 248
Behar
36
Beresheet A
246, 294
Beresheet B
24, 136, 143
Bo
242
Ha'azinu
34, 99
Lech Lecha
168
Noach
125, 127
Pekudei
103, 945
Pinchas
202, 225, 343, 858, 878
Safra Detzniuta
39
Shemot
141, 143
Tazria
32

Trumah
222-224, 302, 328, 921
Vayakhel
313
Vayikra
342
Yitro
525

EITAN

Mishpatim
295-297, 299, 301, 303, 305
Vayechi
432

ELAZAR

Acharei Mot
10, 11, 20-22, 24, 26, 98
Balak
376
Beshalach
85, 91, 172, 200, 262, 293, 298, 307, 327, 346, 375, 378, 383, 407, 414, 429, 444
Chukat
21, 22, 62, 63, 87
Ki Tetze
24
Ki Tisa
47
Naso
81
Pinchas
1, 6, 11, 34, 74, 128, 130, 186, 457
Shemot
56
Shmini
53, 55
Vaera
85
Vayera
494

ELDAD

Beha'alot'cha
137, 138

ELECTRUM

Pekudei
519
Pinchas
196, 266, 282, 313, 341
Trumah
82
Vayera
65
Yitro
235, 310, 311, 312, 315

ELEH (THESE)

Balak
327
Ki Tetze
145
Mishpatim
202, 203, 204, 205, 208
Noach
4
Shemot
269

ELI

Kedoshim
10
Shemot
162
Trumah
406

Vayishlach
214

ELIEZER

Behar
63
Chayei Sarah
66, 169, 170
Emor
269
Pinchas
143, 145, 157
Shemot
254-257
Shlach Lecha
29
Toldot
57, 61, 190, 207
Vayera
23, 32, 33, 35, 38, 39, 133, 143, 144, 361
Vayikra
47

ELIHU

Bo
17
Korach
15
Trumah
733, 734

ELIJAH

Acharei Mot
51, 218, 220, 221
Beresheet A
19, 26, 27, 200
Beresheet B
166
Emor
8
Idra Raba
359, 360, 363
Ki Tetze
15, 16, 24, 82, 104, 107, 125, 127, 133
Ki Tisa
44, 45, 46, 47
Lech Lecha
386, 387, 388, 389
Mishpatim
399, 412, 465, 466
Naso
81, 101, 104
Noach
157, 158
Pekudei
30, 33
Pinchas
36, 146, 267, 354, 480, 482, 487, 552, 553, 558
Prologue
12, 15, 163, 225
Tazria
167
Trumah
789
Tzav
29, 32-34, 41, 74, 75
Vayakhel
44-49, 75, 79, 80, 130, 162, 309, 426
Vayechi
127, 315
Vayera
22, 121, 122, 412, 413

Vayeshev
257, 258, 259, 260
Vayetze
85, 86, 87, 91
Vayigash
72-74, 78-82, 85, 86
Yitro
249, 253

ELIM

Beshalach
317, 394, 439
Bo
228
Emor
111
Idra Raba
5, 248
Vaetchanan
149

ELIMELECH

Balak
99, 100

ELISHA

Balak
186
Beresheet A
256
Beshalach
1-3, 12, 15, 16, 18, 20
Ki Tisa
47
Lech Lecha
56, 262, 263
Miketz
253
Noach
223
Pekudei
70, 668
Pinchas
198, 351
Prologue
115, 116, 117, 118, 163
Tazria
166, 178
Tzav
163
Vayakhel
48
Vayera
398, 413
Vayeshev
257, 258
Vayetze
284
Vayigash
86
Yitro
437

ELISHEBA

Shmini
56, 57, 60

EMASCULATION

Mishpatim
275

EMET (TRUTH)

Mishpatim
408
Prologue
23

Shlach Lecha
121, 123
Vayakhel
47

END OF DAYS

Ki Tisa
37, 38, 41
Noach
355
Pinchas
151
Prologue
240
Vaetchanan
187

ENDLESS

Beresheet A
34, 137

ENDLESSNESS

Beresheet A
1, 2, 29, 134

ENOCH

Acharei Mot
220, 221
Balak
86, 90
Beresheet A
200, 256, 474, 476
Beresheet B
365, 382, 388, 391, 392, 436, 437
Beshalach
232
Bo
111
Kedoshim
64
Lech Lecha
16
Noach
295
Pinchas
85, 771
Prologue
224
Safra Detzniuta
69
Shemot
166
Trumah
364
Vayakhel
439
Vayechi
285
Vayigash
18

ENOSH

Beresheet A
349
Beresheet B
379-382, 384
Ki Tisa
79, 80
Metzora
22
Miketz
234
Pinchas
80
Tazria
106

Trumah
760, 763, 764, 766
Vayechi
612

EPHOD

Pekudei
172, 174, 179, 184-187, 196, 198, 201, 209, 210
Pinchas
712

EPHRAIM

Balak
179
Beha'alot'cha
91, 92, 124, 125
Bemidbar
29-31, 53-55, 59
Beresheet A
249
Lech Lecha
198
Miketz
156, 168
Mishpatim
477, 478
Noach
354-356
Pekudei
178
Pinchas
183, 565, 567, 582
Vayechi
36, 39, 40, 73, 75, 370, 372, 378, 492, 496, 696, 700, 763, 765, 766, 774
Vayigash
8
Yitro
11

EPILEPSY

Prologue
251

ER

Ki Tetze
97
Mishpatim
180, 191, 192, 197
Noach
57
Pekudei
582, 583, 587, 588, 591
Vayakhel
389
Vayechi
192
Vayeshev
150, 151, 153, 154, 183

ERETZ (EARTH)

Beresheet B
36
Mishpatim
117
Vayechi
19

ESAU

Acharei Mot
13, 132, 135, 375, 376
Balak
14, 15, 138, 141, 142, 143, 148, 228, 256, 274, 323, 328

Bechukotai
43
Beha'alot'cha
15, 58
Behar
64, 71
Beresheet A
23, 141, 143-145, 439, 445
Beshalach
59, 307
Bo
151, 157, 197, 206
Emor
20, 55, 217, 219-221, 223, 245
Ki Tetze
17, 111, 112, 121, 123
Ki Tisa
19
Lech Lecha
174
Metzora
54, 55, 56, 58, 59
Miketz
105, 110, 127, 235, 260
Mishpatim
203, 310, 311, 312, 313, 314, 316, 329, 337, 478, 482, 486
Naso
84, 86
Noach
129, 374
Pekudei
190, 954
Pinchas
35b, 35c, 97, 98, 100, 374, 411, 412, 424, 425, 451, 565, 636, 650-652, 677, 679, 703, 740, 743, 881, 882
Shemot
74, 206, 304
Shmini
88, 89
Tazria
56, 57, 58, 164
Toldot
8, 23-27, 30-32, 62, 63, 73-80, 122, 126, 127, 129, 131, 132, 137, 138, 139, 140, 143, 147 -155, 157-159, 161, 165, 166, 172, 175, 176, 180, 185, 188, 192, 194, 195, 199, 202, 203, 205, 206, 208
Trumah
681, 684, 685, 747, 783
Tzav
42, 120
Vaera
147
Vaetchanan
32
Vayechi
112, 266, 274, 306, 604
Vayeshev
13, 143
Vayetze
53, 86, 104, 117, 238, 281
Vayishlach
5, 11, 12, 14, 15, 19-23, 25, 28, 29, 40-43, 48, 58, 59, 60, 68, 70, 92, 95, 104, 106, 110 -112, 117, 120-126, 128, 130, 141, 146, 152, 190, 193, 233, 234, 235, 237, 242, 260
Yitro
240, 241, 388

ESOPHAGUS

Pinchas
365, 370, 439, 440, 441, 442, 445, 451, 531, 636

ESTHER

Behar
67
Chukat
70a, 70b
Ki Tetze
1, 2, 6, 7, 9
Pekudei
831
Tetzaveh
105, 107, 108

ETROG (CITRON)

Emor
282b
Ki Tetze
143, 144, 145
Mishpatim
493, 495, 499
Noach
94, 97
Pinchas
57, 822, 823, 827
Shmini
40
Tzav
108
Vayechi
211, 226, 229, 230
Vayikra
412, 420

EUNUCHS

Vayeshev
171

EVE

Acharei Mot
359, 380
Balak
82
Behar
72
Beresheet A
99, 285, 417, 419-422, 429-431, 440, 450, 455, 458, 464, 465
Beresheet B
198, 220, 221, 285, 286, 324, 331, 332, 350, 416
Beshalach
233
Bo
70, 151, 152
Chayei Sarah
19, 20, 80, 83, 88, 108, 110
Emor
165
Idra Raba
326
Kedoshim
68, 70, 119
Ki Tetze
96
Mishpatim
492
Noach
298, 351
Pekudei
203, 207, 208, 925
Pinchas
62, 448, 587, 629, 739

Prologue
213, 252
Safra Detzniuta
46, 57
Shlach Lecha
75, 133, 134, 135
Tazria
24, 44, 45, 117
Toldot
193
Trumah
172, 181, 188, 194, 207, 215, 517, 760
Vaera
118
Vayakhel
12, 28, 34, 164, 171
Vayera
32
Vayetze
385
Vayikra
189, 320
Vayechi 802

EVENING PRAYER (ARVIT)

Ki Tetze
46
Korach
48
Pinchas
207
Trumah
63
Tzav
47
Vaetchanan
84

EVIL INCLINATION

Acharei Mot
212
Balak
130
Beha'alot'cha
76, 78
Behar
40
Beresheet A
65, 261, 263, 272, 437, 440, 463, 468
Beresheet B
167, 207, 208, 219-221, 290, 393
Beshalach
360
Bo
166, 178, 190, 197, 200, 202, 205-210, 230
Chayei Sarah
180, 181, 206, 212, 213
Ekev
34
Emor
157, 178, 179, 235, 320-322
Ki Tetze
13, 30, 134, 140
Ki Tisa
106
Lech Lecha
76, 78, 81, 85, 86, 90, 92, 300, 301
Miketz
111, 115, 118, 179, 180, 194, 195, 196, 197, 198, 201, 266
Mishpatim
8, 25, 233, 248, 423, 438-441
Naso
42, 83

Noach
36-38, 74, 93, 373
Pekudei
299, 300, 316, 516, 551, 580, 838, 843, 853, 866, 882, 896, 921, 926, 927, 928
Pinchas
51, 53, 126, 167, 170, 171, 220, 240, 245, 250, 266, 378, 414, 416, 485, 486, 488, 601, 658, 659, 689
Prologue
158
Shlach Lecha
101, 103
Tazria
80, 142
Tetzaveh
50, 73, 76
Toldot
52-57, 59, 92, 128, 170, 171
Trumah
443, 444, 447, 517, 669, 671, 675, 678, 747, 883
Tzav
24, 137, 156
Vaera
90, 91, 92, 98
Vaetchanan
75, 77, 149- 153
Vayakhel
466, 470
Vayechi
353, 577, 645
Vayera
56, 240, 314, 316-328, 339 -341, 368, 489, 491
Vayeshev
1, 2, 4, 7-12, 16, 153, 210 -213, 224, 233, 234, 236-238, 240
Vayetze
111-113, 167
Vayigash
110
Vayikra
71, 130, 255, 275
Vayishlach
1-4, 16, 17, 47, 76, 99-101, 185, 186, 188, 189, 195, 196, 271, 274, 277
Yitro
11, 510, 524

EVIL

Acharei Mot
125, 126, 204, 212, 249, 250, 254, 272, 289, 294, 320, 352, 363, 368, 404, 405
Balak
27, 47, 48, 54, 76, 77, 97, 118, 130, 134, 136, 145, 148, 165, 166, 169, 180, 182, 193, 228, 244, 271, 276, 278, 281, 283, 323-325, 333, 385, 387, 388, 390, 392, 393, 394, 396, 397, 432, 449, 473, 480, 482, 485, 486, 487, 488, 489
Bechukotai
9, 10, 11, 13, 15, 23, 25-27, 53, 59
Beha'alot'cha
44, 76, 78, 140, 141
Behar
40, 65-67, 69, 74, 76
Bemidbar
12
Beresheet A
23, 56, 64, 65, 102, 103, 180,

181, 245, 246, 254- 257, 261, 263, 267, 269, 272, 285, 286, 291, 292, 381, 404, 412, 417, 425, 427, 428, 437, 440, 441, 446, 451, 456, 460, 463, 468

Beresheet B
11, 22, 42, 45, 105, 161, 167, 186-190, 192, 195, 196, 207, 208, 219-221, 288, 290, 292, 303, 306, 307, 317, 319, 320, 323, 327, 329, 333-336, 360, 380, 393-398, 402, 435

Beshalach
33, 73, 129, 232, 360, 364, 366, 371, 441, 445-447, 449, 451, 452, 486

Bo
3, 4, 21, 35, 75, 136, 145, 146, 166, 178, 189, 190, 197, 200, 202, 205-210, 230

Chayei Sarah
6, 59, 74, 180, 181, 199, 205, 206, 209, 212, 213, 220, 224, 258

Chukat
70b, 79

Ekev
33, 34

Emor
29, 33, 39, 48, 94, 132, 157, 178, 179, 203, 217, 219, 232-236, 243, 244, 278, 287, 298, 304, 306, 320, 321, 322, 329, 333-335, 338

Ha'azinu
45, 143, 157, 163, 176, 213, 250

Idra Raba
55, 219

Kedoshim
7, 9, 50, 52, 55, 65, 72, 112, 113, 118, 122

Ki Tetze
1-5, 8, 11-13, 20-23, 26, 30, 51, 64, 70, 112, 113, 118, 122-124, 134, 138, 140, 141

Ki Tisa
16, 18, 36, 41, 50, 57, 74, 75, 76, 78, 79, 91, 97, 100, 105, 106, 107, 109, 112, 115, 118

Korach
1, 3, 44

Lech Lecha
47, 58, 68, 76, 78, 81, 85, 86, 88, 90, 92, 175, 178, 191, 192, 280, 300, 301, 358, 403, 406, 473

Metzora
4, 5, 9, 14, 16, 30

Miketz
23, 52, 55-57, 84, 85, 111, 114, 115, 118, 119, 125-127, 131, 136, 137, 151, 175, 178, 179, 180-182, 184, 188, 190, 194-198, 201, 238-241, 243, 244, 264, 266, 267, 268

Mishpatim
8, 25, 29, 30, 41, 167, 172, 179, 180, 184, 187, 210, 211, 233, 234, 238, 245, 248, 265, 266, 267, 319, 320, 322, 332-334, 337, 366, 380, 383, 417, 423, 429, 438, 439, 440 -442, 448-453, 482, 484, 486, 492, 512, 568, 569

Naso
42, 83, 87, 91, 93, 94, 102, 184, 185

Noach
36-39, 41, 44, 48, 57, 74, 90, 93, 105, 116, 119, 184, 197, 198, 213, 214, 221, 244, 247, 258,

348, 351, 354, 373
Pekudei
61, 62, 66, 72, 83, 85-87, 89, 131, 189, 190, 247, 255, 258, 299, 300, 308, 316, 347, 367, 376, 377, 378, 389, 402, 454, 457, 461, 462, 470, 476, 515, 516, 551, 572, 580, 585, 587, 592, 611, 615, 643, 670, 672, 674, 727, 760, 836, 837, 838, 841, 843, 846, 848-851, 853, 864, 865, 866, 875-878, 879, 882, 890, 892, 893, 895, 896, 908, 909, 910, 914, 917, 918, 920-922, 926-928, 943
Pinchas
8, 51, 53, 82, 86, 88, 91, 126, 167-171, 212, 220, 225, 235, 240, 245, 250, 266, 378, 414, 416, 417, 447, 448, 485, 486, 488, 601, 625, 658, 659, 685, 689, 732, 737, 760, 762, 763, 767, 808, 879, 880, 885, 887
Prologue
25, 97, 123, 131, 152, 158, 174, 182, 192, 193, 195, 203, 210, 213, 236, 246, 248, 250, 251, 253, 260
Safra Detzniuta
29, 38, 46, 67
Shemot
21, 73, 81, 173, 262, 289, 305, 307
Shlach Lecha
13, 25, 26, 63, 65, 75, 80, 82, 101, 103, 105, 120, 124, 125, 130, 174, 219, 235, 281, 301, 332, 336
Shmini
20, 99, 100
Tazria
8, 19, 70, 78, 79, 80, 85-87, 89, 90, 94, 130, 142, 143, 180
Tetzaveh
7, 31, 46, 47, 50, 52, 73, 76, 83, 86, 111, 113
Toldot
16, 28, 31, 32, 47, 52-57, 59, 86, 92, 128, 142, 143, 157, 170, 171, 176, 196
Trumah
41, 57, 58, 65, 73, 135, 140, 147, 331, 352, 413, 441, 443, 444, 445, 447, 517, 669, 671-673, 675, 678, 679, 700, 727, 747, 850, 859, 864, 876, 883, 884
Tzav
15, 20, 24, 25, 29, 31, 38, 72, 106, 107, 118, 137, 156
Vaera
90, 91, 92, 98, 114, 116
Vaetchanan
1, 29, 33, 48, 67, 75, 77, 108, 109, 116, 124, 134, 135, 139, 149-153, 185, 187, 194, 196, 197
Vayakhel
1, 2, 4, 10, 13, 163, 174, 198, 201, 244, 273, 382, 389, 466, 467, 468, 470, 472
Vayechi
7, 20, 26, 41, 63, 161, 162, 163, 190, 192-194, 205, 238, 239, 240, 242, 274, 297, 353, 362, 363, 364, 365, 378, 385, 395, 398, 399, 402, 404, 405, 413, 420, 424, 431, 467, 552, 574, 577, 582, 583, 595, 600, 601, 608, 609, 645, 684, 687, 708, 710, 711

Vayera
56, 114, 204, 220, 240, 314, 315-328, 339, 340, 341, 368, 377, 379, 384, 388, 418, 475, 489, 491
Vayeshev
1, 2, 4, 7, 8, 9, 10, 11, 12, 15, 16, 38, 72, 73, 90, 113, 153, 154, 179, 182, 183, 205, 210, 211, 212, 213, 219, 222, 223, 224, 226, 229, 230, 233, 234, 236-238, 240, 266, 269-272
Vayetze
4, 14, 23, 24, 84, 110-113, 167, 178, 183, 278, 279, 280, 283, 311, 348, 381
Vayigash
8, 72-76, 110, 111, 113, 132
Vayikra
71, 74, 120, 121, 127, 130, 212, 227, 235, 249, 253, 255, 269, 270, 275-278, 319, 336, 349, 358, 407, 425, 427, 429 -431, 437, 439
Vayishlach
1-4, 16, 17, 43, 46, 47, 75, 76, 79, 80, 97, 99-101, 108, 117, 125, 182, 185, 186, 188, 189, 195, 196, 250, 266, 271, 274, 277
Yitro
11, 30, 75, 89, 102, 103, 106, 118, 144, 156, 194, 208, 211, 214, 219, 221, 469, 510, 524

EVYATAR

Noach
86, 87
Pekudei
67
Vayechi
831, 832

EXILE

Acharei Mot
9, 28, 61, 178, 182, 183, 204, 275, 285, 337-339, 342, 377
Balak
127, 231, 232, 235, 268, 272, 300, 442, 492, 506, 507
Bechukotai
4, 30, 31, 39, 41, 48, 50, 51
Beha'alot'cha
31, 82, 128
Behar
34
Bemidbar
24, 25, 26, 50
Beresheet A
149, 183, 186-188, 198, 222, 225, 237, 244, 247, 248, 249, 263, 268-270, 272, 274, 276, 277, 279, 284, 287, 288, 356, 449
Beshalach
34, 41, 190, 193, 195, 223, 226, 289, 462
Bo
164, 194, 230
Chayei Sarah
215, 267, 269, 270
Emor
19, 20, 22, 37, 96, 128, 254, 269
Ha'azinu
188, 215, 216, 218, 219, 222, 231, 244

Ki Tetze
22, 28, 41, 45, 46, 50, 56, 60, 63-65, 68, 70, 76, 82, 83, 84, 88, 105, 106, 119, 125, 131
Ki Tisa
16, 17, 20-24, 29, 30, 35, 36
Korach
2, 43
Lech Lecha
182, 186, 449, 475
Miketz
25, 68, 105, 219, 221-224
Mishpatim
204, 205, 371, 373, 376, 378, 452, 474, 480, 482, 488, 490, 492, 495, 497, 498
Naso
25, 86, 90, 95, 99, 188
Noach
206, 289, 291, 355
Pekudei
23, 35, 121, 122, 177, 371, 372, 386, 403, 404, 738, 739
Pinchas
3, 17, 37, 39, 41, 52, 57, 58, 98 -100, 102, 104, 105, 106, 263, 377, 424, 425, 478, 498, 504, 562, 563, 565 -567, 651, 652, 689, 693, 753, 809
Prologue
95
Shemot
5, 8-13, 19, 21, 22, 32, 33, 36, 59, 62, 75, 77, 90-92, 94, 129, 130, 132, 133, 136, 138-144, 146-149, 174, 175, 206, 233, 244, 246, 269 -271, 274, 280, 289, 291, 340, 396
Shlach Lecha
303, 348
Shmini
80, 81, 82
Tazria
1, 2, 54, 62, 64, 65
Tetzaveh
106, 107
Toldot
45, 127, 165
Trumah
79, 272, 325, 485, 486, 488, 551, 586, 593, 631, 684, 742, 859
Tzav
35, 45
Vaera
67, 68, 69, 70, 71, 72, 148, 151, 152
Vaetchanan
111, 131, 184, 185-188, 190
Vayakhel
21, 68, 69, 335, 429, 430, 431, 432, 434, 495
Vayechi
7, 15, 18-25, 33, 34, 36, 37, 39, 40, 41, 51, 52-55, 58, 73, 75, 76, 87, 90, 100, 101, 110, 181, 185, 187, 258, 268, 319, 320, 321, 337, 440, 492, 516, 518, 547, 549, 578, 581, 690, 721, 731, 843, 844
Vayera
157, 441, 443, 446, 449, 450, 452, 454, 476, 487, 510, 511
Vayeshev
17, 18, 65, 66, 68, 81, 104, 107, 251, 252, 270
Vayetze
4, 41, 46, 47, 159, 269, 270, 271, 272, 273, 274, 329, 330

Vayigash
95, 96, 103, 105, 106, 107, 120, 122, 130
Vayikra
48, 49, 78, 81, 102, 114, 253, 265, 267, 286, 290, 292, 293, 297, 344, 347-349, 375-377, 436
Vayishlach
89, 90, 97, 130, 152, 222, 230
Yitro
24, 314, 324, 352

EXPULSION FROM THE GARDEN OF EDEN

Beresheet B
5

EYEBROWS

Ha'azinu
50, 141
Idra Raba
205
Mishpatim
523
Yitro
87, 144, 189, 191, 193, 196, 202, 203, 207, 210, 212, 218, 234

EYES

Acharei Mot
11, 30, 112, 124-128, 199, 278, 280, 350, 392, 397, 412
Balak
1, 2, 43, 44, 46, 47, 57, 59, 169, 172, 182, 195, 196, 202, 214, 217, 219, 228, 282, 287, 321, 322, 323-327, 333, 335, 364, 368, 379, 382, 385, 387 -390, 393, 394, 396, 397, 413, 414, 416, 418, 424, 451, 482, 485-489, 491, 495, 496, 500
Bechukotai
14
Beha'alot'cha
12, 60, 87, 118
Behar
31, 42, 68
Bemidbar
12, 15, 55
Beresheet A
23, 56, 71, 118, 133, 207, 254, 267, 274, 288, 310, 313, 348, 447, 451
Beresheet B
6, 20, 21, 61, 64, 73, 99, 100, 105, 107, 149, 176, 190, 291, 356, 360, 394, 435, 444, 448
Beshalach
18, 59, 67, 83, 87, 113, 140, 146, 298, 342, 358, 384, 407, 459, 462
Bo
125, 129, 137, 231, 241
Chayei Sarah
38, 39, 43, 136, 183, 219, 223, 224, 228, 232
Chukat
57, 59
Ekev
56, 57, 61
Emor
6, 42, 210, 217, 241, 252, 278, 285, 301, 334

Ha'azinu
23, 24, 50, 51, 52, 135-139, 141-145, 157, 158, 160, 250
Idra Raba
40, 41, 42, 44-58, 121, 159, 205-222, 239, 329, 336, 349, 358
Kedoshim
65, 71, 73, 74, 83
Ki Tetze
11, 14, 24, 75, 76, 80, 91, 92, 94, 95
Ki Tisa
1, 78, 106
Lech Lecha
6, 8, 91, 102, 140, 192, 245, 331, 332, 334, 335, 336, 405, 473
Metzora
58, 63
Miketz
49, 50, 134, 165, 209, 214 -216, 269
Mishpatim
34, 64, 68, 93, 113, 123, 143, 144, 208, 210, 211, 212, 245, 288, 293, 340, 342, 418, 421 -427, 432, 433, 462, 499, 522, 523, 580, 581
Naso
51, 112, 116, 119, 183-187
Noach
9, 28, 48, 50, 57, 64, 100, 113, 116, 147, 183, 197 -199, 239, 240, 253, 269, 325
Pekudei
41, 47, 51, 83, 86, 87, 88, 89, 99, 105, 194, 213, 214, 216, 291, 301, 320, 334, 381, 382, 383, 384, 399, 408, 483, 517, 619, 739, 795, 836, 845, 846, 923
Pinchas
69, 126, 139, 145, 167, 168, 177, 184, 248, 290, 297, 301, 303, 305, 307-310, 315, 322, 343, 379, 380, 385, 436, 461, 466, 490, 510, 592, 632, 637, 735, 744, 745, 772, 818, 822, 840, 885
Prologue
7, 49, 53, 60, 63, 66, 92, 97, 147, 157, 171, 174, 236
Safra Detzniuta
6, 14, 28, 30, 33
Shemot
21, 40, 43, 101-103, 109, 112, 113, 188, 236, 238, 239, 258, 313
Shlach Lecha
28, 51, 52, 95, 104, 105, 124, 125, 130, 153, 166, 176, 180, 184, 224-226, 232, 277, 303, 325, 331, 336, 338, 346
Shmini
4, 48, 108
Shoftim
14, 18
Tazria
66, 164, 171
Tetzaveh
79, 85, 127, 144
Toldot
5, 40, 88, 119, 120, 121, 123, 157, 183, 190
Trumah
2, 44, 47, 124, 135, 183, 204, 294, 306, 351, 368, 392, 399, 403, 453, 555, 559, 570, 576, 662, 676, 700, 738, 800, 840,

886, 899
Tzav
27, 28, 62
Vaera
26, 27, 29, 74, 147
Vaetchanan
10, 11, 35, 52, 53, 74, 75, 111, 113, 114, 132, 143, 144, 154, 172, 192
Vayakhel
91, 139, 142, 181, 282, 310, 313, 322, 382, 402, 436, 450-454, 460, 461, 462, 463
Vayechi
63, 67, 81, 100, 110, 115, 124, 141, 148, 151, 169, 237, 251, 271, 301, 338 -345, 366, 406, 448, 470, 473, 479, 497, 499, 511, 632, 655, 661, 662, 775, 847
Vayera
14, 29, 31, 36, 37, 39, 42-48, 132, 167, 181, 231, 234, 271, 328, 411, 441, 465, 495, 507
Vayeshev
73, 115, 155, 169, 207, 210, 218, 240, 249
Vayetze
27, 30, 127, 172, 177, 294, 311, 364, 384, 387
Vayigash
47, 65, 69, 79
Vayikra
18, 68, 241, 266, 334, 349, 361, 386, 387, 444
Vayishlach
83, 194
Yitro
34, 38, 49, 68, 75, 80, 82, 84-92, 97, 98, 100, 102, 103, 108, 109, 113, 118, 121, 152, 166, 168, 171, 175, 180, 181, 189, 200, 203, 205, 207, 209, 210, 211, 214-218, 220, 222, 223, 227, 229, 231, 232, 233, 234, 237, 299, 311, 320, 345, 382, 553, 569

EZEKIEL

Acharei Mot
55, 76, 90, 109, 185, 242, 328
Balak
119, 211, 287, 436
Behar
42
Bemidbar
28
Beresheet A
16, 69, 70, 88, 119, 133, 135, 218, 278, 283, 288
Beshalach
1, 247, 342, 434
Chayei Sarah
8, 140, 148, 158, 161, 270
Chukat
18, 30, 34
Ekev
18, 19, 66
Emor
61, 185, 256
Ha'azinu
37, 141, 238
Idra Raba
67, 172, 324, 336, 351
Ki Tetze
21, 90, 111, 119
Ki Tisa
79, 84, 100
Korach
45, 52

Lech Lecha
188, 199
Metzora
19
Miketz
62
Mishpatim
457, 468, 476, 484, 495, 515, 578
Naso
11, 30, 40, 89, 96, 100, 102, 167
Noach
356
Pekudei
210, 236, 237, 240, 260, 261, 282, 315, 338, 341, 405, 409, 411, 498, 500, 508, 519, 637, 714, 786, 907, 928
Pinchas
79, 80, 117, 160, 171, 176, 179, 187, 196, 221, 248, 249, 253, 256, 266-268, 273, 277, 280, 282, 284, 287, 303, 308, 310, 311, 313, 316, 317, 318, 322, 334, 336, 339, 340, 342, 344, 405, 408, 418, 419, 422, 427, 432, 497, 516, 518, 519, 604, 618, 621, 641, 653, 654, 655, 664, 700, 704, 771, 798, 863
Prologue
95
Safra Detzniuta
9, 11, 25, 48, 67
Shemot
6, 12, 58, 59, 217, 225
Shlach Lecha
48, 156, 270, 295
Shmini
51, 117
Tazria
110, 125
Toldot
15, 56, 64, 86, 186
Trumah
82, 182, 231, 488, 498, 505, 667, 733, 734, 772, 884
Vaetchanan
127, 148, 149, 183
Vayakhel
39, 59, 162, 164, 168, 239, 295, 320, 323, 326, 353, 413, 416, 441, 443
Vayechi
4, 102, 103, 267, 268, 364, 456, 469, 492, 531, 533, 680, 780
Vayera
48, 65, 100, 152, 196, 244, 284-286, 314, 328, 391, 415
Vayeshev
70, 119, 247, 274
Vayetze
46, 47
Vayigash
3, 109, 110, 123, 126, 128
Vayikra
386
Vayishlach
105, 148, 212
Yitro
48, 122, 125, 280, 307, 312, 313-315, 318, 319, 321-327, 329, 405, 490, 516, 571

EZRACHITE

Mishpatim
295, 297, 299, 301

FACE

Acharei Mot
14, 17, 55, 57, 59-61, 76, 77, 126, 128, 186, 191-193, 195, 197, 281, 282, 285, 319, 325, 326, 342, 343, 345, 349-352
Balak
111, 260, 298, 304, 336, 377, 421, 424, 483, 486, 495, 496
Beha'alot'cha
53, 100, 101, 118, 124, 127 -133
Behar
18, 31
Bemidbar
3, 28, 66, 73, 76
Beresheet A
2, 23, 24, 81, 82, 83, 85-89, 98, 99, 100, 119, 121, 122, 130, 131, 146, 156, 165, 228, 238, 240, 241, 245, 273, 277, 330, 331, 350, 419-423, 457, 458, 464, 482
Beresheet B
30, 37, 45, 68, 79, 81, 88, 90, 92, 114, 115, 129, 136, 140, 167, 209, 293, 300, 301, 318, 342, 414, 425, 427
Beshalach
7, 111, 113, 125, 130, 131, 140, 146, 147, 157, 169, 170, 172, 198, 199, 233, 278, 279, 302, 304, 368
Bo
24, 52, 54, 126, 205-208
Chayei Sarah
31, 34, 82, 130, 140, 167, 204, 212, 229
Chukat
17, 18, 33, 34, 82
Ekev
19, 66, 67, 70, 71, 72, 73
Emor
26, 27, 33, 100, 102, 217, 260, 278, 285, 291, 340
Ha'azinu
5, 15, 38, 44, 106, 114, 118, 120, 139, 147, 162, 163, 165, 169, 170, 185, 192, 197, 222, 238
Idra Raba
17, 18, 19, 29, 31, 49, 73, 80, 86, 87, 105, 120, 141-143, 146, 150, 159, 172, 187, 201, 204, 254, 278, 282, 290, 325, 328, 329, 347, 356
Kedoshim
1, 83, 131
Ki Tetze
21, 24, 41, 63, 77, 87, 103, 111, 118, 120, 126
Ki Tisa
7, 8, 19, 53, 55, 107, 108, 114
Korach
14, 21, 36, 52, 57
Lech Lecha
146, 240, 377, 389, 420, 469, 472, 475
Metzora
62
Miketz
41, 46, 62, 107, 145, 194, 222, 248
Mishpatim
14, 99, 101, 125, 167, 177, 181, 300, 340, 363, 420, 425, 457, 476, 483, 524, 526, 531, 570
Naso
11, 20, 33, 42, 43, 151, 169, 180, 189, 196

Noach
44, 45, 55, 74, 75, 77, 78, 81, 99, 100, 104, 106, 131, 152, 181, 193, 202, 207, 211, 236, 238-240, 244, 246, 251, 263 -265, 275, 280, 281, 298, 350, 361, 365, 377

Pekudei
81, 82, 103, 182, 184, 185, 202, 207, 209, 225, 227, 234, 315, 352, 455, 463, 467, 491, 503, 511, 531, 592, 648, 731, 744, 759, 764, 765, 916, 918, 922, 959

Pinchas
35b, 35c, 51, 70, 77, 81, 128, 139, 171, 176, 177, 179, 182, 187, 258, 266, 277, 283, 287, 296, 308, 310, 311, 312, 326, 329, 386, 396, 408, 418, 419, 422, 424, 427, 431, 482, 533 -536, 539-543, 545, 550, 555, 556, 597, 604, 611, 617, 620, 647, 663, 666, 668, 677, 678, 682, 745, 749, 756 -758, 771, 798, 815, 818, 847, 863, 864

Prologue
1, 17, 43, 52, 78, 79, 97, 105, 113, 114, 119, 146, 151, 153, 180, 195, 244

Safra Detzniuta 3, 7, 14, 16, 29, 34, 48, 57, 71, 72

Shemot
213, 251, 254, 259, 276

Shlach Lecha
18, 59, 61, 98, 99, 102, 113, 114, 118, 127, 160, 184, 262, 326

Shmini
18, 19, 20, 51

Shoftim
11

Tazria
43, 44, 70, 73, 110, 115, 129, 130, 143, 147

Tetzaveh
40, 56, 102, 103, 108, 142

Toldot
47, 148, 182

Trumah
45, 120, 166, 407, 431, 435, 483, 526, 527, 618, 619, 680, 681, 685, 747, 759, 813, 824, 840, 899, 918, 923

Tzav
3, 44, 47, 52, 68, 142

Vaera
14, 17, 49, 96, 109, 134

Vaetchanan
1, 11, 26, 142, 163-167, 169

Vayakhel
10, 29, 30, 37, 40, 90, 92, 268, 269, 294, 318, 319, 323, 326, 389, 396, 402, 447-449, 455, 465, 488

Vayechi
43, 67, 69, 70, 71, 100, 101, 103, 158, 192, 194, 200, 342, 386, 389, 390, 392, 554, 633, 827

Vayera
21, 288, 297, 398, 400, 401

Vayeshev
1, 28, 183, 221, 222

Vayetze
26, 40, 108, 177, 202, 312

Vayigash
28, 29, 33, 60, 85, 125 131

Vayikra
76, 100, 109, 135, 137, 156, 218, 221, 244-246, 363
Vayishlach
105, 131, 139, 228, 229, 261
Yitro
7, 17, 68, 93-99, 104-106, 109-114, 118, 131, 132, 148, 171, 180, 181, 183, 198, 211, 212, 220, 225, 227, 230, 280, 282, 297, 310, 313, 329, 330, 381, 404, 408, 421, 423, 424, 426, 427, 429, 459

FAITH

Acharei Mot
106-109, 170, 280, 305
Balak
7, 81, 124, 156, 160, 225, 226, 260, 262, 263, 418, 502
Beha'alot'cha
37, 40, 44, 46, 72
Behar
36, 52-54, 62, 79, 83
Bemidbar
37
Beresheet A
75, 96, 103, 158, 360, 382
Beresheet B
1, 4, 7, 26, 55, 223, 366, 383, 440-442, 445
Beshalach
187, 207, 220, 391-393, 396-400, 466, 468
Bo
35, 77, 81, 103, 123, 124, 185, 229
Chayei Sarah
120, 172, 261, 262
Ekev
12
Emor
41, 49, 64, 121, 130, 131, 141-143, 150, 151, 153, 160, 249, 264, 265, 267, 268, 269, 271, 276-278, 288, 292, 297, 298, 306, 308, 317, 320, 322, 323, 326, 334, 335
Ha'azinu
46, 47, 75, 101, 122, 209
Idra Raba
10, 72, 73, 87, 341, 351
Kedoshim
1-4, 112, 123
Ki Tisa
13
Korach
22, 39, 40
Lech Lecha
107, 161, 166, 178, 179, 193, 199, 200, 211, 254, 257, 274, 320, 428
Metzora
21
Miketz
6, 127, 142, 256, 257, 268
Mishpatim
83, 114, 508, 544, 547
Naso
125, 173, 177
Noach
74, 92, 121, 125, 160, 337, 375
Pekudei
70, 95, 102, 111, 131, 165, 215, 250, 313, 343, 476, 478, 481, 511, 609, 610, 628, 632, 655, 660, 667, 673, 721, 723, 728, 751, 778, 788, 789, 829, 840, 842, 851, 909, 935, 945, 949

Pinchas
231, 332, 338, 502, 511, 521
Prologue
189
Safra Detzniuta
14, 39, 43
Shemot
6, 15, 19, 26, 62, 97, 137, 211
Shlach Lecha
18, 22, 24, 25, 26, 55, 62, 264, 333
Shmini
6, 7, 37, 106
Tetzaveh
75, 133, 134, 136
Toldot
32, 46, 73, 87, 99, 100, 103-105, 109, 110, 118, 119, 128, 133, 146
Trumah
6, 8, 57, 81, 92, 129, 143, 147, 158, 196, 197, 198, 246, 250, 251, 330, 372, 540, 542, 567, 571, 631, 633, 634, 643, 644, 645, 658, 666, 722, 745, 888
Tzav
66, 84, 85, 96, 185-187, 193
Vaera
22, 30, 34, 141
Vaetchanan
73, 95, 108, 121, 129
Vayakhel
66, 67, 68, 106, 141, 167, 187, 188, 226, 253, 254, 373
Vayechi
187, 226, 228, 238, 266, 305, 393, 434, 435, 438-440, 486, 652, 847
Vayelech
33-35, 47, 48
Vayera
49-51, 90, 92, 98, 110, 114, 147, 291, 326, 341, 351-353, 357, 430, 437, 467
Vayeshev
45, 130, 146, 147, 227, 235, 266
Vayetze
15, 18, 20, 22, 59, 81, 106, 115, 118, 279, 282, 311, 319, 320, 356, 357
Vayigash
27, 32, 48, 54
Vayikra
48, 160, 164, 165, 170-172, 174, 179, 229, 329, 353
Vayishlach
18, 129, 141, 143, 233, 234, 235
Yitro
10, 204, 223, 230, 247, 390, 446, 449, 450, 452-454, 457, 458, 460, 461, 466, 473, 507, 529

FALSEHOOD (SHEKER)

Pinchas
106
Tetzaveh
24
Vayigash
4

FAMINE

Emor
78, 79
Ki Tetze
122

Lech Lecha
73, 74, 107
Miketz
13, 15, 67, 68, 104, 183, 238, 244-248, 254, 255
Pekudei
643, 898
Shemot
31, 87
Toldot
72, 83, 94, 95
Vayechi
816
Vayera
18
Vayeshev
17, 106
Vayigash
60, 74
Vayikra
119-121

FASTING

Acharei Mot
17, 267, 272
Balak
225, 226, 327, 328
Beresheet A
103, 421
Beshalach
109
Chukat
70a
Emor
23, 73, 158, 221, 297, 300, 302, 303, 329
Ha'azinu
47
Metzora
20, 21
Miketz
256
Mishpatim
469
Noach
74
Pinchas
31
Shemot
252, 254, 367, 369
Shmini
117
Toldot
194
Trumah
493, 494, 552, 568, 717
Vayakhel
83, 245, 246, 248, 250
Vayechi
217, 221, 318
Vayera
475
Vayetze
196, 197

FEAR

Acharei Mot
2, 4, 5, 15, 54, 65, 67, 74, 84, 92, 198, 206, 213, 351, 354, 363, 397, 400, 407
Balak
47, 56, 67, 153, 206, 268, 270, 275, 289, 318, 322, 323, 327, 352, 353, 357, 377, 389, 393, 486
Bechukotai
25, 50
Beha'alot'cha
16, 103, 105, 106

Behar
10, 38, 39, 55
Bemidbar
1, 16, 25, 39
Beresheet A
159, 185, 186, 197, 346, 348, 350, 372, 412, 457, 476
Beresheet B
2, 7, 93, 146, 150, 176, 178, 187, 188, 191, 194, 289, 293, 317, 385, 398, 443-445
Beshalach
22, 53, 67, 113, 174, 191, 193, 195, 196, 230, 275, 278, 281, 300, 302, 325, 329, 359, 387, 389-391, 399, 420, 443
Bo
2, 11, 15, 24, 25, 31, 35, 37, 120, 181, 198, 206, 208
Chayei Sarah
17, 33, 53, 59, 60, 102, 110, 164, 209, 237
Chukat
88
Ekev
24, 45
Emor
3, 4, 30, 31, 57, 63, 157, 207, 227a, 230, 240, 271, 314, 316, 337
Ha'azinu
7, 8, 105, 159, 247, 254, 256, 260
Idra Raba
3, 6, 7, 42, 54, 64, 65, 67, 68, 120, 125, 141, 153, 243, 260, 262, 265, 266, 299, 322
Kedoshim
11, 12, 15, 26, 27, 29, 34, 37, 42, 43, 60, 61, 64, 93, 106, 123
Ki Tetze
8, 29, 52, 54
Ki Tisa
18, 58, 105, 107, 108
Korach
36
Lech Lecha
36, 60, 61, 77, 113, 192, 270, 280, 288, 314, 406, 407, 409, 432, 444, 472, 473
Metzora
1, 63
Miketz
32, 33, 74, 77, 103, 105, 114, 120, 122, 124, 125, 127, 131, 136, 151, 160, 162, 175, 176, 182, 191, 192, 199, 201, 208, 233, 236, 244, 260
Mishpatim
20, 32, 38, 39, 82, 122, 139, 143, 151, 185, 279, 290, 346, 377, 380, 487, 492, 503, 509, 558, 567, 570
Naso
36, 37, 50, 54, 80, 103, 119, 122, 135, 136, 138, 140, 141, 142, 145, 148, 149, 150, 172
Noach
60, 110, 145, 146, 252-254, 258, 304, 318
Pekudei
3, 4, 50, 51, 52, 86, 100, 192, 262, 263, 267, 334, 365, 461, 481, 521, 626
Pinchas
28, 30, 68, 73, 139, 144, 253, 254, 322, 329, 331, 360, 427,

488, 509, 512, 514, 558, 570, 674, 689, 725, 840, 843

Prologue
29, 33, 56, 82, 85, 98, 106, 108, 113, 115, 118-121, 123, 132, 150, 161, 164 -166, 180, 183, 184, 189, 190-195, 197, 198, 202, 203, 205, 235, 237

Safra Detzniuta
28, 36, 42

Shemot
12, 47, 74, 99, 100, 159, 170, 252, 313, 318, 391

Shlach Lecha
39, 67, 68, 110, 139, 143, 155, 164, 184, 212, 230, 242, 255, 285, 300, 328, 331, 332, 333

Shoftim
10

Tazria
31, 56, 74, 109, 155, 156, 181, 182, 184

Tetzaveh
43, 70

Toldot
68, 99, 100, 105, 137, 159, 187

Trumah
14, 70, 71, 72, 90, 92, 139, 204, 283, 293, 306, 308, 310, 400, 408, 432, 482, 682, 767, 846, 851, 852, 872, 889, 896, 908

Tzav
17, 81, 145-147

Vaera
10, 59, 79, 80, 107, 147

Vaetchanan
1, 29, 32, 44, 67, 99, 100, 116, 117, 132, 135, 165, 167, 169, 171, 172, 189, 190

Vayakhel
25, 101, 108, 120, 151, 152, 223, 228, 253, 273, 331, 371, 412, 413, 414, 415, 416, 417, 418, 425, 437, 439

Vayechi
6, 7, 48, 49, 92, 164, 241, 314, 339, 414, 424, 428, 430, 548, 554, 557-561, 605, 637, 638, 682

Vayelech
19

Vayera
27, 36, 158, 192, 320, 322, 327, 354, 355, 357, 409, 433

Vayeshev
11, 13, 20, 106, 130, 183, 185, 205, 241, 242, 243, 247, 258

Vayetze
14, 66, 67, 78, 79, 80, 152, 2, 46, 251, 302, 378, 382, 383, 389

Vayigash
24, 25, 78, 80

Vayikra
33, 57, 58, 116, 136, 145, 150, 151, 179, 191, 207, 240, 262, 305, 323, 351, 352, 358, 372

Vayishlach
6, 14, 15, 23, 25, 27, 29, 44 -46, 48, 49, 60, 70, 111, 193, 244, 250, 252, 258, 259, 265

Yitro
17, 28, 41, 44, 45, 47, 69, 71, 74, 75, 79, 84, 113, 115, 116, 141, 171, 174, 175, 211, 232, 248, 468, 556, 572

FEMALE

Acharei Mot
25, 57, 59, 120, 135, 171, 219, 304, 328, 355, 357-360, 369, 401-403

Balak
78, 79, 178, 208, 211, 225, 305, 332, 347, 348, 403, 404, 406

Beha'alot'cha
127, 136, 147, 148

Behar
3, 5, 31, 37, 72, 79

Bemidbar
2, 3

Beresheet A
9, 10, 12, 37, 39, 42, 60, 64, 66, 75, 80, 81, 82, 83, 92, 102, 105, 114, 125-127, 144, 149, 150, 157, 165, 171, 217, 243, 244, 308 -313, 317, 331, 343, 357, 364, 371, 374, 395, 396, 415, 416, 420, 421, 423, 424, 435, 441, 445, 449, 466, 467, 470

Beresheet B
16, 19, 25, 47, 64, 76, 98, 106, 119, 121, 129, 137, 158, 159, 172, 175, 200, 207-209, 211, 212, 214, 220, 221, 223 -225, 229, 230, 232, 233, 240, 241, 246, 260-262, 297, 305, 338, 346, 347, 366-369

Beshalach
13, 19, 63, 98, 234, 288

Bo
39, 51, 52, 113, 119, 131, 132, 159, 232, 238

Chayei Sarah
141, 142, 230, 236, 252

Chukat
2, 3, 16, 59, 74, 75, 76

Ekev
41, 42, 67, 68

Emor
68

Ha'azinu
74, 84, 86, 102, 103, 106, 113, 115, 116, 185, 186, 187

Idra Raba
144, 177, 180, 263, 297, 301, 302, 304-306, 308, 309, 310, 313, 314, 317, 323, 324, 325, 326, 339, 340, 341

Kedoshim
23, 24, 62, 63, 69, 124, 126, 130

Ki Tetze
7, 8, 39, 41, 54, 64, 70, 75, 110, 111, 121

Ki Tisa
100

Korach
47

Lech Lecha
23, 46, 59, 78, 99, 107, 126, 204-210, 346, 348, 350, 385, 412, 413, 455

Matot
3

Miketz
157, 158, 229, 230

Mishpatim
105, 106, 132-138, 179, 216, 218, 219, 220, 221, 245, 273, 274, 276, 317, 318, 407, 411, 433, 440, 447, 454, 528, 531, 537, 570, 576

Naso
36, 79, 127, 141, 142, 143, 155, 194

Noach
25, 44, 58, 154, 230, 232, 351
Pekudei
23, 73, 129, 130, 136, 137, 139, 140, 143, 144, 158, 159, 160, 202, 205, 208, 234, 270, 293, 308, 342, 350, 425, 428, 434, 436, 437, 442, 453-455, 458-461, 469, 493-497, 507, 602, 644, 654, 683, 756, 761, 763, 770, 771, 773, 777, 778, 796, 811, 940, 943, 952, 955
Pinchas
201, 209, 212, 318, 353, 416, 468, 517, 537, 609, 639, 730, 731, 737, 743, 797, 820, 828, 878
Prologue
226, 243, 251
Safra Detzniuta
3, 44, 45, 48, 53, 57
Shemot
38, 39, 45, 49, 137, 140, 145, 175, 177, 200
Shlach Lecha
6, 13, 15, 54, 74, 101, 121, 124, 133, 150, 195, 209, 245, 319
Tazria
9, 14, 22, 23, 24, 25, 30, 43, 44, 60, 80, 117, 132, 133
Tetzaveh
8, 45, 67, 110, 142
Toldot
109, 114
Trumah
17, 25, 85, 135, 201, 215, 236, 246, 247, 249, 334-336, 348, 379, 395, 483, 580, 656, 666, 682, 716, 741, 752, 754-757, 760, 861, 875, 894, 922, 923
Vaera
34, 56, 61, 112, 116, 187
Vaetchanan
28, 30, 73, 89, 95, 189
Vayakhel
55, 235, 256, 322-324, 356, 486, 487
Vayechi
119, 177, 290, 378, 379, 381, 468, 469, 537, 568, 572, 586, 612, 620, 661, 662, 718, 720, 731, 739, 743, 748, 749, 755, 756, 759-762, 765, 766, 770, 799, 800, 804-806, 809, 810, 813, 833
Vayelech
7, 41
Vayera
98, 146, 423, 513
Vayeshev
55, 62, 66, 67, 68, 69, 151
Vayetze
7, 23, 24, 30, 31, 33, 45, 73, 91, 94, 115, 116, 119, 133, 191, 220, 227, 260, 261, 265, 266, 279, 283, 288, 289, 291, 294, 313, 328, 329, 338, 361, 378, 384, 385
Vayigash
27-30, 54, 57, 81, 82, 131
Vayikra
57, 64, 72, 73, 93, 94, 96, 101, 156, 265, 289, 315- 318, 320
Vayishlach
82, 204
Yitro
67, 125, 269, 329, 400

FEMALE WATERS (MAYIN NUKVIN)

Balak
439
Beha'alot'cha
20
Beresheet B
16, 47
Beshalach
388
Chukat
75
Emor
86, 91
Lech Lecha
4, 23, 183, 236, 358, 359
Miketz
54
Noach
25, 119
Pekudei
654, 674, 943
Pinchas
79, 81
Shemot
39, 166, 228
Shlach Lecha
83
Trumah
4, 259, 261, 286, 529, 680
Vaera
112
Vayakhel
321
Vayechi
119, 506, 717, 720, 730, 805, 813
Vayera
8, 27, 29

FETUS

Lech Lecha
328
Matot
3
Miketz
87
Vayera
418

FIELD

Beresheet A
141, 233, 234, 235, 236, 237, 261, 274, 285, 290, 302, 418, 426, 447, 458
Chayei Sarah
15, 16, 17, 18, 37, 61, 96, 101, 104, 107, 110, 111, 112, 114, 115, 116, 183, 226
Ki Tisa
15
Lech Lecha
171, 248, 461
Miketz
65
Prologue
41, 259
Vaetchanan
119, 126, 192
Vayera
2, 388, 438
Vayeshev
102, 112, 134, 243
Vayetze
85, 88, 92, 96-98, 106, 108, 190, 201, 203, 204, 211, 212, 228
Vayishlach
41, 137, 150, 237, 259

FIFTY

Acharei Mot
191, 385
Balak
437, 497
Beha'alot'cha
54, 55
Behar
20, 21
Beshalach
39, 40, 57, 58, 255
Emor
175, 177, 259
Idra Raba
187, 191, 195, 200, 241, 315, 362
Ki Tetze
25, 27, 28, 67, 87, 96
Mishpatim
385, 393, 395, 396, 397, 398, 428, 528
Naso
9, 98
Pekudei
161
Pinchas
48, 58, 82, 195, 330, 394, 566, 624, 633, 718, 733, 773, 775, 804, 805, 806, 841
Prologue
48, 239
Shlach Lecha
307
Tetzaveh
25, 27, 67, 70
Trumah
15, 103, 203, 204, 219, 307, 354, 831, 842, 844, 912, 913, 915, 918
Vaetchanan
41, 42, 43, 44
Vayakhel
120, 231, 400
Vayechi
825
Vayera
193, 219, 222, 223
Vayetze
337
Vayigash
70
Yitro
35, 339, 345, 353, 354, 355, 389, 462, 465

FIGS

Beresheet A
289, 452
Lech Lecha
197
Mishpatim
497

FINGERNAILS

Beresheet A
129, 130

FINGERS

Balak
32-35, 42, 197, 416, 489
Beresheet A
129, 130, 321
Ekev
39, 41
Emor
249

Idra Raba
4, 225, 322, 332
Ki Tetze
10, 88
Korach
49
Lech Lecha
262
Naso
158, 171, 174, 175, 176, 177
Pinchas
224, 296, 299, 301, 309, 312, 336, 483, 621, 622, 624, 631, 633, 637, 638
Prologue
2, 12, 16, 173
Shlach Lecha
270
Shoftim
3, 6, 7
Trumah
851
Vayakhel
260-262, 265, 267-269, 273
Vayechi
822
Vayera
399
Yitro
7, 8, 122, 133, 134, 136 -138, 141-144, 148, 161, 370, 371

FIRE

Acharei Mot
6, 13-15, 17-20, 25-27, 69-72, 82, 98, 226, 237, 285, 334, 391, 392, 398
Balak
3, 11, 12, 50, 51, 62, 293, 362, 370, 393, 416, 479, 504
Bechukotai
44
Beha'alot'cha
54, 75, 76, 78, 79, 105, 107, 118, 120-122, 124
Behar
3, 28, 29, 43, 44, 55, 70
Beresheet A
17, 19, 23, 26, 39, 44, 58, 64, 76, 78, 93, 95, 128, 129, 130, 132, 190, 216, 280, 290, 312, 332, 336, 337, 374
Beresheet B
11, 41, 44, 46, 48, 49, 64, 66, 71, 78, 80, 82, 108, 109, 203, 207, 247, 255, 264, 283, 314, 315, 385
Beshalach
52, 54, 55, 111, 113, 147, 157, 158, 161, 184, 209, 258, 298, 299, 301, 302, 353, 484
Bo
162, 188, 204, 241
Chayei Sarah
261
Chukat
71, 72, 80
Ekev
47
Emor
14, 53, 60, 73, 212, 216, 234, 244
Ha'azinu
23, 24, 45, 56, 148, 150, 151, 157, 179, 180, 182, 197, 200
Idra Raba
69, 100, 160, 183, 187, 210, 223, 224, 229, 233, 234, 235, 236, 238, 239, 240

Ki Tetze
119, 120, 121, 140, 145
Ki Tisa
83, 88, 93
Korach
8, 47
Lech Lecha
4, 16, 17, 36, 78, 79, 98, 298, 313, 396, 419, 420, 421
Matot
2
Metzora
10, 11, 39, 42
Miketz
111, 166, 175, 217
Mishpatim
266, 341, 361, 365, 369, 445, 447, 453, 478, 497, 536
Naso
84, 85, 114, 116, 143
Noach
58, 66, 68, 71, 202, 212, 230-236, 238, 243, 309, 330
Pekudei
107, 109, 167, 222, 228, 307, 312, 318, 323, 325, 352, 367, 368, 392, 398, 421, 435, 437, 438, 440, 448, 458, 483, 498, 513, 518, 519, 567, 589, 623, 665, 666, 668, 669, 727, 814, 831, 865, 870, 915, 932
Pinchas
35c, 77, 97, 115, 151, 196, 203, 205, 217, 218, 223, 228, 229, 246, 253, 254, 266, 270, 272, 273, 274, 275, 276, 282, 313-315, 322, 325, 334, 339, 340, 341, 368, 400, 401, 402, 407, 412, 420, 429, 432, 436, 439, 440, 446, 522, 529, 530, 539, 559, 588, 644, 650, 679, 688, 727, 736, 756, 758, 760, 761, 762, 769, 796, 799, 800, 801, 809, 816, 826, 847, 850, 867, 879, 880, 881, 888, 889
Prologue
56, 76, 98, 196, 209, 254, 258
Shemot
18, 79, 81, 86, 102, 113, 116, 134, 135, 219, 225, 234, 237-239, 259, 320, 352, 364, 367-369, 383, 388-391, 396
Shlach Lecha
88, 144, 151, 161, 181, 187, 239, 248, 250, 252, 268, 275, 284, 335
Shmini
38, 52, 58
Shoftim
2, 8, 9, 10
Tazria
53, 76, 80, 130, 178, 179
Tetzaveh
57, 76, 94, 104, 125, 143
Toldot
15, 114, 154, 162, 175
Trumah
27, 82, 236, 278, 335, 387, 392, 426, 427, 428, 429, 439, 443, 444, 447, 448, 450, 452, 453, 454, 455, 457, 553, 607, 702, 703, 709, 711, 873
Tzav
3, 20, 21, 23-27, 37, 48-50, 54, 55, 70, 72-77, 82, 83, 88, 112, 126-129, 131, 134-137, 149, 151, 153, 154, 156, 158 -160

Vaera
33, 34, 35, 36, 37, 38, 39, 40, 42, 43, 44, 45, 46, 47, 50, 64, 86, 96, 107, 108, 109, 153, 174, 196
Vaetchanan
18, 26, 67, 110, 150, 180, 181, 192
Vayakhel
45, 158, 160, 161, 167, 168, 172-174, 234, 257, 258, 259, 260, 261-265, 267, 268, 292-294, 298, 304, 319, 320, 326-328, 330, 331, 332, 334, 337, 365, 412-416, 467, 474
Vayechi
56, 141, 160, 169, 284, 383, 420, 446, 584, 601, 602, 698, 730, 735, 768
Vayera
18, 35, 36, 65, 71, 103, 123, 163-165, 170, 171, 244, 246, 247, 252, 258, 259, 261, 268, 270, 271, 273, 306, 368, 374, 381, 382, 407, 439, 456, 462, 478, 480, 490-493
Vayeshev
2, 131, 145, 148
Vayetze
27, 176, 212, 238, 273, 321, 368, 369, 371, 372
Vayigash
20, 83, 84
Vayikra
28, 64-67, 130, 132, 135, 277-280, 306, 307, 344, 437, 442
Vayishlach
6, 87, 152, 222, 225
Yitro
52, 225, 228, 250, 252, 253, 262, 273, 292, 302, 308, 309, 311, 312, 321, 351, 352, 361, 362, 363, 364, 365, 403, 482, 516, 572

FIRMAMENTS

Acharei Mot
93
Balak
19, 20, 23, 24, 25, 85, 86, 132, 188, 436, 501
Beha'alot'cha
25, 88, 105, 116
Behar
83
Beresheet A
3, 15, 16, 34, 44, 53, 59, 60, 63, 116, 118, 124, 135, 136, 139, 158, 161, 184, 206, 207, 365, 366, 368, 369, 374, 375, 390-392, 396, 397, 400, 402
Beresheet B
49, 55, 60, 65, 69, 81, 112, 113, 154, 155, 161, 162, 167, 274-276
Beshalach
267-271, 275, 296, 299, 302, 337
Bo
42, 69
Chayei Sarah
2, 40, 71, 78, 143, 199
Ekev
65
Emor
195, 197, 296
Ha'azinu
13, 14, 17, 201
Ki Tetze
88

Ki Tisa
10
Lech Lecha
211, 212, 213, 214, 215, 221, 358
Metzora
44
Miketz 78
Mishpatim
13, 61, 209
Naso
7, 90, 178
Noach
261, 264-266, 271
Pekudei
110, 152, 153, 216, 223, 228, 338, 341, 394, 448, 449, 474, 475, 476, 477, 485, 486, 493, 500-503, 562, 569, 576, 589, 605, 607, 609, 695, 852
Pinchas
122, 123, 146, 201, 249, 250, 254, 274, 284, 385, 409, 443, 444, 516-519, 552, 695, 878
Prologue
130, 139, 143, 209
Safra Detzniuta
9, 13, 59, 60
Shemot
1, 2, 51, 79, 86, 110, 112-114, 123, 160, 164, 165, 241
Shlach Lecha
116, 137, 153, 155, 166, 184, 185, 211, 212, 216, 279, 290, 342
Tetzaveh
25, 31, 81, 88, 92
Toldot
115
Trumah
27, 41, 67, 76, 77, 94, 173, 176, 184, 188, 190, 192, 374, 376, 392, 426, 553, 601, 621, 701, 704-709, 711, 712, 717, 746, 749, 750, 751, 753-758, 835, 836, 839, 843, 844, 845, 848, 852, 863
Tzav
48, 49, 107, 125
Vaera
24, 26, 110, 130, 131, 172
Vaetchanan
9
Vayakhel
17, 21, 76, 78, 117, 123, 124, 129, 131, 133, 135-138, 142-148, 175, 283-294, 303-307, 309-312, 314, 316, 317, 320, 323, 324, 331, 339-341, 344-355, 357-365, 368, 371, 376, 438, 441
Vayechi
4, 399, 441, 452, 483, 484, 502, 565
Vayera
61, 281, 393, 409
Vayeshev
196
Vayetze
31, 255, 331, 332, 333, 334, 335, 336
Vayigash
56, 123, 126, 127, 128, 129
Vayikra
134-140, 142, 146, 157, 180, 184, 309, 310
Vayishlach
57

Yitro
129, 130, 131, 146, 147, 183, 184

FIRST FRUITS

Ha'azinu
202
Mishpatim
137, 267, 488, 493, 495, 503, 506, 511, 556, 557, 564
Pekudei
165
Pinchas
767
Prologue
244, 245
Tetzaveh
73

FIRSTBORN

Acharei Mot
10, 11, 230, 232, 284, 322
Balak
14, 124, 146, 331
Beha'alot'cha
6, 7, 9
Behar
78, 79
Beresheet A
198, 459
Beshalach
28, 30, 263
Bo
14, 64, 101, 107, 110, 116, 118-120, 122, 125, 127, 177, 212, 237
Chayei Sarah
65
Ha'azinu
88, 89
Idra Raba
354
Kedoshim
55
Ki Tetze
36, 97
Ki Tisa
32, 38
Lech Lecha
446
Metzora
58
Mishpatim
180, 489
Noach
57
Pinchas
425, 736
Shlach Lecha
119
Toldot
53, 177
Vaetchanan
39, 40, 97, 114, 173, 174
Vayakhel
43, 389
Vayechi
5, 177, 192, 253, 285, 338, 496, 529-531, 538, 544, 545, 551
Vayelech
1
Vayera
316, 323, 324, 339
Vayeshev
151, 154, 183
Vayetze
154, 187
Vayigash
134

Vayishlach
25, 40, 150, 219
Yitro
255, 359, 388, 390, 395, 436, 512

FISH

Acharei Mot
79, 315
Balak
47, 55, 66, 110, 145
Behar
9
Beresheet A
401
Beresheet B
50, 235
Beshalach
82-88, 100, 101, 104, 138, 272
Bo
39, 41, 62, 64, 198
Chayei Sarah
4, 106
Idra Raba
41, 214
Ki Tetze
58, 59, 60
Mishpatim
13, 258, 482, 487
Naso
53, 54
Noach
218, 255
Pekudei
194
Pinchas
126
Prologue
89
Safra Detzniuta
43
Shlach Lecha
124, 125, 272, 314, 342
Shmini
109, 118
Trumah
425
Tzav
147
Vaera
106, 107, 111, 166, 167
Vayakhel
47, 74, 79, 80, 88, 89, 92, 94, 95
Vayechi
705
Vayera 417

FLAME

Acharei Mot
18, 147, 248, 392
Balak
3, 11, 12, 20, 50, 51, 266, 293, 390
Behar
3
Beresheet B
249, 258
Ha'azinu
182
Kedoshim
74
Lech Lecha
9, 19, 20, 104, 237, 238, 396, 421
Metzora
7, 39
Mishpatim
478

Pekudei
406, 499, 709, 865
Pinchas
116, 134, 252, 253, 323, 436, 448, 649, 850
Shemot
113, 114, 116, 383, 388, 390, 396
Shlach Lecha
88, 151, 161, 267, 268
Tazria
53
Toldot
154
Trumah
42, 43, 100, 845
Tzav
24, 37, 54, 126, 131, 134, 151
Vaera
108, 109
Vaetchanan
26
Vayakhel
21, 159, 160, 161, 172, 173, 174, 358
Vayechi
162, 163, 166, 186, 512, 678, 730, 735, 736, 775
Vayera
74, 374, 459, 478
Vayetze
176, 238, 273
Vayikra
379, 394-396
Vayishlach
6, 135, 152
Yitro
52, 224, 228, 292, 572

FLAX

Emor
73
Kedoshim
114, 115, 118, 119, 122, 123
Matot
2
Pekudei
236, 240, 241
Tazria
168

FLESH

Acharei Mot
51, 134, 249, 254, 263, 295, 296, 306, 353, 380, 399
Balak
181
Beha'alot'cha
15
Behar
37
Beresheet A
120, 121, 122, 123, 167, 242, 277, 278, 281, 282, 285, 416, 429, 432, 440, 477, 478, 479, 480
Beresheet B
57, 217, 219, 334, 359, 419, 422, 442
Beshalach
79, 310, 405
Bo
4, 15, 16, 20
Chayei Sarah
38, 39, 42-44, 48
Ekev
43

Emor
308, 309, 323
Idra Raba
8, 108, 324, 363
Kedoshim
63, 121
Ki Tetze
82, 104, 123
Ki Tisa
48, 79, 84, 100
Korach
14, 19, 42, 46
Lech Lecha
290, 298, 302, 336, 388, 393, 394, 410, 414, 439
Matot
3
Metzora
4
Miketz
19, 20, 267
Mishpatim
47, 311, 418, 434, 571, 581
Naso
122, 126, 132
Noach
39, 45, 56, 66, 74, 75, 77, 89, 130, 137, 152, 192, 288
Pekudei
341, 354, 727, 831, 941, 952, 953, 955, 957
Pinchas
60, 89, 126, 160, 161, 162, 488, 568, 572, 600, 639, 761, 800, 801, 811, 830
Prologue
130, 131, 138, 224
Safra Detzniuta
61, 71
Shemot
28, 347
Shlach Lecha
43, 67, 221, 237, 238, 239, 240, 280, 281, 283, 296
Shoftim
13
Tazria
31, 32, 62, 71, 83, 107, 108, 123, 135, 162
Tetzaveh
121
Toldot
5, 29, 56, 162
Trumah
143, 261, 288, 454, 493, 558, 559, 777, 778
Tzav
5, 36, 37, 135, 150, 151
Vaetchanan
149, 180
Vayakhel
209, 274, 334, 387
Vayechi
171, 265, 267, 301, 497, 499, 788
Vayera
40, 136, 217, 218, 249, 250, 314, 318, 396, 415
Vayeshev
39, 72, 135
Vayetze
278
Vayigash
97, 109
Vayikra
107, 230, 236, 286, 412
Vayishlach
148, 149

Yitro
126, 127, 129, 136, 182, 229, 407, 428, 553

FLOOD

Acharei Mot
411, 412
Beresheet A
225, 477
Beresheet B
380, 381, 383, 384, 390, 418, 421, 435
Beshalach
312
Idra Raba
346, 348
Metzora
40
Mishpatim
361
Pekudei
93, 115, 117, 123, 124, 125, 646
Pinchas
34, 169, 702, 891
Shlach Lecha
147, 163, 284
Tazria
68
Tetzaveh
143
Trumah
364, 377
Vaera
16
Vayakhel
39
Vayera
396
Vayigash
18
Vayikra
230

FLOW

Acharei Mot
34, 35, 47, 55, 76, 87, 88, 159, 171, 209, 211, 237, 241, 246, 247, 304, 329, 334, 380, 382, 397, 400, 411
Balak
86, 110, 111, 312, 438, 507
Beha'alot'cha
23, 24, 31, 36, 44, 50, 76, 77, 93, 120, 121
Behar
48
Beresheet A
15, 24, 63, 66, 67, 96, 246, 247, 253, 302, 308, 316, 322, 327, 333, 344, 358, 362, 367, 378, 379, 388, 389, 400, 401, 409, 426, 477
Beresheet B
105, 142, 269, 274, 279, 281, 284, 419-421
Beshalach
141, 142, 352, 357, 395, 410, 430
Bo
235
Chayei Sarah
86, 120, 138, 146, 159, 205, 206
Chukat
27, 28, 74, 75, 77
Ekev
4, 9, 10, 48
Emor
11, 12, 88, 103, 149, 154, 158,

164, 167, 327, 331, 332
Ha'azinu
35, 52, 64, 67, 68, 70, 79, 84, 85, 86, 92, 125, 167, 175, 188, 190, 195, 212, 228
Idra Raba
16, 17, 26, 27, 64, 66, 73, 87, 91, 93, 100, 103, 118, 150, 164, 165, 195, 197, 198, 236, 237, 238, 239, 249, 256, 262, 263, 270, 272, 280, 287, 334
Kedoshim
46, 47, 92
Ki Tetze
72, 74
Ki Tisa
39, 40
Lech Lecha
97, 106, 214, 265, 366, 367
Metzora
40
Miketz
19, 78, 87, 113, 175, 247, 255
Mishpatim
69, 70, 71, 202, 226, 297, 303, 520, 523, 526, 535, 539, 545
Naso
72, 145, 153, 164
Noach
23, 25, 145, 329
Pekudei
1, 10, 226, 228, 265, 266, 271, 412, 493, 624, 630, 653, 705, 710, 756, 767, 793, 821, 900
Pinchas
46, 47, 48, 101, 139, 161, 196, 198, 199, 437, 510, 515, 530, 810, 878
Prologue
40, 43, 94, 95, 219, 222
Safra Detzniuta
15, 17, 28, 39, 43
Shemot
25, 81, 141, 154, 213
Shlach Lecha
35, 36, 63, 78, 79, 89, 91, 111, 115, 155, 156, 157, 162, 164, 166, 178, 179, 253, 257, 261
Tazria
68
Toldot
108, 110, 111, 151
Trumah
169, 170, 188, 189, 190, 192, 197, 241, 291, 292, 355, 373, 376, 402, 534, 535, 557, 656, 749, 752, 777, 812, 823, 896, 903
Tzav
63, 96, 128, 156, 164, 184, 187, 190
Vaera
4, 43, 61, 135, 142, 158
Vaetchanan
21, 37, 39, 54, 58, 59, 89, 122, 123
Vayakhel
310, 311, 313-316, 496
Vayechi
58, 76, 234, 304, 329, 330, 331, 408, 415, 439, 446, 465, 536, 537, 688, 717, 727, 728, 729, 730, 751, 755, 783, 784
Vayelech
34, 39, 40, 46
Vayera
19, 105, 424, 498

Vayeshev
21, 33, 37, 40, 52, 62, 118, 157, 163
Vayetze
67, 94, 99, 189, 267, 306, 310, 318, 323-325, 328, 334, 347, 362, 371
Vayigash
13, 20, 57
Vayikra
29, 31, 103, 104, 149, 163, 172, 182, 221, 246, 290, 344, 350, 351, 360, 418-420, 446
Vayishlach
137, 228
Yitro
485, 520, 521

FLOWER

Idra Raba
87
Pinchas
67, 84
Shlach Lecha
158
Shmini
40

FLOWERS

Prologue
4, 206, 207
Vayera
1, 2

FOOD

Acharei Mot
36, 48, 73, 80, 223
Balak
48, 57, 58, 80, 100, 136, 316
Bechukotai
60
Beha'alot'cha
145, 147, 148
Behar
46, 58, 59, 61, 71, 72
Beresheet A
63, 76, 78, 79, 125, 198, 244, 309, 311, 369
Beresheet B
197, 204
Beshalach
71, 82, 141, 349, 364, 372, 373, 376-382, 384-386, 389, 390, 399, 403, 438
Ekev
24, 25, 32, 50, 63
Emor
30, 31, 32, 120, 185, 186, 217, 219, 334
Ha'azinu
58, 89, 156, 179, 181, 189, 198
Kedoshim
109, 124
Ki Tetze
3, 77, 134
Ki Tisa
48
Lech Lecha
260, 300
Miketz
65, 142, 165
Mishpatim
68, 69, 79, 90, 137, 197, 311, 509, 518, 566, 569, 571, 580
Naso
92

Pekudei
30, 88, 129, 353, 630, 641, 676, 746, 828, 881, 893, 899, 938
Pinchas
79, 81, 89, 91, 154, 245, 265, 282, 331, 345, 346, 347, 349, 350, 366, 411, 418, 423, 424, 425, 426, 439, 441, 442, 515, 530, 544, 605, 636, 655, 658, 692, 694, 695, 696, 759, 762, 783, 853, 881
Prologue
233
Safra Detzniuta
2
Shemot
232, 325, 326
Shlach Lecha
68, 276
Shmini
77, 100, 103, 107, 108
Shoftim
20
Tazria
29, 33
Tetzaveh
74, 75, 77, 138, 139
Toldot
42, 43, 51, 61, 62, 158
Trumah
133, 261, 289, 339, 488, 493, 494, 497, 499, 501, 503, 509, 515-518, 522, 524-527, 556, 557, 560, 561, 567, 777, 782-784, 809, 811, 819, 823, 824, 829
Tzav
41, 68, 148, 149, 192
Vaera
40, 140
Vaetchanan
89, 157
Vayakhel
49, 63, 187, 190, 194, 340, 350, 456, 458, 459, 463, 482
Vayechi
216, 217, 237, 254, 418, 459, 639, 640, 756
Vayera
71, 170, 171, 211, 225, 231, 232, 233, 263, 290, 316, 413
Vayeshev
169, 202, 247, 271
Vayetze
204, 367, 369
Vayigash
55, 64, 65, 67, 71, 116
Vayikra
26, 129, 351, 354, 356, 411, 444, 447
Yitro
17, 74, 444

FOOTSTOOL (EARTH)

Beshalach
481
Mishpatim
406
Pekudei
393, 394
Pinchas
59, 414, 567, 588, 674, 687
Shoftim
16
Trumah
583, 589, 907
Vayechi
15

Yitro
399

FOREHEAD

Acharei Mot
344
Balak
388, 393
Ha'azinu
43-45, 47, 49, 131, 132, 133, 134, 136, 162
Idra Raba
34, 35, 36, 37, 38, 199, 200, 201, 202, 203, 204, 205
Mishpatim
521
Pinchas
362, 363, 712
Safra Detzniuta
6, 28
Shemot
226, 258
Vayechi
625
Vayikra
428
Yitro
68, 75, 77-84, 90, 93, 109, 189, 191-196, 199, 200, 204, 205, 208, 210, 214-218, 222, 227, 230, 234

FOREIGNER

Beresheet A
337
Chayei Sarah
54, 233
Ha'azinu
203
Ki Tetze
10, 46, 47, 134
Lech Lecha
449
Matot
4, 5, 6
Miketz
67
Mishpatim
21, 24-26, 28, 95, 136, 138, 198, 389, 440, 441, 505, 507, 511, 516
Shoftim
8
Vayechi
88, 89
Vayera
211
Vayeshev
195
Vayetze
88, 188

FORESKIN

Beresheet A
64, 364, 383, 434
Chayei Sarah
66
Lech Lecha
45, 47, 290, 343, 397
Miketz
171
Mishpatim
26, 353, 354, 459
Prologue
215, 223, 226
Tetzaveh
47, 48

Vayechi
528
Vayera
6, 8, 161

FORM

Acharei Mot
61, 172, 254, 312, 313, 359
Balak
28, 50, 56, 110, 115-118, 121, 128, 159, 211, 239, 252, 253, 300, 334, 339, 346, 347, 478, 479, 489
Beresheet A
1, 17, 20, 21, 23, 70, 83, 91, 93, 94, 99, 109, 119, 136, 150, 157, 173, 204, 214, 217, 231, 234, 270, 310, 318, 319, 330, 340, 407, 414
Beresheet B
1-4, 8, 9, 53, 88, 95, 103, 189, 237, 310, 349, 372, 423, 435
Beshalach
108, 168, 221, 230, 436
Bo
49, 50, 52, 82, 213-215, 217- 220, 222, 232, 238, 245, 246
Chayei Sarah
42, 105
Chukat
76
Ekev
14, 73
Emor
282
Idra Raba
30, 31, 74, 90, 93, 125, 177, 178, 195, 225, 263, 288, 297, 298, 300, 301, 302, 304, 332, 348
Kedoshim
36, 54, 60, 80, 118
Ki Tetze
4, 32, 33, 37, 42, 51, 63, 69, 81, 88, 131
Ki Tisa
9, 79, 84, 85, 88, 99
Korach
54
Lech Lecha
146, 164, 213, 331, 332, 344
Miketz
158
Mishpatim
114, 183, 214, 316, 405, 541
Naso
34, 35, 36, 42, 43, 52, 55, 59, 147, 191, 196
Noach
230, 231, 238, 252, 254, 258, 270, 325
Pekudei
15, 162, 294, 393, 415, 448, 584, 752, 779, 783, 785, 919, 921
Pinchas
13, 50, 69, 147, 162, 176, 188, 196, 201, 250, 263, 287, 301, 310, 314, 316, 329, 332, 337, 344, 396, 419, 438, 442, 453, 454, 464, 467, 469, 500, 502, 550, 574, 583, 611, 639, 655, 671, 691, 696, 707, 792, 820, 830, 852, 891
Prologue
1, 14, 24, 42, 48, 75, 81, 109, 117, 152, 157, 160, 167, 195, 196, 197, 222

Safra Detzniuta
7, 8, 16, 51, 53
Shemot
48, 149, 177, 178, 218, 224, 272, 350
Shlach Lecha
5, 53, 101, 138, 139, 140, 141, 150, 184, 185, 188, 196, 197, 198, 230, 231, 286, 294, 331
Shmini
2, 3, 5, 47, 48
Tazria
17, 39, 47, 50, 108, 113, 115, 116, 158, 164
Tetzaveh
28, 30, 33
Toldot
3, 110, 164
Trumah
4, 16, 22, 23, 35, 107, 285, 293, 334, 350, 412, 429, 532, 546, 592, 600, 614, 618, 619, 620, 641, 642, 686, 750, 751, 754, 755, 758, 759
Vaera
43, 86
Vaetchanan
20, 21, 54, 111, 188
Vayakhel
168, 196, 292, 301, 323, 324, 383, 443, 444, 487, 491
Vayechi
96, 173, 259, 503, 702, 803
Vayera
96, 98, 299, 300, 301
Vayeshev
48, 65, 218
Vayetze
16, 259
Vayigash
129
Vayikra
17, 51, 158, 171, 172
Vayishlach
122, 241, 266
Yitro
63, 96, 97, 98, 99, 100, 102, 103, 107, 108, 110, 112, 187, 226, 290, 292, 339, 408, 411, 427, 513, 514

FRAGRANCE

Acharei Mot
46, 100, 102, 105, 116, 146, 200, 205, 247, 317, 318, 319, 406, 409
Balak
30, 67, 214
Bechukotai
59
Bemidbar
55
Beresheet A
316
Beresheet B
124, 388, 389
Beshalach
342
Ha'azinu
150, 162
Idra Raba
73, 136, 141, 143, 239, 250
Ki Tisa
31
Mishpatim
42, 46, 427, 492

Naso
143
Pekudei
109, 114, 127
Pinchas
203, 204, 398
Shemot
155, 176, 282-284
Toldot
33, 34, 35, 37, 72, 132
Trumah
24, 126
Tzav
187-189
Vayakhel
276, 277, 300
Vayechi
691
Vayeshev
55, 268
Vayetze
197, 203, 204, 205, 206
Vayishlach
226
Yitro
175
Ki Tetze
27, 28
Ki Tisa
113
Korach
2
Lech Lecha
447
Miketz
99, 100
Mishpatim
364, 365, 510
Pinchas
566, 590, 808, 813
Tetzaveh
70, 71, 73, 102, 108, 125
Vaetchanan
44, 128, 174
Vayechi
217, 406
Vayeshev
208
Vayetze
109, 115

FREEZING

Beha'alot'cha
135
Beresheet A
322, 367
Beresheet B
284
Lech Lecha
4
Vayetze
93

FREEDOM

Balak
173, 217, 219
Beresheet A
478, 479
Chayei Sarah
64, 65, 219, 220, 222
Emor
82, 134, 229, 255, 256, 269, 299
Ha'azinu
86

FROGS

Pinchas
380

Vaera
144, 146, 152, 153, 162, 163, 167
Vayechi
705

FRUIT

Acharei Mot
213, 251
Balak
15, 39, 40, 41, 62, 87, 132, 310, 311, 314, 315
Behar
54, 57
Beresheet A
12, 63, 80, 81, 90, 92, 106, 110, 153, 318, 381, 382, 383, 389, 435, 448, 450
Beresheet B
129, 158, 159, 198, 220, 285, 334, 336, 430
Chayei Sarah
16, 61, 208
Chukat
31
Ekev
30, 42, 75
Emor
149, 150, 156, 264
Ha'azinu
113, 203, 211
Idra Raba
180, 340
Kedoshim
19, 119, 123-127, 129
Ki Tisa
92
Lech Lecha
128, 129, 130, 131, 197, 198, 203, 204, 208, 209, 210, 214, 323
Miketz
65, 76
Mishpatim
137, 166, 167, 170, 265, 267, 278, 280, 490, 493, 494, 496, 497, 498, 499
Noach
4, 12, 19, 20, 72, 73, 172, 307
Pekudei
57, 58, 248, 249, 381, 469, 470, 663, 905
Pinchas
51, 90, 91, 466, 633, 747, 758, 766, 767, 768, 770, 771, 802, 819
Prologue
2, 159, 206, 207, 238, 244, 245
Safra Detzniuta
19, 36, 54
Shemot
3, 259, 263-265
Shlach Lecha
15, 36, 70, 71, 79, 165, 166, 175, 202, 203, 279
Shmini
117
Shoftim
9
Tazria
23
Tetzaveh
42, 110, 130, 131, 132
Toldot
36, 38, 148
Trumah
28, 83, 374, 375, 415, 516, 517, 518, 521, 710, 740, 741, 742, 743, 792, 793, 796

Tzav
68
Vayakhel
325
Vayechi
106, 213, 219, 221, 223, 224, 225, 353, 354, 586, 691, 692, 730, 813
Vayera
1, 26, 328, 331, 418, 424, 425, 426, 427, 428
Vayeshev
22, 214
Vayetze
99, 177, 180, 181, 204, 205
Vayikra
268, 412, 414, 428
Vayishlach
87, 88, 132
Yitro
178, 341

FURNACE

Lech Lecha
36
Vayechi
164
Vayera
18, 30, 268, 312

GABRIEL (ANGEL)

Acharei Mot
76
Balak
90
Beha'alot'cha
74, 101, 118, 120, 121
Bemidbar
27, 29, 31
Beresheet A
70, 191, 249, 250
Beresheet B
51, 166
Bo
200-204, 206
Chayei Sarah
165, 180
Ekev
27
Idra Raba
336
Korach
60
Lech Lecha
9, 291, 361, 396
Miketz
61, 62
Mishpatim
7, 87
Naso
9, 11
Pekudei
199, 200, 236, 237, 238, 357, 659, 660, 664, 665, 780
Pinchas
70, 223, 228, 257, 259, 270, 320, 421, 740, 743, 745
Shemot
180-182, 258, 337
Shlach Lecha
88, 267, 268, 269, 307
Trumah
234, 241, 385, 387, 389
Tzav
8, 9
Vayakhel
51, 53, 260, 298, 299, 300, 323, 326, 339

Vayechi
546, 594
Vayera
49, 53, 55, 56, 74, 75, 171, 275
Vayeshev
83, 84, 85, 87, 105, 256
Vayetze
45, 50, 55, 57, 73
Vayikra
20-24
Yitro
235

GAD

Beha'alot'cha
115, 134
Mishpatim
202
Pekudei
54, 178
Vaera
96
Vayechi
547, 553, 726, 727, 728, 729

GADIEL (SPIRIT)

Pekudei
615
Vayera
276, 277
Vayakhel
146

GADRIHAEL (SPIRIT)

Beresheet B
58

GAI (VALLEY)

Also see Gey

Mishpatim
117

GALL

Beresheet A
266, 267
Pinchas
98, 167, 270, 362, 364, 365, 376, 412, 413, 414, 420, 745
Vayeshev
267

GALLIM

Noach
84, 85

GAMGIMA (SPIRIT)

Pekudei
848

GARDEN OF EDEN

Acharei Mot
34, 160, 207, 209, 210, 258, 260, 261, 264, 266, 269, 270
Balak
155, 214, 216, 218, 370, 488
Behar
3, 70
Beresheet A
100, 243, 256, 257, 259, 260, 316, 432, 468, 472, 473, 478
Beresheet B
1, 3, 5, 6, 8, 9, 12, 14, 26, 49, 178, 233, 313, 361, 363, 379, 410-412, 414

Beshalach
6, 45, 46, 209, 232, 237, 396
Chayei Sarah
55, 88, 95, 96, 143, 147, 148, 168, 242
Emor
331
Ha'azinu
23, 29
Idra Raba
64
Ki Tisa
55
Lech Lecha
5, 9, 14, 94, 95, 100-106, 130-132, 344, 363, 364, 366, 367, 371, 373, 381
Matot
4
Metzora
7, 11, 12
Miketz
140, 141, 238
Mishpatim
26, 54, 57, 58, 67, 88, 89, 90, 106, 107, 116, 153, 158, 222, 430, 431
Noach
26, 34-36, 38, 139-141, 145, 277, 307
Pinchas
2, 120, 125, 127, 167, 177, 528, 558, 614
Prologue
108, 109, 171
Shlach Lecha
4, 10, 50, 53, 56, 93, 175, 177, 182, 191, 199, 204, 231, 264, 265, 291, 292, 293, 297, 305
Tazria
20, 116, 139
Tetzaveh
98, 99
Toldot
14, 34, 140
Tzav
167, 172
Vaetchanan
4, 64
Vayechi
142, 153, 172, 173, 174, 189, 233, 243, 304, 308-312, 327, 330, 348, 349, 351, 454, 455, 460, 570, 572, 693, 727, 801, 853
Vayelech
16, 43
Vayera
63, 78, 242, 243, 244, 248, 292, 393, 404
Vayetze
177
Vayikra
17, 29, 70, 137, 150, 209, 369, 379
Vayishlach
53, 268, 269

GARMENTS

Acharei Mot
189, 260, 290
Balak
20, 21, 30, 246, 247, 438, 439, 489
Beha'alot'cha
59, 60, 62, 64, 142
Behar
27, 41

Beresheet A
20, 21, 109, 120, 121, 123, 166, 167, 182, 183, 288, 350, 454
Beresheet B
9, 10, 19, 58, 423, 424
Beshalach
80, 147, 162, 266, 360
Bo
83, 149, 151-154
Chukat
15, 63, 64, 70a
Emor
11, 12, 16, 17, 18, 19, 20, 25, 50, 51, 109, 152, 171, 172, 218, 232, 233, 287
Ha'azinu
28, 33, 99, 101, 211
Idra Raba
113
Kedoshim
105, 108, 111, 117, 121, 122
Ki Tetze
6, 20, 70, 82
Ki Tisa
42, 57, 101
Lech Lecha
95, 311, 384
Metzora
57
Miketz
36, 64
Mishpatim
13, 48, 49, 58, 70, 73, 85, 89, 90, 93, 95, 96, 104, 116, 337, 338, 434, 450
Naso
117
Noach
143-145, 147, 320-322
Pekudei
164, 165, 166, 167, 168, 169, 171, 172, 199, 200, 226, 238, 352, 354, 513, 522, 523, 524, 891, 915, 929
Pinchas
16, 19, 24, 25, 26, 35, 40, 51, 248, 251, 256, 257, 258, 261, 285, 297, 337, 627, 712, 713, 793, 812
Prologue
14, 15, 16, 20, 109
Safra Detzniuta
4
Shemot
109, 121, 122, 125, 292
Shlach Lecha
125, 228, 230, 232, 235, 240, 265, 275, 309, 321, 322, 324, 328, 334, 338, 348
Tazria
164, 168
Tetzaveh
63
Toldot
131, 132, 134
Trumah
159, 241, 285, 300, 435, 436, 437, 438, 528, 534, 558, 701
Tzav
5, 30-32, 36, 37, 65, 165
Vaera
168
Vaetchanan
7, 33, 34, 100, 196
Vayakhel
43, 45, 48, 151, 175, 271, 272, 275, 277, 300, 301, 302, 308, 309, 315, 327, 495

Vayechi
131-133, 300, 301, 303, 304, 306, 307, 308, 309, 325, 348, 349, 350, 351, 499, 591, 604, 630, 631, 741
Vayera
20
Vayeshev
52, 189, 238, 239
Vayetze
27
Vayigash
134
Vayikra
103, 104, 208
Vayishlach
150, 177, 252
Yitro
127, 128, 129, 249, 250, 415, 501, 502, 551, 571, 572

GATES

Acharei Mot
191, 280, 385
Balak
16, 159, 191, 192, 239, 240, 246, 290, 291, 364
Bechukotai
11
Beha'alot'cha
73
Behar
2, 3, 7, 21
Beresheet A
99, 100, 189, 192, 194, 195, 335, 361, 401, 413, 460
Beresheet B
11, 29, 47, 60, 62, 340, 417
Beshalach
40, 49, 57, 58, 150, 255, 275
Bo
126
Chayei Sarah
10, 60, 88, 98, 134, 137, 150, 232
Chukat
27
Ekev
59, 61
Emor
129, 164, 175, 178, 180, 259
Ha'azinu
17
Idra Raba
88, 191, 200, 241, 315, 354
Ki Tetze
27, 28, 87
Lech Lecha
8, 93, 104, 105, 257, 306, 323, 360, 381, 468
Metzora
6, 8
Miketz
186
Mishpatim
99, 158, 279, 377, 385, 393, 396, 398, 428, 505, 528
Naso
3, 46, 47
Noach
67, 139, 141, 145, 353, 361 -365
Pekudei
158, 236, 406, 481, 483, 485, 488, 489, 490, 512, 514, 535, 537, 538, 539, 540, 542-548, 552, 553, 554, 555, 566, 570, 571, 576, 577, 596, 597, 604, 608, 609, 612, 614, 615, 616, 617, 632, 650, 658, 688, 786, 787, 842, 844, 867, 869

Pinchas
2, 58, 82, 139, 167, 168, 182, 183, 195, 263, 321, 386, 394, 484, 488, 566, 624, 633, 712 -714, 718, 732, 772-776, 839, 841, 873
Prologue
2, 33, 43, 44, 46, 48, 120, 121, 123, 131
Safra Detzniuta
13, 18
Shemot
79, 203, 237, 238, 255, 257
Shlach Lecha
47, 343
Shmini
4, 6
Shoftim
1
Tazria
74, 84
Tetzaveh
114
Toldot
36, 38
Trumah
41, 54, 103, 203, 245, 246, 248, 249, 307, 354, 440, 548, 549, 551, 552, 582, 662, 715, 803, 887, 912, 913, 915, 918
Tzav
29
Vaera
124
Vaetchanan
41-44, 72, 77, 94, 95, 98, 118, 126, 132, 134, 151, 152, 154
Vayakhel
23, 123, 124, 136, 137, 138, 147, 224, 291, 329, 400, 491
Vayechi
28, 121, 163, 394, 473, 527, 542, 584, 585, 683, 691, 692, 693
Vayelech
37, 38, 42, 43
Vayera
35, 51, 147, 151-158, 241, 260, 412, 418, 429, 445
Vayeshev
98, 122, 185
Vayetze
52, 67, 74, 205, 286-290, 337
Vayigash
70
Vayikra
113, 225, 241, 250, 329, 338, 342, 368, 369, 371, 372, 380, 434
Vayishlach
65, 90, 139, 242
Yitro
35, 36, 121, 149, 150, 154, 158, 252, 259, 339, 353 -355, 389, 465

GAZELLE

Prologue
54, 56

GAZRIEL (SUPERNAL MINISTER)

Pekudei
543, 604, 605
Vayera
275
Vayikra
20

GEDARIAH (SPIRIT)

Pekudei
689
Vayakhel
143
Pekudei 618

GEHAZI

Lech Lecha
56
Tazria
166

GEHENOM (HELL)

Acharei Mot
8, 74, 91, 147, 253
Balak
24, 26, 27, 278
Beha'alot'cha
78, 79, 105
Behar
40
Beresheet A
44, 45, 47, 49, 50, 51, 52, 53, 56, 57, 58, 65, 267, 374
Beresheet B
11, 37, 44, 57, 156, 191, 193, 447
Bo
28
Chayei Sarah
59, 99, 126, 134, 135
Chukat
26
Ekev
47
Emor
115, 298
Ha'azinu
28, 45, 244
Kedoshim
6
Ki Tetze
35, 112, 114, 118
Korach
31, 32, 34
Lech Lecha
8, 91, 280, 385, 404, 405, 444
Matot
4
Metzora
11, 38
Miketz
100
Mishpatim
56, 57, 58, 429, 430, 431, 513
Naso
41, 84, 122
Noach
67, 69, 71, 140, 150, 201, 202
Pekudei
100, 484, 540, 677, 701, 838, 839, 842, 902, 928
Pinchas
24, 50, 137, 167, 253, 254, 412, 462, 475, 573, 590, 644, 645, 650
Prologue
138, 190, 254, 255, 259
Shemot
318, 389
Shlach Lecha
24, 193, 197, 322
Tazria
20, 47, 128
Toldot
140, 159, 175

Trumah
70, 180, 335, 426, 439, 440, 443-445, 447, 448, 451, 452, 453, 454, 455, 457, 475, 682
Tzav
172
Vaera
188
Vayakhel
96, 99, 174, 244, 329, 330, 331, 337, 387, 469
Vayechi
44, 169, 170, 190, 193, 300, 347, 583, 584, 585, 601, 602, 603
Vayelech
43, 44, 45, 46
Vayera
193, 195, 200, 242-245, 247, 248, 258-260, 314, 319, 320, 321, 325, 326
Vayeshev
126, 127, 233, 234
Vayetze
27
Vayikra
137, 274-276, 437
Vayishlach
16, 187, 277
Yitro
351, 352, 431, 458, 462

GEMINI

Yitro
238, 239, 241

GERA

Mishpatim
250, 253
Vayetze
136

GEY (VALLEY)

See also Gai
Beresheet B
36, 38

GEZAR DINAYA (SPIRIT)

Pekudei
901

GEZURIYAH (SPIRIT)

Pekudei
687

GIANTS

Beresheet A
224, 231
Beresheet B
424
Mishpatim
482
Shlach Lecha
72, 73, 74
Vayera
418

GIBORIM

Beresheet A
224, 229, 269

GIDEON

Balak
103

GILBOA MOUNTAINS OF

Vayishlach
175

GILGAL

Bechukotai
10

GIRDLE

Balak
258, 261, 262, 263
Pinchas
712

GIZZARD

Pinchas
418, 423

GLASS

Beresheet A
394
Lech Lecha
288
Tetzaveh
136
Vayishlach
253

GOATS

Acharei Mot
9, 111, 116-121, 123, 127, 129-132, 134, 135, 137, 138, 254
Balak
144, 363
Beresheet A
121
Chayei Sarah
18
Ekev
19
Emor
52, 59, 221, 236, 237, 241, 242, 244-248, 271
Pekudei
161, 246-250, 255, 316, 830, 944, 953, 954
Pinchas
374, 378, 379, 534, 597, 672, 673, 679, 681-684, 798, 883
Shmini
49, 50, 107
Tetzaveh
96, 100, 102, 104, 109-111, 113, 138
Toldot
31, 80, 129, 192, 194, 195
Trumah
160, 235, 391, 565, 566, 614, 617, 868
Tzav
24, 40, 42, 43, 143
Vayakhel
55, 359, 360, 382
Vayeshev
140, 141, 142
Vayetze
117, 296, 298, 299
Vayikra
72, 279, 429, 440, 441
Vayishlach
188

GOBLET

Mishpatim
574

Pekudei
599
Shlach Lecha
155
Trumah
856

GODS

Bo
161
Pinchas
734
Prologue
84
Shoftim
6
Vayechi
370

GOG AND MAGOG

Beshalach
290, 312, 459
Vaetchanan
127
Yitro
458

GOLD

Acharei Mot
198
Balak
5, 161, 205, 356, 434, 435
Beha'alot'cha
16
Beresheet A
371
Beresheet B
10, 93, 94, 188, 216, 286
Bo
45, 153
Chukat
1, 65
Ha'azinu
112, 113, 181
Idra Raba
317, 341
Kedoshim
74, 82
Ki Tetze
48
Ki Tisa
9, 71-73, 75, 77, 78, 81-83, 87
Korach
1, 44
Lech Lecha
106, 162, 284, 285, 287
Metzora
56, 58
Miketz
2, 64, 67, 68, 69
Mishpatim
183
Naso
86, 103, 199
Noach
268, 298, 300, 324, 335
Pekudei
18, 19, 60, 62, 67, 68, 70, 74-76, 79, 118, 131, 132, 160, 161, 172, 257, 286, 305, 306, 307, 312, 314, 318, 321, 324, 430, 434, 780, 905
Pinchas
261, 297, 337, 356, 712, 791, 812
Prologue
6, 145

Shemot
9, 10, 97, 319
Shlach Lecha
67, 146, 148, 181, 231, 249, 252, 325, 326
Shmini
84
Tazria
111, 160, 164
Toldot
66
Trumah
60, 157, 160, 161, 227-229, 235, 242, 370, 386-391, 399 -403, 408, 409, 410, 429, 434, 483, 594, 828, 838, 844, 846, 902, 922
Tzav
30, 37, 175
Vaera
34, 35, 42-46
Vaetchanan
65, 66, 93, 168
Vayakhel
55, 57, 73, 164, 166, 446, 447, 448
Vayechi
129, 130, 383, 569, 777, 835, 836, 837, 839
Vayera
144, 252, 254, 318, 329, 333, 337, 388, 463
Vayeshev
134, 277
Vayetze
42, 116
Vayikra
17, 19
Vayishlach
150, 154, 155, 157
Yitro
125, 211, 212, 499, 500

GOLDEN CALF

Acharei Mot
100
Balak
82, 375
Bechukotai
35
Beha'alot'cha
138
Behar
26
Beresheet A
221, 232, 233
Chayei Sarah
82
Ekev
46
Ki Tetze
23
Ki Tisa
66, 83, 93
Mishpatim
361, 362
Noach
36
Pekudei
59, 300, 308, 315, 321
Pinchas
469, 470, 471
Prologue
14
Shmini
31, 32, 34, 35, 45, 46, 49
Vayakhel
6, 157, 480

Vayechi
380, 384

GOLDEN CALVES

Beha'alot'cha
89
Vayechi
366, 723

GOMER

Pekudei
481

GONORRHEA

Vayera
105

GOOD INCLINATION

Bechukotai
25
Beresheet A
180, 272
Beresheet B
207, 208, 286
Bo
178, 197, 200-202, 207, 209, 210, 230
Ekev
34
Kedoshim
7
Ki Tetze
13, 140
Lech Lecha
86
Miketz
111, 179, 180, 195, 198, 201, 266
Mishpatim
438
Naso
42
Pekudei
516, 923, 924
Pinchas
126, 171, 220, 240, 245, 416, 659
Shlach Lecha
233
Tazria
80
Toldot
170, 171
Trumah
669, 883
Vaera
90, 91, 92, 98
Vaetchanan
75, 149, 153
Vayakhel
83
Vayeshev
3, 6, 8, 9, 10
Vayetze
167
Vayigash
110
Vayishlach
2, 3, 4, 271

GOSHEN

Vayigash
129, 135

GRADES

Acharei Mot
1, 34, 47, 49, 76, 79, 82, 83, 88,

90-92, 102, 105, 108, 117, 159, 161-163, 166, 168-170, 189, 209, 220-222, 261, 271, 299-301, 316, 325, 326, 381, 408

Balak

18, 38, 41, 50-54, 86, 110, 124, 133, 135, 158-160, 165, 166, 168, 178, 180, 235, 259, 261, 262, 263, 264, 266, 267, 268, 269, 286, 287, 291, 299, 305, 306, 318, 331, 355, 356, 414, 417-420, 454, 458, 464, 467, 468, 472-475, 483

Bechukotai

6

Beha'alot'cha

23, 24, 28, 29, 45-47, 54, 70, 71, 80, 90, 91, 109, 114, 121, 123, 146-148

Behar

19, 20, 37, 42, 43, 68, 79 -82, 85

Bemidbar

2, 6, 46, 47, 50

Beresheet A

10, 39, 42, 56, 65, 66, 67, 68, 80, 98, 99, 106, 109, 111, 114, 115, 128, 129, 134, 138, 141, 143, 144, 145, 147, 155-157, 161, 162, 165, 169, 176, 202, 203, 206, 221, 222, 231, 274, 302, 308, 310, 312, 333, 344, 356, 357, 364, 366, 382, 394, 396, 399, 407, 412

Beresheet B

20, 22-24, 27, 28, 30, 31, 36, 38, 39, 49, 93, 94, 96-99, 104, 135, 143-145, 159, 163, 242, 273, 275, 288, 292, 341 -343, 422

Beshalach

20, 61, 62, 98, 99, 110, 128, 135, 136, 138, 139, 141-143, 158, 201, 216, 218, 254, 262-265, 267, 272, 292, 323, 326, 461

Bo

36, 37, 41, 56, 64, 103, 111, 118-120, 122, 127, 140, 142, 144, 166, 168, 172, 176, 177, 198, 212, 217, 232, 238, 242

Chayei Sarah

9, 14, 30, 35, 70, 119, 120, 123, 124, 125, 131, 142, 144, 160, 161, 188, 231, 233, 234, 238, 240, 261, 262, 265

Chukat

14, 22, 26, 30, 31, 33, 42, 43, 51, 52, 57, 60, 61, 83

Ekev

2, 4, 6, 10, 13, 38

Emor

52, 54, 58, 86, 87, 88, 90, 91, 114, 130, 135, 136, 138, 139, 152, 154, 158, 227b, 250, 253

Ha'azinu

17, 34, 47, 51, 64, 66, 67, 98, 99, 118, 180, 185, 191, 193, 194, 195, 203, 220

Idra Raba

1, 6, 19, 20, 56, 66, 68, 91, 108, 112, 122, 135, 149, 150, 151, 161, 177, 179, 187, 216, 240, 272, 297, 298, 302, 303, 325, 330, 361

Kedoshim

14, 37, 59, 75, 77, 91, 97

Ki Tetze

27, 28, 46, 57, 67, 88, 101,

115, 117, 144
Ki Tisa
46, 62, 63, 106, 107
Korach
6, 13, 32, 34, 36, 37, 40, 58
Lech Lecha
13, 14, 21, 43, 63, 64, 69-73, 75, 96, 97, 98, 99, 107, 108, 121, 140-143, 146, 147, 149, 152, 153, 154, 157, 160, 161, 164, 165, 167, 168, 169, 172, 185, 193, 194, 200, 228, 229, 230, 239, 241, 245, 246, 251, 255, 257, 271, 272, 273, 274, 276, 304, 305, 319, 324, 335, 337-340, 342, 400, 401, 403, 422, 423, 424, 458
Metzora
38, 42
Miketz
4, 5, 8, 9, 18-24, 26, 30, 35, 52-55, 58, 60, 62, 63, 86, 87, 108, 148, 153, 211, 231, 253, 257
Mishpatim
2, 23, 104, 129, 130, 170, 171, 181, 191, 200, 297, 299, 336, 369, 378, 382, 390, 391, 455, 456, 473, 476, 479, 480, 520
Naso
12, 43, 56, 159, 165, 167, 169, 172, 176, 181
Noach
17, 44, 63, 102, 124, 235, 236, 256, 303, 319, 328, 333, 344, 345, 347, 348, 352, 359, 368, 375
Pekudei
1, 2, 26, 51, 52, 60, 75, 77, 81, 87, 92, 103, 105, 109, 114, 130, 134, 165, 177, 215, 219, 223, 232, 264, 272, 343, 373, 393, 409, 411-415, 424, 427, 435, 444-450, 453-463, 469, 478, 479, 481, 482, 503, 534, 535, 549, 606, 609, 610, 611, 614, 665, 670, 678, 705, 740, 741, 744, 747, 764, 775, 777, 780, 787, 788, 801, 823, 837, 838, 839, 840, 842, 889, 951
Pinchas
76, 104, 137, 139, 142, 157, 185, 187, 193, 194, 225, 226, 233, 253, 291, 383, 396, 406, 411, 417, 446, 448, 449, 462, 482, 484, 491, 502, 530, 541, 543-545, 548, 562, 569, 570, 578, 582, 584, 590, 595, 597, 598, 610, 615, 651, 652, 654, 657, 682, 717, 729, 768, 779, 780, 789, 813, 835, 837, 838, 839, 854, 856, 858, 862, 863, 865, 867
Prologue
8, 9, 19, 20, 21, 78, 92, 93, 95, 97, 100, 118, 120, 140, 144, 147, 199, 205, 223
Safra Detzniuta
13, 24, 29, 39, 57, 58, 63, 66, 71
Shemot
19, 38, 49, 70, 93, 178, 192, 209, 243, 245, 246, 250, 268, 270, 273, 287, 313, 332, 339, 391, 395
Shlach Lecha
12, 18, 24, 54, 56, 89, 93, 94, 98, 99, 115, 120, 122, 123,

125, 126, 149, 152, 155, 156, 157, 242, 245, 256, 262, 281, 310, 312, 320, 339

Shmini
81, 91, 109

Tazria
32, 97, 98, 106, 107, 116, 132

Tetzaveh
20, 25, 54, 64, 111, 115, 116, 118, 120, 126, 129, 131, 132

Toldot
3, 7, 14, 29, 30, 80, 91, 92, 94, 109, 120, 121, 129, 136, 138, 150, 151, 167, 169, 179, 192, 195

Trumah
2, 13, 15, 16, 18, 44, 80, 81, 82, 83, 87, 89, 90, 190, 195, 196, 197, 198, 199, 203, 216, 220, 258, 292, 307, 314, 334, 336, 339, 342, 348, 356, 394, 397, 405, 407, 445, 448, 481, 500, 547, 576, 585, 603, 626, 628, 662, 664, 719, 739, 749, 754, 775, 776, 822, 830, 834, 861, 885, 899, 907, 919

Tzav
4, 35, 78, 80, 102, 123, 128, 185, 186

Vaera
6, 9, 10, 11, 14, 18, 43, 51, 102, 107, 111, 122, 123, 133, 143, 145, 158, 165, 166, 167, 168, 172

Vaetchanan
23, 24, 30, 54, 71, 72, 74, 75, 101, 102, 104, 164, 166, 176, 178, 191

Vayakhel
21, 100, 106, 110, 119, 120, 137, 145, 146, 187, 210, 215, 220, 235, 236, 251-253, 261-264, 266, 267, 283, 357, 376, 390, 418, 419, 425, 435

Vayechi
9, 13, 14, 15, 16, 25, 53, 95, 119, 150, 175, 223, 225, 249, 290, 314, 328, 330, 334, 335, 352, 395, 398, 459, 464, 465, 483, 489, 491, 503, 504, 506, 507, 594, 597, 601, 606, 619, 624, 679, 704, 708, 711, 716, 717, 729, 740, 753, 766, 769, 776, 780, 784, 786, 791, 796, 797, 821

Vayelech
28, 31, 33, 34, 39, 46

Vayera
7, 9-12, 14, 15, 16, 49, 50, 61, 63, 64, 69, 103, 107, 147, 154-157, 159, 161, 188, 189, 199, 203, 210, 222, 239, 256, 281, 330, 331, 334-338, 351, 354, 355, 356, 357, 425, 437, 445, 453, 476, 484, 488, 489, 496, 498, 500, 506

Vayeshev
22, 33, 34, 46, 54, 60, 61, 64, 73, 82, 83, 84, 85, 87, 89, 111, 113, 145, 147, 152, 153, 156, 213, 256, 263, 266, 268, 272, 281

Vayetze
4, 12, 15, 16, 18, 22, 28, 45, 49, 50, 51, 52, 55, 56, 57, 59, 65, 70, 76, 77, 81, 96, 98, 116, 117, 131, 150, 169, 183, 184, 190, 219, 220, 226, 279, 289, 303, 304, 307-309, 312, 317,

319, 320, 321, 322, 336, 345, 347, 348, 351, 352, 353, 355, 358, 391
Vayigash
7, 15, 16, 17, 19, 21, 38, 46, 54, 57, 60, 118, 119
Vayikra
30, 32, 33, 46, 61, 113, 146, 157, 164, 177, 182, 197, 205, 219, 220, 257, 284, 314, 360, 379, 380, 383, 409, 431, 432, 438, 439, 446
Vayishlach
36, 73, 144, 145, 146, 161, 164, 166, 171, 217, 237, 238, 239, 240, 241, 242, 243, 245, 248, 272, 275
Yitro
22, 59, 63, 120, 128, 182, 225, 238, 242, 265, 311, 312, 316, 317, 324, 349, 397, 399, 402, 406, 407, 446, 508, 510, 511, 523, 526, 529, 530, 532, 535, 541, 542, 564

GRASS

Beresheet A
75, 76, 78, 80, 93, 381

GRASSHOPPERS

Beresheet A
431

GRAVE

Beresheet A
273
Chayei Sarah
49, 90, 105, 110, 156, 165, 172, 174
Ki Tisa
98
Lech Lecha
98, 100
Vaetchanan
196
Vayechi
145, 171, 257, 324, 345-347
Vayera
389, 392, 409, 413, 421
Vayeshev
51, 122, 123, 167
Vayetze
290
Vayishlach
201, 210, 214

GREECE

Bo
164
Toldot
188
Yitro
26

GROUND (ARKA)

Beresheet B
36, 38, 343
Mishpatim
117
Prologue
153
Vayetze
222, 227

GROUND

Acharei Mot
249

Balak
161, 191, 278, 331, 468, 496, 504
Bechukotai
45
Bemidbar
50
Beresheet A
233, 234, 236-238, 244, 257, 274, 304, 423
Beresheet B
36, 38, 114, 161, 394, 430, 431
Beshalach
77, 100, 237, 395, 398, 400, 417
Bo
31, 196, 200
Chayei Sarah
155, 179
Chukat
13, 67
Emor
19, 148, 249, 325
Ha'azinu
117, 197
Idra Raba
17, 302, 342
Kedoshim
108
Ki Tetze
1, 97
Ki Tisa
14, 77, 78
Metzora
31
Miketz
194
Mishpatim
64, 117, 118, 143, 279, 308, 408, 429, 490
Noach
60, 181, 211, 243, 307
Pekudei
34, 35, 854, 855, 856, 906, 920, 938
Pinchas
265, 441, 451, 588, 599, 600, 644, 751, 791, 803
Prologue
33
Safra Detzniuta
7
Shemot
39, 81, 105, 128, 264, 276, 290
Shlach Lecha
59, 219, 221, 249, 270
Shmini
116
Shoftim
24
Tazria
80, 113, 169
Tetzaveh
42
Toldot
33, 34, 148
Trumah
558, 559, 742, 766
Tzav
46, 52, 115
Vaera
84
Vaetchanan
10, 30, 164, 165
Vayakhel
201
Vayechi
143, 158, 170, 193, 234, 341, 579, 681, 684, 685

Vayelech
22
Vayera
2, 4, 5, 15, 29, 41, 57, 391, 408
Vayeshev
39, 50, 51, 118, 154, 251
Vayetze
42, 70
Vayikra
93, 237, 242, 446
Vayishlach
29, 117
Yitro
272, 274

GUILT

Balak
74, 275
Behar
30, 46
Beresheet B
394
Beshalach
246
Bo
23, 211
Kedoshim
10
Lech Lecha
303
Noach
163
Pekudei
725, 726
Pinchas
35d, 355, 357, 578
Shemot
71
Shmini
34
Tzav
27, 39, 41, 45, 47, 121
Vayera
117, 241
Vayeshev
162
Vayikra
164, 193, 389

GUTTERS

Vayetze
303, 304, 305, 310, 318, 347, 348, 353

GZARDIA (SPIRIT)

Vayakhel
128

HABAKKUK

Balak
186
Behar
42
Beshalach
1, 20, 22
Idra Raba
7, 243, 246
Ki Tetze
4, 61
Korach
46, 49
Lech Lecha
310
Mishpatim
570
Pinchas
10, 329, 749

Prologue
115, 116, 117, 118
Safra Detzniuta
41
Vayechi
619
Vayera
405
Vayetze
385
Yitro
340

HADAR

Ha'azinu
112, 113
Tetzaveh
130, 132
Vayechi
213, 219, 223, 224, 290, 291

HADARNIEL (ANGEL)

Beresheet B
363
Beshalach
299, 300, 302
Pekudei
518, 519, 525, 526

HADRIEL (SPIRIT)

Vayera
276

HAGAR

Beha'alot'cha
15
Chayei Sarah
254, 256, 257, 258
Shemot
289
Vaera
198, 199
Vayera
141, 463, 464, 465, 466

HAIL

Pekudei
222
Vaera
190, 192
Vayera
480
Vayeshev
145, 148

HAIR

Acharei Mot
78, 79, 127, 250, 251, 312, 402, 403
Balak
177, 386, 494
Beha'alot'cha
52
Beresheet A
361
Beresheet B
347
Ekev
61
Ha'azinu
38, 40, 62, 124-130, 136, 165, 167, 169, 170, 172, 173, 175, 176, 184
Idra Raba
24-31, 33, 37, 48, 72, 74, 75, 76, 77, 79-86, 90, 91, 92, 93, 94, 95, 96, 99-101, 103, 104, 106,

110, 116, 126, 130, 134 -136, 141, 142, 148, 150, 152 -159, 193-198, 200, 201, 205, 235, 238, 250-255, 262, 266, 268, 269, 270, 273, 274, 276, 279, 280, 281, 283, 286, 288, 289-295, 304, 305, 310

Metzora
57

Mishpatim
520

Naso
77, 78, 79, 126, 127, 132, 133, 134

Pekudei
161, 246, 247, 248, 249, 250, 255, 329, 331, 332, 918, 919

Pinchas
126, 212, 685, 741

Prologue
242

Safra Detzniuta
6, 14, 16, 17, 27, 29, 34, 35

Shemot
243

Shlach Lecha
194, 278

Shmini
53

Tazria
96, 119-124, 126, 127, 129, 130, 162

Tetzaveh
111, 113

Trumah
160, 391, 614, 617

Vaetchanan
54

Vayakhel
55, 359, 360, 382

Vayechi
123, 283, 286, 655, 656, 662

Vayera
267, 388, 389, 392

Vayeshev
140, 143, 213, 218, 238, 240

Vayetze
26

Vayishlach
16, 18, 82

Yitro
68, 69, 70, 71, 72, 73, 74, 75, 76, 113, 161, 163, 168, 171, 180, 181, 186-189, 193, 195, 198, 200-205, 207, 208, 211, 212, 214, 216, 219, 220, 222, 230, 234

HALLEL

Emor
137, 138, 139, 174

Ki Tetze
144

Pinchas
192, 302, 823

Tetzaveh
62, 139

Vayechi
506

Vayishlach
270

HAM

Miketz
37, 39

Vayechi
382

HAMAN

Ki Tetze
111
Mishpatim
337
Pekudei
831
Shemot
296
Shlach Lecha
77, 308
Tetzaveh
105, 108
Vaera
71
Vayakhel
22

HAMOR

Vayishlach
146, 147, 150, 151

HANANIAH

Acharei Mot
14-18
Mishpatim
569
Naso
150
Toldot
123

HANDS

Balak
24, 26, 30-34, 42, 45, 50, 58, 67, 70, 83, 84, 99, 109, 122, 124, 134, 171, 196, 197, 202, 203, 204, 223, 229, 253, 260, 261, 265, 267, 268, 282, 301 -303, 328 -330, 351, 353, 368, 383, 386, 398, 427, 451, 460, 461, 489, 491, 495, 505
Bemidbar
5, 36, 41, 42, 51, 55, 56, 61, 70, 71, 77
Beresheet A
53, 56, 62, 73, 145, 153, 173, 175, 215, 223, 243, 255, 262, 263, 264, 273, 281, 289, 312, 321, 430, 442, 446, 450, 467, 472, 475
Chayei Sarah
27, 30, 59, 69, 96, 134, 159, 160, 168, 170, 178, 192, 193, 195, 209, 234, 247, 252, 253
Chukat
13, 19, 36, 45, 88
Ekev
20, 26, 31, 37, 38, 39, 40, 41, 42, 56, 57, 60, 61
Emor
6, 33, 40, 81, 122, 149, 221, 237, 242, 254, 255, 269, 277, 281, 319, 324
Ha'azinu
16, 25, 29, 74, 96, 198, 208, 222, 254
Idra Raba
2, 4, 72, 88, 167, 225, 267, 287, 310, 318, 319, 320, 321, 322, 332
Ki Tetze
18, 28, 45, 56, 69, 72, 88, 104, 136, 139, 145, 146
Ki Tisa
33, 52, 72, 75, 77, 78, 82, 83, 87, 104, 108

Korach
2, 19, 21, 22, 28, 29, 30, 40, 49
Lech Lecha
20, 51, 52, 53, 55, 163, 233, 236, 243, 259, 260, 327, 328, 361, 378, 393, 404, 405, 418, 445, 474
Matot
1, 2
Metzora
11, 35, 36, 37, 40, 41, 42, 54
Miketz
27, 41, 60, 64, 69, 74, 111, 117, 118, 126, 127, 133, 182, 183, 201, 208, 212, 213, 217, 260
Mishpatim
43, 46, 47, 80, 125, 162, 178, 187, 196, 212, 234, 267, 294, 313, 332, 344, 349, 368, 370, 372, 376, 386, 398, 416, 433, 452, 454, 456, 471-473, 475, 476, 489, 507, 540, 580
Naso
2, 4, 51, 94, 97, 98, 100, 103, 114, 115, 151, 153, 154, 155, 156, 162, 164, 171, 173, 175, 183
Pekudei
29, 69, 81, 82, 98, 137, 186, 201, 202, 227, 236, 277, 296, 303, 320, 337, 351, 363, 403, 404, 446, 483, 504, 510, 514, 515, 544, 546, 551, 564, 587, 620, 634, 657, 671, 726, 786 -788, 854, 857, 872, 915, 919, 924, 946
Pinchas
17, 23, 28, 30, 32, 125, 134, 135, 147, 155, 160, 164, 168, 170, 171, 174, 178, 188, 190, 231, 267, 272, 287, 289, 290, 295, 296, 299, 326, 329, 336, 345, 346, 372, 408, 458, 463, 464, 465, 467, 480, 483, 484, 488, 543, 549, 561, 567, 581, 582, 605, 614, 621-623, 631, 634, 637, 638, 649, 651, 657, 679, 681, 703, 715, 724, 728, 736, 753, 754, 782, 789, 822, 823, 849, 872, 874, 876, 880, 888, 889
Prologue
49, 65, 66, 89, 101, 102, 114, 119, 130, 135, 137, 138, 149, 171, 172, 173, 242, 243
Safra Detzniuta
12, 37, 62
Shlach Lecha
27, 28, 29, 57, 87, 146, 165, 199, 224, 225, 234, 240, 246, 264, 280, 297, 336, 337, 338
Shmini
8, 19, 20, 21, 25, 27, 60, 75
Shoftim
4, 6
Tazria
6, 7, 14, 16, 41, 51, 64, 69, 105, 117, 134, 171
Tetzaveh
36, 41, 79, 90, 132
Toldot
13, 26, 27, 39, 45, 121, 123, 131, 137, 188
Trumah
41, 49, 72, 131, 159, 187, 210, 212, 228, 230, 250, 319, 320,323, 328, 411, 417, 446, 460, 461, 462, 463, 466, 499,

520, 521, 523, 537, 569, 595, 617, 653, 655, 657-662, 691, 716, 737, 740, 766, 777, 780-782, 786, 792, 816, 849 -852, 854, 871, 885, 916, 917, 924

Vaetchanan
14, 55, 57, 70, 77, 86, 87, 88, 89, 90, 96, 97, 113, 114, 119, 135, 172, 179, 192, 193, 194

Vayakhel
11, 16, 91, 111, 122, 148, 164, 199, 208, 218, 225, 234, 239, 260, 268, 370, 396, 402, 477

Vayechi
25, 30, 33, 41, 43, 59-63, 71, 72, 87, 96, 108, 115, 126, 148, 159, 173, 188, 191, 192, 208, 215, 228 -230, 265-268, 283, 286, 338, 339, 344, 355, 356, 419, 435, 449, 505, 530, 552, 556, 564, 575, 583, 585, 598, 690, 698, 699, 701, 718, 725, 735, 736, 777, 822, 839, 845, 846, 849, 860

Vayelech
1, 2, 31

Vayera
5, 27, 48, 91, 114, 138, 140, 233, 271, 285, 350, 358, 370, 380, 398, 412, 413, 418, 456, 459, 507, 508

Vayeshev
29, 48, 50, 55, 108, 114-117, 121, 130-133, 135, 136, 142, 162, 181-183, 185, 187, 206, 207, 220, 225, 239, 251

Vayetze
43, 46, 84, 86, 144, 176, 260, 350, 351, 352, 359, 374, 376, 379

Vayigash
9, 23, 80, 116

Vayishlach
7, 8, 30, 36, 42, 47, 62, 63, 70, 83, 110-112, 116, 176, 179, 184, 226, 242, 253, 277

Yitro
1, 2, 4, 5, 6, 10, 21, 23, 31, 68, 122, 124, 133, 136, 137, 143, 148, 150, 151, 154, 157, 158, 161, 164, 165, 171, 176, 180, 181, 197, 213, 228, 249-251, 256, 271, 274, 293, 321, 326, 330, 339, 347, 355, 358, 361, 365, 371, 374, 392, 398, 407, 423-425, 436, 469, 479, 481, 496, 551, 563, 564

HARAN

Chayei Sarah
198, 226

Lech Lecha
16, 17, 26, 27, 30, 31, 36, 40, 42, 44, 47, 57, 59, 61, 200

Vayera
143, 350

Vayetze
1-4, 7, 8, 19, 22, 28, 31, 41, 109, 123, 124, 125, 386

HARIEL (SPIRIT)

Pekudei
618

HARLOTRY

Acharei Mot
78, 281, 285
Beshalach
356, 358
Emor
35, 38
Idra Raba
36, 200
Metzora
15
Mishpatim
453
Naso
85
Pekudei
854, 906, 912, 913
Pinchas
362, 363, 378, 601
Safra Detzniuta
54, 64
Trumah
674, 675

HATRED

Acharei Mot
15
Balak
103, 303, 376, 505
Bechukotai
43
Beresheet A
228
Bo
111
Emor
220
Ha'azinu
160
Idra Raba
265
Kedoshim
100, 105
Ki Tetze
33, 41
Ki Tisa
18, 19
Lech Lecha
3, 215
Miketz
107, 178, 180, 188
Mishpatim
163, 328
Naso
184
Pekudei
442, 903
Pinchas
327, 329, 339, 722
Prologue
174, 200
Shemot
304
Toldot
143
Trumah
4, 540, 541
Vayechi
75, 83, 555, 775
Vayeshev
28, 79-81, 90-92, 102, 131
Vayetze
147, 149, 152
Vayigash
116
Vayishlach
42
Yitro
102, 171, 181, 193, 194, 197,

207, 218

HAVDALAH

Beresheet A
56, 57, 58
Prologue
253, 256

HAWK

Beha'alot'cha
113
Beshalach
67

HEAD

Acharei Mot
21, 24, 75, 104, 108, 109, 121, 138, 147, 165, 180, 214, 312, 320, 330, 332, 335, 349, 385, 387, 407
Balak
4, 5, 25, 43-45, 66, 86, 94, 95, 111, 112, 120, 123, 125, 127, 141, 182, 184, 209, 243, 254, 255, 294, 296, 299, 307, 309, 335-337, 376, 378, 379, 386, 391, 437, 438, 486, 487, 494, 495
Beha'alot'cha
4, 30, 43, 44, 52, 70, 109, 110, 115, 117, 123
Behar
10, 31, 60
Bemidbar
36, 46, 47, 49-51, 55, 56, 70, 71
Beresheet A
3, 6, 7, 16, 27, 33, 34, 113, 114, 118, 135, 138, 139, 185, 192, 203, 204, 225, 264, 281, 299, 307, 361, 368, 374, 413
Beresheet B
25, 32, 44, 58, 116, 118, 124, 221, 315, 321, 325, 341, 343, 347, 364, 370, 418
Beshalach
103, 117, 183, 209, 223-225, 269, 271, 293, 301, 354, 364, 395
Bo
45, 46, 53, 56, 61, 64, 66, 67, 91, 96, 126, 213, 231, 233-235, 244, 245
Chayei Sarah
21, 33, 34, 77, 97, 192, 195, 204, 231, 234, 252, 253
Chukat
28, 29, 47
Ekev
3, 4, 9, 15, 16, 20, 21, 23, 26, 38, 59, 65
Emor
10, 11, 14, 21, 24, 25, 129, 154, 168, 197, 200, 244, 245, 248, 285, 296
Ha'azinu
7, 32, 33, 35, 36, 37, 38, 41, 42, 43, 48, 49, 50, 60-68, 89, 97, 108, 116, 117, 119, 123, 124, 125, 126, 130, 135, 155, 167, 173, 175, 183, 184, 195, 196, 227
Idra Raba
15-17, 19, 20, 21, 22, 24, 26, 27, 34, 40, 48, 74, 90-96, 100-102, 109, 113, 138, 156, 161, 174, 181, 184, 185, 193, 204, 205, 228, 251, 266, 268,

274, 279, 304, 305, 319
Kedoshim
20, 39, 49, 54, 74, 131, 132
Ki Tetze
14, 15, 24, 42, 45, 49, 66, 71, 104, 107, 111, 116, 139
Ki Tisa
8, 61, 72, 76, 79
Korach
40
Lech Lecha
118, 121, 233, 366, 378, 412
Metzora
21, 36, 37, 41, 42
Miketz
94, 106, 108, 109-112, 149, 166
Mishpatim
41, 46, 97, 249, 313, 332, 340, 344, 368, 394, 398, 403, 410-412, 430, 433, 439, 441, 454, 456, 461, 463, 471, 475, 492, 520, 526, 530, 534, 566
Naso
2, 4, 31, 32, 35, 36, 37, 41, 50, 52, 59, 77, 78, 126, 127, 133
Noach
122-125, 127, 261, 264, 271, 274, 278, 279, 284, 296, 328, 335, 338
Pekudei
38, 66, 103, 104, 131, 137, 175, 239, 323, 324, 338, 341, 351, 390, 424, 427, 430, 445, 485, 500, 711, 752, 876, 877, 936, 946
Pinchas
28, 30, 31, 40, 83, 97, 100, 134, 137, 188, 197, 199, 208, 224, 249, 251, 266, 284, 289, 291, 295, 298, 299, 302, 305, 309, 310, 326, 336, 373, 386, 408, 414, 417, 423, 452, 455, 456, 463, 466, 467, 471, 477, 478, 516, 518, 519, 572, 581, 583, 610, 626, 627, 671, 672, 674, 676, 684, 685, 697, 715, 728, 736, 740, 754, 768, 772-776, 781, 783, 788, 789, 795, 816, 848, 849, 852, 853, 855, 871, 872, 873, 874, 875, 876, 889
Prologue
7, 38, 42, 53, 57, 62, 119, 125, 154, 156, 170, 196, 237, 242, 243
Safra Detzniuta
4, 5, 6, 9, 12, 24, 27
Shemot
62, 63, 122, 236, 238, 239, 250, 259, 260, 275, 276, 320
Shlach Lecha
24, 84, 87, 88, 89, 111, 113, 115, 137, 140, 146, 148, 149, 150, 160, 165, 167, 169, 174, 176, 177, 183, 185, 186-188, 190, 192, 204, 205, 206, 209, 210, 213, 215, 221, 223, 229, 231, 232, 244, 245, 251, 254, 263, 283, 289, 306, 338
Shmini
12, 53-55, 64, 73, 97, 118
Tazria
94, 96, 119, 120, 121, 124, 126, 127, 128, 129, 130, 179
Tetzaveh
11, 29, 30, 83, 84, 104, 120, 135
Toldot
13, 24, 25, 50, 52, 58, 60, 87,

88, 95, 104, 113, 161, 169
Trumah
46, 110, 188, 189, 191, 228, 233, 326, 377, 382, 396, 397, 401, 403, 408, 489, 490, 497, 521, 528, 534, 544, 552, 577, 578, 579, 580, 583, 584, 588, 589, 615, 619, 629, 630, 653 -655, 658, 659, 767, 774, 792, 799, 853, 902, 903
Tzav
2, 12, 42, 58, 62, 69, 164
Vaera
46, 80, 83, 84, 85, 86, 104, 106, 123, 124, 159
Vaetchanan
7, 9, 10, 37, 38, 54, 55, 77, 86-88, 90, 91, 96, 97, 98, 100, 106, 116, 119, 157, 158, 165, 191
Vayakhel
23, 40, 65, 87, 97, 111, 143, 146, 149, 208, 279, 320, 323, 324, 326, 339, 345, 349, 417, 438, 441, 469
Vayechi
4, 35, 50, 123, 126, 133, 182, 206, 207, 284, 329, 331, 333, 334, 335, 351, 355, 405, 412, 445, 464, 485, 512, 613, 650, 655, 656, 659, 662, 673, 718, 722, 735, 762, 764, 783, 784, 785, 802, 839, 840
Vayera
57, 110, 154, 167, 235, 267, 337, 376, 388, 389, 392, 437, 438, 456, 481
Vayeshev
9, 252, 253, 269, 270, 271
Vayetze
6, 11, 22, 24, 28, 30, 42, 52, 84, 202, 222, 260, 289, 318, 323, 324, 325, 339, 352
Vayigash
9, 123, 128
Vayikra
2, 6, 9-11, 13, 14, 19-24, 59, 93, 103, 113, 148, 149, 223, 242, 304, 322, 332, 337, 361, 384
Vayishlach
45, 62, 82, 119, 128, 155, 156, 176, 205, 259
Yitro
23, 69, 75, 81, 113, 121, 161 -163, 190, 194, 200, 203, 211, 223, 251, 266, 270-272, 274 -276, 321, 322, 392, 400, 414, 418, 419, 439, 448, 503, 529, 536, 537

HEALTH

Beha'alot'cha
1
Beresheet B
106
Ha'azinu
118
Kedoshim
11
Miketz
237
Pekudei
603
Pinchas
109, 112, 215, 375, 401
Shlach Lecha
67
Trumah
524

HEART

Balak
7, 69, 87, 126, 183, 184, 188, 197, 200, 203, 281, 292, 305, 374
Bemidbar
12, 15, 70, 75, 76
Beresheet A
255, 266, 274, 283, 352, 369
Chayei Sarah
88, 89, 94, 122, 193, 194, 195
Chukat
80, 81, 83
Ekev
38
Emor
15, 100, 102, 124, 128, 196, 204, 218, 266, 290, 292, 293, 334, 335
Ha'azinu
1, 16, 26, 27, 34, 76, 91, 108, 158
Idra Raba
32, 72, 73, 86, 148, 241, 247, 306, 324, 329, 346
Ki Tetze
46, 80, 91, 97, 104, 108
Ki Tisa
21, 70, 85, 99
Korach
17, 18, 19, 22
Lech Lecha
1, 6, 96, 119, 120, 146, 181, 301, 337, 416, 429, 434, 435, 473, 475
Matot
1
Metzora
36
Miketz
16, 34, 44, 52, 53, 64, 130, 183, 185, 197, 201, 209, 210, 212, 266, 267, 268
Mishpatim
95, 99, 101, 123, 143, 144, 172, 232-234, 248, 251, 259-262, 282, 356, 357, 367, 369, 422-426, 432, 489, 499, 553, 554, 569
Naso
12-15, 37, 50, 118, 145, 149, 190
Pekudei
4, 56, 176, 276, 291, 439, 441, 471, 515, 584, 619, 667, 768, 775, 795, 816, 832, 911, 912, 920
Pinchas
68, 69, 77, 80, 81, 95, 97, 152 -155, 167, 168, 184, 204, 209, 210, 211, 213-215, 219, 220, 232, 265, 267, 268, 271, 273, 275, 276, 296, 322, 324, 327, 340, 359, 365, 374, 375, 379 -381, 400, 401, 402, 403, 405, 407, 411, 412, 422 -428, 430, 432, 434, 436 -438, 449, 465, 471, 525, 548, 551, 575, 665, 667, 711, 723, 734, 796, 822, 823, 841, 889
Prologue
103, 104, 149, 203, 208, 218, 232, 235
Safra Detzniuta
16, 43
Shlach Lecha
22, 25, 59, 66, 77, 84, 85, 87-91, 131, 138, 175, 261, 296, 297, 303, 332, 338, 345, 346

Shmini
49, 50, 61
Shoftim
11
Tazria
7, 69, 89, 90, 103, 141, 142, 146, 181
Tetzaveh
3, 22, 105
Toldot
40, 41, 56-62, 84, 124, 125
Trumah
1, 34, 37, 38, 39, 55, 76, 137, 139, 141, 144, 145, 148, 151, 152, 172, 204, 246, 351, 352, 363, 366, 384, 385, 439, 440, 493, 494, 495, 518, 541, 552, 572, 591, 627, 634, 652, 660 -662, 668, 669, 679, 714, 727, 747, 881-883
Vaetchanan
9, 29, 95, 97, 139, 140-142, 149, 153, 170, 174
Vayakhel
7, 8, 16, 42, 51, 54, 58, 71, 72, 107, 108, 111, 112, 114, 115, 117, 120-122, 127, 132, 139, 153, 154, 156, 223, 225, 228, 253, 255, 309, 335, 365, 366, 368, 421, 440, 456, 457, 460, 463, 464-466, 473
Vayechi
1, 3, 9, 10, 77, 88, 92, 157, 209, 226, 237, 239, 346, 352, 390, 393, 419, 456, 515, 522, 530, 633, 634, 635, 678, 714, 730, 731, 737, 739
Vayelech
32, 37, 42
Vayera
38, 84, 91, 121, 122, 128, 239, 284, 314, 317, 358, 435, 506
Vayeshev
15, 40, 98, 154, 166, 247, 273, 275, 281
Vayetze
127, 167, 168, 169, 189, 317, 337, 340, 350, 384
Vayigash
97
Vayishlach
17, 46, 72, 73, 74, 97, 101, 198, 220, 231, 267, 271

HEAVEN

Acharei Mot
51, 61, 63, 83, 219, 220, 251, 270, 285, 291, 301, 314, 319, 329, 406
Balak
12, 23, 25, 104, 105, 142, 144, 152, 190, 191, 241, 320, 343, 362, 364, 366, 382, 396, 413, 417, 423, 424, 436, 459, 503
Beha'alot'cha
3, 139, 146-148
Behar
10
Bemidbar
11
Beresheet A
11, 48, 50, 67, 116, 118, 124, 135, 158, 216, 218, 229, 232, 246, 304-311, 317, 325, 328, 329, 330, 339, 343, 345, 347, 358, 375, 376, 390, 391, 392, 396, 400, 402, 438, 468, 476

Beresheet B
42, 63, 65, 76, 77, 130, 161, 162, 167, 179, 244, 373, 375, 406, 424
Beshalach
67, 96, 114, 116, 117, 258, 267, 302, 368, 376, 380, 395, 482, 483
Bo
6, 105, 108, 153, 171, 174, 198, 211, 225, 235
Chayei Sarah
17, 81, 98, 110, 161, 162, 215, 216, 268
Chukat
80
Ekev
10, 45, 65
Emor
70, 112, 131, 146, 230, 260a, 272, 276
Ha'azinu
13, 33, 34, 35, 58, 117, 144, 224-227, 231, 234, 238, 259
Idra Raba
123, 149, 229, 336, 351, 353
Kedoshim
10, 29, 38, 44, 50, 59, 106, 109
Ki Tetze
6, 97, 100
Ki Tisa
5, 8, 22, 43, 69, 74, 83
Korach
15
Lech Lecha
4, 70, 180, 192, 243, 277, 283, 286, 317, 343, 358, 376, 383, 386, 391, 392, 469, 473, 475
Metzora
26, 45
Miketz
10, 17, 25, 26, 41, 78, 81, 133, 151, 167, 250, 258
Mishpatim
8, 9, 34, 85, 155, 204, 209, 264, 268, 363, 392, 405, 406, 407, 408, 424, 428, 463
Naso
53, 135, 136, 137, 192
Noach
2, 59, 160, 163, 194, 212, 265, 339, 342, 344, 353, 371
Pekudei
6, 8, 12, 14, 23, 50, 89, 129, 192, 211, 212, 218, 222, 255, 271-273, 334, 382, 393, 394, 511, 512, 518, 559, 570, 665, 686, 692, 729, 751, 788, 791, 812, 813, 819
Pinchas
42, 49, 56, 58, 64, 65, 121-123, 193, 202, 227, 267, 304, 334, 373, 390, 396, 409, 444, 469, 487, 491, 501, 503, 621, 632, 674, 702, 761, 778, 784, 788, 811, 831, 852, 855, 858, 867, 871
Prologue
1, 7, 9, 10, 48, 61, 63, 66, 68, 69, 95, 145, 166, 209, 219, 259
Safra Detzniuta
7, 8, 13, 58, 71
Shemot
2, 11, 12, 53, 59, 85, 89, 101, 115, 129, 132, 142, 164, 250, 258, 263, 266, 268, 294, 297, 307, 311, 327, 348, 373, 393, 396

Shlach Lecha
40, 62, 73, 132, 229, 264
Shmini
5, 44, 100, 103
Shoftim
2, 16
Tazria
8, 13, 74, 150
Tetzaveh
72, 98
Toldot
36, 47, 116, 127, 133, 136, 144, 148-152, 154, 186
Trumah
141, 143, 195, 207, 315, 333, 355, 417, 478, 537, 538, 589, 618, 622, 634, 639, 701, 751, 753, 807, 906, 913, 916, 918
Tzav
45, 48, 56, 57, 68, 94, 150, 175, 178, 182
Vaera
6, 25, 55, 91, 130, 180
Vaetchanan
3, 62, 112, 162, 175, 180
Vayakhel
43, 44, 46, 47, 50, 51, 78, 98, 101, 130, 225, 252, 283, 292, 321, 324, 363, 466
Vayechi
15, 36, 63, 71, 79, 96, 115, 120, 124, 175, 176, 180, 181, 256, 307, 308, 333, 407, 408, 437, 438, 443, 565, 569, 596, 640, 660, 661, 667, 689, 707, 752, 754, 772, 779, 781, 782
Vayelech
4, 30
Vayera
19, 74, 88, 128, 207, 208, 230, 233, 234, 252, 256, 259, 278, 281, 284, 285, 372, 477, 481
Vayeshev
51, 86, 94, 110, 129, 215, 218, 258
Vayetze
46, 52, 58, 67, 70, 71, 74, 128, 153, 224, 226, 236, 271, 284, 295, 331, 334, 392
Vayigash
42, 66, 69, 70, 78, 82, 94, 108, 111
Vayikra
98, 132, 178, 180, 182, 184, 222, 284, 332, 341, 401, 413, 445
Vayishlach
38, 41, 57, 89, 132, 143, 174, 215, 216, 232, 242, 243
Yitro
13, 23, 127, 249, 250, 278, 279, 282, 299, 335, 336, 338, 351, 382, 388, 393, 394, 398, 399, 402, 403, 433, 494, 560, 570, 572, 574, 575

HEAVENS

Acharei Mot
50, 54, 61, 95, 222, 329, 334
Balak
19, 207
Beha'alot'cha
3, 63, 147
Beresheet A
9, 10, 11, 13, 50, 52, 53, 207, 214-217, 219, 222, 226, 232, 312, 339, 388, 396, 401, 410
Beresheet B
33, 34, 50, 65, 73, 79, 159,

175-177, 179, 241, 246, 268, 343, 362, 366, 367, 372, 373, 392, 443

Beshalach
96, 100, 116, 130, 267, 310, 364, 374, 376, 378, 384, 483

Bo
69, 104, 108, 150, 171, 174

Chukat
36

Ekev
5, 26, 35

Emor
54, 90, 149

Ha'azinu
1, 6, 7, 8, 19, 21, 22, 144, 227

Idra Raba
9, 120

Kedoshim
99

Ki Tisa
6

Korach
35

Lech Lecha
4, 216, 226, 310, 311, 313, 316, 392, 469

Metzora
26

Miketz
17, 84, 86

Mishpatim
85, 209, 311, 408, 546

Naso
33, 39, 53, 168

Noach
41, 44, 163, 204, 211, 367

Pekudei
13, 45, 217, 218, 219, 222, 255, 646, 788

Pinchas
58, 65, 124, 126, 127, 147, 150, 177, 193, 199, 202, 213, 226, 248, 305, 383, 408, 443, 445, 487, 577, 606, 657, 674, 678, 778, 847, 871, 878

Prologue
11, 12, 16, 46, 56, 59, 64, 65, 66, 67, 73, 107, 127, 128, 130, 141-143, 145, 151, 152, 159, 161, 163, 165, 167, 178, 186, 195, 205

Safra Detzniuta
58

Shemot
12, 17, 18, 47, 66, 68, 85, 242, 258, 266, 311, 324, 347, 359

Shlach Lecha
41, 140, 211, 238, 239, 259

Shmini
44

Shoftim
16

Toldot
134

Trumah
18, 49, 75, 184, 186, 190, 192, 194, 195, 201, 206, 208, 258, 550, 701, 702, 703, 770, 785, 812, 832, 906, 907

Tzav
107, 182

Vaera
6, 180

Vaetchanan
58, 111, 112, 138, 198

Vayakhel
14, 75, 253, 254, 283, 284, 289, 360, 363, 364, 410

Vayechi
130, 175, 176, 180, 406, 437, 438
Vayera
2, 40, 100, 103, 122, 152, 177, 252, 253, 269, 270, 271, 273, 274, 278, 279, 281, 282, 285, 286, 414, 478, 513
Vayeshev
66, 145, 147, 148, 214, 215, 218
Vayetze
191
Vayigash
12, 41, 42, 43, 44, 70, 108
Vayikra
258, 259, 268, 444-446
Yitro
127, 146, 148, 183, 245, 250, 252, 253, 286, 321, 322, 336, 340, 347, 383, 398, 399, 401, 402, 442, 484, 497

HEAVE-OFFERING

Mishpatim
136, 138

HEBER

Balak
221
Beresheet A
286

HEBREW ALPHABET

Acharei Mot
303
Beresheet A
11, 34
Beresheet A
34
Beresheet B
348
Ekev
29, 41
Korach
49
Miketz
241
Mishpatim
298, 359
Noach
22
Pekudei
134, 139, 142, 181, 791
Pinchas
129, 184, 200, 611, 739
Pinchas
792
Prologue
23, 116
Safra Detzniuta
40
Shlach Lecha
288, 289
Tetzaveh
24, 122
Trumah
102, 106, 110, 113, 114, 477, 616, 618, 619, 620, 622, 882
Vayakhel
212
Vayetze
261, 264
Vayikra
155, 157
Yitro
26, 138, 139

HEBREW LETTERS

Acharei Mot
25-27, 49, 91, 132, 150, 151, 157, 161-163, 171, 184-186, 190, 303, 332, 384, 386-390, 392
Balak
8, 72, 73, 74, 75, 76, 77, 114, 159, 170, 271, 276, 277, 469
Beha'alot'cha
33-37, 39, 40, 78, 80, 150
Behar
17, 18, 20
Beresheet A
6, 8, 9, 11, 13, 14, 15, 27, 30, 31, 32, 34, 43, 59-62, 65, 83, 89, 97, 103, 115, 117, 134, 137, 173-175, 183, 195, 197, 199, 203, 207, 209, 223, 224, 234, 235, 236, 238, 250, 251, 270, 271, 279, 295, 305, 310, 311, 318-320, 324, 328, 329, 373, 374, 386, 414, 415, 458, 471
Beresheet B
1, 86, 106, 109, 259, 291, 310, 348, 371, 372, 377-379, 435
Beshalach
75, 112, 134, 135, 164, 165 -168, 171, 173, 211, 255, 257, 298, 300, 339
Bo
213-215, 218
Chayei Sarah
110, 161, 192, 194, 195
Chukat
17, 74
Ekev
19, 27, 29, 41, 43, 48, 53, 65, 68, 74
Emor
40, 64, 66, 67, 68, 282
Ha'azinu
7, 53, 54, 61, 73, 75, 78, 79, 82, 83, 87, 132, 133, 180, 181, 225, 258
Idra Raba
23, 203, 229, 249
Kedoshim
51, 62, 118
Ki Tetze
14, 19, 25, 28, 35, 57, 67, 77, 90, 96, 98, 111, 117, 127, 141, 145
Ki Tisa
8, 106
Korach
28, 46, 48-50, 52, 53, 55, 57
Lech Lecha
66, 79, 213, 308, 310, 343, 383, 442
Metzora
14, 21, 22
Miketz
158, 205, 206, 240, 241, 242
Mishpatim
13, 69, 182, 184, 203, 206, 214, 215, 298, 304, 305, 310, 359, 365, 379, 381, 382, 384, 388, 391, 393, 396, 397, 408, 411, 414, 428, 433, 446, 468, 471, 492, 531, 532
Naso
12, 28, 31, 33, 36, 37, 39, 48, 64, 158, 161, 162, 163, 164, 165, 170, 178
Noach
22, 178

Pekudei
6, 22, 23, 109, 134-140, 142-144, 179-182, 188, 209, 264, 265, 267-275, 292-294, 374, 505, 506, 519, 520, 559-561, 602, 784, 785, 791, 798, 804, 807, 808, 811, 812, 817, 820, 826

Pinchas
46, 48, 50, 51, 58, 63, 68, 69, 70, 103, 106, 129, 139, 174, 178, 183, 184, 186, 187, 188, 190, 192, 196, 200, 201, 202, 222, 223, 224, 228, 229, 230, 243, 248, 255, 258, 261, 262, 268, 269, 271, 278, 282, 287, 289, 292, 293, 297, 298, 302, 303, 306, 307, 308, 309, 312, 324, 340, 341, 344, 368, 371, 405, 419, 432, 438, 448, 451, 453, 454, 455, 466, 467, 481, 482, 485, 489, 492, 504, 580, 585, 600, 601, 603, 608, 611, 617, 621, 622, 624, 628, 630, 641, 646, 647, 649, 668, 688, 712, 713, 731, 733, 739, 749, 750, 757, 763, 771, 792, 805, 812, 814, 815, 819, 820, 840, 841, 843, 845, 846, 848, 851, 864, 867, 870, 872, 873, 885, 886, 890, 892

Prologue
3, 7, 8, 9, 11, 14, 15, 17, 18, 20, 22, 23, 24, 25, 30, 33, 35, 36, 38, 39, 40, 46, 47, 48, 62, 86, 87, 95, 97, 116, 117, 133, 145, 205, 212, 213, 214, 237, 242

Safra Detzniuta
10, 22, 27, 31, 36, 38, 40, 49, 52, 62, 71

Shemot
112, 118, 136, 139, 151, 153, 177, 207, 257, 313, 370

Shlach Lecha
5, 6, 7, 33, 121, 122, 144, 152, 153, 174, 181, 248, 269, 286, 287, 288, 289, 308, 345

Shmini
12, 57

Shoftim
4, 5, 19, 23

Tetzaveh
6, 7, 9, 13, 14, 15, 21, 22, 24, 25, 33, 122, 141

Toldot
146, 169, 177

Trumah
8, 23, 48, 75, 76, 102-107, 109, 110, 112-114, 131, 132, 135, 189, 191, 209, 238, 242-245, 317, 320, 322, 340, 372, 373, 375, 429, 470, 471, 472, 476, 477, 478, 505, 555, 574, 577, 583, 584, 585, 595, 601, 603, 604, 606, 607, 608, 609, 610, 612, 613, 615-622, 624, 629, 699, 700, 702, 720, 758, 761, 762, 763, 765, 817, 818, 861, 880, 882, 912, 913

Tzav
35, 42, 57, 68, 139, 156, 157, 160, 161

Vaera
8, 112, 180, 192, 193

Vaetchanan
37, 38, 64, 92, 93, 94, 95, 109, 117

Vayakhel
11, 69, 77, 130, 131, 133, 168, 180, 211, 212, 218, 296-299, 302, 304, 305, 311, 324, 339, 340, 343, 344, 345, 346, 347, 348, 349, 350, 351, 352, 353, 355-358, 361, 376, 381, 382, 400, 408, 447, 448, 465, 470, 484
Vayechi
18, 19, 62, 63, 95, 202, 203, 204, 205, 294, 437, 448, 523, 567, 612, 772, 781, 859
Vayelech
39
Vayera
66, 67, 96, 98, 196, 207, 208, 283, 442, 446, 451, 452, 458, 460
Vayeshev
153
Vayetze
28, 30, 31, 73, 153, 209, 230, 232, 259, 260, 261, 262, 264, 265, 266, 281, 337, 345
Vayigash
2, 4, 5, 91
Vayikra
1-5, 13, 15-17, 19, 22-25, 146, 152, 155-159, 176, 282, 283, 285, 331, 337
Vayishlach
123, 246
Yitro
8, 26, 73, 84, 87, 89, 94-97, 99, 105, 106, 109-114, 119, 138, 139, 149, 150, 187, 202, 210, 222, 228, 235, 253, 364, 365, 372, 374, 375, 507, 521, 534, 535, 536, 537, 541, 542, 543, 544, 545

HEBRON

Chayei Sarah
46, 47, 69
Lech Lecha
64, 65
Shlach Lecha
38, 39, 59, 60, 61
Trumah
466
Vaera
176-178, 181
Vayera
16

HEEL

Beresheet A
202
Chayei Sarah
34
Miketz
127
Mishpatim
202, 309, 312, 313, 315, 492
Tetzaveh
84
Toldot
26, 27, 31, 133

HEIFER

Balak
238
Beha'alot'cha
53
Chukat
18, 26

Pekudei
315, 323-325, 327
Pinchas
185, 590
Trumah
20
Vayera
376, 377, 379, 380
Vayigash
79, 112, 113, 115, 116, 117
Vayikra
219

HEIMAN (SPIRIT)

Acharei Mot
145, 150

HELL (GEHENOM)

Acharei Mot
8, 74, 91, 147, 253
Balak
24, 26, 27, 278
Beha'alot'cha
78, 79, 105
Behar
40
Beresheet A
44, 45, 47, 49-53, 56-58, 65, 267, 374
Beresheet B
11, 37, 44, 57, 156, 191, 193, 447
Bo
28
Chayei Sarah
59, 99, 126, 134, 135
Chukat
26
Ekev
47
Emor
115, 298
Ha'azinu
28, 45, 244
Kedoshim
6
Ki Tetze
35, 112, 114, 118
Korach
31, 32, 34
Lech Lecha
8, 91, 280, 385, 404, 405, 444
Matot
4
Metzora
11, 38
Miketz
100
Mishpatim
56, 57, 58, 429, 430, 431, 513
Naso
41, 84, 122
Noach
67, 69, 71, 140, 150, 201, 202
Pekudei
100, 484, 540, 677, 701, 838, 839, 842, 902, 928
Pinchas
24, 50, 137, 167, 253, 254, 412, 462, 475, 573, 590, 644, 645, 650
Prologue
138, 190, 254, 255, 259
Shemot
318, 389
Shlach Lecha
24, 193, 197, 322

Tazria
20, 47, 128
Toldot
140, 159, 175
Trumah
70, 180, 335, 426, 439, 440, 443-445, 447, 448, 451-455, 457, 475, 682
Tzav
172
Vaera
188
Vayakhel
96, 99, 174, 244, 329, 330, 331, 337, 387, 469
Vayechi
44, 169, 170, 190, 193, 300, 347, 583-585, 601, 602, 603
Vayelech
43, 44, 45, 46
Vayera
193, 195, 200, 242, 243, 244, 245, 247, 248, 258, 259, 260, 314, 319, 320, 321, 325, 326
Vayeshev
126, 127, 233, 234
Vayetze
27
Vayikra
137, 274-276, 437
Vayishlach
16, 187, 277
Yitro
351, 352, 431, 458, 462

HEPHZIBAH

Shlach Lecha
298, 304

HESHBON

Balak
10, 11, 12
Pinchas
139

HEZEKIAH

Balak
276, 287
Beshalach
7, 420
Chayei Sarah
229
Miketz
124, 206, 207
Noach
145, 146
Prologue
58, 180
Shemot
169
Shoftim
11
Trumah
120, 899-901
Vaetchanan
1, 11
Vayechi
386, 387, 389, 390-392
Vayigash
40

HIDDEN BOOK (SAFRA DE'TZNIUTA)

Beshalach
82, 180
Ha'azinu
53, 93

Idra Raba
14, 53, 73, 126, 149, 173, 220, 223, 242, 250, 259, 267, 285, 289, 294, 311, 323, 326, 332, 339, 343
Safra Detzniuta
1, 3, 73
Tazria
116
Vaetchanan
37
Vayera
457 Hidden Book (Safra de'tzniuta)
Trumah
925
Yitro
357

HIGH PRIEST

Behar
18
Beresheet B
183
Emor
12, 13, 21, 24, 25, 28, 38, 160, 251, 256
Ki Tisa
37
Lech Lecha
84, 93, 102
Pekudei
162-164, 174, 176, 179, 182, 199, 225, 226, 327
Pinchas
712, 716
Trumah
404, 405, 596, 598, 713
Tzav
138, 143, 168
Vayechi
129, 131, 132, 133
Vayetze
6
Yitro
41

HIND

Beshalach
43, 47
Ha'azinu
38
Mishpatim
202, 485
Pinchas
581, 690-693, 695
Shemot
160, 161
Shlach Lecha
183
Vayechi
553, 759, 767
Vayeshev
70
Vayetze
144
Vayikra
367

HIPS

Balak
258, 261, 262, 263

HIRE

Ki Tetze
45, 49
Lech Lecha
247

Vayetze
215, 229, 231

HITTITES

Mishpatim
243, 244
Shlach Lecha
65

HOLINESS (KEDUSHAH)

Acharei Mot
26, 41, 82, 84, 87, 96, 109, 135, 176, 289
Balak
7, 75, 79, 80, 82, 107, 137, 162, 417, 418, 426, 431
Bechukotai
5, 7, 9
Beha'alot'cha
66-68, 74
Behar
10, 34
Bemidbar
46
Beresheet A
38, 47, 48, 56, 123, 146, 199, 228, 287, 365, 382, 435, 455
Beresheet B
43, 48, 192, 195, 210, 228, 305, 306, 328, 337, 380, 422
Beshalach
6, 8, 13, 71, 74, 273, 317, 419, 437
Bo
9, 16, 31, 34, 88, 122, 165, 231, 235, 237
Chayei Sarah
17, 61, 75, 125, 133, 256, 262
Ekev
37, 39, 47, 56
Emor
10, 13, 24, 34, 36, 42, 45, 54, 83, 87-90, 102-106, 109-111, 114, 115, 117, 125, 126, 127, 226, 325
Ha'azinu
60, 202, 203, 204, 205, 211
Idra Raba
149, 160, 340, 344
Kedoshim
4, 13, 14, 17, 23, 25, 115, 116, 118, 119, 128
Ki Tetze
51, 70, 117
Ki Tisa
57, 82, 91, 93, 99, 110, 117
Korach
9, 10
Lech Lecha
67, 75, 78, 179, 196, 233, 326, 442
Metzora
18, 48, 51, 57, 58
Miketz
21, 53, 127, 136, 231, 246, 247, 248, 254
Mishpatim
27, 137, 138, 265, 268, 310, 324, 325, 327, 328, 348, 371, 414, 486, 500-508, 510, 511, 512, 516, 556, 563, 571
Naso
108, 109, 124, 130, 134, 145, 156, 157, 159
Noach
2, 148, 295, 335, 336, 343,

348, 352, 365
Pekudei
35, 40, 49, 64, 74, 84, 85, 86, 89, 91, 92, 120-122, 131, 158, 159, 238, 246, 247, 248, 253, 259, 279, 286, 300-333, 336, 347, 354, 363, 374, 378, 416, 420-424, 455, 460, 464, 468, 470, 471, 479, 481, 516, 541, 553, 564, 572, 573, 581, 609, 610, 654, 675, 677, 727, 747, 809, 823, 831, 835, 839, 840, 844, 849, 869, 880, 883, 885, 886, 888, 889, 892, 900, 907, 909, 910, 933, 934
Pinchas
35d, 63, 109, 135, 192, 213, 217, 298, 421, 432, 625, 638, 651, 652, 712, 717, 719, 732, 740, 760, 800, 801, 863, 864, 894
Prologue
80, 169, 216, 227, 247, 251, 252, 257
Safra Detzniuta
38, 64
Shemot
3, 28, 73, 74, 195, 262, 329, 393, 394
Shlach Lecha
38, 101, 275
Shmini
15, 83, 85, 87, 102, 115-117
Tazria
29, 38, 83, 87, 121, 136, 138, 140, 141, 146, 149, 173, 175 -177
Tetzaveh
40, 42, 44, 46, 48, 55, 56, 58- 61, 64, 87, 98, 140
Toldot
6, 24, 26, 27, 73, 150
Trumah
35, 37, 55, 57, 60, 99, 143, 167, 168, 173, 174, 235, 261, 274, 392, 468, 506, 568, 829, 852, 869
Tzav
4, 5, 8, 15, 74, 104-106, 107, 128, 157
Vaera
7, 94, 104, 107, 108, 111, 118, 120
Vaetchanan
96, 119, 172
Vayakhel
3, 127, 167, 178, 189, 255, 257, 258, 262, 359, 377, 382, 383, 394, 410, 416, 417, 435, 483
Vayechi
8, 43, 51, 68, 95, 102, 131, 132, 197, 315, 378, 379, 382, 631, 704, 711, 712
Vayelech
16, 17, 18, 19, 28
Vayera
37, 85, 86, 161, 278, 291, 307, 330, 351, 414, 416, 417, 439
Vayeshev
154, 227
Vayetze
15, 23, 101, 148, 179, 184, 279, 289, 355, 358
Vayigash
39, 60, 65, 111, 120, 130, 133
Vayikra
56-58, 68, 97, 198, 204, 321, 423, 425, 433, 437

Vayishlach
38, 39, 109, 115, 144, 145, 147, 233
Yitro
8, 9, 10, 40, 50, 51, 52, 110, 205, 474, 476, 516, 546, 548, 549

HOLY LAND

Acharei Mot
177, 234, 290, 291-294
Balak
440, 504
Beha'alot'cha
134, 137
Bemidbar
23, 25
Beresheet A
150, 151, 152, 153, 155, 156, 273, 287
Beshalach
226
Chayei Sarah
211
Ekev
64
Emor
239
Ki Tetze
83
Ki Tisa
100
Lech Lecha
73, 145, 183, 187, 190
Miketz
215
Mishpatim
66
Noach
169, 170, 173, 206, 317, 364
Pekudei
837
Prologue
5, 102
Shemot
100, 152
Shlach Lecha
76, 174
Toldot
100
Trumah
64, 68, 269, 270, 271, 274-276, 278, 281-283, 365, 460, 462-466, 468, 473, 486, 561, 567, 568, 769, 821, 822, 896, 907
Vaera
15, 58, 173, 203
Vaetchanan
129, 137, 162
Vayechi
51, 64, 73, 109, 336, 528, 548, 551, 728, 729
Vayera
434
Vayeshev
52, 53, 56, 112, 128, 251, 270
Vayetze
49, 77, 121, 240, 241, 249, 250, 271, 312
Vayigash
12, 108
Vayikra
43
Vayishlach
9, 244
Yitro
263, 264

HOLY NAME

Acharei Mot
47, 84, 86, 168-170, 183, 184, 188, 197, 277, 288, 296, 300, 303, 336, 358, 384, 389 -392

Balak
35, 37, 199, 327, 385, 396, 476

Bechukotai
17, 18, 19, 20, 21, 23, 24

Beha'alot'cha
33, 40, 71, 150

Bemidbar
31, 57, 76

Beresheet A
6, 65, 81, 114, 115, 197, 210, 241, 263, 318, 319, 365, 397

Beresheet B
33, 77, 188, 189, 259, 291, 433

Beshalach
42, 44, 75, 90, 160, 164, 168, 173-175, 276-279, 298, 300, 339, 396, 424, 425, 454

Bo
77, 82, 169, 213, 217

Chayei Sarah
115, 83

Ekev
1, 22

Emor
57, 66, 67, 86, 92, 134, 145, 188, 312, 313, 317, 318, 319, 320

Ha'azinu
33, 54, 82, 170, 192, 206, 213, 214, 241

Idra Raba
248, 259, 261, 263, 271

Kedoshim
13, 18

Ki Tisa
74, 106, 107

Korach
1, 5, 9

Lech Lecha
66, 294, 303, 308, 322, 469

Miketz
47

Mishpatim
48, 304, 343, 536, 542, 543, 544

Naso
62, 64, 67, 68, 71, 110, 123, 158, 160-162, 170, 171, 177, 179, 188

Noach
97, 349, 352, 357

Pekudei
13, 22, 23, 25, 27, 77, 113, 116, 123, 140, 164, 174, 184, 217, 244, 250, 264, 268, 269, 274, 292, 504-508, 510, 579, 705, 706, 710, 717, 730, 748, 779, 780, 783, 784, 787, 788, 790, 794, 795, 807, 811, 817, 820, 826

Pinchas
11, 353, 391, 467, 542, 548, 626

Prologue
3, 24, 32, 48, 101, 117, 237, 240, 242, 243

Safra Detzniuta
42, 43, 65

Shemot
26, 28, 47, 53, 118, 123, 133, 136, 139, 151, 153

Shlach Lecha
5, 6, 43, 44, 72, 199, 286, 338, 344

Shmini
7, 81, 82, 86, 103
Tazria
173, 174, 175, 176, 180
Tetzaveh
4, 7, 13, 14, 15, 22, 40
Toldot
182
Trumah
8, 32, 48, 76, 98, 105, 107, 108, 132, 184, 186, 319, 325, 358, 372, 470, 477, 604, 648, 659, 903, 912, 913
Tzav
123, 192
Vaera
8, 74, 98, 206
Vaetchanan
38, 40, 43, 44, 75, 81, 98, 107-109, 116, 118, 132, 146, 149, 154, 175, 183
Vayakhel
97, 130, 133, 262, 334, 347, 352, 353, 355, 356, 361, 363, 364, 400, 401, 409, 411, 434, 440, 447, 465, 470, 482
Vayechi
14, 37, 38, 42, 85, 211, 266, 317, 443, 453, 485, 486, 567, 581, 626, 627, 628, 629, 636, 648, 678, 720, 794, 796, 825, 826
Vayelech
34, 35
Vayera
64, 278, 281, 305, 346, 442, 446, 452
Vayeshev
279
Vayetze
30, 64, 158, 159, 167, 262
Vayikra
6, 48, 51, 70, 94-97, 102, 103, 111, 113, 115, 147, 148, 152, 161, 166, 167, 171-173, 182, 200, 221, 324, 342, 368, 427, 448
Yitro
6, 27, 42, 235, 430, 439, 441 -443, 484, 497, 498, 505, 510, 511, 519, 522, 523, 526, 545, 548

HOLY OF HOLIES

Acharei Mot
45, 53, 198, 199, 255, 297
Beha'alot'cha
74
Beresheet A
369, 375
Beresheet B
137, 139, 142
Chayei Sarah
240, 267
Ha'azinu
60
Idra Raba
19, 112, 150, 151, 156, 171, 222
Korach
26
Mishpatim
31, 61, 501
Naso
187
Noach
286
Pekudei
41, 349-354, 359, 366, 394, 732, 734, 735, 752, 753, 755, 756, 766, 795-797, 818

Pinchas
19, 85
Prologue
169
Safra Detzniuta
59
Shemot
37, 38
Shlach Lecha
87, 89
Trumah
316, 319, 355, 357, 359, 561, 567, 600, 821
Tzav
2-5, 11, 19, 67, 135, 158
Vayakhel
18, 249, 253
Vayechi
397, 409, 436, 445
Vayigash
33
Vayikra
113
Yitro
9

(HOLY) TEMPLE

Acharei Mot
8, 55, 120, 288
Behar
23, 27, 28, 33, 34
Beshalach
121, 236, 240, 297, 326, 334-336, 481
Bo
34
Kedoshim
30, 50, 61, 123
Noach
99, 100, 206, 241, 245, 273, 274, 319, 324
Prologue
9, 18, 33, 94, 95
Shemot
37, 38, 61, 62, 64, 81, 121, 125, 142, 369
Shlach Lecha
184, 185
Trumah
261, 313-317, 325, 345, 357, 472, 473, 475, 477, 525, 527, 568, 686, 690, 769, 784, 903, 907
Tzav
175
Vaera
33, 50

HONEY

Acharei Mot
210
Balak
317, 460
Chukat
1
Emor
223
Ki Tetze
48
Ki Tisa
100
Korach
1
Lech Lecha
203
Pekudei
454, 910

Pinchas
348, 379, 423, 544, 552, 553, 558, 594, 596, 616
Prologue
88
Safra Detzniuta
2
Shlach Lecha
13, 35, 63, 78, 79
Shmini
67
Trumah
492
Vayakhel
171
Vayechi
624, 641
Vayera
226
Vayetze
177, 369
Vayikra
26, 29, 33, 34, 98

HOREB

Ha'azinu
1
Ki Tisa
46, 109

HORSES

Acharei Mot
51
Balak
179, 448
Beresheet A
199
Beshalach
63, 228, 229
Bo
228, 229
Kedoshim
1, 4, 5, 15
Ki Tetze
4, 66
Lech Lecha
218
Naso
99
Pekudei
782
Pinchas
44, 253, 293, 749, 759, 762
Tazria
138
Tzav
60, 70
Vaera
191
Vayechi
267, 681, 706, 708
Vayigash
34, 83
Vayikra
227
Vayishlach
263

HOSEA

Beshalach
1
Ki Tisa
43
Vayechi
519

HOSTS

Acharei Mot
84, 88, 177, 179, 219

Balak
104, 117, 190
Beha'alot'cha
101
Behar
81, 83, 84
Bemidbar
7, 21, 53
Beresheet A
40, 75, 110, 116, 151, 179, 401, 457
Beresheet B
68, 69, 80, 82, 89, 91-95, 98, 109, 124, 176, 179, 268
Beshalach
98, 177, 209, 262, 263, 293, 301-304, 309, 340
Bo
6, 121, 211
Chayei Sarah
157, 158, 159, 160, 161, 193
Ha'azinu
58, 189, 190, 195
Idra Raba
292, 339
Kedoshim
56, 128
Ki Tisa
6, 28, 32
Lech Lecha
313
Metzora
29
Mishpatim
13, 209, 244, 298, 311, 380, 464, 465, 466, 467, 530
Naso
33, 56, 104, 137, 138, 160
Noach
263, 371
Pekudei
96, 221, 563, 569
Pinchas
13, 81, 83, 126, 210, 212, 220, 226, 316, 423, 449, 456, 515, 517, 518, 534, 535, 538, 541, 547, 578, 659, 692, 711, 717, 764, 778, 837, 867
Prologue
12, 16, 19, 20, 91, 93, 128, 161, 167, 219, 251, 252, 256, 257
Shemot
11, 12, 34, 36, 47, 57, 59, 61, 85, 107, 115, 133, 152, 222, 223, 268, 321, 322
Tazria
4
Tetzaveh
133
Trumah
11, 130, 131, 265, 807, 835
Tzav
126
Vaera
55, 170
Vaetchanan
62, 118, 176
Vayakhel
15, 51, 54, 55, 58, 138, 147, 286
Vayechi
408, 443, 587, 704, 707, 726, 727, 806, 820, 821
Vayera
122, 438
Vayeshev
200, 202
Vayikra
345, 370
Vayishlach
6

Yitro
128, 129, 146, 182, 356, 383

HOUSE

Beresheet A
7, 8, 98, 117, 125, 127, 148, 149, 154, 186, 279, 280, 293, 298, 300, 327, 328, 370, 374, 375, 379, 401
Chayei Sarah
16, 106, 128, 156, 157, 250, 259, 267, 270
Ki Tisa
25, 32, 33, 37, 41, 111
Lech Lecha
15, 30, 32, 39, 90, 115, 136, 182, 262, 284, 369, 370, 403, 419, 421, 422, 423, 426, 461, 464, 471
Miketz
20, 137, 142, 181, 192, 199, 203, 208, 213, 224, 248
Prologue
18, 106, 114, 134, 177, 183, 184, 202
Tetzaveh
64, 70, 74, 102
Vaetchanan
8, 72-77, 98, 106-109, 114, 117, 132-135, 151, 152, 154, 168, 171, 175, 179, 187, 197
Vayera
48, 101, 197, 225, 227, 229, 235-237, 257, 362, 366, 372, 431, 463, 479
Vayeshev
13, 49, 78, 98, 116, 118, 145, 171, 204, 207, 236, 237
Vayetze
28, 31, 33, 34, 35, 39, 42, 67, 71, 74, 76, 77, 81, 82, 83, 84, 97, 138, 147, 148, 153, 230, 238, 241, 242, 247, 248, 249, 293, 338, 339, 389
Vayigash
34, 35, 97, 104, 110
Vayishlach
8, 9, 41, 118, 131, 132, 133, 137, 138, 140, 142, 152, 173, 175, 203, 204, 253

HUNDRED

Acharei Mot
126, 191, 192
Balak
34, 72
Beresheet A
205, 206, 475
Beresheet B
351
Beshalach
109, 199, 268, 274, 299, 301
Bo
141
Chayei Sarah
1, 14, 21, 23, 24
Chukat
76
Emor
29, 221, 239
Ha'azinu
19, 207
Idra Raba
15, 37, 187, 206, 226, 240, 307, 322
Kedoshim
77

Ki Tetze
1
Ki Tisa
62
Korach
48, 49, 52
Lech Lecha
11, 14, 43, 90, 109, 257, 344
Mishpatim
150, 344, 434
Noach
60, 74
Pekudei
19, 79, 87, 97, 108, 111, 114, 118, 120, 130, 205, 242, 255, 278, 289, 375, 417, 429, 440, 446, 490, 696, 702
Pinchas
55, 59, 82, 257, 291, 292, 330, 389, 394, 498, 701, 713, 748, 749, 791, 865
Safra Detzniuta
62
Shemot
4, 50, 54, 55, 63, 148, 149, 296, 318
Shlach Lecha
97, 115, 141, 180, 210, 290
Tazria
162
Tetzaveh
25, 26, 116, 117, 118
Toldot
68, 69, 71, 102, 133
Trumah
15, 23, 219, 264, 354, 843, 848, 867
Tzav
79
Vaera
201
Vaetchanan
181
Vayakhel
14, 106, 144, 145, 154, 155
Vayechi
19, 20, 21, 24, 655
Vayelech
6
Vayera
26, 149, 398
Vayetze
298
Vayishlach
43, 131
Yitro
4, 332, 462, 512, 513, 514, 569

HYSSOP

Bo
77, 189
Chukat
23
Metzora
17, 18, 19
Shemot
265
Tazria
112
Tzav
180
Vayechi
210
Yitro
278

IDOLATRY

Acharei Mot
54, 115, 232, 271, 289, 290, 95,

298, 301
Balak
81, 222, 223, 385, 395
Bechukotai
13
Beha'alot'cha
150
Behar
49, 64, 69-71
Bemidbar
46, 51
Beresheet A
119, 122, 230, 265, 267, 285, 291, 432, 444, 445
Beresheet B
11, 17, 19, 170, 210, 211, 242
Beshalach
42, 244, 421
Bo
75, 76, 196, 229
Chayei Sarah
163, 257
Emor
287, 326
Ha'azinu
9, 29, 160, 215
Idra Raba
4
Kedoshim
48, 65, 72, 78, 79, 80, 122
Ki Tetze
2, 13, 21, 35, 37, 41, 123
Ki Tisa
9, 80
Lech Lecha
35, 36, 151, 174-176, 235, 434
Miketz
85, 119, 168, 174, 203, 237, 250, 267, 268
Mishpatim
37, 38, 41, 242, 449, 491, 546, 547, 565
Naso
18
Noach
183, 321, 356, 357
Pekudei
363, 365
Pinchas
68, 115, 117, 192, 375, 412, 413, 474, 475, 526, 573, 702, 721 -729, 734, 736, 767
Prologue
227
Shemot
28, 62, 64, 89, 93, 170, 195, 205, 230, 322, 365
Shlach Lecha
300
Shmini
49, 115
Tazria
147, 156, 160, 178
Tetzaveh
49, 50, 55, 56, 58, 60, 61
Toldot
73, 74
Trumah
441, 488, 631, 814, 869, 896, 902, 903, 914
Tzav
15, 17, 193
Vaera
63
Vaetchanan
120
Vayakhel
470
Vayechi
95, 105, 185, 195, 196, 198,

353, 366, 370, 378, 385, 412, 578, 579, 587, 588, 590, 591, 604, 610, 630, 631, 723
Vayera
91, 108, 109, 110, 113, 200, 253, 334, 352, 466, 467, 470, 471
Vayeshev
80
Vayetze
360, 375, 378, 380, 381
Vayigash
65, 67, 68
Vayikra
71, 181, 218
Vayishlach
154, 155, 156, 157, 177, 249
Yitro
11, 42, 57, 427, 428, 431, 433, 435, 513, 516, 517, 554

IDRA RABA

Ha'azinu
25, 29, 30, 34, 91, 95, 108, 109, 138, 149, 170, 171

IGAEL (SPIRIT)

Pekudei
583

IGERET

Bechukotai
26
Beresheet B
355

ILLNESS

Chayei Sarah
45
Miketz
22, 209, 210, 212
Prologue
260
Tetzaveh
74
Vaetchanan
123, 142, 153, 160, 183, 187, 189
Vayechi
36, 191, 192, 206, 333, 334, 361, 363, 365, 676, 680
Vayera
32, 36, 200
Vayigash
72, 76
Vayishlach
119

IMA

Beha'alot'cha
20, 21, 24, 29, 30
Behar
16, 17, 21, 79
Beshalach
144, 161-163, 172, 239, 244, 255, 428, 429
Bo
126

IMAGES

Beresheet A
81, 89-92, 95, 97, 158, 240, 242
Chayei Sarah
42, 249

Ki Tisa
78, 80
Lech Lecha
271, 288, 329, 330, 331, 336
Miketz
23
Prologue
13, 155
Vayeshev
245, 246
Vayetze
51, 375, 376, 377, 378
Vayishlach
154

IMMANUEL

Vayechi
20

INCENSE

Acharei Mot
6, 43, 45, 46, 49, 55, 69, 70, 199
Balak
2, 4, 6, 136
Bechukotai
9
Beha'alot'cha
1, 22, 50, 51
Behar
27, 39
Bo
147
Chayei Sarah
77
Emor
15, 260b, 290, 293
Korach
13, 22, 24, 27
Lech Lecha
185, 303
Noach
235
Pinchas
203, 206, 795
Shemot
366
Shlach Lecha
179
Shmini
37, 38
Trumah
160, 398
Tzav
52, 84, 85, 152-154, 180
Vayakhel
55, 466-479, 481, 482, 483, 484
Vayechi
419, 420, 421
Vayera
122, 123, 126, 507
Vayikra
65, 67, 104, 165, 177, 314
Vayishlach
227
Yitro
125, 249

INCEST

Acharei Mot
343, 393
Balak
385, 391
Behar
49, 71, 72
Beresheet A
265-269, 291, 432, 444, 445
Kedoshim
17

Noach
2, 382
Pekudei
856
Pinchas
45, 245, 475
Prologue
132
Trumah
6, 814
Vayechi
79, 178
Vayeshev
189
Vayetze
152
Vayikra
71
Yitro
554

INFERTILITY

Beresheet A
461
Beshalach
9, 12
Emor
69, 248
Lech Lecha
320, 321, 471
Mishpatim
109, 110, 114-116, 118, 120, 125, 130, 133, 134, 175, 181, 191, 195, 215, 222, 228, 274, 276, 334
Pinchas
51, 92, 580
Shlach Lecha
132, 204
Toldot
22, 55
Trumah
795, 796
Tzav
42
Vaera
198
Vayechi
82, 270, 388
Vayera
138, 140, 413
Vayeshev
173, 174
Vayetze
49, 147, 148, 200, 230, 248
Vayikra
346, 419

INFINITE

Idra Raba
137
Ki Tetze
72, 73
Pinchas
575, 805, 878
Trumah
834

INFINITY (EIN SOF)

*see also Endless Light

Acharei Mot
75, 248
Behar
36
Beresheet A
246, 294
Beresheet B
24, 136, 143

Bo
242
Ha'azinu
34, 99
Lech Lecha
168
Noach
125, 127
Pekudei
103, 945
Pinchas
202, 225, 343, 858, 878
Safra Detzniuta
39
Shemot
141, 143
Tazria
32
Trumah
222, 223, 224, 302, 328, 921
Vayakhel
313
Vayikra
342
Yitro
525

INFINITY

Acharei Mot
75, 248
Beresheet B
24, 270
Pekudei
102, 103, 360, 361, 471, 771, 795, 945, 949, 951
Pinchas
655, 858, 878
Shemot
141, 143
Trumah
9, 222, 223, 224, 302, 328, 921
Vayakhel
313, 419, 421, 425, 428, 481, 482
Vayelech
33
Vayikra
342
Yitro
525

INTERCOURSE

Beresheet A
102, 455
Mishpatim
25, 410
Prologue
133, 134, 251, 252
Vayechi
262
Vayera
327, 328
Vayeshev
203
Vayetze
136, 185
Vayishlach
216, 217

IRA

Balak
179, 405

IRIEL (SPIRIT)

Pekudei
549, 551

Vayera
277
Pekudei
583, 584
Vayeshev
209, 284
Vayetze
190

IRON

Acharei Mot
361
Balak
494
Beha'alot'cha
76
Beresheet B
273, 283
Chayei Sarah
81
Ha'azinu
114
Metzora
11
Miketz
38
Mishpatim
202, 228
Noach
323, 327, 333
Pekudei
131, 151, 433
Pinchas
361, 390, 488
Trumah
124, 308, 353, 364, 911, 919, 925
Vaera
34, 35, 43, 45, 46, 106
Vaetchanan
150
Vayechi
54, 287, 313

ISAAC

Acharei Mot
13, 74, 75, 147, 182, 184, 251, 385
Balak
85, 141, 145, 146
Bechukotai
47
Beha'alot'cha
30, 36, 37, 39, 40
Behar
64, 71, 73
Bemidbar
5, 52, 58
Beresheet A
23, 141, 197, 346, 433
Beresheet B
25, 134
Beshalach
53, 54, 59, 158, 200, 248, 338, 404
Bo
13, 14, 111, 123, 154-156, 201
Chayei Sarah
26, 164, 183-186, 199, 200, 217, 226, 238, 245, 246, 248 -253, 255, 256, 258, 259, 260, 261, 262, 263
Chukat
73, 86
Ekev
17, 62
Emor
189, 190, 192, 196, 197, 198,

199, 201, 217, 218, 219, 220, 263, 279, 281, 289

Ha'azinu
121, 227

Idra Raba
35

Kedoshim
77

Ki Tetze
19, 20, 71, 136, 140

Ki Tisa
54

Lech Lecha
76, 197, 201, 254, 272, 288, 323, 326, 453, 454, 457, 458, 459, 460, 466

Metzora
26, 36, 55, 56, 57, 62, 63

Miketz
98, 105, 227

Mishpatim
295, 481, 484

Naso
2

Noach
13, 24, 154, 282, 374

Pekudei
301, 302, 305, 712, 716, 718 -721, 724, 800, 801

Pinchas
35b, 35c, 65, 70, 97, 99, 100, 207, 329, 344, 350, 352, 360, 368, 425, 435, 460-465, 479, 480, 482, 560, 567, 575, 579, 615, 651, 652, 657, 672, 677, 844, 881-883

Prologue
177, 178, 179, 184

Shemot
120, 150, 290, 387

Shlach Lecha
2, 133, 134, 135, 168, 267

Shmini
31, 32, 43, 44, 48, 51, 72, 88

Tetzaveh
115, 125, 142

Toldot
1, 6-9, 13-15, 18-24, 32, 33, 40, 46, 47, 49, 55, 66, 75, 76, 77, 79, 95- 98, 100-103, 106, 118-121, 126, 129, 130, 132, 134, 135, 139, 140, 147, 153, 156, 159, 160, 167, 169, 173 -175, 185, 194, 195, 197

Tzav
48, 49, 76, 77, 82, 88, 96, 112, 114, 116, 135, 187

Vaera
1, 13, 14, 17, 19, 21, 28, 32, 51, 73, 74, 200, 201

Vaetchanan
46

Vayakhel
66, 215, 253, 258, 275, 379

Vayechi
35, 48, 49, 93, 119, 219 -221, 223, 224, 266, 269, 277, 330, 355, 357, 374, 377, 422, 433, 516, 517, 539, 640, 649, 783, 802

Vayelech
23, 24

Vayera
14, 22, 28, 29, 60, 90, 97, 141, 142, 146, 159-166, 188, 306, 330, 363, 401, 461-463, 466, 468, 469, 487, 489, 491 -495, 497, 498, 501-508, 512, 513

Vayeshev
20, 46, 112, 141, 142
Vayetze
21-23, 33, 48, 59, 60, 61, 62, 83, 158, 211, 212, 262, 268, 296, 313, 354, 372, 373, 382, 383
Vayigash
44, 119
Vayikra
33, 116, 191, 192, 216, 291, 295, 304-308, 352, 421
Vayishlach
13, 54, 55, 56, 60, 67, 111, 143, 225, 226, 228, 233, 234
Yitro
338, 380, 461

ISAIAH

Balak
77
Beshalach
1
Emor
18
Ha'azinu
6, 7, 8
Idra Raba
9
Ki Tetze
81
Tetzaveh
7
Vayechi
387
Vayelech
19

ISH BOSHET

Vaera
178

ISHMAEL

Balak
138, 145, 148
Behar
64, 65, 70
Chayei Sarah
36, 258
Ki Tetze
17, 113, 123
Lech Lecha
326
Mishpatim
482, 486
Naso
84, 86, 198
Pinchas
35c, 97, 99, 100, 269, 567, 650, 651, 652
Shemot
16, 18, 289
Toldot
6
Vaera
198, 199, 200, 201, 202, 203, 204, 205
Vayera
145, 304, 463, 469, 472
Vayigash
8
Yitro
407, 422, 423, 424, 425, 426

ISRAEL

Bemidbar
6, 7, 8, 13, 15, 17, 18, 19, 21, 23, 25, 26, 28, 37, 40, 45, 46, 50, 51, 53, 54, 55, 65, 77
Beresheet A
198

Chukat
46
Emor
29
Ki Tetze
110, 111
Korach
2, 10, 37, 40, 43, 45, 46, 49, 53, 58
Safra Detzniuta
30
Shemot
204
Vayechi
5-8, 12-16, 25, 35, 50, 88, 100, 110, 111, 134, 245, 249, 250, 333-335, 351, 366, 370, 488, 490, 491, 496, 855
Vayeshev
74
Vayetze
18, 28, 154
Vayigash
118, 119
Vayishlach
113, 119, 165-167, 169, 171, 172, 203, 217

ISSACHAR

Ki Tetze
5
Beha'alot'cha
25-27
Mishpatim
200, 202
Vayechi
663, 664, 674, 675, 681, 682, 685, 687, 688, 690, 691, 692, 694, 774
Vayetze
160, 162, 196, 197, 198, 228, 232

ITAI

Vayishlach
156

ITAMAR

Acharei Mot
10, 11, 20
Shmini
53, 55

IVTZAN

Mishpatim
193

IZHAR

Korach
1
Vayechi
563

JACOB

Acharei Mot
12-18, 74, 107, 112, 132, 182 -184, 193, 238, 251, 298 -300, 305, 310, 385
Balak
15, 33, 48, 50, 51, 53, 54, 85 -88, 143, 144, 256, 268, 270, 275, 321, 347, 349, 406, 464, 467, 468, 469, 470, 473-475, 483, 488, 490
Beha'alot'cha
15, 37, 39, 40, 80

Behar
71-73
Bemidbar
5, 6, 51, 52
Beresheet A
55, 141-146, 148-155, 157, 186, 188, 197, 202, 249, 359, 433, 439, 467
Beresheet B
25, 132, 159, 238, 240, 397, 419
Beshalach
52-54, 69, 81, 96, 97, 104, 109, 168, 193, 195, 197, 198, 200, 207, 276, 307, 349, 440, 475
Bo
111, 123, 141, 148, 157, 197, 200, 201
Ekev
62
Emor
29, 57, 77, 79, 80, 150, 182, 197, 200, 202, 217, 218, 219, 220, 221, 223, 279, 282a, 289, 330
Ha'azinu
9, 93, 121, 122, 135, 210, 218, 222, 223, 228, 236, 238, 240, 246
Idra Raba
4, 58, 89, 97, 153, 231, 232, 353
Kedoshim
75-77, 81, 106, 107
Ki Tetze
43, 55, 71, 110, 111, 115, 140
Ki Tisa
20, 54
Lech Lecha
83, 174, 198, 201, 219, 220, 227, 229, 254, 272, 288, 368, 370, 372, 384, 445, 457, 459, 465, 471
Metzora
52-56, 58, 61, 62
Miketz
11, 12, 13, 15, 37, 38, 39, 47, 67, 84, 92, 93, 98, 101-105, 127, 172, 214, 227, 228, 235, 236, 238, 248, 260
Mishpatim
62, 186, 203, 210, 211, 213, 295, 309-313, 315, 316, 324, 327, 328, 337, 338, 390, 465, 478, 481, 492, 531, 554, 564
Noach
13, 17, 129, 158, 272, 274, 278, 279, 283, 284, 330, 357, 374
Pekudei
23, 175, 190, 224, 228, 231, 394, 412, 415, 648, 707, 710, 711, 713, 739, 748, 749, 766, 767, 768, 800, 801, 954
Pinchas
35b, 35c, 51, 70, 94, 97, 100, 191, 193, 208, 234, 235, 237, 240, 329, 339, 344, 360, 368, 370, 374, 412, 414, 425, 482, 544, 557, 562, 563, 567, 575, 578, 579, 580, 594, 597, 609, 610, 630, 651, 652, 653, 676, 677, 679, 684, 713, 716, 719, 747, 748, 844, 845, 857, 882
Prologue
10, 84, 184
Safra Detzniuta
12

Shemot
1, 13, 14, 36, 38, 48, 50-52, 54-57, 59, 61, 62, 65, 67, 74, 120, 149, 168, 209, 210, 214, 215, 228, 229, 231, 233, 243, 244, 248, 249, 266-271, 273, 275, 280, 286, 290, 302, 326, 388

Shlach Lecha
117, 118, 119, 120, 121, 123, 132-135, 168, 212, 225, 326

Shmini
42, 43, 44, 58, 88

Shoftim
10

Toldot
6, 9, 13, 15, 22-30, 32, 37, 47, 55, 61-63, 71, 73, 74, 76 -80, 82, 103, 121, 126, 127, 129, 132, 133, 134, 136, 137, 139-143, 147, 148, 150 -154, 156, 158, 160, 162, 164, 165, 167, 169, 172-176, 180, 184, 185, 186, 187, 188, 191, 192, 194-203, 205

Trumah
1, 4, 6, 7, 12, 13, 69, 123, 141, 142, 143, 144, 243, 283, 308, 318, 352, 353, 364, 378, 380, 491, 492, 510, 514, 585, 631, 681, 684, 782, 794, 829, 847, 860, 888-892, 895, 898, 908, 909, 911, 913, 914, 919, 920, 923

Tzav
42, 96, 112, 176, 187

Vaera
1, 13, 14, 17, 18, 19, 21, 28, 32, 51, 73, 74, 99, 116, 148

Vaetchanan
13, 14, 32, 92, 171

Vayakhel
66, 68, 215, 235, 236

Vayechi
1, 2, 3, 4, 5, 6, 8-12, 14, 15, 18, 20-24, 29, 35, 38, 39, 45, 47, 48, 49, 50, 64, 70, 71, 74, 75, 84, 89, 93, 98, 104, 105, 109-116, 119, 128, 177, 195, 223, 224, 245, 249, 251, 254-256, 259, 260, 262-267, 269 -274, 294, 305, 306, 330, 336, 337, 339, 352, 357, 375, 377, 378, 385, 395, 404, 405, 427, 446, 447, 490, 492, 505, 513, 516-520, 525 -530, 538, 539, 540, 541, 544, 545, 550, 553, 555, 557-560, 562, 563, 574, 640, 649, 652, 656, 659, 674, 689, 712, 725, 729, 763, 777, 779, 783, 801, 802, 807, 808, 813, 814, 816, 821, 822, 852, 853, 855, 858

Vayera
14, 21-24, 26-29, 57, 77, 90, 188, 248, 255, 382, 410, 422, 451, 468, 469, 476, 477, 479, 485-487, 493, 495-498, 500, 501, 505, 512, 513

Vayeshev
1, 12, 13-15, 17, 20-24, 29, 46, 68, 71, 76, 80, 81, 96, 102, 103, 141, 142, 143, 203, 217

Vayetze
1-4, 7, 8, 12, 17-20, 22, 28, 29, 31, 33, 41-43, 48, 49, 52, 53, 58-65, 71, 75, 80, 81, 86, 89, 90, 91, 95, 97, 103, 104, 105, 109, 120, 122-128, 131, 132, 135,

137, 138, 140, 149, 151-153, 158, 185, 186, 196, 207, 210, 211, 213, 214, 216, 228, 229, 232, 238-240, 246 -252, 262, 281, 292-301, 303, 307, 308, 310-312, 316 -323, 346, 347, 353, 354, 357, 378-384, 386, 387, 389, 390, 392, 393

Vayigash
31, 44, 77, 113, 116-118, 131, 132

Vayikra
5, 33, 116, 191, 192, 284, 306-308, 310, 314, 332, 346, 351, 352

Vayishlach
1, 5, 9, 10, 12-16, 19-23, 25, 28-30, 32-34, 36, 40-45, 48-51, 54-56, 58, 60, 67, 68, 69, 70, 74, 75, 84, 88, 95, 96, 99, 100, 104, 105, 107, 110 -113, 115-117, 119, 122, 125 -131, 141-143, 146-149, 151, 152, 154, 157 -161, 163, 165, 167, 169-172, 190-193, 195, 197, 199, 201, 203-205, 216, 217, 218, 220, 221, 226, 228, 233, 234, 235, 242, 244, 245, 248, 250, 252

Yitro
14, 56, 58, 236, 240-242, 246, 247, 259, 260, 261, 265, 269, 281, 338, 348, 359, 380, 407, 451, 454, 457, 461, 477, 494

JEALOUSY

Balak
97, 148, 330, 376

Beresheet A
458

Beresheet B
338, 348, 351

Chayei Sarah
214

Emor
148

Lech Lecha
388

Metzora
38, 39

Miketz
250

Mishpatim
369

Naso
82, 83, 84

Noach
154, 197

Pekudei
206

Pinchas
468, 530

Shemot
26, 121

Shlach Lecha
70

Tazria
128

Tetzaveh
57

Trumah
5

Vayakhel
321

Vayechi
610, 733, 734

Vayera
467

Vayigash
85, 87
Vayikra
199
Vayishlach
41, 117
Yitro
429, 431, 516

JEHOIADA (YEHOYADA)

Chayei Sarah
222
Prologue
91, 114, 146
Toldot
11
Vayera
209
Vayigash
52

JEHOSHAPHAT

Bo
96
Lech Lecha
177
Miketz
123
Noach
53
Yitro
382

JERED

Beresheet B
382, 387
Lech Lecha
16
Trumah
364
Vayechi
285
Vayigash
18

JEREMIAH

Acharei Mot
15, 32, 33, 40, 75, 86, 144, 147, 275, 291, 301, 305, 329, 333, 335, 342
Balak
50, 73, 87, 128, 268, 273, 405
Bechukotai
29
Bemidbar
50
Beresheet A
216, 358, 379, 385
Beresheet B
37, 343, 370, 373
Beshalach
1
Bo
3, 120, 136, 212, 230
Chayei Sarah
198, 208, 239, 268
Emor
22, 39, 54, 56, 106, 158, 226, 275
Ha'azinu
38, 86, 118, 202, 231
Idra Raba
29, 36, 40, 65, 123, 125, 149, 200, 307
Kedoshim
65, 67, 106, 111
Ki Tetze
55, 61, 139
Ki Tisa
18

Lech Lecha
180, 198, 277, 343, 391, 410, 461, 466, 469
Metzora
59, 60
Miketz
71, 219, 221, 224
Mishpatim
32, 34, 86, 137, 182, 212, 228, 267, 406, 488, 490, 503, 506, 518, 573
Naso
13, 110
Noach
2, 57, 83, 86, 160, 194, 206, 291, 312, 313, 329
Pekudei
90, 165, 282, 365, 372, 825
Pinchas
191, 242, 315, 325, 339, 362, 563, 690, 747, 748, 760, 767, 800, 838, 844, 872
Prologue
84, 85, 151, 152, 159, 161, 165-167, 196
Safra Detzniuta
15, 21, 60, 73
Shemot
10, 47, 109, 127, 199, 201, 204-206, 256, 262, 309, 387
Shlach Lecha
211, 301, 310, 317
Shmini
97, 117
Shoftim
10
Tazria
150, 154, 173
Tetzaveh
57
Toldot
88, 131, 187, 208
Trumah
281, 355, 404, 406, 502, 586, 770, 847, 889, 896, 903
Tzav
54, 55
Vaera
146
Vaetchanan
120, 121, 130, 156, 190
Vayakhel
21, 98, 163, 496
Vayechi
5, 12, 22, 31, 77, 81, 164, 261, 287, 304, 321, 336, 368, 392, 422, 496, 600, 627, 667, 814, 833
Vayelech
46
Vayera
45, 46, 101, 306, 356, 389, 390, 396, 470, 479, 496
Vayeshev
57, 128, 129, 218
Vayetze
84, 180, 186, 232, 389
Vayigash
102, 103, 112
Vayikra
49, 178, 181, 222, 227, 265, 273, 289, 343, 351, 352, 388
Vayishlach
223, 249, 253
Yitro
341, 345, 350, 382, 477, 500, 574

JERICHO

Shemot
128
Shlach Lecha
16
Vayikra
125

JEROBOAM

Beha'alot'cha
89
Beshalach
421
Ha'azinu
29
Ki Tetze
21
Vayechi
366, 370, 378, 385, 723

JERUSALEM

Acharei Mot
61, 175, 277, 288, 377, 381
Balak
114, 501
Bemidbar
21, 23, 24
Beresheet A
279, 280
Beresheet B
17
Beshalach
149, 250, 286, 292, 309, 310, 311, 337, 462
Bo
126
Chayei Sarah
45, 98, 113, 151, 270
Ekev
63, 64
Emor
17, 26, 98
Ha'azinu
142, 143, 145, 146, 193, 194
Idra Raba
219, 220
Ki Tisa
98, 99
Lech Lecha
93, 105, 181, 402, 403, 407-409, 422, 425
Metzora
15, 28, 59, 60
Miketz
109, 205, 206
Mishpatim
254, 255, 263, 264, 266, 453, 489, 502, 506, 546
Naso
80, 192
Pekudei
40, 224, 300, 347, 371, 380, 382, 657
Pinchas
17, 148, 151, 152, 442, 746
Prologue
9
Safra Detzniuta
28
Shemot
92, 128, 133, 156, 233, 290, 292, 374
Shlach Lecha
86, 136, 252, 253, 257, 304
Shmini
10, 11, 12
Tetzaveh
97, 98

Toldot
34, 39, 65, 145
Trumah
561, 784, 901
Tzav
102, 103, 181
Vaera
151, 178, 204
Vaetchanan
53, 131
Vayakhel
64, 333, 377, 454, 495
Vayechi
13, 21, 64, 77, 79, 86, 174, 175, 342, 442, 548, 551, 575, 597, 676, 679, 680, 689, 723, 800, 839
Vayera
286, 293, 394, 395, 396, 397, 398, 399, 481, 483
Vayeshev
98, 99, 100, 147
Vayetze
43, 85, 244, 360
Vayigash
32, 89, 105, 106
Vayikra
82, 132, 136, 205, 253, 334, 348, 364, 402, 406
Vayishlach
122
Yitro
336, 481

JERUSALEM, CELESTIAL

Naso
188
Vaetchanan
53
Vayechi
442
Vayetze
85
Vayigash
89

JERUSALEM, TERRESTRIAL

Chayei Sarah
150
Emor
98
Idra Raba
341
Lech Lecha
93
Naso
188
Shemot
293
Vaetchanan
53
Vayechi
79, 442, 689
Vayeshev
100
Vayetze
85

JESSE

Shoftim
24

JESURUN

Vayishlach
244, 245, 246, 247

JETHRO

Balak
2, 60, 221, 222, 223
Beresheet A
286
Naso
16, 18
Pekudei
281
Pinchas
61
Shemot
56, 214, 215, 230, 358, 371, 377
Vayakhel
5
Vayetze
251, 252
Vayikra
125, 128
Yitro
1, 14, 15, 20, 22, 24, 26, 27, 28, 39-43, 46, 47, 54-57, 60

JOAB

Balak
387
Mishpatim
241, 252, 253
Pinchas
383, 491

JOB

Acharei Mot
51, 75, 101, 144, 146, 168, 210, 215, 290, 349
Balak
159, 280, 287, 468
Beresheet A
80, 120, 167, 250, 267, 288, 301, 308, 314, 320, 334, 354, 372, 393
Beshalach
190, 191
Bo
9-12, 14, 15, 18, 23-25, 27-30, 33, 35
Chayei Sarah
32, 41, 48, 137
Chukat
10
Ekev
22, 55
Emor
4, 50, 94, 230, 233, 238, 240, 242
Ha'azinu
38, 71, 113, 139, 156, 179, 181, 242
Idra Raba
39, 126, 127, 211, 241, 273, 280
Ki Tetze
26, 72, 98, 100, 101
Ki Tisa
111
Korach
15, 18, 19, 42-44
Lech Lecha
4, 8, 37, 39, 51, 77, 212, 285, 410, 411
Metzora
1, 8
Miketz
1, 2, 41, 42, 131, 134, 136, 233
Mishpatim
49, 56, 135, 162, 163, 265, 333, 373, 375, 432, 434, 500, 528, 531, 532

Naso
111
Pekudei
78, 128, 325, 360, 476, 547, 555, 613, 643, 722, 848, 859, 894, 895, 898, 905, 923
Pinchas
34, 43, 50, 53, 63, 67, 74, 88, 93, 120, 161, 163, 164, 223, 351, 352, 354, 435, 486, 487, 489, 530, 575, 599, 613, 639, 841
Prologue
8, 48, 72, 73, 95, 220, 221
Safra Detzniuta
30
Shemot
152, 159, 247, 266, 292, 326
Shlach Lecha
1, 7, 35, 74, 240, 295
Shmini
1, 9, 18, 92
Tazria
14, 21, 55, 94, 119, 150, 156
Tetzaveh
41, 45, 46, 47, 48, 55, 90, 141
Toldot
43, 113, 178, 183
Trumah
157, 288, 295, 297, 389, 442, 594, 660, 733-735, 742, 764, 848, 861
Vaera
42, 77, 159, 205
Vaetchanan
25, 188, 196
Vayakhel
24, 87, 143, 228
Vayechi
44, 46, 112, 147, 171, 302, 303, 444, 445, 452, 569, 580, 658, 728, 777, 812, 820, 835, 842, 843
Vayelech
16, 29, 30, 44, 45
Vayera
43, 106, 191, 211, 212, 230, 242, 296
Vayeshev
12, 25, 32, 52, 86, 177, 178, 196, 200, 203, 225, 283
Vayetze
189, 208, 223, 256, 286, 290, 364
Vayigash
43, 109
Vayikra
58
Vayishlach
137, 182, 246
Yitro
43, 44, 47, 53, 126, 182, 250, 288, 393

JOKSHAN

Chayei Sarah
199

JONAH

Beha'alot'cha
90
Beshalach
82-88
Chayei Sarah
1, 3, 7
Ki Tisa
95

Lech Lecha
180, 187, 190
Naso
27
Noach
218
Pekudei
189, 192, 194
Shlach Lecha
150
Trumah
821
Vayakhel
47, 74, 79, 81, 83, 87, 89, 92, 94, 95
Vayechi
520
Vayelech
45
Vayera
417

JORDAN RIVER

Beha'alot'cha
134
Beresheet A
62
Shlach Lecha
176

JOSEPH

Acharei Mot
112, 214
Balak
56, 84, 86, 89, 321, 322, 323, 324, 325, 342, 354, 356, 376, 403
Beha'alot'cha
38, 42, 82
Beresheet A
148, 149, 150, 151, 186, 226, 234, 364
Beresheet B
135
Beshalach
41, 42, 113
Bo
13, 232, 234
Chayei Sarah
61, 97
Emor
289
Idra Raba
55, 232
Ki Tetze
6, 21, 48, 56, 62, 64
Lech Lecha
80, 198, 291, 398
Metzora
45
Miketz
7-9, 12, 13, 15, 16, 18, 19, 31, 32, 34-36, 38, 39, 57-60, 63-65, 67, 69, 77, 78, 79, 82, 83, 84, 92, 93, 101, 106, 107, 113, 114, 126, 130, 133, 144-147, 156, 157-159, 162, 164, 166, 167, 172, 174, 177, 182-185, 189, 192, 199, 201, 202, 208, 214-216, 228, 238, 245, 247, 248
Mishpatim
129-132, 201, 316, 387, 435, 478, 479, 481, 483, 484
Noach
3, 267, 268
Pekudei
87, 189, 190, 415, 740, 741,

742, 743, 748, 749, 766, 767, 768

Pinchas
16, 18, 446, 565-567, 610, 651, 652, 676, 677, 684, 722, 723, 724, 734, 745, 764

Prologue
5, 84

Shemot
87, 149, 158, 268, 269, 275, 281

Shlach Lecha
97, 105, 119, 136, 174, 198, 224, 225

Toldot
6, 65, 67, 154, 174

Trumah
282, 352, 353, 355, 550, 551, 898

Vaera
20, 146, 154

Vayakhel
384, 493, 494

Vayechi
20, 26, 28, 35, 36, 37, 45, 64, 84, 88, 91, 112-116, 145, 251, 253, 254, 260, 262, 264, 265, 267, 268, 334, 338, 339, 344, 366, 370-373, 375, 378, 405, 490, 493, 505, 544, 553, 598, 729, 763, 764, 765, 766, 770, 775 -778, 783, 785, 855, 858, 859

Vayera
216, 239, 327, 478, 480

Vayeshev
14, 18, 21, 22, 23, 24, 29, 68, 70 -74, 80-82, 90, 91, 95, 96, 102, 103, 104, 106-108, 130, 131, 137-140, 144, 149, 195, 203, 204, 206-208, 210, 212, 213, 218, 219, 230, 234, 253, 254, 255, 257, 261, 262, 263, 265, 268, 269, 270, 271, 272

Vayetze
133-139, 163, 165, 166, 187, 234, 238-240, 246, 249, 292

Vayigash
22, 23, 25, 26, 31, 32, 45, 61, 62, 67, 69, 77, 113, 116, 117, 118, 121, 122, 123, 129, 131

Vayikra
217-219, 220, 446

Vayishlach
54, 55, 56, 57, 148, 149, 152, 193, 194, 219, 221, 227, 228

Yitro
22, 99, 212, 507

JOSHUA

Acharei Mot
78, 114

Balak
16, 19, 25, 97, 99, 270

Bechukotai
36

Beha'alot'cha
138, 139

Beresheet A
145, 394

Beresheet B
242, 298, 299, 304, 308, 309

Beshalach
192, 214, 330, 331, 457, 460 -464, 469, 470, 472

Bo
171

Chukat
41, 42

Ekev
64
Emor
187, 188, 237
Ha'azinu
4, 5, 237
Kedoshim
45
Ki Tisa
47, 112, 116, 119
Lech Lecha
394
Naso
196
Pinchas
23, 24
Prologue
164
Safra Detzniuta
63
Shemot
128
Shlach Lecha
16, 17, 31, 33, 34, 38, 69-71, 115, 232, 234, 235, 309, 321
Trumah
689
Tzav
33
Vaetchanan
2, 15, 163, 166, 167, 169
Vayakhel
4, 10, 12, 13, 78, 169, 396, 400, 402
Vayechi
519, 672, 673
Vayelech
4-6, 12, 13, 14, 23, 24
Vayera
367, 368, 370, 373
Vayikra
44

JOSIAH

Bechukotai
27, 28
Chayei Sarah
42
Yitro
382

JUBILEE

Acharei Mot
187, 241
Behar
7, 8, 13, 16, 20, 21, 25, 63
Beresheet A
153, 154, 157
Beresheet B
182, 196, 243
Beshalach
40, 56, 57, 58
Bo
69, 160, 174, 238
Chayei Sarah
65
Emor
177
Ha'azinu
11
Idra Raba
191
Lech Lecha
384, 447, 463, 464
Mishpatim
221, 222, 288, 365, 393, 396, 397, 501, 510, 511, 532
Naso
98

Safra Detzniuta
72, 73
Shlach Lecha
314
Tetzaveh
71
Toldot
49, 68
Trumah
245, 348, 354, 357, 403, 912
Vaera
3, 4, 65
Vaetchanan
44, 94, 128
Vayakhel
318
Vayechi
648, 650, 657, 659
Vayetze
7, 83, 84, 130, 131, 140, 141, 142, 148, 149, 151
Vayigash
70
Vayikra
428
Yitro
24, 353, 354, 355, 356, 389, 396

JUDAH

Acharei Mot
14, 281, 285, 286
Balak
132, 238
Beha'alot'cha
47
Bemidbar
29, 30, 31
Beresheet A
234, 249
Beresheet B
394, 435
Chayei Sarah
13
Ha'azinu
246
Ki Tetze
97
Lech Lecha
64, 308
Miketz
122-124, 185, 206, 215
Mishpatim
180-184, 186, 187, 190-194, 196, 198, 199, 200, 309, 475, 483, 485
Naso
150
Noach
57, 319
Pekudei
8, 36, 47, 54, 55, 69, 178, 298
Pinchas
651
Trumah
253, 257, 480, 586, 849, 850, 899, 901
Vaera
93, 95, 178
Vayakhel
5, 389
Vayechi
51, 287, 529, 544, 546, 553 -555, 564, 567, 569, 574, 575, 577, 581, 647, 655, 694, 696 -699, 701, 702, 724, 773, 774
Vayelech
24
Vayera
297,307

Vayeshev
144, 149, 150, 151, 152, 154, 155, 177, 183, 191, 193
Vayetze
41, 158, 159, 160, 162, 168, 169, 170, 175
Vayigash
1, 22, 23, 25, 26, 31, 61
Vayikra
124,125,364
Yitro
380, 383, 384

JUDGES

Acharei Mot
147, 196, 348
Balak
99, 263, 377, 378
Behar
12
Beresheet A
432
Beresheet B
104, 105, 118, 301, 317
Beshalach
9, 169, 190
Bo
197, 214
Emor
280, 283
Idra Raba
329
Kedoshim
98, 99
Ki Tisa
74, 115
Metzora
4
Mishpatim
431, 435, 518, 536
Naso
74, 104
Noach
98, 99
Pekudei
538, 717, 721, 723
Shemot
69, 85
Shoftim
1, 14, 18, 21, 23
Tetzaveh
77, 120
Trumah
231, 382, 811
Vaera
94
Vayechi
229, 363, 364
Vayera
383, 386
Vayeshev
26, 226, 246
Vayikra
118, 409
Yitro
279, 417

JUDGMENT

Acharei Mot
1, 37, 39, 40, 54, 59, 71, 73, 75, 78, 79, 84, 104, 105, 108, 112-114, 116, 118, 120, 121, 123, 129, 139, 146-148, 151, 152, 154, 157, 158, 161, 163, 180, 193, 205, 237, 241, 244, 247, 251, 285, 287, 289, 295, 298-300, 308, 320, 327, 348, 382, 396, 400, 402, 403, 405
Balak
17, 18, 21, 23, 89, 124, 147,

228, 239, 240, 245, 259, 262, 263, 273, 274, 275, 315, 316, 329, 375, 393, 395, 408, 411, 412, 417, 423, 428, 429, 431, 445, 466, 476, 480

Bechukotai
17, 21, 25, 42, 44, 47, 53, 55

Beha'alot'cha
10, 12, 14, 17, 19, 28, 36, 37, 41, 44, 51, 52, 55, 92, 123, 124

Behar
2

Bemidbar
3, 47, 48, 58, 63, 67, 75

Beresheet A
50, 101, 144, 146, 173, 193, 197, 214, 330, 390, 401, 460 -462

Beresheet B
1, 6, 11, 21, 40, 43, 46, 48, 58, 61, 62, 78, 93, 94, 104-106, 110, 111, 114, 134, 136, 140, 149, 156, 255, 283, 311, 313-315, 317, 340, 381, 383, 385, 387, 390, 400-402, 404, 405, 408, 426, 427, 432, 434

Beshalach
9-11, 69, 75-81, 115, 123, 127, 128, 159, 169, 170, 228, 264, 281, 326, 327, 365, 376, 379, 404-406, 429, 430, 432, 433, 454, 455, 484

Chayei Sarah
6, 7, 8, 25, 41, 67, 85, 239, 240, 243, 246, 247, 261, 270

Chukat
3, 19, 21, 22, 24, 25, 32, 35, 84

Ekev
1, 17, 39, 50

Emor
5, 18, 32, 40, 52, 126, 128, 146, 157, 190-193, 196, 197, 199-203, 205, 206, 208, 209, 210, 215, 217, 219, 227a, 256, 292, 302, 314, 333, 335, 338

Ha'azinu
10, 38, 39, 41, 44, 45, 47, 56, 57, 59, 98, 101-103, 105, 106, 107, 111, 113, 116, 117, 123, 126, 133, 139, 142, 145, 148b, 149, 163, 164, 167, 168, 172 -174, 177, 182, 194, 238

Idra Raba
35, 37, 58, 71, 98, 105, 106, 109, 118, 132, 135, 155, 171, 173, 175, 183, 196, 199-201, 203, 204, 220, 221, 227-229, 235, 245, 266, 275-277, 279, 280, 287, 299, 308, 309, 310, 313-317, 320, 322, 323, 325, 326, 327, 333, 337, 340, 341

Kedoshim
8, 58, 62, 64, 65, 97, 98, 99, 108

Ki Tetze
28, 54, 61, 85, 89, 120, 140, 143

Ki Tisa
18, 51, 95, 96, 103

Korach
12, 15, 16, 17, 18, 20, 24, 25, 31, 39

Lech Lecha
8, 9, 31, 47, 50, 81, 91, 107, 148, 216, 254, 300, 325, 361, 362, 363, 370, 373, 375, 376, 377, 406, 450, 459

Matot
1-5
Metzora
1, 4, 9, 15, 26, 28, 30, 31, 34, 35, 48, 50, 53, 54, 55, 56, 57
Miketz
14, 85, 110, 119, 126, 168, 169, 172, 173, 174, 176, 193, 194, 198, 202, 208, 226, 227, 228, 231
Mishpatim
1, 38, 246, 247, 260, 261, 284, 291, 329, 336, 338, 357, 430, 431, 432, 437, 438, 445, 446, 447, 448, 450, 456, 477, 504, 513, 515, 517, 518, 519, 521, 522, 523, 524, 536, 537, 548, 564, 566
Naso
2, 21, 24, 25, 61, 62, 64, 70, 71, 72, 79, 112, 114, 119, 122, 125, 127, 128, 133, 138, 145, 146, 150, 151, 164, 170, 172, 173, 190, 191
Noach
18, 51-53, 58-60, 71, 80, 98, 99, 104, 112, 114, 116, 134, 151, 152, 163, 176, 177, 185, 188, 203, 205, 210, 211, 215, 216, 221-224, 235, 243, 258, 282, 310, 335, 348, 351, 358, 359, 367, 368, 380, 386, 387
Pekudei
3, 11, 37, 50, 59-62, 67, 69, 94, 117, 123-125, 136, 183, 196, 237, 247, 248, 260, 268, 269, 287, 302, 305, 322, 325, 328, 332, 335, 353, 374, 376, 428, 447, 455, 461, 462, 483, 520, 521, 540, 542, 547, 552, 574, 587, 588, 590, 593, 596, 597, 598, 604, 614, 617, 630, 658, 661, 669, 697, 701, 716, 718 -727, 760, 792, 806, 807, 858, 867, 869, 870, 878, 895, 924, 929, 935, 945
Pinchas
28, 30, 68, 108, 111, 183, 199, 203, 204, 206, 255, 275, 314, 337, 344, 350-355, 358, 359, 360, 369, 371, 374, 402-404, 406, 407, 427, 434, 451, 457, 460, 461, 463, 479, 513, 560, 567, 583, 590, 591, 615, 634, 649, 672-674, 688, 689, 702, 726, 728, 732, 735, 736, 750, 757, 798, 813, 816, 819, 820, 850, 859, 860, 867, 880, 881, 887, 888
Prologue
1, 98, 102, 148, 156, 199, 200, 201, 203, 260
Safra Detzniuta
5, 7, 27, 28, 29, 45, 46, 70
Shemot
18, 31, 41, 42, 44, 73, 74, 81, 85, 86, 94, 115-117, 128, 150, 168, 193-195, 201, 202, 261, 262, 311, 313, 316-323, 326, 342, 343, 346-349, 356, 361, 365, 376, 383-385, 387 -389, 391
Shlach Lecha
1, 68, 89, 95, 120, 124, 151, 161, 191, 193, 240, 269, 290, 301, 308, 313, 315, 321, 322, 335

Shmini
12, 19, 25, 43, 44, 55, 57, 63, 65, 76, 82, 88, 95, 96, 114
Shoftim
3, 4, 14, 15
Tazria
46, 54, 55, 58, 64, 90, 94, 118-120, 122, 123, 126, 131, 133, 137, 163, 164, 165
Tetzaveh
41, 77, 87, 88, 89, 90, 92, 93, 111, 113, 120, 125, 126, 128, 129, 141, 142, 143
Toldot
18, 24, 47, 48, 82, 122, 130, 179, 180, 197
Trumah
6, 30, 43, 70, 157, 158, 165, 167, 168, 200, 204, 230, 231, 233, 234, 295, 320, 321, 352, 388, 393, 399, 400, 409, 410, 412, 426, 429, 430, 431, 443, 452, 456, 457, 459, 481, 483, 484, 512, 513, 547, 550, 551, 552, 603, 617, 618, 663, 672, 776, 777, 785, 814, 815, 848, 849, 853, 855, 856, 858, 860, 911, 913, 919, 920, 921
Tzav
1, 23, 38, 64, 76, 77, 82, 85, 88 -94, 96, 114-119, 127, 136, 159, 183
Vaera
9, 11, 12, 30, 77, 90, 91, 93, 102, 106, 107, 108, 109, 113, 114, 115, 131, 135
Vaetchanan
24, 48, 52, 53, 105, 176, 177, 186
Vayakhel
22, 29, 33, 85, 88, 97, 163, 167, 172-174, 234, 243, 246, 274, 320, 348, 355, 356, 358, 412, 413, 414, 468, 469, 473, 475, 476, 487
Vayechi
7, 12, 13, 14, 15, 21, 57, 60, 61, 75, 76, 82, 83, 92, 95, 102, 106, 160, 163, 166, 167, 185, 186, 190, 202, 204, 205, 224, 228, 229, 236, 239, 242, 286, 287, 315, 316, 345, 353, 355, 356, 358, 359, 361, 364, 421, 422, 433, 435, 463, 468, 469, 470, 476, 477, 512, 552, 557, 559, 563, 580, 591, 604, 605, 631, 632, 633, 641, 647, 655, 662, 666, 712, 776, 820, 837, 843
Vayelech
6, 7, 8, 29, 30
Vayera
30, 51, 55, 75, 128, 129, 146, 167-169, 180, 191, 202, 203, 205, 206, 207, 215, 216, 219, 238, 247, 249, 250, 256, 257, 258, 259, 261-263, 265, 268-272, 278, 279, 281, 284-286, 300, 312, 324, 330, 333, 346, 354, 361, 366, 369-372, 375, 381-387, 423, 425, 453, 472, 474, 475, 485, 486, 490-492, 502
Vayeshev
15, 16, 17, 19, 20, 25, 26, 32, 57, 75, 76, 77, 78, 109, 111, 112, 120, 141, 147, 148, 186, 266
Vayetze
3, 14, 28, 31, 79, 80, 81, 83, 84, 85, 93, 94, 101, 102, 106, 141,

212, 260, 273, 284, 286, 304, 309, 340, 345, 346, 347, 348, 349, 383

Vayigash
47, 92, 115, 133, 134

Vayikra
11, 13, 35, 40, 52, 53, 110, 111, 120, 152, 159, 160, 162, 163, 174, 176, 197-199, 210, 214, 218, 221, 223, 233, 247-250, 252, 270, 277-279, 294, 299, 303, 306-308, 310, 312-314, 325, 331, 332, 338, 339, 343, 352, 362, 380-382, 401-406, 409-411, 420, 421, 429, 442

Vayishlach
24, 65, 144, 147, 169, 175-177, 190-192, 199, 209, 210

Yitro
39, 76, 80, 131, 135, 147, 159, 209, 228, 261, 281, 287, 288, 291, 308, 339, 435, 458, 482, 501, 510

JUNIPER

Chayei Sarah
208

Vayetze
180

JUPITER

Beresheet B
69, 82

Ha'azinu
14

Ki Tetze
116

Pinchas
737, 739

KADDISH

Mishpatim
20

Trumah
57, 731

KADMIEL (SPIRIT)

Pekudei
699

Vayetze 73

KADSHIEL (SUPERNAL MINISTER)

Beresheet B
4

Vayera
27

Vayikra
22

KAFTZIEL (SPIRIT)

Beha'alot'cha
118

Pekudei
548, 549, 552

Pekudei
541

Vayera
276

KARSHIEL (SPIRIT)

Pekudei
531

Vayera
275

KARTANA (PHYSICIAN)

Ha'azinu
248, 253, 254

KASIRIYAH (SPIRIT)

Pekudei
696

KATFIRA

Vaera
124

KEDUMIEL (SUPERNAL MINISTER)

Beresheet B
43
Pekudei
50
Vayera
27
Vayikra
14

KEDUMIYAH (SPIRIT)

Pekudei
622, 696

KEDUSHAH (HOLINESS)

Acharei Mot
26, 41, 82, 84, 87, 96, 109, 135, 176, 289
Balak
7, 75, 79, 80, 82, 107, 137, 162, 417, 418, 426, 431
Bechukotai
5, 7, 9
Beha'alot'cha
66-68, 74
Behar
10, 34
Bemidbar
46
Beresheet A
38, 47, 48, 56, 123, 146, 199, 228, 287, 365, 382, 435, 455
Beresheet B
43, 48, 192, 195, 210, 228, 305, 306, 328, 337, 380, 422
Beshalach
6, 8, 13, 71, 74, 273, 317, 419, 437
Bo
9, 16, 31, 34, 88, 122, 165, 231, 235, 237
Chayei Sarah
17, 61, 75, 125, 133, 256, 262
Ekev
37, 39, 47, 56
Emor
10, 13, 24, 34, 36, 42, 45, 54, 83, 87, 88, 89, 90, 102-106, 109-111, 114, 115, 117, 125, 126, 127, 226, 325
Ha'azinu
60, 202, 203, 204, 205, 211
Idra Raba
149, 160, 340, 344
Kedoshim
4, 13, 14, 17, 23, 25, 115, 116, 118, 119, 128
Ki Tetze
51, 70, 117

Ki Tisa
57, 82, 91, 93, 99, 110, 117
Korach
9, 10
Lech Lecha
67, 75, 78, 179, 196, 233, 326, 442
Metzora
18, 48, 51, 57, 58
Miketz
21, 53, 127, 136, 231, 246, 247, 248, 254
Mishpatim
27, 137, 138, 265, 268, 310, 324, 325, 327, 328, 348, 371, 414, 486, 500-508, 510, 511, 512, 516, 556, 563, 571
Naso
108, 109, 124, 130, 134, 145, 156, 157, 159
Noach
2, 148, 295, 335, 336, 343, 348, 352, 365
Pekudei
35, 40, 49, 64, 74, 84-86, 89, 91, 92, 120, 121, 122, 131, 158, 159, 238, 246, 247, 248, 253, 259, 279, 286, 300, 330-333, 336, 347, 354, 363, 374, 378, 416, 420-424, 455, 460, 464, 468, 470, 471, 479, 481, 516, 541, 553, 564, 572, 573, 581, 609, 610, 654, 675, 677, 727, 747, 809, 823, 831, 835, 839, 840, 844, 849, 869, 880, 883, 885, 886, 888, 889, 892, 900, 907, 909, 910, 933, 934
Pinchas
35d, 63, 109, 135, 192, 213, 217, 298, 308, 421, 432, 625, 638, 651, 652, 712, 717, 719, 732, 740, 760, 800, 801, 863, 864, 894
Prologue
80, 169, 216, 227, 247, 251, 252, 257
Safra Detzniuta
38, 64
Shemot
3, 28, 73, 74, 195, 262, 329, 393, 394
Shlach Lecha
38, 101, 275
Shmini
15, 83, 85, 87, 102, 115, 116, 117
Tazria
29, 38, 83, 87, 121, 136, 138, 140, 141, 146, 149, 173, 175, 176, 177
Tetzaveh
40, 42, 44, 46, 48, 55, 56, 58, 59, 60, 61, 64, 87, 98, 140
Toldot
6, 24, 26, 27, 73, 150
Trumah
35, 37, 55, 57, 60, 99, 143, 167, 168, 173, 174, 235, 261, 274, 392, 468, 506, 568, 829, 852, 869
Tzav
4, 5, 8, 15, 74, 104-107, 128, 157
Vaera
7, 94, 104, 107, 108, 111, 118, 120
Vaetchanan
96, 119, 172
Vayakhel
3, 127, 167, 178, 189, 255, 257,

258, 262, 359, 377, 382, 383, 394, 410, 416, 417, 435, 483
Vayechi
8, 43, 51, 68, 95, 102, 131, 132, 197, 315, 378, 379, 382, 631, 704, 711, 712
Vayelech
16-19, 28
Vayera
37, 85, 86, 161, 278, 291, 307, 330, 351, 414, 416, 417, 439
Vayeshev
154, 227
Vayetze
15, 23, 101, 148, 179, 184, 279, 289, 355, 358
Vayigash
39, 60, 65, 111, 120, 130, 133
Vayikra
56-58, 68, 97, 198, 204, 321, 423, 425, 433, 437
Vayishlach
38, 39, 109, 115, 144, 145, 147, 233
Yitro
8, 9, 10, 40, 50-52, 110, 205, 474, 476, 516, 546, 548, 549

KEMUEL (ANGEL)

Acharei Mot
392
Beshalach
298

KENITES

Pinchas
61
Yitro
56

KESHER

Pinchas
106, 368

KESTIMON (SPIRIT)

Prologue
155

KETER

Acharei Mot
171, 224, 332-334, 389, 408
Balak
420
Beha'alot'cha
90, 91, 93
Behar
18, 19, 32, 37
Beresheet A
170, 173, 203, 204, 225, 252, 253, 313, 340, 347
Beresheet B
7
Beshalach
224, 274, 386, 395, 435
Bo
40, 41, 43, 64, 65, 218, 220, 222, 236
Chayei Sarah
23, 24, 169
Ekev
60
Emor
154, 249, 250
Ha'azinu
33, 35, 36, 41, 42, 63, 65, 116,

124
Idra Raba
16, 18, 20, 24, 31, 40
Kedoshim
37, 42, 58, 59
Ki Tetze
90, 117
Korach
39
Lech Lecha
79, 257
Mishpatim
379, 428, 470, 501, 523, 528, 531
Naso
15, 36
Noach
99, 122-124
Pekudei
266, 360, 361, 673, 946, 947
Pinchas
191, 192, 211, 226, 452, 505, 569, 570, 572-574, 576, 655, 665, 670, 682, 687, 754, 805, 818, 841, 842, 846, 848, 849, 852-854, 865, 873, 875, 877, 878
Prologue
62, 146, 186
Safra Detzniuta
6, 26, 40, 49, 60
Shemot
258
Shlach Lecha
343
Shmini
13
Shoftim
15
Tazria
32
Tetzaveh
15
Trumah
363, 546, 584
Tzav
12, 13, 37, 38, 62, 79, 192
Vaera
143
Vaetchanan
91, 144, 146, 173, 174, 191
Vayakhel
101, 137, 190, 196, 204, 284, 285, 345
Vayechi
63, 769
Vayera
68
Vayeshev
46
Vayikra
103, 148, 151, 156, 157, 162, 166-168, 171, 174, 177, 245 -247, 260, 285, 332, 341, 342, 360, 428
Yitro
223, 334, 337, 370, 468, 486, 529

KETURAH

Chayei Sarah
187, 196, 257, 258, 263
Vayeshev
161

KEY

Acharei Mot
76, 82, 193, 311

Balak
124
Beresheet A
475
Beresheet B
47, 362, 392
Beshalach
208-210, 482
Chayei Sarah
168
Idra Raba
167
Lech Lecha
14, 207, 313, 360, 361
Miketz
217
Mishpatim
226, 303-305, 322
Noach
67, 353
Pekudei
291, 504, 510, 526, 634
Pinchas
606, 712, 713, 714
Prologue
42, 44-46
Safra Detzniuta
13
Shemot
54, 55, 66
Shlach Lecha
261, 264
Shmini
59
Trumah
49, 131, 604, 886
Vayakhel
131, 132, 148, 486
Vayechi
284, 556
Vayera
138-140, 412, 418
Vayeshev
48
Vayetze
176, 268
Yitro
235, 236, 522

KIDDUSH

Ekev
37
Emor
127
Pinchas
629
Prologue
82
Shlach Lecha
297

KIDNEYS

Ha'azinu
190
Lech Lecha
119, 120
Mishpatim
426, 535
Pinchas
97, 213, 407, 426, 427, 429

KIDRON

Mishpatim
256

KINGDOM

Beresheet A
72, 117, 118, 119, 316

Chayei Sarah
191
Ki Tisa
13
Lech Lecha
70, 265, 308, 398, 399, 401, 408, 409
Miketz
57, 78, 81, 83, 132, 205, 250, 252, 253
Prologue
166, 167
Tetzaveh
98, 111
Vaetchanan
3, 53, 78, 88, 89, 92, 94, 95
Vayera
16, 239, 280, 338
Vayeshev
69, 194
Vayetze
158, 284
Vayigash
65, 66, 77, 110, 111
Vayishlach
89, 108, 130, 175, 267

KIRYAT ARBA

Chayei Sarah
46, 47, 62, 69

KISSES

Acharei Mot
67
Balak
66, 116, 124
Beresheet B
125, 127, 130, 132, 136, 141
Chayei Sarah
68
Emor
333
Ha'azinu
12
Idra Raba
355
Kedoshim
54
Ki Tetze
108
Miketz
64
Mishpatim
61, 62, 466, 489, 551, 552, 554
Noach
238
Pekudei
638, 648, 649, 651, 652, 679, 704, 708, 766, 910, 914, 917
Pinchas
716, 719
Prologue
88
Safra Detzniuta
17
Shemot
122, 127, 332
Shlach Lecha
203, 306
Toldot
47, 49
Trumah
44, 368, 369, 371-374, 376, 378, 379, 380, 674
Vaetchanan
10
Vayakhel
111, 112, 129, 132, 134, 135,

137, 142
Vayechi
236
Vayeshev
106, 107
Vayetze
25
Vayishlach
123

KLIPOT (SHELLS – NEGATIVITY)

Balak
5, 15, 70, 79, 81, 169, 399, 474, 490
Beresheet A
40, 104, 105, 106, 109, 110, 118, 184, 186, 223, 225, 226, 229, 251, 256, 257, 289, 411, 435, 445, 462
Beresheet B
40, 42, 286, 287, 305, 346, 354
Chayei Sarah
9, 19, 67, 72, 73
Ekev
29
Emor
132, 157, 255
Ha'azinu
248
Idra Raba
2, 336
Ki Tetze
3, 6, 8, 63, 70, 72, 73, 81
Lech Lecha
42, 47, 147, 148, 149, 233, 305, 405
Metzora
56, 57, 58
Miketz
2
Mishpatim
8, 265, 266, 267, 377, 403, 418, 420, 421, 426, 556
Noach
64, 116, 251, 335, 340, 343-345, 363-365
Pekudei
74, 158, 248, 923
Pinchas
97, 100, 248, 263, 264, 266, 267, 269, 271, 284, 591, 652, 653, 655, 730, 731, 738, 739, 894
Shemot
39, 73, 116, 259, 261, 332, 360, 361
Shlach Lecha
123, 124, 157
Shmini
84
Shoftim
4, 20
Tazria
154
Trumah
57, 58, 81, 83, 200, 236, 268, 391, 392, 506, 523, 760
Tzav
29, 41, 57, 69, 70, 78, 127, 132, 156
Vaera
108, 109, 158
Vayakhel
162, 165, 170, 177, 274, 407

Vayechi
316, 321, 383, 473, 560, 580, 597, 628, 705, 706
Vayera
439, 458
Vayetze
4, 23, 81, 289
Vayikra
136, 140
Vayishlach
25, 34, 135, 146
Yitro
390

KNIFE

Toldot
159

KOH

Bo
116
Lech Lecha
322, 323, 324, 325, 456, 457, 466
Pinchas
845
Shemot
207
Trumah
244, 320, 322
Vaera
30
Vaetchanan
93, 141, 172, 177
Vayetze
110, 111
Vayishlach
189
Yitro
261

KOHATH

Beresheet A
234
Korach
1, 26
Vayechi
563

KOLYAH

Vayera
370

KORAH

Balak
375
Beresheet A
46, 47, 48, 49, 50, 52-54, 57, 58
Korach
1, 3, 4, 5, 8, 12
Vayechi
563
Vayetze
253

KOZBI

Vayechi
562

KRASHIHAEL (SPIRIT)

Pekudei
699

KRASPIHAEL (SPIRIT)

Pekudei
689

KRIAT SH'MA

Balak
29, 30
Ki Tetze
30, 96, 142
Mishpatim
394, 396, 397, 398, 428
Trumah
231, 232, 651

KRISHIEL (SPIRIT)

Pekudei
622

KTATARIHAEL (SPIRIT)

Pekudei
694

KUSHITE

Chayei Sarah
198
Trumah
62

LABAN

Balak
338, 400, 422
Bechukotai
12, 13
Beha'alot'cha
15, 58
Behar
63, 72
Beshalach
440
Chayei Sarah
180, 181, 264
Emor
151
Ki Tisa
76
Metzora
52, 62
Mishpatim
564
Pinchas
240
Shemot
52
Shlach Lecha
29
Toldot
16, 18, 52, 53, 54, 82, 199, 207
Vayechi
112
Vayera
346
Vayeshev
13
Vayetze
123, 130, 138, 246, 250-252, 292, 296, 298-301, 319, 321, 337, 353, 356, 375, 378, 380, 381, 382, 383
Vayishlach
5, 9, 21, 22, 23, 28, 30, 32, 33, 34, 36, 40-42, 49, 70
Yitro
56

LABYRINTH

Vayetze
17, 18

LADDER

Ha'azinu
199

Naso
52, 53
Pekudei
390
Pinchas
343, 430, 432, 433, 438, 646, 837
Vayetze
46, 47, 52-54, 59, 60, 69, 70, 74
Vayikra
284
Vayishlach
162

LAISHA

Noach
84-86

LAMBS

Acharei Mot
297
Beha'alot'cha
7, 69-71, 74
Behar
29
Bo
101, 160, 161, 163, 164, 176, 177, 230
Chayei Sarah
244
Ekev
19
Emor
183, 241, 257
Korach
52
Mishpatim
196
Pekudei
323, 324, 943
Pinchas
93, 207, 229, 244, 246, 560, 664, 675, 678, 703, 706, 717, 721, 725, 729, 735, 806, 888, 889, 890
Shemot
232, 320, 375, 376, 386
Shmini
49
Tetzaveh
72
Trumah
405
Tzav
42, 143
Vaera
150
Vayechi
417, 553, 715
Vayera
142, 503
Vayetze
298, 299, 319
Yitro
272

LAMP

Mishpatim
451
Trumah
574

LAMPS

Balak
7, 209, 313, 354
Beha'alot'cha
1, 4, 11, 20, 22, 23, 48, 49

Beresheet A
335
Beshalach
7, 8
Chukat
65, 66
Ekev
6, 9, 24, 33, 36, 49, 65
Emor
14, 15, 290, 293
Ha'azinu
183
Ki Tetze
92, 95
Mishpatim
491
Pekudei
17, 61, 242
Pinchas
40, 115, 820
Shemot
245
Shlach Lecha
181, 208
Shmini
27, 54
Shoftim
23, 24
Tazria
137
Toldot
107
Trumah
80, 119-122, 124, 579, 746
Vayakhel
106, 114, 169, 191, 194, 262, 268, 309
Vayechi
419
Vayeshev
224
Vayetze
174
Vayikra
165
Yitro
23

LAND OF YISRAEL

Bo
13, 175
Lech Lecha
33, 161, 187, 394
Noach
41, 169, 208, 209, 242, 279, 300, 363, 366
Pinchas
230, 426, 632
Shemot
144
Trumah
179, 275, 277, 282, 461, 468, 471, 561, 821, 867
Vaera
195
Vayechi
75, 84, 323, 413, 551
Vayeshev
51
Vayetze
3, 28, 45, 49, 122, 173, 174, 292
Vayishlach
234
Yitro
263

LAWS OF PRIESTS

Bo
135

LEAH

Balak
321, 322
Beresheet A
55, 68, 186
Beresheet B
159
Chayei Sarah
256
Ki Tetze
111
Lech Lecha
73
Mishpatim
182
Noach
116
Pinchas
609, 754, 776
Shemot
333
Shlach Lecha
132, 133, 134, 135, 136
Toldot
54
Trumah
4, 5, 13, 909
Vaera
146, 147, 149
Vayechi
262, 263, 264, 270-274, 550, 751, 802
Vayeshev
72
Vayetze
105, 126, 127, 131, 132, 139, 140-143, 145, 147, 149, 151, 152, 155, 157, 166, 185, 186, 196, 204, 206, 212, 215, 216, 217, 228, 230, 234, 236, 242, 243, 337
Vayishlach
42, 60, 144, 193, 194, 200, 203, 204, 220
Yitro
236

LEAVEN

Acharei Mot
240
Bo
166-168, 178
Emor
131, 134, 137, 157
Ki Tetze
134, 135
Pinchas
377, 744
Tetzaveh
49, 50, 73
Vaetchanan
163, 197

LEAVES

Beresheet B
16, 17, 195, 224, 311, 330, 379, 380, 397, 398, 413
Mishpatim
341, 342
Vaetchanan
132

LEBANON

Acharei Mot
34, 282, 318
Balak
310, 312, 334

Beresheet A
293, 295, 338, 428, 431
Beshalach
123
Chayei Sarah
183, 226
Ekev
63
Ha'azinu
84, 150, 205, 227, 228
Lech Lecha
125, 127
Metzora
17
Pinchas
77, 82, 241, 348, 437
Shemot
14, 19, 20, 60-64
Tazria
112
Toldot
9
Trumah
20, 25-30, 32
Vaetchanan
121
Vayetze
337
Vayikra
266, 267

LEMUEL

Vayechi
811, 812

LENTILS

Toldot
63, 77, 79

LEOPARD

Chayei Sarah
198

LEPERS

Balak
289, 291, 386, 388
Beha'alot'cha
76, 77
Behar
46
Metzora
1, 4, 13, 14, 16
Tazria
86, 170, 171, 178
Tzav
155
Yitro
267

LEPROSY

Balak
386, 387, 388, 391, 392, 393
Chukat
70b
Ekev
48
Metzora
12, 15, 49
Naso
77, 79
Pekudei
72
Pinchas
53, 375
Tazria
71, 87, 88, 90, 91, 93, 107, 136, 137, 144, 148, 157, 168, 175

Tzav
42
Vayera
105

LEVANA (SPIRIT)

Beresheet B
65-67, 69, 70, 76

LEVIATHAN

Beresheet A
408, 409
Beshalach
101, 143, 145
Ki Tetze
66, 67
Mishpatim
272, 273
Shlach Lecha
273
Toldot
43, 44, 45
Vayechi
774

LEVIRATE MARRIAGE

Acharei Mot
287
Beresheet A
279
Chukat
9, 12
Ki Tetze
98
Korach
18
Matot
6
Mishpatim
110, 112, 118, 120, 130, 131, 138, 193, 195, 395
Pinchas
45, 87, 613, 614
Shlach Lecha
189
Vayeshev
155, 168, 173, 174, 177, 192, 194

LEVITES

Acharei Mot
21, 198
Beha'alot'cha
52-54, 74, 111
Behar
26, 27, 38, 39
Bemidbar
16, 30, 52, 53
Beresheet B
141, 265
Beshalach
240
Chayei Sarah
267
Chukat
3, 73
Ekev
20
Emor
1, 36
Ha'azinu
203
Idra Raba
149
Ki Tetze
57, 77
Ki Tisa
6

Korach
3, 12, 13, 23, 24, 35, 37, 38, 39, 40
Lech Lecha
58, 303
Mishpatim
365, 388, 451
Naso
9, 126, 132, 156, 157
Noach
90, 119, 121
Pekudei
25, 165, 351, 359, 770, 943, 945
Pinchas
37, 204, 211, 220, 298, 541, 542, 548, 555, 595, 640, 652, 802
Shemot
331-333
Shlach Lecha
14, 256
Shmini
62
Shoftim
24
Tazria
123, 127
Tetzaveh
34, 35, 38
Toldot
130
Trumah
91, 307, 321
Tzav
2, 11, 68, 122, 123, 130, 136
Vaera
85, 86
Vaetchanan
13
Vayechi
94, 696, 718, 719, 792, 825
Vayera
163, 435, 436
Vayeshev
43, 263
Vayetze
37, 38, 39, 151, 198
Vayikra
110, 111, 313, 314
Vayishlach
149, 150, 172, 272

LIGHT

Vayera
12, 13, 22, 27, 38, 40, 45, 46, 59, 60, 161, 172, 235, 244, 393, 409, 422, 458
Acharei Mot
62, 75-77, 79, 83, 84, 120, 145, 146, 149, 156, 190, 193, 195, 200, 236-238, 251, 258, 354, 409, 412
Balak
5, 44, 52, 75, 76, 80, 110, 128-131, 140, 143, 144, 146, 147, 156, 158, 172, 195, 206, 208, 209, 217, 248, 313, 326, 354, 355, 419, 420, 422, 442, 476, 501
Bechukotai
2, 29
Beha'alot'cha
2, 3, 5, 10, 11, 20-22, 37, 51, 79, 88, 99, 102, 108, 120, 121, 148
Behar
25, 29, 37, 38, 48, 55, 64, 65, 66, 79

Bemidbar
1, 17, 19, 20, 32, 39
Beresheet A
1, 7, 15, 16, 17, 21, 28-38, 40-43, 66, 67, 98, 101, 103, 107, 108, 110, 114, 116, 118, 120, 125-128, 131, 132, 137, 140-142, 158, 161, 165, 166, 167, 176, 178, 180-183, 206, 230, 231, 258, 281, 299, 308, 312, 313, 316, 320, 322, 323, 324, 326, 330, 331, 332, 334, 335, 344, 348-353, 356, 357, 377, 378, 388-392, 394, 396, 400-404, 413, 431, 447, 450, 454
Beresheet B
5, 12, 14, 15, 18, 19, 22, 30, 31, 33, 35, 40, 46, 48, 49, 59, 60, 63-65, 67, 70, 73-75, 78 -81, 84 -89, 91, 93, 94, 97, 103, 106, 115, 126, 131, 136, 138, 139, 142-153, 157, 160, 163, 169, 176-178, 198, 199, 202, 212, 214, 249-260, 262 -266, 268-271, 281, 287, 288, 290, 306, 309, 330, 343, 378, 379, 397, 410, 412, 421, 446
Beshalach
48, 52, 137, 160, 172, 180, 215, 224, 235, 255, 274, 275, 282, 296, 297, 302, 328, 395, 429, 430, 480, 482-484
Bo
1, 55-58, 61, 66, 102, 108, 110, 128, 153, 218, 222, 236, 239
Chayei Sarah
17, 30, 40, 89, 101, 105, 106, 129, 154, 155, 158, 159, 160, 161, 168, 169, 205, 206, 209, 234
Chukat
7, 40, 42, 44, 51, 59, 65
Ekev
6, 10, 17, 23, 24, 31, 33, 47, 49
Emor
3, 4, 8, 14, 20, 27, 58, 60, 88, 90, 94, 95, 132, 136, 176, 183, 203, 205, 207, 224, 227a, 255, 282a, 287, 290
Ha'azinu
33, 34, 35, 38, 39, 42, 49, 63, 68, 69, 98, 99, 100, 114, 123, 124, 133, 139, 174, 196, 197, 233
Idra Raba
15, 17, 18, 33, 38, 44, 45, 48, 51, 53, 58, 63, 80, 87, 118, 138, 142, 143, 147, 186, 187, 196, 218, 246, 263, 271, 273, 280, 282, 285, 289, 290, 359
Kedoshim
7, 36, 45-47, 54, 55, 63, 92
Ki Tetze
3, 51, 85, 88, 92, 95, 119
Ki Tisa
6, 7, 9, 10, 105, 116, 118, 119
Korach
41
Lech Lecha
8, 20, 37, 38, 39, 67, 76, 99, 103, 112, 114, 115, 151, 155, 157-161, 163, 213, 221, 241, 247, 251, 310, 311, 312, 360, 361, 374, 376, 389, 413, 420, 459, 476
Metzora
41, 60

Miketz
25, 26, 72, 73, 98, 99, 225, 227, 228, 230, 233, 234, 237, 238, 241
Mishpatim
69, 85, 105, 126, 183, 200, 202, 296, 297, 324, 343, 403, 475, 476, 523, 524, 525, 526, 527, 528, 529, 530, 531, 532, 536, 539, 580, 581
Naso
44, 90, 95
Noach
18, 25, 35, 47, 50, 67, 84, 85, 116, 123, 125, 127, 142, 145, 146, 195, 219, 236, 241, 242, 245, 247, 268, 296, 344, 345, 350, 367
Pekudei
4-10, 27, 59, 75, 76, 78, 79, 101, 103, 118, 127, 146, 147, 162, 168-170, 180, 181, 198, 224-227, 234, 239, 266, 268, 286, 348, 351, 378, 395, 430, 482, 492, 499, 507, 508, 511, 517, 518, 520, 526, 531, 534, 537, 557, 558, 560, 561, 562, 566, 603, 626, 655, 656, 658, 659, 660, 663, 696, 709, 710, 761, 768, 772, 773, 790, 792, 866, 933, 934, 947, 948, 950
Pinchas
40, 41, 102, 115-117, 122, 126, 131, 134, 174, 192, 211, 213, 225, 226, 232, 239, 246, 253, 314, 323, 343, 348, 361, 384, 385, 396, 444, 498, 538, 560, 564, 569, 596, 619, 627, 644, 645, 648, 657-659, 662, 669, 677, 689, 690, 696, 737, 777, 790, 816, 824, 829, 877, 878
Prologue
2, 14, 15, 16, 40, 43, 45, 49, 53, 54, 58, 59, 90, 92, 95, 99, 102, 108, 110-112, 119, 153, 154, 185, 186, 198, 201, 202, 209, 210, 212, 220, 224, 251, 256, 258
Safra Detzniuta
10, 11, 16, 26, 37, 38, 61, 62, 66, 70
Shemot
1, 4, 14, 19, 79, 81, 82, 97, 112-114, 126-129, 137, 142, 143, 155, 159-163, 187, 191, 208, 213, 224, 238, 240, 245, 251, 279, 310, 366, 383, 384
Shlach Lecha
7, 23, 31, 53, 54, 102, 104, 112, 114, 124, 140, 141, 142, 143, 144, 151-153, 157, 158, 161, 176, 181-185, 187, 189, 196, 197, 198, 201, 206-208, 225, 230, 241, 242, 244, 248, 270, 272, 277, 279
Shmini
99, 100
Shoftim
8, 13, 23, 24
Tazria
16, 40, 54, 55, 59, 62, 84, 91, 96, 101, 102, 105, 137
Tetzaveh
2, 5, 6, 7, 18, 32, 40, 46, 48, 86, 88, 96, 136, 142, 144, 145, 146

Toldot
12, 27, 31, 48, 70, 107, 118, 119, 120, 133, 134, 182, 194
Trumah
3, 7, 9-11, 13, 17, 22, 24, 26, 29, 30, 41, 63, 74, 80, 97, 101, 124-126, 160, 162, 165, 166, 185, 186, 191, 198, 200, 202, 206, 207, 216, 232, 241, 251, 252, 259, 260, 261, 265, 268, 269, 273, 283, 289-291, 293, 296, 304, 305, 311, 333, 336, 361, 362, 364, 365, 370, 374, 376, 379, 380, 381, 394, 395, 397, 400, 414-416, 423, 427, 428, 474, 480, 531, 532, 542, 551, 557, 569, 598, 611, 619, 639, 659, 701, 702, 703, 704, 726, 728, 729, 732, 736-743, 745, 746, 748-751, 753, 754-758, 766, 776, 838, 841, 842, 849, 855, 859, 862, 880
Tzav
27, 28, 42, 49, 51, 52, 158, 165-167, 172
Vaera
23, 24, 25, 26, 43, 123, 133, 134, 141, 179, 181, 187
Vaetchanan
10, 15, 34, 39, 91, 110
Vayakhel
12, 13, 24, 46, 55, 75, 109, 118, 124, 125, 143, 153, 160, 161, 165, 167, 169-171, 175, 180, 205, 210, 220, 225, 257-264, 266-269, 275, 280, 285, 286, 288, 294, 295, 296, 297, 298, 307, 309, 311, 312, 314, 317, 319-322, 325, 331-333, 349, 354, 362, 368, 391, 396, 410, 438, 448, 454, 465, 477, 481, 486, 489
Vayechi
5, 18, 22, 30, 39, 42, 43, 44, 51, 56, 57, 58, 59, 103, 208, 218, 315, 350, 415, 437, 452, 462, 465, 472, 483, 484, 502, 503, 504, 511, 512, 523, 565, 566, 589, 682, 727, 767, 829, 830, 838
Vayelech
5
Vayeshev
5, 41, 42, 44, 46, 47, 51, 55, 63, 65, 66, 146, 169, 203, 224, 275
Vayetze
3, 4, 18, 23, 24, 30, 46, 52, 65, 133, 161, 177, 179, 180, 192, 193, 194, 237, 277, 311, 312, 318, 339, 340, 362
Vayigash
15, 21, 33, 43, 45, 103, 130
Vayikra
74, 83, 132, 142, 179, 225, 241, 260, 382, 383, 435, 449
Vayishlach
12, 42, 56, 57, 75, 89-94, 96, 115, 134, 136, 223, 225, 258, 265
Yitro
9, 23, 32, 36, 38, 48, 49, 50, 51, 53, 87, 113, 134, 223, 235-238, 280, 288, 305, 311, 318, 381, 413, 439, 440, 465, 505, 510, 513, 539, 541, 543, 572

LIGHTS

Acharei Mot
146, 154, 159, 237, 248, 304,

311, 329, 374, 385-387, 411, 412
Balak
7, 208, 209, 342, 355, 356, 437, 439
Beha'alot'cha
22-24, 39
Bemidbar
17, 19, 60
Beresheet A
55, 68, 98, 101, 110-112, 118, 119, 124, 128, 135, 142, 158, 161, 176, 322, 344, 367, 377, 390-394, 396, 400, 412, 431
Beresheet B
1, 9, 10, 12, 15-19, 22, 25, 30, 64, 65, 75, 77, 78, 85-90, 92, 95, 98, 103-107, 110, 117-119, 126-128, 130, 131, 136, 145, 190, 212, 249, 250, 265, 269, 271, 272, 274-277, 279-285, 288, 292, 293, 339, 419
Beshalach
49, 208, 209, 221, 437, 483
Bo
56, 71, 108
Chayei Sarah
72, 73, 129, 205
Ekev
7, 9, 35, 36, 61, 65
Emor
21, 45, 164, 179, 192, 224, 250, 257
Ha'azinu
33, 42, 49, 69, 98, 99, 100, 101, 118, 119, 120, 127, 163, 195
Idra Raba
11, 17, 34, 186, 211, 264, 290, 315, 321, 361
Kedoshim
94
Ki Tetze
87, 89, 113
Ki Tisa
5, 104, 107, 108
Korach
34
Lech Lecha
12, 114, 147, 159, 161
Metzora
40, 56
Miketz
10, 99, 135
Mishpatim
60, 71, 263, 336, 455, 526-529, 534, 535
Noach
99, 100, 104, 125, 269
Pekudei
2, 4, 10, 81, 82, 97, 102, 111, 145, 147, 148, 153, 157, 164, 181, 182, 183, 224, 227, 264, 268, 279, 287, 360, 361, 391, 514, 531, 534, 560, 598-602, 621, 626, 640, 642, 645, 655, 662, 664, 665, 674, 678, 718, 724, 756, 792, 822, 924, 949
Pinchas
2, 70, 123, 167, 168, 174, 217, 239, 256, 268, 280, 281, 337, 375, 409, 510, 546, 628, 629, 645, 677, 691, 703, 708, 709, 712, 715, 717, 718, 719, 739, 795, 824
Prologue
4, 186, 209, 212, 254, 258
Safra Detzniuta
3, 5, 26, 52

Shemot
1, 4, 5, 47, 114, 118, 148, 160, 233, 247
Shlach Lecha
5, 6, 105, 129, 156, 157, 161, 190, 202, 271, 272, 333
Shmini
6, 27
Tazria
64, 91, 92, 94
Tetzaveh
9, 13, 32, 122, 124, 125, 136
Toldot
120, 196
Trumah
8, 9, 125, 186, 192, 194, 198, 199, 201, 202, 231, 233, 260, 341, 361, 370, 381, 394, 399, 427, 434, 552, 555, 576, 753, 880
Tzav
13, 51, 121, 152, 172, 190
Vaera
25, 26, 105, 106, 127, 130, 134, 156, 161, 187
Vaetchanan
37, 43, 192
Vayakhel
78, 165, 166, 183, 200, 257, 260-263, 275, 280, 293, 294, 298, 307, 311, 314-316, 320, 322, 324, 340, 341, 357, 362, 416, 447, 463
Vayechi
218, 311, 409, 419, 449, 463, 464, 465, 475, 483, 484, 503, 509, 511, 659, 729
Vayera
61, 64, 296, 297, 298, 353, 422
Vayeshev
42, 43, 46, 148
Vayetze
5, 7, 17, 115, 120, 175, 192, 333, 338
Vayigash
45, 70, 84, 103-105, 108
Vayikra
85, 87, 103, 132, 165, 184
Vayishlach
12, 75, 133, 134, 137
Yitro
33, 36, 223, 236, 237, 238, 240, 334, 339, 413

LIKENESSES

Acharei Mot
76, 185, 260
Balak
50, 51
Bemidbar
7, 28, 38
Beresheet A
16, 69-71, 88, 93, 135, 162, 166, 167, 177, 197, 413, 470
Beresheet B
1, 4, 6, 30, 63, 66, 172, 349, 350, 351
Beshalach
238, 265, 271
Bo
152, 215, 219
Chayei Sarah
42, 43, 158
Chukat
9
Emor
13, 14, 25, 28, 29, 34, 35, 47, 97, 98, 126, 151, 214, 284

Idra Raba
172, 179, 180, 232, 351
Ki Tetze
77
Ki Tisa
56, 57, 58
Miketz
23, 79, 81
Mishpatim
316, 476, 515
Naso
31, 41, 42, 55
Noach
252, 261, 265, 266, 271, 272, 280
Pekudei
199, 206, 209, 211, 317, 338, 341, 411
Pinchas
79, 128, 175, 188, 225, 249, 253, 256, 259, 284, 343, 419, 485, 497, 500, 519, 611, 771, 859, 863
Prologue
233
Safra Detzniuta
9, 43, 48, 51
Shlach Lecha
110, 275, 276
Shmini
3, 22
Tazria
45, 49, 60, 97, 110, 115, 127, 168
Tetzaveh
22, 34, 133
Toldot
163
Trumah
4, 29, 82, 231, 266, 413, 531, 558, 560, 759, 762, 875
Tzav
75, 82, 129, 170
Vaera
115, 149
Vaetchanan
34
Vayakhel
228, 301, 323, 326, 441-444
Vayechi
4, 469, 610, 731, 766, 826
Vayelech
1
Vayera
284
Vayeshev
54, 157, 161
Vayetze
168, 214, 261
Vayigash
123, 128
Vayikra
93-96, 138, 139, 143
Vayishlach
105
Yitro
10, 62, 66, 67, 282, 313, 317, 327, 427, 428, 433, 490, 491, 516, 517

LILIT

Acharei Mot
360, 362-366
Beresheet A
268, 393, 408, 416, 417, 421
Beresheet B
354, 355
Emor
39

Ki Tetze
113, 123
Mishpatim
43, 319, 320, 377, 452
Naso
92
Pekudei
207, 920
Pinchas
168, 270, 327, 331, 353, 362, 364, 375, 376, 409, 410, 424
Prologue
251
Safra Detzniuta
38
Tetzaveh
120
Trumah
682
Vayikra
315, 316, 319-321, 323
Vayishlach
76, 79

LILY

Beresheet A
298
Emor
330, 332, 333
Ha'azinu
10, 11, 12, 176
Ki Tetze
51
Ki Tisa
31, 32
Naso
4
Prologue
1, 2
Shmini
39, 40
Toldot
18
Vaetchanan
66
Vayechi
232, 234, 235, 236

LINEN

Kedoshim
105, 108, 111, 114, 117, 121, 122
Miketz
64
Pekudei
132, 187, 199, 224, 226, 236, 237, 247, 248, 250, 255, 259, 354
Shlach Lecha
124
Tazria
168
Trumah
160, 234, 402
Tzav
5
Vaera
168
Vaetchanan
34
Vayakhel
55
Vayechi
129

LINTEL

Beha'alot'cha
7-9

Bo
74, 77, 81-83, 191
Emor
130

LION

Acharei Mot
67, 76, 407
Balak
210, 252, 253, 476, 477, 478, 479, 492
Beha'alot'cha
101, 102, 104-106, 114, 116, 117, 120
Bemidbar
28
Beresheet A
81-84, 87, 89, 121, 191
Beresheet B
67, 79, 88
Beshalach
269
Bo
204-206
Ekev
19, 41, 67, 68, 69, 72
Ha'azinu
238
Idra Raba
172, 263
Ki Tetze
77
Korach
57
Lech Lecha
123
Mishpatim
143, 193, 195, 196, 197, 199, 283, 370, 445, 475, 476, 480, 481, 483, 485
Naso
42, 54
Noach
12, 85, 199, 212, 265
Pekudei
561, 562
Pinchas
70, 218, 260, 270, 329, 407, 408, 418, 419, 422, 424, 485, 533, 539-541, 545, 567, 597, 604, 617, 620, 647, 651, 666, 749, 769, 863, 864
Prologue
96, 97
Safra Detzniuta
67
Shemot
252, 259, 313
Shlach Lecha
26, 64, 118, 213, 250
Tazria
115
Trumah
308-310, 396, 526, 801
Tzav
47, 68, 129, 131, 138
Vaetchanan
189, 190
Vayakhel
326
Vayechi
279, 286, 358, 430, 431, 553, 554, 577-579, 657, 681, 702, 724, 829, 842, 843
Vayeshev
237, 241
Vayetze
73, 282

Vayikra
279, 435
Yitro
96, 97, 103, 104, 107, 111, 213, 225, 280, 282, 327

LIPS

Balak
66, 210, 221, 362, 364, 376, 379
Beresheet A
189, 190, 372
Beresheet B
125
Bo
26, 111
Chukat
70b, 72
Emor
145, 333
Ha'azinu
12, 96, 154, 155, 157, 169, 170, 176, 178
Idra Raba
170, 253, 287
Ki Tisa
100
Lech Lecha
79, 119, 120
Metzora
44
Mishpatim
382, 398, 446, 527-529
Naso
6, 14, 29, 112, 137, 160
Noach
331
Pekudei
454, 647, 653, 795, 910
Pinchas
182, 196, 261, 265, 277, 278, 280, 281, 338, 341, 404, 434, 443, 719, 822
Prologue
170
Safra Detzniuta
16, 17, 34, 39, 43
Shemot
20, 356
Shlach Lecha
75, 296
Shmini
14, 68, 70, 99
Shoftim
4
Tazria
85
Toldot
138, 141, 181
Trumah
149
Tzav
28, 118, 149, 182
Vaera
66
Vaetchanan
158
Vayakhel
68, 69, 171, 366
Vayechi
236, 671, 673
Vayetze
26
Vayikra
337
Yitro
68, 115, 170, 171, 180, 214, 219, 221, 256

LIVER

Beresheet A
265, 266, 267
Naso
13
Pekudei
924
Pinchas
97, 98, 209, 210, 212, 214-216, 220, 270, 362, 363, 364, 374, 375, 376, 378, 379, 410-414, 422, 424, 425, 440, 889
Toldot
58, 59, 60, 61, 62
Trumah
493, 494, 495
Vayakhel
122
Vayera
340

LIVING CREATURES

Acharei Mot
255
Balak
309
Beha'alot'cha
100, 101, 111, 116-118, 124
Beresheet A
83, 84, 88, 89, 91, 133-135, 139, 192, 264, 274, 366, 368, 369, 405
Beresheet B
160, 165, 170, 171
Beshalach
95, 236, 271
Bo
213
Chayei Sarah
140, 234
Chukat
30
Emor
185, 186
Ha'azinu
37, 141
Ki Tetze
42, 77, 127
Korach
57
Metzora
19
Mishpatim
5, 11, 13, 429, 445, 457, 460, 481, 483
Naso
42
Noach
72, 192, 258
Pekudei
210, 339, 405, 409, 410
Pinchas
123, 263, 270, 316
Prologue
4, 232
Safra Detzniuta
11, 25, 50, 67
Shemot
200
Shlach Lecha
295, 319
Shmini
77, 106
Tazria
22, 81
Tetzaveh
140
Trumah
30, 82, 211, 213, 385, 711

Tzav
82, 83
Vayakhel
295, 296, 323
Vayechi
439, 621, 681, 774, 787, 836
Vayetze
272
Vayigash
123
Vayikra
2, 185, 186, 277, 279-281, 317, 424
Yitro
311, 327, 506, 511, 515

LOCK

Acharei Mot
82, 410
Balak
435
Beha'alot'cha
73
Bo
69
Emor
185, 206, 208
Ha'azinu
124, 126, 167
Idra Raba
25, 29, 31, 100, 105, 106, 110, 193-196, 198, 251, 268, 273, 305
Mishpatim
405
Naso
126, 133
Prologue
42, 44, 45, 121
Shemot
54
Shlach Lecha
120, 124, 257, 258, 261
Shmini
59
Tazria
121
Trumah
57, 58, 552, 715, 848, 860

LOCUSTS

Ki Tetze
58

LOINS

Balak
258, 261, 262, 263
Ki Tetze
90
Mishpatim
290
Pinchas
316
Vayeshev
98

LOT

Chayei Sarah
151, 181
Lech Lecha
17, 36, 42, 46, 50, 56, 59, 76, 85, 86, 88, 92, 174-176, 178 -180, 191, 192, 234
Toldot
52, 53, 54
Vaera
196

Vayakhel
40
Vayera
75, 168, 169, 173, 182-185, 187, 225-229, 235, 236, 238, 241, 256, 266, 287, 288, 295, 307, 308, 312 -314, 317, 319, 320, 322, 325, 326, 329, 333, 339, 362
Vayetze
172

LOVE

Acharei Mot
31, 46-49, 56, 65, 115, 144, 155, 171, 213, 216-218, 273, 295, 369, 377, 378, 381, 413
Balak
88, 92, 114, 115, 128, 140, 235, 263, 294, 336, 389
Bechukotai
40, 42, 43, 49, 59
Beha'alot'cha
6, 21, 23, 35, 128, 129
Behar
12, 14
Bemidbar
12, 15, 20, 21
Beresheet A
51, 52, 53, 193, 195-197, 221
Beresheet B
21, 24, 122-124, 127, 128, 133, 217, 220, 243, 306
Beshalach
47, 49, 59, 63, 64, 70, 109, 152, 157, 207, 239, 240, 245, 247, 252, 255, 281, 362, 387, 389, 391, 393
Bo
6, 25
Chayei Sarah
45, 46, 190, 251, 252
Chukat
20
Ekev
62
Emor
26, 38, 111, 127, 129, 149, 159, 160, 208, 215, 227, 273, 275
Ha'azinu
2, 49, 76, 84, 85, 98, 210, 216, 221, 227
Idra Raba
7, 32, 36, 97, 137, 153, 278, 284, 285
Kedoshim
74, 76, 77, 94, 100
Ki Tetze
4, 29, 37, 59
Ki Tisa
25, 31, 54, 117, 118
Korach
8, 28, 36, 40
Lech Lecha
3, 226, 275, 281, 436, 454
Matot
6
Metzora
10, 37, 38, 40, 41, 42
Miketz
38, 70, 71, 178
Mishpatim
61, 97, 99, 102, 220, 282, 286, 330, 368, 369, 466, 477, 497, 500, 518, 519, 551, 554, 558
Naso
10, 37, 38, 46-50, 52, 59, 105,

110, 135, 136, 138, 140 -142, 164, 183

Noach
102, 110, 154, 232, 239-241

Pekudei
43, 62, 83, 87, 128, 202, 351, 414, 468, 632, 635, 636, 640, 645, 646, 649, 651-654, 659, 667, 679, 699, 714, 726, 748, 751, 793, 805, 923

Pinchas
52, 85, 104, 155, 381, 398, 455, 505, 517, 548, 553, 558, 596, 677, 690, 715, 716, 825, 831, 844, 854, 865, 873, 891

Prologue
60, 176, 183, 184, 198-203, 228

Shemot
61, 133, 199, 324

Shlach Lecha
6, 92, 111, 154, 183, 211, 214, 265

Shmini
39, 82, 91, 92, 100, 119

Shoftim
24

Tazria
60, 70, 71, 72, 73, 88, 145

Tetzaveh
24

Toldot
18, 23, 35, 46, 49, 57, 96, 181, 182, 184

Trumah
4, 6, 44, 54, 91, 130, 139, 153, 156, 168, 188, 319, 320, 323, 325, 340, 342, 344, 347, 371 -378, 382, 415, 491, 493, 540, 545, 591, 652, 659-663, 668, 670, 671, 673, 675, 738, 739, 777, 798, 879

Tzav
1, 2, 31, 54, 149, 151, 156, 165, 176, 186

Vaera
90, 98, 100, 101, 159

Vaetchanan
46, 47, 68, 69, 70, 85, 91, 136, 138, 140, 141, 144, 145, 146, 147, 173, 197

Vayakhel
151, 153, 224, 413, 415, 417, 418, 425, 439

Vayechi
21, 22, 30, 58, 89, 107, 175, 243, 410, 435, 493, 509, 676-678, 680, 688, 719, 732 -737, 739, 744, 745, 748, 775, 792, 806, 838, 839

Vayera
29, 36, 160, 313, 326, 349, 364, 390, 393, 399, 407, 494

Vayeshev
26, 41, 74, 80, 81, 90, 91, 209, 285

Vayetze
84, 115, 129, 207, 208, 209, 217, 232, 302

Vayigash
17, 43, 106, 119, 133, 134

Vayikra
39, 99, 116, 191, 198, 224, 258, 290, 292, 384

Vayishlach
223, 269

Yitro
21, 79, 80, 91, 98, 99, 104, 244, 281, 292, 356, 406

LULAV

Emor
282b
Ki Tetze
143, 144, 145
Mishpatim
457
Naso
176
Pinchas
302, 304, 821-823, 827
Shlach Lecha
344
Tetzaveh
132
Trumah
710, 711
Tzav
108, 110, 111
Vayechi
211, 226, 229, 230

LUNGS

Ekev
65
Ki Tetze
119
Mishpatim
457
Pinchas
97, 267, 270, 273, 276, 277, 278, 279, 365, 367, 400, 401, 403, 405, 407, 423, 426-428, 431, 436, 437, 442, 449

LUPINUS

Beshalach
311

LUZ

Vaetchanan
196
Vayechi
64

MAASSIYAH

Vayera
370

MACHALAT

Bechukotai
26
Behar
65
Beresheet B
355

MACHLON

Mishpatim
175, 180, 191

MACHPELAH

Chayei Sarah
93, 104, 106, 111, 112, 114 -116
Shlach Lecha
132, 133, 136, 285
Vayechi
172, 254, 269, 270, 329, 331
Vayetze
243
Vayishlach
234

MAH (WHAT)

Ki Tetze
20

Ki Tisa
68
Korach
49
Mishpatim
483
Pinchas
791
Trumah
15, 16, 17

MAHALALEL

Trumah
364, 760, 764, 765

MAIDENS

Acharei Mot
48
Behar
46
Beresheet A
127, 277
Beshalach
349
Emor
31, 172
Kedoshim
109
Mishpatim
336
Pekudei
128, 129, 283, 828
Pinchas
692, 738, 739, 759, 795
Shemot
197, 202, 326
Shlach Lecha
316
Trumah
31, 129, 138, 142, 289, 340, 343, 344, 361
Vayakhel
194
Vayera
29, 232
Vayeshev
202
Vayetze
256
Yitro
17

MALACHI

Naso
148

MALE

Acharei Mot
57, 59, 120, 135, 171, 173, 187, 219, 304, 328, 355, 360, 401, 402
Balak
78, 79, 178, 208, 211, 332, 403
Balak
406
Beha'alot'cha
47, 127
Behar
31, 79
Bemidbar
2, 3, 33, 37
Beresheet A
10, 12, 39, 60, 64, 66, 80 -83, 92, 105, 125, 127, 144, 165, 171, 178, 217, 308 -310, 312, 317, 343, 357, 364, 371, 388, 395, 415, 416, 423, 470
Beresheet B
64, 76, 98, 106, 119, 129, 137,

139, 158, 159, 172, 175, 200, 209, 211, 212, 220, 221, 223 -225, 229, 230, 232-234, 241, 246, 261, 288, 297, 305, 347, 366-370

Beshalach
22, 63, 354

Bo
16, 40, 53, 87, 112, 113, 126, 131, 132, 134, 159, 232, 238

Chayei Sarah
141, 142, 230, 236, 252

Chukat
2, 3, 16, 74, 76

Ekev
67, 68

Emor
176

Ha'azinu
74, 84, 85, 102, 103, 112, 113, 115, 116, 139, 183-187, 189 -191, 193, 195

Idra Raba
144, 177, 180, 297, 301, 304, 307-309, 311, 317, 318, 323, 324, 325, 339, 340, 341

Kedoshim
23, 24, 69, 124, 130

Ki Tetze
64, 70, 110, 111

Ki Tisa
46, 100

Lech Lecha
46, 59, 99, 103, 107, 126, 204-210, 346, 348, 350, 412, 413, 455, 457, 460, 462, 463

Matot
3, 4

Miketz
157, 158, 230

Mishpatim
105, 106, 132, 133, 134, 136, 137, 184, 218, 219, 220, 245, 273, 274, 276, 317, 318, 407, 409, 411, 440, 447, 454, 457, 528, 531, 537, 539, 576

Naso
36, 79, 141, 142, 143, 155, 194

Noach
25, 44, 58, 103, 154, 230 -232, 310, 351, 379

Pekudei
23, 129, 136, 137, 139, 140, 143, 144, 158, 159, 160, 202, 208, 234, 270, 293, 308, 342, 350, 424, 425, 427, 434, 436, 437, 453, 454, 458, 460, 469, 493, 495, 497, 507, 602, 644, 654, 683, 756, 761, 763, 770, 771, 773, 776-778, 796, 811, 877, 940, 952, 955

Pinchas
201, 209, 212, 318, 362, 363, 416, 468, 630, 639, 730, 731, 737, 740, 820, 828, 878

Prologue
17, 215, 226

Safra Detzniuta
3, 44, 45, 48, 53, 57

Shemot
38, 49, 200

Shlach Lecha
6, 101, 121, 124, 133, 150, 171, 206, 209, 267, 319

Tazria
9, 10, 14, 22-25, 27, 43, 60, 61, 80, 106, 117, 132, 133

Tetzaveh
8, 45

Toldot
109
Trumah
17, 25, 85, 135, 195, 201, 215, 236, 246, 247, 249, 333, 334, 336, 348, 379, 395, 483, 580, 656, 666, 716, 741, 752, 761, 861, 875, 894, 922, 923
Tzav
42
Vaera
56, 61, 112, 116, 187
Vaetchanan
30, 73, 89, 95
Vayakhel
55, 218, 225, 235, 256, 323, 324, 356, 487
Vayechi
94, 119, 177, 290, 375, 378, 379, 381, 468, 469, 537, 568, 572, 586, 612, 620, 661, 662, 718, 720, 731, 739, 743, 748, 755, 756, 759-762, 764-767, 770, 771, 799, 800, 804, 805, 809, 810, 813, 833
Vayelech
7, 28, 41
Vayera
98, 423, 513
Vayeshev
55, 62, 66, 67, 68, 69, 151
Vayetze
7, 23, 24, 28, 30, 31, 33, 45, 73, 91, 115, 116, 119, 133, 191, 209, 220, 227, 260, 261, 266, 269, 279, 283, 288, 289, 291, 298, 299, 313, 329, 337, 338, 378, 384, 385
Vayigash
27-30, 54, 57, 81, 82, 131
Vayikra
57, 64, 72, 73, 93, 94, 96, 101, 156, 167, 221, 265, 289, 315, 317, 318
Vayishlach
204
Yitro
67, 125, 329, 400

MALE WATERS (MAYIN DUCHRIN)

Vayera
29

MALKAM

Vayishlach
155, 156

MALKIEL (SPIRIT)

Pekudei
504, 538, 539, 541, 542, 703, 869
Vayera
275, 276

MAMRE

Vayera
17, 18, 26, 27, 30

MANDRAKES

Toldot
33, 34, 35, 37
Vayechi
691

Vayetze
190, 196, 197, 199, 200, 201, 203, 205, 206, 214, 229

MANNA

Balak
420
Beha'alot'cha
134, 146
Beshalach
364, 372, 373, 376, 380, 393, 395-397, 401, 407, 453
Ekev
64
Emor
260a
Ha'azinu
117
Idra Raba
17
Ki Tisa
49, 68
Lech Lecha
445
Pinchas
81, 450
Prologue
88
Trumah
557, 632
Vayechi
126
Vayelech
4
Vayikra
446, 447
Yitro
444, 445

MANOAH

Prologue
111
Vayera
73, 74
Yitro
72

MARA

Beha'alot'cha
85

MARAH

Beresheet A
261
Beshalach
347, 349
Naso
65, 66, 87
Pinchas
270

MARRIAGE

Balak
30
Beresheet A
152, 305, 446
Chayei Sarah
16, 215, 234, 259
Chukat
12
Ekev
32
Ki Tetze
1, 29, 97, 103
Ki Tisa
33

Korach
18
Lech Lecha
350, 352, 353, 471
Matot
4, 5,6
Mishpatim
21, 24, 26, 28, 68, 71, 79, 90, 108, 123, 125, 148, 154, 155, 157, 160, 162, 163, 171, 172, 195, 198, 223, 224, 225, 239, 276, 277, 284, 323, 391
Naso
61, 130
Pinchas
45, 327, 336, 614
Prologue
125, 168
Shlach Lecha
312
Toldot
15
Trumah
126, 137-139, 344, 345, 347, 349, 731, 788, 893
Vaetchanan
120, 157
Vayechi
51, 77, 82, 157, 271, 272, 274, 387, 391, 401, 495, 620, 637
Vayelech
7, 8, 9, 11
Vayera
327
Vayeshev
165, 172, 173
Vayetze
43, 44, 48, 52, 62, 63, 65, 68, 124, 128, 135, 142, 188, 386
Vayikra
41
Vayishlach
49
Yitro
434

MARS

Balak
142
Beresheet B
69, 94
Ha'azinu
14
Ki Tetze
112, 114, 120, 121
Pinchas
35b, 270, 737, 739

MATA (ANGEL)

Vayechi
52
Vayera
128

MATANA

Mishpatim
363

MATCH-MAKING

Trumah
818, 819

MATRED

Ha'azinu
112, 113

Toldot
190

MATRON

Acharei Mot
36, 37, 116
Balak
437
Bechukotai
40, 41, 51
Beha'alot'cha
73
Bemidbar
26
Beresheet B
216
Emor
154, 159, 170, 171, 172, 173, 226, 254-256, 258
Idra Raba
341
Ki Tetze
4, 6, 30, 35, 39
Metzora
24
Mishpatim
372, 442, 443, 450, 452, 465
Naso
61
Pinchas
163-165, 170, 406
Shemot
92
Shlach Lecha
317
Shmini
52
Tazria
28
Trumah
152, 716
Tzav
99, 156
Vaera
9, 13, 67, 159
Vayechi
557, 558, 559, 617, 618, 647, 676, 693, 716, 744, 745, 747, 770, 774, 798, 838
Vayetze
202
Vayikra
152
Yitro
455, 472, 474-476

MATZOH

Pinchas
732, 737-739, 741, 743, 746

MAYIN DUCHRIN (MALE WATERS)

Vayera
29

MAYIN NUKVIN (FEMALE WATERS)

Balak
439
Beha'alot'cha
20
Beresheet B
16, 47
Beshalach
388
Chukat
75

Emor
86, 91
Lech Lecha
4, 23, 183, 236, 358, 359
Miketz
54
Noach
25, 119
Pekudei
654, 674, 943
Pinchas
79, 81
Shemot
39, 166, 228
Shlach Lecha
83
Trumah
4, 259, 261, 286, 529, 680
Vaera
112
Vayakhel
321
Vayechi
119, 506, 717, 720, 730, 805, 813
Vayera
8, 27, 29

MAZAL

Acharei Mot
372, 410-412
Beresheet B
110, 114
Beshalach
88, 89
Chayei Sarah
36
Ha'azinu
58-61, 63, 64, 66, 69, 78, 90, 94, 109, 117, 167, 172-174
Idra Raba
149, 150, 151
Miketz
113
Pekudei
630, 631
Pinchas
64
Safra Detzniuta
16, 17, 56
Shemot
72
Toldot
20
Vayera
424, 425
Vayeshev
34
Vayetze
199, 200, 229, 267, 269, 274, 291
Vayigash
55, 57

MEAL OFFERING

Behar
28, 29, 45
Emor
145, 148, 150, 151, 183
Kedoshim
10
Mishpatim
260
Naso
15
Noach
121
Pinchas
656, 657, 766, 767, 769, 770,

771, 778, 803, 804, 806
Tzav
121
Vayechi
666, 668
Vayera
117
Vayikra
130, 199

MEALS

Balak
40, 70, 89, 92, 120, 210
Ekev
18, 20, 25, 31, 37, 38, 45, 48, 50, 51, 52, 62, 63, 64
Emor
104, 108, 118-120, 122-125, 145, 147, 148, 150, 151, 152, 183, 278, 297
Ha'azinu
46, 47
Idra Raba
364
Ki Tisa
46
Mishpatim
260, 566
Naso
15
Pekudei
31, 33, 626, 892
Pinchas
543, 602, 604, 608, 610, 618, 619, 635, 637, 638, 656, 657, 766, 767, 769-771, 778, 803, 804, 806
Prologue
2
Shlach Lecha
297
Tetzaveh
102
Toldot
41, 45
Trumah
280, 487, 488, 489, 490, 498, 500-502, 571, 588, 731, 768, 769, 773, 777-780, 782, 783, 786
Vayakhel
172, 187, 188, 190, 456, 457, 458, 459, 461, 462
Vayechi
227, 636, 666, 668
Vayera
117, 129, 170
Vayigash
53
Yitro
437, 438, 446-458, 461, 466, 531

MEDICINE

Ha'azinu
248, 253, 256, 259
Miketz
68
Tetzaveh
74, 75, 77

MEDITATION

Acharei Mot
227
Bemidbar
66
Beresheet B
47, 53, 265
Ki Tetze
25, 142

Lech Lecha
243
Pinchas
207, 667, 796
Tzav
146
Vaetchanan
61-66, 78-80, 85, 86, 87, 90
Vayechi
44
Vayetze
261
Vayikra
312, 448
Vayishlach
72, 73, 74
Yitro
45

MEHETABEL

Idra Raba
180, 316, 317

MEHITAVEL

Ha'azinu
112, 113

MEI ZAHAB

Ha'azinu
112, 113

MEIDAD

Beha'alot'cha
137, 138

MELCHIZEDEK

Balak
157
Emor
45
Ha'azinu
101
Lech Lecha
237, 240, 241, 255, 257

MENASHE, KING OF JUDAH

Balak
376
Beresheet B
21
Pekudei
178
Vayechi
36, 39, 40, 73, 75, 370, 372, 492
Vayigash
8
Yitro
382

MENORAH

Mishpatim
451
Trumah
574

MERCURY

Beresheet B
69
Ha'azinu
14
Ki Tetze
117
Pinchas
737, 739

MERCY

Acharei Mot
1, 106, 107, 115, 138, 156 -158, 160, 161, 165, 183, 184, 196, 247, 258, 262, 264, 266, 267, 272, 275, 282, 308, 396

Balak
17, 18, 89, 124, 260, 268, 309, 367, 411, 476

Beha'alot'cha
8-10, 19, 36, 37, 39, 41, 44, 78, 92, 93, 118

Behar
15

Bemidbar
75

Beresheet A
3, 82, 101, 112, 126, 173, 193, 214, 219, 221, 222, 467

Beresheet B
1, 2, 6, 46-48, 55, 156, 383, 401, 408, 432, 434

Beshalach
66, 75-81, 182, 249, 317, 328, 379, 406, 455

Bo
78-80, 82, 83, 85, 92, 106, 113, 137, 142, 145, 146, 205

Chayei Sarah
25, 141, 195

Chukat
10, 68

Ekev
22, 50, 60

Emor
40, 52, 53, 74, 190, 191, 193, 195-197, 201-203, 218, 227a, 292, 304, 314, 333, 335, 338, 339

Ha'azinu
38, 39, 44, 45, 57, 59, 102, 117, 127, 128, 139, 142, 163, 168, 172, 174, 177, 194, 205

Idra Raba
33, 41, 88, 97, 98, 105, 132, 137, 155, 196, 197, 220-222, 227, 228, 240, 245, 246, 275, 276, 277, 307, 308, 313, 317, 341

Ki Tetze
17, 27, 47, 54, 55, 80, 82, 85, 86, 88, 89, 118, 120

Ki Tisa
25, 50, 58

Korach
31, 46, 55

Lech Lecha
107, 171, 251, 254, 325, 353, 354, 427

Matot
1, 2, 3

Metzora
35, 53-55

Miketz
32, 33, 125, 231

Mishpatim
133, 230, 231, 277, 278, 281, 286, 456, 477, 515, 519, 522, 548

Naso
21, 26, 27, 64, 90, 138, 162, 164, 170, 191

Noach
67, 100, 104, 112-114, 164, 180 -184, 188, 216, 219, 337

Pekudei
9, 11, 41, 43, 50, 60, 61, 118,

123, 124, 231, 335, 574, 645, 724, 806, 807

Pinchas
52, 68, 190, 203, 204, 206, 243, 255, 285, 286, 326, 333, 337, 344, 352, 357, 358, 367, 369, 386, 387, 394, 396, 402, 408, 428, 434, 505, 599, 615, 634, 646, 672, 673, 674, 688, 689, 697, 758, 820, 850, 858-860, 882

Prologue
1, 15, 118, 176, 177, 233, 235, 236

Safra Detzniuta
8, 18, 54, 60

Shemot
44, 47, 256, 342, 361, 384

Shmini
11, 25, 42, 43, 44, 57, 76, 82, 88, 89, 96

Shoftim
15

Tazria
20, 46, 94, 118, 122, 129, 131, 137, 164

Tetzaveh
92, 95, 120, 143

Toldot
47, 48

Trumah
86, 99, 110, 123, 230-232, 284, 287, 295, 331, 332, 382, 399, 409, 460, 466, 483, 484, 547, 603, 714, 716, 777, 784, 856, 913, 918-920

Tzav
92, 94, 137, 159

Vaera
11, 90, 113, 114, 115

Vaetchanan
24, 39, 48, 52, 53, 176, 177

Vayakhel
132, 155, 224, 225, 449

Vayechi
7, 13, 14, 15, 26, 57, 59, 60, 61, 89, 236, 239, 242, 315, 319, 320, 325-328, 330, 331, 332, 469, 631, 660, 778, 781

Vayelech
11

Vayera
124, 125, 128, 173, 203, 205-207, 218, 219, 255, 256, 260, 264, 312, 313, 361, 379, 382, 383, 384, 385, 386, 387, 473, 485, 486, 502

Vayeshev
25, 46, 86, 147, 148, 266

Vayetze
38, 80, 81, 83, 84, 260, 315, 345

Vayigash
133

Vayikra
51-53, 111, 156, 159, 160, 174, 195, 198, 199, 223, 234, 236, 237, 239, 244, 247-250, 260, 261, 280, 331, 338, 339, 343, 371, 380, 382, 421, 447

Vayishlach
45, 169, 183

Yitro
147, 261, 279, 281, 282, 286, 287, 292, 387, 477, 501-503, 512, 518, 537

MERIT

Acharei Mot
2, 13, 17, 19, 96, 97, 133, 144, 207, 219, 225-228, 291-293, 353, 356, 396, 411, 412
Balak
46, 60, 61, 179, 220, 225, 293, 352, 367
Bechukotai
28, 61
Beha'alot'cha
5, 142, 144, 146
Behar
13, 59, 61
Beresheet A
153, 186, 260, 283, 324
Beresheet B
7, 10, 15, 21, 56, 93, 102, 105, 118, 169, 176, 177, 199, 231, 296, 345, 398, 404, 435
Beshalach
68, 69, 75, 144, 145, 196, 249, 295, 325, 339, 357, 451
Bo
1, 21, 23, 91, 96, 126, 138, 143, 201, 202, 211, 230
Chayei Sarah
44, 45, 49, 97, 125, 132, 138, 197, 207, 210, 218, 219
Chukat
50, 57, 58, 62, 68
Emor
145, 164, 168, 173, 260a, 260b, 261, 263, 282a
Ha'azinu
47, 79, 117, 132, 211
Idra Raba
54, 55, 58, 126, 186, 329
Ki Tetze
4, 18, 51, 54, 56, 105
Ki Tisa
41, 120
Lech Lecha
61, 82, 83, 94, 95, 111, 132, 177, 253, 281, 282, 284, 286, 313, 317, 404, 411, 468
Metzora
9
Miketz
13, 14, 15, 39, 69, 74-77, 226, 254
Mishpatim
11, 12, 13, 59, 76, 77, 89, 112, 117, 216, 221, 222, 281, 392, 483, 548, 569, 575
Naso
41, 47, 57, 137, 147, 167
Noach
1, 38, 63, 117, 146, 174, 179, 187, 228, 232
Pekudei
32, 381, 400, 483, 484, 524, 546, 551, 563, 567, 593-597, 603, 630, 631, 641, 712, 716, 721-726, 746, 792, 848, 849, 883, 884
Pinchas
14, 55, 64, 108, 177, 484, 578, 579, 592, 767
Prologue
49, 110
Safra Detzniuta
67
Shemot
3, 32, 33, 35, 69, 71, 72, 97, 130, 133, 136, 171, 203, 205, 206, 233, 290, 330, 339

Shlach Lecha
52, 57, 63-66, 93, 187, 201, 214, 254, 307, 308, 322
Shmini
43
Tazria
5, 8, 22, 24, 109, 181, 182
Toldot
41, 69, 73, 119, 148, 196
Trumah
35, 37, 39, 41, 50, 51, 58, 79, 173, 182, 259, 306, 307, 311, 404, 421, 424, 468, 473, 492, 509, 512, 513, 529, 535, 567, 588, 663, 672, 679, 729, 730, 767, 799, 801, 815, 816, 913
Tzav
93, 135
Vaera
19, 28, 148, 203
Vaetchanan
51, 105, 129, 184, 198
Vayakhel
63, 439
Vayechi
37, 41, 161, 162, 163, 180, 227, 240, 255, 257, 297, 302, 304, 331, 363, 474, 478, 500, 505, 511, 512, 638, 725, 823
Vayelech
2, 31
Vayera
75, 169, 170, 172, 185, 239, 294, 426, 427, 429
Vayeshev
10, 12, 27, 34, 36, 88, 126, 132, 186, 188, 221, 285
Vayetze
15, 99, 138, 204, 366, 367, 370
Vayigash
17, 18, 55, 63
Vayikra
203, 353, 425, 437, 445
Vayishlach
44, 50, 58, 68, 116, 187, 216, 244
Yitro
152, 263, 264, 289, 346, 351, 397, 423, 425, 477

MERODACH BALADAN

Miketz
205

MESOPOTAMIA

Balak
136, 154

Pinchas
383, 491

MESSIAH, THE

Acharei Mot
32, 211-214
Balak
179, 219, 262, 340, 341, 342, 343, 384, 404, 501, 504, 505
Beha'alot'cha
91, 92
Beresheet A
234, 245, 262, 283
Beresheet B
15-19
Beshalach
218, 220, 226, 289, 290, 294, 311, 312, 459

Chayei Sarah
31
Ha'azinu
55
Idra Raba
64-66, 68, 121
Kedoshim
50
Ki Tetze
4, 21, 48, 56, 62, 77
Lech Lecha
135, 172, 399
Mishpatim
387, 399, 475, 477-479, 481, 483-485, 487
Naso
29, 95, 100
Noach
290, 291, 319
Pekudei
299, 639, 757
Pinchas
183, 271, 455, 487, 546, 565, 567, 573, 582, 651, 652, 745, 747
Prologue
57-60, 88, 119
Shemot
96, 99-104, 106-111, 117 -119, 121-124, 127-132, 136, 150
Shlach Lecha
45, 136, 141, 142, 144, 146, 147-150, 165, 174, 191, 193, 214, 288, 289, 298
Toldot
64, 65, 145, 146, 148, 149, 152, 154, 186
Trumah
25, 98, 383, 859, 860
Tzav
172
Vaetchanan
14, 189
Vayakhel
334, 335, 336, 337, 371, 432, 455, 493
Vayechi
1, 35, 36, 38, 45, 61, 71, 73, 92, 548, 551, 576, 587-590, 630, 631
Vayera
158, 200, 254, 297, 307, 310, 311, 377, 460, 478, 480
Vayeshev
191, 194, 274
Vayikra
268, 385, 388
Yitro
23, 175, 212, 297, 299

METATRON

Acharei Mot
52, 56, 71, 72, 76, 153
Balak
25, 54-56, 86, 90, 132, 233
Beresheet A
133, 200, 256, 257, 262, 263, 272, 273
Beresheet B
309
Beshalach
139, 461, 462, 464, 480, 484
Bo
203
Chayei Sarah
12, 66, 67, 155-157, 159, 161, 163, 165, 174, 178
Chukat
29

Emor
113, 186
Kedoshim
51, 55, 56
Ki Tetze
4, 5, 26, 27, 31, 45, 48, 49, 50, 51, 75, 100, 101, 137-139
Ki Tisa
119
Korach
60
Lech Lecha
313, 361, 449, 450, 451
Mishpatim
2, 5, 9, 10, 383, 391, 415
Naso
35
Pekudei
500
Pinchas
36, 39, 41, 80, 85, 103, 198, 199, 200, 201, 221, 228, 248, 250, 251, 257-260, 263-266, 283, 284, 286, 293, 297, 316, 318, 343, 344, 584, 587, 771, 808, 874
Prologue
55, 56, 59
Safra Detzniuta
69
Shlach Lecha
34, 116, 121, 142, 244, 246, 264, 294
Toldot
144
Trumah
84, 85, 90, 297, 314, 596 -598, 689, 800, 922
Tzav
58, 64, 67
Vaera
103
Vayakhel
281
Vayechi
52, 54, 56, 284, 285, 397, 398, 467, 572
Vayera
192
Vayeshev
7, 48, 49, 54, 64, 65
Vayetze
71-74, 105

METHUSELAH

Beresheet B
382

MEZAHAB

Idra Raba
180, 317

MEZUZAH

Ki Tetze
137
Pinchas
295, 732, 851, 873, 876
Vaetchanan
72-77, 98, 99, 105, 109, 117 -119, 132, 134
Vayechi
603

MI (WHO)

Balak
8, 18, 327
Beresheet A
30, 313-315

Lech Lecha
212, 213, 215
Mishpatim
202-206
Pekudei
105
Prologue
7, 8, 9, 10, 12, 14-21, 48
Trumah
2, 219, 250, 251
Vayakhel
50

MICHAEL (ANGEL)

Balak
90
Beha'alot'cha
74, 101, 102
Bemidbar
27, 29, 31
Beresheet A
70, 82, 191, 249
Beresheet B
51, 59, 166
Beshalach
157
Bo
201, 203-205, 212
Chayei Sarah
150
Ekev
27, 67
Korach
60
Lech Lecha
93, 102
Metzora
12
Mishpatim
87, 371
Naso
9, 10, 85, 138, 194
Pekudei
162, 163, 199, 357, 524, 655-657, 660, 664, 665, 780
Pinchas
70, 188, 223, 228, 257, 259, 270, 320, 421, 745
Shemot
258
Shlach Lecha
88, 307
Toldot
140
Trumah
233, 234, 241, 385, 387, 389, 598
Tzav
8, 9, 84, 138, 143
Vayakhel
51, 53, 260, 295, 297, 323, 326, 339
Vayechi
50, 546
Vayera
49, 53, 54, 70, 72, 171, 275
Vayetze
73
Vayikra
9, 11, 12, 14, 17, 20
Yitro
10, 235

MIDIANITES

Balak
284, 285
Naso
16
Pinchas
157, 233

MIDNIGHT

Acharei Mot
148, 149, 152, 153, 206, 210
Balak
155
Bechukotai
19, 34
Beha'alot'cha
7
Behar
3
Beresheet B
48, 49
Beshalach
28, 45, 49, 274
Bo 93,
98, 99, 101, 105-107, 109, 113-115
Chayei Sarah
242, 243
Emor
31, 130, 312
Kedoshim
18
Ki Tisa
61
Lech Lecha
5, 9, 130, 132, 134, 363, 366, 368, 369, 370, 371, 373-377
Metzora
33
Mishpatim
138
Naso
1, 4
Noach
273
Pinchas
4, 12, 84, 141, 579, 696
Prologue
171
Shlach Lecha
5, 182, 201, 267
Tazria
40, 139
Toldot
14
Trumah
73, 84, 175, 181, 182, 312, 725, 837, 876, 878, 879
Vaera
100, 159, 161
Vaetchanan
4, 8, 98, 155
Vayakhel
14, 19, 195, 282, 338
Vayechi
137, 166, 441, 460, 463, 466, 487, 683, 693
Vayelech
17, 18
Vayera
63
Vayigash
34, 35, 38, 39, 40, 46, 47, 48
Vayikra
163, 200-202, 366, 369, 372, 374, 395, 396, 398, 399, 406, 435
Vayishlach
257, 267, 268

MIDYAN

Balak
16, 27, 60, 61, 62, 93, 94, 96, 97, 161, 173, 221-223, 267, 282, 284 -286, 398, 500

Bechukotai
8
Shemot
209, 232, 358, 371, 377
Yitro
1, 22, 26

MILCAH

Chayei Sarah
177

MILK

Beresheet B
113
Ha'azinu
51
Idra Raba
206
Mishpatim
523, 556, 562, 564, 565, 566, 568, 569
Pekudei
642
Pinchas
161, 162, 348, 349, 423, 544, 552, 553, 594, 596, 616, 639
Safra Detzniuta
28
Shemot
130
Shlach Lecha
35, 63, 78, 79, 258, 265
Trumah
35
Vayechi
624, 632, 796
Vayera
115
Vayetze
369
Vayikra
26, 29, 33, 34, 288

MINCHAH

Acharei Mot
147
Beresheet A
141
Beshalach
404
Bo
93
Chayei Sarah
226
Ha'azinu
45, 47, 133
Idra Raba
35
Ki Tetze
45
Ki Tisa
61
Pekudei
302, 546
Pinchas
207
Shemot
383, 384, 387, 388
Toldot
106
Trumah
547, 548
Vaera
161
Vaetchanan
84
Vayakhel
234, 236, 237

Vayechi
421, 422, 715
Vayeshev
76
Vayigash
98
Yitro
463

MIRACLE

Acharei Mot
52, 143
Balak
97, 186, 232, 294, 295, 302, 304, 308, 312, 357, 362, 364, 368
Beha'alot'cha
21, 49
Behar
60, 61
Beshalach
17, 94, 201, 206, 215, 218, 239, 340, 424, 425, 430
Bo
101, 125, 129, 180-182
Emor
329
Ha'azinu
3
Idra Raba
360
Kedoshim
83
Ki Tisa
34, 37, 60
Lech Lecha
117
Metzora
62
Miketz
187, 189
Naso
66
Noach
324, 327, 332, 357
Pekudei
182, 193, 194, 371, 372, 404, 610, 930
Pinchas
158, 161
Prologue
110, 114
Shemot
91, 106, 132, 133, 150
Shlach Lecha
151, 348
Shoftim
10
Trumah
263, 343, 424, 632, 780, 884, 900
Tzav
163
Vaera
57, 125
Vayakhel
48, 49, 69, 70, 429
Vayechi
63, 396, 424, 428, 449, 607
Vayera
343, 344, 362, 370-373
Vayeshev
132, 207, 259
Vayetze
218, 221
Vayigash
83
Vayikra
144, 350, 352, 355

Vayishlach
49, 158, 160
Yitro
27, 31, 41, 47, 209, 374

MIRIAM

Balak
392
Chayei Sarah
13, 63, 68, 224
Chukat
35, 36, 37, 38, 39, 40, 67
Emor
260a, 261
Ki Tisa
47, 49
Mishpatim
363
Shemot
333-335, 338
Shlach Lecha
116, 199
Trumah
461, 462
Vayelech
2

MIRROR

Acharei Mot
315, 345
Balak
48, 52, 110, 248
Beresheet A
193, 394
Beresheet B
20, 153, 203, 213, 291, 293
Beshalach
55
Chayei Sarah
45
Ki Tetze
89, 90, 94
Ki Tisa
108
Lech Lecha
271, 288, 335, 338, 339, 340, 341
Miketz
62
Noach
142, 143, 145
Pekudei
16, 17, 19, 135, 162, 170, 184, 185, 236, 268, 348, 394, 478, 919, 920
Pinchas
173, 174
Shemot
33
Trumah
61, 252, 259, 260, 551, 840
Tzav
37
Vaera
26, 28, 29, 75
Vaetchanan
20, 31, 164, 165
Vayakhel
448
Vayechi
2, 461, 462, 471, 590, 829
Vayera
24, 47, 48, 59, 499, 500
Vayeshev
83
Vayetze
17, 51, 259
Vayishlach
51, 105, 129

Yitro
66, 313, 322, 323, 328, 329, 558

MISARSANIYAH (SPIRIT)

Pekudei
703

MISHAEL

Acharei Mot
14-18
Mishpatim
569
Noach
357
Toldot
123

MISHNAH

Balak
246, 385
Beresheet A
189, 261, 471
Chayei Sarah
9, 94, 140, 141, 143, 152, 170, 185, 188, 191, 197
Ekev
19, 21, 25, 29, 32, 38, 41, 48, 50, 57
Emor
185, 186
Ki Tetze
4, 6, 7, 12, 32, 33, 47, 48, 49, 52, 54, 58, 59, 60, 61, 63, 66, 67, 75, 76, 81, 100, 101, 116, 133
Korach
47, 49, 55, 60
Lech Lecha
380, 381, 448, 458
Mishpatim
385, 386, 391, 402, 406, 411, 413, 420, 438, 446, 448, 457, 461, 477, 487, 493, 569
Naso
12, 95
Pekudei
525, 731, 732, 734, 735, 818
Pinchas
51, 52, 57, 180, 181, 197, 247, 250, 282, 321, 332, 367, 376, 408, 413, 414, 434, 451, 452, 478, 487, 492, 494-496, 500, 503, 562, 563, 581, 593, 597, 602, 604, 606-608, 622, 626, 635, 663, 686, 703, 751, 759, 763, 764, 773, 787, 788, 790, 791, 803, 809, 819, 832, 847, 872
Shlach Lecha
99, 335
Shmini
118, 119
Shoftim
11, 12, 15, 20
Toldot
41, 48, 53, 57, 58, 64, 68
Vaetchanan
191
Vayechi
36, 285, 301
Vayelech
25, 32, 41
Vayera
66
Vayetze
176

MOAB

Balak
4, 9, 13, 16, 27, 60, 61, 62, 64,

65, 67, 93, 94, 96, 98, 99, 101, 223, 252, 253, 255, 265, 267, 282, 284, 285, 286, 287, 292, 336, 338, 372, 422, 425

Ha'azinu
132

Miketz
123

Prologue
94, 95, 230

Vayera
297, 309, 334, 335, 336

MOCHIN

Acharei Mot
76, 77, 101, 102, 159, 160, 166, 169, 226, 244

Balak
124, 159

Beha'alot'cha
3, 73, 92

Behar
8, 17

Bemidbar
18

Beresheet A
30, 38, 63, 66, 67, 73-75, 78, 217, 221, 238, 239, 243, 244, 248, 256, 296, 297, 298, 299, 300, 304-306, 311, 319, 327, 329, 333, 334, 336, 337, 342, 354, 355, 358, 360, 361, 362, 366, 367, 373, 374, 377, 378, 380, 381, 383, 384, 387, 393, 399, 414, 423, 426, 436, 439, 469

Beresheet B
2, 29, 163, 164, 180, 202, 211, 233, 244, 289, 419

Beshalach
205, 225, 317, 349, 411

Bo
108, 126, 147, 170, 232, 235

Chayei Sarah
2, 14, 23, 65

Chukat
74

Emor
11, 40, 100, 102, 127, 128, 133, 134, 152-154, 169, 218, 255

Ha'azinu
41, 88, 210

Idra Raba
135, 150, 261, 262, 263, 271, 298, 302, 303, 308, 320, 321

Kedoshim
20, 35, 95

Ki Tetze
139, 140, 143, 144

Ki Tisa
6

Lech Lecha
8, 10, 12, 73, 107, 112, 214, 239, 240, 310, 311, 312, 366, 367, 375, 447, 460

Metzora
36, 41

Mishpatim
3, 77, 129, 137, 379, 402, 435, 553

Naso
28

Noach
18, 19, 25, 47, 65, 84, 101, 250, 300, 302, 303, 310, 333

Pekudei
23, 27, 49, 81, 102, 103, 172, 222, 245, 264, 271, 775, 796, 801, 804, 881

Pinchas
243, 272, 336, 365, 370, 383, 455, 484, 510, 566, 591, 670, 712-714, 789, 811, 871-873, 875, 876
Safra Detzniuta
53, 72
Shemot
15, 46, 68, 137, 176, 212, 240, 258, 328, 329, 363
Shlach Lecha
156
Shmini
117
Tazria
3, 8, 68, 93
Tetzaveh
26, 63, 69, 92, 134, 142
Toldot
115, 136, 169
Trumah
2, 4, 12, 17, 125, 132, 133, 134, 139, 184, 241, 355, 360, 368, 407, 529, 654, 689, 690, 798
Tzav
167
Vaera
61
Vaetchanan
28, 37, 38, 49, 55, 58, 96, 97, 174
Vayakhel
100, 101, 183, 362, 397, 432
Vayechi
5, 37, 98, 119, 180, 217, 237, 334, 447, 456, 461, 476, 477, 542, 560, 577, 614, 656, 661, 662, 705, 827
Vayera
13, 278, 382, 498
Vayeshev
107, 275
Vayetze
6, 7, 15, 82, 120, 190, 206, 232, 392
Vayigash
12
Vayikra
44, 149, 156, 165, 170, 305, 337, 448
Yitro
125, 418, 488, 525, 526, 546

MOON

Acharei Mot
89, 91, 145, 196, 263, 366, 406, 408, 409
Balak
6
Bechukotai
22, 29, 36, 39
Beha'alot'cha
4, 57, 70, 139, 148
Behar
29
Bemidbar
9
Beresheet A
37, 39, 101, 103, 110, 113, 126, 128, 153, 154, 155, 277, 281, 390, 396, 401-404, 478, 479
Beresheet B
57, 65, 69, 161-164, 211, 296, 297, 302, 303, 306- 309, 397
Beshalach
160
Bo
158-160, 169-171, 174, 175, 187
Chayei Sarah
30, 67, 167, 205, 206

Chukat
34, 38, 39, 40, 41, 42, 44, 46, 59, 87
Ekev
16, 44
Emor
132, 134, 139, 151, 180, 181, 187, 190, 205, 206, 209, 224, 257
Ha'azinu
14, 15, 17, 204
Idra Raba
362, 363
Kedoshim
45, 46, 63
Ki Tetze
32, 84, 112-114, 118, 120
Ki Tisa
6, 110, 111, 115-119
Korach
41
Lech Lecha
114, 223, 224, 361, 384
Metzora
60
Miketz
73, 80, 112, 113, 134
Mishpatim
573
Naso
13, 14, 55, 196
Noach
35, 66, 101-106, 108, 129, 149, 169, 245, 247, 251, 319, 361, 362, 364, 365
Pekudei
27, 222, 224, 234, 235, 279, 281, 336, 348, 378, 503, 549, 550, 579, 734, 757, 812, 871, 920, 924, 940, 953
Pinchas
126, 136, 139, 236, 360, 444, 671, 674, 675, 676, 677, 678, 679, 683, 684, 686, 687, 688, 689, 690, 706, 717, 720, 737, 739, 777
Prologue
104, 139, 164
Shemot
1, 14, 107, 155, 174, 191
Shlach Lecha
8, 31, 53, 54, 112, 124, 142, 205, 311
Shmini
50, 90
Shoftim
14, 15
Tazria
16, 62, 76, 77, 78
Tetzaveh
2, 3, 31, 32, 34, 38, 40, 83, 88, 90-92, 116, 118, 122, 124
Toldot
6, 10, 12, 13, 25, 27, 31, 128, 168, 196
Trumah
2, 3, 107, 168, 171, 200, 203, 205, 209, 212, 221, 294, 301, 304, 313, 333, 347, 355, 361, 362, 381, 551, 581, 753, 843, 859
Tzav
48
Vaera
130, 134, 135
Vaetchanan
15
Vayakhel
10, 13, 78, 200, 221, 333,

396-400, 402, 489
Vayechi
208, 276, 281, 286, 288, 289, 290, 310, 311, 335, 359, 502, 540, 564-566, 574, 589, 590, 597, 614, 615, 619, 673, 702, 781, 793, 807, 808, 813, 829, 830-834, 840, 841
Vayelech
4, 5, 6, 12, 14
Vayera
40, 384, 385, 405, 406
Vayeshev
6, 21, 22, 32, 38, 39, 40, 42, 44, 45, 47, 48, 55, 63, 68, 152, 272, 275
Vayetze
16, 55, 57, 58, 128, 346, 354, 385
Vayigash
108, 130
Vayikra
132, 184, 354
Vayishlach
12, 57, 64, 75, 80, 90, 93, 94, 163
Yitro
212, 225, 379, 380, 381, 382, 383, 384, 402, 505

MORDECAI

Ki Tetze
7
Shlach Lecha
230, 231

MOREH

Lech Lecha
68, 80

MORNING

Acharei Mot
146, 148-150, 153-156, 217, 344
Balak
59, 215, 294, 350, 351, 352, 354, 356, 407, 476
Bechukotai
53
Beha'alot'cha
28, 92
Behar
4, 34
Bemidbar
44, 57, 58, 67, 73
Beresheet A
95, 126, 127, 191, 242, 356, 363, 450
Beresheet B
41, 46, 49, 61, 151, 152
Beshalach
6, 47, 48, 51, 53, 58, 112, 274, 391, 404, 405, 412, 413
Bo
81, 84, 134
Chayei Sarah
238, 239, 243, 244, 246
Ekev
64
Emor
95, 282a
Ha'azinu
47, 233
Kedoshim
84
Ki Tetze
115
Ki Tisa
96

Korach
12, 48
Lech Lecha
223, 224, 362, 378, 399, 416, 446, 450, 476
Metzora
7, 8, 45, 46, 51
Miketz
27, 33, 117, 124, 225-230, 232, 237
Mishpatim
15, 296, 297, 393, 405, 407, 428, 473, 475, 476, 480, 484, 518
Naso
5
Noach
81, 282
Pekudei
90, 113, 392, 523, 626, 923
Pinchas
58, 207, 229, 240, 244, 246, 255, 285, 336, 345, 384, 387, 444, 498, 517, 560, 564, 566, 567, 580-582, 657, 692-696, 795, 835, 850, 855
Prologue
125, 127, 171, 183
Shemot
79, 159-161, 279, 324, 384-387
Shlach Lecha
1, 7, 181, 184, 192, 270, 297, 335, 336, 338
Shmini
1, 8, 9
Tazria
55
Tetzaveh
52
Toldot
165, 166, 198
Trumah
61, 74, 77, 78, 85, 86, 90, 91, 121, 231, 232, 247, 248, 683, 684, 764, 815-817, 893, 908
Tzav
23, 25, 47, 76, 126, 152, 153, 193
Vaera
2, 100, 159, 160, 161
Vaetchanan
5, 6, 8, 84, 89, 98
Vayakhel
24, 124, 234, 238, 255, 256, 266, 373, 475
Vayechi
57, 65, 208, 358, 377, 414, 415, 417, 418, 419, 452, 453, 464, 487, 715, 789, 790, 791, 794, 795
Vayera
101, 197, 217, 257, 311, 318
Vayeshev
76, 117, 181, 184, 187, 200
Vayetze
126, 310, 372
Vayigash
53, 98
Vayikra
74, 165, 367, 378-383, 436
Vayishlach
83, 93, 94, 137, 256, 257, 268
Yitro
284, 288, 289, 524

MOSES

Acharei Mot
1, 11, 12, 30, 38, 39, 51, 68,

70, 97, 100, 167-169, 211, 302, 355, 391, 392
Balak
8, 10, 11, 32, 33, 34, 50-53, 60, 93, 94, 95, 96, 97, 98, 99, 101, 135, 139, 150, 162, 171, 186, 187, 191, 237, 238, 242, 247, 248, 268, 269, 270, 288, 291, 300, 376, 377, 378, 380, 386, 392, 447, 499
Bechukotai
35, 36, 37, 52
Beha'alot'cha
1, 38, 39, 42, 56, 89, 91, 94, 127, 130, 132, 136-139, 145-150
Behar
1, 74
Bemidbar
1, 8, 11
Beresheet A
45, 46, 47, 48, 49, 145, 147-150, 152-155, 157, 208, 209, 221, 222, 223, 234, 236, 237, 238, 239, 243, 248, 250, 254, 262, 263, 273-278, 281, 282, 284- 288, 290, 348, 349, 350, 457, 478, 479
Beresheet B
60, 127, 134, 255, 257, 293 -295, 299, 303, 304
Beshalach
2, 24, 29, 31, 39, 41, 42, 68, 82, 88, 91, 157, 167, 174, 180, 188, 192, 203, 206-208, 210-214, 216, 219, 221, 222, 240, 283, 298-300, 302-304, 314, 334, 343, 344, 350, 364, 403, 412, 413, 420, 423, 424, 433, 457, 458, 460, 461, 463, 465-467, 469, 473, 474, 485
Bo
1, 36-38, 109, 111, 112, 114, 116, 117, 161, 173, 186
Chayei Sarah
68, 84, 129, 195, 221
Chukat
1, 35, 37, 38-42, 62-64, 67, 69, 70b, 71, 77, 84, 85, 87, 88, 90
Ekev
29, 43, 45, 61, 64
Emor
1, 57, 260a, 262, 266, 279, 289, 318, 319, 325
Ha'azinu
1, 2, 3, 4, 5, 6, 7, 8, 19-22, 61, 174, 207, 214, 229, 239, 241, 245
Idra Raba
9, 98, 120, 125, 231, 232, 233, 278, 321, 353
Kedoshim
1, 35, 37, 45, 55, 65
Ki Tetze
14, 18, 19, 20, 31, 68, 73, 75, 77, 80, 81, 82, 87, 118, 120, 131
Ki Tisa
1, 43, 45, 46, 47, 49, 52, 53, 58 -60, 63, 65, 69, 70, 71, 74, 94, 96, 102, 103, 107, 109, 113, 116
Korach
3, 8, 9, 11, 12, 14, 20, 22, 27
Lech Lecha
395, 396, 397
Metzora
1, 22, 23, 24
Miketz
36, 43, 44

Mishpatim
96, 201, 303, 361, 363, 364, 372, 373, 376, 378, 383, 385, 386, 398, 415, 476, 480, 481, 483, 484, 528, 555, 557, 558, 559, 560, 561, 572, 574, 575
Naso
1, 16, 33, 67, 145, 164, 193, 194, 195, 196, 197
Noach
13, 14, 90, 144, 175, 179, 180, 182-187, 375
Pekudei
8, 12, 14, 15, 17, 18, 20, 23, 24, 29, 33, 34, 35, 47, 48, 69, 83, 87, 108, 163, 184, 272, 275, 283, 284, 285, 295, 296, 299, 300, 310, 338, 340, 341, 343-348, 370, 372-375, 379, 386, 388-390, 398, 399, 400, 401, 402, 404, 413 -417, 421, 422, 473, 534, 565, 651, 653, 774, 788, 874, 901, 958
Pinchas
1, 55, 60, 75, 103, 130, 131, 133, 140, 142, 165, 177, 181, 185, 194, 252, 258, 260, 291, 302, 306, 329, 342, 356, 406, 446, 470, 471, 473, 482, 490, 498, 515, 566, 574, 581, 582, 632, 643, 651, 652, 678, 792, 803, 818
Prologue
66, 99, 101, 162, 164
Safra Detzniuta
55, 71
Shemot
56, 58, 61, 120, 185, 188, 193, 194, 196, 197, 199, 200, 209, 210, 228-230, 232, 251, 318, 331, 333, 334, 338, 339, 358, 371, 373-382, 388-393, 395, 396
Shlach Lecha
1, 8, 9, 10, 12, 14, 15, 17, 30, 31, 33, 34, 35, 38, 72, 76, 82, 92, 112-116, 128, 196, 199, 298, 307, 309, 310, 313-316, 318, 320
Shmini
34, 53, 93, 94, 98
Shoftim
9, 23
Tazria
1, 109
Tetzaveh
4, 34, 35, 37, 38
Toldot
29, 41, 164
Trumah
1, 85, 209, 210, 216, 242, 243, 262, 263, 265, 314, 325, 342, 343, 345, 346, 349, 366, 367, 404, 405, 406, 407, 410, 411, 412, 413, 416, 424, 461, 462, 479, 511, 548-551, 553, 563, 564, 575, 587, 591, 596, 597, 623, 632, 633, 689, 806, 815, 887, 888, 904
Tzav
33, 36-38, 87, 98, 153, 171
Vaera
1, 9, 10, 11, 12, 17-19, 23, 24, 26, 28, 29, 51, 57, 58, 65, 67-71, 72, 82, 84, 87, 88, 90, 97, 99, 117, 128, 142, 154
Vaetchanan
9, 12-15, 20, 22, 27, 28, 30, 31,

92, 101-104, 163, 164, 165, 166, 167, 169
Vayakhel
1, 4, 5, 8, 9, 10, 11, 13, 36, 37, 42, 43, 45, 51, 69, 119, 157, 215, 217, 227, 229, 396, 402, 479, 480
Vayechi
2, 14, 35, 91, 99, 369, 386, 420, 473, 519, 520, 521, 529, 552, 555-560, 563, 611, 612, 615-620, 672-674, 724, 725, 746, 758
Vayelech
1-5, 12, 13, 14, 20, 25, 27-29, 31, 33
Vayera
48, 117, 120, 121, 123, 126, 127, 140, 219, 220, 221, 374, 390, 506
Vayeshev
16, 139
Vayetze
19, 35, 38, 89, 90, 91, 95, 97, 122, 248, 251, 252, 270, 273
Vayigash
72, 73, 76
Vayikra
1-4, 7, 8, 16, 18, 25, 26, 28, 42, 46, 47, 50, 89-91, 125, 126, 128, 167, 235, 243, 274, 286, 296, 330, 335, 337, 385, 386, 387, 427
Vayishlach
62, 64, 105, 107, 149, 150, 165
Yitro
1, 13, 18, 22, 24, 25, 39, 51, 52, 54, 55, 56, 57, 60, 172, 173, 175, 179, 181, 206, 244, 245, 249, 252, 253, 257, 258, 260, 263, 313, 320, 323, 328, 329, 348, 376, 410, 435, 464

MOUNT ARARAT

Beha'alot'cha
13, 14, 18
Noach
82
Pinchas
884

MOUNT EBAL

Vayeshev
111

MOUNT GERIZIM

Vayeshev
111

MOUNT HOR

Chukat
67
Ki Tisa
106, 109, 112
Shlach Lecha
103, 231

MOUNT HOREB

Ki Tisa
106, 109, 112
Pekudei
116
Shemot
60, 379, 388
Shlach Lecha
103, 231

MOUNT MORIAH

Shemot
292
Vayera
494
Vayikra
32

MOUNT OF OLIVES

Mishpatim
249

MOUNT SINAI

Acharei Mot
100
Balak
105, 247
Beha'alot'cha
62
Behar
1
Beresheet A
290, 312, 350, 453
Beresheet B
287, 290, 294, 298, 299, 302, 372, 374, 377, 378
Beshalach
57, 363
Chayei Sarah
83
Emor
57, 165, 324
Idra Raba
120, 353
Ki Tetze
42
Ki Tisa
74, 106, 112, 113, 115, 119
Lech Lecha
202, 249, 278, 315, 335, 421, 429
Mishpatim
359
Naso
98
Noach
88, 233, 244, 260
Pekudei
115, 313
Pinchas
291, 313, 342, 546, 758, 816, 843
Prologue
4
Shemot
16, 62, 64, 284, 388
Shlach Lecha
103
Trumah
325, 368, 370, 424, 553, 766
Vaera
64, 68, 70, 71
Vayakhel
10, 217, 223, 226
Vayechi
120, 384, 616
Vayeshev
164
Vayetze
70
Vayikra
92, 229
Yitro
243, 283, 284, 285, 286, 289, 312, 313, 318, 358, 362, 383, 384, 402, 573, 575

MOUNT ZION

Vayechi
174, 450

MOUNTAINS

Balak
8, 46, 80, 140, 165, 209, 295, 384, 421, 422, 425, 494, 497, 498
Bemidbar
19, 26
Beresheet A
19, 26, 76, 254, 302, 312, 426
Chayei Sarah
9, 71, 81, 97, 232, 264
Chukat
28, 63, 67
Ekev
29, 63
Emor
16, 52, 195, 324
Ha'azinu
180
Idra Raba
357, 362
Ki Tetze
61, 74, 79, 83
Ki Tisa
7, 37, 39, 41, 46, 63, 73
Lech Lecha
70, 264
Metzora
35
Miketz
175, 186, 224
Mishpatim
96, 289-293, 295, 302, 307, 308, 322, 335, 336, 344, 361, 489, 531
Naso
98, 99, 112, 189, 194
Noach
60, 62, 64, 82, 117, 144
Pekudei
15, 27, 61, 158, 163, 224 -226, 228, 229, 238, 265, 279, 307, 398, 399, 565, 780, 781, 782, 874, 897, 898
Pinchas
78, 147, 264, 267, 342, 378, 390, 579, 686, 696, 697, 698, 699, 884, 885, 886, 887, 894
Prologue
112, 113, 119, 156, 196
Safra Detzniuta
2, 68
Shemot
10, 14, 16, 20, 235, 253, 256, 257, 292, 306, 379-381, 388
Shlach Lecha
19, 20, 110, 111, 298, 303, 304
Shmini
50, 77, 93
Tazria
69, 152
Toldot
43, 57, 155, 204, 208
Trumah
158, 237, 238, 544, 549, 550, 551, 560, 563, 564, 565, 838, 916, 918
Vaetchanan
26, 131, 187
Vayakhel
16, 18, 45, 117, 159, 162, 227, 380
Vayera
44, 76, 91, 295, 320, 326, 339, 341, 420, 494
Vayeshev
111, 240

Vayetze
221, 234, 236
Vayigash
69, 84, 105,
Vayechi
164, 280, 282, 423, 424, 428, 487, 616, 623, 679, 680, 836
Vayishlach
130, 132, 175, 259, 263, 265, 266
Yitro
57, 58, 59, 60, 61, 245, 259, 294, 330, 343, 345, 351, 358, 439

MOZNIYA (SPIRIT)

Pekudei
617, 618

MYRIADS

Beresheet B
108
Beshalach
199
Pinchas
77, 78
Shemot
110
Tazria
26
Trumah
11, 264, 446
Vaera
85
Vayechi
465
Vayetze
258, 262
Vayishlach
136, 241

MYRRH

Balak
464
Bo
156
Ha'azinu
180
Idra Raba
287
Korach
50
Metzora
11
Mishpatim
427, 428, 531
Pekudei
653
Pinchas
348, 423, 544, 552, 576, 594, 596, 616
Shemot
292, 366
Tetzaveh
1
Trumah
398
Vayakhel
318
Vayera
494
Vayikra
26, 29, 32, 34
Vayishlach
223, 226
Yitro
362

MYRTLE

Beresheet A
57
Emor
282b
Ki Tetze
143, 144, 145
Noach
94, 97
Pinchas
822
Shemot
363
Trumah
710, 711, 796
Tzav
108, 110, 187, 188
Vayakhel
276, 277
Vayechi
211
Vayikra
420

NAAMAH

Acharei Mot
360, 361, 365
Balak
60, 61
Beresheet A
102, 466
Beresheet B
353-355, 357
Prologue
157
Vayetze
136

NABAL

Vayishlach
118

NADAB AND ABIHU

Mishpatim
577, 580
Vayetze
29

NADAB

Acharei Mot
6, 10, 11, 19-22, 24, 25, 69, 97, 98
Pinchas
11, 35d, 71-74
Shmini
36, 37, 52, 55, 61
Tzav
156
Vaera
86, 87
Vayikra 64, 65, 67

NAFTALI

Beha'alot'cha
118, 123
Mishpatim
202, 485
Pekudei
178
Vayechi
553, 759, 767

NAHSHON

Beha'alot'cha
146

NAKEDNESS

Acharei Mot
316, 317, 320, 327, 329, 336, 338, 341, 357, 369, 370, 372, 377, 379, 383, 393, 397
Balak
382
Behar
49, 63
Beresheet A
268, 269, 270, 284, 286 -289, 291, 451
Beshalach
357
Chayei Sarah
86
Idra Raba
313
Ki Tetze
47
Miketz
205, 207
Mishpatim
104, 110, 115, 116, 118, 452
Noach
74, 310
Pinchas
73
Prologue
251
Safra Detzniuta
12, 32
Shlach Lecha
189
Trumah
4, 6, 439, 923
Tzav
38
Vayakhel
270, 276
Vayechi
178, 301, 302
Vayikra
254-256
Yitro
357

NAOMI

Balak
100
Beresheet B
431
Vaetchanan
152

NATHAN

Shlach Lecha
298

NAVOT

Vayeshev
276, 277, 278, 279, 280

NAZARITES

Mishpatim
568
Naso
124, 125, 127- 132

NEBAIOTH

Vayera
411

NEBO

Ki Tetze
79

NEBUCHADNEZZAR

Beshalach
311
Miketz
27, 28, 60
Mishpatim
569
Noach
356, 357
Pekudei
131
Prologue
236
Trumah
896, 901, 902
Vayakhel
162
Vayera
368, 388

NECHO

Bechukotai
27, 28

NEFESH (SOUL)

Acharei Mot
205, 215, 216, 236, 255, 258, 259, 262-264, 267, 274
Beresheet A
94, 109, 258, 274, 405, 408, 450, 454
Beresheet B
169, 212, 378, 379
Chayei Sarah
140
Emor
58, 61, 287
Kedoshim
4, 5
Ki Tetze
51, 55, 108
Korach
17, 42, 45
Lech Lecha
47, 76-78, 96, 97, 98, 99, 100, 103, 146-160, 167, 193, 194, 205, 208-210, 245, 246, 273
Metzora
46
Mishpatim
11-13, 23, 95, 107, 108, 158, 467
Naso
36, 37, 128, 131
Noach
25, 50, 62-64
Pekudei
638
Pinchas
39, 371, 568, 569, 570, 571, 572, 607, 612, 613, 633, 670, 716, 717, 790
Prologue
216
Safra Detzniuta
38, 39, 51
Shemot
23
Shlach Lecha
221, 237, 319
Shmini
77, 104
Tazria
26, 69, 81, 84, 86, 116
Tetzaveh
53, 54
Toldot
91, 107

Trumah
268, 284, 286-293, 295-306, 458, 531, 591
Tzav
62-65, 68-71, 140, 141, 146 -148, 187-189
Vaera
48
Vaetchanan
3, 195
Vayakhel
91, 97, 113, 114, 192, 193, 270, 271, 275, 277, 278, 369, 405, 409
Vayechi
309-312, 319, 324, 325, 327, 328, 331, 343, 345 -348, 360, 361, 363
Vayera
56, 92, 267, 315-317, 322, 323, 339
Vayeshev
35, 36
Vayetze
165, 179
Vayigash
15-17, 19-22, 80, 81, 82, 84
Vayikra
185, 263, 317, 318, 422, 424 -426, 430, 432, 438-440
Yitro
60, 226, 227

NEFILIM

Beresheet A
224, 226, 228, 269, 464, 466, 467, 468
Beresheet B
423, 424
Idra Raba
345
Safra Detzniuta
63, 65
Shlach Lecha
40, 73
Vayera
418

NEGEV

Beresheet B
223
Emor
265, 266
Lech Lecha
72, 140, 143, 160, 161, 165, 168, 193
Shemot
279
Shlach Lecha
38, 59, 65, 80-82
Vaera
176

NESHAMAH (SOUL)

Acharei Mot
255, 256, 258, 261-264, 267, 274
Behar
66
Beresheet A
109, 258
Beresheet B
211, 212
Chayei Sarah
140, 141
Emor
58
Idra Raba
136, 138, 140

Kedoshim
70
Ki Tetze
108
Korach
17, 19, 42, 45
Lech Lecha
47, 48, 76-79, 96, 98, 103, 153-157, 159-161, 167, 193, 273
Mishpatim
11, 12, 23, 24, 95, 105-107, 110, 111
Naso
36
Pinchas
569, 572, 589, 607, 624, 625, 630, 635, 760, 817
Safra Detzniuta
51
Shlach Lecha
238
Tazria
81, 83-86, 116
Tetzaveh
53, 54, 55
Toldot
107
Trumah
284, 286-293, 298, 301-304, 306, 530, 591
Tzav
50, 57, 62, 64, 68-71, 140, 141, 146-148, 187
Vayakhel
184, 202, 243, 255, 270, 278, 297-300, 404-407
Vayechi
309, 311, 312, 320, 328, 331, 348, 359, 360-363
Vayera
56, 267, 315
Vayetze
189
Vayigash
15-19, 21
Vayikra
263, 318, 422-424, 430, 433 -435, 437, 438
Yitro
128

NESHIYAN (OBLIVION)

Beresheet B
36, 38

NESIRA (SPIRIT)

Pekudei
930, 931

NEST

Acharei Mot
193
Balak
212, 217, 219, 221, 361
Beresheet A
17
Beresheet B
334
Emor
70
Ha'azinu
237, 238
Ki Tetze
47, 60, 119
Lech Lecha
415
Naso
16, 59

Pinchas
53, 54, 387, 492, 494, 495, 498, 751, 787, 791
Safra Detzniuta
25, 46, 67
Shemot
99, 105, 108-111, 121, 122, 125-129
Shmini
14
Tetzaveh
70
Vayikra
125
Vayishlach
132
Yitro
279, 281, 559

NETZACH

Bo
40, 225

NIATZIRIEL (SPIRIT)

Pekudei
859

NILE

Beresheet A
350
Beshalach
42
Shemot
322
Vaera
129, 137
Vaetchanan
161
Vayechi
816
Vayera
292

NIMROD

Bo
151
Lech Lecha
37, 38
Noach
320, 321, 338
Pinchas
35c
Toldot
24, 131

NINEVEH

Naso
27

NINTH OF AV (MONTH)

Shlach Lecha
81, 273
Vayishlach
103, 104

NISHYAH (FORGETFULNESS)

Mishpatim
117

NOAH

Beha'alot'cha
88, 89
Beresheet A
70, 222, 481
Beresheet B
381, 417, 427-431, 435-437

Bo
111
Chayei Sarah
19
Idra Raba
349
Ki Tetze
55
Lech Lecha
142, 301
Noach
1, 3, 5-19, 26, 27, 30-32, 34, 38, 61, 71-75, 77, 79-81, 88, 92, 93, 113, 115, 131-133, 137, 151, 154, 156, 164, 165, 167, 174-177, 180, 181, 184, 187, 189, 190, 194, 200 -202, 212-216, 221, 224, 225, 228, 229, 232, 244, 245, 248-250, 256, 258, 259, 261, 267, 292, 293, 296, 297, 301, 302, 307, 308, 310, 311, 374
Pekudei
115, 117, 124, 311, 480, 481
Pinchas
34, 168, 170, 828, 829
Shlach Lecha
147, 150, 169, 170, 172
Tetzaveh
143
Toldot
49, 93
Trumah
364, 766
Vayakhel
39, 41
Vayechi
382, 574, 760
Vayera
5, 218, 219, 257, 396, 445
Vayeshev
72, 77, 267
Vayetze
21, 22, 278
Vayikra
230, 236-238, 283

NOD

Beresheet B
343-345
Vayishlach
261

NOGAH (SPIRIT)

Ha'azinu
14
Pekudei
122, 158, 159, 160, 238, 556

NORTH

Acharei Mot
76, 149
Balak
434
Beha'alot'cha
2, 4, 7, 108, 118, 125
Behar
3, 40
Bemidbar
29-31, 33, 35-37, 53, 56, 58, 59, 63-65
Beresheet A
81, 89, 249, 302, 413
Beresheet B
51, 71, 81, 82, 90, 207
Beshalach
100, 137, 274
Chukat
45, 46, 67

Ekev
31, 37, 49, 50, 66
Emor
39
Idra Raba
210
Lech Lecha
7, 9, 162, 363
Metzora
7
Noach
66, 101, 263, 265
Pekudei
38, 141, 142, 178, 351, 502, 511, 512, 531, 537, 553, 585, 658, 659, 680, 684, 686, 689, 694, 814
Pinchas
204, 268, 319, 582, 634, 686, 705, 708, 713, 714, 798, 821, 847
Shemot
113
Shlach Lecha
4, 271, 301, 302, 303
Tazria
40
Tetzaveh
8
Toldot
12, 15
Trumah
22, 65, 66, 73, 82, 157, 277, 278, 519, 521, 610, 612, 615, 683, 709, 876
Tzav
2, 77, 132
Vaera
35-38, 40-42, 95, 109, 157, 158, 159
Vaetchanan
4, 191, 193
Vayakhel
12, 21, 159, 162, 163, 293, 342, 348, 353, 354, 358
Vayechi
118, 136, 162, 166, 461, 463, 464, 466, 509, 533, 553, 569, 652, 653, 683, 694, 711, 768, 777, 847
Vayera
461, 478, 512
Vayeshev
155, 158
Vayetze
2, 11, 31, 32, 81, 84, 92, 93, 116, 168, 170, 264, 306
Vayigash
32
Vayikra
53, 163, 369, 395, 435
Vayishlach
136
Yitro
16, 17, 307, 516

NOSE

Behar
31, 42
Beresheet A
240
Chayei Sarah
178
Emor
46
Ha'azinu
55, 56, 57, 147, 148a, 148b, 149, 150, 157, 160, 162
Idra Raba
62-64, 66-71, 76, 78, 126, 134,

204, 223-226, 230, 233 -235, 238, 239, 253, 283, 286
Mishpatim
524
Naso
52
Noach
234, 235, 238
Pinchas
203, 204, 301, 309, 325, 329, 428, 559
Safra Detzniuta
6, 16, 21, 29, 34, 61
Shemot
302
Vaetchanan
43
Vayechi
67
Yitro
105, 180, 186, 196, 200, 202, 203, 218

NUKVA

Acharei Mot
102, 161, 328
Beha'alot'cha
37
Beresheet B
28, 29, 33, 35, 134, 135, 151, 159, 164, 169, 172, 175, 179 -181, 184, 200, 202-204, 206 -208, 210, 211, 221, 232, 233, 238, 240-246, 254, 257, 259, 261, 262, 264, 267-269, 271, 272, 300, 302-304, 306 -309, 311, 361, 366, 370, 375, 397, 405, 410, 411, 420, 421
Beshalach
21, 22, 24, 28, 53, 98, 99, 110, 137, 238, 275
Bo
35, 105
Chayei Sarah
1, 2, 7, 10, 15, 30, 65, 67, 193, 205, 224, 230, 231, 234-236, 241, 242, 246, 252- 256
Chukat
2
Ekev
45
Emor
314
Ha'azinu
84, 150, 180, 184, 187, 188
Lech Lecha
4, 7, 12-15, 19, 20, 25, 33, 43, 70, 74, 75, 78, 99, 101, 103, 107, 127-129, 151, 152, 164-169, 172, 173, 179, 183, 194, 232, 233, 236, 240-243, 246, 251, 254, 255, 257, 271, 272, 274, 277, 304, 308, 310, 312, 319, 322, 323, 325, 337-342, 373, 374, 375, 403, 445, 446, 449, 451, 462
Metzora
12
Miketz
2, 10, 11, 17, 18, 20, 26, 32, 40, 52, 53, 62, 72, 73, 77, 78, 79, 80, 86, 87, 88, 108, 110, 112, 113, 134, 136, 140, 141, 162, 211, 218, 228, 250-252, 254-258, 268
Mishpatim
130, 137, 181, 182, 183, 184,

219, 323, 414, 457, 496, 531, 536, 537

Noach
16-18, 22, 23, 26, 27, 62, 67, 85, 98-104, 106, 107, 112, 113, 116, 128, 129, 134, 143, 145, 149, 170, 172, 173, 231, 232, 241, 243, 245, 249, 250, 259, 283, 284, 297, 300-302, 319, 326, 332-334, 362, 379, 380

Pinchas
517

Prologue
10, 42

Safra Detzniuta
4, 13, 20, 21, 26, 38, 43, 46, 48, 52, 57, 67

Shemot
1, 20, 39, 80, 81, 139, 149-151, 154, 155, 158, 161-166, 174-176, 192, 200, 201, 228, 265, 324, 329, 332, 391

Shmini
66, 93

Tazria
25, 30, 40

Tetzaveh
2-5, 34

Toldot
6, 10-13, 15, 18, 25, 27, 29, 31, 32, 103-106, 112, 116-118, 121, 128, 135, 136, 144, 168, 182, 184, 185, 204

Trumah
42, 341, 342, 519, 520, 521, 666, 758, 759

Tzav
27, 102, 189

Vaera
5, 17, 49, 56, 75, 76, 103, 149

Vaetchanan
28

Vayakhel
235, 255, 256, 419, 428

Vayechi
13, 43, 96, 106, 108, 118, 119, 132, 135, 138, 139, 151, 174, 175, 176, 181, 183, 219, 220, 222, 224, 226, 233, 234, 238, 240, 276, 277, 281, 284-286, 289, 290, 291, 307 -309, 314, 335, 348, 351, 379, 380, 394, 395, 397, 408, 416, 435, 436, 437, 438, 440, 444, 445, 448, 458, 459, 463, 464, 469, 470 -472, 475-477, 480, 481, 486, 490, 491, 509, 510, 540, 543, 546, 568, 570-575, 586, 588, 589, 590, 591, 594, 596, 597, 599, 600, 604, 612, 614-619, 622, 630-636, 640, 641, 647, 648, 650-652, 654, 655, 656, 658-660, 667-669, 674, 676-680, 689, 693, 697, 698, 708, 711, 715, 716, 727, 730, 731, 742-745, 748, 750 -757, 759, 761, 762, 764, 765, 767, 770, 773-777, 779, 781, 785, 787, 791, 792, 793, 794, 797-800, 805 -813, 819, 826-829, 832-835, 838-840

Vayelech
41

Vayera
7-16, 20, 50-53, 63, 64, 69, 70, 92, 98, 175, 267, 268, 270, 278, 279, 281, 284, 300, 302, 332, 354, 355, 356, 361, 423, 425,

427, 438-441, 444, 445, 447 -451, 453, 492, 513

Vayeshev
20-22, 32, 33-35, 37, 39, 40, 42-48, 54, 55, 62, 68, 69, 83, 85, 100, 106, 145, 146, 148, 152, 159, 200, 202, 246, 256, 263, 266, 272, 275, 282

Vayetze
1-5, 7-12, 16, 18, 19, 23, 30 -33, 35, 42, 45-47, 50, 51, 52, 55, 57, 59, 60, 62, 67, 70, 76, 79, 80, 81, 82-85, 87, 90-100, 105, 106, 115, 119, 120, 128, 130, 133, 134, 139, 148, 150, 158, 161, 163, 165, 168, 173, 177, 191, 193, 195, 201, 202, 203, 204, 207, 209, 211, 212, 224, 225, 226, 230, 231, 241, 242, 254, 260, 266-271, 274, 282, 291, 292, 306, 311, 319, 320, 324, 327 -330, 334, 335, 339, 340, 345, 346, 347, 353, 354, 356, 362, 363, 365, 371, 373, 387

Vayigash
7, 8, 9, 12-15, 20, 21, 22, 27, 31, 32, 38, 42, 44, 45, 46, 49, 54, 57, 59, 60, 63, 64, 65, 66, 67, 69-71, 81, 82, 84, 90, 100 -105, 115, 119, 127-130

Vayishlach
12, 45, 57, 62, 64, 66, 71, 73, 88, 105, 129, 131-135, 137, 140, 141-143, 159, 161-163, 199, 258, 265, 270

Yitro
327, 350, 379, 400, 487, 489, 505

NUTS

Beresheet A
104

Pekudei
248, 663

Shemot
259, 260

OATH

Behar
31

Beresheet A
200, 231

Beresheet B
383

Beshalach
27, 41, 42, 327

Chayei Sarah
160, 161, 162, 174, 176

Idra Raba
284

Ki Tetze
50, 125, 126, 133

Lech Lecha
399

Miketz
37

Mishpatim
228, 258, 259, 400-407, 409, 475, 489

Naso
101, 104

Noach
353, 360, 369, 371, 384

Pekudei
895

Pinchas
34, 36, 106, 371, 490, 809 -811

Prologue
59
Vayakhel
49
Vayechi
21, 440
Vayera
396
Vayeshev
96
Vayetze
209, 383
Vayikra
213, 253
Yitro
520, 521, 523-526

OBADIAH

Balak
14, 505
Emor
70
Ki Tetze
119
Lech Lecha
262
Mishpatim
478
Pinchas
605
Toldot
154, 208
Vayakhel
130
Vayetze
238
Vayishlach
106, 130, 152, 236

OBLIVION (NESHIYAN)

Beresheet B
36, 38

OCEAN

Prologue
25, 89

OFFERING

Acharei Mot
6, 27, 69, 70, 179, 250, 410
Balak
71-74, 80, 81, 197, 202, 317, 396, 462, 463, 472, 478
Beha'alot'cha
11
Behar
1, 2, 5, 28-30, 34, 38, 40, 44 -47, 49
Beresheet A
80, 199, 458
Beresheet B
141, 264, 335-337, 437
Beshalach
467
Bo
13, 14, 31-33
Chayei Sarah
18, 77
Chukat
24, 33
Emor
49, 53, 60, 150, 159-162, 178, 179, 183, 185, 244, 288
Ha'azinu
165, 169
Idra Raba
73, 79, 80, 86, 136, 141, 143, 159, 234, 235, 250, 254, 284

Kedoshim
10, 122
Ki Tetze
45
Korach
13, 48, 49, 50, 51, 53, 55
Lech Lecha
84, 98, 298, 299, 302, 303, 305
Metzora
42
Mishpatim
21, 25, 28, 260, 261, 470
Naso
9, 15, 199
Noach
99, 121, 130, 184, 188, 228, 230-233, 240, 245, 250
Pekudei
74, 103, 131, 322, 349, 352 -356, 359, 364, 366, 367, 369, 421, 455, 464, 691, 770, 831, 850, 851, 943, 945
Pinchas
203, 205, 246, 325, 418, 419, 446, 471, 476, 532, 540, 547, 656, 667, 669, 670, 673, 674, 679, 682, 756, 760-762, 769, 796, 799, 801, 806, 826, 835, 836, 838, 850, 879 -881, 883, 888
Prologue
179, 245
Safra Detzniuta
16, 50
Shemot
364, 366-369
Shlach Lecha
23, 105, 131, 297, 335
Shmini
31-34, 38, 46-51, 83, 88
Shoftim
8
Tazria
35, 36, 106, 107, 123
Tetzaveh
40, 42-47, 72, 73, 109
Toldot
19
Trumah
1, 13, 14, 18, 19, 34, 38, 60, 63, 65, 148, 150, 151, 153-156, 161, 227, 229, 262, 263, 266, 278, 363, 366, 368, 384, 385, 386, 405
Tzav
1, 3-6, 19, 20, 26, 27, 35, 39 -42, 45, 72, 84, 121, 130 -132, 134, 143, 157, 180, 190
Vaera
31, 49
Vaetchanan
64, 65
Vayakhel
8, 52, 55, 58, 61, 63, 71-73, 98, 107, 114, 117, 471
Vayechi
76, 129, 619, 620, 621, 622, 624, 668, 715, 716, 718, 719, 723, 759, 761, 789, 797
Vayera
117, 120, 126, 385, 481, 503, 507
Vayeshev
141
Vayetze
368, 369, 371, 372, 373
Vayigash
29, 122

Vayikra
28, 50, 51, 54, 62-65, 68-70, 72 -74, 97, 98, 108-111, 117, 118, 122-124, 128-131, 134, 178, 190, 193, 195, 197-199, 280, 283, 299-301, 335, 341, 391, 403, 415, 417, 428, 429, 440, 441
Vayishlach
214, 215, 222
Yitro
405

OFFERING, DAILY

Bechukotai
9
Behar
28
Chayei Sarah
244, 245
Emor
14
Pinchas
522
Toldot
106
Tzav
55
Vaetchanan
84
Vayechi
13, 417, 715
Vayetze
368, 371, 372

OG

Balak
7, 8, 398
Chukat
86, 87, 88
Vayechi 54

OIL

Acharei Mot
34, 46, 47, 49, 87, 88
Balak
44, 59, 438
Beha'alot'cha
22, 50, 99
Behar
27, 38
Beshalach
207, 225, 354, 400, 401
Bo
111
Chayei Sarah
65
Ekev
1, 23
Emor
10-12, 14, 21, 25, 154, 290, 293
Ha'azinu
59, 165, 166, 175, 190, 220
Idra Raba
73, 87, 89, 113, 164, 249, 256, 275, 279
Korach
55
Lech Lecha
262-266, 464
Mishpatim
202, 388, 532, 535, 536
Noach
121, 284, 296
Pekudei
31, 33, 129, 454, 557, 560, 756, 914, 945

Pinchas
70, 77, 81, 247, 620, 638, 660 -664, 806, 850
Safra Detzniuta
2, 17, 72
Shlach Lecha
111
Shmini
27, 53, 54, 64, 65, 91, 92
Toldot
21
Trumah
160, 171, 241, 394, 395, 397, 398, 489, 490, 492, 508, 528, 534, 535
Tzav
85, 137, 152, 153, 162-165, 168, 184, 187
Vayakhel
55, 171, 368
Vayechi
133, 633, 758, 793, 856, 857
Vayera
19
Vayetze
26
Vayigash
45
Vayikra
103, 165, 193, 196, 197, 199, 418
Yitro
121, 400, 439

OLIVE

Ekev
22, 23, 47
Emor
290
Mishpatim
344, 345, 490
Naso
80
Pinchas
602-604, 611, 616, 617
Prologue
254
Shlach Lecha
150
Trumah
499, 539
Vayera
431, 432, 433

OMER

Balak
71, 74
Behar
29
Beshalach
403
Emor
146, 148, 150, 159, 162, 163, 174, 178, 183, 185, 186
Idra Raba
191
Pinchas
804
Shemot
257
Tetzaveh
65, 66
Trumah
191, 195, 196
Vaetchanan
44
Vayechi
126

ONAN

Mishpatim
191, 192, 197
Vayeshev
151, 154, 155

ONE (ECHAD)

Beresheet A
126, 138
Ekev
52, 55
Ki Tetze
97, 104
Mishpatim
405, 407, 436, 463
Pinchas
183, 300, 397, 453, 454, 455, 603, 646, 654, 710, 711, 754, 846, 870, 871
Prologue
204, 205
Shlach Lecha
95
Shoftim
16
Trumah
135, 629
Tzav
142, 144
Vaetchanan
64
Vayetze
315
Vayikra
100

ONIMTA

Balak
495, 497

ONKELUS

Beresheet B
12

ORAL LAW

Beha'alot'cha
85
Behar
41
Beresheet B
180
Pekudei
350, 351, 729, 738
Pinchas
57, 663, 764
Shmini
93
Vayakhel
99, 103, 215, 218
Vayechi
632, 641, 686, 781

ORIEL (LION)

Prologue
97

ORLAH

Lech Lecha
45
Mishpatim
77, 78

ORNAMENTS

Balak
151, 433, 436

Beresheet B
291, 294, 295, 298, 303, 304, 309, 310
Emor
287
Idra Raba
87
Ki Tisa
106, 109, 112, 113, 116, 119
Mishpatim
450
Noach
90, 91
Pekudei
116
Pinchas
792, 794, 871
Prologue
6, 127
Shlach Lecha
103, 231
Trumah
401, 529
Vaera
112
Vayigash
93

ORPAH

Balak
387

OTHER SIDE

Acharei Mot
41, 54, 84, 104, 126, 132, 134, 135, 138, 230, 232, 251, 252, 284, 285, 290, 293, 319, 320, 335, 406
Balak
15, 35, 38, 39, 74-78, 81, 82, 87, 125, 137, 141, 151, 208, 209, 211, 228, 257, 282, 283, 286, 370, 394, 403
Bechukotai
13, 14, 19
Beha'alot'cha
6, 67, 68
Behar
19, 48, 49
Bemidbar
14
Beresheet A
56, 57, 58, 120, 122, 123, 146, 229, 245, 260, 261, 404, 435
Beresheet B
306, 311
Beshalach
109-111, 187, 273, 437, 439
Bo
4, 12, 21, 24, 27, 28, 31-35, 188, 193, 195
Chayei Sarah
17-20, 126
Chukat
24, 26
Emor
27, 39, 54, 217
Idra Raba
303, 312, 325, 344
Kedoshim
54, 74, 112, 115, 116, 118, 119
Ki Tetze
38, 91
Ki Tisa
3, 41, 65, 69, 76, 83, 84, 88, 90, 93, 99, 101, 105, 117
Korach
45, 47

Lech Lecha
322
Metzora
15, 44
Miketz
20, 52, 135, 141, 204
Mishpatim
27, 28, 29, 30, 41, 45, 46, 47, 50, 66, 77, 78, 167, 170, 187, 220, 221, 265, 270, 271, 275, 324, 325, 327, 329, 330, 332, 337, 338, 348, 349, 351, 354, 434, 445, 449, 562, 564, 567
Naso
17
Noach
37, 118, 131, 251, 338, 348, 349, 351, 354-357, 363, 364, 380
Pekudei
20, 64, 66, 74, 75, 85, 89, 121, 203, 248, 310, 311, 320, 321, 329, 332, 335, 337, 347, 353, 363, 365, 368-370, 374, 375, 379, 387, 388, 390, 419 -424, 428, 429, 432-434, 436, 437, 445, 448, 453, 458 -460, 463 -466, 468, 469, 478, 480, 481, 484, 488, 515, 521, 540-542, 553, 565, 572, 573, 579, 580, 588, 604, 607, 610, 611, 616, 627, 632, 643, 656, 657, 658, 668, 669, 671, 674, 677, 688, 690, 691, 704, 723, 725-728, 736, 746, 826, 828-831, 836 -838, 840, 842-844, 853, 866, 869, 882, 883, 885, 886, 892, 896, 899, 900, 907, 916, 925, 952
Pinchas
93, 109, 111, 135, 137, 192, 216, 217, 219, 233, 253, 254, 298, 366, 389, 417, 421, 424, 509, 531, 581, 590, 614, 650, 677, 681, 682, 684, 685, 879, 881, 884, 886, 887, 892, 893, 895
Prologue
25, 97, 137, 203, 211, 212, 224, 227, 228, 249, 250, 251, 252
Safra Detzniuta
38
Shemot
3, 70, 73, 138, 155, 185
Shlach Lecha
62, 119, 238, 240, 244, 246, 280, 281
Shmini
37, 38, 68, 84, 111, 112, 114
Shoftim
5
Tazria
18, 141, 143, 150, 153, 173, 180
Tetzaveh
23, 24, 40, 43, 44, 45, 46, 47, 48, 52, 55, 61, 83, 88, 90-92, 95, 97, 100, 102, 108, 110, 111, 113
Toldot
27, 165
Trumah
36, 40, 41, 47, 51, 57, 58, 63, 64, 73, 84, 133, 135 -139, 141 -143, 163, 165, 167, 209, 231, 236, 277, 283, 353, 392, 463 -465, 475, 522, 525, 562, 563, 565, 566, 683, 700, 752, 773, 782, 783, 865-870, 872, 873, 876, 877

Tzav
15, 17, 21, 22, 25, 41, 127, 128
Vaetchanan
121
Vayakhel
10, 12, 20, 177, 179, 195, 200, 203, 273, 274, 359, 360, 369, 370, 377, 381, 382, 383, 386, 387, 394, 404, 406, 408, 466, 468, 470, 472
Vayechi
31, 199, 345, 378, 379, 380, 381, 382, 402-404, 410, 413, 694, 829, 852, 860
Vayera
82, 91, 267, 306, 307, 482
Vayeshev
225, 232, 237, 275
Vayetze
3, 23, 72, 100, 179, 184, 279-281, 289, 353
Vayigash
6, 39, 60, 65, 73, 75, 108, 133, 134
Vayikra
182, 197, 198, 425, 442
Vayishlach
13, 48, 109, 139, 144, 277
Yitro
8, 11, 12, 14, 27, 39, 44, 48, 50, 51, 82, 100, 102, 107, 129, 136, 241, 516

OVED

Mishpatim
175, 176, 177, 179, 180, 193
Vayeshev
193, 207

OX

Acharei Mot
76, 355
Balak
27, 28, 246, 404, 406, 491
Beha'alot'cha
53, 101, 118-121, 124
Behar
9
Bemidbar
28
Beresheet A
80, 81, 82, 83, 84, 85, 89, 121, 191
Beshalach
42, 269, 437, 440, 441
Bo
204-206
Chukat
18, 26, 29
Ekev
19, 41, 67, 69, 70
Emor
71
Ha'azinu
238
Idra Raba
172, 263
Kedoshim
118
Ki Tetze
21, 43, 62, 64, 77
Ki Tisa
56-58, 84, 85, 88, 99-101
Korach
52, 57
Lech Lecha
431
Mishpatim
196, 445, 447, 476, 479, 481, 483

Naso
11, 42, 54
Pekudei
315, 317
Pinchas
70, 260, 270, 318, 329, 407, 408, 418, 419, 424, 533, 534, 535, 536, 539, 540, 541, 543, 545, 567, 590, 597, 604, 617, 620, 647, 651, 666, 677, 745, 749, 769, 798, 857, 863, 864
Prologue
155
Safra Detzniuta
67
Shemot
67, 73, 74, 259
Shlach Lecha
118, 119, 120, 125, 275, 276
Shmini
31, 32, 33, 51
Tazria
115
Tetzaveh
138, 139, 140
Trumah
526
Tzav
47, 56, 58, 60, 68, 143
Vaera
49, 96
Vayakhel
326
Vayechi
554, 621, 622, 624, 652, 702, 757, 770
Vayera
318
Vayetze
11, 73
Vayikra
54, 218, 219, 221, 405
Vayishlach
24, 41, 145, 147, 148, 149 -151
Yitro
96, 97, 108, 111, 225, 280, 282, 327

PADAEL (ANGEL)

Beresheet B
47

PADDAN-ARAM

Toldot
16

PALANQUIN

Beresheet A
15, 16, 293, 296
Trumah
19-33, 917

PALM TREE

Beshalach
394, 439
Ha'azinu
113
Idra Raba
180, 340
Ki Tetze
145
Ki Tisa
44
Lech Lecha
125, 126
Mishpatim
576
Pinchas
281

Shemot
128
Tetzaveh
132, 133
Vayakhel
5
Vayechi
213, 219, 223, 224
Vayikra
125, 264, 265, 412-414, 420
Yitro
56

PARTZUFIM

Beresheet A
68, 373
Noach
47
Trumah
9
Vayetze
24

PASSOVER

Acharei Mot
7, 297
Behar
29
Beshalach
30
Bo
78, 80, 81, 185-187, 189, 191, 192, 194
Emor
122, 126
Mishpatim
477
Pinchas
567, 703, 721, 731, 739, 748, 828, 857, 879
Tetzaveh
48, 49
Toldot
128
Trumah
158, 162, 904
Tzav
64
Vayechi
353
Vayelech
4
Vayetze
224

PATCHIEL (SPIRIT)

Pekudei
684
Vayera
276

PATRIARCHS

Acharei Mot
183, 258, 276, 385, 411
Balak
88, 90, 334, 465
Beha'alot'cha
29, 33, 38, 40-43, 46
Bemidbar
52
Beresheet A
143, 192, 467
Beresheet B
13, 26, 414
Beshalach
27, 52, 53, 69, 75, 96, 97, 164, 168, 172, 173, 175, 198 -200, 210, 313, 314, 338

Chayei Sarah
69, 151, 245, 254
Chukat
47, 86
Ekev
9, 20, 27, 62
Emor
154, 188, 192
Ha'azinu
11, 212
Idra Raba
158, 318, 319, 363
Kedoshim
21
Ki Tetze
70, 71, 94, 115, 116, 140, 146
Ki Tisa
37, 39
Lech Lecha
65, 95, 104, 288, 426, 454
Miketz
38, 81, 94, 99, 112
Mishpatim
23, 446
Naso
149
Noach
84, 187
Pekudei
23, 140, 393, 800, 802, 803, 810
Pinchas
35b, 35c, 70, 83, 97, 100, 101, 102, 127, 181, 298, 317, 329, 344, 455, 482, 498, 586, 652, 749, 776, 803, 814, 824, 844, 855, 857, 863
Prologue
5, 6, 25, 183
Safra Detzniuta
40
Shemot
109, 279, 290
Shlach Lecha
31, 32, 38, 39, 133, 168, 285, 304, 307
Tazria
91, 187
Toldot
101, 110, 135, 169
Trumah
108, 109, 110, 287, 317, 323, 325, 328, 329, 569, 577, 579, 580, 782, 888, 911
Tzav
47, 96
Vaera
14, 19, 22, 23, 26, 28, 34, 51, 73, 75, 79, 176, 177, 179, 181, 186, 187
Vaetchanan
51, 53, 54
Vayakhel
53, 54, 180, 182, 211, 215, 251
Vayechi
93, 220, 259, 265, 269, 270, 294, 329-332, 352, 353, 407, 432, 771, 783, 802 -804, 826, 848, 853
Vayelech
48
Vayera
16, 20, 22, 23, 28, 29, 391, 487, 493, 512
Vayetze
48, 262
Vayigash
44, 69

Vayikra
231, 232, 247, 296, 304, 329, 449
Vayishlach
50, 55, 117, 163
Yitro
244, 395

PEACE

Acharei Mot
26, 27, 37, 61, 66, 69, 71, 89, 90, 92, 105, 110, 117, 144, 181, 189, 308, 356
Balak
59, 160, 263, 272, 394
Bechukotai
24, 26, 55
Behar
15, 47
Bemidbar
20, 22
Beresheet A
40, 45, 52, 186, 251, 293, 317, 324, 377, 382, 449
Beresheet B
52, 157, 192-194, 199, 213, 227, 228, 264
Beshalach
69, 70, 75, 78, 81, 252, 295, 316, 318, 325
Bo
95, 96
Chayei Sarah
37, 49, 61, 142, 143, 151, 152
Ekev
19, 60
Emor
2, 49, 129, 146, 251, 252, 273, 311, 338
Ha'azinu
76, 109, 181, 200
Idra Raba
296, 357
Kedoshim
118, 120
Ki Tetze
79, 82
Ki Tisa
18, 45, 46
Korach
5, 6, 7, 8, 22, 27
Lech Lecha
2, 20, 40, 164, 182, 222, 232, 303, 356, 430, 432
Metzora
27
Miketz
9, 32, 33, 42, 53, 54, 57, 96, 97, 101, 129, 139, 168, 169, 170, 188, 206, 207, 226, 261, 262, 264
Mishpatim
123, 124, 149, 260, 264, 290, 306, 321
Naso
62, 63, 80, 104, 169, 172
Noach
9, 110, 111, 148, 161, 235
Pekudei
26, 43, 232, 353, 414, 491, 528, 671, 709, 726, 736, 751, 821, 921, 922
Pinchas
22, 26, 113, 128, 131, 140, 198, 223, 304, 305, 490, 563, 647, 814, 831, 839, 864
Prologue
84, 150, 154

Safra Detzniuta
1, 37
Shemot
55, 168, 233, 311, 329
Shlach Lecha
185
Shmini
12, 32, 33, 35, 51, 57
Tazria
35, 85, 87, 133, 150, 156
Toldot
41, 59, 94, 170, 171, 172, 180
Trumah
25, 28, 33, 41, 45, 88, 101, 112, 171, 201, 252, 257, 316, 341, 359, 389, 419, 420, 428, 532, 687, 688, 702, 748, 785, 798, 855, 901, 923
Tzav
4, 39, 40, 96, 98, 121, 186
Vaera
4, 30, 31, 39, 182, 183, 185, 188, 189
Vaetchanan
64
Vayakhel
88, 115, 116, 117, 198, 203, 225, 297
Vayechi
231, 242, 351, 810, 842
Vayelech
26
Vayera
20, 28, 29, 492, 504, 505
Vayeshev
65, 104, 106, 121, 227
Vayetze
20, 76, 77, 80, 81
Vayigash
31, 61, 65, 87, 108
Vayikra
83, 119, 127, 134, 146, 154, 164, 165, 178, 190-192, 194, 195, 199, 206, 231, 232, 280, 282, 284, 314, 341, 352, 356
Vayishlach
118, 270
Yitro
140, 169, 190, 192, 575

PEACE-OFFERING

Behar
47
Lech Lecha
430, 432
Mishpatim
260
Pekudei
921, 922
Pinchas
839, 864
Shmini
32, 33, 51
Tazria
35
Tzav
39, 40, 121
Vayikra
134, 164, 165, 178, 190, 192, 194, 195, 199, 282, 341

PEARLS

Chayei Sarah
223
Mishpatim
192, 211, 369
Pinchas
56, 140, 337

Trumah
599, 871
Vayakhel
281, 441
Vayechi
670, 741, 777
Vayetze
10, 12, 14, 43, 73, 341, 343, 392
Yitro
533, 534, 538-540, 542-545

PEDAEL (SPIRIT)

Pekudei
554, 555, 613
Vayera
275
Vayetze
73
Pekudei
684

PENIEL

Pinchas
482
Pinchas
482
Vayishlach
96

PEOR

Balak
395
Pekudei
65
Pinchas
35d
Vayera
331, 332, 334, 335

PERETZ

Mishpatim
180, 191, 192, 197

PERSIMMON

Prologue
58

PESAGNIYAH (SPIRIT)

Vayakhel
132

PETACHIYAH (SPIRIT)

Vayakhel
134

PHARAOH, THE

Acharei Mot
227
Balak
84, 393
Bechukotai
27, 28
Beshalach
1, 27-29, 63, 65, 67, 75, 105, 111, 113, 128, 129, 131, 186-188, 191, 202, 211, 259, 261, 263, 264, 266, 267, 273, 422, 481
Bo
1, 4, 15, 17, 35, 36, 38, 109, 117-119, 122
Ki Tetze
4, 9, 12
Ki Tisa
65
Lech Lecha
108, 115, 117, 122, 123, 136, 137, 138, 139

Miketz
9, 16, 18, 22-24, 26, 27, 30, 32, 34, 36, 42-44, 57-60, 63-65
Naso
30, 145
Shemot
87, 88, 123, 195, 202, 228, 295, 345
Shlach Lecha
170, 196, 197, 263, 315
Shmini
104
Tazria
184, 185
Trumah
98, 894
Tzav
59
Vaera
9, 66, 67, 69, 82, 84, 100, 104, 116, 118, 120, 122, 144, 153- 155, 162
Vayechi
598
Vayera
366
Vayeshev
253, 271
Vayetze
89
Vayigash
97, 104, 117, 121, 122, 132 -134
Yitro
13, 18, 25, 43, 507

PHILISTINES

Balak
1, 257, 301, 372, 386, 387, 388
Bechukotai
12
Beshalach
1, 27
Ekev
27
Mishpatim
30
Naso
131
Toldot
101
Trumah
364
Vayechi
725
Vayera
357, 358
Vayetze
21, 22

PHYSICIAN KARTANA

Ha'azinu
248, 253, 254

PILLAR

Acharei Mot
34, 35, 88, 211, 214, 233, 388
Balak
20, 21, 33, 127, 128, 155, 320, 362, 364
Beha'alot'cha
44
Beresheet A
15, 16, 38, 40, 45, 80
Beresheet B
72, 83, 95, 97, 135
Beshalach
52, 54, 55, 138, 157, 158, 172

Bo
113, 227
Emor
45, 154, 270
Idra Raba
1, 6, 166, 167, 169, 331, 361
Ki Tetze
20, 46, 51, 67, 69, 70, 102, 116, 117, 140
Ki Tisa
9, 42
Lech Lecha
4, 101, 105, 128, 129
Metzora
21
Miketz
135
Mishpatim
12, 27, 296, 305, 341, 382, 396, 404, 406, 408, 429, 460, 467
Noach
8, 170-173, 273, 274, 278, 279, 283, 284
Pekudei
108, 111, 118, 122, 129, 175, 219, 220, 289, 290, 407, 408, 429, 434, 500, 504, 509, 510, 531, 582, 608, 665, 680, 682, 684, 686, 687, 689, 692, 694, 699, 729, 740, 833, 834
Pinchas
202, 329, 354, 449, 592, 716, 873
Prologue
46, 49, 52, 55, 113
Shemot
79, 98, 101-103, 164, 174, 217, 219, 237, 258
Shlach Lecha
173, 178, 179, 180, 181, 243, 244, 247, 248, 249, 250, 251, 252, 253, 254, 267, 284, 335
Tetzaveh
8, 9, 10, 12, 16, 17, 18, 20, 21, 99
Toldot
197, 204
Trumah
77, 341, 391, 423, 424, 459, 529, 582, 594, 687, 688, 733, 748, 794, 795, 797, 897, 925
Tzav
117, 184
Vaera
16, 110
Vaetchanan
51
Vayakhel
306, 307, 316, 317, 318, 319, 320, 466, 470
Vayechi
132, 173, 174, 222, 225, 322, 444, 446, 447, 542
Vayera
267, 288, 412
Vayeshev
145
Vayetze
13, 28, 59, 81, 82, 175, 318, 392
Vayigash
64
Vayikra
281, 282, 420
Vayishlach
13, 136, 201, 222, 223

PILLAR OF CLOUD

Beshalach
157, 158

Emor
270
Mishpatim
341
Trumah
423, 424
Vayishlach
136

PILLAR OF FIRE

Balak
128, 362, 364
Beshalach
52, 54, 55, 157, 158
Emor
270
Mishpatim
341
Shemot
98, 102, 103
Shlach Lecha
173
Vayishlach
223

PINCHAS

Acharei Mot
21-26, 98
Balak
161, 173, 174, 175, 177, 180, 181
Beresheet B
222, 235, 258, 259
Emor
148
Ki Tetze
24, 79, 82, 125
Ki Tisa
45, 46, 47
Naso
81
Noach
161
Pinchas
1, 6, 11, 16, 20-22, 26, 34, 35d, 36, 71, 73, 74, 128, 129, 130, 131, 140, 142, 156, 157, 232, 233, 457, 460, 462, 463, 464, 465, 467-469, 474, 479-483, 489
Shlach Lecha
16
Shoftim
24
Tzav
34
Vaera
85, 86, 87
Vayigash
87

PIPES

Beresheet B
278
Pekudei
149, 151, 152, 155, 156
Pinchas
820

PISHON (RIVER)

Beresheet A
250
Bo
45
Chayei Sarah
146, 147
Lech Lecha
106, 107

Shemot
158
Vaera
47
Yitro
341

PITUT (SPIRIT)

Pekudei
845, 846, 848

PLAGUES

Acharei Mot
358
Balak
195, 315, 385, 386, 392
Beresheet A
248
Beresheet B
187, 347
Beshalach
202, 266, 310, 311
Ekev
48
Emor
329
Kedoshim
83
Ki Tisa
2, 3
Korach
27
Lech Lecha
117, 136, 138
Metzora
4, 48-50
Naso
145
Noach
79
Pekudei
91, 205, 864, 865, 890, 891
Pinchas
246, 376, 460, 469, 474, 479, 704, 726, 733, 736
Prologue
170
Shemot
73
Shmini
55
Tazria
71, 87, 88, 90, 91, 93, 107, 108, 117, 135, 136, 137, 143, 144, 148, 153, 157, 158, 161, 168, 175, 176, 177, 185, 186
Tzav
153
Vaera
85, 132, 145, 153, 170, 190, 191
Vayakhel
467, 473, 476
Vayechi
420, 822
Vayera
120, 122-124, 127, 293, 366
Vayikra
243
Vayishlach
75, 79, 80, 81, 150
Yitro
13 planets
Balak
142, 501

PLANETS

Beresheet A
396, 397, 401
Beresheet B
69, 82, 84, 94, 112, 124

Ekev
65
Ha'azinu
14
Idra Raba
149, 150
Ki Tetze
70, 112-114, 116-123
Mishpatim
460
Noach
96
Pinchas
35b, 270, 478, 737, 738, 739, 820
Prologue
11
Vayera
254, 290
Yitro
130, 184

PLANTS

Beresheet A
77, 237, 401, 428, 430, 431, 433, 469

POINT

Acharei Mot
4, 26, 41, 88, 113, 171, 180, 192, 197, 201, 237
Balak
74, 77, 114, 115, 118, 128, 156, 176, 226, 347
Beha'alot'cha
67
Bemidbar
26
Beresheet A
2, 3, 5, 7, 9, 10, 13, 31, 32, 33, 34, 38, 43, 44, 66, 68, 107, 108, 128, 136, 204, 209, 211, 212, 213, 308, 325, 331, 357, 387
Beresheet B
6, 164, 221, 253, 362, 363, 365, 371, 405
Beshalach
172
Chayei Sarah
51, 158, 176
Chukat
66
Ekev
18, 28, 39
Emor
165, 310
Ha'azinu
69
Idra Raba
6, 77, 79, 118, 130, 316
Kedoshim
101, 102, 127-129
Ki Tisa
41, 58
Lech Lecha
23, 25, 27, 31, 174, 257
Metzora
17, 57
Miketz
86
Mishpatim
301, 363, 366, 370, 384, 386, 406, 538, 541, 559
Naso
40
Noach
11, 36, 63, 85, 101, 122, 125,

184, 201, 212, 235, 252, 271, 310, 319, 345

Pekudei
38, 39, 41, 42, 360, 362, 416, 417, 419, 424, 426, 428, 429, 439, 769, 776, 817, 929

Pinchas
11, 181, 202, 208, 295, 298, 317, 349, 363, 428, 470, 502, 545, 566, 586, 588, 590, 649, 650, 672, 687, 690, 707, 715-717, 720, 758, 795, 863, 892

Prologue
2, 13, 42, 85, 98

Shemot
38, 115, 242, 332

Shlach Lecha
5, 130, 131, 186, 188, 206, 221, 251, 257, 258, 259, 261, 294, 306, 340

Tetzaveh
8, 11, 17, 18, 19, 20, 33, 36, 97, 98, 99

Toldot
155

Trumah
3, 219, 233, 263, 363, 561, 567, 580, 583, 588, 589, 603, 654, 656, 659, 660, 683, 751, 853, 858

Tzav
12, 14

Vaera
52, 106, 107, 108

Vaetchanan
87, 89, 91

Vayakhel
101, 102, 105, 106, 137, 161, 164, 177, 178, 179, 180, 181, 182, 183, 186, 189, 191, 196, 204, 212, 214, 237, 262, 264, 311-313, 318, 319, 320, 321, 324-326, 338, 339, 344, 367, 368, 372, 401, 422, 430

Vayechi
20, 22, 218, 287, 309, 342, 353, 409, 445, 449, 782

Vayera
48, 188, 399

Vayeshev
146

Vayetze
27, 70, 131, 150, 209, 214, 314, 333

Vayikra
348

Vayishlach
5, 69, 129

Yitro
76, 84, 114, 120, 170, 176, 204, 219, 376, 421, 514

POISON

Beresheet A
261, 262

Vayechi
598

POLE

Mishpatim
384

Shoftim
5, 17

POMEGRANATE

Balak
357, 359, 435, 436

Beha'alot'cha
107

Pekudei
197
Pinchas
712

POOR

Beresheet A
15, 187, 188, 189
Ki Tisa
4
Lech Lecha
260, 287
Miketz
138
Prologue
36, 88, 175, 176, 177, 178, 179, 233, 234, 235, 236, 242, 260
Vaetchanan
148, 149
Vayera
158, 167, 226, 263, 285, 294
Vayeshev
3, 6
Vayigash
62, 63, 64, 65, 66
Vayishlach
61, 62, 63, 64, 65, 66, 88

POTIPHAR

Miketz
35
Pinchas
16, 19
Vayeshev
195, 213
Vayetze
138

POTTAGE

Toldot
61-63, 77, 79

POX

Beresheet A
248

PRAISE

Acharei Mot
11, 102, 118, 145, 146, 148, 151, 152, 277, 288, 382, 408
Balak
51, 68, 73, 106, 107, 108, 111, 156-158, 164, 165, 186, 207, 216, 266, 281, 352, 355, 418, 423, 484, 489, 490, 507
Bechukotai
19, 61
Beha'alot'cha
111, 126, 128
Behar
4, 16
Bemidbar
11, 56, 57, 58, 65, 66, 67
Beresheet A
345, 348, 449
Beresheet B
31, 39, 53, 91, 218, 345, 359, 408, 414, 448
Beshalach
3, 24, 25, 46, 47, 50, 216, 222, 314
Bo
132, 159, 179, 180-182
Chayei Sarah
151
Chukat
42, 48, 51, 54, 77

Ekev
21
Emor
93, 109, 127, 129, 141, 143, 144, 243, 244, 245, 329
Ha'azinu
17, 28, 31, 55, 148
Idra Raba
70-72, 98, 165, 226, 233, 250, 354
Kedoshim
18, 28, 124, 127
Ki Tetze
2, 37
Ki Tisa
12, 108
Korach
11
Lech Lecha
5, 245, 318, 391, 394
Metzora
7, 8, 36
Miketz
123
Mishpatim
12, 34, 39, 54, 114, 181, 186-188, 190, 192, 195, 196, 227, 230, 446, 467, 524, 571
Naso
4, 5, 46
Noach
30, 33, 149, 220, 262, 286, 305, 306
Paqudei
217-222, 231, 232, 276, 577, 581, 832
Pinchas
3, 118, 190, 191, 192, 206, 345-347, 350, 385, 404, 435, 443, 550, 575, 719, 804, 820
Prologue
18, 29, 120, 124, 140, 141, 144, 161, 171, 183
Shemot
29, 45, 47, 159, 241, 242, 324
Shlach Lecha
4, 79, 127, 156, 167, 199, 213, 348
Shmini
39, 40, 71
Shoftim
19
Tazria
41, 56
Tetzaveh
24, 65
Toldot
1, 4, 46
Trumah
40, 54, 55, 77, 78, 83, 93, 95, 96, 97, 98, 99, 103, 104, 106, 112, 114, 126, 135, 207, 208, 209, 211-214, 219, 220, 221, 223, 241, 253, 256, 257, 258, 293, 294, 316, 324, 325, 327, 343, 344, 360, 371, 372, 377, 378, 379, 462, 493, 549, 575, 675, 681, 686, 687, 692, 694, 695, 696, 697, 698, 809, 816, 823, 833, 863, 865, 867, 873, 874, 880-883, 885, 895, 923
Tzav
62, 80, 192
Vaera
100, 110, 133, 160-162
Vaetchanan
4, 7, 12, 20, 172

Vayakhel
16, 24, 25, 126, 208, 210, 211, 213, 214, 410, 411, 495, 496
Vayechi
91, 95, 99, 351, 379, 451, 452, 478, 479-481, 486, 506, 521, 527, 564, 567, 574, 714, 720, 792, 817, 819, 820, 824, 826, 828
Vayelech
16, 17, 20, 28, 31, 34
Vayera
9, 497
Vayeshev
99, 194, 198, 200
Vayetze
74, 82, 141, 159, 167, 169, 170, 175, 230, 255, 277
Vayigash
48, 49, 52, 91
Vayikra
18, 55-57, 59, 60, 81, 142, 200-203, 205, 206, 333, 339, 371, 379, 380
Vayishlach
69, 158, 267, 270, 271, 273
Yitro
16, 21, 264, 331, 340, 355, 503, 505, 528, 544

PRAYER

Acharei Mot
40, 133, 147, 198, 200, 201, 227, 247, 258, 269, 271, 281, 332, 411, 412
Balak
7, 51, 111, 112, 133, 161, 186-192, 197, 198, 200-209, 216, 239, 249, 252, 254, 256, 268, 331, 338, 350, 351, 352, 354, 356, 439
Bechukotai
9, 10, 21
Beha'alot'cha
10, 19, 92, 136, 138, 145, 147, 150
Behar
23, 33, 34, 44, 58, 75, 80, 82
Bemidbar
58, 68, 69, 71-74
Beresheet A
42, 56, 57, 77, 141, 184-192, 194-196, 198, 199, 201, 208, 209, 242, 244, 249, 289
Beresheet B
14, 47, 60-62, 70, 82, 86, 92, 95, 97, 101, 131, 141, 146, 193, 194, 224, 226, 265, 439
Beshalach
1, 16, 21, 22, 66, 69, 87, 89, 116, 178, 276, 278, 283, 301, 303, 332, 335-337, 359, 384, 385, 390, 392, 404, 409, 411, 467, 479
Bo
93, 155, 156, 235
Chayei Sarah
37, 38, 96, 101, 109, 174, 178, 226, 229-240, 243, 244, 245
Chukat
82
Ekev
9, 10, 15, 16, 48, 59
Emor
137, 176, 185, 218, 220, 221, 223, 228, 251, 252, 255, 279, 299

Ha'azinu
16, 25, 44, 126, 155, 158, 174, 254, 259
Idra Raba
4, 10, 35, 70, 130, 132, 146, 199, 240
Kedoshim
44
Ki Tetze
25, 45, 49, 50, 51, 56, 105, 129, 132, 140, 142
Ki Tisa
15
Korach
48, 59
Lech Lecha
86, 87, 112, 113, 123, 173, 176, 292, 323, 398, 409, 450
Metzora
16, 20, 43, 44, 45
Miketz
42, 80, 210, 211, 212, 224, 260, 263
Mishpatim
54, 114, 133, 206, 263, 286, 382, 395, 396, 409, 426, 427, 496, 525, 561
Naso
2, 4, 7, 12, 173, 177, 199
Noach
67, 121, 122, 184, 185, 256, 282, 283
Pekudei
29, 189, 190, 344, 351, 355, 362, 364, 473, 485-490, 501, 502, 510, 532, 546-548, 554, 555, 568, 570, 575-577, 579, 591, 620, 621, 648, 650, 679, 768, 774, 775, 786, 787, 789-791, 794, 811, 815, 826, 827, 830, 832, 848, 886, 943, 945, 946
Pinchas
39, 41, 106, 180, 181, 182, 192, 206, 207, 211, 214, 235, 241, 243, 250, 261, 279-282, 293, 304, 305, 306, 311 -313, 315, 319-323, 325, 326, 335, 337, 338, 340-342, 345, 347, 348, 349, 350, 368, 404, 424, 425, 451, 492, 542, 547, 548, 549, 550, 562-567, 569, 576, 577, 578, 579, 580, 583, 592, 596, 610, 621, 636, 643, 657, 719, 753, 754, 758, 780, 783, 785, 789, 803, 804, 807, 812, 818, 821, 823, 829, 831, 838, 855, 880, 881, 882
Prologue
82, 163, 183, 184, 219, 253, 254, 256
Safra Detzniuta
6, 29, 39, 40, 41, 42
Shemot
24, 134, 162, 203, 207, 253, 256, 278, 279, 340, 354, 356, 368, 369, 387
Shlach Lecha
1, 31, 32, 38, 76, 83, 130, 131, 142, 207, 216, 307
Shmini
14, 34
Shoftim
4
Tazria
134, 181, 182
Tetzaveh
65, 106, 120
Toldot
20-22, 55, 62, 75, 105, 114, 137, 154, 158

Trumah
43, 44, 45, 52, 61, 63, 69, 70, 72, 76, 78, 85, 86, 90, 93, 94, 95, 97, 103, 114-117, 119 -121, 123, 156, 164, 166, 210, 220, 223, 225, 247, 287, 361, 362, 386, 500, 501, 545, 546, 547, 550, 681, 694, 695, 696, 697, 714, 715, 716, 773, 785, 809
Tzav
2, 6, 14, 16, 27, 28, 47, 149
Vaera
12, 112, 199
Vaetchanan
8-10, 12, 32, 84, 112, 158, 171
Vayakhel
107, 108, 109, 111, 121-123, 128, 132, 134, 136-140, 142 -151, 154, 155, 198, 199, 207, 208, 212, 214, 215, 221, 224, 225, 244, 256, 309, 365, 366, 403, 408, 409, 410, 411, 412, 430, 476-478, 483
Vayechi
30, 75, 97, 145, 146, 227, 265, 266, 267, 271-274, 318, 320, 324, 326, 327, 336, 361, 386, 390, 393, 394, 406, 415, 416, 417, 419, 421, 422, 426, 464, 506, 513-516, 520, 608, 646, 647, 713, 714, 715, 720, 844
Vayelech
37
Vayera
107, 115, 182, 200, 206, 220, 221, 229, 235, 236, 410, 417, 439
Vayeshev
32, 50, 60, 92, 221, 255, 257
Vayetze
101, 189, 196, 206, 283, 302, 346, 378
Vayigash
40, 54, 91, 97, 98, 99, 100, 101
Vayikra
32, 33, 37, 113, 116, 238, 239, 243, 253, 302, 311, 312, 339, 362, 418, 448, 449
Vayishlach
44, 45, 49, 50, 58, 61-66, 69, 70, 74, 127, 128, 159, 164, 215, 242, 251, 255-258, 273
Yitro
2, 4, 5, 7, 152, 176, 400, 414, 418, 463, 464, 511, 548, 563

PRECEPTS

Acharei Mot
3, 61, 227, 310
Balak
30, 74, 121, 123, 216, 470
Bechukotai
16, 18
Behar
16, 20, 24-27, 30, 45, 50, 75
Bemidbar
22
Beresheet A
57, 180, 183, 185, 195-197, 219, 260, 261, 288, 383, 432, 444, 445
Beresheet B
186, 226, 228, 230, 413
Bo
231

Chayei Sarah
135, 208
Chukat
61, 86
Ekev
63
Emor
84, 178, 183
Ha'azinu
125, 127
Idra Raba
33, 197
Kedoshim
20, 34, 36, 41-44, 47, 48, 51, 52, 56, 58, 60, 66, 96, 97, 100, 114
Ki Tetze
3, 24, 25, 29, 37, 43, 45, 47, 51, 52, 54, 57, 58, 89, 95, 96, 97, 98, 103, 106, 136, 140
Korach
44, 45, 46, 48, 51, 55, 59
Lech Lecha
14, 379, 471
Miketz
132, 171, 249
Mishpatim
2, 92, 104, 112, 318, 372, 380, 387, 388, 391, 428, 433, 434, 444, 454, 456, 457, 458, 460, 461, 462, 466, 470, 471, 472, 493, 496, 497, 498, 499, 542, 557
Naso
35, 37, 47, 49, 50, 52, 59, 81, 113
Noach
254, 260
Pekudei
70, 231, 235, 310, 514, 522, 594, 836, 874, 883, 907
Pinchas
72, 91, 92, 205, 223, 250, 291-296, 299, 319, 320, 323, 325, 326, 332, 337, 342, 366, 432, 492, 493, 504, 561, 574, 611, 637, 639, 678, 738, 768, 787, 795, 798, 801, 827, 831, 838, 850, 859, 872, 873, 881
Prologue
188, 189, 194, 195, 197, 198, 202, 204, 208, 215, 219, 223, 228, 233, 235, 237, 244, 245, 246, 247
Shemot
233
Shlach Lecha
197, 198, 321, 322, 324, 328, 335, 343, 347, 348
Shoftim
1, 2, 5, 6, 8, 11, 18, 19, 21
Tazria
20
Toldot
69, 73, 74, 84, 104, 124, 170, 171
Trumah
34, 152, 576, 650, 662, 663, 666, 721, 722, 723, 724, 726, 728, 729, 737, 745
Tzav
28, 31, 37, 39, 44, 46, 50, 51, 54, 56-61, 68, 108, 135, 136, 155
Vaera
55, 56, 57, 58, 60, 61, 62, 63, 64, 80, 126
Vaetchanan
119, 135, 155
Vayakhel
121, 122, 127, 150-156, 244, 308, 309, 338, 410, 412, 415,

459, 463
Vayechi
211, 295, 349, 382, 425, 498, 603, 610
Vayera
8, 18, 174, 245, 328, 387
Vayeshev
236, 237
Vayetze
220, 325
Vayikra
109, 110, 190, 192, 196, 208, 213, 274, 335, 390, 393, 439
Vayishlach
103, 227
Yitro
317, 406, 513, 514, 526, 551, 562, 563

PREGNANCY

Beresheet A
30, 308, 349, 350, 382
Chayei Sarah
7
Ki Tisa
24
Lech Lecha
206
Prologue
133
Vayechi
20, 468
Vayera
325
Vayetze
250

PRIESTS

Acharei Mot
5, 10, 20, 22, 26, 37, 44, 53, 55, 84, 120, 122, 124, 126, 127, 132-134, 176, 180, 181, 188, 189, 194, 197, 198, 200, 201, 247, 355
Balak
16, 25, 34, 71, 93, 157, 195, 386, 396
Beha'alot'cha
11, 22, 49, 52, 53, 74
Behar
26-29
Bemidbar
15, 52
Beresheet A
147
Beresheet B
141, 265
Beshalach
120-124, 277, 467, 477
Chayei Sarah
267
Chukat
21, 22
Ekev
11, 16, 17, 19, 20, 38
Emor
1-3, 9-11, 13-15, 21, 24, 25, 28, 29, 34, 36, 38, 41, 47, 48, 151, 237, 248, 249, 251, 252, 293
Ha'azinu
194, 203
Idra Raba
113, 114, 138, 149
Kedoshim
13, 78, 101, 121, 122, 131
Ki Tetze
24, 57, 77, 124, 125
Korach
3, 12, 13, 23, 24, 26, 27, 46, 47, 51

Lech Lecha
241, 242, 256, 303
Metzora
12, 16, 17, 18, 19, 24, 25
Miketz
141, 217
Mishpatim
21, 23, 24, 25, 26, 28, 31, 134, 186, 188, 189, 388, 451, 464, 500
Naso
9, 10, 18, 60-64, 67, 68, 70, 72, 81, 85, 124, 125, 129, 137, 138, 142, 143, 144, 146, 151-160, 162-165, 170 -183, 185, 192
Noach
86, 87
Pekudei
67, 80-82, 182, 197, 199, 209, 227, 229, 327, 351, 354, 359, 362-365, 524, 736, 770, 784, 785, 906, 943, 945
Pinchas
6, 11, 20, 21, 23, 34, 85, 128, 130, 157, 184, 211, 220, 232, 233, 246, 261, 297, 298, 542, 548, 555, 593, 595, 652, 712, 751, 795, 802
Shemot
58, 230, 332, 358, 371, 377
Shlach Lecha
111, 232, 309, 321, 325, 327
Shmini
27, 29, 30, 32, 33, 35, 37, 38, 41, 45, 49, 52, 54, 55, 60, 61, 62, 64, 65, 66, 91, 96
Tazria
71, 88, 108, 123, 133-137, 143, 158, 159, 165
Trumah
241, 324, 404, 406, 517, 518, 555, 598, 733, 746
Tzav
68, 76, 82, 122, 177, 180, 191
Vaera
117, 175
Vaetchanan
13
Vayakhel
106, 151, 154, 448, 449, 470
Vayechi
268, 419, 718, 719, 792, 830, 831
Vayelech
42
Vayera
353, 367, 368, 370, 415, 435, 436, 484, 507
Vayeshev
43, 173, 189, 263
Vayetze
36, 37, 38, 39
Vayikra
90, 92, 96, 110, 111, 119, 122, 123, 164, 286, 294, 295, 297 -301, 312-314, 330, 389, 390, 392
Vayishlach
172, 214, 215, 272
Yitro
1, 9-12, 14, 15, 20, 22, 26, 264, 384

PRISON

Miketz
32, 34, 35, 40, 41, 42
Vayera
388, 389

PROPHECY

Acharei Mot
324
Balak
210, 248
Beha'alot'cha
92, 147, 149
Behar
41, 42
Beresheet A
143, 145, 193, 283
Chayei Sarah
2, 148
Idra Raba
125
Ki Tetze
81, 94, 120
Ki Tisa
94
Lech Lecha
187, 188
Miketz
218
Mishpatim
324, 423, 465, 477
Naso
196
Noach
15
Pekudei
236, 534, 608, 729, 730, 740, 741, 817
Pinchas
171, 417, 581, 652
Shemot
58, 83, 217, 395
Shlach Lecha
320
Trumah
80, 81, 342, 404, 405, 511-513, 796, 804, 805, 822
Vaera
9
Vaetchanan
190
Vayechi
1-3, 9-11, 532, 593, 594, 650, 811, 812
Vayera
65, 391
Vayeshev
82, 83, 89, 256
Vayetze
44, 45, 46, 50, 70
Vayikra
175, 333
Vayishlach
105, 107
Yitro
314

PROPHETS

Acharei Mot
214
Balak
119, 139, 160, 162, 165, 169, 186, 206, 238, 248, 414, 418, 426
Beha'alot'cha
90, 91, 93, 139, 146, 147, 149
Behar
37, 41, 42
Beresheet A
145, 175, 433
Beresheet B
134

Beshalach
1, 2, 14, 15, 20-22, 24, 207, 208, 212, 247, 340, 342, 421, 434
Bo
110, 111, 216
Chayei Sarah
144, 145, 148
Chukat
40, 90
Ekev
19, 40, 44
Emor
45, 93
Ha'azinu
3, 6, 29, 178, 229
Idra Raba
72, 98, 113, 125, 157, 232, 243, 293
Ki Tetze
86, 91, 120, 122, 139
Ki Tisa
16, 47, 77
Lech Lecha
137, 185, 187
Metzora
19, 21
Miketz
30, 218
Mishpatim
200, 382, 423, 425, 487
Naso
100, 148
Noach
146, 223
Pekudei
111, 478, 480, 533-535, 608, 729, 740, 817
Pinchas
104, 174, 177, 185, 251, 287, 329, 332, 372, 450, 456, 482, 485, 574, 838, 872
Prologue
5, 114, 162
Safra Detzniuta
40
Shemot
6, 83, 84, 200, 212, 390, 392, 394, 395
Shlach Lecha
128, 156, 196, 199, 309, 310, 320
Shmini
94
Shoftim
10
Tazria
166
Tetzaveh
6, 7, 37, 51
Trumah
80, 81, 404, 406, 424, 510, 512-514, 550, 586, 589, 591, 686, 733, 796, 804, 822
Tzav
29, 33, 37, 158, 185
Vaetchanan
30, 101, 102, 104, 164, 165, 178
Vayakhel
225, 235
Vayechi
2, 369, 473
Vayelech
27
Vayera
48, 65, 177, 200, 240, 359, 368, 398, 506

Vayeshev
82, 83, 94, 258, 276
Vayetze
45, 107, 254
Vayigash
86
Vayikra
1, 175, 241, 327, 343, 386
Vayishlach
105, 106, 107
Yitro
26, 52, 312, 313, 318, 323, 328, 329, 464, 571

PROSECUTION

Acharei Mot
49, 115, 118, 129, 253
Balak
353, 369
Beresheet A
103, 184, 197
Beresheet B
21, 60, 93
Emor
206, 207, 209, 216, 217, 221, 223, 227b, 238-240, 242, 244, 246, 271, 273
Ha'azinu
7, 49, 130, 131, 137, 148a, 201
Idra Raba
1, 129
Korach
21
Miketz
190, 191, 193
Noach
104, 106, 121
Pekudei
336, 656, 725, 727
Pinchas
355, 357, 531, 881
Prologue
96
Shlach Lecha
65, 68, 120, 253, 255, 334
Trumah
167, 761, 782
Vaetchanan
105, 109, 115, 160
Vayakhel
33, 82, 85-88, 198, 199
Vayechi
818
Vayera
132, 383
Vayikra
279, 311, 372

PUNISHMENT

Beresheet A
56, 100, 101, 180-182, 372, 437, 461, 463
Chayei Sarah
49, 50
Ha'azinu
8, 29, 132, 134, 177, 217, 246, 251
Ki Tetze
1, 11, 25, 35, 40, 46, 76
Ki Tisa
58
Lech Lecha
91, 176, 177, 254, 259, 283, 388, 403, 408, 417, 472, 473, 475
Miketz
15, 52, 55, 74, 85, 100, 103, 115, 151

Mishpatim
114, 117, 249, 256, 287, 309, 347, 371, 439, 462, 580
Prologue
21, 136, 166, 190, 192, 193, 195, 197, 255
Shoftim
18
Tetzaveh
76, 101
Toldot
2, 43, 174, 191
Vaetchanan
29, 42, 67, 161, 183, 187, 196
Vayechi
170, 192, 205, 274, 300, 324, 327, 388, 471, 508, 604, 637, 638, 642, 704, 822
Vayelech
7, 29, 42, 45, 46
Vayera
87, 166, 178, 182, 190, 191, 195, 219, 245, 246, 248, 258-261, 265, 269, 285, 293, 314, 320, 322, 369, 373, 377, 383, 434, 472-475, 486, 489
Vayeshev
28, 72, 128, 141, 150, 277, 280
Vayetze
14, 88, 90, 100, 278, 283, 342, 348, 380
Vayishlach
191, 192, 195, 197, 209, 214, 219, 249

PURIFICATION

Acharei Mot
115, 119, 122, 133, 153, 180, 195, 241, 242, 244-247, 284, 290, 291, 403
Balak
22, 255, 274, 275, 332, 370, 373
Beha'alot'cha
52, 69, 77-79, 87
Behar
30, 70, 71
Bemidbar
70
Beresheet A
18, 19
Beresheet B
9, 230, 357
Beshalach
26
Bo 35, 77
Chayei Sarah
17, 72, 83, 85, 262
Chukat
18, 21, 22, 24, 25, 28, 33-35
Ekev
56, 60
Emor
163-167, 170, 172, 174, 175, 256
Ha'azinu
84, 86, 211
Idra Raba
127
Kedoshim
9, 11, 15, 64
Ki Tisa
43, 70
Korach
22, 38
Lech Lecha
18, 89, 90, 119, 120, 144, 161, 269

Metzora
11, 17-19, 25, 27, 32, 45, 49, 50
Miketz
91, 116, 155
Mishpatim
36, 54, 55, 111, 322, 478, 489, 567
Naso
73, 74, 86, 89, 109, 132, 157
Noach
63, 104, 201, 381, 382
Pekudei
310, 313, 314, 316, 523, 600, 610, 673, 840, 905, 921
Pinchas
30, 35c, 102, 523, 625, 684, 812
Prologue
96, 192
Safra Detzniuta
6, 22
Shemot
33, 144, 152, 293
Shlach Lecha
53, 64, 118
Shmini
21, 34, 35, 45, 49, 50, 109, 117
Tazria
107, 121, 122, 123, 125, 132, 136, 148, 159, 163, 165, 175
Tetzaveh
58, 60, 112-114, 120, 129
Toldot
52, 54, 66, 124, 171
Trumah
157, 178, 448, 449, 507, 727, 752, 754
Tzav
29, 72, 193
Vayakhel
76, 95, 96, 302, 304, 327, 328, 329-332, 333, 410, 466, 472, 479, 483
Vayechi
141, 210, 382, 384, 390, 391, 528, 546
Vayera
107, 108, 111, 112, 260, 379, 507
Vayeshev
36, 117, 119, 177
Vayetze
18, 321, 353
Vayigash
16
Vayikra
27, 92, 210, 278, 302, 415
Vayishlach
4, 79
Yitro
258, 278, 510

PURPLE

Beresheet A
4
Ha'azinu
184
Matot
1
Vayechi
129, 309
Vayera
388, 389, 392
Vayetze
17, 26

QUEEN OF SHEBA

Balak
183, 184

RABBI AKIVA

Beresheet A
250, 251, 252, 255
Beresheet B
20, 360
Chayei Sarah
220
Pekudei
654, 666, 671
Pinchas
198, 334, 343, 648, 733, 878
Shemot
168, 171, 254-256, 259-262
Vayera
23, 25, 34, 35, 36, 37, 40

RABBI SHIMON DEATH OF

Ha'azinu
23-30, 95-97, 196-201

RACHEL

Balak
50, 321, 322, 324, 325
Behar
72
Beresheet A
55, 69, 70, 186, 364
Beresheet B
132, 159, 214
Chayei Sarah
13, 224, 252, 256, 268
Ha'azinu
121, 122
Ki Tetze
111
Lech Lecha
73
Miketz
219
Mishpatim
62, 182, 183, 554
Noach
116
Pekudei
648, 711
Pinchas
544, 594, 609, 677, 716, 719, 776
Shemot
109, 127, 128, 204-206, 228, 229
Shlach Lecha
119, 132, 136
Toldot
54
Trumah
4, 5, 378, 380, 909
Vaera
116, 146, 148-152
Vayakhel
235
Vayechi
81, 83, 85, 113, 260, 262- 264, 270, 272, 273, 332, 338, 392, 538, 550, 729
Vayera
403
Vayeshev
56
Vayetze
95, 103, 105, 127, 128, 130, 131, 133, 138-140, 142, 143, 145, 147, 150, 166, 185, 187,

196, 199, 204, 206, 209, 215, 216, 228, 230, 238, 241, 242, 243, 246-250, 253, 267, 269, 274, 291-293, 337, 378, 380

Vayigash
103

Vayikra
335, 343, 345, 346, 446

Vayishlach
42, 60, 173, 175, 190-195, 197-199, 203, 204, 220, 221

Yitro
14

RACHMIEL (ANGEL)

Beresheet B
55

RAGSHIEL (SUPERNAL MINISTER)

Vayikra
24

Vayikra
22

RAHAV

Balak
145, 147, 148

Pinchas
650

Prologue
56

Trumah
814

RAIN

Acharei Mot
58, 60, 218, 271

Bechukotai
20

Beha'alot'cha
139, 146

Beresheet A
65, 233, 313, 418, 419, 420, 422, 423

Beshalach
267, 364, 374, 384

Bo
171

Emor
42, 131, 146, 260

Ha'azinu
21, 58, 117

Idra Raba
9

Miketz
227, 228

Mishpatim
388

Noach
55, 266

Pekudei
31, 32, 519

Pinchas
334, 344, 401, 435, 437, 665, 697

Prologue
163

Shemot
254

Tetzaveh
72

Toldot
49, 57, 114

Trumah
405, 521

Vaera
91

Vaetchanan
48, 161, 162
Vayakhel
48, 49, 287, 305
Vayechi
103, 318, 469, 752
Vayera
2, 139, 293, 412, 413, 421, 424
Vayeshev
214, 215, 216, 217
Vayetze
226
Vayigash
78
Vayikra
236, 444
Vayishlach
105
Yitro
249, 292

RAINBOW

Beresheet A
69, 70, 71, 72
Beshalach
476-480
Kedoshim
78
Mishpatim
96
Noach
261, 266-270, 289-291
Pinchas
34, 35a, 35b, 35c, 37, 38, 39, 41, 51, 334, 337, 344, 583, 584
Prologue
5
Shemot
81
Shmini
12
Toldot
15
Vayechi
174, 315
Vayera
52, 53, 447
Vayikra
238, 239

RAMA

Vayigash
102

RAMAH

Balak
50
Vaera
146, 151

RAPE

Ki Tetze
12, 13

RAPHAEL (ANGEL)

Beha'alot'cha
101, 124
Vayakhel
53
Vayetze
73

RATZON

Beresheet B
125, 127, 131, 132, 136

RAVENS

Balak
359, 458, 472
Beha'alot'cha
88, 89
Idra Raba
100, 110
Mishpatim
405
Safra Detzniuta
27
Shlach Lecha
68
Vayakhel
79

RAZIEL (SUPERNAL MINISTER)

Beresheet B
361
Noach
373
Pekudei
649, 654, 655, 664
Vayera
275
Vayetze
73
Vayikra
11

REBECCA

Chayei Sarah
13, 177, 180, 182, 185, 186, 224-226, 248-251, 255, 256, 259
Emor
218
Lech Lecha
76
Mishpatim
337
Pekudei
301, 302, 305, 724
Pinchas
242, 279, 328, 567, 776, 882
Toldot
15-18, 20, 22, 49, 55, 56, 74, 97, 126-129, 131, 132
Vayechi
306, 802
Vayetze
65

RED

Acharei Mot
79, 281, 311, 315, 318, 353, 355
Balak
256, 435, 437
Beha'alot'cha
53, 121
Beresheet A
1, 23, 70, 72, 207, 277, 278, 281
Beresheet B
27, 64, 65, 76, 84, 89, 115, 252, 273
Beshalach
88, 171, 388, 476, 478
Bo
78, 79, 82, 83, 206, 232
Chukat
18, 21, 26, 35, 84
Ekev
61
Emor
333
Ha'azinu
10, 131, 138, 139, 140, 162

-164, 176, 179, 184, 189

Idra Raba
57, 58, 142, 185, 186, 202, 208, 210, 213-215, 217, 222, 224, 235, 254, 287, 290, 305

Ki Tetze
54, 114, 120

Ki Tisa
9

Lech Lecha
196, 201, 340

Matot
1,3

Metzora
19, 35, 55, 58, 59

Mishpatim
96, 515, 522, 523, 531, 534

Naso
143

Noach
102, 266, 269-271, 302

Pekudei
151, 164, 165, 307, 323-325, 356, 398, 430, 448, 449, 458, 574, 633, 848

Pinchas
35a, 35b, 35c, 51, 68, 185, 193, 270, 344, 420, 584, 590, 629, 688, 822

Prologue
1

Safra Detzniuta
25, 26, 28, 34

Shemot
4, 41, 81, 125, 194, 361, 364 -367, 369, 385

Shlach Lecha
124, 157, 248, 252, 284, 314

Tazria
70, 120, 131, 163, 164, 165

Tetzaveh 94

Toldot
15, 24, 61, 62, 79

Trumah
160, 233, 234, 235, 387, 392, 400, 428-431, 818, 844, 846

Tzav
7, 69

Vaera
26, 106, 113, 131

Vayakhel
36, 55, 252, 293, 303, 414

Vayechi
235, 469, 470, 471, 475, 508, 604, 632

Vayera
45, 52, 53, 96, 269

Vayeshev
49, 83

Vayetze
23, 26, 117, 190, 308, 309, 316, 391

Vayikra
140, 219, 223, 427

Vayishlach
11, 237, 241

Yitro
87, 109, 127, 144, 163, 164, 165, 168, 195, 207-210, 215, 216, 218, 222, 225, 229-233, 360, 362, 535, 536

RED COW

Acharei Mot
353, 355

Chukat
21, 26, 35

RED SEA

Beshalach
181
Ekev
50
Trumah
96, 810-815, 818
Vayechi
822
Vayelech
7
Vayera
279, 372
Vayigash
55, 58
Yitro
571, 573

REDEMPTION AND SALVATION

Acharei Mot
60, 183, 225
Balak
179, 245, 368, 507
Behar
17, 22, 24, 25
Bemidbar
39
Beresheet A
153, 231
Beresheet B
18, 283
Beshalach
41, 42, 53, 57, 68, 187, 197-200, 219, 226, 239, 241, 244, 250
Bo
125, 132, 189, 190, 212
Chayei Sarah
235
Chukat
83
Emor
37
Ha'azinu
91
Ki Tetze
4, 20, 28, 47, 54, 61, 68, 69, 85, 103
Korach
43, 45
Miketz
17, 209, 212, 213
Mishpatim
220, 388, 390, 393, 395, 397, 399, 473, 477, 479, 480
Naso
29, 89, 98-102, 188
Noach
262, 292
Pekudei
50, 177, 276, 277, 281, 554, 886
Pinchas
28, 41, 105, 106, 127, 151, 373, 401, 498, 564, 567, 624, 698, 701, 703, 708, 743, 747-749, 767
Prologue
2, 27, 246
Shemot
95, 183, 206, 280
Shlach Lecha
298
Tazria
186, 187
Tetzaveh
7

Toldot
49, 68, 70
Trumah
43, 44, 225, 325, 545, 546, 586, 684, 859, 893, 894
Tzav
70
Vaera
54
Vaetchanan
188, 189
Vayakhel
70, 225, 429, 430, 432-434
Vayechi
15, 18, 21, 22, 50, 54, 74, 78, 79, 84, 92, 104, 394, 682, 712, 725
Vayera
120, 253, 399, 400, 452, 454, 487
Vayeshev
14, 113
Vayetze
362, 363
Vayigash
48, 50, 51, 68
Vayikra
179, 267, 447
Vayishlach
45, 91, 275
Yitro
17, 26, 27, 501, 502

REFAEL (ANGEL)*

*See also Raphael

Acharei Mot
76
Balak
90, 351
Bemidbar
27, 29, 31
Beresheet A
70, 249
Beresheet B
51, 167, 365
Bo
201, 203, 204
Korach
60
Mishpatim
87
Pekudei
660, 662, 664, 665, 780
Pinchas
223, 257, 259, 270, 401, 421
Shemot
258
Shlach Lecha
88
Trumah
241, 385, 388, 390
Vayakhel
51, 260, 296, 297, 323, 326, 339, 341
Vayera
49, 53, 74, 171, 275

REFAIM

Beresheet A
224, 230, 231, 269

REHOBOTH

Idra Raba
315

REINCARNATION

Behar
64

Beresheet A
222, 267, 285
Beresheet B
189
Chukat
55
Ekev
44
Ki Tetze
103
Lech Lecha
353, 354
Mishpatim
1, 351, 477
Pinchas
7, 45, 46, 50-53, 59, 63, 67, 87, 614
Vayeshev
179, 180
Yitro
518

REMARRIAGE

Mishpatim
155

REMEMBER AND KEEP

Bechukotai
53, 54
Beresheet B
200

REPENTANCE

Acharei Mot
38, 96, 244-247, 253, 266, 267, 272, 332, 333, 340, 345, 346, 352, 394, 411
Balak
7, 18, 193, 201, 318, 326, 327, 328, 336, 351, 352, 479
Behar
68, 73
Beresheet A
173, 179, 180, 258, 260, 262, 286, 463
Beresheet B
14, 21, 22, 57, 341, 342, 345, 390, 404, 405, 435
Beshalach
65, 308
Bo
21, 137, 184, 230
Chayei Sarah
197, 198
Chukat
68
Emor
23, 193, 202, 205, 213, 221, 224, 227a, 227b, 230, 280, 317
Ha'azinu
246, 249
Idra Raba
1, 88, 204
Kedoshim
67, 101, 132
Ki Tetze
31, 47, 52, 106
Ki Tisa
22-24, 29, 36, 43, 44
Korach
31, 33
Lech Lecha
1, 35, 36, 48, 77, 79, 90, 108, 270, 310
Metzora
13, 16, 18, 27
Miketz
120, 200, 253
Mishpatim
56, 66, 228, 229, 231-234, 236,

237, 249, 251, 358, 377, 378, 386, 439, 443, 463, 497

Naso
22-31, 38, 46, 47, 48, 58, 59, 90, 118, 122

Noach
45, 52, 57, 63, 74, 137, 150, 151, 196, 312

Pekudei
71, 335, 486, 487, 489, 547, 548, 569, 570, 586, 587, 668

Pinchas
30, 48, 52, 138, 266, 319, 381, 529, 569, 613, 749, 807, 812, 827

Prologue
144, 181

Shemot
28, 78, 169, 203-205, 294

Shlach Lecha
54

Shmini
92

Tazria
46, 47, 73

Tetzaveh
129

Toldot
2, 70, 71, 86, 146

Trumah
50, 51, 79, 295, 388, 432, 439, 440, 442, 898, 899

Tzav
123, 129, 138-141, 144, 172

Vaera
192

Vaetchanan
2, 153, 160, 184

Vayakhel
96, 97, 360, 388, 439, 475

Vayechi
15, 69, 179, 194, 202-204, 206, 209, 297, 301

Vayera
128, 131, 178, 200, 223, 298, 326, 386, 454

Vayeshev
139, 236, 250

Vayetze
381

Vayigash
63

Vayikra
211, 212, 250, 252, 256 -258, 260, 261, 271, 274 -276, 280, 329, 402, 405, 409, 410

Vayishlach
43

Yitro
48, 145, 155, 156, 164, 165, 169, 197, 233

REPTILE

Miketz
186

RESURRECTION

Acharei Mot
294

Balak
273, 364

Behar
31

Beresheet A
95, 230, 273

Beshalach
216, 290, 311

Chayei Sarah
12, 31, 53, 99, 156, 163-165,

173, 187, 197, 198, 203, 204, 207, 208, 210, 211, 212, 270
Chukat
13
Emor
50, 51
Ha'azinu
35
Idra Raba
63
Ki Tetze
81
Lech Lecha
135
Mishpatim
114, 116, 117, 213, 271
Noach
13, 76, 152, 208, 209, 357
Pekudei
806, 939
Pinchas
158, 160162, 166, 173, 635
Prologue
115, 118
Shemot
152, 154, 217
Shlach Lecha
130, 136, 226, 227, 237
Shmini
68
Tazria
128, 187
Toldot
49, 51, 64-67, 69-71, 107
Trumah
325, 564
Vaera
126
Vaetchanan
28, 148, 191, 196
Vayakhel
91, 94, 95, 493, 494
Vayechi
18, 84, 86, 303
Vayera
133, 135-137, 139, 248, 249, 262, 265, 390, 396, 401, 404, 406, 409, 410, 413, 421
Vayeshev
57-60, 63, 122
Vayishlach
201, 210, 212, 213, 253

REUBEN

Beha'alot'cha
112, 115
Beresheet A
55, 249, 459
Miketz
164
Mishpatim
181, 183, 200
Vayechi
75, 262, 263, 264, 529-531, 538, 544-551, 655, 691, 696, 699, 701, 729, 774
Vayera
49
Vayeshev
23, 130, 131, 133-135, 137 -139
Vayetze
155, 156, 158, 159, 160, 162, 170, 186, 187, 190, 201, 202, 214
Vayishlach
203-205, 217, 218, 219, 220

REVENGE

Acharei Mot
340, 396

Balak
96, 98, 179, 232, 373
Beshalach
28, 66, 228, 244, 311
Bo
82, 83, 125
Chayei Sarah
31
Emor
16, 239
Ha'azinu
131, 168, 175, 242, 243
Idra Raba
07, 212, 333
Ki Tetze
109
Korach
60
Lech Lecha
215
Miketz
133, 166, 229
Noach
134
Pekudei
447, 571, 572
Shemot
122, 123
Shmini
104, 114
Vaera
77
Vaetchanan
181, 183
Vayakhel
386
Vayechi
579
Vayera
253, 254, 415, 416
Vayetze
88
Vayikra
121, 408
Yitro
102

RIB

Beresheet A
279, 416
Beresheet B
201, 203, 205, 213, 241

RIGHTEOUS

Acharei Mot
9, 17, 29, 34-36, 51, 75, 154, 173, 182, 207-210, 217, 221, 228, 231-233, 258-260, 262, 264, 265, 269-271, 273, 274, 276, 278, 285, 319, 320, 348, 351, 369, 381, 388, 391, 396, 412, 413
Balak
19, 23, 132, 155, 180, 185, 213, 214, 219, 220, 316, 322, 350, 506, 507
Bechukotai
10, 29, 53, 61
Beha'alot'cha
29, 31, 36, 38, 42, 64, 70, 78, 89, 93, 150
Behar
4, 16, 37, 38, 53, 62, 63, 67, 68
Bemidbar
40, 77
Beresheet A
3, 40, 52, 75, 118, 148, 151, 155, 167, 181, 188, 199, 203,

235-237, 244, 246, 326, 339, 352, 358-360, 362, 364, 379 -382, 384, 385, 395, 405, 456, 470, 471, 481

Beresheet B
5-8, 10, 15, 16, 22-24, 49, 52, 54, 59, 61, 70, 82, 86, 97, 131, 135, 140, 141, 147, 150, 169, 176, 178, 209, 300, 301, 352, 370, 371, 376, 382, 387, 390, 391, 414, 419, 431, 435, 440, 443, 446, 448

Beshalach
11, 45, 46, 49, 68, 142, 145, 150, 157, 158, 170, 174, 188, 190, 216-218, 240, 280, 281, 286, 325, 328, 330, 353, 355, 356, 358, 363, 383, 392, 407, 420, 422, 454, 463

Bo
4, 22, 27, 29, 39, 57, 94, 98, 100, 136-138, 145, 146, 197, 202, 206, 225, 232, 234

Chayei Sarah
36, 40, 51, 53, 55-61, 70, 94, 95, 96, 99, 117, 121 -123, 136, 143, 149, 164, 168, 209, 210, 224, 231, 242

Chukat
51, 58, 68, 80, 81

Ekev
4, 9, 23, 46

Emor
1, 3, 4, 30-32, 42, 56, 57, 62, 63, 90, 94, 203, 233, 276, 279, 282a, 291, 292, 313, 316

Ha'azinu
17, 28, 29, 30, 34, 35, 40, 79, 95, 103, 105, 107, 110, 113, 117, 132, 161, 207, 210, 254

Idra Raba
9, 10, 15, 17, 30, 33, 52, 201, 218, 230, 240, 248, 328, 329, 331, 362, 363, 364

Kedoshim
4, 9, 62-64, 76, 78, 92, 93, 130, 133, 134

Ki Tetze
12, 13, 44, 50, 67, 98, 99, 113, 116, 127, 129, 132, 138

Ki Tisa
1, 4, 47, 114, 120

Korach
21, 25, 34, 49

Lech Lecha
5, 6, 8, 9, 50, 54, 55, 80, 84, 88-90, 94, 105, 122, 123, 125 -132, 148, 170, 198, 203, 219, 226, 227, 253, 256, 309, 317, 332, 348, 357, 362, 363, 364, 367, 370, 371, 378, 379, 380, 381, 408, 428, 444, 467

Metzora
6, 7, 10, 11, 13, 46, 51, 62

Miketz
7, 9, 15, 17, 18, 32, 35, 45, 46, 53, 57, 69, 72, 79, 82, 119, 125, 129, 148, 149, 151, 153, 154, 155, 166, 175, 182, 184, 207, 219, 228, 247, 249, 259, 264, 265

Mishpatim
3, 5, 6, 31, 46, 65, 67, 75, 79, 82, 125, 136, 201, 227, 231, 237, 243, 265, 334, 370, 381, 384, 385, 386, 389, 390, 395, 396, 404, 406, 410, 411, 435, 438,

439, 441, 454, 458, 475, 480, 498, 531, 532, 537, 540, 547

Naso
21, 41, 46, 54, 199

Noach
1, 3, 6, 8, 9, 13, 14, 16, 17, 19-21, 23, 25, 26, 39, 44, 65, 68, 69, 71-73, 76, 83, 92, 127, 131, 133, 136, 137, 140, 141, 143 -147, 153-155, 166, 169, 170, 172-176, 187, 190, 201, 206, 216, 267, 268, 275, 277, 300, 304, 310

Pekudei
4, 5, 6, 58, 64, 78, 81, 88, 89, 171, 182, 248, 337, 343, 365, 461, 467, 485, 491, 493, 522, 525, 565, 576, 582, 583, 616, 631, 671, 679, 704, 706, 728, 733, 740, 741, 742, 743, 745, 747, 749, 762, 763, 842, 865, 880, 924, 933, 951, 956

Pinchas
2, 8, 9, 10, 15, 17, 35a, 38, 40, 52, 78, 79, 81, 83, 91, 93-96, 98, 99, 100-102, 106, 108-113, 132, 134, 137, 138, 141, 142, 164, 171, 177, 190, 191, 193, 195, 213, 247, 261, 278, 288, 289, 293, 294, 306, 316, 328, 332, 334, 354, 361, 376, 414, 416, 443, 444, 446-450, 452, 458, 459, 482, 486, 533, 535, 564 -567, 571, 574, 583, 585, 610, 628, 654, 655, 662, 664, 689, 719, 732, 738, 739, 741, 746, 759, 777, 821, 839, 851, 852, 855, 858, 865, 871, 873, 895

Prologue
26, 29, 52, 57, 60, 62, 105, 106, 108, 109, 110, 129, 132, 164, 171

Safra Detzniuta
11, 13, 40

Shemot
8, 39, 47, 68, 78, 96, 107, 109, 118, 120, 121, 133, 146, 158, 163, 166-174, 176, 181, 182, 185, 186, 193, 200, 207, 208, 222, 223, 228, 241, 250, 252, 253, 256, 257, 370, 389

Shlach Lecha
30, 52, 66, 98, 99, 102, 128, 129, 137, 139, 154, 198 -201, 203, 204, 207, 208, 231, 232, 235, 291, 293, 300, 305, 306, 313, 318, 333, 334, 341, 346

Shmini
12, 15, 16, 22, 42, 68, 81, 92

Shoftim
4, 12, 16, 24

Tazria
3, 14, 20, 40, 51, 61, 68, 77, 78, 118, 139, 179

Tetzaveh
41, 89, 130, 132

Toldot
6, 11, 14, 21, 39-42, 44, 46, 69, 71, 72, 83, 86, 87, 88, 89, 90, 91, 95, 96, 107

Trumah
17, 20, 25, 39, 40, 44, 48, 49, 73, 87, 89, 90, 110, 151, 152, 155, 175, 176, 178, 180, 204, 208, 252, 257, 279, 280, 286, 297, 300, 306, 307, 308, 309, 355, 364, 383, 385, 414, 457, 458, 479, 529, 538, 550, 551, 555,

557, 562, 612, 618, 619, 675, 677, 680, 690, 738, 740, 741, 776, 777, 793, 797, 811, 812, 830, 878, 879, 880, 888, 924

Tzav
18, 45, 62, 63, 89, 93, 96, 112, 145, 147, 148, 166

Vaera
20, 30, 31, 79, 94, 100, 115, 148

Vaetchanan
4, 23, 25, 35, 77, 129-131, 135, 145, 177, 190

Vayakhel
6, 18, 22, 23, 51, 67, 88, 120, 134, 142, 149, 195, 213, 225, 244, 282, 296, 301, 307, 312, 313, 317, 321, 322, 325, 332, 338, 362, 367, 368, 370, 371, 373, 383, 385, 386, 387, 388, 391, 393, 394, 439, 443, 444, 446, 447, 451, 455, 457, 463

Vayechi
6, 77, 105-107, 109, 112, 140, 141, 142, 155, 161, 168-170, 180, 189, 194, 209, 219, 221, 225, 226, 247, 250, 265, 271, 274, 299, 300, 303, 304, 312, 314, 320, 324, 326, 327, 351, 354, 358, 363, 365, 367, 369, 373, 400, 404, 408, 425, 430, 431, 439, 440, 442, 454, 455, 461, 462, 466, 475, 506, 514, 537, 542, 585, 640, 662, 668, 676, 683, 690, 693, 725, 730, 743, 747-751, 753, 760, 761, 763, 764, 766, 777, 783, 786, 793, 806, 854, 860

Vayelech
16, 17, 20, 33, 37

Vayera
13, 20, 21, 23, 27, 30, 31, 41, 58, 63, 119, 129, 131, 136, 177 -180, 186, 191, 192, 193, 196, 199, 200, 208, 209, 210, 218, 219, 221, 222, 239, 244, 249, 257, 267, 318, 323, 367, 369, 370, 392-394, 398, 399, 401, 404, 410, 411, 417, 419, 424, 425, 473, 474

Vayeshev
1, 10, 11, 12, 15-17, 19, 22, 26 -31, 35, 36, 40-42, 50, 61, 67, 69, 102, 132, 140, 143, 145, 170, 172-174, 179, 180, 189, 205, 207-209, 212, 219, 239, 240, 243, 245, 253, 258, 264, 278, 279, 284, 285

Vayetze
101, 119, 133-135, 137-139, 141, 143, 164, 165, 166, 177, 239, 244, 264, 280, 283, 323, 324, 325, 327, 330, 331, 362, 364, 374

Vayigash
3, 5, 18, 31, 32, 45, 61, 63 -66, 70, 79, 89, 129

Vayikra
60, 61, 92, 98, 100, 115, 131, 144, 161, 176, 177, 205, 209, 231, 233, 234, 238-241, 244, 264, 265, 270-273, 276, 277, 278, 283, 284, 292, 293, 311, 324, 341, 368, 369, 372, 379, 423, 434-436, 446, 447

Vayishlach
40, 44, 45, 47, 57, 66, 74, 91, 120, 134, 169, 196, 197, 214, 227, 244, 268, 269, 272, 278

Yitro
19, 53, 63, 64, 102, 116, 121, 149, 165, 174, 181, 184, 187

-189, 192, 193, 195, 197, 199, 201, 213, 221, 228, 237, 240, 333, 334, 399, 400, 468, 510, 550, 562

RING

Beresheet A
319, 344
Chayei Sarah
178
Lech Lecha
465
Mishpatim
48, 343, 345
Prologue
23

RIVER JORDAN

Beresheet A
62
Lech Lecha
56, 178

RIVER OF FIRE (DINUR)

Beha'alot'cha
105, 120
Beresheet A
58
Beresheet B
44, 108, 109
Bo
162
Miketz
175, 176
Pekudei
368, 523, 559, 623, 624, 628, 654
Shemot
86, 352
Shlach Lecha
53, 88
Trumah
447
Tzav
21, 73, 127, 128
Vayakhel
304, 331, 332
Vayechi
162
Vayikra
278

RIVERS

Acharei Mot
30, 33-35, 101, 147, 159, 160, 166, 168, 171, 172, 209, 238, 304, 380, 382, 411
Balak
154, 160, 394, 396, 438
Beha'alot'cha
30, 31, 44, 88, 105, 120, 121
Bemidbar
63
Beresheet A
58, 96, 220, 246-250, 256, 260, 269, 297, 298, 303, 311, 316, 327, 336, 342, 367, 376, 388-401, 426, 436, 477
Beresheet B
44, 50, 108-110, 114, 281, 283, 364
Beshalach
42, 86, 116, 117, 141, 142, 184, 225, 239, 255, 410, 411, 424, 481
Bo
10, 37, 40-48, 50, 56, 58, 60, 62-64, 67, 68, 71, 73, 162, 224, 235

Chayei Sarah
138, 143, 146, 147, 148, 206
Chukat
27, 28
Ekev
48
Emor
11, 103, 154, 158, 164, 165, 167, 170, 187-190, 241, 250, 331, 332
Ha'azinu
67, 79, 80, 85, 86, 96, 156, 188, 205, 212, 226, 227, 228
Idra Raba
23, 118, 189, 277, 315, 362
Kedoshim
92
Ki Tetze
72
Lech Lecha
106, 107, 129, 189, 396, 423, 448
Metzora
40
Miketz
9, 18, 19, 20, 62, 78, 87, 113, 175, 176
Mishpatim
86, 105, 166, 226, 296, 297, 301, 483, 523, 539, 578
Naso
72
Noach
4, 5, 11, 84, 145, 173, 302, 336
Pekudei
1, 58, 99, 271, 368, 411, 414, 493-495, 523, 559, 623, 624, 628, 630, 637, 638, 654, 711, 732, 756, 798
Pinchas
17, 30, 47, 48, 101, 196, 198, 248, 380, 530, 654, 655, 766, 768, 891
Prologue
40, 58, 95, 96, 109, 219, 222
Safra Detzniuta
17, 39
Shemot
1, 9, 32, 58, 86, 158, 190, 191, 195-197, 202, 259, 322, 352
Shlach Lecha
53, 88, 177, 183, 253, 315, 316
Shmini
77, 79
Tazria
13, 53, 68, 124
Toldot
108, 115
Trumah
20, 24, 45, 183, 188, 200, 208, 355, 376, 377, 402, 447, 742, 820, 823
Tzav
21, 63, 73, 96, 109, 110, 112, 127, 128
Vaera
16, 47, 104, 105, 106, 107, 108, 109, 111, 122, 123, 128, 129, 131, 135-137, 144, 146, 153, 156, 158, 164, 165, 166, 167, 175
Vaetchanan
59, 122, 123, 142, 146, 162
Vayakhel
20, 95, 304, 310, 311, 313, 314, 315, 316, 326, 327, 331, 332
Vayechi
25, 57, 58, 162, 182, 234, 268,

282, 304, 534, 605, 727, 728, 783, 784
Vayelech
39, 40
Vayera
211, 292, 424
Vayeshev
21, 33, 37, 52, 157, 159, 160
Vayetze
46, 47, 93, 94, 178, 181, 267, 289, 305, 324, 334, 347
Vayigash
13, 20, 57, 64, 65, 81
Vayikra
29, 31, 37, 38, 88, 103, 132, 134, 151, 153-155, 159, 168 -170, 172, 174, 197, 204, 246, 267, 272, 278, 290, 331, 350, 351, 418, 448
Vayishlach
68, 137, 217, 228
Yitro
25, 64, 95, 326, 341, 400, 485

ROBBERS

Ki Tisa
89
Miketz
259, 260, 264
Vaetchanan
32, 36
Vayera
419

ROCK

Acharei Mot
7, 92, 104, 193
Balak
59, 182, 308, 316, 318, 465
Beresheet A
263, 287
Beshalach
90, 424-433, 444
Bo
214
Chayei Sarah
20
Ha'azinu
206, 228, 244
Kedoshim
2
Ki Tetze
60, 61, 72-76
Lech Lecha
181, 248, 327, 328, 336, 337
Miketz
17
Mishpatim
61, 74, 116, 118, 222, 223, 306, 383
Noach
12
Pekudei
564, 602, 727
Pinchas
26, 72, 107, 315, 333, 492, 494, 498, 499, 521, 699
Prologue
101, 102
Shlach Lecha
220, 303
Tazria
37, 39
Tetzaveh
92
Toldot
83
Trumah
538, 566

Vaera
, 5, 8
Vaetchanan
149
Vayakhel
144
Vayechi
122, 429
Vayera
457
Vayeshev
126
Vayetze
100, 222, 362
Vayikra
240, 268, 350
Yitro
224, 345, 352, 520, 521

ROCKS

Acharei Mot
315
Balak
339, 344, 465, 466
Beresheet A
19, 241
Beshalach
152
Bo
214
Chayei Sarah
9
Idra Raba
153
Ki Tisa
73
Noach
64
Pekudei
897
Pinchas
158, 264, 573
Prologue
113
Shemot
99
Shlach Lecha
217
Shmini
97
Tzav
83
Vayakhel
162
Vayera
409
Vayetze
42, 221
Vayikra
88, 427, 433
Vayishlach
135
Yitro
345

ROD

Beresheet A
262, 263, 320
Beresheet B
187
Beshalach
90, 91, 93, 424
Ki Tetze
73, 88
Mishpatim
384, 386, 548
Pinchas
361, 699, 724, 733, 808
Prologue
101, 102, 149

Shemot
262, 304, 308, 372
Shlach Lecha
72, 315
Tazria
156
Vaera
100, 104
Vayeshev
205
Vayetze
278, 316

RODS

Ekev
65
Vayetze
296, 300, 303, 304, 307, 308, 311, 314, 317, 318, 341, 346- 349

ROME

Balak
502
Pinchas
740, 743-746
Shemot
81, 116
Tazria
171
Vaera
175, 205
Vayakhel
496
Vayera
480, 481
Vayikra
319

ROOSTER

Balak
184, 495
Behar
3
Lech Lecha
9, 368, 369
Metzora
7
Prologue
171
Shlach Lecha
267, 268
Vayakhel
14, 21
Vayechi
163, 164, 165, 166, 167
Vayikra
379, 394-397

ROPE

Chayei Sarah
236
Ki Tetze
119
Miketz
128
Mishpatim
121, 149
Prologue
70
Shoftim
6
Vayera
357
Vayigash
126

ROSH HASHANAH

Acharei Mot
196
Beha'alot'cha
10
Beresheet A
461, 470
Beshalach
9, 12, 21
Bo
5
Emor
118, 120, 126, 205, 206, 215, 217, 221, 224, 227a
Ki Tetze
136, 143, 145, 146
Pekudei
588, 722, 726, 883, 885
Pinchas
27, 30, 351, 352, 355, 358, 360, 364, 678, 827
Shlach Lecha
219
Tetzaveh
77, 87, 125, 129, 141, 142
Trumah
707
Tzav
59
Vayakhel
33
Vayechi
202, 229, 353, 355, 356
Vayera
146, 381, 384, 385, 386
Vayeshev
226
Vayetze
284
Vayikra
302, 311
Vayishlach
176

RUACH (SOUL)

Acharei Mot
205, 215, 216, 255, 256, 258, 260, 262-264, 266, 267, 274
Balak
78
Beresheet A
18, 94, 109, 258, 274
Beresheet B
130, 212, 379
Emor
58, 287
Idra Raba
138, 139, 140
Ki Tetze
51, 108
Korach
19, 42, 45
Lech Lecha
76-78, 96, 98-104, 146, 152 -161, 167, 193, 239, 273, 363
Mishpatim
11, 12, 23, 24, 105, 106, 107, 108, 110
Naso
36, 37
Noach
25, 62-64
Pekudei
638
Pinchas
39, 271, 405, 572, 607, 790
Prologue
109

Shemot
163
Shlach Lecha
221, 237
Shmini
104
Tetzaveh
53, 54
Trumah
268, 284-293, 298-304, 306, 458, 531, 591, 607
Tzav
3, 62-65, 68-71, 140, 143, 144, 146-148, 188, 189
Vaera
48
Vaetchanan
195
Vayakhel
46, 47, 48, 96, 113, 122, 123, 135, 184, 186-188, 191, 192, 193, 196, 270, 275, 401
Vayechi
309-312, 319, 320, 325, 327, 328, 331, 348, 360, 361, 363
Vayera
267
Vayetze
189
Vayigash
15-17, 19, 20-22
Vayikra
263, 317, 422, 424, 430, 432, 433, 437, 438
Yitro
224, 225, 226, 227

RUMIEL (SUPERNAL MINISTER)

Vayikra
11

RUTH

Acharei Mot
287
Balak
60-62, 98, 99, 252
Lech Lecha
399
Mishpatim
334, 476
Prologue
236
Vaetchanan
126, 152
Vayechi
57
Vayera
311, 336
Vayeshev
191, 193, 194

SAADIEL (SPIRIT)

Pekudei
682

SABBATICAL YEAR

Behar
8
Emor
177
Lech Lecha
384
Shlach Lecha
264
Tetzaveh
71
Trumah
403
Vaera
3, 4

Vayechi
648
Vayetze
3, 7, 8, 130, 131, 133, 134, 140, 142, 148, 150

SACHSICHA (SPIRIT)

Pekudei
875

SACRIFICE

Acharei Mot
9, 13, 28, 45, 49, 119, 123, 133, 247, 249, 250, 409, 410
Balak
193, 221, 317, 396, 454, 472, 478, 479
Beha'alot'cha
27, 48, 53, 79
Behar
5, 28, 29, 31-34, 39, 41, 43-45, 48, 50, 71
Beresheet A
77, 80, 233, 424
Beresheet B
25, 141, 263, 264, 334, 337, 411, 431, 437
Beshalach
30, 277
Bo
13, 177, 186, 187, 191, 194
Chayei Sarah
198, 261
Emor
16, 38, 39, 46, 48, 62, 69, 130, 146, 159, 161, 174, 183, 184, 185, 272, 274, 288
Ha'azinu
148b
Kedoshim
10, 116, 119
Ki Tetze
40, 46, 136
Ki Tisa
97
Lech Lecha
84, 98, 102, 298, 301, 303, 304, 380, 425, 426, 430-432, 436, 469
Metzora
12, 42
Miketz
106, 109, 110, 111, 222
Mishpatim
260, 261, 268, 275, 312, 450, 468, 469, 547
Naso
9, 58
Noach
88, 107, 118-120, 127, 129, 131, 189, 227-229, 232, 240, 244, 245, 250
Pekudei
65, 66, 73, 115, 356, 358, 359, 363, 364, 421, 452, 524, 559, 672, 720, 817, 831, 921, 922, 942, 944, 946, 951, 953, 955, 956
Pinchas
203, 206, 207, 209-211, 213, 214, 216-219, 221-224, 229, 230, 244, 245, 323, 325, 342, 374, 379, 381, 399, 418, 419, 421, 422, 424, 440, 446, 522 -525, 527-529, 531-537, 539-543, 545, 547 -549, 552, 559, 560, 561, 595, 597, 658, 667, 670, 674, 676, 679, 681, 682, 683, 721, 722, 725, 731,

751-753, 756, 760-762, 765, 769, 796, 797, 799, 800, 802, 804, 826, 828, 837, 838, 879, 880, 881, 883, 885, 886, 888, 889, 890

Prologue
96, 178

Shemot
369, 374

Shlach Lecha
86, 87

Shmini
30, 31, 32, 83

Tazria
36, 107, 108, 133

Tetzaveh
45, 48, 140

Toldot
19, 88

Trumah
63, 588, 589, 651, 879

Tzav
4, 6, 7, 10, 15, 16, 22, 24, 26-29, 47, 55, 69-71, 84-86, 98 -100, 121, 123, 128-136, 138, 139, 149, 150, 154, 180, 186, 189, 191

Vaera
205

Vaetchanan
66, 84, 119

Vayakhel
152, 258, 327, 337, 371, 379, 380, 410, 472, 477, 478

Vayechi
20, 231, 419, 421, 604, 620, 715, 718-720, 723, 788, 790, 791, 792, 794, 795, 796, 797, 843

Vayera
116, 117, 131, 142, 379, 433, 435, 497, 498, 507

Vayeshev
43, 98, 251, 267

Vayetze
368, 369, 371

Vayigash
29, 119

Vayikra
28, 30, 40, 50, 52, 53, 70, 72 -74, 117, 123, 128, 129, 134, 178, 190, 193, 195, 314, 442

Vayishlach
161, 229

SAFSIRITA (SPIRIT)

Pekudei
850

SAHADIEL (SPIRIT)

Pekudei
486, 487

SAKAFORTAYA (SPIRIT)

Pekudei
867

SALT

Beha'alot'cha
86, 87

Behar
28

Ha'azinu
181

Pinchas
637, 664

Shmini
88
Trumah
418
Vayechi
666-668
Vayera
262, 288
Vayetze
59

SAMAEL

Acharei Mot
79, 359
Balak
141-145, 147, 148, 228, 274, 275, 276
Behar
43
Beresheet A
175, 184, 291, 437, 438, 439, 445, 446, 458, 464, 465
Beresheet B
45, 349
Beshalach
155, 156, 460, 463
Bo
202, 203, 209, 228
Ekev
28
Emor
222, 236, 245
Kedoshim
48, 51
Ki Tetze
13, 26, 35, 39, 41, 96, 97, 111, 119, 138
Korach
47, 48
Lech Lecha
76, 78
Mishpatim
8, 84, 313, 371, 380, 383, 385, 407, 429, 430
Naso
13, 42, 84
Pekudei
299, 304, 308, 375, 389, 390, 424, 439, 454
Pinchas
118, 209, 210, 212, 214-216, 220, 362, 363, 364, 374, 378, 379, 410, 412, 414, 416, 424, 562, 573, 577, 578, 580, 593, 650, 679, 681, 682, 683, 808, 831, 883, 891, 892
Shemot
175
Shoftim
2, 5, 6-9, 14, 17, 19, 20
Tetzaveh
83, 120
Toldot
25, 80, 161, 172, 192, 193, 195-198
Trumah
586
Tzav
57, 61
Vayechi
378, 379, 380
Vayetze
23, 28, 85, 86, 288, 313
Vayishlach
80, 88, 101, 103, 104, 110, 114-116, 188

SAMSON

Balak
178
Chayei Sarah
40, 42
Naso
130
Vayechi
703, 704, 709, 725

SAMUEL

Balak
24, 90, 101, 113, 179, 221, 369, 386, 387, 388, 464
Beresheet A
63, 143, 145, 146, 147, 148, 167, 187, 211, 263, 304, 359
Chayei Sarah
27, 59, 222
Chukat
20, 54
Ekev
7, 27, 54
Emor
54, 69, 97, 118, 141, 274, 280
Ha'azinu
55, 56, 92, 120, 123, 147, 158, 177, 240
Idra Raba
69, 204, 223, 231, 232, 312, 322
Ki Tetze
76, 120
Ki Tisa
56
Korach
32
Lech Lecha
64, 172, 327, 393, 403, 407, 408
Metzora
23, 46, 58
Miketz
14, 28, 122, 227
Mishpatim
104, 180, 240, 241, 242, 249, 251, 255, 256, 324, 325, 328, 376
Naso
16, 58, 100
Pekudei
90, 186, 187, 231, 260, 587, 837, 859
Pinchas
14, 138, 183, 263, 338, 344, 356, 453, 459, 494, 522, 558, 572, 653, 674, 754, 832, 870, 875, 877
Prologue
91, 92, 94, 96-103, 104, 134, 135, 136, 164, 170
Safra Detzniuta
41, 60, 72
Shemot
355
Shlach Lecha
101, 336
Tazria
6, 37, 69, 128, 164
Toldot
11, 19, 20, 136
Trumah
1, 211, 229, 299, 303, 404 -407, 442, 464, 497, 510, 512, 527, 537, 556, 667, 689, 700, 781, 799, 914, 922
Vaetchanan
10, 31, 52, 152, 166

Vayakhel
1, 2, 4, 5, 120, 377
Vayechi
141, 424, 480, 687, 756, 844
Vayelech
31, 34, 36, 45
Vayera
23, 209, 243, 336, 337, 359, 361, 413, 427, 440, 506
Vayeshev
188, 207, 277
Vayetze
64, 111, 362, 376
Vayigash
52, 79, 100
Vayishlach
7, 20, 88, 118, 155, 198, 214
Yitro
100, 286, 288, 321, 360, 383, 401, 502

SANCTIFICATION

Balak
88, 107-109, 193, 196, 197, 199
Chukat
22
Ekev
6, 49
Emor
91, 93, 144
Ki Tisa
6
Mishpatim
464
Naso
180
Noach
357
Pekudei
109, 532, 577, 791, 809-812, 823, 826, 828, 880, 881
Pinchas
63, 308, 625, 712
Prologue
248, 250
Prologue
254, 258, 259
Shlach Lecha
297
Tetzaveh
68
Trumah
115
Trumah
52, 54-56, 57, 94, 115-119, 121, 124
Vayakhel
214, 252, 254, 435
Vayechi
443
Vayechi
85
Vayeshev
116

SANCTUARY

Acharei Mot
5, 130, 180, 334, 402
Behar
33
Bemidbar
57
Beresheet A
387
Beshalach
48-51, 146, 149, 275, 276, 309
Bo
98, 237

Chayei Sarah
190
Emor
25
Ha'azinu
13
Idra Raba
149, 150, 151
Kedoshim
30
Ki Tisa
4
Korach
26, 49, 54
Metzora
22, 25, 32, 59
Mishpatim
564, 575, 579
Naso
105
Noach
21, 43, 190
Pekudei
25, 35, 42, 97, 159, 163-165, 217, 297, 343
Pinchas
147, 477, 682, 683, 812, 848, 877, 879
Prologue
80, 82, 85, 183
Safra Detzniuta
41
Shemot
6, 38, 213
Shlach Lecha
87, 193, 196-200, 202, 203, 257, 263, 270-272, 278, 297
Shmini
38, 66
Tazria
29, 92, 93, 96
Tetzaveh
17, 18, 46, 102, 103
Trumah
261, 365, 374, 376, 378, 404, 568, 579, 713, 870, 872, 905
Vaetchanan
67
Vayechi
131, 449
Vayelech
1
Vayetze
108
Vayigash
3
Vayikra
41, 113, 178, 190, 203, 204, 363
Vayishlach
139
Yitro
255, 256

SANDALFON

Acharei Mot
52, 56
Balak
54, 55, 56
Beshalach
301, 302
Ki Tetze
102
Pekudei
500, 501, 505, 782
Pinchas
754

Trumah
922
Tzav
64
Vaera
103
Vayakhel
148
Vayechi
397, 398, 572
Vayetze
105
Vayishlach
44

SANEGORYAH (SPIRIT)

Pekudei
632

SANGADIEL (SPIRIT)

Pekudei
540, 542, 860, 868

SANGIRYA (SPIRIT)

Trumah
66

SANHEDRIN

Acharei Mot
11
Behar
30
Idra Raba
232
Pekudei
724, 725
Pinchas
61, 383, 455, 461, 632
Shlach Lecha
86, 89
Shoftim
21, 22, 23
Trumah
382, 625
Tzav
176
Vaetchanan
13
Vayakhel
358, 453
Vayechi
655, 656
Vayikra
313, 334-337, 386

SANSANIYA (SPIRIT)

Pekudei
596, 597, 604, 605

SANURIYA (SPIRIT)

Pekudei
544

SAPIR (SPIRIT)

Beresheet B
63-65, 67, 69, 70, 76, 135

SAPPHIRE

Beresheet B
63-65, 67, 69, 70, 76, 135
Beshalach
208, 481, 482
Miketz
134

Mishpatim
576, 579
Noach
261, 266, 271
Pekudei
239, 338, 341, 380, 384, 478, 492, 496, 559, 680, 686, 740, 741, 743, 749, 781, 790, 821
Pinchas
249, 253, 255, 256, 519
Prologue
128
Trumah
231
Tzav
64
Vayakhel
441
Vayechi
4, 8, 12, 17
Vayigash
128
Vayikra
139
Yitro
364, 367, 368

SARAH

Balak
393
Beresheet A
461
Beresheet B
231
Chayei
1, 9, 13, 14, 19, 20, 21, 23, 25, 26, 36, 46, 47, 48, 62, 63, 68, 69, 90, 94, 99, 108, 109, 110, 185, 248, 249, 250, 252, 253, 254, 256, 258, 259, 260
Ki Tetze
9, 12
Lech Lecha
17, 46, 58, 59, 76, 77, 109 -111, 114, 117, 123, 126, 136 -138, 140, 200, 454, 455
Mishpatim
41
Pekudei
715
Pinchas
776
Prologue
178, 179
Shlach Lecha
119, 133, 134, 135, 204, 210, 245, 246
Tazria
184, 185
Tetzaveh
25
Toldot
22
Vaera
155, 196, 198, 199
Vayechi
802
Vayera
54, 97, 99, 102, 106, 115, 132, 133, 135, 140, 141, 146-150, 159, 343, 345, 348, 366, 367, 388, 392, 394, 399-401, 403, 406, 412, 423-425, 453, 462-467, 469, 471
Vayetze
267, 268, 274
Vayikra
304

SARTAYA (SPIRIT)

Pekudei
862

SATAN, THE

Balak
28
Beresheet A
437
Beresheet B
167
Bo
8-10, 13, 14, 16, 33, 34
Chukat
26
Emor
243
Lech Lecha
44
Miketz
1, 2, 210
Noach
376
Pekudei
838, 843, 848, 853
Pinchas
93, 353, 366, 370, 378, 590
Prologue
174, 176
Shlach Lecha
235, 236, 240
Vayechi
577
Vayera
367, 368, 369, 370, 373-375, 381, 384, 385, 387
Vayeshev
225, 279
Vayetze
103
Vayikra
275
Vayishlach
197

SATURN

Beresheet B
69
Ha'azinu
14
Ki Tetze
70, 112-114, 118, 122, 123
Pinchas
270, 737, 739

SAUL

Acharei Mot
395
Balak
221
Beresheet A
147
Beshalach
122, 124
Chayei Sarah
40, 42
Idra Raba
315
Lech Lecha
64
Miketz
107
Naso
16
Noach
87
Pekudei
67, 837

Shemot
355
Trumah
510, 512, 513
Vaera
178
Vayakhel
1, 5, 6
Vayechi
424, 832
Vayelech
10, 11
Vayigash
79
Vayikra
125, 127, 330
Vayishlach
61, 174, 175, 243
Yitro
360

SCALES

Balak
263
Beresheet A
321, 387
Ki Tisa
73
Lech Lecha
22, 23, 369, 370
Mishpatim
27, 29, 41, 45, 46, 48, 103, 258, 277, 348
Pekudei
615-618, 683, 876-878, 880, 883
Safra Detzniuta
3, 5, 10, 11, 22, 52
Vayechi
662

SEA OF GALILEE

Bechukotai
34
Beha'alot'cha
26, 47
Beshalach
104
Trumah
19
Vaera
16

SEA OF KINERET

Shlach Lecha
342
Trumah
425
Vaera
16

SEA OF SUF

Beshalach
30, 128, 265, 273, 344
Yitro
47

SEAL

Beresheet A
319
Mishpatim
304, 343, 364, 367-369
Prologue
23, 57
Vayechi
68, 203, 228, 730, 731, 737, 739

SEAS

Acharei Mot
30, 34, 75-77, 79, 129, 154, 315, 361, 398
Balak
7, 47, 145, 168, 171, 229
Bechukotai
34
Beha'alot'cha
26, 27, 30, 31, 39, 47, 90
Bemidbar
58
Beresheet A
59, 62, 96, 99, 100, 254, 298, 300-302, 308, 311, 315, 360, 362, 371, 376, 377, 379, 380, 401, 409
Beresheet B
50, 168, 201, 279-282, 284, 293, 409, 417
Beshalach
30, 63, 67, 77, 83, 84, 86, 88, 89, 93, 94, 99-104, 110, 112, 113, 128, 137-139, 141 -143, 178, 179, 181, 184, 206, 211, 228, 229, 247, 254, 256, 259-261, 264 -267, 272, 273, 340, 343, 344, 371, 434
Bo
41, 46, 70, 71, 73, 198, 220, 221, 223, 224, 235
Chayei Sarah
1-4, 7, 32
Chukat 73
Emor
165, 234, 235, 239, 242, 248
Ha'azinu
198, 228
Idra Raba
41, 97, 109, 118, 152, 214
Kedoshim
83
Ki Tetze
18, 43, 54, 58-60, 66, 67, 109, 128
Ki Tisa
43, 108
Lech Lecha
12, 213, 214, 215, 396
Miketz
98, 101
Mishpatim
13, 87, 121, 122, 139, 149, 178, 185, 192, 194, 200, 213, 282, 289, 375, 482, 483, 487
Naso
27, 39, 53, 54, 71, 72
Noach
21, 53, 171-173, 185, 217 -220, 255, 339, 344
Pekudei
1, 2, 93, 94, 105, 127, 157, 189, 190, 193, 194, 271, 297
Pinchas
8, 47, 48, 101, 198, 199, 253, 254, 274, 318, 413, 575, 733, 740, 743, 805, 839
Prologue
9, 40, 56, 59, 89, 156, 157, 187, 219
Safra Detzniuta
9, 43
Shemot
123, 134, 135, 194-196, 313, 323, 342, 343, 359

Shlach Lecha
74, 88, 124, 125, 183, 199, 211, 212, 252, 253, 258, 259, 261, 272, 284, 285, 314, 315, 342
Shmini
35, 118
Tazria
13, 68, 94, 111
Tetzaveh
113, 120
Toldot
43, 72
Trumah
19, 98, 200, 325, 343, 424-426, 429, 632, 699, 742, 771, 813, 814-818, 831
Tzav
80, 112, 124, 147
Vaera
16, 47, 49, 103, 107, 111, 130, 131, 156-158, 164, 186, 189, 204
Vaetchanan
149
Vayakhel
14, 16, 21, 74, 77, 79, 86, 88, 394
Vayechi
25, 57, 58, 88, 341, 484, 534, 542, 553, 572, 574, 605, 643, 652-654, 663-665, 667, 668, 669, 675, 705-707, 732, 757, 798
Vayera
39, 241, 332, 371, 372
Vayetze
11, 93, 227, 387
Vayigash
55, 58
Vayikra
88, 124, 134, 143, 144, 319-321, 386, 388, 427
Vayishlach
74, 121, 122
Yitro
47, 358, 497

SEASONS

Beresheet A
396
Lech Lecha
304, 446, 448
Miketz
25
Vaetchanan
48
Vayera
138, 159, 403, 423
Vayigash
65

SEFER YETZIRAH (BOOK OF FORMATION)

Ki Tetze
34, 35
Ki Tisa
4
Trumah
707
Vayera
274

SEIR

Balak
138-140, 143, 144, 153, 505
Emor
54, 56, 223
Miketz
123

Shemot
16, 18
Trumah
79, 81, 83, 90
Vayeshev
112

SEMEN

Balak
183, 184
Behar
65, 69
Beresheet B
357
Beshalach
4
Chayei Sarah
152
Ekev
22
Emor
33, 154
Ha'azinu
190
Kedoshim
71
Ki Tetze
135
Miketz
115
Mishpatim
198
Noach
2, 57, 162
Pekudei
854, 855, 861
Trumah
67
Vaera
77
Vayechi
191, 192, 193, 194
Vayeshev
154, 182, 183

SENNACHERIB

Bo
101

SERACH

Shlach Lecha
198, 263

SERAPH

Beha'alot'cha
6
Beresheet B
78
Pekudei
622
Pinchas
503

SERAPHEL (SPIRIT)

Pekudei
622

SERAPHIM

Beresheet B
77, 78, 108, 166
Pekudei
251, 252, 253, 254
Pinchas
448

SERPENT

Acharei Mot
79, 80, 180, 210, 212, 214, 359, 401-406
Balak
82, 178, 181, 183, 184, 255, 276, 279, 294, 379, 380
Behar
60, 72
Bemidbar
50
Beresheet A
64, 175, 184, 199, 202, 262, 263, 285, 290, 291, 320, 404, 434, 437, 438, 440-442, 453, 455
Beresheet B
78, 112, 113, 161, 219, 283 -287, 290-292, 294, 295, 297, 298, 303, 306-308, 319, 320, 323, 331-333, 336, 341, 349, 416, 422
Beshalach
183, 218, 424
Bo
69-73
Chayei Sarah
19, 31, 32, 33, 34, 68, 69, 71-74, 76-80, 83, 84, 86, 87, 205, 206, 220
Chukat
17, 70b, 72
Emor
165, 222, 329
Ha'azinu
103
Idra Raba
326
Kedoshim
48, 55, 130
Ki Tetze
31, 58, 61, 96
Ki Tisa
106, 107, 109, 112, 115, 116, 118, 119
Korach
46
Lech Lecha
42, 44-48, 68, 76, 78, 79, 81, 85, 142, 396
Metzora
4
Miketz
186, 187, 193
Mishpatim
15, 147, 222, 242, 259, 313, 316-320, 322, 323, 330, 334, 377, 482, 492, 537, 564
Naso
72, 73, 83, 84, 86, 92
Noach
88-92, 99, 103-107, 244, 245, 247, 298, 299, 301, 311, 341
Pekudei
117, 203, 205, 299, 308, 313, 322, 426, 442, 454, 469, 476, 528, 551, 552, 836, 872, 876 -879, 894, 895, 901, 905, 936, 937, 938, 940
Pinchas
51, 89, 209, 210, 318, 331, 378, 416, 485, 486, 498, 562, 573, 587, 593, 650, 696, 698, 699, 700, 708, 808, 853
Prologue
156, 210
Safra Detzniuta
9, 46, 68
Shemot
70, 175, 302

Shlach Lecha
75, 80, 103, 105, 130, 217 -220
Shmini
14, 15, 119
Shoftim
6, 9, 19, 20
Tazria
32-34, 83, 85, 86, 93-95
Tetzaveh
84, 87
Toldot
25, 26, 28, 30-32, 43, 50, 52, 138, 139, 141-143, 148, 191 -193, 195, 196
Trumah
333-336, 410-413, 430, 431, 482, 586, 760, 871, 872
Tzav
57
Vaera
100, 104-109, 116, 118-120, 122, 123
Vayakhel
1, 2, 4, 12, 171, 407, 488, 490 -492
Vayechi
378-381, 384, 704-712, 722 -724
Vayera
331, 334, 377, 379, 384
Vayeshev
9, 38, 152, 272
Vayetze
21, 23, 25, 112, 116, 288, 313
Vayikra
232, 242, 325
Vayishlach
26, 27, 28, 76, 80, 85, 86, 108 -110, 114, 140, 146, 147, 156
Yitro
30, 77, 168, 272, 274-276

SETH

Acharei Mot
369
Bemidbar
4
Beresheet A
456, 481
Beresheet B
348-350, 365, 371, 372, 376, 378
Bo
111
Chayei Sarah
42, 43
Idra Raba
339
Metzora
22
Mishpatim
316
Pekudei
206
Trumah
759, 760, 762, 763, 764
Vayechi
612

SEVEN

Acharei Mot
48, 91, 233, 324, 355, 388
Balak
6, 85, 281, 314, 331, 382, 396, 453, 454

Bechukotai
46-48, 50, 55
Beha'alot'cha
20, 43, 45, 46, 49, 73, 88
Behar
7, 16-19, 21, 29, 72
Bemidbar
56
Beresheet A
34, 44, 64, 65, 131, 184, 193, 194, 207, 216, 306, 365, 397, 403, 432, 444, 445, 468
Beresheet B
4, 39, 44, 53-55, 62, 69, 72, 105, 164, 269, 271, 272, 278 -282, 325, 343, 361
Beshalach
19, 121, 267, 270
Bo
141, 167, 199, 221, 225
Chayei Sarah
1, 14, 23, 25, 35, 48, 70, 169, 206
Chukat
22
Ekev
34, 48, 65
Emor
16, 21, 23-25, 52, 53, 60, 68-70, 137-140, 149, 155, 162, 163, 164, 166, 175, 177-181, 249-260, 264, 265, 270-272, 276, 277, 282b, 288, 302
Ha'azinu
13, 14, 17, 41, 138, 139, 206, 230
Idra Raba
1, 66, 68, 97, 172, 175, 177, 178, 180, 209, 210, 211, 314, 357, 358, 360
Kedoshim
74, 88
Ki Tetze
72, 122, 143-145
Ki Tisa
37, 58
Korach
41
Lech Lecha
13, 41-43, 64, 65, 90, 128, 211, 212, 213, 215
Metzora
40, 42
Miketz
19, 20, 21, 22, 135, 256, 257, 258
Mishpatim
83, 117, 200, 303, 336, 427, 428, 433, 471, 533
Naso
53, 61
Noach
55, 69, 172, 247, 260
Pekudei
65, 97, 108, 111, 114, 118, 120, 130, 146, 148, 156, 157, 191, 217, 218, 224, 244, 282, 283, 313, 435, 474, 475, 789, 790, 795, 836, 838, 839, 842, 878, 936
Pinchas
69, 246, 291, 302, 336, 436, 443, 506, 517, 592, 632, 675, 737, 738, 739, 769, 778-780, 795, 804-806, 814, 815, 819, 820, 824, 826-829, 879, 888, 890

Prologue
7, 153
Safra Detzniuta
7, 22, 26, 44, 57, 66, 67
Shemot
101, 126, 127, 141, 142, 163 -165, 197, 245, 287, 290, 314
Shlach Lecha
6, 61, 86, 88, 89, 113, 128, 139, 180, 210, 255, 260, 270, 276, 296, 316, 323, 339, 341
Shmini
26-30, 45, 59
Shoftim
18, 20
Tazria
26, 44, 45, 49, 97-99
Tetzaveh
62, 63, 67, 68, 72, 117, 118, 120, 128, 134-136, 138, 140
Trumah
31, 49, 94, 114, 125, 138, 330, 387, 391, 399, 401, 403, 405, 406, 445, 575-577, 618, 630, 662, 687, 704, 708, 709, 758, 788, 791, 792, 798, 846, 848, 849, 912, 913
Tzav
78, 108-110, 113, 114, 168 -172, 191
Vaera
16, 128, 166, 172, 173, 176, 178, 179, 180, 181
Vaetchanan
21, 125, 126
Vayakhel
38, 96, 103-105, 109, 147 -149, 204, 219, 220, 236, 246, 251, 492
Vayechi
21-23, 139, 145, 151, 171, 172, 227, 291, 346, 444, 448, 506, 568, 584, 605, 655, 661, 662, 679, 771, 772, 773, 810
Vayelech
1, 34
Vayera
16, 104, 105, 112, 124, 281, 389, 478, 480
Vayeshev
47, 51, 145, 196
Vayetze
13, 14, 19, 83, 96, 128-131, 140-142, 219, 223, 380
Vayigash
86
Vayikra
75, 134-136, 141, 142, 145, 157, 209, 283, 335, 337, 413, 414, 416-419
Vayishlach
29, 117, 120, 236
Yitro
68, 211, 212, 465, 523, 534 -536, 539, 557

SEVENTEEN

Pekudei
151
Trumah
352
Vayechi
1, 113-115, 245, 656
Vayeshev
24

SEVENTY

Acharei Mot
79, 191-193, 211, 212, 214, 388

Balak
4, 9, 10, 314, 501, 502
Beha'alot'cha
137, 148
Bemidbar
6
Beresheet B
41, 103-106, 118, 168, 179, 361
Beshalach
19, 160, 162, 163, 176, 309, 315, 316, 394, 438, 439
Chayei Sarah
35, 36, 70, 143
Emor
22, 23, 69, 70, 151, 155, 171, 247, 272-274, 288, 300, 302, 303, 326
Ha'azinu
14, 30, 236
Idra Raba
232
Ki Tetze
7, 17
Ki Tisa
31
Lech Lecha
42, 43, 90, 125, 126, 196, 197, 291, 344
Metzora
42
Miketz
47, 135
Mishpatim
2, 303, 473, 474, 475, 531, 533, 577
Naso
58
Pekudei
131, 278, 598, 599, 601, 626
Pinchas
16, 33, 55, 134, 185, 190, 269, 302, 308, 353, 355, 453, 455, 461, 506, 593, 629, 632, 642, 698, 700, 701, 712, 713, 802, 826, 827, 833, 834, 884-886, 888-890
Prologue
82
Shemot
66, 286, 290
Shlach Lecha
12, 61, 86, 88, 124, 125, 259
Tetzaveh
117-120, 138-140
Toldot
85
Trumah
49, 50, 125, 158, 283, 368, 382, 586, 624, 625
Tzav
176
Vaetchanan
13, 20, 58, 113, 114
Vayakhel
144, 147, 159, 160, 162, 204, 246, 251, 254, 255, 290, 291, 358
Vayechi
138, 156, 409, 501, 502, 655, 656, 803
Vayera
268, 269, 270, 271, 274, 278, 279, 281, 284
Vayikra
265, 337
Vayishlach
52, 53, 55, 162, 236
Yitro
285, 345, 413, 465, 522, 540

SEVENTY-TWO

Acharei Mot
303, 388, 404
Balak
169
Beha'alot'cha
33, 35, 36, 38, 41-43, 46, 72
Beresheet A
43, 236
Beresheet B
361
Beshalach
134, 135, 137, 160, 163-168, 171, 174, 176, 177, 300, 482
Bo
56
Ekev
49, 72
Idra Raba
232
Ki Tetze
17
Korach
52
Lech Lecha
66
Mishpatim
388
Pekudei
268, 278, 600, 602, 603, 621, 623, 718
Pinchas
69, 106, 190, 256, 258, 268, 269, 271, 285, 302, 305, 307, 308, 340, 341, 455, 629, 632, 647, 711, 713, 718, 747, 749, 750, 823
Prologue
116, 117
Shemot
69
Shlach Lecha
288
Shoftim
21, 23
Tetzaveh
14, 15, 21, 25, 28, 29
Trumah
105, 107, 108, 110-112, 382, 471, 625, 912
Tzav
176
Vaetchanan
58, 63
Vayakhel
420
Vayechi
409
Vayera
274, 278, 279, 283, 458, 477
Vayikra
337, 427
Yitro
545

SHABBAT

Acharei Mot
7, 263, 366, 388, 408, 410
Balak
239, 305, 306, 446
Bechukotai
39, 54
Behar
5, 6, 8, 14-16, 29
Beresheet A
56-58, 128-132, 189, 192, 199, 278, 355, 396
Beresheet B
57, 185, 188, 191-200, 228,

229, 345, 377, 378
Beshalach
70-74, 211, 386, 408, 415, 416, 418, 419
Bo
124
Chayei Sarah
173, 248
Chukat
26, 59
Ekev
17, 22, 31-35, 37, 38, 44, 45, 47, 48, 62
Emor
23, 53, 60, 61, 110, 111, 115, 117-127, 162, 174, 182, 183, 294, 295, 297, 299, 300, 302, 303
Ha'azinu
45, 46, 47, 133, 186, 192
Idra Raba
35, 324, 325, 358, 362, 363, 364
Kedoshim
19, 26, 30, 32-34, 79, 80
Ki Tetze
16, 20, 37, 70, 114-116, 118, 122
Korach
6, 7, 45
Lech Lecha
105
Miketz
100, 140
Mishpatim
3, 5, 6, 67, 79, 89, 359, 360, 364, 401, 456, 458
Naso
34, 38, 39, 93
Noach
19, 66, 361, 362, 364, 365
Pekudei
545, 550, 622-625, 628, 675, 676, 691, 700, 890, 892
Pinchas
62, 209, 298, 319, 452, 484, 495, 561, 568, 569, 571 -573, 583, 584, 587, 589 -591, 593, 608, 618, 620, 621, 629, 644, 645, 669, 670, 799, 800, 806, 828, 830, 854
Prologue
4, 23, 34, 75, 78-83, 101, 148, 247, 249, 250, 252-257
Shemot
156, 210, 363, 370
Shlach Lecha
11, 12, 53, 54, 111, 112, 116, 142, 205, 290, 292, 293, 295, 297, 305, 306
Tazria
17, 36, 117, 140
Toldot
38
Trumah
32, 70, 103, 112, 113, 114, 164, 165, 167, 169, 170, 172, 173, 175, 176, 178, 180-184, 188, 191, 205, 206, 207, 213 -216, 218-220, 280, 285, 293, 294, 319, 325, 450, 451, 452, 455, 456, 517, 547, 548, 558, 717, 729, 785
Tzav
55, 56-58, 60-62, 64-66, 187, 188
Vaera
188
Vaetchanan
110

Vayakhel
157, 158, 173, 174, 175, 176, 178-183, 186, 188, 189, 191-195, 198, 199, 201, 202, 204, 207-209, 216, 217, 219, 220, 229, 230, 231, 233, 234, 236-240, 243, 244, 245, 248-250, 252, 254, 256-258, 264-266, 270, 276, 277, 278, 290, 307, 318, 333, 457, 459

Vayechi
310, 311, 348, 509, 565, 585, 614, 754, 755

Vayelech
26, 27

Vayera
32, 40, 244, 248, 328, 356, 412, 445, 483, 508

Vayeshev
39, 57

Vayikra
37, 183, 253, 274

Vayishlach
262, 263

Yitro
444, 446-448, 450-453, 455-457, 459, 460, 463-469, 472, 474, 475, 482, 494, 508, 512, 527-532, 534, 538, 544-546, 548, 549

SHACHNIEL (SPIRIT)

Pekudei
692

Vayera
277

SHADAI

Acharei Mot
358

Balak
169, 172, 424

Bemidbar
49, 54

Beresheet A
25, 26

Bo
218

Chukat
29

Ki Tetze
30, 31, 50, 137, 138

Korach
16

Lech Lecha
271, 272, 274, 288, 290, 341, 437, 441, 442, 443, 444

Noach
261, 262

Pekudei
640, 641, 714, 767, 793

Pinchas
36, 39, 294, 295, 316, 318, 344, 484-486, 488, 732, 763, 817, 839, 851, 867, 873, 874, 876

Prologue
24

Safra Detzniuta
40

Toldot
199

Trumah
613, 615, 735

Tzav
58

Vaera
1, 13, 14, 17, 18, 23, 28, 32, 75, 76

Vaetchanan
109, 116, 117, 118

Vayechi
63, 64, 66, 778, 780, 781, 811
Vayera
68, 70, 188
Vayeshev
25
Vayetze
51, 71
Vayikra
176

SHADES

Beresheet A
1, 224, 230

SHADOW

Balak
7, 177, 296, 307
Beha'alot'cha
21, 108, 121
Beresheet A
320
Beresheet B
37, 414
Chayei Sarah
45
Emor
264, 265, 267-269, 271, 276, 278
Idra Raba
273
Lech Lecha
197, 198, 202
Miketz
1, 2
Noach
75
Pekudei
36, 53, 56, 57, 59, 427, 428, 439, 838, 908
Pinchas
83, 490, 817, 829
Prologue
65, 66
Shemot
2
Shlach Lecha
68
Tazria
21
Tetzaveh
80, 136, 137
Trumah
33, 296, 297, 479
Tzav
182
Vaetchanan
188
Vayechi
44, 143, 146, 147, 197, 198, 200, 201, 206-209, 359, 360, 361
Vayera
43, 388
Vayeshev
205, 206
Vayetze
286-289
Vayigash
66
Vayikra
267
Vayishlach
274

SHAMASHIEL (SPIRIT)

Pekudei
541

SHAMAYIM (HEAVEN)

Idra Raba
229
Mishpatim
408
Pinchas
847

SHAMIEL (SUPERNAL MINISTER)

Pekudei
682
Vayikra
24

SHAMSHIEL (SPIRIT)

Beha'alot'cha
112
Vayakhel
145
Vayera
275

SHARON

Beresheet A
298
Vayechi
232, 233, 234

SHAVUOT

Behar
29
Ekev
34, 65
Emor
110, 126, 140, 142, 143, 157, 163-167, 177, 178, 180, 183, 184
Ki Tetze
143, 145
Pinchas
766, 828, 857
Prologue
125, 129, 139, 140
Tetzaveh
68, 75
Vayechi
353, 354, 356

SHECHEM

Lech Lecha
48, 68, 80
Miketz
161, 162
Vayakhel
494
Vayechi
112, 562
Vayeshev
13, 95, 102, 134
Vayishlach
146, 147, 150, 151, 154

SHECHINAH

Acharei Mot
52, 53, 56, 57, 63, 65, 67, 92, 107, 155, 182, 211, 275, 292, 295, 339, 340, 342, 373, 383, 388, 397
Balak
38, 43-45, 50, 223, 231, 234, 235, 271, 272, 278, 281, 298, 300-302, 426, 460, 506
Bechukotai
30, 31, 32, 35, 37, 39, 57, 59
Beha'alot'cha
46, 66, 75, 128, 129, 132

Behar
16-19, 21, 22, 24, 31-39, 44-46, 69, 70
Bemidbar
24, 29, 53, 54, 55, 56
Beresheet A
48, 149, 152, 160, 173, 175, 178, 179, 182, 183, 187, 189, 195, 198-200, 211, 218, 221, 232, 234, 236-239, 242-247, 258, 260, 268, 269, 272, 274, 276, 279, 282, 292, 337, 433, 434, 474
Beresheet B
25, 26, 31, 61, 223-229, 231, 232, 234, 235, 246, 262-265, 296, 297, 303, 312, 313, 388, 396-398, 411, 418, 429, 439, 440, 444
Beshalach
25, 27, 52, 64, 98, 125, 156-158, 212, 301, 329, 336, 357, 434, 453, 461, 462, 464, 476, 478, 480-484
Bo
147, 155, 172, 179, 194
Chayei Sarah
1, 16, 17, 18, 68, 170, 171, 191, 194, 195, 215, 221, 237, 248, 267, 268, 269, 270
Chukat
7, 26
Emor
2, 6, 20, 33, 37, 40, 276
Ha'azinu
26, 110, 216, 218, 220, 222, 223, 231, 245
Idra Raba
149, 232
Kedoshim
36, 56, 57, 107, 114
Ki Tetze
2, 7, 8, 9, 11, 15, 24, 25, 28, 37-39, 41, 47, 48, 50, 51, 56, 57, 60, 62, 69, 70, 71, 93, 100, 102, 105, 106, 108, 117, 118, 119, 125, 129, 132, 134, 140, 142, 143, 146
Ki Tisa
1, 15, 55, 56
Korach
44, 45, 48, 51, 53, 58
Lech Lecha
15, 48, 80, 82-84, 111-113, 123, 181, 182, 184-191, 197, 202, 209, 247, 269, 296, 312, 313, 372, 381-383, 411, 412, 420, 442
Metzora
2, 3, 10, 18, 19
Miketz
33, 35, 39, 52, 82, 84, 92, 93, 96, 101, 108, 157, 158, 160, 215, 218, 219, 222-224
Mishpatim
3, 7, 9, 14, 66, 91, 167, 202, 380, 398, 401, 405, 408, 414-417, 419, 422, 426, 429, 433, 434, 440-442, 444, 446, 449, 450, 455-458, 460, 464, 466, 467, 471-475, 478, 506, 551, 562, 572, 574, 577, 581
Naso
31, 33, 42, 105, 106, 107, 108, 121, 144, 171, 175-177, 179, 188, 189, 193-196
Noach
17, 39, 40, 128, 154, 169, 186, 199, 204-207, 237, 248, 250,

269, 276, 358, 383
Pekudei
34, 42, 66, 73, 81, 88, 177, 179, 212, 230, 317, 338, 473, 628, 653, 825, 833, 854, 900, 957
Pinchas
4, 5, 16, 17, 102, 119, 120, 126, 131, 134, 137, 159, 166, 172, 181, 182, 186, 243, 245, 248, 251, 252, 274, 280, 281, 287, 288, 293, 298, 299, 302, 305, 307, 320, 322, 323, 325-329, 331-333, 335, 336, 343, 353, 364, 368, 372, 381, 383, 398, 413, 414, 426, 430, 443, 444, 479, 491-496, 498, 504, 505, 520, 535, 562, 563, 572, 574, 580, 583, 588-593, 605, 626, 628, 641, 653-655, 657, 660, 663, 751, 752, 755, 758, 760, 770, 771, 787, 788, 803, 804, 827, 830-833, 835, 851, 852, 854, 856, 873, 884
Prologue
56, 146, 228, 231, 232
Safra Detzniuta
10
Shemot
13, 19, 24, 28, 31, 45, 46, 48, 50, 55, 57-59, 61, 63, 64, 90, 96, 130, 131, 133, 184, 185, 187, 188, 191-193, 199, 201, 203, 233, 237, 244, 247, 248, 259, 268-272, 275, 332, 333, 338, 362
Shlach Lecha
16, 17, 34, 39, 87, 88, 154, 170-172, 203, 298, 304, 307, 308, 313, 328, 341
Shoftim
15, 22, 24
Tazria
3, 4, 35, 82, 83, 139, 145, 148, 149
Tetzaveh
1, 3
Toldot
8, 9, 32, 39, 40, 49, 76, 89, 96, 97, 99, 100, 125, 126, 135, 140, 156, 159, 168, 173, 181, 185, 188, 199
Trumah
39, 56, 76, 87, 89, 105, 116, 120, 122, 143, 144, 147, 264, 265, 266, 267, 268, 314, 324, 366, 384, 385, 386, 539, 564, 575, 581, 582, 589-592, 594, 595, 629, 630, 680, 685, 699, 706, 707, 716, 722, 771, 788, 789, 791, 802, 808, 809, 821 -824
Tzav
28, 38, 45, 46, 50, 136, 148, 149, 158, 182
Vaera
112, 113, 114, 183
Vaetchanan
10, 11, 15, 32, 102, 110, 131, 137, 141, 155, 156, 163, 183
Vayakhel
20, 64, 71, 72, 73, 117, 126, 242, 280, 307, 389, 394, 412, 413, 429, 431, 432
Vayechi
15, 20, 25, 35, 37, 51, 53-56, 64, 77, 82, 83, 84, 88, 91, 95, 100, 101, 103, 106, 107, 115 -118, 187, 192, 194, 228, 256, 258, 268, 285, 321, 332-334, 337,

342, 385, 389, 390, 391, 392, 423, 425, 426, 427, 428, 492, 517, 518, 538, 539, 540, 552, 553, 557-560, 577, 579, 581, 612, 649, 652, 653, 661, 735, 737, 757, 763, 765, 766, 780, 801, 814, 859, 860

Vayelech
1, 18, 33

Vayera
13, 20, 24, 29, 30, 36, 41, 45, 49, 53, 56, 57, 58, 59, 61, 72, 96, 98, 140, 147, 148, 152, 159, 171, 176, 188, 189, 202, 224, 228, 229, 235, 287, 345, 348-350, 352, 353, 357, 359, 362, 401, 402, 430, 433, 434, 440, 506, 510, 511, 512

Vayeshev
14, 29, 65, 70, 81, 95, 96, 97, 99, 104, 107, 138, 203, 205, 206, 251, 252

Vayetze
46, 47, 48, 64, 65, 66, 110, 111, 124, 247, 248, 271-274, 293, 321, 361, 389

Vayigash
46, 48, 66, 106, 107, 118, 120

Vayikra
8, 9, 41, 46, 63, 84, 99, 221, 226, 265, 279, 284, 344, 346 -348, 363-365, 426, 427, 443

Vayishlach
5, 6, 7, 8, 9, 11, 14, 18, 60, 102, 119, 162, 164, 165, 173-175, 179, 180, 189, 203, 204, 205, 216, 217, 218, 223, 224, 225

Yitro
27, 54, 55, 56, 57, 60, 61, 179, 180, 223, 245, 263, 298, 319, 322-326, 340, 350, 363, 388, 395, 402-404, 417, 432, 448, 471, 481, 487

SHEEP

Acharei Mot
67, 103, 105, 122

Balak
50, 246

Beresheet A
121

Bo
10, 95, 96, 101, 161, 162, 177, 198, 230

Chayei Sarah
224

Ekev
19

Emor
52, 59

Kedoshim
119

Ki Tisa
67, 68

Lech Lecha
431

Mishpatim
469, 495

Noach
119

Pinchas
221, 534, 597, 798

Shemot
230, 371, 373-377, 379, 385
Toldot
54
Trumah
810
Vaera
100, 150, 190, 191, 193
Vaetchanan
184-186
Vayechi
353, 355, 597, 621, 624
Vayera
318
Vayetze
31, 92, 95, 98, 101, 127, 298, 299, 375
Vayikra
54, 72, 279
Vayishlach
150

SHEKELS

Beresheet A
387
Chayei Sarah
98
Emor
29
Idra Raba
15, 20
Ki Tetze
1, 25, 27, 28
Ki Tisa
4
Korach
54
Naso
199
Pekudei
91, 97, 108, 118
Pinchas
848, 877
Toldot
102
Trumah
573, 579, 581, 588
Vayikra
178, 190
Yitro
125

SHEKER (FALSEHOOD)

Pinchas
106
Tetzaveh
24
Vayigash 4

SHELAH, SON OF JUDAH

Vayeshev
150, 151, 154, 192

SHELLS (KLIPOT)

Balak
5, 15, 70, 79, 81, 169, 399, 474, 490
Beresheet A
40, 104, 105, 106, 109, 110, 118, 184, 186, 223, 225, 226, 229, 251, 256, 257, 289, 411, 435, 445, 462
Beresheet B
40, 42, 286, 287, 305, 346, 354
Chayei Sarah
9, 19, 67, 72, 73
Ekev
29

Emor
132, 157, 255
Ha'azinu
248
Idra Raba
2, 336
Ki Tetze
3, 6, 8, 63, 70, 72, 73, 81
Lech Lecha
42, 47, 147, 148, 149, 233, 305, 405
Metzora
56, 57, 58
Miketz
2
Mishpatim
8, 265, 266, 267, 377, 403, 418, 420, 421, 426, 556
Noach
64, 116, 251, 335, 340, 343-345, 363-365
Pekudei
74, 158, 248, 923
Pinchas
97, 100, 248, 263, 264, 266, 267, 269, 271, 284, 591, 652, 653, 655, 730, 731, 738, 739, 894
Shemot
39, 73, 116, 259, 261, 332, 360, 361
Shlach Lecha
123, 124, 157
Shmini
84
Shoftim
4, 20
Tazria
154
Trumah
57, 58, 81, 83, 200, 236, 268, 391, 392, 506, 523, 760
Tzav
29, 41, 57, 69, 70, 78, 127, 132, 156
Vaera
108, 109, 158
Vayakhel
162, 165, 170, 177, 274, 407
Vayechi
316, 321, 383, 473, 560, 580, 597, 628, 705, 706
Vayera
439, 458
Vayetze
4, 23, 81, 289
Vayikra
136, 140
Vayishlach
25, 34, 135, 146
Yitro
390

SHELOMITH

Emor
310, 312, 318

SH'MA YISRAEL

Balak
29, 30, 37, 199, 476
Beresheet A
196, 242, 289
Chayei Sarah
230
Ha'azinu
89
Ki Tetze
25, 67

Korach
48
Mishpatim
384, 393, 394, 395, 397, 428
Pinchas
57, 255, 280, 283, 285, 290, 292, 295, 334, 336, 337, 339, 348, 404, 453-455, 581, 596, 718, 753, 754, 788, 789, 795, 803, 804, 821, 835, 845, 850, 857, 870, 873, 875
Prologue
204, 205, 206, 241
Shemot
207
Shoftim
4, 5, 16
Trumah
121, 125, 127, 132, 135, 142, 145, 246-249, 623-625, 629, 652-654, 659, 731
Tzav
69, 151
Vaetchanan
46, 58, 71, 78, 79, 80, 84-88, 90, 91, 95, 101, 104, 154, 173
Vayakhel
420, 429
Vayetze
6, 233, 302
Vayishlach
255, 256

SHEOL

Balak
370
Korach
32, 34
Miketz
74, 76
Mishpatim
369
Pekudei
838, 896, 902
Pinchas
136, 137, 138, 267, 270
Vayakhel
89, 244
Vayechi
585, 733, 734
Vayelech
44, 45
Vayeshev
227

SHEPHERD

Acharei Mot
134, 211
Balak
233, 243, 244, 276
Beha'alot'cha
72, 86, 94
Behar
16, 63, 74
Beresheet A
202, 285
Beshalach
68, 207, 332
Bo
10, 95, 177
Chukat
25
Ekev
18, 19, 24, 38, 44
Emor
13, 37, 38, 40, 84, 158, 173, 205, 227, 241, 270, 282

Kedoshim
5, 6, 36, 37, 50, 54, 55, 99
Ki Tetze
1, 15, 16, 17, 24, 26, 42, 45-48, 55, 60, 62, 65, 67, 72, 74, 77-79, 85, 87, 88, 89, 90, 95, 107, 108, 109, 131, 133, 134
Ki Tisa
5, 6, 103
Korach
41, 43, 60
Mishpatim
370, 398, 403, 413, 415, 417, 444-446, 465, 466
Naso
8, 27, 80, 101, 102, 104, 173
Pekudei
176
Pinchas
36, 55, 59, 85, 86, 93, 94, 95, 102, 125, 166, 167, 177, 186, 194, 195, 204, 207, 215-217, 221, 230, 237, 239, 295, 296, 364, 365, 369, 370, 373, 375, 376, 401, 402, 406, 407, 410, 411, 415, 416, 422, 423, 435, 436, 442, 443, 474, 475, 491, 499, 500, 501, 503, 519, 560, 564, 566, 574, 575, 581, 582, 588, 592, 599, 600, 605, 609, 611, 612, 615, 645, 646, 651, 652, 654, 656, 657, 662, 663, 667-670, 677, 678, 683, 700, 704, 708, 709, 717, 722, 723, 732, 733, 736, 737, 742, 744, 760, 766, 767, 769, 786, 787, 796, 803, 814, 819, 824
Shemot
120, 229, 371-373, 375, 376
Shlach Lecha
306, 323
Shmini
117
Shoftim
10, 22
Tazria
30
Toldot
204
Trumah
146, 548, 550, 564, 572, 574, 587, 589, 591, 808, 810, 823
Tzav
33, 38, 39, 42, 43, 71, 122, 123, 135, 149, 159
Vaera
54, 100
Vayakhel
65
Vayechi
375, 395, 457
Vayera
221
Vayetze
95, 127, 251, 315
Vayikra
77, 274, 292
Vayishlach
41
Yitro
522, 527, 550

SHESHAI

Shlach Lecha
32, 39, 40, 60

SHEVNA

Balak
276

SHIELD

Acharei Mot
276, 339
Balak
75, 81, 97, 232, 278, 432
Beresheet A
103
Beresheet B
7
Ekev
27
Idra Raba
128
Kedoshim
77
Ki Tetze
117
Lech Lecha
81, 118, 121, 270, 280, 319, 321
Mishpatim
403
Pekudei
77, 573
Pinchas
720
Shemot
27
Shmini
42, 43
Vaera
134
Vayakhel
111
Vayetze
340
Vayikra
184, 383
Vayishlach
274
Yitro
179

SHIELDS

Beha'alot'cha
96
Ha'azinu
164
Idra Raba
2, 107, 294
Lech Lecha
122, 445
Mishpatim
403
Pekudei
571
Trumah
161, 200, 353, 452, 554
Vayechi
283
Vayetze
390
Vayigash
89, 92

SHILOH

Beresheet A
234
Mishpatim
484
Pekudei
395
Pinchas
651, 652
Vayechi
581

SHIM'I

Mishpatim
250-254, 256-259

SHIPS

Acharei Mot
75, 76
Balak
168, 228
Beresheet A
409
Beresheet B
50, 51
Beshalach
100, 101, 138, 141, 143, 211, 256
Chayei Sarah
32
Mishpatim
121, 185, 200
Naso
19
Prologue
18z8
Vayakhel
81-83, 86
Vayechi
643, 665, 675
Vayikra
143, 144
Yitro
72

SHITTIM

Bechukotai
10
Shlach Lecha
71
Vaetchanan
197

SHMAYAHEL (SPIRIT)

Pekudei
703

SHMINI ATZERET

Behar
29
Emor
140, 155, 156, 288
Ki Tetze
144
Pinchas
33, 832, 894
Tetzaveh
138, 140, 141

SHOE

Balak
256
Chukat
4, 5, 7-9, 11-13, 15
Ki Tetze
99, 102, 103
Vayikra
399, 435

SHOFAR

Acharei Mot
82
Beha'alot'cha
10, 19
Behar
25
Beresheet A
199, 210, 212, 304
Beshalach
174, 337
Bo
1
Emor
82, 187, 190-194, 202-206,

215, 218
Kedoshim
104
Ki Tetze
140, 141, 145
Korach
56
Metzora
39
Naso
13-15, 176
Pekudei
215, 335, 352, 589, 590, 722
Pinchas
105, 364, 365, 367, 369-371, 435, 668, 813, 827, 882, 883
Prologue
239, 240
Shlach Lecha
219
Shmini
58, 59
Shoftim
14, 15
Tetzaveh
88, 91, 92, 94
Trumah
584
Tzav
3
Vaetchanan
26, 127, 128
Vayakhel
32, 33
Vayechi
507, 509, 735
Vayera
381, 382, 384, 387
Vayeshev
226
Vayigash
105
Vayikra
84-86, 88, 302-304, 308, 309, 311, 312
Yitro
294, 295, 300-305, 312

SHEWBREAD

Lech Lecha
262, 267
Trumah
178, 516, 572

SHUA

Chayei Sarah
13

SHUNAMIT

Balak
186

SICHON

Chayei Sarah
12

SIHON

Balak
7, 9, 10, 11, 12, 398

SILENCE

Beresheet A
30, 449
Prologue
18, 137, 164

SILKWORM

Beresheet A
4

SILVER

Balak
5
Beha'alot'cha
87, 100, 117, 126
Behar
70
Beresheet B
418
Beshalach
42, 370
Bo
212
Chayei Sarah
98
Chukat
60
Emor
29, 234, 235
Idra Raba
15, 341
Kedoshim
64
Ki Tetze
1, 25, 27, 28, 135
Korach
43
Lech Lecha
162
Miketz
67, 68, 69
Mishpatim
400
Naso
85, 86
Pekudei
18, 19, 74, 76, 79, 83, 86, 87, 97, 118, 131, 132, 160, 431, 432, 434, 780, 924
Pinchas
401, 709, 838
Shemot
97, 319
Shlach Lecha
67
Shmini
95
Tazria
111, 160
Toldot
66
Trumah
60, 157, 160, 227-229, 242, 370, 386, 387, 389, 390, 391, 399, 401, 403, 408, 409, 670, 828, 902, 924, 925
Vaera
34, 35, 43, 44, 45, 46
Vaetchanan
93
Vayakhel
55, 57, 73
Vayechi
129, 130, 132, 835, 837, 839, 840, 841
Vayera
144, 407, 409
Vayeshev
134
Vayishlach
150, 154, 157
Yitro
499, 500

SIMEON

Miketz
126, 163-166, 172, 174
Vayechi
75, 552, 554, 555, 557, 562
Vayetze
155, 157, 158, 159, 160, 162, 170

SIN

Acharei Mot
6, 9, 26, 29, 41, 44, 84, 115, 117, 119, 122, 129-134, 138, 139, 143, 181, 194-197, 201, 213, 223, 224, 237, 242-247, 267, 285, 292, 329, 333, 338, 341, 344, 345, 353, 377, 383, 394, 397, 399-402, 405, 406
Balak
75, 76, 77, 123, 125, 139, 193 -195, 201, 229, 243, 245, 246, 264, 270, 274, 275, 284, 302, 315, 328, 329, 330, 336, 351, 366, 373, 375, 380, 389
Bechukotai
25, 28, 29, 30, 45,- 48, 50
Beha'alot'cha
80, 81, 89, 119
Behar
24, 26, 28, 30, 40, 68, 69
Bemidbar
41, 73, 74, 75
Beresheet A
100, 162, 163, 164, 166, 167, 177-180, 182, 183, 221, 227, 232, 233, 254, 255, 261, 286, 287, 290, 292, 323, 412, 437, 438, 439, 440, 445, 447, 448, 454, 459, 461, 477
Beresheet B
16, 21, 104, 150, 161, 187, 225, 227, 228, 283, 289, 290, 296 -299, 302, 304, 309, 310, 318, 333, 336, 340, 371, 372, 374 -377, 388, 390, 394, 396-399, 407, 413-418, 434, 436, 440
Beshalach
33, 100, 119, 122-124, 190, 218, 246, 260, 390, 427, 433, 486
Bo
26, 96, 137, 138, 143, 146, 183, 184, 197, 199, 206, 208, 209, 211
Chayei Sarah
59, 68, 70, 82, 85, 108, 109, 110, 220, 221, 257
Chukat
40, 44
Emor
165, 179, 193, 207, 227b -235, 248, 251, 255, 308, 309, 315, 320-323, 326, 337
Ha'azinu
65, 244, 254, 256
Idra Raba
1, 8, 10, 63, 97, 126, 152, 201, 229
Kedoshim
1, 10, 48, 50, 52, 66, 67, 91, 101-103, 122
Ki Tetze
13, 21, 52, 111
Ki Tisa
27, 30, 43, 56, 70, 92, 93, 98, 100, 112, 113, 115, 116, 118
Korach
16, 36, 46

Lech Lecha
52, 53, 89, 90, 91, 92, 197, 248, 251, 299, 302, 303, 362, 407
Metzora
11, 14, 15, 30, 32
Miketz
1, 2, 35, 64, 77, 85, 103, 114, 120-122, 124, 125, 128, 129, 131, 179, 180, 201, 202, 204, 207, 208, 243
Mishpatim
2, 56, 238, 239, 240, 241, 244, 245, 248, 249, 322, 335, 347, 348, 349, 351, 355, 357, 362, 383, 420, 443, 451, 477, 509, 521, 580
Naso
1, 8, 16, 20, 22, 23, 28, 29, 47, 48, 58, 83, 86, 87, 101, 103, 128, 135
Noach
28, 29, 35, 36, 40, 45, 49, 52, 56, 57, 69, 74, 82, 83, 89, 93, 100, 105, 119, 120, 133, 141, 150, 151, 161-163, 176, 183, 191, 194, 196, 204, 207, 222, 228, 232, 244, 245, 251, 252, 254, 256-258, 308, 312-314, 318, 319, 337, 381
Pekudei
3, 5, 67, 73, 180, 181, 263, 306, 308, 313, 315, 316, 321, 322, 327, 328, 332, 333, 371, 447, 481, 488, 551, 552, 553, 567, 569, 570, 585-587, 612, 616, 618, 657, 671, 745, 757, 826, 829-831, 848, 878, 882, 883, 885, 886, 893, 905, 923, 937, 943, 944
Pinchas
9, 10, 28, 31, 38, 53, 75, 76, 87, 96, 98, 99, 100, 102, 108, 109, 111, 113, 148, 170, 171, 212, 222, 225, 228, 230, 269, 270, 354, 355, 356, 364, 376, 378, 379, 448, 472, 473, 485, 522-524, 528, 529, 570, 643, 672, 673, 679, 682, 683, 688, 797, 809, 812, 827, 836, 881, 883
Prologue
21, 26, 33, 70, 71, 96, 97, 98, 101, 102, 131, 135, 136, 192, 202, 210, 260
Safra Detzniuta
7, 16, 32, 51
Shemot
18, 28, 91, 145, 167, 170, 172, 173, 201, 204, 250, 256, 301, 349, 361, 364
Shlach Lecha
11, 12, 42, 43, 53, 69, 75, 107, 167, 229, 283, 289, 303
Shmini
2, 24, 25, 29, 31-35, 45-47, 49, 50
Shoftim
12, 13
Tazria
20, 23, 31, 64, 79, 89, 92, 93, 94, 95, 106, 131, 142, 150, 156, 163, 181
Tetzaveh
46, 58, 110, 114, 121
Toldot
2, 52, 56, 57, 133, 146, 148, 152
Trumah
157, 270, 293, 432, 449, 473, 476, 481, 482, 507, 720, 727, 765, 766, 768, 811, 814, 898, 923

Tzav
24, 27, 29, 38-43, 45-47, 90, 121, 145, 146, 193
Vaera
90, 91, 96, 113, 125
Vaetchanan
34, 152, 172, 196, 197
Vayakhel
6, 63, 82, 83, 86, 91, 253, 275, 337, 389, 408, 416, 480, 483, 490
Vayechi
7, 13, 18, 22, 25, 36, 39, 41, 51, 75, 178, 194, 202, 203, 241, 261, 264, 287, 296-301, 303, 331, 380, 384, 390, 403, 410, 411, 514, 523, 561, 571, 573, 704, 734, 763, 851
Vayelech
8, 10, 19
Vayera
108, 117, 118, 132, 179, 180, 191, 195, 213, 220, 286, 302, 323, 327, 373, 379, 386, 454, 473, 475, 489, 491
Vayeshev
1, 28, 36, 139, 140, 179, 181, 182, 195, 210, 214, 222, 224 -226, 236, 244, 246, 248, 249, 250, 251
Vayetze
78-80, 88, 90, 283, 285
Vayigash
28, 29, 63, 106, 110
Vayikra
50, 71, 106-108, 112, 118, 119, 122, 124, 130, 164, 165, 193, 195, 207, 209, 210, 213, 214, 218, 224, 235, 250, 251, 255, 256, 263, 273, 275, 276, 279, 286, 293-295, 297-301, 312, 315, 325, 334, 338-341, 349, 387, 389, 390, 393, 401-406, 409, 414, 419, 422, 429,440
Vayishlach
1, 2, 49, 108, 183, 186, 205, 214, 218, 259
Yitro
49, 74, 75, 204, 306, 331, 393, 394, 396, 428, 492, 518

SINAI

Acharei Mot
20, 229
Balak
138, 139, 140
Beha'alot'cha
56, 57
Behar
14
Bemidbar
1, 8
Beshalach
57, 363
Chayei Sarah
195
Chukat
1
Ekev
45
Emor
186, 324
Kedoshim
45, 80
Ki Tetze
14, 15, 19, 42, 73

Ki Tisa
74, 115
Lech Lecha
249
Mishpatim
415
Pekudei
109, 114, 115
Pinchas
102, 313, 343, 498
Shemot
14, 16, 379
Shlach Lecha
103
Trumah
83, 766
Tzav
33
Vayakhel
45
Vayechi
99
Vayera
38
Vayetze
70
Vayikra
1, 3, 4, 86, 228
Yitro
283, 312, 320, 321, 346, 363, 401, 402, 570, 571

SINEW

Behar
37
Beresheet B
273
Bo
199, 200
Matot
3
Mishpatim
418, 434
Pinchas
89, 126, 160, 161, 374
Safra Detzniuta
35
Trumah
723
Vayishlach
99-101, 103, 104, 107, 114 -116
Yitro
110, 126, 127, 128, 129

SINGING

Acharei Mot
2, 7, 8, 47, 53-55, 151, 155, 199, 243
Balak
128, 299, 300, 304
Beha'alot'cha
7, 35, 55, 111
Behar
26, 39
Beresheet A
248
Beresheet B
31, 43, 46, 49, 265, 345, 409
Beshalach
25, 47, 213, 215, 216, 219-222, 224-226, 230, 239, 241, 242, 244, 289, 311, 339-342, 408
Chayei Sarah
27, 28, 29, 30, 31, 243
Chukat
77

Ekev
32
Emor
107, 144, 149, 150, 228, 252
Korach
23
Lech Lecha
132, 365, 452, 460-462
Miketz
33, 109
Mishpatim
382
Naso
9, 11
Noach
119, 121, 168, 262
Pekudei
98, 128, 129, 351, 498, 532, 770, 943, 945
Pinchas
106, 118, 191, 268, 269, 555, 698, 715
Shemot
40, 42, 43, 242, 324, 327, 328, 330-333, 335
Shlach Lecha
151, 155, 199, 200, 211, 244, 246, 247
Shmini
9, 64, 65
Shoftim
24
Tazria
41
Toldot
136, 137
Trumah
95, 98, 99, 101, 103, 211, 212, 214-216, 219, 256, 307, 313-319, 321, 323-325, 327, 338, 339, 340, 341, 342, 343, 362, 378, 415, 686, 687, 713, 818
Tzav
2, 14, 122, 123, 126
Vayakhel
25
Vayechi
82, 93, 94, 117, 230, 414, 416-418, 433, 443, 449, 450, 452, 453, 608, 824, 825, 828, 833, 838
Vayelech
17, 26, 27, 28, 31, 47, 49
Vayera
1, 3, 6, 8, 400
Vayetze
101, 253, 255, 256, 340
Vayigash
69
Vayikra
42, 43, 55, 109, 110-112, 115, 224, 333, 442
Vayishlach
269
Yitro
16, 544

SIN-OFFERING

Acharei Mot
130, 131
Behar
28, 30
Beshalach
246
Emor
179
Kedoshim
10

Noach
100
Pekudei
313, 315, 322
Pinchas
672, 673, 679, 682, 683, 836, 883
Shmini
31, 33, 34, 46, 47, 49, 50
Tzav
27, 29, 39, 40, 42, 43, 121
Vayera
117

SISERA

Balak
1
Beshalach
62, 156
Vaetchanan
180, 181, 183

SISRA

Bechukotai
12
Lech Lecha
393
Tazria
6
Toldot
98
Vayakhel
78

SIXTH DAY, THE

Behar
57
Beresheet A
117, 326, 412, 461
Beresheet B
160, 173, 175
Beshalach
414
Ki Tetze
116
Metzora
42
Pinchas
123, 825, 826, 886
Prologue
4
Tazria
114
Trumah
30
Vayakhel
80
Vayera
445
Vayeshev
57
Vayigash
1
Yitro
369

SKATUFA (SPIRIT)

Pekudei
918

SKIN

Acharei Mot
127
Behar
37
Beresheet A
120, 167, 183, 364, 454
Beresheet B
57, 293

Bo
149
Chayei Sarah
198
Idra Raba
73, 120
Kedoshim
63
Ki Tetze
82
Ki Tisa
71, 107
Mishpatim
418, 434, 566
Noach
152, 320
Pekudei
877-879
Pinchas
126, 155, 160-162, 375, 639
Safra Detzniuta
71, 72
Shlach Lecha
120, 217, 238
Shoftim
13
Tazria
62, 71, 107, 108, 135, 162
Trumah
179
Tzav
42
Vaetchanan
33, 34, 96
Vayakhel
360
Vayechi
89, 90
Yitro
82, 93, 126, 127, 129, 130, 138, 142-144, 146, 147, 182 -186, 194, 200, 214, 227, 553

SLAVERY

Acharei Mot
230
Balak
205, 493
Bechukotai
43
Behar
9, 11, 14, 25, 46, 63
Beresheet A
188, 273
Beshalach
190
Bo
119, 163
Chayei Sarah
65
Ekev
42
Emor
82
Ha'azinu
86, 244
Ki Tisa
74
Lech Lecha
385
Mishpatim
391, 395, 413, 447
Naso
95, 99
Noach
301, 311
Pekudei
404
Pinchas
221, 245, 734, 808

Prologue
239, 240
Shemot
76, 77, 250, 289, 308
Toldot
62, 80, 171, 188, 192
Tzav
58, 59
Vaetchanan
42, 44, 114, 128, 174
Vayakhel
225, 407
Vayechi
92, 255, 821, 822
Vayera
326
Vayeshev
103, 104
Vayigash
76
Vayikra
85
Yitro
389

SMOKE

Acharei Mot
51
Beresheet A
80, 215, 222, 312, 424
Beresheet B
44, 141, 263, 264
Bo
113, 147
Ekev
35
Ha'azinu
55, 56, 147-151, 157
Idra Raba
69, 223, 224, 226, 230, 233, 234, 235, 238, 239
Mishpatim
427, 524
Noach
67, 68, 121, 233-236, 241 -243
Pekudei
363, 424-427, 435, 436, 438, 439, 440, 770, 945
Pinchas
203, 204, 205, 206, 211, 438, 559, 758, 816
Prologue
169
Safra Detzniuta
45
Shemot
364
Shlach Lecha
116
Tazria
66, 169
Trumah
65-68, 72, 277, 278
Tzav
15, 52-54, 128, 132, 190
Vayakhel
317, 319, 320, 466, 467, 470, 472
Vayechi
174, 715, 716, 792
Vayera
268, 312
Vayishlach
222-225, 229
Yitro
182, 321, 362, 363

SNOW

Beresheet A
17

Mishpatim
74, 189, 283
Prologue
98
Vayechi
601-605
Vayera
36

SODOM AND AMORAH (GOMORRAH)

Lech Lecha
56, 88, 179
Noach
111-113, 175
Pekudei
123, 124, 712
Pinchas
401, 637
Trumah
364
Vayera
55, 72, 75, 130, 166, 168, 170, 181, 182, 189-191, 193, 200, 203, 205, 207, 211-213, 218, 224, 235, 238, 241, 247, 250, 251, 256, 258, 259, 262, 265, 266, 273, 284-286, 292-295, 312, 333
Yitro
403

SODOMY

Vayera
415

SOIL (ADAMAH)

Beresheet B
36
Mishpatim
117, 118

SOIL

Balak
289, 291
Beresheet A
413
Beresheet B
36
Chayei Sarah
211
Chukat
22
Kedoshim
124
Mishpatim
351
Pekudei
905
Prologue
56, 206
Shlach Lecha
118
Trumah
449
Vaetchanan
76
Vayechi
860
Vayera
136
Yitro
226

SOLOMON

Acharei Mot
7, 61, 71, 83, 89-91, 140, 141, 264, 271, 279, 324-326, 353, 367, 374, 390

Balak
44, 114, 137, 163, 182, 183, 439, 469
Beha'alot'cha
141
Bemidbar
53, 56
Beresheet A
104, 280, 293, 296, 466, 467
Beshalach
97, 148, 152, 214, 296, 318, 335, 448, 451
Chayei Sarah
198, 264
Chukat
38, 40, 43, 48, 52, 54, 55, 60
Ekev
64
Emor
127, 170, 180, 181, 259
Ha'azinu
15, 17, 84, 86, 104, 181, 204
Idra Raba
66, 250
Kedoshim
132
Korach
10, 29, 30
Lech Lecha
76, 164, 266, 307
Miketz
48, 50, 51, 132, 139, 243
Mishpatim
77, 123, 124, 150, 252, 254, 255, 256, 258, 298, 300, 306, 314, 331, 332, 339-343, 346, 348, 349, 352, 353, 422, 427, 492, 566
Naso
76
Pinchas
148, 185, 327, 355, 386, 389, 390, 391, 429, 442, 507, 508, 740, 814, 824
Shlach Lecha
13, 18, 21-23, 25-27, 61, 220, 221, 322
Tazria
15, 75, 76, 96, 97, 100, 141
Toldot
5, 116, 145, 171
Vaetchanan
74, 179, 183
Vayechi
157, 275, 276, 281, 289, 290, 291, 292, 322, 333, 335, 351, 403, 597, 648, 650, 651, 662, 702, 708, 787, 810, 811, 832, 834, 835, 837, 838, 840, 841, 847
Vayelech
26
Vayera
256, 310, 311
Vayeshev
5, 9, 98, 191, 194
Vayetze
13, 55, 57, 58, 254, 344
Vayikra
12, 33, 44, 151, 212, 220, 294, 322
Vayishlach
131, 188

SORCERY

Acharei Mot
249, 252, 254, 272, 405
Balak
2, 3, 5, 6, 28, 135, 136, 154,

161, 171, 175, 176, 182, 254, 255, 282, 286, 402, 406, 410, 411, 414, 422, 423, 427, 431, 453, 461, 472, 474, 481-484, 486, 497

Bechukotai
11, 12, 13

Behar
2

Beresheet A
452

Beresheet B
311, 379, 380, 381, 424

Beshalach
440

Bo
76, 119, 120, 127

Chayei Sarah
74, 80, 81, 83-87, 263, 264

Ha'azinu
256, 258, 260

Ki Tisa
75, 83

Mishpatim
564

Pekudei
319, 320, 861

Shlach Lecha
221

Shmini
106

Tazria
16, 17, 160, 170

Tetzaveh
110

Trumah
36, 852, 854

Vaera
53, 166, 170

Vayakhel
467, 468

Vayetze
252, 298

Vayishlach
22, 23, 32, 34, 37, 77

Yitro
46

SOTAH

Mishpatim
256, 323

SOUL (NEFESH)

Acharei Mot
205, 215, 216, 236, 255, 258, 259, 262-264, 267, 274

Beresheet A
94, 109, 258, 274, 405, 408, 450, 454

Beresheet B
169, 212, 378, 379

Chayei Sarah
140

Emor
58, 61, 287

Kedoshim
4, 5

Ki Tetze
51, 55, 108

Korach
17, 42, 45

Lech Lecha
47, 76, 77, 78, 96, 97, 98, 99, 100, 103, 146-160, 167, 193, 194, 205, 208, 209, 210, 245, 246, 273

Metzora
46

Mishpatim
11-13, 23, 95, 107, 108, 158, 467
Naso
36, 37, 128, 131
Noach
25, 50, 62-64
Pekudei
638
Pinchas
39, 371, 568, 569, 570, 571, 572, 607, 612, 613, 633, 670, 716, 717, 790
Prologue
216
Safra Detzniuta
38, 39, 51
Shemot
23
Shlach Lecha
221, 237, 319
Shmini
77, 104
Tazria
26, 69, 81, 84, 86, 116
Tetzaveh
53, 54
Toldot
91, 107
Trumah
268, 284, 286-293, 295-306, 458, 531, 591
Tzav
62-65, 68-71, 140, 141, 146 -148, 187-189
Vaera
48
Vaetchanan
3, 195
Vayakhel
91, 97, 113, 114, 192, 193, 270, 271, 275, 277, 278, 369, 405, 409
Vayechi
309-312, 319, 324, 325, 327, 328, 331, 343, 345- 348, 360, 361, 363
Vayera
56, 92, 267, 315, 316, 317, 322, 323, 339
Vayeshev
35, 36
Vayetze
165, 179
Vayigash
15-17, 19-22, 80-82, 84
Vayikra
185, 263, 317, 318, 422, 424 -426, 430, 432, 438, 439, 440
Yitro
60, 226, 227

SOUL (NESHAMAH)

Acharei Mot
255, 256, 258, 261-264, 267, 274
Behar
66
Beresheet A
109, 258
Beresheet B
211, 212
Chayei Sarah
140, 141
Emor
58
Idra Raba
136, 138, 140
Kedoshim
70

Ki Tetze
108
Korach
17, 19, 42, 45
Lech Lecha
47, 48, 76, 77-79, 96, 98, 103, 153-157, 159-161, 167, 193, 273
Mishpatim
11, 12, 23, 24, 95, 105, 106, 107, 110, 111
Naso
36
Pinchas
569, 572, 589, 607, 624, 625, 630, 635, 760, 817
Safra Detzniuta
51
Shlach Lecha
238
Tazria
81, 83-86, 116
Tetzaveh
53, 54, 55
Toldot
107
Trumah
284, 286-293, 298, 301-304, 306, 530, 591
Tzav
50, 57, 62, 64, 68-71, 140, 141, 146-148, 187
Vayakhel
184, 202, 243, 255, 270, 278, 297, 298, 299, 300, 404-407
Vayechi
309, 311, 312, 320, 328, 331, 348, 359, 360, 361, 362, 363
Vayera
56, 267, 315
Vayetze
189
Vayigash
15, 16, 17, 18, 19, 21
Vayikra
263, 318, 422-424, 430, 433-435, 437, 438
Yitro
128

SOUL (RUACH)

Acharei Mot
205, 215, 216, 255, 256, 258, 260, 262-264, 266, 267, 274
Balak
78
Beresheet A
18, 94, 109, 258, 274
Beresheet B
130, 212, 379
Emor
58, 287
Idra Raba
138, 139, 140
Ki Tetze
51, 108
Korach
19, 42, 45
Lech Lecha
76-78, 96, 98-104, 146, 152-161, 167, 193, 239, 273, 363
Mishpatim
11, 12, 23, 24, 105, 106, 107, 108, 110
Naso
36, 37
Noach
25, 62-64
Pekudei
638

Pinchas
39, 271, 405, 572, 607, 790
Prologue
109
Shemot
163
Shlach Lecha
221, 237
Shmini
104
Tetzaveh
53, 54
Trumah
268, 284-293, 298-304, 306, 458, 531, 591, 607
Tzav
3, 62-65, 68-71, 140, 143, 144, 146-148, 188, 189
Vaera
48
Vaetchanan
195
Vayakhel
46, 47, 48, 96, 113, 122, 123, 135, 184, 186-188, 191-193, 196, 270, 275, 401
Vayechi
309-312, 319, 320, 325, 327, 328, 331, 348, 360, 361, 363
Vayera
267
Vayetze
189
Vayigash
15-17, 19-22
Vayikra
263, 317, 422, 424, 430, 432, 433, 437, 438
Yitro
224, 225, 226, 227

SOUL, THE

Acharei Mot
31, 94-96, 98, 140, 142-144, 170, 202-208, 211, 215, 216, 218-223, 225, 236, 237, 239, 240, 252-256, 265, 272, 274, 292-294, 316, 351, 386, 393, 408
Balak
24, 26, 104, 180, 181, 191, 193, 196, 198, 199, 200, 202, 213, 214, 217, 230, 260, 290, 312, 337, 366, 367, 370, 371, 374, 382
Bechukotai
25, 32, 43, 57, 59
Beha'alot'cha
3, 20, 61-63, 66, 76, 78, 79, 88, 141, 142, 144, 146
Behar
20, 34-37, 40
Bemidbar
42, 43, 45, 66, 67, 73-76
Beresheet A
3, 37, 40, 49, 75, 90, 96, 154, 155, 162, 164, 167, 218, 222, 223, 228, 233, 235, 236, 252, 258, 262, 267, 273, 282, 283, 285, 286, 288, 291, 309, 337, 382, 384, 405, 413, 415, 440, 477
Beresheet B
2, 5, 6, 8-10, 12, 16, 19, 21, 22, 27, 28, 44, 52, 54-59, 136-138, 142, 145, 167, 170, 171, 186, 195, 196, 198, 212, 228, 229, 319, 320, 322, 333, 341, 358, 413
Beshalach
17, 19, 49, 71, 218, 235, 236,

246, 321, 324, 325, 347, 367 -370, 376, 377, 379, 381, 392, 403, 486

Bo
16, 39

Chayei Sarah
4, 5, 15, 16, 39, 44-46, 48-54, 56, 59, 61, 70, 94, 95, 96, 124, 126, 130-135, 142, 143, 149-153, 155, 156, 158, 159, 160, 162-165, 169, 174, 176, 177, 179, 183-185, 187, 197, 198, 203, 204, 207, 211, 212, 213

Chukat
52, 64

Ekev
44

Emor
5-8, 126, 151, 227b, 235

Ha'azinu
45, 110, 161, 185, 190, 213, 253

Idra Raba
6, 138, 232, 302, 303, 312, 326, 327, 328, 342, 354, 355

Kedoshim
1, 5, 24, 32, 33, 46, 52, 55, 57, 58, 64, 70, 78, 84-88, 95, 126

Ki Tetze
11, 13, 25, 27, 30, 31, 34, 47, 110, 128, 134

Ki Tisa
25, 31, 54, 55, 82

Korach
14

Lech Lecha
6, 8, 13, 14, 15, 40, 42-47, 51, 59, 61, 81, 82, 84-86, 88-90, 94, 95, 112, 129-132, 135, 146, 151, 152, 198, 200, 203, 204, 206, 207, 244-246, 258, 280, 302, 328, 332, 346, 348, 350, 353, 354, 359, 362, 404, 407, 410, 411, 413

Matot
5, 6

Metzora
9-13, 37, 46, 62, 63

Miketz
1, 4, 24, 74, 86, 87, 88, 113, 149, 154, 171, 175, 176, 192, 193, 194

Mishpatim
1-9, 23-32, 41, 42, 44, 47, 50-65, 67, 68, 70, 73, 77, 78, 79, 88-90, 92, 95, 99, 103-105, 107, 111, 116, 134, 234, 348, 427, 448, 455, 467, 531, 552, 567

Naso
6-8, 31, 34, 35, 52, 83, 84, 85, 110, 119, 123, 128, 167

Noach
8, 13, 20, 23, 25, 26, 38, 50, 78, 96, 130, 134, 139, 142, 143, 145, 170, 191, 209, 218, 275, 302

Pekudei
58, 91, 159, 166, 167, 171, 200, 204, 396, 458, 483, 484, 488, 493-497, 513, 514, 522-524, 529, 550, 552, 556, 558-560, 567, 570, 587, 616, 638, 639, 646, 647, 650, 654, 667, 671, 672, 674, 677, 679, 700, 704, 727, 747, 748, 753, 756, 757, 761-763, 766-768, 771-773, 819, 820, 837, 841, 842, 844, 845, 847, 854, 858, 913, 916,

917, 926, 937, 949, 955

Pinchas
7, 9-15, 26, 35d, 44, 45, 48-50, 53-55, 59, 71, 73, 74, 76, 79, 83, 101, 105, 115-117, 124, 126, 130, 164, 165, 170-180, 182, 218, 219, 220, 265, 281, 293, 343, 349, 364, 371, 406, 486, 491, 539-541, 550, 612, 614, 625, 633, 648, 691, 731, 747, 812, 824, 859, 861, 862, 869, 878

Prologue
18, 96, 105, 110, 118, 137, 182, 201, 215, 216, 219, 220, 222, 223, 224, 231, 232, 260

Safra Detzniuta
19, 57, 60

Shemot
3, 47, 65, 107, 149, 156, 166, 176, 179-181, 200, 228, 233, 237, 242, 257, 274, 286, 309, 310, 318, 333, 363, 371, 391

Shlach Lecha
3, 5, 16, 17, 22, 24, 53, 93, 188, 201-204, 206, 207, 217, 222, 230, 235, 259, 281, 290 -295, 299, 305, 306, 318, 319, 330, 334

Shmini
3, 77, 99, 100, 101, 102, 104, 105, 110-113, 114, 116

Shoftim
20

Tazria
1, 16, 17, 20, 23, 24, 26-29, 50, 68, 82, 86, 94, 141, 142, 183

Tetzaveh
55, 58, 59, 60, 118, 119, 120, 140

Toldot
34, 35, 36, 37, 38, 40, 46, 48, 49, 57, 68, 83, 89, 90, 91, 106, 107, 115, 117, 131, 138

Trumah
17, 20, 24, 25, 31, 37, 39, 45-51, 67, 71, 72, 103, 123, 166, 168, 173, 174, 176, 177, 178, 179, 180, 181, 182, 183, 204, 217, 218, 219, 230, 231, 261, 274, 275, 276, 279, 281, 282, 283, 284, 286, 288, 289, 299, 303, 305, 438, 439, 440, 448, 453, 454, 459, 466, 481, 528, 535, 556, 557, 558, 590, 591, 641, 642, 652, 660, 661, 662, 668, 670, 724, 761, 764, 793, 820, 830, 885

Tzav
38, 50, 139, 145, 147, 176

Vaera
18, 48, 50, 60, 98, 101, 126

Vaetchanan
6, 9, 10, 13, 69, 139, 140, 141, 142, 172

Vayakhel
16-18, 22, 23, 62, 81, 83, 91, 97, 113-115, 117, 151, 154, 183, 184, 185, 195, 197, 205, 206, 209, 213, 275-278, 296, 301, 302, 304, 305, 306, 308-310, 314-321, 325, 327-333, 335, 337, 338, 362, 367-373, 385, 388, 404, 436, 490, 491

Vayechi
25, 113, 141, 143, 146, 150,

162, 164, 170-174, 217, 299, 300, 304, 312, 328, 336, 337, 354, 358, 360, 368, 388, 442, 470, 475, 497, 498, 499, 512, 517, 534, 535, 536, 537, 545, 561, 562, 582-585, 603, 609, 640, 656, 658, 676 -678, 683, 730, 740-745, 747-750, 806, 813, 852, 854, 858, 860

Vayelech
7, 11, 38, 42

Vayera
19-21, 23-25, 28-31, 40, 41, 43, 56, 63, 78, 79, 92, 115, 116, 119, 122, 126, 129, 132, 133, 136, 137, 146, 155, 191-193, 195, 199, 243, 244, 251, 260, 263, 318, 326, 333, 340, 367, 368, 375, 377-379, 389, 391- 393, 396, 404, 405, 409, 424, 425, 429, 479, 482, 483

Vayeshev
1, 26, 27, 28, 32, 33, 35-39, 50, 52, 59-62, 64, 68, 86-88, 114, 115, 120, 122, 156 -162, 169, 188, 242, 243, 276, 284

Vayetze
27, 92, 93, 94, 99, 112, 113, 164, 165, 177, 178, 179, 181, 184, 188, 204, 347, 350, 351, 369, 377

Vayigash
12-15, 17, 57, 73-75, 81, 97, 114, 134

Vayikra
36, 93, 95, 96, 98, 130, 131, 185, 207-210, 213, 214, 277, 278, 286, 287, 290, 296, 311, 317, 365, 368, 402, 422, 424, 425

Vayishlach
53, 83, 178, 181, 186, 198, 208, 210, 266

Yitro
60, 64, 66, 95, 121, 126, 178, 223, 250, 283, 342, 343, 346, 377, 378, 417, 428, 429, 431, 455, 459, 460, 464, 468, 475, 481, 501, 503, 518, 556, 563, 572

SOULMATES

Beresheet A
283

Lech Lecha
208, 352, 353, 354

Mishpatim
6, 120, 155, 156, 157, 240

SOUTH

Acharei Mot
76

Balak
351, 353, 434

Beha'alot'cha
2, 4, 112, 113, 125, 126

Bemidbar
29-37, 53, 56, 58-65

Beresheet A
81, 82, 89, 249, 302, 413

Beresheet B
51, 71, 81, 82, 90, 242

Beshalach
100, 137

Chukat
45, 46, 67

Ekev
31, 49, 66, 67
Idra Raba
211
Lech Lecha
7, 72, 143, 162, 167, 168, 221, 273, 363
Mishpatim
340
Noach
101, 263, 265
Pekudei
140, 141, 142, 178, 265, 511, 512, 523, 531, 537, 542, 584, 655, 680, 682, 686, 687, 692, 713, 814
Pinchas
204, 271, 319, 505, 582, 686, 705, 708, 712, 714, 718, 821, 847
Shemot
114, 160
Shlach Lecha
56, 72, 163, 164, 178, 270, 271, 302, 303
Tetzaveh
8
Toldot
12, 15
Trumah
22, 42, 77, 130, 610, 612, 615, 709, 843, 844, 876, 877
Tzav
35, 77, 145
Vaera
35-38, 40, 41, 43, 96, 156-159
Vaetchanan
173, 174, 193
Vayakhel
12, 132, 133, 139, 175, 293, 294, 344, 354
Vayechi
118, 136, 461, 463, 464, 504, 509, 533, 553, 652, 653, 694, 699, 767, 768, 777, 847
Vayera
342, 461, 512
Vayeshev
200
Vayetze
2, 11, 31, 32, 81, 92-94, 115, 168, 170, 202, 204, 205, 264, 306
Vayikra
137, 163, 164, 371, 380
Vayishlach
136

SPEARS

Beresheet A
481
Ekev
25, 27, 28
Ki Tetze
140, 141
Mishpatim
257, 376
Pinchas
157, 464, 465, 467, 480, 728
Prologue
34, 101, 102, 149

SPICES

Acharei Mot
208
Balak
116, 148, 149, 464
Bechukotai
9, 58

Beshalach
396
Bo
147, 149, 153
Chukat
3
Ekev
56
Emor
172, 293
Ha'azinu
162, 165, 169
Idra Raba
250, 254
Korach
50
Metzora
11
Mishpatim
427, 428, 531
Pinchas
348, 400, 423, 544, 552, 576, 594, 596, 616
Safra Detzniuta
14, 16, 25, 33
Shemot
2, 176, 220, 235, 237, 242, 366
Shlach Lecha
178, 179
Tetzaveh
1
Trumah
99, 126, 160, 181, 318, 398, 838
Vayakhel
55, 300, 471, 479
Vayechi
856
Vayera
44, 507
Vayetze
234, 236
Vayikra
26, 29, 32, 163

SPIES

Acharei Mot
78
Balak
375
Emor
266
Ki Tetze
1, 11
Miketz
147
Safra Detzniuta
63
Shlach Lecha
9, 10, 17, 27, 31, 32, 38, 70-72, 75, 76, 92
Vaera
176, 177
Vayera
220

SPINAL CHORD

Pinchas
821

SPINNING

Matot
2
Vayishlach
252

SPLEEN

Beresheet A
266, 267
Pinchas
97, 99, 270, 375, 376, 409, 410, 424, 429

SPOONS

Korach
54

SRAYAH

Balak
179

STAFF

Acharei Mot
285
Balak
429, 431, 445
Beresheet A
234, 263
Beshalach
17, 349
Ki Tetze
31, 76
Mishpatim
376, 383, 384, 386
Pinchas
728, 736
Prologue
102
Shemot
196
Shlach Lecha
72, 165
Shmini
23
Toldot
39
Vaera
84, 104, 116-119, 121, 125, 126, 128, 142, 154
Vayakhel
66
Vayechi
14, 581
Vayera
398
Vayeshev
205

STANDING PRAYER (AMIDAH)

Balak
198, 200, 205
Bemidbar
73
Beresheet A
189, 244
Chayei Sarah
232, 234, 235
Emor
176
Ki Tetze
45, 49, 129, 132
Mishpatim
114, 395, 396
Pekudei
790, 797, 811
Pinchas
41, 261, 281, 282, 304-306, 312, 338, 349, 350, 564, 566, 569, 583, 596, 610, 719, 789, 821, 855
Trumah
43, 45, 54, 115-117, 121, 225, 247, 546, 785

Vayakhel
109, 111, 256, 411
Vayechi
394
Vayigash
9
Vayikra
32, 33

STARIEL (SPIRIT)

Pekudei
682

STARS

Acharei Mot
146
Balak
1, 104, 501-504
Bemidbar
11
Beresheet A
3, 116, 127, 314
Beresheet B
49, 113, 164
Beshalach
267
Chayei Sarah
71
Ekev
44
Emor
70, 315
Ha'azinu
167
Idra Raba
79
Kedoshim
45, 46
Ki Tetze
32, 40, 84, 112-115, 117, 119
Ki Tisa
10
Lech Lecha
27, 322-324, 328, 449
Metzora
8
Mishpatim
212, 336, 460, 473, 564
Pekudei
54, 55, 161, 216, 222, 223, 503, 514, 562, 817
Pinchas
58, 59, 64-66, 139, 334, 383 -385, 478, 496, 498, 580, 581, 692
Prologue
19, 21, 139
Safra Detzniuta
25
Shemot
1, 101, 102, 112-114, 159, 160, 266
Shmini
1, 9
Tazria
40, 150
Toldot
6, 98, 115
Trumah
660, 708, 831, 832, 834- 847, 849-860, 863
Vaera
24, 130, 159
Vaetchanan
180-182
Vayakhel
24, 78, 159, 160-162, 210, 253,

286, 410
Vayechi
218, 353, 452
Vayera
83, 244, 246, 252, 253, 353, 478
Vayeshev
196, 198, 200, 203
Vayetze
131, 150, 332, 333
Vayigash
94
Vayikra
13, 135, 156, 157, 348, 371, 379, 380
Vayishlach
137, 240
Yitro
43, 130, 133, 135, 146, 183, 184, 288

STATURIYAH (SPIRIT)

Pekudei
492-494, 496, 500, 506-508, 680, 681

STERILIZATION

Mishpatim
273, 274

STONE

Acharei Mot
100, 104, 105, 309, 312
Balak
24, 113, 242, 388
Beha'alot'cha
70, 76
Beresheet A
118, 201-203, 205, 264
Beresheet B
63
Beshalach
29, 83, 208, 304, 321, 423, 424, 465, 481, 482
Chukat
47
Ekev
27, 28, 46
Ha'azinu
138
Idra Raba
209, 214, 273, 319, 324
Ki Tetze
14, 71-75
Ki Tisa
4
Lech Lecha
164, 166, 167, 306, 435
Miketz
1, 2, 94
Mishpatim
104, 108, 164, 222, 576, 579
Naso
70
Noach
261, 271, 273, 274, 278-281, 283, 284, 286, 323, 326, 332
Pekudei
38, 46, 175, 176, 177, 179, 231, 233, 260, 338, 341, 382, 465, 478, 496, 559, 564, 680, 686, 727, 740, 741, 743, 749, 781, 790, 821, 838, 882
Pinchas
14, 249, 253, 255, 256, 264, 519, 592, 631, 648, 649, 650, 653, 674
Prologue
185

Shemot
214, 215, 229, 319, 379, 393
Shlach Lecha
137, 208
Shmini
93
Shoftim
7
Tazria
148
Tetzaveh
93-96
Toldot
90, 204
Trumah
231, 471, 579
Tzav
64, 70
Vaera
47, 125, 163
Vaetchanan
186
Vayakhel
11, 369, 441
Vayechi
4, 17, 125, 141, 287, 445-449, 454, 456, 457, 764, 777, 802
Vayelech
23, 24
Vayera
299, 301, 303, 337
Vayeshev
284
Vayetze
81, 82, 93, 94, 96, 100-104, 190
Vayigash
128
Vayikra
139
Yitro
343, 364, 368, 431, 519, 521, 569

STONES

Balak
68, 242, 391, 434, 468, 489
Beresheet A
21, 22, 24, 252, 253, 255
Beresheet B
10, 13, 216, 269, 270, 279
Beshalach
67, 134, 135, 151, 152, 231, 256, 481
Ekev
25, 27
Emor
171
Idra Raba
17
Ki Tetze
43, 63
Lech Lecha
433-435, 452, 465
Metzora
49
Miketz
134
Mishpatim
211, 259, 369, 450
Noach
75
Pekudei
132, 146, 157, 174-179, 182, 289, 380, 381, 382, 384
Pinchas
9, 61, 89, 208, 264, 337, 557, 648, 653, 878
Prologue
196

Shemot
39, 93, 257, 258, 322
Shlach Lecha
20, 146, 249
Tazria
149, 153, 159, 175, 176
Trumah
160, 241, 242, 398, 476, 670, 838, 841, 871
Vaera
47, 125, 137
Vaetchanan
93, 168
Vayakhel
11, 284
Vayechi
456, 457, 458, 839
Vayera
33, 144, 267, 268, 480, 496
Vayetze
10, 11, 30, 42, 82, 343
Vayikra
391, 392
Vayishlach
155
Yitro
345, 367, 368, 370, 372

STORK

Vayetze
338, 339

STREAMS

Acharei Mot
34, 35, 37, 46, 87, 101, 105, 207, 209, 246, 334, 374, 385
Balak
116, 310, 312, 314
Beha'alot'cha
23, 24, 30, 31
Beresheet A
190, 249, 250, 251, 259, 317, 333, 380, 426
Beresheet B
44, 50, 281
Beshalach
410
Bo
38, 40, 71, 221, 225
Chayei Sarah
94, 226
Chukat
28, 29, 77
Emor
44, 102, 170, 331
Ha'azinu
33, 59, 80, 96, 156, 166, 227, 228
Idra Raba
73, 273
Kedoshim
19, 94
Ki Tetze
85, 128
Lech Lecha
189, 214, 366, 367, 416
Mishpatim
86
Noach
84, 85, 145, 173
Pekudei
51
Pinchas
161, 437
Prologue
219
Safra Detzniuta
63
Shemot
46, 134, 158, 371

Shlach Lecha
20, 115
Shmini
13, 54
Toldot
9, 111
Tzav
74
Vaera
104, 122, 128, 129, 144, 164, 165, 167
Vaetchanan
59, 121, 123
Vayakhel
104, 326
Vayechi
162, 536, 658
Vayetze
11, 236
Vayigash
64
Vayikra
278
Yitro
341, 465

STRENGTH

Acharei Mot
134, 150, 193, 208, 227, 228, 340
Balak
8, 113, 117, 198, 232, 252, 254, 257, 262, 275, 279, 367, 428, 429, 449, 476, 491, 492
Bechukotai
20
Beha'alot'cha
39, 54, 112
Behar
15, 45, 48
Bemidbar
22, 35
Beresheet A
47, 70, 144, 146, 197, 323, 401, 421
Beresheet B
15, 42, 49, 69, 120, 211, 238, 345, 396, 397, 402, 405, 444
Beshalach
107, 112, 222, 227, 230, 239, 241, 242, 244, 255, 305, 307, 317, 328, 454
Bo
7, 27, 51, 60, 70, 120, 181
Chayei Sarah
201, 213
Chukat
24, 51, 62
Emor
18, 100, 160, 189, 192, 194, 196, 199, 266
Ha'azinu
96
Idra Raba
256, 289, 294, 295
Kedoshim
37, 38, 58, 73, 108, 126, 132
Ki Tetze
98, 107
Ki Tisa
46, 76, 89, 90
Korach
28, 29, 30
Lech Lecha
26, 74, 172, 318, 327
Miketz
53, 74, 75, 89, 90, 136, 199, 201
Mishpatim
42, 43, 121, 122, 242, 279, 283, 290, 296, 300, 306, 315, 316, 320, 358, 490

Noach
148, 308, 351, 355, 370
Pekudei
26, 50, 160, 270, 276, 291, 299, 307, 312, 314, 373, 436, 457, 461, 745, 767, 804, 855, 900, 923
Pinchas
100, 101, 134, 135, 137, 180, 188, 215, 223, 253, 289, 346, 370, 438, 474, 511, 523, 554, 611, 657, 873, 883, 886
Prologue
75, 217, 248
Shemot
74, 130, 297, 327-330
Shlach Lecha
2, 57, 64, 84, 137, 150, 238
Shmini
57
Tazria
30, 77, 78
Tetzaveh
5, 83, 110, 142
Toldot
9, 12, 54, 55, 59, 106, 122, 124, 125, 165, 172, 197
Trumah
57, 62, 90, 221, 224, 233, 284, 309, 310, 387, 444, 466, 509, 538, 554, 562, 565, 567, 618, 620, 678, 679, 684, 687, 757, 758, 760, 761, 764, 773, 802, 817, 840, 845
Tzav
25, 78
Vaera
2, 7, 9, 40, 45, 157, 189
Vaetchanan
55, 173
Vayakhel
47, 77, 286, 288, 378, 404, 407, 456
Vayechi
33, 61, 62, 72, 139, 262, 415, 464, 476, 477, 520, 521, 529, 544, 547, 549, 551, 560, 579, 587, 641, 694, 697, 699, 709, 712, 776, 829, 835, 837
Vayelech
3
Vayera
4, 212, 361, 363, 366, 383, 441, 509
Vayeshev
45, 56, 146, 184, 210, 212
Vayetze
23, 34, 35, 71, 109, 110, 111, 271
Vayigash
59, 70, 124
Vayikra
53, 136, 206, 221, 231, 292, 308, 332, 380, 396, 409, 411
Vayishlach
20, 28, 36, 93, 94, 104, 106, 108, 149, 178-181, 189
Yitro
44, 181, 355, 561, 575

STURIYAH (ANGEL)

Vayetze
73

SUBSTANCE (YESH)

Pinchas
504, 505, 865

Trumah
738
Vayechi
688
Vayetze
209, 232

SUFFERING

Balak
273
Beha'alot'cha
87
Beresheet A
52, 186, 263
Chayei Sarah
67, 164
Ekev
54, 55
Ha'azinu
118
Idra Raba
285
Ki Tetze
21, 54
Ki Tisa
2, 16, 18, 21, 29, 35, 36
Korach
36
Lech Lecha
117
Miketz
105
Mishpatim
191, 192, 231, 290, 384, 386, 474, 524
Pinchas
94, 367, 504, 751
Shlach Lecha
229
Shoftim
11
Toldot
45
Tzav
140
Vaetchanan
142, 187
Vayakhel
334
Vayechi
1, 13, 20, 171, 316, 321, 547, 666, 668, 687, 775
Vayera
21, 146, 510
Vayeshev
11-13, 28-31, 35, 36, 38, 40, 41, 179
Vayikra
193
Vayishlach
97, 130
Yitro
415

SUGADYAH (SPIRIT)

Pekudei
689

SUICIDE

Ki Tetze
11

SUKKOT

Emor
69, 70, 110, 126, 137, 138, 140, 143, 155, 223, 270- 272, 276, 277, 279, 288
Ki Tetze
143, 144

Metzora
42
Noach
106, 107
Tetzaveh
62, 134, 136-139
Vayechi
204, 205, 215, 227, 353, 356
Vayishlach
131, 141, 142, 176

SUN

Acharei Mot
62, 145, 156, 175, 409
Balak
6, 80, 308
Bechukotai
11, 22, 36
Beha'alot'cha
2, 4, 35, 57, 70, 102, 103, 108, 112, 121, 125, 139, 140, 148
Bemidbar
34, 35
Beresheet A
110, 113, 114, 126, 127, 128, 142, 189, 277, 394-396, 402, 403, 479
Beresheet B
70, 112, 161-164, 211, 216, 297, 306
Beshalach
49, 83, 169, 318, 323, 325, 445
Bo
56, 78, 94, 164, 174, 175
Chayei Sarah
30, 205, 206, 209, 238, 239
Chukat
33, 36-44, 46, 49, 50, 51, 52
Ekev
44
Emor
4, 132, 134, 205, 224, 331
Ha'azinu
14, 17
Idra Raba
120
Kedoshim
45, 46, 63, 84, 88
Ki Tetze
32, 45, 84, 85, 87, 112, 114, 117, 118, 120
Ki Tisa
7-10, 61, 62, 73, 75, 111, 118
Korach
28, 41
Lech Lecha
114, 223, 347, 350, 360, 450
Metzora
13, 60
Miketz
50, 72, 73, 80, 112, 113, 134, 227, 228, 233, 235, 236, 237
Mishpatim
137, 331, 332, 339, 350, 403, 404, 497
Naso
69
Noach
101, 169, 247, 362
Pekudei
27, 59, 77, 222, 224, 234, 279, 281, 307, 314, 348, 378, 503, 507, 607, 675, 734, 940
Pinchas
35c, 59, 75, 76, 107, 114, 126, 207, 236, 238, 239, 240, 344, 409, 444, 498, 658, 676, 678, 689, 695, 717, 720, 737, 739,

817, 820, 887
Prologue
51, 104, 112, 139, 142, 144, 164, 185
Shemot
1, 14, 27, 115, 155, 160, 251
Shlach Lecha
1, 2, 8, 19, 25, 31, 54, 110, 124, 151, 244, 262
Shoftim
14
Tazria
62, 63, 64, 76
Tetzaveh
2, 3, 34, 36, 38
Toldot
6, 10, 12, 13, 25, 39, 133, 168
Trumah
2, 3, 29, 42, 52, 62, 78, 80, 198, 199, 203, 208, 209, 212, 213, 221, 301, 347, 361, 381, 551, 560, 753, 843, 844, 859, 899, 900
Tzav
173, 175
Vaera
25, 130, 161
Vaetchanan
15
Vayakhel
13, 25, 75, 78, 145, 210, 221, 282, 331, 396, 402
Vayechi
12, 275, 293, 359, 449, 451, 485, 540, 564-566, 589, 619, 673, 730, 793, 807, 808, 829, 830, 835-837, 839, 840, 841
Vayelech
4, 5, 6, 12, 14
Vayera
27, 40, 405, 409, 445
Vayeshev
21, 22, 32, 42, 44, 47, 55, 63, 65, 68, 146, 155, 159, 179, 196, 203, 221
Vayetze
1, 2, 5, 7, 9, 12, 13, 15, 16, 32, 271, 385
Vayigash
94, 108, 130
Vayikra
132, 184, 241, 244, 267, 278, 383
Vayishlach
12, 64, 88, 90, 93, 94, 96, 97, 256, 258
Yitro
43, 225, 288, 383, 505

SUPERNAL BOOK

Shmini
93
Trumah
186, 206

SUPERNAL FORMS

Beresheet B
9
Vayechi
702

SURIYAH (SPIRIT)

Pekudei
633

SWORD

Acharei Mot
72, 73, 108, 309, 314-316

Balak
68, 70, 76, 81, 106, 113, 147, 161, 181, 252, 316, 427, 451, 468
Bechukotai
26, 27
Beresheet A
100, 101, 266, 289, 481
Beresheet B
94, 118, 119, 283, 314-316
Beshalach
147, 148, 152, 215, 256, 359, 360, 464, 469, 473
Ekev
25, 26, 27, 28
Emor
6, 207, 338
Idra Raba
2, 226
Ki Tetze
141
Korach
46
Lech Lecha
104
Metzora
1, 4, 30, 31, 35
Miketz
221
Mishpatim
173, 241, 242, 244, 257, 258, 398, 430
Naso
70, 115, 118
Noach
41, 90, 162
Pekudei
376, 377, 571, 642, 727, 859, 875, 897, 904, 915, 916
Pinchas
98, 120, 218, 270, 364, 414, 485, 728
Prologue
34, 197
Shemot
347-349, 365, 393
Shmini
118
Shoftim
2, 3, 4
Toldot
43, 179, 180
Trumah
744
Tzav
87
Vaera
77-79, 112, 114, 115, 131, 143
Vaetchanan
170, 180, 192
Vayechi
30, 172, 242, 284, 469, 572, 604, 643-647, 708
Vayera
271
Vayetze
26, 27, 31, 176, 340, 390, 391
Vayikra
21, 196, 326
Vayishlach
147
Yitro
25, 271

TABERNACLE

Bechukotai
30, 31, 32, 39
Beha'alot'cha
93, 95, 99, 111, 116, 118
Bemidbar
6, 7, 8, 9

Beresheet A
420
Beresheet B
192, 194-198, 296, 297, 304, 308, 309
Beshalach
334
Bo
89
Ki Tisa
119
Korach
50
Noach
106, 169
Pekudei
1, 2, 7, 8, 11-15, 17, 19-23, 25, 26, 28, 29, 33-37, 42, 44, 48, 49, 52-55, 57, 59, 60, 68, 69, 83, 84, 87, 97, 107, 131, 132, 159, 160, 161, 211, 212, 216, 240, 241, 249, 251, 255, 258, 259, 260, 272-275, 283, 284, 285, 286, 290-292, 294 -299, 338, 340 -343, 345-348, 370, 372-374, 376, 377, 379, 386, 388-392, 395-402, 404, 413, 414, 417, 641, 680, 682, 684, 692, 906, 957
Shemot
33
Tetzaveh
2-4, 13, 135, 136
Trumah
240, 244, 314, 503, 573, 581, 596, 597, 598, 599, 600, 613 -616, 618-621, 664, 665, 666, 689, 690, 699, 703, 706, 707, 788, 806, 807, 842, 844, 848
Vaetchanan
13

TABLE

Acharei Mot
85, 109, 110
Balak
38, 66, 67, 68, 69, 83, 92, 136, 137, 154, 229, 438
Bechukotai
9
Beresheet A
316, 335
Beresheet B
401
Beshalach
4, 5, 7, 8, 71, 414, 415
Bo
24
Ekev
18-21, 24, 31, 32, 37, 44, 48-52, 62
Emor
108, 109, 118, 119, 123, 125, 152, 175, 277, 278, 279
Ha'azinu
46
Ki Tetze
77
Ki Tisa
5, 38, 39
Lech Lecha
262, 267, 284
Miketz
142
Mishpatim
197, 451
Noach
110
Pekudei
257, 625, 626, 627, 890-892

Pinchas
548, 605, 617, 618, 620, 621, 634-636, 641, 755, 757, 762, 783, 834, 872
Tetzaveh
101, 103
Trumah
119-124, 485, 488-491, 495, 496, 497, 498, 503-509, 515 -519, 521, 522, 524-527, 535, 556, 557, 560, 568, 571-574, 770, 772, 773
Tzav
163
Vayakhel
172, 175
Vayechi
157, 636, 675, 845, 848
Vayera
431, 432, 433, 434
Vayetze
44
Vayikra
328
Yitro
121, 437, 438, 446, 447, 450, 455

TABLETS

Acharei Mot
100
Bechukotai
9
Bemidbar
29
Beresheet A
241, 254, 287, 289, 478
Beresheet B
200
Beshalach
35, 36, 304
Chayei Sarah
220
Ekev
19, 45, 46
Emor
184
Idra Raba
149
Ki Tetze
14, 69
Korach
2
Mishpatim
359-361, 364, 372
Noach
89
Pinchas
631, 842
Prologue
104
Shemot
189
Shmini
93
Tetzaveh
71
Tzav
57
Vaera
25
Vayakhel
11
Vayechi
457
Vayikra
87
Yitro
212, 343, 345, 364-370, 372, 374, 431, 569

TAHARIEL (ANGEL)

Beresheet B
41
Pekudei
483, 844
Vayera
276

TALIT

Beresheet A
185, 189, 350
Miketz
259, 260

TALMAI

Shlach Lecha
32, 39, 40, 60

TAMAR

Acharei Mot
277-280, 285, 287
Bo
113
Vayakhel
453
Vayeshev
189-194

TAMMUZ

Prologue
135

TANYA

Ki Tetze
60
Mishpatim
305
Pinchas
491

TARMOD

Mishpatim
344
Pinchas
389, 390

TASKIFA (SPIRIT)

Pekudei
856

TAURUS

Miketz
164

TEARDROPS

Beresheet A
254

TEMPLE, THE

Acharei Mot
176, 179, 288, 295, 326, 331, 333, 334
Balak
221, 230, 317, 504
Bechukotai
9, 29
Beha'alot'cha
25
Behar
23, 27, 28, 30, 34, 38, 39, 45, 75
Beresheet A
3-7, 29, 30, 66, 107, 108, 186, 189, 220, 231, 233, 246, 254, 280, 292, 371, 413, 415
Beresheet B
29, 284, 295, 308, 370, 397

Beshalach
121, 236, 240, 297, 326, 332, 334-336, 407, 480, 481
Bo
34
Chayei Sarah
124, 128, 129, 185, 191, 194, 201, 240, 265, 267, 268, 270
Chukat
57
Ekev
36, 40, 47
Emor
14, 16, 48, 160, 248, 254
Ha'azinu
13, 103
Idra Raba
341, 360
Kedoshim
40, 123
Ki Tetze
77
Ki Tisa
109, 118
Korach
9, 26, 27
Lech Lecha
184, 186-190, 227, 422, 424, 426
Metzora
59
Miketz
72, 215-223
Mishpatim
66, 169, 170, 263, 264, 265, 266, 293, 450, 491
Naso
9, 28, 29
Noach
43, 47, 49-51, 54
Pekudei
10, 27, 40, 42, 43, 46, 98, 170, 282, 291, 309, 370, 394, 395, 397, 414, 474, 491, 639, 734, 735, 736, 737, 749
Pinchas
19, 31, 40, 58, 106, 142, 143, 147-151, 319, 321, 322, 333, 440, 442, 524, 580, 617, 679, 700, 701, 708, 712, 713, 717, 718, 743, 744, 752, 787, 788, 795, 802
Prologue
18, 42, 43, 93, 94, 119, 139, 183, 184, 239
Safra Detzniuta
41
Shemot
38, 64, 115, 141-143, 146, 147, 149, 164, 179, 292
Shlach Lecha
4, 6, 17, 86, 87, 89, 164, 176, 177, 185, 243, 257, 265, 273
Shmini
96
Tazria
66, 80, 92, 93, 146, 177,
Tetzaveh
6, 7, 40, 112
Toldot
32, 65, 154
Trumah
313-315, 393, 472, 473, 525, 527, 686, 907
Tzav
5, 67, 79, 84, 172, 175
Vaera
33, 50
Vaetchanan
100, 144, 185, 188

Vayakhel
7, 16, 18, 20, 37, 42, 169, 225, 241, 300, 306, 318, 336, 377, 401, 422, 423, 424, 431
Vayechi
13, 52, 56, 74, 77, 95, 156, 180, 181, 380, 392, 422, 441, 442, 443, 689
Vayera
116, 253, 396, 441, 443
Vayeshev
43, 44, 56, 65, 66, 98, 99, 270
Vayetze
19, 41, 55, 271, 273, 329, 330, 359
Vayigash
14, 32, 33, 66, 88, 90, 93-96, 102, 106, 110, 130
Vayikra
12, 44, 113, 116, 253, 298, 314, 344, 348, 349, 363, 425
Vayishlach
104, 122, 215, 230
Yitro
58, 510

TEMPLE, DESTRUCTION OF

Beresheet B
16

TEN

Acharei Mot
81, 82, 248, 249, 252, 304, 386, 389, 394, 411
Balak
314, 403, 404, 406
Beha'alot'cha
46, 67, 90, 103
Behar
18, 36, 37, 44, 76
Bemidbar
57
Beresheet A
5, 29, 82, 173, 175, 187, 194, 199, 205, 295, 317, 325, 340, 341, 347
Beresheet B
7, 20, 57, 67, 92, 143, 325
Beshalach
122, 146, 161, 266, 269, 299, 339
Bo
42, 47, 122, 141, 218, 221, 222, 227
Chayei Sarah
24, 25, 35, 168, 169, 170
Ekev
30, 31, 34, 37, 38, 41, 43, 44, 48, 57, 59
Emor
23, 228, 257, 258, 280, 300
Ha'azinu
73, 243
Idra Raba
24, 88, 97, 107, 150, 151, 184, 187, 193, 206, 226, 231, 240, 273, 292, 307, 321, 322, 350, 357
Kedoshim
16, 34, 38, 79, 80, 83
Ki Tetze
24, 34, 35, 37, 57, 87, 90, 96, 129, 131, 132, 141, 145
Ki Tisa
4, 35
Korach
49, 52, 53, 54, 55, 56

Lech Lecha
7, 90, 117, 125, 257, 312, 381, 428
Miketz
174
Mishpatim
66, 163, 303, 359, 445, 470, 471, 498, 517, 528, 533, 571
Naso
15, 59, 106-108, 176-178, 199
Noach
55, 175, 256, 358
Pekudei
87, 122, 146, 217, 246, 249, 252, 253, 566, 569, 575, 654, 672, 674, 677, 826
Pinchas
48, 57, 58, 105, 195, 221, 224, 243, 247-249, 251, 252, 268, 269, 271, 287, 330, 343, 370, 371, 394, 483, 502, 506, 548, 570, 572, 574, 587, 603, 620, 622-624, 628, 632, 640, 641, 649, 655, 682, 705, 707, 708, 713, 733, 749, 759, 771, 805 -807, 816, 818, 826, 829, 839 -842, 846, 848, 865, 877, 878
Safra Detzniuta
40, 62
Shemot
113, 121, 141, 148, 243-245, 249, 287, 310, 326, 343, 391
Shlach Lecha
61, 88, 142, 199, 290
Shmini
106
Shoftim
24
Tazria
170, 185
Tetzaveh
20, 25, 26, 30, 33, 116, 117, 118, 120, 141
Toldot
71
Trumah
23, 56, 57, 87, 89, 103, 105, 106, 109, 115, 125, 160, 203, 219, 296, 325, 368, 553, 554, 555, 570, 648, 662, 664, 692, 698, 699, 703, 706, 707, 708, 798, 881, 884, 899, 912
Tzav
28, 39, 55, 155, 160
Vaera
143, 145, 166, 173
Vaetchanan
22, 69, 70, 138, 154, 179, 192
Vayakhel
38, 60, 106, 147, 185, 204, 234, 251, 284, 358, 398
Vayechi
20, 126, 285, 502, 655, 822
Vayera
68, 69, 126, 194, 196, 197, 198, 219, 222, 223, 274, 281, 283, 354, 386, 402, 444, 445, 450
Vayeshev
54, 95
Vayetze
12, 70, 81, 128, 300, 301
Vayigash
15, 96, 121
Vayikra
140, 155-157, 162, 166, 177 -179, 190, 303, 337, 413, 414, 417
Vayishlach
34, 35, 103, 184, 236

Yitro
2-4, 6, 8, 13, 124, 125, 180, 235, 317, 366, 371, 400, 465, 496, 497, 504, 542, 569

TEN COMMANDMENTS

Acharei Mot
394
Behar
76
Bo
227
Kedoshim
16, 79, 80
Mishpatim
470
Pinchas
842
Trumah
325, 368, 554
Tzav
155
Vaetchanan
138, 154
Vayera
194, 197
Yitro
317, 569

TENTS

Acharei Mot
61, 181, 182, 188, 280
Balak
32, 114, 233, 243, 244, 291, 488, 490
Bechukotai
9, 35, 36
Beha'alot'cha
26
Bemidbar
1, 8, 30, 53
Beresheet A
140
Beresheet B
227, 228, 231, 296, 297, 303, 304
Beshalach
462
Bo
89-91
Chayei Sarah
19, 129, 248, 250, 259, 260
Emor
173, 279
Idra Raba
219
Ki Tetze
66, 69
Ki Tisa
109, 110, 111, 116, 118, 119
Korach
26, 35
Lech Lecha
56, 70, 82, 88, 142, 166, 179
Metzora
22
Miketz
109
Mishpatim
338, 365, 434
Naso
9, 157, 193
Noach
93, 308
Pekudei
10, 44, 284, 285, 300, 346, 387, 392, 480, 957, 958
Pinchas
252

Prologue
142
Shemot
18, 227, 233, 359
Shlach Lecha
42
Shmini
26
Tazria
150
Toldot
61, 93, 194
Trumah
198, 199, 243, 416, 424, 587, 614, 689, 909, 914
Tzav
170
Vaetchanan
28, 92, 166, 167, 169
Vayakhel
359, 382
Vayechi
612, 614, 618, 664
Vayelech
13
Vayera
5, 11-13, 27, 29, 41, 50, 51, 98, 99, 102, 115, 119, 132, 147, 148, 156-159, 228, 266
Vayeshev
112, 267
Vayetze
21, 65, 216, 228, 296
Vayikra
7, 8, 16, 25, 26, 28, 50, 225, 292
Vayishlach
42, 60, 204, 214

TERAH, ABRAHAM'S FATHER

Ha'azinu
237
Lech Lecha
16, 17, 35, 36, 38, 40
Toldot
86
Vayera
106, 200

TERAH

Behar
64, 69, 70
Shemot
169
Vaera 196

TESTIMONY

Acharei Mot
57, 138, 382
Balak
395
Beha'alot'cha
16
Bemidbar
28
Beresheet A
337
Beresheet B
3
Emor
41, 43, 57, 211, 219
Ha'azinu
88, 93, 107, 162
Ki Tetze
14, 100
Lech Lecha
362

Miketz
140
Mishpatim
240, 526
Pekudei
1, 12, 14, 19, 21-23, 25, 26, 29, 33, 48, 173, 174, 284, 285, 392, 755, 935
Pinchas
16, 193, 356, 383, 393, 444, 491
Safra Detzniuta
67
Shemot
34, 250
Shlach Lecha
334, 337, 343
Shoftim
11, 15, 16, 17, 20
Tazria
20
Trumah
204
Tzav
184
Vaera
125
Vaetchanan
58, 100
Vayakhel
252, 253, 254
Vayechi
164, 296, 357, 362, 458, 562, 680
Vayelech
22
Vayera
239, 336, 337
Vayeshev
101, 181
Vayetze
168, 237
Vayikra
217
Vayishlach
31, 134
Yitro
99, 100, 106, 373, 494

TETRAGRAMMATON

Acharei Mot
1, 157, 158, 161-163, 166, 169, 170, 174, 184, 190, 191, 212, 277, 288, 328, 332, 335, 336, 371, 385, 386, 389, 396
Balak
49, 80, 116, 344
Beha'alot'cha
49, 50, 93
Beshalach
75, 188, 241, 258, 435
Ekev
66
Emor
25, 40, 64, 66-68, 88, 102, 184, 185, 188, 313, 314, 317, 323
Ha'azinu
7, 53, 61, 75, 82, 84, 190, 220
Idra Raba
172, 227, 229, 232, 233, 244, 245, 261-263, 266, 271, 297, 300, 317, 329
Ki Tetze
19, 57, 71, 74, 77, 85, 93, 99, 101, 102, 117, 126, 128, 129, 133, 137, 138, 144, 145
Ki Tisa
65, 66

Lech Lecha
319
Miketz
11, 43, 44, 108
Mishpatim
12, 13, 37, 69, 71, 258, 260, 304, 364, 365, 378, 379, 382, 405, 436, 445, 467, 468, 470, 471, 472, 489, 498, 539, 549
Naso
13, 28, 30, 31, 36, 37, 38, 41, 48, 52, 55, 58, 102, 165, 167, 173
Pinchas
35d, 42, 43, 44, 50, 51, 58, 63, 70, 78, 106, 177-179, 187, 188, 191, 195, 201, 202, 221-225, 228, 229, 243, 246, 255, 260-262, 268, 269, 271, 280, 282, 283, 287-289, 291, 292, 294, 295, 297, 303, 305 -308, 311, 312, 320, 322, 323, 325, 333-335, 337, 340, 341, 342, 344, 371, 405, 419, 432, 434, 482, 483, 484, 489, 492, 502, 530, 569, 572, 573, 574, 584, 585, 603, 604, 606, 608, 609, 611, 612, 616, 617, 620, 627, 633, 640, 641, 646, 647, 649, 657, 666, 668, 670, 674, 678, 688, 712, 713, 717, 733, 734, 738, 749, 752, 756, 757, 758, 769, 789, 790, 809-813, 815, 821, 837-840, 846, 848, 851, 856, 860, 864, 866 -868, 872, 874, 876, 877, 888, 889
Prologue
26, 48, 85, 211, 237, 238, 239
Shemot
44, 141-147, 149-155, 313
Shlach Lecha
5, 11, 36, 96, 129, 262
Tazria
13, 28, 91
Tetzaveh
5, 8, 14-17, 19, 20, 25, 26, 28, 32, 33, 36, 143
Tzav
140, 142, 143, 146
Vaera
29
Vaetchanan
12, 20, 37, 38, 40, 43, 44, 59, 60, 78, 80, 81, 83, 86, 87, 91, 118, 146, 175, 177
Vayakhel
43, 69, 100, 120, 347, 351- 353, 355, 356, 357, 360, 361, 363, 364, 365, 376, 383, 397 -401, 422, 443, 464, 481, 484
Vayechi
37, 38, 43, 59, 60, 63, 87, 96, 175, 672, 752
Vayetze
18, 30, 65, 71, 74, 87, 158, 167, 169
Vayikra
52, 104, 132, 139, 146, 152, 153, 158-161, 169, 170, 172, 174, 175, 221, 248, 278-282, 284, 285, 306, 331, 421, 428

TEVEL (WORLD)

Beresheet B
36, 38, 54
Beshalach
127
Mishpatim
117, 118
Prologue
159

Vayikra
138, 139

TFILIN

Bechukotai
21
Beha'alot'cha
92
Behar
10
Bemidbar
68, 70, 71
Beresheet A
185, 197, 199, 289
Beshalach
388
Bo
231, 234, 235, 244- 246
Chayei Sarah
189, 190-193, 195, 234
Ekev
65
Ha'azinu
89, 119, 138
Idra Raba
271
Kedoshim
20, 21
Ki Tetze
25, 45, 104, 132, 136, 137, 139, 140, 142
Korach
45
Lech Lecha
308
Metzora
36, 37, 40, 42
Mishpatim
394, 454, 456, 458, 461, 471
Pekudei
184, 329, 331, 332
Pinchas
285, 289, 334, 484, 754, 788, 795, 830, 871, 872, 873, 874, 876, 877
Prologue
237, 238, 242, 243
Shlach Lecha
126, 338
Tazria
134
Toldot
104, 105
Trumah
230, 651, 653, 654, 655, 658, 659
Tzav
56, 57, 59
Vaetchanan
6, 7, 37, 38, 40, 41, 43, 44, 46-49, 55, 57, 60, 86-91, 96-100, 119, 173, 174
Vayakhel
127, 151, 410
Vayechi
603
Vayera
33
Vayetze
6, 302, 318
Vayigash
9
Vayishlach
62, 63
Yitro
75, 236, 418, 512

THESE (ELEH)

Balak
327

Ki Tetze
145
Mishpatim
202, 203, 204, 205, 208
Noach
4
Shemot
269

THIGH

Acharei Mot
74, 315
Balak
261
Beresheet A
142-146, 249, 289
Beshalach
104, 359, 360, 479
Bo
199, 200
Chayei Sarah
159, 160
Ekev
39
Emor
160, 161
Idra Raba
310
Metzora
35
Miketz
235
Mishpatim
200, 201, 302, 324-327, 329, 330, 337, 338
Naso
73, 88
Pekudei
462, 518, 729, 731-733, 735, 737, 738, 740, 741, 816, 817, 819
Pinchas
316, 408, 433, 456, 544, 580, 594
Tazria
51, 53
Toldot
197
Trumah
402, 576, 710, 795
Vaera
95, 96
Vayechi
30, 265, 266, 267, 643, 645, 646, 696, 697, 698, 700, 711
Vayeshev
50
Vayetze
29, 52
Vayikra
199
Vayishlach
13, 96, 97, 99, 100, 104, 105, 107, 108, 111, 116, 146
Yitro
204

THIRTEEN

Acharei Mot
106-108, 184, 315
Balak
363, 368
Beha'alot'cha
13
Beresheet A
112, 126
Beresheet B
67
Chayei Sarah
141, 195

Chukat
77
Emor
148
Ha'azinu
39, 41, 49, 59, 166, 174
Idra Raba
18, 20, 72-74, 87-89, 96-99, 110, 112, 120, 121, 147, 164, 165, 233, 249, 267, 275, 278, 282
Ki Tetze
17
Lech Lecha
42, 45-47, 284
Mishpatim
76, 77, 78, 283, 284, 354, 355, 463
Naso
162, 164
Pekudei
551-553, 826, 872, 923
Pinchas
256, 257, 259, 262, 286, 288, 291, 297, 299, 300, 367, 393, 394, 396, 397, 646, 826
Prologue
1
Safra Detzniuta
7, 14, 15, 17, 18, 36, 56, 66
Shlach Lecha
6, 92, 262, 339, 341
Tetzaveh
20, 128
Toldot
17
Trumah
99, 100, 110, 242, 376, 377, 398, 403, 662, 663, 913
Vaera
104
Vaetchanan
142
Vayakhel
41, 155
Vayechi
660
Vayera
64, 472, 473
Vayeshev
3
Vayetze
44, 245, 315
Vayikra
156, 419
Yitro
205, 332, 407, 512, 537, 569

THIRTEEN ATTRIBUTES OF MERCY

Acharei Mot
106-108, 184
Beresheet A
112, 126
Ha'azinu
39, 59
Idra Raba
278
Ki Tetze
17
Naso
164
Pinchas
286, 367, 394, 396, 646
Prologue
1
Trumah
100, 110
Vayakhel
155

Vayechi
660
Vayetze
315
Vayikra
156
Yitro
512, 537

THORNS

Pekudei
24
Shoftim
9

THOUGHT

Acharei Mot
44, 281
Balak
95, 143, 148, 153, 168, 250, 251, 278, 327, 376, 455, 461, 474
Bechukotai
29, 41
Beha'alot'cha
24, 56, 146
Beresheet A
30, 55, 114, 136, 137, 139, 197, 201, 286, 287, 297, 303, 354, 355, 410
Beresheet B
143, 239, 385, 393, 397
Beshalach
188, 246
Bo
18, 75, 117, 121, 154
Chayei Sarah
24, 170
Chukat
83, 86, 87
Ha'azinu
153
Kedoshim
53, 54
Ki Tetze
145
Ki Tisa
26, 71, 94
Lech Lecha
119, 120, 310, 378, 409
Miketz
9, 40, 64, 152, 206, 263
Mishpatim
8, 18, 83, 150, 267, 282, 283, 295-297, 345, 380, 381, 398, 467, 468, 470, 471, 570
Naso
14, 15, 112
Noach
123-127, 228, 232, 235, 314, 328-331
Pekudei
9, 101, 102, 103, 104, 106, 266, 360, 363, 367, 577, 673, 674, 772, 823, 824, 832-834, 943, 947-951
Pinchas
136, 223, 271, 308, 324, 327, 474, 489, 665, 667, 668, 780, 813
Prologue
5, 13, 14
Safra Detzniuta
41
Shemot
10, 53, 80, 139, 239, 256, 268, 296, 298, 317, 358, 396
Shlach Lecha
22, 30, 38, 77, 164, 191

Shmini
58, 59, 65
Shoftim
7
Tetzaveh
8, 15, 22, 101
Toldot
47, 62, 99, 140, 184
Trumah
109, 301, 539, 592, 593, 900
Tzav
12, 15, 20, 29, 49, 69, 71, 72
Vaera
53, 119
Vayakhel
3
Vayechi
164, 262, 264, 338, 390, 550, 729, 768, 769
Vayera
32, 97, 220, 227, 317, 324, 328, 383, 507
Vayeshev
23, 124, 131
Vayetze
19, 20, 44, 88, 124, 131, 140, 166, 182, 185, 187-189, 300, 314, 370
Vayikra
70-74, 124, 235
Vayishlach
23, 28, 43, 49, 118, 125, 220
Yitro
84, 125, 141, 193, 304, 338

THREAD

Acharei Mot
153, 217, 351
Beresheet B
125
Beshalach
47, 274
Bo
61, 62
Idra Raba
148, 150, 213, 214, 215
Lech Lecha
132, 365
Miketz
33, 42
Noach
217, 219
Pekudei
236, 240, 241, 647, 653
Pinchas
4, 297, 689, 730, 741, 746
Prologue
137
Safra Detzniuta
34
Shemot
160
Shlach Lecha
270, 329, 335
Shmini
8
Tazria
41, 59
Toldot
18
Trumah
415, 416
Vaetchanan
99
Vayakhel
159, 408
Vayechi
671, 672, 673
Vayeshev
240

Vayigash
51
Vayikra
372, 398, 399, 435
Vayishlach
269
Yitro
48, 228, 232

THRESHING

Vayechi
815, 822, 850
Vayera
436

THRONE

Acharei Mot
13, 17, 59, 71, 185, 196, 210, 308
Balak
289, 363, 469
Bechukotai
19, 60
Beha'alot'cha
17, 18, 40
Behar
33-36
Beresheet A
85-87, 89-91, 97, 117, 118, 131, 223, 231
Beresheet B
21, 250, 251, 418
Beshalach
53, 139, 297, 304, 369, 485
Bo
118, 119, 140, 227, 228
Chayei Sarah
2, 4, 51, 150, 158, 169
Chukat
49
Ekev
9, 58, 70-72, 74, 75
Emor
56, 90, 149, 190, 195, 196, 202, 210, 215, 227a, 247, 257
Ha'azinu
17, 98, 101, 192
Idra Raba
2, 14, 60, 61, 66, 169, 172, 319, 351
Kedoshim
38, 39, 99, 128
Ki Tetze
19, 42, 109, 127, 139
Ki Tisa
104
Korach
36
Lech Lecha
33, 155, 156-159, 183, 255, 306
Metzora
59, 60, 63
Miketz
45, 206
Mishpatim
11, 343, 345, 442, 460, 489, 515, 519
Naso
12, 13, 14, 52, 53, 179
Noach
18, 98, 134, 216, 261, 271, 272, 286
Pekudei
9, 10, 11, 38, 43, 195, 198, 338, 340, 341, 343, 393, 394, 411, 412
Pinchas
79, 164, 171, 187, 200, 202, 249, 251, 253, 255-258, 284, 285, 337, 358, 402, 403, 407,

408, 421, 427, 428, 430, 438, 519, 533, 539-541, 543, 545, 547, 549, 619, 630, 667, 669, 674, 687, 703

Prologue
31, 77, 86, 95, 124, 186

Safra Detzniuta
48

Shemot
44, 110, 111, 122, 217, 219, 240, 243, 258

Shlach Lecha
118, 151, 328, 332, 334, 340, 342

Shmini
95, 96

Tazria
97, 110, 111, 114

Tetzaveh
88, 128, 139

Toldot
25, 139

Trumah
51, 119, 123, 163, 164, 167, 176, 193, 211, 213, 230, 231, 233, 286, 290, 295, 385, 426, 481, 483, 528, 589, 738, 901, 922

Tzav
45, 64, 116, 159, 172-175

Vaera
104, 134

aetchanan
26, 105

Vayakhel
56, 58, 213-215, 218, 222, 233, 281, 285, 290, 291, 292, 326, 327, 441, 442, 443

Vayechi
4, 8, 12, 15, 17, 35, 40, 42, 48, 52, 56, 60, 82, 87, 151, 202, 259, 269, 331, 334, 407, 567, 613, 623, 649, 652, 666, 689, 693, 702, 708, 711, 770, 787, 790, 838

Vayera
15, 16, 22, 23, 26, 96, 267, 284, 375, 382, 389, 392, 404

Vayeshev
149

Vayetze
5, 40, 57, 159, 175, 364, 365, 392

Vayigash
128, 129

Vayikra
139, 277, 279, 280, 310, 330

Yitro
23, 174, 282, 377, 379, 380, 399, 490, 505, 506, 509, 511, 540-543, 548

TIKUN (CORRECTION)

Acharei Mot
105

Balak
274

Bechukotai
20, 42, 43

Beha'alot'cha
53

Beresheet A
234, 250, 280, 281, 332

Beresheet A
252, 273

Beresheet B
16, 157, 184, 187, 362

Bo
50

Idra Raba
1, 170, 178, 300, 330, 349,

350, 351
Korach
3
Lech Lecha
75
Mishpatim
138, 176, 203, 350
Naso
188
Noach
73
Noach
73, 244
Pekudei
381, 484, 491, 752, 765, 878, 955
Pinchas
1, 76, 222, 228, 231, 232, 235, 284, 313, 322, 334, 509, 512, 542, 556, 567, 605, 636, 674, 705, 727, 892
Shlach Lecha
125, 258, 340
Tetzaveh
89
Toldot
146
Toldot
148
Trumah
115
Tzav 29, 34, 38, 41, 117
Vaera
126
Vayechi
21, 648, 650, 657, 658
Vayechi
42
Vayeshev
45, 173, 176
Vayigash
17, 29
Vayikra
115, 256
Vayishlach
159
Yitro
165, 518

TISHREI (MONTH)

Mishpatim
298, 304, 477, 479
Tetzaveh
122

TITHING

Balak
79
Beshalach
207
Bo
212
Ekev
30
Korach
51, 53
Lech Lecha
243, 257
Mishpatim
388, 489, 493, 495, 499
Pekudei
84
Pinchas
713
Prologue
244, 245
Shmini
88
Vayakhel
106

Vayikra
119

TORAH

Acharei Mot
2, 3, 8, 31, 32, 60, 61, 67, 70, 85-87, 92-94, 100, 106, 110, 111, 118, 140, 144, 147, 153, 155, 206, 207, 211, 213, 227-229, 243, 257, 265-271, 275-278, 288, 295-303, 305, 307-310, 322, 336, 341, 343, 346-349, 351, 354, 363, 368, 383, 389, 394, 400, 407, 410

Balak
20, 37, 57, 63, 92, 123, 126, 130, 131, 138, 139, 140, 141, 142, 143, 145, 146, 150, 151, 153, 155, 164, 210, 220, 221, 232, 233, 234, 238, 295, 313-319, 333, 335, 338, 361, 365, 367, 375, 376, 393, 415, 418, 432, 439, 443, 476, 490, 492, 494, 500

Bechukotai
9, 16-20, 34

Beha'alot'cha
1, 5, 12-16, 20, 21, 26-28, 41, 55, 57-60, 62-64, 67, 71, 77, 79, 81, 82, 86, 88, 90, 92, 102, 122, 140, 141

Behar
1, 21, 22, 25, 41, 43-45, 50, 63, 66, 75, 81

Bemidbar
6, 7, 8, 9, 21, 22, 45

Beresheet A
8, 16, 34, 50, 53, 123, 181-183, 195, 198, 216-219, 229-231, 233, 237, 238, 239, 250-252, 254, 256, 260-264, 271, 272, 274, 287, 288, 289, 290, 324, 347, 350, 394, 458, 470, 478, 479

Beresheet B
29, 30, 43, 56, 86, 169, 177-181, 199, 201-204, 222, 229, 236, 238, 240, 297, 298, 303, 308, 324, 325, 360, 371, 377-379, 438, 441, 442

Beshalach
28, 35, 40, 43-47, 50, 57, 58, 70, 92, 104, 109, 209, 224, 251-253, 274, 295, 296, 302, 305-307, 329, 331, 345, 346, 348, 361, 362, 373-375, 377, 382, 383, 387, 391-393, 397, 425, 435, 445, 454, 455

Bo
1, 2, 4, 97, 121, 124, 139, 158, 205, 206, 208, 212, 217, 227

Chayei Sarah
13, 26, 61, 64, 83, 84, 86, 94, 116, 141, 142, 169, 172-174, 177, 212, 214, 219, 220, 222, 223, 227, 242, 247, 269

Chukat
1-6, 16, 25, 50, 52, 61, 85

Ekev
8, 18, 19, 22, 29, 37, 42, 43, 45, 49, 50, 55, 63

Emor
7, 26, 31, 32, 43, 45, 55-57, 58, 84, 85, 93, 124, 127, 131, 133, 138, 143, 145, 147, 149, 150, 153, 155, 158, 163, 164, 165, 166, 167, 168, 173, 175, 177, 184, 185, 186, 188, 258, 281, 296, 305, 309, 320, 323

Ha'azinu
1, 3, 14, 16, 18, 20, 62, 73,

127, 208, 235, 241, 243, 255, 259

Idra Raba
1, 3, 5, 10, 13, 33, 59, 100, 113, 120, 147, 149-151, 170, 191, 193, 197, 249, 336

Kedoshim
1-4, 10-14, 16, 18, 19, 26, 28, 33, 35, 41, 44, 45, 47, 48, 52, 53, 55, 56, 62, 66, 79, 81, 92 -97, 123, 131, 132

Ki Tetze
3, 4, 14, 16, 18, 26, 30, 32-34, 37, 51, 52, 54, 57, 58, 64, 66, 72, 78, 81, 82, 89, 92, 93, 95, 100, 105, 106, 115-117, 122, 129, 132, 136, 140, 143, 145, 146

Ki Tisa
13, 14, 15, 16, 17, 23, 24, 54, 68, 77, 78, 83, 104, 112, 120

Korach
1, 2, 8, 35, 36, 39, 42, 43, 45, 47, 48, 50, 59

Lech Lecha
1, 4, 6, 8, 9, 14, 77, 80, 90, 129, 132, 134, 135, 146, 163, 179, 195, 202, 203, 227, 260, 278, 280-282, 284-289, 292, 297, 310, 315, 335, 355, 356, 364, 366, 369, 378, 379, 389, 390, 416, 417, 418, 420, 421, 429, 452

Metzora
1, 2, 3, 4, 7, 12-15, 18, 20, 21, 33, 46

Miketz
3-6, 26, 33, 52, 56, 83, 95, 96, 98, 111, 129-133, 137, 138, 139, 143, 151, 177, 178, 190, 192, 195, 198, 211, 225, 238, 240, 241, 249, 262

Mishpatim
2, 16, 18, 20, 21, 22, 51, 53, 73, 81, 93, 97, 98, 99, 100, 101, 102, 104, 112, 143, 144, 168, 254, 303, 304, 305, 323, 327, 361, 374, 375, 382, 384, 391, 392, 403, 410, 411, 413, 418, 429, 431, 434, 438, 439, 449, 454, 456-458, 460, 461, 470, 473, 491, 496 -499, 501, 505, 509, 513, 517, 520, 528, 542, 543, 553, 557, 577, 581

Naso
7, 11, 15-20, 22, 37, 38, 44, 45, 48-52, 65, 86, 92, 94-100, 110, 113, 134, 137, 160, 189, 193

Noach
1, 32, 36, 39, 40, 91-93, 96, 111, 138, 225, 227, 254, 260, 273, 275-277, 285, 292, 295, 311, 328, 345, 357, 376, 379, 383, 386

Pekudei
13, 50, 54, 61, 70, 109-112, 114, 176, 180, 188, 195, 230, 235, 258, 269, 270, 276, 301, 310, 349, 350, 355, 365-367, 502, 514, 522, 525, 559, 560, 564, 568, 586, 594, 608, 631, 693, 695, 698, 706, 724, 729, 732, 735, 749, 856, 873, 874, 880, 888, 903

Pinchas
1-4, 13, 23, 33, 36, 40, 55, 56, 60, 64-66, 68, 69, 84, 91, 92, 94, 103, 107, 114-118, 132, 143, 146, 159, 172, 184, 185, 192,

193, 198, 199, 205, 217, 222, 234, 240, 241, 244, 250, 265, 274, 284, 286, 289, 291-293, 308, 310, 313, 314, 315, 319, 320, 323, 325, 329, 332, 342, 353, 370, 372, 379, 403, 404, 446, 451, 484, 492, 495, 498, 504, 506, 511, 514, 515, 546, 563, 570, 571, 575, 579, 600, 601, 604, 606, 612, 619, 625, 627, 628, 630, 631, 634-637, 640, 641, 648, 663, 702, 709, 751, 759, 760, 761, 764, 766, 767, 768, 773, 774, 777, 780, 792, 793, 803, 804, 805, 832, 838, 841, 847, 848, 857, 873, 886

Prologue

4, 6, 23, 41, 48, 57, 58, 59, 61, 63-68, 70-74, 88, 90, 91, 105, 106, 112, 119, 124 -126, 128, 130, 132, 139, 140, 144, 145, 171, 172, 180, 181, 188, 194, 195, 197, 215, 216, 217, 218

Safra Detzniuta

14, 42

Shemot

14, 16-18, 60, 62, 64, 65, 84, 88, 105, 130, 168, 188 -190, 194, 197, 198, 202, 216, 233, 237, 241, 242, 251, 257, 261, 262, 270, 283, 284, 296, 302, 328 -330, 338, 340, 370

Shlach Lecha

4, 14, 19, 20, 23, 27, 28, 29, 41-44, 52, 55-64, 67, 68, 83, 93, 95, 99, 102, 110, 113, 130, 138 -144, 147, 149, 151, 168, 183, 186, 188, 194, 197, 198, 216, 231, 254, 259, 294, 295, 305, 306, 309, 314, 317, 324

Shmini

1-4, 6, 7, 8, 9, 14, 19, 62, 67 -70, 73, 74, 79, 93, 94, 118

Shoftim

10, 13, 20

Tazria

6, 40, 74, 85, 89, 111, 140, 167, 168, 171, 178, 181

Tetzaveh

12, 21, 24, 27, 37, 38, 57, 58, 67, 69, 71-73, 76-78, 80, 85, 86, 99, 119, 144

Toldot

1-5, 8, 14, 45, 46, 61, 62, 74, 104, 118, 124, 125, 146, 170, 171, 181-184, 189, 190

Trumah

19, 35, 53, 58, 78, 79, 96, 97, 147-149, 159, 162, 196, 203, 204, 207, 244-246, 319, 325, 326, 334, 352, 368, 369, 383, 386, 415, 417, 421-424, 443, 452, 454, 455, 497, 498, 505 -508, 536, 537, 538, 540, 542, 543, 548, 549, 550-555, 560, 578, 586, 587, 594, 595, 623, 632, 635-640, 643, 644, 645, 648, 649, 650, 666, 685, 721 -726, 728-732, 735, 736, 737, 743, 745, 747, 766, 767, 772, 773, 778, 779, 787, 799-802, 817, 821, 828, 878, 880, 893, 895, 897, 924

Tzav

1, 18-20, 26, 27, 31-35, 37, 38, 43, 44, 46, 50-52, 54, 56, 59, 60, 66, 68, 71, 72, 121, 122, 135 -137, 143, 145, 146, 149, 150, 172, 182, 184-186

Vaera

20, 29, 32, 54, 58, 62-64, 68, 71,

74, 83, 89, 95, 100-102, 114, 121, 126, 138, 141, 182, 183, 186, 187, 198, 206

Vaetchanan
1, 2, 5, 8, 13, 17, 21, 22, 26, 32, 41, 55, 67, 68, 81-83, 92, 94, 95, 98, 101, 103, 105, 107, 126, 138, 143, 153-160, 162, 169, 170, 171, 173, 184, 185

Vayakhel
14, 26, 38, 98, 99, 102-105, 118, 141, 144, 150, 152, 154, 155, 207, 208, 215, 217, 219-228, 231, 234-237, 244, 275, 282, 304, 305, 308, 321, 336-338, 361, 372, 375, 376, 405, 412, 415, 438, 440, 445, 450, 454, 455, 460, 462, 463, 485, 496

Vayechi
18, 19, 35, 77, 91, 92, 94, 97, 99-101, 104, 110, 124, 126, 145, 148, 149, 152, 154, 159, 188, 210, 227, 293, 295, 317-321, 327, 331, 335, 349, 357, 381, 382, 388, 410, 425, 427, 428, 442, 455, 466, 487, 498, 525, 526, 528, 531, 561, 570, 592, 632, 641-643, 648, 660, 663, 670, 671, 674, 675, 681, 682, 684-694, 698, 725, 730, 738, 781, 846

Vayelech
20, 21

Vayera
23, 34, 35, 37-39, 64, 66, 88, 116-119, 128, 193, 194, 195, 197, 200, 230, 245, 248, 283, 318, 326, 376, 390, 402, 412, 430, 434, 439, 440, 511

Vayeshev
42, 58, 120-129, 156, 162-164, 170, 185, 188, 194, 219, 220 -224, 227, 235-237, 241, 243, 251, 252, 284

Vayetze
19, 43, 44, 62, 70, 85, 86, 87, 109-111, 119, 142, 168, 171, 175, 196, 197, 209, 218, 231, 232, 275, 276, 311, 322, 325, 341-344, 361, 384

Vayigash
1, 2, 10, 35, 40, 41, 47, 48, 51, 118

Vayikra
44-46, 70, 77, 86-88, 90-92, 109, 112, 115, 124-126, 129, 133, 142, 144, 145, 166, 177-179, 181, 190, 196, 198-202, 206, 208, 209, 214-216, 263, 274, 292, 293, 324, 333, 334, 336-338, 342, 353, 356-358, 366, 370, 372-374, 379, 384, 387, 388, 394, 396, 398, 399, 405, 435, 437, 439, 443

Vayishlach
46, 47, 49, 83, 101-103, 108-112, 116, 121, 179, 180, 181, 182, 189, 206-213, 218, 227, 244, 257, 266, 269, 274

Yitro
15, 16, 20, 23, 26, 42, 54, 62, 67, 73, 76, 79, 80, 82, 86, 90, 95, 108, 115, 152, 157, 159, 162, 170, 175, 190, 194, 200, 238, 239, 242, 244, 257, 283, 285, 287, 293, 299, 312, 331, 332, 346, 348, 351-353, 355, 356, 361, 365, 378, 385-387, 389, 391, 392, 394, 397, 401, 406, 407, 410-412, 414, 419, 428-431, 434, 436, 441, 462, 465, 468, 469, 471, 472, 475, 477, 478, 479, 489, 494, 496

-498, 507, 508, 512, 513, 527, 528, 532, 537, 541, 542, 551 -554, 559, 566, 567, 568, 569, 570, 574, 575

TOWER

Balak
242, 434, 438
Beresheet A
229, 349, 471
Beresheet B
422
Ha'azinu
188
Ki Tetze
40
Lech Lecha
93, 467
Miketz
234
Mishpatim
14, 150
Noach
32, 33, 335, 339-342, 344 -347, 349-351, 353-355, 358 -360, 365, 377, 384, 387
Prologue
88, 89, 143
Shemot
116
Shlach Lecha
137-141, 143, 145-147, 151, 262
Trumah
582, 600, 601
Vayera
270
Vayigash
89, 90
Vayikra
22
Vayishlach
16
Yitro
213, 513

TRACHEA

Pinchas
275, 365-367, 405, 430, 433, 435-438, 636

TREE

Acharei Mot
33, 79, 184, 200, 295, 317, 318, 369, 371, 382
Balak
34, 58, 61, 62, 76, 77, 79, 129, 309, 314-316, 318, 320, 334
Bechukotai
21, 23, 34
Beha'alot'cha
1, 2, 44, 81, 86, 92, 96, 136, 143, 144
Behar
60, 62, 65
Bemidbar
18, 28, 41, 43-45, 62, 67, 73 -75
Beresheet A
63, 80, 81, 90, 92, 179, 198, 233, 235, 244-246, 253-258, 261, 262, 265, 266, 269, 271, 285, 286, 318, 381 -383, 389, 425, 426, 427, 432, 433, 435, 436, 438 -448, 450, 452, 458, 468, 476, 477, 478, 482
Beresheet B
161, 189, 198, 210, 220, 254, 267, 285-288, 290, 302, 307, 310, 314, 333, 336, 364, 371, 372, 374, 375, 377, 413, 416

Beshalach
97, 132, 147, 148, 176, 231, 232, 315-317, 348, 349, 351, 385, 394, 437-439, 483
Bo
70, 97
Chayei Sarah
205, 207, 208, 213, 220
Chukat
3, 44, 50, 52
Ekev
30, 75
Emor
7, 52, 142, 143, 151, 153-158, 165, 184, 186, 222, 227a, 272, 334-340
Ha'azinu
9, 11, 89, 113, 189, 198, 236
Idra Raba
142, 232, 248, 340, 362
Kedoshim
15, 19, 51, 53, 55, 56, 68, 81, 92, 95, 112, 118, 124
Ki Tetze
3-5, 8, 12, 13, 20, 26, 71, 123, 138-140
Ki Tisa
41, 44, 105, 106, 115, 118
Korach
1, 14, 27, 28, 33, 44
Lech Lecha
10, 15, 43, 45, 103, 125, 126, 196, 197, 199, 201, 202
Metzora
8, 17, 20, 58
Miketz
4-6, 49, 138, 209, 211, 213, 214, 238
Mishpatim
15, 24, 29, 71, 79, 81, 84, 85, 105, 128, 130, 131, 176, 177, 179, 180, 209, 237, 259, 280, 281, 344, 345, 378, 383, 384, 417, 430, 431, 438, 442, 455, 460, 480, 490, 492, 493, 495, 496, 498, 499, 531, 576
Naso
67, 80, 83, 87, 88, 90, 91, 93-95, 98, 125
Noach
50, 72, 73, 88, 92, 93, 258, 308, 319, 351, 379
Pekudei
26, 41, 57, 63, 92, 304, 469, 746, 757, 776
Pinchas
45, 48, 50, 51, 67, 82, 90, 91, 159, 168, 189, 263, 271, 281, 297, 335, 339, 394, 416, 417, 446, 447, 448, 510-515, 589, 591, 613, 625, 628, 655, 689, 690, 751, 760, 762, 766-772, 791, 800, 808, 875, 880
Prologue
2, 71, 92, 107, 113, 123, 180, 181, 219, 220, 232, 244, 245, 248, 249
Safra Detzniuta
7, 17, 19, 36, 46, 51, 57, 60, 67
Shemot
2-5, 105, 128, 179, 220, 253, 256, 257, 262-264, 303, 304, 306
Shlach Lecha
10, 13, 15, 35-37, 58, 69, 75, 98, 105, 130, 150, 203, 206, 238, 290, 291
Shmini
77, 83, 99, 100
Shoftim
8-10

Tazria
8, 23, 66, 70, 112, 116
Tetzaveh
130-132
Toldot
84, 92, 138, 141, 148, 149, 164, 191
Trumah
19, 20, 21, 22, 23, 125, 126, 131, 148, 194, 226, 332, 354, 355, 376, 539, 744, 792
Tzav
38, 54, 110, 165, 167
Vaera
114, 115, 116
Vaetchanan
1, 3, 13, 22, 28, 33, 59, 66, 113, 194, 196, 197
Vayakhel
275, 488
Vayechi
124, 135, 153, 213, 219, 220, 223, 224, 237, 238, 240-244, 301, 304, 334, 353-356, 384, 560, 571-573, 586, 591, 607, 609, 629, 672, 708, 752, 753, 805
Vayera
109-114, 230, 329, 331, 428, 431, 432
Vayeshev
58, 244
Vayetze
22, 85, 109, 177-181, 198, 308, 309, 314, 316, 392, 393
Vayigash
63, 74, 80, 81, 82, 84
Vayikra
150, 264, 265, 282, 325, 412-414, 420, 427, 441
Vayishlach
47, 48, 86, 132, 133, 179
Yitro
177, 178, 395, 465, 518

TREE OF KNOWLEDGE OF GOOD AND EVIL

Beha'alot'cha
86
Emor
165, 186, 222, 227a, 335, 337-339
Ki Tisa
41, 115, 118
Mishpatim
29, 81, 383, 438, 442
Pinchas
762, 808, 880
Trumah
332
Vayechi
242, 243, 301, 384, 572
Vayetze
22

TREE OF LIFE

Acharei Mot
295
Balak
34, 58, 315
Bechukotai
21, 23, 34
Beha'alot'cha
1, 2, 44, 81, 92, 96, 136, 143
Behar
62
Bemidbar
41, 43, 44, 45, 62, 73, 74

Beresheet A
63, 198, 245, 255-258, 262, 269, 271, 425, 426, 476-478
Beresheet B
288, 290, 307, 314
Beshalach
97, 132, 147, 148, 232, 348
Chayei Sarah
205, 220
Chukat
3, 50, 52
Emor
142, 143, 158, 184, 186, 334-336, 340
Idra Raba
248
Kedoshim
51, 53, 55, 95, 112
Ki Tetze
12, 138, 139
Ki Tisa
105, 106, 118
Korach
1, 27, 28, 44
Lech Lecha
15, 43, 103
Metzora
20
Miketz
4, 5, 6, 138, 209, 211, 213, 214
Mishpatim
24, 71, 79, 84, 85, 237, 378, 384, 417, 430, 431, 438, 442, 455, 496, 498
Naso
90, 91, 94, 95, 98
Noach
88, 93
Pekudei
26
Pinchas
82, 263, 271, 394, 589, 591, 625, 628, 690, 762, 766, 768, 800, 808, 880
Prologue
123, 180, 181, 249
Shemot
2, 3, 179, 304
Shlach Lecha
10, 13, 15, 36, 58, 203, 238, 290, 291
Shmini
83, 99, 100
Shoftim
8-10
Toldot
191
Trumah
125, 131, 148, 194, 226, 332, 354, 355, 744, 792
Tzav
54, 165
Vaetchanan
1, 22, 28, 194
Vayechi
153, 237, 240, 244, 560, 572, 672, 708, 752, 805
Vayera
113, 114, 230, 428
Vayeshev
58
Vayetze
85, 109, 177-181, 198, 392
Vayigash
63, 74, 80, 81, 82
Vayishlach
47, 48, 179
Yitro
177, 395

TRIBES

Acharei Mot
112, 382
Balak
75, 95, 176, 179, 323, 324, 376
Beha'alot'cha
49, 115, 123
Bemidbar
27, 28, 30
Beresheet A
54, 249
Beshalach
199, 207
Chukat
40
Kedoshim
126
Ki Tetze
76, 77
Korach
23
Lech Lecha
15, 83
Miketz
38, 69, 82, 157, 158, 201, 202, 208, 226
Mishpatim
196, 202, 483
Naso
156
Noach
158, 199
Pekudei
8, 21, 23, 36, 37, 47, 54, 69, 172-175, 178-181, 269, 298
Pinchas
73, 469, 471, 749
Shemot
34, 35, 52, 53, 91, 118, 146 -148, 250, 257, 266, 267, 269, 270, 272, 274, 275, 280, 332
Shlach Lecha
243
Shoftim
1
Toldot
6
Trumah
4, 144, 476, 480, 551, 587, 849
Vaera
95, 146
Vaetchanan
13
Vayakhel
64, 119, 494
Vayechi
28, 80, 251, 260, 270, 458, 492, 554, 562, 574, 575, 653, 654, 669, 680, 695, 703, 712, 724, 728, 757, 766, 770, 773, 774, 798, 799
Vayera
200
Vayeshev
81, 97, 101, 144, 177
Vayetze
49, 105, 126, 127, 158, 166, 186, 196, 197, 217, 231, 237, 240, 241, 247, 248, 249, 250, 272, 292, 386, 387
Vayigash
31, 61, 95, 96, 118, 135
Vayishlach
5, 173, 205, 218, 220, 243
Yitro
206, 316, 333, 541

TRUTH (EMET)

Mishpatim
408

Prologue
23
Shlach Lecha
121, 123
Vayakhel
47

TUBAL-CAIN

Acharei Mot
360, 361

TULIP

Beresheet A
298
Emor
330, 331, 333
Vayechi
232-236

TUMIEL (SPIRIT)

Pekudei
619, 623
Vayera
275

TUMIHAEL (SPIRIT)

Pekudei
684

TUMIM

Pekudei
183-185, 268
Pinchas
575

TURTLE

Beresheet B
31
Prologue
4
Vayikra
42, 44, 45

TURTLEDOVE

Beresheet B
31
Prologue
4
Vayechi
92-94, 96
Vayera
1, 3, 8

TWELVE

Acharei Mot
106, 107, 293, 382, 386, 392
Balak
75, 366, 433
Beha'alot'cha
38, 49
Bemidbar
6, 27, 30
Beresheet A
27, 97, 126, 471
Beresheet B
25, 67, 81, 91, 111, 126-128, 130
Beshalach
298, 315, 394, 438, 439, 483
Bo
28
Chayei Sarah
50, 135, 253, 255, 256
Chukat
77
Ekev
19, 39
Emor
16, 151

Ha'azinu
39, 257
Idra Raba
97, 158, 232
Ki Tetze
18, 43, 124
Korach
57, 58, 59
Lech Lecha
7, 10, 15, 42, 43, 83, 219, 227, 360
Miketz
135, 159, 164
Mishpatim
158, 196, 202, 203, 450, 463, 483
Naso
165, 197, 198
Noach
158, 199, 266
Pekudei
172-176, 178, 179, 181, 242, 249, 253, 255, 288, 290, 484, 504, 582, 583, 588, 592, 597, 621, 655, 664, 678, 682, 684, 686, 687, 689, 692, 694, 842
Pinchas
70, 297, 303, 305, 603, 617 -619, 668, 713, 748, 749, 750, 756-758, 826
Prologue
33
Safra Detzniuta
8
Shemot
5, 65, 66, 102, 103, 114, 115, 117, 118, 128, 129, 131, 146 -149, 154, 247, 249, 250, 256, 270-272, 276, 313
Shlach Lecha
124, 174, 243, 262, 287
Tetzaveh
14, 15, 20, 21, 28, 29
Toldot
6, 13, 22, 23
Trumah
4, 41, 99, 105, 110, 241, 242, 283, 398, 403, 526, 527, 599, 631, 662, 699, 700
Vaera
18, 35, 47, 49
Vaetchanan
13, 20
Vayakhel
15, 21, 51, 54, 55, 58, 112, 122, 130, 133, 138, 300, 347, 352, 382
Vayechi
155, 264, 324, 325, 348, 456, 458, 459, 538, 553, 557, 601, 647, 649, 651-654, 657-660, 674, 679, 680, 697, 757, 763, 765, 766, 770, 773, 774, 777, 798, 799
Vayera
64, 65, 246, 260
Vayeshev
70, 72
Vayetze
10-12, 73, 82, 145, 161, 164, 166, 202, 234, 239, 241, 242, 246-249, 255, 272, 292, 293, 389
Vayikra
11, 12, 14, 20, 22-24, 33
Vayishlach
143, 173-175, 203, 205, 216-218
Yitro
225, 512, 514, 515, 525, 541, 542

TWELVE STONES

Ki Tetze
43
Lech Lecha
83
Noach
158
Pekudei
172, 175, 179
Trumah
241, 398
Vaera
49
Vayetze
10, 82

TWELVE TRIBES OF ISRAEL

Acharei Mot
107, 382
Balak
75
Bemidbar
6, 27
Chayei Sarah
253
Idra Raba
158, 232
Korach
59
Lech Lecha
219, 227
Miketz
164
Mishpatim
196, 202, 203
Noach
199
Pekudei
172-175, 178, 181
Pinchas
668, 749
Prologue
33
Shemot
5, 66, 146-149, 154, 249, 250, 270-272
Toldot
6, 13, 22, 23
Trumah
241, 283, 631
Vaera
18, 47
Vaetchanan
13
Vayechi
458, 538, 553, 557, 647, 651-654, 674, 679, 757, 763, 766, 770, 773, 798, 799
Vayeshev
70, 72
Vayetze
145, 161, 166, 241, 242, 246, 247, 248, 249, 292, 293, 389
Vayikra
33
Vayishlach
143, 173-175, 205, 217, 218
Yitro
541, 542

TWINS

Ha'azinu
183
Idra Raba
217
Pinchas
445
Tazria
44

Yitro
240, 241, 242

TZADIKIM (RIGHTEOUS)

Prologue
26

TZADKIEL (SUPERNAL MINISTER)

Beha'alot'cha
102
Pekudei
522, 524
Pinchas
401
Vayera
275
Vayetze
73
Vayikra
9, 10

TZADOK

Vayetze
43, 44

TZAFTZAFIYAH (SPIRIT)

Pekudei
703

TZALMON (SPIRIT)

Pekudei
932
Vayechi
603

TZARFAT

Vayera
412

TZELYAH

Balak
176-178, 180

TZIDON

Mishpatim
200
Vayechi
664, 665, 696

TZIPOR

Balak
1, 2, 212, 222, 223, 287, 292, 397

TZIPORAH

Balak
60, 61
Beresheet A
157
Lech Lecha
397
Vayetze
95

TZITZIT

Bemidbar
68, 71
Beresheet A
183, 189, 289
Kedoshim
114, 115, 123
Ki Tetze
25, 45
Miketz
259, 265
Mishpatim
461

Pinchas
45, 250, 257, 288, 292, 298, 334
Shlach Lecha
125, 126, 321, 322, 324, 327-329, 332-335, 339, 341, 343, 345, 347, 348
Toldot
104
Trumah
230, 231
Tzav
64, 136
Vaetchanan
6, 7, 73, 98, 99, 100, 119
Vayakhel
127, 410
Vayechi
603
Yitro
512

TZIYAH (DRYNESS)

Beresheet B
36, 37
Mishpatim
117

TZRUYAH

Mishpatim
252

UNITY

Acharei Mot
58, 64, 65, 82, 84, 109, 170, 176, 320, 372, 373
Balak
344
Behar
34
Bemidbar
58, 70
Beresheet A
199, 255, 271, 397, 399, 434
Beresheet B
24, 62, 70, 77, 95, 139, 262 -264
Beshalach
240, 276-280
Chukat
39
Emor
14
Ha'azinu
85
Idra Raba
114, 150
Kedoshim
37, 80
Ki Tetze
30, 142
Lech Lecha
169, 305
Metzora
41
Mishpatim
183, 369, 384, 394, 396, 403, 457, 458, 463, 515, 523
Noach
306, 334, 368
Pekudei
34, 139, 144, 265, 349, 350, 393, 395, 503, 525, 590, 602, 705, 758, 762, 764, 768, 769, 770, 779, 809, 810, 823, 932
Pinchas
63, 179, 187, 191, 193, 202, 241, 255, 280, 282, 283, 288, 290, 308, 311, 312, 314, 328, 334, 337, 339, 340, 393, 397, 434, 448, 454, 456, 542, 544,

548, 565, 711, 718, 740, 753, 778, 789, 845, 846, 850, 870
Prologue
38, 204, 205, 206, 207, 230, 241
Safra Detzniuta
56
Shemot
158, 260
Shlach Lecha
14, 156
Shmini
3, 59, 92
Tetzaveh
4, 35, 40, 48
Trumah
44, 121, 132, 133, 142, 546, 547, 581, 624, 625, 628, 629, 645, 652, 653, 654, 655, 656, 658, 659, 666
Tzav
10
Vaera
99
Vaetchanan
61, 63
Vayakhel
151, 153, 257, 321, 322, 345, 418-420, 424, 425, 426, 427, 428, 470, 477, 481
Vayechi
85, 212, 219, 378, 395, 621, 622
Vayelech
32
Vayeshev
107
Vayetze
33, 62, 261, 327
Vayigash
28, 54, 100
Vayikra
37, 39, 51, 99, 100, 102, 115, 167
Yitro
505, 508

UNIVERSE

Balak
7, 59, 101, 420
Beha'alot'cha
31
Bemidbar
19, 28, 41, 43, 44, 49, 54, 56, 60
Beresheet A
167, 410
Beresheet B
428
Bo
217
Chayei Sarah
125, 177
Ekev
65
Emor
55, 84
Ha'azinu
248
Idra Raba
52, 61, 80, 86, 88, 124, 143, 144, 339
Ki Tetze
48, 131, 133
Ki Tisa
6, 10, 44, 60
Korach
5, 35
Lech Lecha
118, 225

Metzora
61
Mishpatim
32, 52, 151, 159, 185, 247, 277, 355, 356, 361, 374, 454
Naso
19, 20, 22, 23, 24, 26, 42, 53, 173, 194
Noach
384
Pekudei
38, 45
Pinchas
130, 380, 575, 859-861, 863, 865, 866, 877
Prologue
82, 128, 132, 134, 136, 176, 178
Shemot
61, 236
Shlach Lecha
199
Toldot
38, 178
Trumah
265, 814, 898
Vaera
15
Vaetchanan
96
Vayakhel
225, 254, 332, 374
Vayechi
27, 41, 44, 108, 151, 368, 435, 444, 446, 539
Vayera
117, 193, 195, 198, 389
Vayeshev
42, 145, 146, 157, 242
Vayetze
11, 14, 258
Vayigash
10, 11, 41, 64, 65
Vayikra
92, 134, 138
Yitro
343, 443

URFANIEL (SPIRIT)

Pekudei
511, 512, 517-521, 525, 526, 531, 791

URIAH THE HITTITE

Mishpatim
242, 243, 244

URIAH

Acharei Mot
395
Mishpatim
239, 241, 242, 243, 244
Prologue
133, 134, 136

URIEL (ANGEL)

Acharei Mot
76
Balak
90, 479
Beha'alot'cha
101, 112
Bemidbar
27, 29, 31
Beresheet A
190
Beresheet B
50, 51, 167

Korach
60
Pekudei
663, 664, 665, 780
Pinchas
223, 228, 421
Shemot
258
Shlach Lecha
88
Trumah
241, 385, 387, 390
Tzav
129-131, 134
Vayakhel
51, 53, 260, 296, 326
Vayera
49, 73
Yitro
235, 236, 238

URIM

Naso
144
Pekudei
183-185, 268
Pinchas
575

UZZIAH

Balak
393

VALLEY (GEY)

Beresheet B
36, 38

VALLEY

Balak
421, 458
Beresheet B
36, 38, 398
Idra Raba
360
Ki Tetze
83
Miketz
186, 217, 218
Mishpatim
117
Noach
66, 355
Pinchas
107
Shlach Lecha
41
Trumah
19, 563
Vaetchanan
196, 197
Vayechi
234, 236
Vayeshev
205, 206

VANITY

Balak
346
Beshalach
318, 319, 322
Bo
103, 136, 140, 142-145
Chayei Sarah
152
Ha'azinu
104
Korach
28
Miketz
72, 128

Mishpatim
34
Naso
41, 53
Noach
342
Pekudei
670
Pinchas
60
Prologue
70
Shemot
163, 164, 166, 169, 170, 172, 174
Tazria
75, 76, 98
Vayera
470
Vayetze
13-16
Vayishlach
249

VENUS

Beresheet B
69, 84, 124
Ha'azinu
14
Ki Tetze
119, 120
Pinchas
737, 739

VERTEBRAE

Pinchas
305, 821
Tetzaveh
29

VESSELS

Acharei Mot
389
Balak
149, 190, 495
Bechukotai
9
Beha'alot'cha
76, 78
Beresheet A
33, 301, 328
Beresheet B
130, 210, 212, 323, 418
Beshalach
334, 403
Bo
50, 220-223, 225-227
Ekev
19, 27, 33
Emor
10, 34, 46, 50, 287
Idra Raba
11, 47
Kedoshim
123
Ki Tetze
128, 129, 134, 140
Korach
23, 44
Lech Lecha
265, 284, 285, 287, 369, 431
Mishpatim
97, 108, 109, 110, 115, 116, 125, 130, 135, 139, 141, 145, 146, 158, 173, 451, 536
Noach
48, 344
Pekudei
52, 159, 235, 674

Pinchas
219, 554, 715, 737, 738, 739, 798, 853
Prologue
17, 46, 171, 175
Shemot
2, 118, 322
Shlach Lecha
53, 182, 189
Shmini
95
Tazria
33, 154
Trumah
267, 276, 363, 520, 573, 575, 578, 580, 581, 611, 903
Tzav
67, 163
Vaera
112
Vaetchanan
37, 168, 195-197
Vayakhel
103, 274, 375, 455
Vayechi
131, 301, 742, 756
Vayera
272, 299-302
Vayeshev
116, 118, 134
Vayetze
40, 347
Vayikra
7, 88, 120, 415
Vayishlach
154
Yitro
416, 526

VINE

Acharei Mot
213, 305
Balak
40, 41, 84, 87, 405
Beresheet A
245
Beresheet B
124
Ha'azinu
231
Lech Lecha
182, 466
Mishpatim
490, 497
Naso
75, 77
Noach
307, 319
Pekudei
645
Pinchas
660
Shlach Lecha
323
Trumah
792, 793, 821
Vayechi
582, 586-588, 592, 596, 599, 600, 625-627, 629
Vayera
306, 431
Vayeshev
262, 263
Vayikra
227

VINEYARD

Acharei Mot
63

Balak
442
Beresheet A
337
Idra Raba
1
Ki Tetze
46
Lech Lecha
452, 461, 462, 463, 465
Mishpatim
490, 568
Naso
44, 131
Noach
307, 308
Pekudei
900
Pinchas
747
Shemot
39
Tazria
65
Vayakhel
377
Vayechi
184, 657
Vayeshev
268, 277, 280
Vayikra
242

VINEYARDS

Acharei Mot
63
Balak
431-433, 441, 442
Bemidbar
51
Lech Lecha
307
Mishpatim
453
Pekudei
900
Tazria
63, 65
Trumah
516
Vayechi
181
Vayeshev
277

VIRGIN

Ki Tetze
1, 14, 22, 23, 25, 27, 62
Ki Tisa
38
Matot
5
Mishpatim
221, 336
Vaetchanan
124, 125, 126
Vayechi
579
Vayera
353
Vayigash
107

VISION

Beresheet A
141
Lech Lecha
271, 272, 274, 276, 288, 290, 294, 295, 338, 339, 340, 341,

342
Miketz
61-63, 149, 217, 218
Prologue
50
Vayera
7, 9, 45, 46, 65
Vayeshev
82, 83, 86, 89, 105
Vayetze
48, 49, 50, 51, 57, 172
Vayigash
45, 119

VOICE

Beresheet A
9, 10, 11, 19, 24, 26, 211, 213, 290, 333, 354, 355, 359, 360, 388, 410, 448, 449
Chayei Sarah
6, 9, 10, 55, 232, 243, 247, 268
Ki Tisa
18, 75, 105
Lech Lecha
6, 9, 77, 283, 309, 313, 316, 317, 357, 358, 359, 364, 376, 403
Miketz
62, 148, 219, 221
Prologue
4, 9, 18, 53, 57, 59, 112, 113, 138, 187, 196
Tetzaveh
52, 131
Vaetchanan
18, 20-22, 26, 102, 104, 191
Vayera
1, 3, 8, 10, 11, 36, 128, 140, 214, 215, 381, 382, 398, 421, 422, 442, 467, 469, 471, 475, 513
Vayeshev
145, 147, 148, 210, 282, 283
Vayetze
18, 19, 86, 131, 221
Vayigash
84, 85, 97, 99, 100-105
Vayishlach
110-112, 136, 269

VOID

Balak
142, 153, 324
Beha'alot'cha
51
Beresheet A
17, 214, 231, 318, 330
Beresheet B
35, 36, 38, 42, 160
Bo
50, 52
Chukat
5, 68
Emor
297
Idra Raba
1, 5, 325
Ki Tetze
63
Ki Tisa
106
Miketz
26
Mishpatim
285, 336, 407
Pekudei
912
Pinchas
264, 371, 396

Prologue
1, 167, 195, 196, 197
Safra Detzniuta
3, 7, 8
Shlach Lecha
239
Tetzaveh
141
Trumah
537, 538, 540, 543, 618
Vayechi
559, 560
Vayera
439, 440

VOW

Acharei Mot
346
Behar
28
Beresheet A
223
Miketz
37
Mishpatim
402-404, 409
Naso
72, 105, 124, 132
Pekudei
922
Pinchas
371, 809, 810, 811
Shemot
280
Tzav
55
Vayeshev
96, 138
Vayetze
75
Vayigash
118
Vayikra
124
Vayishlach
191, 195, 197
Yitro
192, 525, 526

WAGONS

Vayigash
106, 112, 116, 117, 121, 122

WALLS

Acharei Mot
225, 226
Balak
214-216, 242, 443-445, 502
Bechukotai
40, 41
Behar
22
Bemidbar
20
Beresheet A
280, 394
Beshalach
7, 9, 279
Bo
126
Chayei Sarah
229
Emor
17
Ha'azinu
111, 188
Idra Raba
360

Lech Lecha
93, 105
Metzora
17, 60
Mishpatim
35, 39, 263, 264, 265, 266, 281, 283, 405, 547
Naso
116
Pekudei
40, 260
Pinchas
8, 151, 894
Prologue
180
Shemot
64
Shlach Lecha
140, 164, 270, 304, 320
Shoftim
11
Tazria
112
Trumah
80, 120, 899
Vaera
125, 155
Vaetchanan
1, 11
Vayakhel
333, 362
Vayechi
146, 386, 389, 390, 392, 473, 737, 770, 775
Vayeshev
37, 171
Vayikra
358, 359
Yitro
49, 51, 273, 313, 319, 333, 470, 480, 481

WALNUT

Beresheet B
129
Ekev
45

WAR

Acharei Mot
65, 73, 315
Balak
8, 68, 106, 113, 238, 257, 262, 263, 313, 392, 503
Beha'alot'cha
26, 27, 102, 108, 112
Beresheet A
223, 231
Beshalach
7, 63, 75, 80, 81, 152, 154, 251, 252, 256-259, 309, 311, 444, 454-457, 459, 460, 464, 465, 468, 485, 486
Bo
38, 101, 199
Chayei Sarah
17
Ekev
28
Emor
17, 338
Ha'azinu
136, 173, 175
Idra Raba
294
Ki Tetze
27, 43, 44, 47
Lech Lecha
118, 234
Metzora
29

Miketz
120, 124, 150, 260
Mishpatim
7, 239, 289, 290, 294, 296, 321, 526
Naso
13, 149
Noach
18, 367
Pekudei
437, 562, 571
Pinchas
106, 179, 190, 242, 383, 491, 578, 579, 581, 728
Prologue
34, 86, 133, 135
Safra Detzniuta
66
Shemot
101, 104, 113, 191, 323
Shlach Lecha
7, 311
Shmini
43, 57
Tazria
109, 110, 118, 124
Toldot
202
Trumah
869
Vaera
204, 205
Vaetchanan
32, 106, 171, 179, 180, 181
Vayakhel
1, 10, 12, 33, 378
Vayechi
60, 61, 72, 84, 85, 86, 87, 92, 242, 548, 549, 551, 575, 577, 643, 706, 726
Vayera
266, 313, 362, 363, 449, 481
Vayeshev
110, 237, 238, 239
Vayetze
280
Vayikra
127, 408
Vayishlach
30, 168, 177, 250
Yitro
209, 213, 458

WASHING

Chayei Sarah
181
Ekev
20, 31, 37-40, 56, 57, 60
Ha'azinu
51, 137
Lech Lecha
259, 260
Miketz
117, 118, 175
Mishpatim
523
Prologue
134, 171, 172
Tetzaveh
114
Toldot
52
Vayechi
591, 630, 631, 666
Vayera
115, 236
Vayeshev
114, 115, 116, 117

WATCHMAN

Beshalach
249
Bo
133
Lech Lecha
93, 105
Pekudei
106
Pinchas
498, 819
Toldot
166
Trumah
78, 79, 84, 85, 90, 686, 690
Vayakhel
333
Vayetze
87
Vayikra
375-378
Vayishlach
140
Yitro
481

WATER

Acharei Mot
34, 82, 101, 140, 142-144, 160, 206, 208, 209, 211, 238, 241, 242
Balak
32, 35, 47, 55, 66, 86, 87, 88, 89, 110, 145, 231, 255, 309, 310, 312, 314, 320, 489, 490, 507
Beha'alot'cha
23, 43, 77-79, 120, 122
Behar
19
Beresheet A
17, 22, 209, 218, 233, 247, 249, 252, 253, 255, 256, 301, 302, 327, 333, 336, 337, 342, 344, 359, 365, 367, 372, 400, 401, 436
Beresheet B
48, 49, 70, 71, 82, 142, 154, 165, 169, 262, 269-272, 274, 279, 285, 323, 383
Beshalach
92, 93, 112, 134, 136, 182, 209, 239, 267, 327, 345 -347, 394, 425, 426, 430-433, 437, 439, 444, 453
Bo
46, 54, 56, 65, 72, 73, 143, 203, 204, 220, 221, 241
Chayei Sarah
63, 94, 138, 145, 146, 147, 148, 166, 172, 173, 174, 176, 178, 205, 224, 225, 226, 261
Chukat
24, 25, 28, 34, 37, 75, 77
Ekev
42, 48, 57, 65
Emor
161, 164, 172, 216, 229, 234, 256, 261, 327, 331, 332
Ha'azinu
67, 79, 80, 85, 96, 112, 113, 179, 226, 227
Idra Raba
8, 229, 360
Kedoshim
19
Ki Tetze
18, 58, 63, 64, 72, 73, 75, 76,

81, 82, 84, 122, 140, 145
Ki Tisa
49
Korach
47, 50
Lech Lecha
4, 73, 78, 79, 129, 189, 260, 369, 416, 423, 448
Metzora
11, 39, 42
Miketz
35, 166, 183, 185
Mishpatim
86, 166, 211, 256, 361, 362, 363, 374, 375, 476, 497, 499, 523, 539, 546
Naso
58, 60, 64, 66, 67, 68, 70, 71, 72, 87, 88, 132, 156
Noach
4, 22, 24, 58, 59, 71, 96, 97, 109, 135, 179, 181, 193, 202, 212, 330, 336
Pekudei
2, 51, 63, 117, 146, 147, 149, 152, 265, 326, 327, 328, 352, 354, 507, 518, 589, 665, 666, 745, 756, 814, 837, 881, 906, 907, 943
Pinchas
18, 32, 46, 79, 97, 98, 114, 121, 159, 166, 201, 217, 219, 223, 228, 253, 270, 272-274, 276, 315, 402, 420, 424, 426, 436, 437, 441, 448, 516, 588, 620, 625, 628, 637, 638, 648, 654, 664, 680, 690, 691, 697, 699, 727, 736, 809, 825, 847, 867, 878, 886, 889-893
Prologue
76, 171, 205
Safra Detzniuta
15, 39, 59, 60
Shemot
39, 68, 71, 141, 213-215, 219, 224, 225, 227, 230, 251, 322, 371, 391
Shlach Lecha
19, 20, 156, 162, 163, 164, 165, 239, 252, 253, 257, 258, 284
Shmini
58, 62-64, 79, 96, 117
Shoftim
12
Tazria
76, 80, 99, 123, 125
Tetzaveh
94, 99, 144
Toldot
10, 15, 41, 103, 104, 108, 109, 110, 111, 114, 115, 164
Trumah
27, 30, 169, 171, 188, 189, 200, 261, 426-428, 471, 520, 521, 523, 606, 607, 632, 702, 703, 709, 711, 746, 749, 750, 751, 754-757, 758, 816, 838, 916
Tzav
3, 5, 27, 49, 52, 63, 110, 112, 114-116, 124, 150, 193
Vaera
16, 32, 33, 34, 35, 36, 37, 38, 39, 40, 43-47, 50, 88, 95, 97, 103, 105, 129, 130 -132, 142, 144, 153, 156 -158, 165, 174, 175
Vaetchanan
26, 76, 106, 121-123, 162, 181, 184, 185, 186, 191, 197

Vayakhel
48, 49, 60, 76, 77, 292, 293, 294, 304, 310, 311, 314, 316, 405, 486, 487, 489
Vayechi
160, 215, 217, 218-222, 225, 234, 268, 341, 353, 356, 446, 530, 536, 537, 544, 546, 548, 550, 551, 669, 688, 699, 705, 727, 729, 736, 768, 792, 800, 816
Vayelech
1, 34
Vayera
36, 105, 107, 111, 112, 115, 116, 163-165, 171, 211, 246, 258, 259, 261, 273, 305, 306, 381, 382, 393, 424, 462, 490, 491, 492, 493
Vayeshev
56, 58, 59, 61, 116, 118, 119, 120, 127, 130, 148, 157, 163, 217
Vayetze
31, 47, 90, 91, 92, 93, 94, 95, 98, 122, 124, 133, 305, 306, 316, 318, 334, 346, 347, 353, 362, 372, 387
Vayigash
20, 64, 65
Vayikra
22, 135, 146, 149, 153, 181, 182, 197, 204, 247, 263, 267, 272, 280, 290, 291, 322, 365
Vayishlach
137, 188
Yitro
64, 225, 250, 252, 253, 290, 292, 302, 316, 326, 341, 519, 521

WATERS

Acharei Mot
35, 209, 238, 411, 412
Balak
255, 310, 311, 312, 439, 490
Beha'alot'cha
20, 21, 31, 39, 42, 78, 81, 86
Behar
19, 22
Beresheet A
18, 24, 44, 53, 59-62, 63, 66, 67, 73-75, 218, 229, 244, 261, 262, 298, 301, 302, 308, 309, 313, 317, 321, 322, 327, 333, 334, 336, 342, 360, 362, 365-370, 372-380, 388, 389, 405, 409, 411, 423-426, 436
Beresheet B
16, 19, 47, 98, 154, 157-159, 165, 169, 260, 272, 281, 282, 284, 364, 384, 385
Beshalach
90, 156, 239, 260, 261, 312, 348, 388, 426, 437, 439
Bo
39, 40, 58, 59, 63, 65, 68, 220, 224
Chayei Sarah
143, 208
Chukat
30, 69, 73, 75
Ekev
10, 56
Emor
158, 160, 163, 164
Ha'azinu
67, 79, 85, 96, 226
Idra Raba
118, 317

Ki Tetze
74, 84
Lech Lecha
4, 12, 23, 78, 129, 183, 236, 358, 359, 366
Metzora
40
Miketz
19, 54, 62
Mishpatim
85, 166, 361, 362, 363, 374, 497, 531
Naso
65, 67, 68, 70, 72-74, 87, 88
Noach
4, 24, 25, 27, 58-60, 80, 96, 97, 119, 127, 134, 135, 148, 149, 151, 152, 173, 181, 186, 200, 202, 213, 217, 261, 292, 339, 341
Pekudei
1, 2, 39, 139, 148, 150, 157, 646, 654, 674, 768
Pinchas
18, 34, 79, 122, 123, 124, 169, 198, 199, 201, 220, 247, 253, 267, 276, 315, 396, 435, 437, 451, 510, 511, 513, 516, 528-531, 535, 639, 648, 650, 654, 690, 825, 827, 831, 878, 885-887, 891
Prologue
2, 4, 56, 95, 96, 187, 205, 215, 218, 219, 222, 224, 226
Safra Detzniuta
7, 9, 38, 39, 43, 60
Shemot
39, 67, 68, 71, 72, 166, 228, 229, 256, 257, 371
Shlach Lecha
74, 83, 155, 157, 162, 163, 164, 212, 253, 261, 268, 284, 297
Shmini
59, 77, 79
Shoftim
12
Tetzaveh
129
Toldot
9, 72, 108, 115
Trumah
4, 27, 74, 169, 170, 192, 217, 259, 261, 286, 376, 377, 426, 427, 431, 529, 621, 622, 680, 742, 749, 751, 752, 758, 771, 782, 813, 820, 829, 830, 912, 916
Tzav
49, 96, 109, 112, 124, 125
Vaera
111, 112, 128-130, 142, 143, 156, 158, 164
Vaetchanan
120-123, 146, 161, 162, 184
Vayakhel
43, 48, 76, 313, 321, 322
Vayechi
96, 234, 506, 536, 631, 716, 717, 730, 736, 749, 805, 813
Vayelech
46
Vayera
8, 27, 29, 33, 107, 161, 371, 393, 396, 421
Vayeshev
21, 274
Vayetze
91, 94, 133, 181, 261, 267, 314, 345

Vayikra
70, 134, 146, 149, 180-182, 185, 230, 236, 238, 267, 271, 288, 388
Vayishlach
121
Yitro
249, 250, 341, 519, 520-522

WELL

Acharei Mot
103-105, 246
Balak
306, 310, 312, 323
Bechukotai
47
Beha'alot'cha
29, 30, 37, 39, 43
Beresheet B
2, 61, 62, 87, 126, 142, 190, 197, 339, 340, 392, 423, 436
Chayei Sarah
166, 172, 174, 200, 218, 224, 226
Chukat
35, 37, 39, 73, 74, 76, 77, 79
Emor
260a, 261, 262, 263
Ha'azinu
227
Idra Raba
55
Ki Tetze
5, 6, 12, 13, 124
Ki Tisa
49
Miketz
35
Mishpatim
363, 374, 375
Naso
153
Noach
22-24, 27
Pekudei
81, 82, 177, 756, 764
Pinchas
159, 437
Safra Detzniuta
39
Shemot
209, 210, 213-215, 227, 228, 232, 360
Shlach Lecha
2
Toldot
8, 9, 11, 103-106, 109, 110
Trumah
169, 170, 171, 188, 857
Tzav
114, 116
Vaera
104
Vaetchanan
121, 122, 123, 124, 186
Vayakhel
402
Vayechi
219, 220, 222, 224, 510, 536, 537, 764, 770, 775
Vayelech
23, 24, 34, 40, 47, 48
Vayera
63
Vayeshev
56, 163
Vayetze
4, 19, 31, 88, 90, 91-103, 106, 108, 122, 124-126, 347, 362, 363

Vayikra
181, 365, 421
Vayishlach
194

WELLS

Acharei Mot
358
Balak
507
Ki Tisa
3
Naso
55
Pinchas
8, 9
Trumah
465, 604
Tzav
116
Vaera
104, 105
Vayechi
199, 218
Vayeshev
2
Vayetze
133

WEST

Balak
45, 434
Beha'alot'cha
4, 108, 124
Bemidbar
29-31, 33, 36, 53, 54, 56, 59, 64
Beresheet A
81, 89, 413, 414
Beresheet B
50, 51, 71, 81, 82, 90, 189, 242
Beshalach
100, 137, 233
Chayei Sarah
238, 239
Ekev
66
Ki Tisa
73
Lech Lecha
162, 222
Mishpatim
143
Noach
263, 265
Pekudei
178, 531, 537, 555, 586, 660, 662, 663, 680, 684, 686, 689, 694, 814
Pinchas
319, 686, 705, 708, 821
Shlach Lecha
271
Tetzaveh
8
Trumah
22, 604, 610, 612, 846, 877
Tzav
77
Vaera
35, 40
Vayakhel
12, 136, 293, 294, 343, 354
Vayechi
118, 492, 504, 533, 540, 546, 652, 653, 696, 765, 767, 847
Vayera
458, 512
Vayetze
2, 3, 5, 7, 8, 11

Vayikra
24
Vayishlach
199

WHALE

Prologue
59, 226
Shemot
191

WHAT (MAH)

Ki Tetze
20
Ki Tisa
68
Korach
49
Mishpatim
483
Pinchas
791
Trumah
15, 16, 17

WHEAT

Balak
72, 74, 76, 77, 78, 79
Ekev
30
Ki Tetze
3, 4
Mishpatim
488, 489
Pinchas
264, 265, 417, 598, 658
Safra Detzniuta
2

Vayakhel
463
Vayetze
190, 201, 204

WHEEL

Balak
436
Beresheet A
77, 133
Chayei Sarah
140, 141, 234
Chukat
30
Ekev
43
Mishpatim
5, 11, 13
Pekudei
3, 16, 156, 210, 253, 287 -290, 339, 405, 409, 410, 413, 490, 498, 499, 504, 531, 536, 562, 563, 565, 566, 571, 574, 623, 786, 790, 797
Pinchas
46, 202, 273, 274, 348
Prologue
200, 202
Vayechi
507-512
Vayera
299, 301, 303
Vayetze
311
Vayishlach
88

WHITE

Acharei Mot
201, 281, 311, 318

Balak
435, 437, 495
Beha'alot'cha
28, 107, 121, 122, 135
Beresheet A
1, 23, 70, 72, 86, 183, 207, 277, 281
Beresheet B
27, 63, 65, 67, 73, 74, 76, 79, 84, 89, 115, 249-253, 255, 256, 258-260, 262-264, 273
Beshalach
4, 6, 171, 299, 388, 476, 478
Bo
78, 79, 113, 205, 207, 212, 232
Chukat
84
Emor
212, 251, 333
Ha'azinu
10, 35, 51, 52, 117, 131, 137-141, 143, 162 -164, 179, 184, 195, 205
Idra Raba
14, 17, 20, 24, 40, 42, 46, 47, 48, 51, 56, 57, 58, 72, 73, 86, 96, 100, 108, 142, 147, 159, 174, 181, 184-186, 188, 208, 216-218, 220, 228, 269, 270, 277, 290
Kedoshim
7
Ki Tetze
92, 120
Ki Tisa
79
Lech Lecha
19, 20, 158, 159, 201, 340, 462
Matot
1, 3, 4
Mishpatim
96, 365, 450, 461, 515, 522, 523, 531, 532, 534
Naso
86, 89, 143
Noach
266, 269-271, 302
Pekudei
109, 151, 165, 198, 286, 398, 517, 574, 633, 709
Pinchas
35a, 35b, 35c, 51, 68, 126, 193, 255, 261, 264, 270, 285, 290, 297, 334, 337, 344, 420, 584, 629, 688, 712, 812, 822, 850, 873
Prologue
1, 209
Safra Detzniuta
14, 26
Shemot
41, 81, 194, 361, 364-367, 369, 385
Shlach Lecha
124, 157, 166, 181, 248, 252, 314, 322, 335
Shoftim
13
Tazria
105, 108, 131, 162, 163, 165
Tetzaveh
94
Toldot
15, 52, 54, 66
Trumah
43, 62, 157, 233, 234, 259, 260, 331, 332, 338, 428, 480, 481, 528, 534, 595
Tzav
70, 136

Vaera
26, 113, 131
Vaetchanan
191
Vayakhel
161, 252, 293, 303, 368, 414
Vayechi
235, 341, 469, 470, 471, 475, 508, 632
Vayera
36, 45, 52, 53, 267, 269
Vayeshev
49, 65, 83, 266, 268, 269, 270
Vayetze
26, 30, 308, 309, 315, 316, 347
Vayikra
140, 223, 427
Vayishlach
11
Yitro
49, 86, 88, 89, 91, 92, 104, 135, 205, 207, 222, 223, 225, 229, 237, 360-362, 364, 365, 535, 536

WHO (MI)

Balak
327
Beresheet A
301
Lech Lecha
212
Mishpatim
202, 204, 208, 397, 427
Pinchas
466
Trumah
2, 6, 15
Vayakhel
50
Vayera
27, 418

WICKED

Acharei Mot
37, 84, 147, 151, 158, 180, 253, 259, 271, 290, 294, 316, 319, 320, 348, 396
Balak
26, 47, 78, 97, 137, 161, 162, 165, 168, 173, 175, 176, 178, 180, 185, 193, 249, 251, 252, 253, 254, 255, 260, 266, 267, 276, 279, 281, 286, 292, 304, 321, 322, 324, 325, 350, 389, 390, 393, 408, 413, 418, 430, 459, 483, 493, 505
Bechukotai
9, 10
Beha'alot'cha
10, 36, 64, 78, 87, 105
Behar
68
Beresheet A
98, 122, 123, 167, 291, 352, 374, 456, 462, 470
Beresheet B
44, 54, 147, 148, 156, 187, 285, 294, 295, 315, 316, 336, 386, 387, 390, 395, 398, 400, 404, 409, 418, 435, 443, 447, 448
Beshalach
17, 33, 59, 170, 189-191, 257, 391, 393, 406, 427
Bo
18, 22, 26, 28, 56, 71, 136 -138, 145, 146, 151, 197, 202, 206

Chayei Sarah
6-8, 11, 12, 76, 99, 197, 198, 206
Chukat
6, 15, 54
Ekev
34, 35, 41
Emor
4, 94, 115, 203, 233, 244, 279
Ha'azinu
28, 118, 127, 129, 131, 132, 135, 160, 163, 211-214, 242
Idra Raba
199, 200, 210, 227, 229, 230, 240, 320, 321, 328, 333, 344
Kedoshim
82, 133
Ki Tetze
13, 26, 65, 83, 96, 97, 113, 121, 124, 125
Ki Tisa
74, 75, 76
Korach
34, 60
Lech Lecha
1, 2, 17, 21, 35-38, 54-56, 87-90, 116, 148, 176, 179, 251, 254, 269, 379, 380
Metzora
4, 26-28, 30, 32, 38
Miketz
2, 43, 54, 100, 137, 233, 234, 264
Mishpatim
180, 231, 232, 235, 248, 260, 320, 448, 479, 485, 521
Naso
17, 21, 27, 33, 40, 41, 42, 44, 45, 47, 89, 100, 102, 121, 184, 185
Noach
14, 51, 52, 55, 57, 61, 66, 69, 76, 78, 82, 83, 136, 137, 141, 150, 152, 163, 166, 173-176, 178, 189-193, 201-207, 215, 229, 339, 340, 382
Pekudei
3, 5, 61-64, 78, 248, 303, 326, 363, 376, 377, 461, 462, 466, 484, 670, 712, 733, 746, 836, 838, 839, 842, 867, 886, 925, 932, 935, 958
Pinchas
9, 10, 34, 50, 52, 53, 60, 108, 138, 146, 171, 190, 245, 269, 327, 331, 339, 354, 375, 412, 414, 416, 451, 469, 486, 573, 583, 643, 645, 702, 709, 740, 746, 860
Prologue
5, 192, 195, 196, 251, 259
Shemot
111, 152, 163, 167-173, 175, 185, 208, 292, 318, 370, 389, 393
Shlach Lecha
3, 24, 26, 89, 91, 206, 208, 307, 308, 331
Shmini
16, 20, 21, 22, 24, 95
Shoftim
5, 12, 15
Tazria
20, 75, 78, 79, 89, 128, 156, 167
Tetzaveh
89, 90
Toldot
16, 25, 39, 67, 74, 76, 83, 86, 91, 101, 102
Trumah
40, 41, 46-51, 70, 143, 180,

279, 364, 439, 440, 443 -447, 449-454, 457, 458, 677, 678, 684, 773, 776, 777, 811, 812, 814, 818

Tzav
51, 59, 78, 92, 93, 98, 117

Vaera
30, 31, 91, 92, 115, 126, 147, 148, 176, 188, 205

Vayakhel
22, 88, 95, 244, 334, 335, 389, 391, 394, 412, 413

Vayechi
44, 69, 162, 169, 190, 191, 192-194, 248, 258, 259, 264, 303, 304, 364, 474, 512, 583, 584, 585, 592, 594, 596, 598, 609, 733, 734

Vayelech
43

Vayera
27, 130, 179, 184, 190, 191, 192, 218, 241, 244, 245, 248, 257, 273, 294, 320, 322, 323, 324, 325, 346, 360, 361, 362, 363, 366, 369, 370, 411, 416, 419, 472, 473, 474, 475

Vayeshev
32, 52, 154, 180, 183, 207, 214, 235, 240, 262, 269

Vayetze
78-80, 94, 294, 341, 364

Vayigash
63, 65

Vayikra
1, 119, 234, 247, 270, 278

Vayishlach
85, 86, 118, 121, 122, 124, 169, 193, 194, 207

Yitro
118, 211, 240, 392, 510

WICKEDNESS

Acharei Mot
37, 84, 147, 151, 158, 180, 253, 259, 271, 290, 294, 316, 319, 320, 348, 396

Balak
26, 47, 78, 97, 137, 161, 162, 165, 168, 173, 175, 176, 178, 180, 185, 193, 249, 251, 252, 253, 254, 255, 260, 266, 267, 276, 279, 281, 286, 292, 304, 321, 322, 324, 325, 350, 389, 390, 393, 408, 413, 418, 430, 459, 483, 493, 505

Bechukotai
9, 10

Beha'alot'cha
10, 36, 64, 78, 87, 105

Behar
68

Beresheet A
98, 122, 123, 167, 291, 352, 374, 456, 462, 470

Beresheet B
21, 44, 54, 147, 148, 156, 187, 285, 288, 294, 295, 315, 316, 336, 386, 387, 390, 393 -395, 398, 400, 404, 409, 418, 435, 443, 447, 448

Beshalach
17, 33, 59, 170, 189-191, 257, 391, 393, 406, 427

Bo
18, 22, 26, 28, 56, 71, 111, 136-138, 145, 146, 151, 197, 202, 206

Chayei Sarah
6-8, 11, 12, 76, 99, 197, 198, 206
Chukat
6, 15, 54
Ekev
34, 35, 41, 42
Emor
4, 33, 94, 115, 203, 233, 244, 279
Ha'azinu
28, 118, 127, 129, 131, 132, 135, 160, 163, 211, 212-214, 242
Idra Raba
199, 200, 210, 227, 229, 230, 240, 320, 321, 328, 333, 344
Kedoshim
67, 82, 133
Ki Tetze
13, 26, 65, 83, 96, 97, 113, 121, 124, 125
Ki Tisa
74-76, 105
Korach
16, 34, 60
Lech Lecha
1-3, 17, 21, 35, 37, 38, 54-56, 87-90, 116, 148, 176, 179, 251, 254, 269, 379, 380
Metzora
4, 26, 27, 28, 30, 32, 38
Miketz
2, 43, 54, 100, 137, 233, 234, 264
Mishpatim
180, 231, 232, 235, 248, 260, 320, 448, 479, 485, 521
Naso
17, 21, 27, 33, 40-42, 44, 45, 47, 89, 100, 102, 121, 184, 185
Noach
14, 51, 52, 55, 57, 61, 66, 69, 76, 78, 82, 83, 136, 137, 141, 150, 152, 163, 166, 173-176, 178, 189-193, 201-207, 215, 229, 339, 340, 382
Pekudei
3, 5, 61-64, 78, 248, 260, 303, 326, 363, 376, 377, 461, 462, 466, 484, 670, 712, 733, 746, 836, 838, 839, 842, 867, 886, 925, 932, 935, 958
Pinchas
9, 10, 34, 50, 52, 53, 60, 108, 138, 146, 171, 190, 245, 269, 327, 331, 339, 354, 375, 412, 414, 416, 451, 469, 486, 573, 583, 643, 645, 702, 709, 740, 746, 860
Prologue
5, 192, 195, 196, 251, 259
Shemot
111, 152, 163, 167-173, 175, 185, 208, 292, 318, 370, 389, 393
Shlach Lecha
3, 24-26, 89, 91, 206, 208, 307, 308, 331
Shmini
16, 20, 21, 22, 24, 95
Shoftim
5, 12, 15
Tazria
20, 75, 78, 79, 89, 128, 156, 167
Tetzaveh
89, 90
Toldot
16, 25, 31, 39, 54, 67, 74, 76, 83, 86, 91, 101, 102

Trumah
40, 41, 46-51, 70, 143, 180, 279, 364, 439, 440, 443 -447, 449-454, 457, 458, 677, 678, 684, 773, 776, 777, 811, 812, 814, 818
Tzav
51, 59, 78, 92, 93, 98, 117
Vaera
30, 31, 91, 92, 115, 126, 147, 148, 176, 188, 205
Vayakhel
22, 88, 95, 244, 334, 335, 386, 389, 391, 394, 412, 413, 439
Vayechi
44, 69, 162, 169, 190-194, 248, 258, 259, 264, 303, 304, 364, 474, 512, 583-585, 592, 594, 596, 598, 609, 733, 734
Vayelech
43
Vayera
27, 130, 179, 184, 190-192, 218, 241, 244, 245, 248, 257, 273, 294, 320, 322-325, 346, 360-363, 366, 369, 370, 411, 416, 419, 472-475
Vayeshev
7, 25, 32, 52, 154, 180, 182, 183, 207, 214, 235, 240, 262, 269
Vayetze
78-80, 94, 279, 294, 341, 364
Vayigash
63, 65
Vayikra
1, 119, 234, 247, 270, 278
Vayishlach
85, 86, 118, 121, 122, 124, 169, 193, 194, 207
Yitro
103, 118, 211, 240, 392, 510

WIDOW

Mishpatim
21, 108, 125, 130, 134, 139, 149, 156, 157, 197, 198, 514
Vaetchanan
126, 157
Vayeshev
189
Vayigash
72, 74

WILLOW

Emor
282b
Tetze
143, 144, 145
Mishpatim
84, 85
Noach
94, 97
Pinchas
822
Shemot
265
Shlach Lecha
344
Tetzaveh
132
Tzav
108, 110, 114-118
Vayechi
211, 213, 221-225

Vayikra
420

WIND

Acharei Mot
51, 149
Balak
20, 78, 168, 211, 228, 419, 501
Beha'alot'cha
7, 39, 59, 101, 102, 122
Behar
3
Bemidbar
32
Beresheet A
18, 19, 24, 25, 26, 89, 336, 337, 367, 371, 409
Beresheet B
49, 50, 71, 90, 92, 116
Beshalach
100, 101, 134, 138, 229, 267, 274, 318, 319, 322, 325
Bo
53-56, 66, 67, 103, 198
Chukat
45-47, 75
Ekev
65
Emor
216
Ha'azinu
55, 180, 228
Idra Raba
67, 68
Ki Tetze
140
Lech Lecha
10, 22, 39, 40, 100, 237, 363
Metzora
7
Mishpatim
24, 87, 149, 468
Naso
41, 112, 117
Noach
55, 66, 264, 265, 277, 330
Pekudei
133, 167, 589, 655, 928, 932
Pinchas
84-86, 88, 100, 223, 228, 264, 267-271, 273, 275, 334, 377, 396, 400, 401, 405, 407, 420, 428, 432, 435, 436, 438, 449, 487, 525, 867
Prologue
43
Safra Detzniuta
7, 21, 61
Shemot
66, 157, 217, 218, 225, 226, 254, 259
Shlach Lecha
4, 24, 97, 229, 282, 284, 290
Shmini
8, 14
Tazria
76, 99
Toldot
12, 64, 114, 162
Trumah
73, 82, 236, 281, 795, 855, 873, 876, 912
Tzav
41, 74, 83, 117, 132
Vaera
32, 33, 38, 158, 159
Vaetchanan
4, 26, 43

Vayakhel
12, 43, 44-46, 48, 75, 162, 163, 167, 172, 174
Vayechi
31, 118, 160, 164, 166, 446, 461, 463, 466, 531-533, 683, 768, 848
Vayera
93, 167, 268, 381, 459
Vayeshev
271
Vayetze
11, 14, 16, 31, 32, 173, 233, 258, 262-264, 278, 306, 392
Vayigash
82, 125, 127
Vayikra
135, 163, 201, 369, 380, 395, 435
Vayishlach
75, 211, 212, 268
Yitro
16, 17, 225, 226, 249, 250, 290, 292, 302, 307, 311, 312, 343, 367, 516

WINDOWS

Balak
1, 6, 188, 191, 209
Bechukotai
12, 41
Beshalach
336
Ha'azinu
55
Idra Raba
63, 64
Ki Tisa
8
Mishpatim
116, 204, 426, 427, 433
Noach
59
Pekudei
574, 583, 588, 589, 591, 592, 934
Pinchas
204, 702
Shemot
160
Toldot
98
Trumah
843, 844, 848-851, 853-860
Vaetchanan
43
Vayechi
120, 154, 671

WINE

Acharei Mot
31, 102, 213
Balak
40, 85-89, 91, 92
Beha'alot'cha
23, 64
Beresheet A
57, 456
Beshalach
368, 482
Chayei Sarah
19
Ekev
18, 37, 49, 62
Emor
103, 124, 127, 218, 243, 244
Idra Raba
22, 170, 279, 359

Ki Tisa
57
Korach
24
Lech Lecha
142, 237, 241, 255, 265, 303
Metzora
26, 27, 42
Miketz
95, 198
Mishpatim
388, 491, 553, 568, 574
Naso
11, 124-129
Noach
93, 239, 240, 296, 307, 309, 310, 374
Pekudei
62, 480, 481, 515, 599, 925
Pinchas
68, 69, 77, 80, 217, 348, 349, 403, 423, 424, 441, 448, 544, 552, 553, 594, 596, 616, 628-630, 632, 677, 748, 756, 761, 825, 882
Prologue
253, 256
Shlach Lecha
275
Shmini
61-72, 81-87, 91-93, 96
Toldot
42, 45, 46, 49, 93, 130, 136, 144, 148
Trumah
35, 381, 382, 502, 792, 856
Tzav
68, 150
Vaera
138, 139, 141
Vayakhel
22, 255
Vayechi
112, 591, 597, 624, 630-634, 636, 704, 792, 796, 845, 846
Vayera
5, 163, 308, 316, 318, 323-325, 331, 334
Vayeshev
247, 264, 267
Vayetze
21-23, 25, 27, 201, 324, 369, 384
Vayikra
26, 29, 33, 34, 36, 38, 197, 198, 354
Vayishlach
19, 41
Yitro
424

WINEPRESS

Lech Lecha
468
Mishpatim
413, 414
Vayechi
591

WISDOM

Acharei Mot
4, 34, 89-91, 101, 103, 140, 141, 195, 211, 213, 227 -229, 288, 303, 304, 325, 326, 354, 355, 380, 386, 407, 410
Balak
1, 4, 48, 72, 162, 163, 169, 237, 265, 313, 314, 326, 398, 403,

409, 411, 416, 430, 432, 448, 449, 451, 454

Beha'alot'cha
19, 50, 113

Behar
10

Bemidbar
4, 17

Beresheet A
45, 160, 249, 253, 293, 298, 370, 385, 472-474, 476

Beresheet B
3, 172, 177, 248, 259, 288, 289, 317, 361, 362, 379 -381, 383, 384, 437

Beshalach
60, 61, 125, 188, 189, 235, 237, 279, 318, 319, 341, 374, 377, 448, 454, 460, 466

Bo
4, 38, 118, 126, 136, 140, 142, 212, 223, 224

Chayei Sarah
137, 139, 144-147, 149, 156, 177, 178, 194, 201, 215, 223, 226, 264

Chukat
25, 27, 40, 48-52, 55

Ekev
8, 49, 58

Emor
31, 77, 232, 311

Ha'azinu
15-18, 55, 57, 71, 73, 81, 87, 90, 91, 95, 109, 121, 152, 158, 162, 188, 204, 207-210, 235, 259

Idra Raba
2, 52, 63-65, 67, 68, 94, 102, 190, 218, 222, 272, 280, 282, 296, 348, 349, 350

Kedoshim
12, 14, 35

Ki Tetze
7, 52, 54, 72, 73, 75, 113

Ki Tisa
8, 63, 103, 104, 105

Korach
10, 29, 30, 31, 32, 34, 44

Lech Lecha
22, 23, 29, 30, 63, 65, 71, 75, 76, 77, 112, 141, 143, 154, 157, 162, 165, 168, 179, 211, 274, 297, 321, 322, 331, 345, 378, 421, 423

Miketz
18, 52, 74, 76, 131, 136

Mishpatim
22, 40, 124, 126, 127, 251, 254, 345, 375, 392, 422, 424, 468, 500, 501, 503

Naso
102, 134, 177

Noach
35, 138, 245, 256, 304, 343, 348, 349, 353, 372-378, 384

Pekudei
13, 14, 36, 50, 56, 178, 189, 243, 244, 248, 250, 255, 258, 291, 293, 360, 526, 527, 529, 530, 533, 790, 791

Pinchas
3, 27, 103, 136, 137, 153, 185, 204, 271, 332, 367, 383, 391, 394, 405, 427, 433, 438, 507, 508, 515, 530, 570, 571, 606, 628, 678, 722, 811, 824, 839, 841, 858, 871

Prologue
40, 48, 62-64, 67, 91, 107, 110, 111, 120, 121, 125, 149, 166,

189

Safra Detzniuta
1-3, 11, 32, 54, 64, 65, 73

Shemot
1, 82, 84, 151, 174, 191, 201, 208, 251, 262-264, 328 -330, 343, 358, 362, 391

Shlach Lecha
18, 21, 55, 61, 77, 95, 129, 163, 224, 250, 323, 345

Shmini
73, 114

Tazria
11, 12, 96-98, 101-103, 104, 157, 158

Tetzaveh
2, 3, 72, 81

Toldot
3, 17, 22, 28, 31, 32, 40, 80, 92, 94, 96, 98, 99, 103, 112, 117, 181-185, 189, 190

Trumah
5, 250, 350-353, 363, 419, 421, 422, 469, 478, 497, 528, 544, 553-555, 558, 572, 706, 708, 735, 838, 847, 871, 885, 915

Tzav
12, 35, 146

Vaera
49, 111, 122, 123, 139, 140, 165, 167-169, 195

Vaetchanan
35, 191

Vayakhel
119, 120, 122, 158, 186, 195, 228, 252, 284, 347, 375, 396, 400, 402, 440, 443

Vayechi
104, 120, 125, 165, 183, 275 -278, 280, 281, 290, 292, 322, 323, 335, 339, 522-524, 532, 541, 597, 670, 811, 819

Vayera
11, 39, 80, 89, 151, 153, 158, 283, 315, 345, 350, 445, 455, 456, 458, 459, 476, 498

Vayeshev
6, 9, 46, 60, 69, 89, 145, 156, 189, 261, 266

Vayetze
13, 55, 68, 69, 177, 190, 194, 208, 217, 247, 253, 270, 302, 303, 312, 326, 337, 344

Vayigash
41, 42

Vayikra
1, 84, 142, 150, 152, 154, 312, 331, 333, 386, 387, 444

Vayishlach
20, 219, 276

Yitro
26, 32, 34, 38, 83, 84, 93, 94, 97, 114, 127, 149, 172, 178, 179, 180, 181, 183, 184, 187, 228, 265, 277, 278, 299, 312, 386, 390, 537

WITCHCRAFT

Acharei Mot
249, 252, 254, 272, 405

Balak
2, 3, 5, 6, 28, 135, 136, 154, 161, 171, 175, 176, 182, 254, 255, 282, 286, 402, 406, 410, 411, 414, 422, 423, 427, 431, 453, 461, 472, 474, 481-484, 486, 497

Bechukotai
11, 12, 13

Behar
2
Beresheet A
452
Beresheet B
311, 379-381, 424
Beshalach
440
Bo
76, 119, 120, 127
Chayei Sarah
74, 80, 81, 83-87, 263, 264
Ha'azinu
256, 258, 260
Ki Tisa
75, 83
Mishpatim
564
Pekudei
319, 320, 861
Shlach Lecha
221
Shmini
1z06
Tazria
16, 17, 160, 170
Tetzaveh
110
Trumah
36, 852, 854
Vaera
53, 166, 170
Vayakhel
467, 468
Vayetze
252, 298
Vayishlach
22, 23, 32, 34, 37, 77
Yitro
46

WITNESSES

Acharei Mot
388
Beshalach
163
Emor
210, 211, 212
Ha'azinu
47
Idra Raba
9, 232
Kedoshim
106
Miketz
162
Naso
42
Pinchas
204, 455, 646
Prologue
9, 133
Shlach Lecha
336, 337, 338
Shoftim
11, 14, 16, 17, 18, 19, 20
Tazria
162
Toldot
46, 78
Trumah
47, 382, 625
Tzav
176
Vaetchanan
58, 126, 143
Vayakhel
358
Vayechi
27, 164, 358

Vayelech
22-24, 29
Vayeshev
248, 249
Vayetze
381
Vayishlach
31
Yitro
110, 174, 175, 417, 493

WOLVES

Mishpatim
484
Pinchas
93
Vayechi
553, 787, 788

WOMB

Beresheet A
288, 301, 314
Lech Lecha
212, 328, 453
Prologue
232, 238, 239, 240
Vaetchanan
39
Vayera
418, 426, 427
Vayetze
199, 291
Vayishlach
244

WOMEN

Acharei Mot
25, 26, 78, 211, 226, 278, 279, 281, 393, 394, 397, 400, 403, 405, 406, 411
Balak
46, 94, 123, 173, 224, 232, 235, 236, 243, 261, 284, 315, 321, 322, 326, 327, 419, 499
Bechukotai
19, 58
Beha'alot'cha
52, 76, 78, 123
Behar
28, 30, 46, 48
Bemidbar
8, 15, 23
Beresheet A
104, 114, 152, 179, 223, 228, 269, 273, 279, 282, 361, 435, 438, 441, 445-448, 458, 461, 466, 470
Beresheet B
7, 133, 139, 198, 199, 203, 209, 213, 217, 218, 220, 234, 302, 314, 338, 347, 424
Beshalach
2, 3, 9, 10, 12, 32, 48, 234, 356-358, 481
Bo
24, 112, 198
Chayei Sarah
7, 13, 14, 17, 20, 26, 32, 33, 62, 80, 83-86, 110, 139, 142, 173, 176, 214, 216, 256, 259
Chukat
7, 11, 12, 13, 25, 66
Ekev
30
Emor
1, 33-35, 38, 147, 148, 160 -162, 164, 175, 178, 179, 306, 310, 312, 313, 318, 319, 334,

336, 339
Ha'azinu
84, 191, 229, 231, 232, 247
Idra Raba
310, 317
Kedoshim
28, 68, 70-72, 114
Ki Tetze
1, 8, 12, 13, 29, 50
Ki Tisa
19, 24, 33, 39, 40, 44, 100
Korach
18, 28, 44
Lech Lecha
59, 99, 110, 111, 114, 115, 142, 200, 329, 353, 385
Matot
1-5
Metzora
4, 28, 30
Miketz
87
Mishpatim
130, 133, 141, 147, 148, 154, 155, 157, 158, 160, 162, 170, 171, 173, 174, 184, 197, 198, 222-225, 277, 278, 284, 317 -320, 322, 323, 330, 352, 371, 377, 454, 474, 566
Naso
16, 20, 22, 23, 60, 61, 67, 68, 74, 78, 79, 80, 83, 88, 92, 130, 143
Noach
45, 101, 164, 223, 309, 316, 376
Pekudei
30, 32, 207, 285, 365, 371, 381, 454, 479, 549, 685, 688, 711, 746, 860, 864, 865, 871, 888, 896, 906, 909, 910, 912
Pinchas
16, 51, 53, 55, 57, 104, 126, 140, 157, 181, 192, 233, 327, 331, 362, 459, 463, 469, 551, 593, 600, 684, 685, 687, 693, 702, 710, 797, 852
Prologue
213
Safra Detzniuta
54, 64
Shemot
18, 24-26, 32-35, 91, 172, 186, 192, 247, 330, 334
Shlach Lecha
116, 134, 135, 171, 190, 196 -200, 217, 222, 241, 263-265, 282, 312
Shmini
38, 39
Tazria
1, 4, 5, 9-11, 21, 23-25, 37, 42, 44, 48, 49, 60, 61, 93, 94, 108, 118, 146, 162
Tetzaveh
65, 66
Toldot
39, 98, 193
Trumah
62, 333, 413, 578, 625, 673, 729, 730, 754, 779, 818, 821, 894
Tzav
9, 17, 156-158, 161
Vaera
114, 116, 154
Vaetchanan
126

Vayakhel
9, 12, 26, 28, 30, 34-38, 80, 91, 108, 171, 218, 372, 451, 455, 479, 485
Vayechi
20, 237, 240, 243, 264, 290, 403, 494, 495, 572, 733
Vayelech
7, 9, 11
Vayera
106, 108, 133, 138, 140, 146, 150, 165, 326-328, 346, 398, 412, 413, 418, 421, 431, 439, 447
Vayeshev
58, 61, 62, 134, 165, 189 -191, 193, 219, 224
Vayetze
49, 57, 147, 148, 183, 230, 248, 249, 294, 375, 391
Vayigash
25, 74, 82, 93
Vayikra
65, 186, 220, 274, 286, 292, 293, 315, 322, 323, 325-329, 346, 353, 408, 412
Vayishlach
25, 141, 157, 194, 214, 215
Yitro
22, 164, 166, 216, 240, 283, 286, 316, 350, 434, 435, 495

WOOD

Beresheet A
295
Ha'azinu
9
Mishpatim
515
Shoftim
8, 10
Vaetchanan
66
Vayechi
210, 460
Vayera
218

WOOL

Ha'azinu
62
Idra Raba
24, 29, 100, 110, 279
Kedoshim
105, 108, 111, 114, 115, 117 -119, 122, 123
Matot
2
Naso
133
Safra Detzniuta
6, 22
Tazria
168
Trumah
230, 231
Vaera
113, 168

WORLD (TEVEL)

Beresheet B
36, 38, 54
Beshalach
127
Mishpatim
117, 118
Prologue
159

Vayikra
138, 139

WORLD TO COME, THE

Acharei Mot
105, 108, 109, 115, 144, 208, 228, 255, 294, 348, 350-352, 391, 396, 413
Balak
155, 373
Bechukotai
15, 60, 61
Beha'alot'cha
1, 5, 41, 51, 60, 71, 99, 142, 150
Behar
66, 83
Bemidbar
38, 56, 58, 65, 77
Beresheet A
152, 228, 240, 335, 351 -353, 384, 398
Beresheet B
59, 97, 137, 196, 323, 445, 446, 448
Beshalach
43, 144, 220, 226, 227, 312, 325, 339, 383, 407, 452, 486
Bo
1, 100, 179, 202
Chayei Sarah
38, 40, 61, 94, 117, 137, 151, 158, 174, 181, 196, 198, 219, 222
Chukat
34, 50, 68, 83
Ekev
10, 16, 17
Emor
4, 36, 54, 62, 83, 94, 126, 133, 145, 161, 169, 175, 218, 223, 232, 278, 282a, 305, 314, 323, 326, 340
Ha'azinu
9, 26, 35, 40, 79, 91, 97, 117, 146, 166, 192, 226, 253
Idra Raba
15, 17, 33, 66, 69, 115, 135, 160, 169, 170, 221, 247, 248, 280, 312, 329, 352, 356, 361, 364
Kedoshim
51, 53, 91, 92, 120
Ki Tetze
44, 47
Ki Tisa
120
Korach
1, 30, 31, 34, 42, 43
Lech Lecha
150, 170, 281, 282, 286, 321, 366, 367, 381, 414, 428, 429, 445
Matot
4, 6
Metzora
3, 27, 51
Miketz
4, 69, 70, 73-77, 96, 99, 128, 129, 143, 184, 191, 232, 251 -254, 269
Mishpatim
64, 69, 71, 83, 364, 392, 397, 404, 409, 410, 411, 417, 422, 426, 538
Naso
25, 41
Noach
1, 2, 13, 68, 127, 136, 143, 210
Pekudei
4, 5, 62, 64, 70, 78, 80, 81, 139,

233, 278, 291, 337, 349, 350, 362, 365, 461, 468, 470, 525, 530, 536, 556, 557, 558, 581, 584, 590, 593, 616, 675, 676, 695, 704, 706, 728, 739, 746, 751, 753, 760, 777, 815, 820, 827, 835, 849, 881, 910, 924, 935, 951, 956

Pinchas
33, 52, 174, 345, 605, 607, 635, 731, 752, 774, 871, 872

Prologue
4, 33, 52, 60, 106, 108, 190

Safra Detzniuta
42

Shemot
3, 60, 68, 133, 176, 357, 375, 376

Shlach Lecha
13, 25, 26, 27, 41, 42, 93, 95, 110, 201, 214, 290, 292, 334

Shmini
68, 83, 85-87, 92, 99, 111, 113, 115

Tazria
89, 167, 179

Tetzaveh
27, 89, 96, 98, 102, 103, 146

Toldot
4, 26, 36, 86, 91, 95, 106, 113, 154

Trumah
6, 41, 53, 58, 59, 102, 103, 104, 111, 112, 122, 145, 147, 149, 173, 252, 259, 306, 311, 331, 337, 348, 383, 414, 473, 500, 508, 509, 534, 554-557, 560, 564, 578, 582, 588, 595, 598, 601-603, 606, 656, 675, 676, 679, 724, 727, 738, 739, 755, 758, 820, 830, 877, 880, 892, 895

Tzav
1, 14, 18, 29, 65, 100, 166

Vaera
8, 115, 183, 187

Vaetchanan
25, 66, 87, 89, 123, 133, 135

Vayakhel
31, 70, 98, 103, 114, 180, 182, 211, 238, 249, 250, 269, 278, 280, 313, 373, 388, 398, 411, 415, 417, 418, 419, 448, 463, 464, 469, 475, 484

Vayechi
37, 53, 69, 105, 153, 194, 209, 227, 244, 300, 303, 358, 387, 388, 475, 675, 688, 694, 749, 751, 752, 786, 827, 846

Vayelech
16, 34, 37, 38, 46

Vayera
31, 44, 193, 230, 247, 262-264, 284, 294, 316, 319, 324, 420, 426, 428, 467

Vayeshev
10-12, 27, 28, 35, 36, 41, 120, 125, 139, 167, 169-172, 175, 178-180, 182, 185, 186, 188, 209, 220, 221, 228, 285

Vayetze
88, 111, 209, 232, 261, 340, 344, 366, 374

Vayigash
17, 23, 43, 45, 102

Vayikra
71, 217, 224, 278, 339, 425, 428

Vayishlach
46, 78, 92, 116, 128, 207, 244, 278
Yitro
21, 53, 95, 121, 170, 175, 332, 333, 397, 411, 428, 430, 431, 460, 466, 489, 507, 568

WORLDS

Acharei Mot
48, 76, 273
Balak
311, 312
Beha'alot'cha
63
Behar
33-35, 37, 41-43
Beresheet A
63, 77, 83, 109, 110, 114, 164 -166, 180-182, 256, 257, 260, 263, 272, 282, 302, 401, 407, 445, 470
Beresheet B
29, 33, 39, 53, 60, 69, 76, 131, 268, 420
Beshalach
225, 273, 411
Bo
47, 227
Chukat
29
Emor
58, 158
Ha'azinu
187, 189, 190, 195, 224, 228
Idra Raba
20, 177, 179, 340
Kedoshim
52, 56, 57, 61
Ki Tetze
27, 30, 37, 38, 43, 138, 139
Ki Tisa
82
Korach
9
Lech Lecha
214, 449
Miketz
20
Mishpatim
2, 5, 6, 7, 8, 11, 61, 336, 351, 352, 403, 415, 442, 443, 455, 578
Naso
10
Noach
61, 62
Pekudei
1, 2, 210, 222, 251, 339, 729, 737, 781, 821, 906
Pinchas
57, 223, 225, 230, 283, 294, 316, 348, 456, 502, 515, 692, 700
Safra Detzniuta
63
Shemot
1, 137, 310
Shlach Lecha
48, 345
Tazria
4
Trumah
94, 114, 138, 175, 176, 235, 286, 287, 340, 343, 361, 393, 396, 493-495, 530, 531, 532, 757, 759
Tzav
57, 64, 65, 75, 172

Vaera
34, 103
Vaetchanan
21
Vayakhel
102-104, 136, 137, 142, 143, 148, 275, 283-285, 292, 306, 318, 321
Vayechi
118, 119, 284, 285, 397, 408, 568, 716, 753, 806
Vayera
232
Vayetze
92, 116, 120, 148, 160, 163, 242, 262, 305, 306, 310, 318, 335, 337
Vayikra
36, 149, 152, 282, 433, 434
Yitro
10, 327, 328, 329

WORM

Beresheet A
4
Vayera
136
Vayishlach
250, 251, 252

WORMWOOD

Beresheet A
266
Vayetze
180

WRAPPING

Beresheet A
294
Ekev
59
Ha'azinu
28, 197
Ki Tetze
45, 130
Ki Tisa
78
Mishpatim
21
Vaetchanan
98
Vayechi
741
Vayigash
85
Vayishlach
51

WREATH

Ekev
60, 71
Vayishlach
45

WRITTEN LAW

Balak
220
Ekev
18
Noach
272
Pekudei
350, 729
Pinchas
764
Shmini
93

Vayakhel
103, 218, 237
Vayechi
686

YAAHADONAHI (SPIRIT)

Pekudei
507, 508

YACHIN

Ki Tetze
121

YEAR

Acharei Mot
39, 115, 218, 353, 357, 412
Balak
7, 34, 39, 215, 219, 363, 366, 368, 371, 381, 382, 481
Bechukotai
47
Beha'alot'cha
10, 54-57, 112
Behar
6, 7, 12, 13, 15-17, 20, 21, 29, 52, 57, 72
Bemidbar
8, 9, 16
Beresheet A
63, 64, 102, 118, 425, 461, 470, 478
Beresheet B
163, 196, 243-245, 348, 351, 358, 359, 362, 422
Beshalach
9, 12, 19, 21, 23, 109, 197, 199, 268, 301
Bo
5, 21, 40, 48, 51, 159, 163, 166 -168, 175
Chayei Sarah
1, 14, 20, 21, 23-26, 35, 36, 62, 63, 70, 121, 173, 185
Chukat
22
Ekev
24, 51
Emor
16, 22, 23, 55, 177, 183, 239, 255, 300, 302, 303
Ha'azinu
19, 86, 134, 142, 144, 145, 207, 234, 244
Idra Raba
13, 137, 191, 214, 221, 244, 246
Kedoshim
85, 124, 125-129
Ki Tetze
43, 122, 133
Ki Tisa
67, 68
Lech Lecha
42, 43, 45-47, 62, 64, 65, 109, 125, 126, 327, 344, 345, 356, 357, 437, 439, 440, 458
Miketz
1, 8, 10, 16, 18, 26, 105, 238, 243-248, 255
Mishpatim
2, 76, 77, 78, 129, 135, 218, 285, 354, 355, 359, 388, 391, 393, 395, 396, 474, 493, 544, 546, 547
Naso
9, 68, 98, 139
Noach
74, 98, 106, 132, 133, 137,

223, 245

Pekudei
99, 121, 122, 205, 278, 335, 469, 470, 551-553, 699, 872, 878, 883-885, 923, 924

Pinchas
82, 106, 134, 302, 330, 351, 358, 366, 394, 530, 653, 675, 678, 701, 706, 746-749, 770, 790, 827, 828, 857, 881, 888, 889

Prologue
22, 72, 89, 103, 115, 118, 129, 143, 144, 150, 159, 185

Safra Detzniuta
8, 60, 62

Shemot
87, 141-143, 148, 149, 151, 152, 154, 190, 269, 276, 291, 293, 294, 296, 370

Shlach Lecha
42, 61, 124, 154, 168, 177, 210, 219, 270

Shoftim
14, 16

Tazria
170, 171

Tetzaveh
25, 71, 77, 84, 87, 118, 119, 126-128

Toldot
15, 17, 21, 36, 47, 49, 66-71, 85

Trumah
157, 161, 295, 307, 352, 354, 355, 562, 565, 637, 707, 735, 887

Tzav
63, 113, 119

Vaera
58, 60-62, 107, 110, 176, 178, 179, 180, 181, 201

Vaetchanan
44, 107, 134, 184

Vayakhel
12, 33, 230, 246, 380, 492

Vayechi
1, 19, 20, 21-24, 35, 39, 96, 113-116, 138, 139, 202, 245, 293, 323, 353, 355, 501, 502, 564, 565, 605, 656, 725, 771 -773, 803, 825

Vayelech
6

Vayera
16, 17, 42, 102, 129, 133-135, 142, 149, 196, 216, 231, 384, 398, 441, 445, 446, 450, 455, 472-474, 477, 478, 480, 489, 508

Vayeshev
3, 24, 57, 91, 226

Vayetze
7, 8, 19, 43, 85, 128-131, 140 -142, 148, 149, 151, 250, 284

Vayigash
80, 112

Vayikra
85, 134, 140, 221, 252, 264, 265, 267, 302, 311, 335, 337, 413, 414

Vayishlach
23, 28, 49, 52-57, 81, 103, 104

Yitro
179, 205, 235, 249, 270, 291, 353, 354, 378, 389, 396, 407

YECHIDAH

Beresheet A
252

Naso
36
Trumah
591

YECHONYAH

Mishpatim
228

YEHADANIEL (SPIRIT)

Pekudei
687

YEHADRIEL (SPIRIT)

Balak
306
Pekudei
562

YEHIRAEL (SPIRIT)

Pekudei
583, 586, 587, 593

YEHODIAM

Trumah
48

YEHODIYAH (SPIRIT)

Pekudei
692

YEHOSHEVA

Pekudei
67

YEHOTZEDEK

Balak
19
Vayera
367

YEMIM

Vayishlach
260, 261, 263

YESH (SUBSTANCE)

Pinchas
504, 505, 865
Trumah
738
Vayechi
688
Vayetze
209, 232

YESHIVAH

Acharei Mot
269, 270
Balak
19-25, 86, 132, 233, 340, 343, 366
Behar
74
Beresheet A
200
Beshalach
121
Chayei Sarah
21, 97, 188
Ha'azinu
110
Kedoshim
36, 49
Ki Tetze
15, 24, 25, 42, 48, 49
Ki Tisa
55

Korach
48
Mishpatim
46
Prologue
59, 176
Shemot
246
Shlach Lecha
93, 95, 99, 106, 109, 111, 112, 116, 121, 124, 128, 137, 142, 150, 160, 165, 169, 174, 176, 177, 186-188, 190 -193, 195, 204-206, 209, 210, 215, 221, 223, 224, 229, 244, 245, 253-255, 259, 262, 263, 264, 265, 271, 289, 294, 306
Trumah
593
Vayechi
673
Vayera
402

YETZIRAH

Acharei Mot
273
Balak
311, 312
Beha'alot'cha
63
Behar
33, 35, 41, 43
Beresheet A
63, 77, 83, 109, 114, 260, 282, 302, 401, 407, 445, 470
Beresheet B
29, 76, 268, 420
Beshalach
225, 273, 411
Chukat
29
Emor
58, 158
Ha'azinu
187, 189, 190, 195, 224, 228
Idra Raba
20, 177, 179, 340
Kedoshim
57
Ki Tisa
82
Korach
9
Lech Lecha
214
Mishpatim
11, 336, 403, 578
Naso
10
Noach
61, 62
Pekudei
1, 2, 210, 222, 339
Pinchas
223, 225, 230, 283, 294, 456, 502, 515, 692, 700
Safra Detzniuta
63
Shemot
1, 137, 310
Shlach Lecha
48, 345
Tazria
4
Trumah
287, 493, 494, 495, 531, 532
Tzav
57, 64, 65

Vaera
34, 103
Vaetchanan
21
Vayakhel
148, 306, 321
Vayechi
118, 119, 285, 408, 716, 753, 806
Vayera
232
Vayetze
92, 116, 120, 148, 160, 242, 262, 305, 306, 310, 318, 335, 337
Vayikra
149, 152, 282, 433
Yitro
10, 327, 328, 329

YIBUM

Vayera
40

YIFTACH

Mishpatim
243

YISHAI

Acharei Mot
238
Balak
96, 344
Beresheet A
304
Beresheet B
416
Lech Lecha
173, 266
Mishpatim
175, 177, 179
Pekudei
26, 28, 231
Trumah
860, 914
Yitro
380

YISRAEL SABA

Acharei Mot
64, 87, 166, 167, 386
Balak
156, 157, 347, 348
Beshalach
69
Bo
232
Chukat
27, 28
Ha'azinu
48, 166
Lech Lecha
212
Mishpatim
527
Noach
235
Pekudei
10, 14, 92, 95, 96, 97
Pinchas
542, 548, 670
Safra Detzniuta
31, 32
Shlach Lecha
54
Tetzaveh
135

Toldot
106
Trumah
7, 155, 625, 628
Vaetchanan
46, 58
Vayakhel
102-104, 255, 324, 420, 421
Vayechi
491, 551
Vayikra
168-170, 172
Yitro
541

YISRAEL-SABA AND TEVUNAH

Beresheet A
9, 67, 108, 109, 307, 336, 413
Vaetchanan
10, 42, 96, 157

YOACH

Balak
276

YOFIEL (SUPERNAL MINISTER)

Balak
238
Beha'alot'cha
102
Pekudei
526, 531
Vayera
275
Vayetze
73
Vayikra
12

YOM KIPPUR

Acharei Mot
9, 28, 29, 111, 118, 119
Balak
326, 329, 332
Beshalach
71
Bo
160
Emor
126, 203, 221, 224, 226, 227b, 228, 234, 238, 243, 250, 253, 271
Lech Lecha
240
Mishpatim
409
Noach
105
Pinchas
30, 31, 33, 366, 678, 807, 827, 883
Tetzaveh
96, 106, 108, 109, 112, 114, 120
Toldot
31, 80, 129
Trumah
161
Tzav
28
Vayakhel
220
Vayechi
203, 217, 229
Vayera
223, 381, 385, 386

Vayeshev
226
Vayikra
250, 256, 302
Vayishlach
176, 188

YUD HEI VAV HEI (YHVH)

Acharei Mot
1, 157, 158, 161-163, 166, 169-171, 174, 183, 184, 190, 191, 212, 277, 288, 328, 332, 335, 336, 371, 385, 386, 389, 396
Balak
49, 80, 116, 118, 124, 127, 128, 156, 157, 158, 344, 369, 411, 469
Bechukotai
13
Beha'alot'cha
49, 50, 93
Behar
7, 20, 39, 41, 47, 48
Bemidbar
28, 31, 32, 33, 74
Beresheet A
11, 25, 26, 27, 32, 36, 60, 62, 67, 73, 89, 97, 114, 115, 126, 134, 173-175, 185, 192, 194-197, 206-208, 210, 221, 222, 236, 240, 247, 268, 269, 270, 271, 277, 279, 282
Beresheet B
29, 33, 135, 159, 202, 432, 433
Beshalach
75, 188, 241, 258, 435
Bo
210, 213, 218
Chayei Sarah
115, 160, 194, 224, 241
Ekev
12, 19, 38, 41
Emor
25, 40, 64, 66-68, 88, 102, 184, 185, 188, 313, 314, 317, 323
Ha'azinu
7, 53, 61, 75, 82, 84, 190, 220
Idra Raba
172, 227, 229, 232, 233, 244, 245, 261, 262, 263, 266, 271, 297, 300, 317, 329
Kedoshim
36, 51, 57
Ki Tetze
19, 57, 71, 74, 77, 85, 93, 99, 101, 102, 117, 126, 128, 129, 133, 137, 138, 144, 145
Ki Tisa
65, 66
Korach
40, 52, 53, 55, 57-59
Lech Lecha
99, 240, 246, 308, 319, 337, 340, 341, 342, 455
Metzora
19
Miketz
11, 43, 44, 108
Mishpatim
12, 13, 37, 69, 71, 260, 304, 364, 365, 378, 379, 382, 390, 398, 405, 435, 436, 445, 467, 468, 470, 471, 472, 489, 498, 506, 539, 549
Naso
13, 28, 30, 31, 36, 37, 38, 41, 48, 52, 55, 58, 64, 102, 165, 167, 173

Noach
112, 114, 164, 165, 249
Pekudei
13, 27, 77, 123, 164, 172, 188, 195, 217, 261, 292, 293, 294, 355, 505-507, 710, 748, 778, 779, 783-785, 790, 811, 822, 826
Pinchas
35d, 42, 43, 44, 50, 51, 58, 63, 70, 78, 106, 177-179, 187, 188, 191, 195, 201, 202, 221-225, 228, 229, 243, 246, 255, 260-262, 268, 269, 271, 280, 282, 283, 287-289, 291, 292, 294, 295, 297, 303, 305, 306-308, 311, 312, 320, 322, 323, 325, 333-335, 337, 340 -342, 344, 371, 405, 419, 432, 434, 482-484, 489, 492, 502, 530, 569, 572-574, 584, 585, 603, 604, 606, 608, 609, 611, 612, 616, 617, 620, 627, 633, 640, 641, 646, 647, 649, 657, 666, 668, 670, 674, 678, 688, 712, 713, 717, 733, 734, 738, 749, 752, 756-758, 769, 789, 790, 809, 810, 811, 812, 813, 815, 821, 837-840, 846, 848, 851, 856, 860, 864, 866 -868, 872, 874, 876, 877, 888, 889
Safra Detzniuta
19, 21, 23, 40-42, 44, 49, 52, 58, 60, 65, 69, 73
Shemot
44, 141-147, 149-155, 313
Shlach Lecha
5, 11, 36, 96, 129, 262, 308, 317
Shmini
44
Shoftim
5, 7
Tazria
13, 28, 91
Tetzaveh
5, 8, 14-17, 19, 20, 25, 26, 28, 32, 33, 36, 143
Toldot
182, 184
Trumah
8, 9, 107, 110, 132, 185, 186, 205, 377, 382, 398, 434, 477, 579, 604, 611, 634, 645, 649, 650, 652, 654, 666, 703, 720, 823, 881
Tzav
27, 28, 68
Vaera
5, 11-14, 18, 23, 29, 58, 75, 90, 112-114
Vaetchanan
12, 20, 37, 38, 40, 43, 44, 59, 60, 78, 80, 81, 83, 86, 87, 91, 118, 146, 175, 177
Vayakhel
43, 69, 100, 120, 347, 351 -353, 355-357, 360, 361, 363-365, 376, 383, 397, 398, 399, 400, 401, 422, 443, 464, 481, 484
Vayechi
37, 38, 43, 59, 60, 63, 87, 96, 175, 672, 752
Vayera
10, 64, 65, 68, 189, 256, 278, 279, 281, 305, 425, 442, 444, 446, 451, 452, 453
Vayetze
18, 30, 65, 71, 74, 87, 158, 167, 169
Vayigash
41

Vayikra
6, 51, 52, 104, 132, 139, 146, 152, 153, 158-161, 169, 170, 172, 174, 175, 221, 248, 278 -282, 284, 285, 306, 331, 421, 428
Vayishlach
169, 171
Yitro
327, 442, 510-512, 536, 537

YUMBRUS

Balak
174

YUNUS

Balak
174
Ki Tisa
61, 75, 83

ZACHAR

Bo
126
Pinchas
209
Shlach Lecha
167
Shmini
93
Tetzaveh
62
Vayetze
269

ZAHARIEL (SPIRIT)

Pekudei
557-562
Vayera
276

ZARKA

Balak
374, 379, 380
Beresheet A
201, 212
Pinchas
668
Shoftim
5

ZEBULUN

Beha'alot'cha
25-28, 47
Beshalach
104
Mishpatim
200, 202
Vaera
95
Vayechi
643, 647, 663-665, 669, 674, 675, 694, 696, 774
Vayetze
160, 162

ZECHARIAH

Naso
148

ZECHUT (SPIRIT)

Beresheet B
102, 103, 106, 107, 109, 114, 118, 134
Pekudei
595, 598, 600, 602, 618, 619, 621, 626, 640

ZEDEKIAH

Chayei Sarah
42
Shmini
90
Vayera
370

ZEH (THIS, MASC.)

Balak
248
Beha'alot'cha
147
Beshalach
145, 221, 363
Bo
112, 132, 159
Chukat
16
Ekev
19
Lech Lecha
400
Mishpatim
310, 388
Pekudei
745
Pinchas
618, 707
Shlach Lecha
72
Toldot
177
Trumah
816
Tzav
98-100
Vayechi
91, 92, 94-99
Yitro
187

ZEIR ANPIN

Acharei Mot
1, 26, 27, 33, 34, 37, 46, 49, 56, 59, 62-64, 71, 72, 74, 77, 83, 101, 102, 104, 108, 109, 115, 147, 153-156, 162, 163, 169 -173, 175, 176, 179, 180, 184, 185, 189-194, 197, 205, 209 -211, 214, 226, 238, 244, 251, 277, 295, 304, 305, 308, 319, 324, 328-330, 332, 334, 335, 337, 369-374, 377, 380-382, 385-389, 408-411
Balak
34, 38, 41, 52, 53, 56, 73, 81, 86, 88, 89, 110, 111, 114, 116, 124, 125, 128, 156, 157, 159, 232, 239, 248, 259, 260, 300, 301, 311, 312, 331, 332, 334, 340, 342-344, 347, 348, 349, 394, 396, 433, 437, 438, 439, 440, 464, 469, 506, 507
Bechukotai
16-24, 47, 48, 53, 56
Beha'alot'cha
2-4, 6, 9, 10, 24, 25, 29, 30, 35-38, 49, 52, 57, 63, 70, 71, 96-99, 121, 125, 127, 131, 132, 136, 143, 144, 147, 148
Behar
10, 13, 47, 53, 54, 62, 79-83, 85
Bemidbar
7, 8, 18, 22, 23, 27, 32, 37, 41, 44, 56, 58, 64, 68, 71, 73, 74
Beresheet A
8, 11, 15, 16, 30, 34, 35, 36, 38, 39, 40, 42, 43, 49, 50, 53, 60,

62, 63, 66-70, 73, 74, 80 -82, 85, 87, 89, 90, 95, 97, 109, 111, 112, 114, 116, 118, 125, 126, 142, 149, 150, 153 -155, 157, 160, 164, 175, 195, 198, 199, 202, 203, 204, 207, 230, 233, 235, 236, 242, 244, 245, 246, 247, 256, 258, 268, 273, 276, 279, 282, 293, 296, 298, 304, 305, 307, 309, 310, 311, 312, 317, 325, 327, 329 -333, 336, 337, 339, 341, 343, 344, 346, 353, 354, 357, 359, 360, 362, 364, 370, 373, 375, 376, 377, 379-385, 392, 394, 396, 398, 399, 402, 403, 404, 407, 410, 413, 414, 420, 423, 424, 426, 428, 431, 434 -436, 441, 442, 445, 448, 449, 461, 466, 467, 469, 470, 477, 479

Beresheet B

4, 7, 19, 29, 33, 35, 63, 97, 130-136, 151, 153, 159, 162 -164, 169, 175, 179-181, 184, 186, 196, 200, 202-204, 210, 213, 214, 232, 233, 236, 238, 240, 242, 244, 246, 257 -259, 262, 264, 268-272, 278, 279, 293, 300, 302, 304, 306, 307, 311, 325, 361, 366, 370, 375, 397, 419

Beshalach

21, 49, 53, 55, 58, 97, 98, 101, 102, 109, 110, 116, 117, 121, 122, 127, 132, 137, 141-143, 148, 150, 151, 153, 157, 172, 180, 211, 212, 221, 224, 225, 227, 238, 241, 250, 258, 274, 275, 296, 315, 330, 331, 348, 352, 372, 374, 376, 380, 394, 395, 424, 426, 428, 435, 436, 438, 458, 467, 482, 483

Bo

42, 44, 56, 57, 87, 90, 105, 106, 108, 112, 116, 131, 134, 147, 171, 174, 232, 233, 235, 243, 246

Chayei Sarah

15, 17, 30, 65, 171, 205, 206, 224, 230, 234, 235, 246, 252, 253, 254, 255, 256, 268

Chukat

2, 3, 15, 18, 19, 26, 28, 29, 36-38, 39, 42, 44, 46, 49, 50, 51, 52, 57, 67, 73, 74, 77, 87

Ekev

2, 3, 4, 7, 9-14, 18, 22, 26, 29, 30, 39, 45, 49, 50, 61

Emor

12, 13, 14, 20, 21, 27, 32, 40, 43, 45, 57, 62-64, 67, 68, 84-88, 90-93, 95, 97, 98, 100, 101, 102, 105, 106, 111, 113 -115, 117, 127, 131, 132, 133, 134, 138, 139, 141-143, 146, 149-151, 153-158, 160, 163, 164, 165, 167, 170, 173, 175, 176, 178, 182, 184-186, 190, 192-195, 202, 205, 206, 209, 224-226, 253, 255, 257 -259, 260a, 263, 272, 284, 299, 302, 331, 334, 335

Ha'azinu

8, 12, 13, 15, 17, 35, 40, 44, 47, 48, 50-55, 57, 58, 59, 61, 62, 66-69, 71-73, 75, 77, 80 -85, 87-90, 92, 93, 101, 103, 106, 108, 109, 116-119, 123, 126, 127, 135, 138, 142, 144, 147, 149-151, 161-163, 165, 166, 172-175, 183-185, 187, 189, 191, 194, 195, 210, 220, 224-228, 236, 238

Idra Raba
5, 16, 17, 19, 20, 23, 26, 30, 32, 33, 35, 37, 39, 40, 41, 42, 45, 48, 51-54, 56-59, 63, 64, 65, 69, 71, 86, 87, 88, 92, 93, 94, 96, 97, 98, 100, 110, 113, 126, 127, 133, 139, 140, 143, 145-147, 150, 153, 155-158, 161, 162, 171, 172, 178, 181 -183, 185-190, 193-197, 199 -202, 205, 208, 216, 218, 219, 221 -223, 225, 227-230, 232, 233, 235, 236, 240-250, 256, 257, 261, 267, 269-273, 275, 278-282, 284-286, 288, 290 -292, 294, 295, 297-305, 308, 309, 315, 317, 323, 324, 329, 333, 337, 339, 340, 344, 345, 346, 363

Kedoshim
18-20, 30, 32, 33, 35, 38, 41, 47, 51, 52, 61-64, 77, 92, 95, 97, 107, 109, 124-129

Ki Tetze
18, 19, 35, 46, 51, 52, 68, 69, 88, 89, 92, 93, 95, 100, 102, 104, 125, 126, 140, 143-145

Ki Tisa
4, 6, 33, 58, 106, 108, 111, 115, 117, 118

Korach
11, 28, 50, 56, 59

Lech Lecha
4, 7, 10, 11-13, 15, 19, 20, 25, 43, 72, 90, 99, 102, 103, 107, 128, 129, 143, 152, 164, 166, 167, 172, 197, 232, 233, 236, 237, 239, 240, 241, 242, 246, 257, 277, 308, 310, 311, 312, 337, 446, 447, 448, 451, 462

Matot
6

Metzora
21, 24, 26, 29, 34, 36, 37, 40, 42, 46, 55, 58, 60

Miketz
2, 4, 10, 11, 17, 18, 32, 39, 40, 72, 73, 79, 80, 83, 108, 112, 113, 134, 140, 141, 157, 211, 218, 268

Mishpatim
7, 12, 13, 24, 76, 77, 79, 96, 105, 123, 124, 129, 130, 134, 136, 137, 166, 177, 181, 182, 183, 186, 201, 202, 209, 218, 237, 303, 305, 367, 378, 388, 403-406, 408, 410, 414, 429, 434, 435, 438, 442, 446, 454, 455, 456, 457, 467, 480, 496, 498, 499, 511, 520, 521, 524 -526, 528-531, 549, 550, 553, 578

Naso
2, 10, 11, 12, 14, 15, 26, 28, 36, 38, 48, 49, 60, 61, 72, 98, 125, 127, 139, 142, 143, 160, 162, 164, 167, 172, 173, 176, 192, 195, 199

Noach
18, 22, 23, 26, 44, 62, 67, 73, 99, 101-104, 112, 113, 116, 128, 129, 134, 143, 145, 159, 165, 170, 172, 231, 232, 249, 272, 282, 283, 296, 297, 300 -302, 330, 332, 333, 362

Pekudei
1, 2, 10, 14, 27, 35, 41, 50, 54, 58, 77, 97, 99, 105, 106, 107, 111, 112, 114, 118, 123, 124,

126, 129, 130, 135, 137, 138, 146, 148-150, 162, 164, 172, 173, 174, 176, 184-186, 196, 197, 209, 210, 211, 212, 215, 217-219, 221-227, 234, 255, 259, 264, 265, 267, 268 -272, 277, 279, 283, 284, 290, 293, 295-298, 340-343, 345, 348-350, 352, 355, 357, 372, 373, 394, 404, 408, 411, 412, 414, 475, 477, 493, 494, 495, 503, 533-535, 589, 630, 638, 653, 672, 674, 714, 716 -718, 730, 732, 734, 736, 743, 744, 756, 762, 763, 766, 768, 775, 778-780, 783, 798 -801, 811, 821, 822, 834, 953

Pinchas

29-32, 35b, 35c, 35d, 36, 38, 39, 44, 46, 47, 48, 57, 58, 63, 70, 79, 82, 83, 115, 136, 141, 142, 172, 178, 179, 183, 184, 187, 193, 196, 197, 198, 199, 201, 202, 209, 211, 213, 220, 222, 236, 237, 240, 246, 251, 255, 259, 260, 263, 271, 272, 280, 281-284, 288, 289, 291, 294, 297, 300, 302, 303, 308, 310, 316, 323, 324, 329, 331, 335, 336, 337, 343, 344, 353, 370, 371, 394, 400, 405, 406, 408, 412, 421, 444, 449, 455, 456, 461, 484, 492, 510-519, 521, 528, 530, 532, 533, 540, 542 -545, 549, 561-563, 565, 567, 569, 572, 574, 576, 582 -585, 589, 591, 598, 604, 606, 609, 610, 617, 619, 628, 646, 647, 648, 654, 655, 657, 661, 662, 667, 669-674, 676, 677, 678, 682, 684, 687, 689-691, 705, 706, 707, 710, 712, 714 -717, 719, 720, 733, 738, 749, 753, 754, 755, 756, 758, 760, 766, 768, 774, 777, 780, 782, 783, 788-790, 805, 810, 811, 813 -815, 820, 823, 827, 835, 837

Prologue

10, 16, 40, 41, 78, 79, 82, 107, 128, 130, 140, 142, 143, 168, 204, 206, 207, 209, 210, 219, 222, 232, 241, 242, 249

Safra Detzniuta

7, 10, 12, 13, 15, 21-24, 26, 27, 28, 35-38, 41, 43, 44, 49, 52, 53, 57, 59-62, 65, 66, 67, 69, 71, 72

Shemot

1, 3, 4, 19, 20, 38, 44, 45, 47, 48, 55, 68, 80, 81, 117, 131, 139, 140, 146, 147, 158, 161 -165, 179, 199, 200, 210, 211, 217, 233, 243, 244, 258, 298, 310, 324, 332, 339, 359, 391, 393

Shlach Lecha

1, 2, 4-8, 11, 1-15, 31, 36, 37, 46, 47, 54, 58, 61, 62, 83, 87, 89, 90, 91, 124, 126, 138, 145, 151, 154-157, 177, 184, 185, 203, 229, 238, 239, 242, 244, 246, 262, 267, 290, 291, 307, 311, 317, 318, 323, 325 -327, 333, 342-346, 348

Shmini

3, 5-7, 9, 12, 13, 27, 28, 37, 38,

41, 51, 52, 59, 60, 66, 72, 77, 81, 83-86, 90, 93, 94, 96, 99-101, 103, 104, 117

Shoftim
4, 8-10, 13, 16, 19, 20, 23

Tazria
3, 7, 8, 14, 23, 27, 29, 30, 41, 45, 57, 63, 64, 91, 92, 97, 109, 114, 118, 124, 125, 132, 133, 134

Tetzaveh
2-6, 14, 26, 28, 32, 33, 34, 36, 53, 62, 65-69, 72, 73, 75, 76, 92, 126, 135, 139, 140

Toldot
6, 10-13, 18, 20, 25, 29, 31, 96, 107, 116, 135, 144, 151, 168, 182-184, 204

Trumah
3, 4, 16, 17, 25, 26, 27, 28, 31, 42, 44, 61, 85, 99, 101, 106, 107, 108, 109, 110, 112, 114, 116, 117, 119, 120, 122, 124, 125-139, 141-144, 149, 150, 152, 156, 163, 164, 169-171, 184, 186-195, 198, 201, 205 -219, 221-223, 227, 228, 229, 231, 233, 243, 247-249, 251, 252, 256, 258-261, 265, 267, 268, 286, 289-292, 302, 316, 332, 333, 336, 340-348, 354, 355, 356, 357, 359, 360, 361, 362, 367, 371, 373, 375, 378, 380, 381, 385, 395, 397, 398, 399, 401, 403, 419, 429, 493, 494, 495, 505, 526, 527, 550, 551, 558, 569, 575, 577-585, 588, 589, 594, 598, 600, 601, 603, 604, 613, 624, 625, 628, 629, 634, 645, 648, 649, 651, 655-659, 666, 680, 687, 688, 690, 702, 703, 704, 708, 709, 710, 711

Tzav
1-3, 8, 9, 35, 37-42, 44-46, 52-54, 58, 62-65, 68, 75-77, 83, 85, 91, 98-100, 102, 103, 109, 139, 140, 142, 145, 146, 149-151, 157, 165, 167, 168, 178-181, 184, 185, 189, 190

Vaera
2, 4-6, 9-11, 14, 16, 17, 23-30, 34, 44, 51, 56, 61, 62, 64, 67, 68, 69, 72, 73, 75, 76, 78, 81, 88, 99, 104, 114, 130, 131, 149, 150, 151, 156, 158, 159, 179, 180, 187, 189

Vaetchanan
4, 5, 6, 12, 13, 18, 20, 21, 22, 24, 26-28, 30, 31, 34, 37, 43, 45, 46, 49-51, 54, 55, 56, 59, 60, 70, 71, 72, 78, 80-82, 92, 95, 96, 97, 102, 104, 112, 113, 117, 129, 147, 155-157, 159, 166, 174, 177, 189, 190, 192, 194, 195

Vayakhel
13, 22, 24, 50-53, 56, 58, 59, 60, 100, 110, 140, 141, 149, 155, 177, 180, 194, 195, 207, 210, 214, 219-222, 233, 235-237, 253, 255, 256, 262, 269, 292, 293, 300, 304, 316, 323-325, 345, 355, 356, 361, 363, 365, 368, 375, 376, 383, 386, 396, 397, 401, 402, 417, 418, 420, 421, 423, 424, 428 -432, 434, 443, 479, 481, 486, 489

Vayechi
13, 15, 20, 25, 35, 37, 43, 51, 54, 63, 64, 75, 96, 107, 117,

118, 132, 174-176, 180, 181, 183, 187, 217, 219, 228, 237, 238, 240, 285, 291, 307, 314, 329, 331, 354, 355, 374, 375, 379, 380, 407, 408, 416, 437, 438, 446, 454, 458, 459-461, 464, 465, 485, 486, 489 -491, 502, 506, 509, 521, 523, 537, 540, 551, 560, 562, 567, 568, 569, 577, 586, 589-591, 594, 612, 615-618, 622, 630, 632 -634, 636, 640, 641, 648, 650, 661, 678, 680, 689, 693, 697, 698, 716, 725, 730, 731, 743-745, 748-757, 762, 767, 771, 779-781, 783-785, 789 -795, 797, 798, 799, 803 -806, 808-810, 813, 835, 837, 839-841, 859

Vayelech
4, 5, 16, 27, 28, 30, 31, 33, 36, 41, 47, 48

Vayera
7, 8, 10-15, 20, 28, 52, 53, 57, 58, 63, 65, 92, 267, 268, 269, 270, 271, 278, 279, 281, 284, 300, 355, 382, 424, 425, 439, 444, 445, 449, 451, 453, 482, 512, 513

Vayeshev
20-22, 32, 42, 44, 55, 62, 65, 66, 68, 83, 104, 106, 145, 263, 264, 272, 275, 282

Vayetze
1, 4-7, 9, 12, 16, 23, 30-32, 45, 46, 47, 50, 52, 55, 62, 70, 76, 79, 83-86, 91, 96, 98, 105, 115, 128, 133, 134, 139, 148, 150, 173, 177, 179, 191, 198, 207, 209, 211, 212, 220, 224, 226, 230, 236, 241, 259, 260, 267 -269, 272, 274, 282, 291, 292, 316, 317, 320, 327, 329, 330, 331, 361, 362, 371, 373, 384

Vayigash
7, 12, 13, 15, 20-22, 27, 31, 41-43, 57, 59, 66, 69, 70, 81, 100-103, 105, 128-130

Vayikra
5, 6, 13, 15, 29-31, 34, 36, 43 -46, 48, 58-61, 67, 70, 74, 75, 85, 89-91, 96, 101-104, 108, 113, 132, 150, 152, 154, 156, 170-172, 176, 180, 183, 184, 192, 201, 205, 223, 225, 226, 228, 229, 231, 232, 245-248, 253, 258, 260, 266, 267, 270 -272, 280, 281, 283, 287, 291, 292, 296, 297, 299, 301, 317, 329, 331, 332, 335, 337, 341, 343-346, 352, 360, 366, 369, 371, 373, 377, 380, 381, 400, 413-415, 417-420, 426, 428, 445, 446, 448, 449

Vayishlach
12, 37, 51, 62, 64, 88, 105, 108, 129, 131-133, 137, 138, 143, 161, 163, 258

Yitro
64, 65, 67, 95, 96, 97, 223 -225, 239, 246, 253, 265, 279, 282, 300, 303-305, 321, 323, 327, 328, 335, 336, 338, 350, 356, 359, 360, 379, 382, 383, 385, 388, 391-395, 399, 400, 403, 404, 418, 436, 448, 449, 451, 453, 456, 457, 462, 465, 487, 489, 505, 506, 511, 529, 530, 532, 540, 542, 546 -549, 559, 560, 561, 564

ZELOPHEHAD

Balak
375, 376, 379
Korach
7

ZERACH

Mishpatim
191, 192, 197

ZEVULIEL (SPIRIT)

Vayakhel
136, 137

ZIBEON

Vayishlach
260, 264

ZILPAH

Trumah
352
Vayeshev
70

ZIMRAN

Chayei Sarah
199

ZIMRI

Vayechi
562

ZION

Acharei Mot
51, 174, 175, 231, 234, 277, 288, 374-376
Balak
391, 439, 507
Beha'alot'cha
80, 150
Bemidbar
17, 19
Beresheet B
17
Beshalach
250, 286, 292, 296
Emor
22, 127, 170, 259
Ha'azinu
142, 146, 191-195, 231
Idra Raba
52, 218, 220
Lech Lecha
264, 422, 425
Metzora
59
Miketz
269
Mishpatim
123, 124, 263, 264, 266, 453, 502, 506, 581
Naso
80, 103, 189, 192
Noach
349
Pekudei
38, 41, 382, 383, 735, 816, 818
Pinchas
17, 742, 746
Prologue
65, 67
Shemot
9, 10, 125, 156, 292
Shlach Lecha
61, 297, 298, 303, 304

Shmini
10, 11, 13
Toldot
155, 208
Trumah
52, 56, 117, 121, 138, 307, 310
Tzav
101-103, 167, 181-183
Vaera
4
Vaetchanan
53, 131
Vayakhel
20, 317, 319, 454, 496
Vayechi
77, 157, 174, 175, 342, 430, 800, 803, 804, 810
Vayera
394, 395, 396, 397, 483
Vayeshev
146, 147
Vayetze
41, 244, 360
Vayigash
32
Vayikra
44, 60, 132, 133, 204, 205, 304, 352
Vayishlach
130
Yitro
299, 336, 356, 503

ZODIAC

Ekev
35
Prologue
11

ZOHAR

Beha'alot'cha
88-89
Beresheet A
308, 331, 347, 470
Beresheet B
2, 73, 76, 134
Bo
176
Naso
90
Noach
382
Pekudei
637
Pinchas
575, 657, 749
Prologue
116
Shemot
59, 351
Shlach Lecha
88, 105
Trumah
132, 171, 403, 404, 474, 520, 648, 758
Vayakhel
339
Vayechi
29, 39
Vayera
38, 39, 201, 220, 229, 255
Vayetze
31

ZOT (THIS, FEM.)

Acharei Mot
5, 41, 44, 53, 64, 84, 85, 87,

107, 235, 348, 411
Balak
300
Bechukotai
56
Beshalach
145, 153, 280, 281, 470
Bo
112, 113, 117, 159
Chukat
16
Ha'azinu
216, 219, 220, 242, 243
Korach
45
Lech Lecha
400, 401, 402, 403
Metzora
23
Miketz
162
Naso
143, 145
Noach
281
Pekudei
308
Pinchas
707, 838, 852
Shlach Lecha
312, 348
Shmini
88, 102, 104
Toldot
68
Trumah
2, 6
Tzav
1, 21, 35, 98-101, 121, 162,
164, 177
Vayechi
91, 92, 95, 379
Vayikra
114, 214, 230, 238, 415

NOTES